ENCYCLOPEDIA OF
Outdoor &
Wilderness
Skills

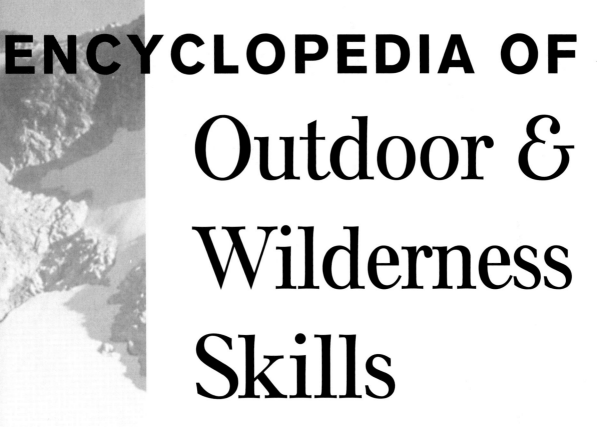

ENCYCLOPEDIA OF
Outdoor & Wilderness Skills

CHRIS TOWNSEND   **ANNIE AGGENS**

RAGGED MOUNTAIN PRESS / McGRAW-HILL
Camden, Maine • New York • Chicago • San Francisco •
Lisbon • London • Madrid • Mexico City • Milan • New Delhi •
San Juan • Seoul • Singapore • Sydney • Toronto

The McGraw·Hill Companies

1 2 3 4 5 6 7 8 9 0 DOC DOC 0 9 8 7 6 5 4 3

Copyright © 2003 by Ragged Mountain Press
All rights reserved. The publisher takes no responsibility
for the use of any of the materials or methods described
in this book, nor for the products thereof. The name
"Ragged Mountain Press" and the Ragged Mountain
Press logo are trademarks of The McGraw-Hill
Companies. Printed in the United States of America.

Library of Congress Cataloging-in-Publication Data
Townsend, Chris, 1949–
    Encyclopedia of outdoor and wilderness skills / Chris
Townsend and Annie Aggens.
            p.   cm.
Includes bibliographical references and index
ISBN 0-07-138406-5 (pbk. : alk. paper)
1. Outdoor life—Encyclopedias. 2. Wilderness
survival—Encyclopedias. I. Aggens, Annie M. II. Title.
    GV191.3 .T69 2003
    796′.03—dc21   2002156672

Questions regarding the content of this book should be
addressed to
Ragged Mountain Press
P.O. Box 220
Camden, ME 04843
www.raggedmountainpress.com

Questions regarding the ordering of this book should be
addressed to
The McGraw-Hill Companies
Customer Service Department
P.O. Box 547
Blacklick, OH 43004
Retail customers: 1-800-262-4729
Bookstores: 1-800-722-4726

Illustrations by Christopher Hoyt unless otherwise
indicated. Chapter opening art by Carolyn Kasper. Photo
page ii by Chris Townsend.

Contents

Editorial Board

The following outdoor specialists have reviewed this book to ensure it is as complete and accurate as possible.

HOLLY BEATIE remembers camping in the Sierra Nevada since the age of three. She has spent over thirty years learning and mastering many forms of skiing and backcountry travel. As America's female biathlon pioneer, in 1984 she won the U.S.'s first world championship medal. Holly keeps her wilderness skills honed as a member of the Tahoe Nordic Search and Rescue Team and leading nature hikes around the Lake Tahoe area.

MARK JOHNSON has nearly twenty years of experience in desert hiking and exploration in North America and Africa. A frequent writer and lecturer on desert hiking, travel, and camping, he has been published in a number of print and online publications, including *Four Wheeler* and *The Survivor*. Mark's first book, *The Ultimate Desert Handbook*, is the first complete manual on desert hiking and exploration (Ragged Mountain Press, 2003).

JACK HEGARTY is a lifelong photographer and Registered Maine Master Guide. His guiding and photographic treks have taken him to Greenland, Baffin Island, Alaska, Europe, Africa, and South America. He has also directed and produced award-winning outdoor films, such as those in the North American Outdoorsman series, and films for ABC American Sportsman.

SHIRLEY FORTIER

About the Authors

CHRIS TOWNSEND, author of *The Backpacker's Handbook* (in its third edition), *Backpacker's Pocket Guide*, and *The Advanced Backpacker* as well as numerous other books and articles, is one of the world's best-known and experienced rough-terrain hikers. His most notable adventures include a 1988 trek spanning the 1,600-mile length of the Canadian Rockies, a 1,000-mile walk through the Yukon, and a monumental 3,000-mile expedition from Canada to Mexico along the Continental Divide Trail. He has also undertaken extensive treks in Europe and long ski tours everywhere from the High Sierra to the Canadian Rockies, the Yukon, Lapland, Spitsbergen, and Greenland.

ANNIE AGGENS fits the mold of the modern-day voyageur. Vying at the top of her "things-she-would-rather-be-doing" list are canoeing the rivers of the Canadian subarctic and climbing the crags of the Rockies. Annie has led many expeditions throughout the Northwest Territories, Nunavut, Saskatchewan, and British Columbia. She has also skied to the North Pole and guided several dog-sledding trips. When her toes get cold she warms up by guiding sea kayaking trips in the warmer climates of the Mediterranean and Central America. Annie has served as the director of an adventure travel company and has instructed for the National Outdoor Leadership School, the American Canoe Association, and many other organizations. She regularly lectures on organizing paddling expeditions, adventure travel, and the history of Arctic exploration.

Acknowledgments

Many people contributed valuable information and considerable expertise to the *Encyclopedia of Outdoor and Wilderness Skills*. Without their help, this book would be incomplete.

Special thanks go to the following individuals: Joanne Aggens, Lorenz Aggens, Bill Barklay, Amy Duchelle, Keith Garvey, John Gookin, Cliff Jacobson, Dirk Jensen, Dr. David Johnson, Peter McClelland, Bob Peterson, Harry Rock, Matt Snider, Lieutenant Commander Paul Steward, John Stoddard, Rick Sweitzer, Mike Tuttle, and Chuck Weber.

The following organizations provided valuable information: American Canoe Association, American Canyoneering Association, American Long Distance Hiking Association–West, American Mountain Guides Association, American Whitewater, British Canoe Union, Federal Communications Commission, Leave No Trace, National Association for Search and Rescue, National Outdoor Leadership School, National Park Service, Wilderness Medical Associates, and U.S. Coast Guard.

Introduction

Wilderness is the natural state of our planet. It is where we came from and where many of us return whenever we can in order to renew ourselves by experiencing nature in all its forms. Reasons for visiting the wilderness are many: excitement, adventure, challenge, escape, contemplation, solitude, and more. How we achieve these varies enormously. Hiking, backpacking, skiing, canoeing, climbing, and mountain biking are all ways to enjoy the wilderness. All require different technical skills and equipment but also the same awareness of nature and the same knowledge of how to protect both yourself and the wilderness so neither comes to harm.

Between us, the authors (Chris and Annie), we have spent many years living, teaching, and guiding groups in the wilderness. Our lives revolve around wilderness activities. We are dedicated to promoting these activities and to working for the future of the wilderness, both for its own sake and so that those who come after us will be able to enjoy the outdoors in the same way.

In this book, we discuss the various outdoor activities and all that they entail. We have also provided information on the skills and equipment required to carry them out safely and enjoyably, without causing damage to the environment. Imagine that you are able to have a conversation with an expert in kayaking or ski touring. What would you want to know? Would you be interested in the technicalities, such as equipment or technique? What about the level of difficulty or comfort? Maybe you would want to know the best way to get some experience? We continually asked ourselves these questions as we wrote each subject in this book. As a result, this *Encyclopedia* is packed with practical information. It provides the inside scoop on 450 outdoor- and wilderness-related topics.

Like a standard encyclopedia, our entries are thorough yet short enough that any one can be read in a few minutes. This makes the *Encyclopedia* easy to use as a reference for a specific topic as well as an armchair adventure that is easy to pick up and put down. In some instances, where further reading would be beneficial, we've directed you to additional resources (see complete information on these in the resources section).

The book is intended to be entertaining and interesting—a way to find out about activities, techniques, equipment, and more that you may never have heard of or know little about. It's a book to dip into at random to see what you find—a cornucopia of wilderness lore that we hope will inspire and stimulate you to undertake more adventures in the outdoors. One of the delights of encyclopedias is that in looking up one entry you are distracted by an adjacent one and discover something you didn't know or had never thought about before—an adventure in words, as it were.

As in conversation, your thoughts may drift from one topic to another. You may open the *Encyclopedia* to read about ice climbing and find yourself, hours later, learning how to bake fresh bread on your backcountry stove. Along the way, you might have discovered how to plan an expedition, the best way to survive in cold water, what a bivouac is, and why they're notoriously uncomfortable. *Note:* To help you navigate, cross-references to names of other entries appear in **boldface** type within an entry.

There are two things this book is not. First—and this is important—it is not a one-on-one instructional. The information presented here is meant to empower you with knowledge, not actual skills. You are responsible for investing the time, energy, and sweat it takes to acquire good skills and wilderness-worthy common sense. Second, the *Encyclopedia* is not the final word in wilderness living. There are, and will always be, differing opinions regarding technique and equipment. Be skeptical of people who suggest that their way is the only way to do something. In reality, there are many ways to experience the wilderness, and the sense of discovery that accompanies life on the trail is half the fun. Even after thousands of days of living in the backcountry, we both learn something new each time we head out. You'll discover that the only rules written in stone here are those pertaining to your safety and to the preservation of the wilderness.

Whether you are going out for a weekend or a multimonth expedition, the wilderness demands that you come prepared and ready to handle a myriad of possibilities. We hope the *Encyclopedia* helps prepare you for the expected and unexpected alike. We also hope you have as much fun reading it as we have had writing it. Happy trails!

Annie Aggens
Chris Townsend

ABBEY, EDWARD

Edward Abbey (1927–1989) was a passionate, eloquent writer who devoted his life to the preservation of the American Southwest. Abbey authored 21 books, including *The Monkey Wrench Gang* and *Desert Solitaire*, which are favorites among preservationists. To many people, Abbey came across as a radical environmentalist. His Monkey Wrench Gang, a fictional group of eco-terrorists who blow up dams, inspired a generation of environmentalists. His other writings reflect the beauty of the natural world he loved. Abbey grew up in the Appalachian Mountains. At age 17 he hitchhiked west, discovering in the **desert** a world that captivated his heart. For the rest of his life, he fought, both in words and action, to save the deserts of the southwestern United States from development. He died at age 62 and is buried at an undisclosed location in the Cabeza Prieta National Wildlife Refuge, which is part of the lower Sonoran Desert in Arizona.

AID CLIMBING

Aid climbing is a form of **rock climbing** in which you rely on **artificial protection** and **fixed protection** to hold your weight while you ascend a vertical rock face. Aid climbing was born out of the desire to climb rock that simply didn't have the **handholds** or **footholds** for **free climbing**. As rock climbing techniques have improved, the climbing community has seen many traditionally aided routes become free routes.

Aid climbing is a very specialized discipline that requires plenty of training, a technical understanding of artificial protection placement, and an array of specialized equipment. Some of the protection used in aid climbing is designed to bear the static weight of a climber and may not hold up to the force of a fall. Because of the "sensitivity" of some placements, aid climbers make slow, calculated moves up a route.

Aid climbers may find themselves spending multiple days on a route, particularly if it is a big wall (see **big-wall climbing**). This adds a certain degree of difficulty, as quick descents are usually out of the question. In addition, you could find yourself having to endure poor **weather** while you cling to the side of a rock a thousand vertical feet above the ground.

ALCOHOL

For some people, an alcoholic beverage is the last thing they would bring into the **wilderness**. For others, it is the perfect ending for a delicious meal. Whatever your preferences, you should understand the effects alcohol has on your body—and the special considerations for drinking alcohol in the backcountry.

Alcohol is a central nervous system depressant: it slows your body's major functions. In a setting that requires us to be acutely aware of our surroundings, alcohol diminishes **judgment**, dulls motor-sensory skills, and tampers with our emotional well-being. If you are going to drink, the best time is at the end of the day when you have no tasks ahead of you. Keep in mind that in the backcountry, sometimes all it takes is a stumble over a rock or a fall into a river to create an emergency.

Some people bring alcohol to "warm themselves up" when the temperature gets low. In reality, alcohol does just the opposite—in fact, it can even advance **hypothermia**. A vasodilator, alcohol opens your blood vessels, allowing blood to flow closer to the surface of your skin (which is why you sometimes get flush when you drink). Having your blood so close to your skin cools it much faster, lowering your body temperature. You may feel warmer, but in reality your core temperature is dropping. It is much better to rely on physical activity and appropriate **clothing** to warm up.

If you decide to travel with alcohol, first make sure your destination permits alcohol to be consumed, and then consider the best way to carry it. Many local, state, and **national parks** do not allow glass containers. Most people will decant their favorite beverage into a metal flask or a plastic bottle, such as a water bottle. If you are in bear country, your alcohol is "scented food" and should be stored as such (see **bears**).

ALLERGIC REACTIONS

Imagine this scenario: You're walking through the woods with two friends when you unexpectedly step on a fallen beehive. Suddenly, hundreds of bees are swarming around you. You quickly turn and run away. When you reach a safe distance, you take inventory and discover that you have been stung four times. The stings are burning, but otherwise you feel OK. The friend immediately behind you has been stung twice on her fingers, and her hand is quite swollen. Your other friend has been stung only once, on his knee. Although his knee is swelling, he has worse problems. He

begins to itch all over, red hives appear on his arms and face, and he is complaining that his throat feels tight. You can see that he's beginning to have difficulty breathing. He is having an allergic reaction to the bee sting. What should you do?

> "Every time I wear a Band-Aid, I have a reaction to the adhesive. It causes my skin to itch. If I leave the Band-Aid on for several days, I develop blisters. While it can be bothersome, I'm not too concerned about this allergy. My friend on the other hand cannot go near a poison ivy plant without developing a rash that itches uncontrollably. Still, even poison ivy isn't too much of a threat."—AA

An allergic reaction occurs when a person comes in contact with a substance to which he has an allergy. Common reactions occur from stinging **insects**, certain **foods**, and even medications. While some reactions go virtually unnoticed, others can be life threatening. Many people are aware of their allergies and can predict the severity of a reaction. Other people, who have never been exposed to a substance, will not be able to predict whether they will have an allergic reaction. Some allergies are passed from generation to generation, but this is not a sure way to determine whether you are allergic to a particular substance. Allergens (the toxins that create allergic reactions) can be introduced to a person's body in three ways: injection (a bite or sting), ingestion (swallowing or inhaling something), or absorption (touching a substance or rubbing against it). Once you have been subjected to an allergen, your body will try to fight it by producing antibodies, which are the body's natural defense against foreign intruders. However, some toxins may make your body produce the wrong kind of antibodies. When this occurs, your body falls prey to its own defense mechanisms, and you have an allergic reaction. You may develop a rash, a runny nose, or itchy eyes. If the reaction is more severe, you may experience swelling or **blisters**. You may also feel sick to your stomach.

Some allergies are simply an annoyance, while others present serious health concerns. The most worrisome reactions in the **wilderness** are those that cause a life-threatening condition called *anaphylactic shock*, or *anaphylaxis*. Anaphylaxis can become fatal in a matter of minutes. It is caused by a severe reaction that affects a person's entire body, including the respiratory system. Left untreated, a person in anaphylactic shock will likely develop breathing difficulties that lead to respiratory failure, followed shortly by death. Because anaphylaxis can occur in a matter of moments, you must be prepared to deal with such a crisis immediately.

The first step in treating anaphylaxis is to know how to recognize it. Not everyone who is allergic to a toxin will develop a reaction severe enough to cause anaphylaxis. Anaphylaxis occurs when you have a systemic reaction—in other words, one that affects your whole body. In the example at the beginning of this entry, the bees stung three people. The first person simply experienced burning and the second had dramatic local swelling, but the third person developed a reaction that affected his entire body. The first two reactions are common, and each remained local to the site of the sting. The third person was stung on the knee but developed hives on his arms and face and had difficulties breathing—all signs that the reaction had become life threatening.

An anaphylactic reaction will usually occur within 5 to 15 minutes of exposure to an allergen. This does not allow you much time to react, particularly if you are not near your **first-aid kit**! At the first signs that a reaction has become systemic, you need to administer a drug called *epinephrine* into the subcutaneous tissues of the patient. This requires you to have two things: first, the epinephrine, and second, the training to administer it. Epinephrine is a prescription drug that usually comes in premeasured doses, so all you have to

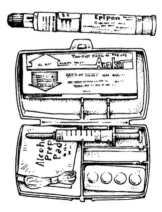

Epi-Pens (top) and Ana-kits (bottom) are used to treat anaphylactic reactions.

know is where and how to give the injection. Although easy, the process does require specialized training. Improper use of epinephrine can be dangerous. People who are aware that they are likely to experience an anaphylactic reaction to a toxin will often carry their own emergency dose. If this is the case, they should always know exactly where it is located, and they should also tell you: if they can't administer the drug to themselves, you may be the only person who can do it for them. If you give someone epinephrine, you should always follow it up with a dose of Benadryl.

When **planning a trip** into the backcountry, be sure you know what your traveling companions are allergic to and how severe their reactions may be. Plan ahead and be prepared for the nuances of common allergies with the appropriate prescription medications and such over-the-counter drugs as Benadryl. While Benadryl may make you drowsy, it can often alleviate the symptoms of some allergic reactions. If you are planning a very remote trip, obtain training in anaphylaxis and carry some epinephrine. While the likelihood that you will need such a drug is minimal, it's well worth carrying a few doses just in case.

ALTIMETERS

An altimeter, a device that tells you the height of your location, can be useful for both navigation and weather forecasting (see **weather**).

Altimeters measure air pressure. As air pressure lessens with height, an altimeter converts the amount of pressure to calculate the altitude. Of course, the fact that air pressure also changes with the weather must also be taken into account. If the pressure drops, the altimeter will indicate that you are higher than you actually are. If the pressure rises, the altimeter will indicate that you are lower than you actually are. To be as accurate as possible, an altimeter should be reset whenever you know the exact height by referring to a **map** or trail guide, such as on a summit, on a pass, or by a lake.

For navigation and for timing a mountain hike, an altimeter can help keep track of altitude so you will know how fast you are ascending or descending and can easily find your position on a topographic map (see **navigation**). An altimeter can also tell you when you need to change direction. For example, if you're descending a gentle ridge that you want to leave when you reach 5,500 feet and descend more steeply down one side, keeping an eye on the altimeter will show you when you have reached that height. This can be particularly useful in mist, dense **forest**, or featureless terrain.

For weather forecasting, you simply need to check whether the altimeter is giving accurate readings. A reading on the high side means the pressure is dropping and stormy weather may be on the way; if it's on the low side, pressure is building and the weather should improve or stay fair. Rapid changes in either direction mean faster changes in the weather and often also strong **winds**. The easiest way to use an altimeter for forecasting is when you're in one place for a long period, such as in camp. Many altimeters can keep a record of changes over a period of time so—for example, in the morning you can see what has happened overnight. With most altimeters, you can change the readings to give the actual air pressure rather than the height, if you wish to track the changes this way.

Modern electronic altimeters usually have other features, including the ability to tell you your rate of ascent or descent and to record the total ascent, descent, and time for a trip (although keep in mind that any big changes in the weather can make ascent totals inaccurate).

ALTITUDE SICKNESS

The higher the altitude, the lower the atmospheric pressure. This means less oxygen in the blood. The body can adjust to this, at least at altitudes below 18,000 feet, but it takes time. Up to 8,000 feet, problems rarely occur, but above that many people start to notice the effects. Breathlessness and a need to walk more slowly than usual, especially uphill, are normal at first, especially if you ascend to high altitudes quickly. More unpleasant is acute mountain sickness (AMS), the symptoms of which include headaches, loss of appetite, dizziness, nausea, and vomiting. To avoid or at least reduce AMS, gain height slowly (no more than 1,000 feet a day above 14,000 feet) and drink plenty of fluids (**dehydration** makes the condition worse). Spending a few days at a moderate altitude (6,000 to 8,000 feet) can help too. (If AMS does occur, it

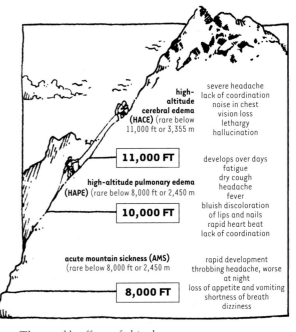

The possible effects of altitude.

can be relieved by descending—you certainly shouldn't ascend any higher. AMS should disappear in a few days.) Keep in mind that altitude increases dehydration, and dehydration manifests more quickly in arid desert peak climbing.

If the symptoms worsen rather than fade, descend immediately, as it could mean you are suffering from high-altitude cerebral or pulmonary edema, a buildup of fluid in the brain or the lungs that can kill.

Fitness doesn't affect altitude illnesses, so being very fit doesn't mean you can safely ascend more rapidly than someone who is unfit. Nor does altitude always affect people the same way each time they climb. You may have only mild effects on one trip yet feel awful on another.

ANCHORS

Anytime you use a **rope** for technical **rock climbing**, **mountaineering**, **canyoneering**, **caving**, or **rappelling**, you will need to build an anchor. An anchor is the part of a rope system that fixes the rope to the rock, **snow**, or **ice**. Because such a wide variety of outdoor activities employs ropes, it's good to have a basic understanding of anchors.

An anchor can be found at different places inside of a rope system. For example, when rappelling or **top roping**, the anchor will be at the top of the pitch and the rope will hang down from the anchor. When **multi-pitch climbing**, the anchor may be at the bottom of the pitch, below the lead climber. An anchor that secures a whitewater rescue rope may be tied around a submerged boulder. Regardless of the anchor's location, its goal remains the same: to attach the rope to a fixed object so it remains secure, even under tremendous tension.

An anchor can be as simple as a piece of webbing tied around a big tree, which is one type of natural protection. If you don't have natural protection nearby, you will have to rely on **artificial protection**, which can be placed in rock, snow, or ice. Either type of protection must be placed with precision to ensure adequate safety. By combining several pieces of well-placed artificial or natural protection, you can build a solid anchor. From your anchor, you can hang a rope, belay a climber, or execute a **rescue**. When building an anchor, keep four things in mind: adequate protection, equal load distribution, direction of pull, and redundancy.

Adequate Protection

Finding adequate protection isn't always easy. If you are surrounded by healthy trees or big, sturdy boulders, consider yourself lucky. Before you use them, however, be sure to evaluate them for structural integrity (see **natural protection**). If you are using natural protection for your anchor, it is ideal to rely on at least two different points of protection. For example, you might choose to sling a tree and also a boulder or to sling two boulders. If you are placing artificial protection, you'll want to have at least three different pieces to combine to create one anchor. Having this many pieces adds redundancy to your anchor, which will keep you safe in the off chance that something unexpectedly fails. Never attach your rope directly to your anchor. Instead, always use a **carabiner** (a locking biner is best) between the rope and the anchor. The frictional heat created when two pieces of rope rub against each other is enough to melt through either piece completely. In addition, a rope attached directly to an anchor increases the likelihood that the anchor will become dislodged.

Equal Load Distribution

Because a good anchor employs several points of protection, you need to consider how they should be connected. Your goal when connecting protection is to have each piece equally weighted when under tension; this type of anchor is called an *equalized anchor*. The simplest way to accomplish this task is to run a separate **sling** from each pro (that's short for *protection*) to the locking carabiner. This technique is simple, but it can take time to adjust each sling to the appropriate length. In addition, this technique does not always allow for a change in the direction of pull. Instead, many climbers will connect their pro using a technique that is self-equalizing even when the direction of pull changes. This means that no matter how the rope moves, the pro will always be weighted equally.

To create a self-equalizing anchor, connect all your protection with one large loop of webbing and clip a locking biner to the loop. Now take a section of webbing in between two pieces of pro and twist it 180 degrees, creating a small loop. Clip the same locking biner through this loop so that it is now attached to the same piece of webbing in two places. Repeat the process as necessary for each piece of protection.

As is, the self-equalizing technique is handy, but if one piece of your protection fails, it may shock load your system. Shock loading occurs when the system is suddenly presented with excess slack, allowing the loaded rope to drop. Even though this drop may only be a few feet, it can be a severe shock to the remaining pieces of protection. To prevent shock loading, take the self-equalizing anchor and tie an **overhand knot** just above the locking biner.

An equalized anchor. The angle between each piece of protection should be less than 90 degrees; any angle greater will add dangerous strain to the anchor.

Anytime you connect multiple pieces of protection, you need to consider the angle that separates each piece. Locate the point where the two pieces of protection come together (usually at the locking carabiner); from this point, the angle between each piece of protection should be no more than 90 degrees. Ideally, your protection should be close enough together that the angle between them is relatively small (30–60 degrees). If your pieces of protection are more than 90 degrees apart, you begin to place unnecessary strain on each piece.

Direction of Pull

Now that your anchor is coming together, check it to ensure that it is adequate for the anticipated direction of pull. This is critical. An anchor that

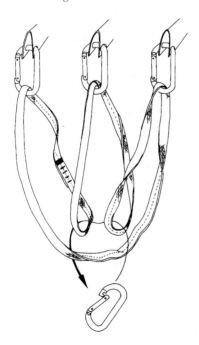

Equalizing an anchor ensures that each piece of protection is equally weighted.

works great in a downward direction of pull may fail completely if it is pulled to the side or from above. To test for the anticipated direction of pull, pull on the anchor's locking carabiner. Do the pieces of protection get equal tension?

Redundancy

The last thing you need to double-check is the redundancy in your anchor. Ask yourself the following questions: What would happen if one piece of protection pulled out or failed? What would happen if a carabiner broke? What would happen if a piece of webbing failed? A redundant system provides safety despite a failure.

Because your life depends on the quality of the anchor that you build, it is essential that you do it right. Reading about anchor-building techniques is not enough; you must get your hands dirty with hours of practice (preferably supervised) before you even consider building your own anchors. Furthermore, various circumstances can require advanced techniques and special considerations. For more information on anchor building, consider reading the following books: *The Complete Climber's Handbook*, by Jerry Cinnamon; *Climbing Anchors*, by John Long; and *Mountaineering*, edited by Don Graydon and Kurt Hanson.

APPALACHIAN TRAIL

The Appalachian Trail was the first designated National Scenic Trail and is America's most famous long-distance trail. Along with the **Pacific Crest** and **Continental Divide** Trails it forms part of the **Triple Crown**, awarded by the American Long Distance Hiking Association–West to hikers who complete the three great trails. First conceived by Benton MacKaye in 1921, the trail was finally completed in 1937. It runs continuously for some 2,160 miles (the exact distance varies from year to year due to trail relocations) from Springer Mountain in Georgia along the crest of the Appalachian Mountains to Mount Katahdin in Maine. Every year several thousand hikers set out to walk the whole trail in one go,

known as *thru-hiking*. However, only two hundred or so succeed each year. The first thru-hike was achieved by Earl Shaffer in 1948. Half a century later he returned and thru-hiked the trail again. Many thousands more people hike short sections of the trail, which is easily accessible from many cities.

The Appalachian Trail is a forest trail, sometimes dubbed the "long green tunnel," with only a few sections, such as that in the White Mountains of New Hampshire, above timberline. It's also known as the "people's trail" due to the large numbers who hike it, many starting on the same dates. Towns along the way organize "trail days" and other events for the annual influx of hikers.

The trail is for hikers only, not equestrians or mountain bikers. White **blazes** mark the entire route. There are many shelters along the way, roughly a day's walk apart. This doesn't mean it is an easy walk, however, as there are many steep climbs and some rough and rocky terrain. Most thru-hikers spend five to six months on the trail.

For more information, consult the Appalachian Trail Conference.

ARTIFICIAL PROTECTION

In the early days of climbing, enthusiastic and daring British climbers would flock to the cliffs created when railroad beds were cut deep into hillsides. Stories tell how climbers would unscrew the bolts from the railroad ties and use them as protection for their lead climbers—a daring venture to say the least! Luckily, the evolution of artificial protection, or *pro*, has provided the climbing community with a full range of finely engineered devices that can be used in just about any situation. Nowadays, artificial protection can be categorized as passive pro, spring-loaded pro, and fixed pro. The first two are discussed below; for the third, see **fixed protection**.

Passive Protection

Passive protection is any kind of protection with no moving parts. Common types of passive pros are nuts, hexes, and tri-cams. Passive pro can be further divided into pieces that wedge and pieces that cam. Most climbers don't distinguish much between these, but to be technical, you should understand the difference. A wedging pro, like a stopper or nut, will fit into a constricting crack. The piece is set so that it only becomes more and more wedged when tension is placed in the anticipated direction of pull. Passive protection, which is built to cam like a hexcentric (or *hex* for short), differs only slightly. These pieces can be used in constricting cracks as well as cracks that are parallel. In a parallel crack, a camming device, such as the hex or tri-cam, will rotate under tension into one side of the crack, allowing the piece to lock into place.

Many different types of passive protection can be found on the market. As a general rule, the bigger the piece, the stronger it is. The reason for this is that bigger pros have more surface area, and when placing protection you want to have as much surface contact as possible between the rock and the pro. Needless to say, this guideline is true only if the protection is well placed. The strongest protection in the world won't do you any good if you don't know how to judge adequate placement.

Available in a variety of shapes and sizes, all passive protection is designed to wedge or cam into cracks. The first four biners show various nuts and the biner on the far right shows hexcentrics.

Spring-Loaded Protection

Any protection that is mechanical, or has moving parts, is spring loaded. Most spring-loaded devices are camming devices and are referred to as *SLCDs* (spring-loaded camming devices). Common SLCDs are Camalots, made by Black Diamond; Friends, made by Wild Country; and the TCU, also known as the *three-cam unit*, manufactured by Metolius. SLCDs use three or four cams that individually rotate on an axis. When you pull a trigger on the piece's stem, the cams retract, allowing you to place the piece in a narrow crack. Once you let go of the trigger, the cams release, allowing them to expand in the crack. Because the cams can expand to varying degrees, the SLCD is very versatile and easy to place. Spring-loaded wedging devices are less common. These pros use the same concept of an axle controlled by a trigger, but instead of retracting cams, they retract wedges. The invention of spring-loaded devices (mainly SLCDs) brought climbing to new heights, literally.

Placing Protection

Learning to place solid protection, either passive or spring loaded, takes time. It is worth seeking out a skilled climber who can teach you how to evaluate your placement. This is important stuff: not only will your life depend on your ability to place solid protection, but so too will the life of your climbing partner. A well-placed pro is achieved by first choosing the right piece of gear for a specific crack or pocket and then finding the absolute best placement inside the crack. As already mentioned, one of the most important ingredients in placing solid protection is getting lots of surface area contact between the rock and the pro. While each type of protection requires familiarity to place it correctly, the following guidelines can be used for general pro placement.

• Determine the quality of the rock. In the big picture, how does the rock look? Is it a solid rock face, or are you using a flake? Is there a chance

ANNIE AGGENS

A correctly placed spring-loaded camming device with a quickdraw: the cams are equally retracted to mid-range, and they have good surface contact. The device is placed far enough into the crack that it won't accidentally pop out but is close enough to the surface to retrieve easily.

that any part of the rock could become loose? Upon close examination of the rock, are there many crystals that prevent firm surface contact with your pro? Is there lichen or dirt in the crack? If so, you may want to look elsewhere.

• Is the crack constricting? Flaring? Is it a parallel crack? This will determine what type of protection you use. Remember to look for constricting cracks if you are going to use any type of a wedging pro, such as a stopper.

• Determine the most likely direction of pull, and then place your pro accordingly. Remember to plan for a certain amount of outward pull. Avoid placing pros near the edge of a crack. Rather, opt for a position inside the crack, but not so far in that it is difficult to assess the piece or remove it.

• If the stem of your pro is rigid, such as on a Friend, avoid placing it in a horizontal position that could subject the stem to torque. Instead, find a position that points the stem in the anticipated direction of pull.

• If using an SLCD, be careful not to place it in too small of a crack. This will cause you to overcam the device by pulling back too far on the trigger. An overcammed pro has compromised strength and is difficult to retrieve. The cams on an SLCD are most effective when deployed 10 to 50 percent.

• Use a quickdraw (a short piece of webbing with biners on either end) or a **sling** (with biners) to connect the rope to your protection. A rope should never be clipped directly to a piece of protection, as drag on the rope could alter the position of the pro, possibly rendering it useless.

• Make sure that you are able to retrieve your protection. Not only is it expensive, but leaving gear behind becomes an eyesore and can be dangerous for those who follow.

AURORA BOREALIS

Look in the sky! Is it a UFO? Ah, it's the aurora borealis! The aurora borealis (from the Latin for "northern dawn"), also known as the *northern lights*, is a luminous display that dances across the sky in the northern **latitudes**. It is a beautiful and seemingly mysterious exhibition of light that has mesmerized humans since the beginning of time. As a full spectrum of colors play in the sky, the observer is treated to a truly amazing optical phenomenon.

The aurora has ignited many colorful myths about why it exists and what power it possesses. An old Inuit tradition states that the aurora is the highest level of heaven. In the aurora, no **snow** falls, it is never stormy, and animals are easily caught. Another legend advises women to avoid going outside bareheaded when the aurora is present, lest the aurora come down and grab their hair. One last legend, believe it or not, says that you should protect yourself from the aurora by carrying a **knife** and, if possible, throwing frozen dog excrement and urine in its general direction. The traditional Greek term for the aurora is *pluvia sanguinea*, or "blood rain." The traditional Chinese term is *thien lieh*, or "cracks in heaven." Needless to say, our relationship with the aurora is enduring and fascinating.

The aurora is simply particles in the ionosphere that get charged by electrons found in solar rays. Like a neon sign, the particles light up when they become charged. The color of the light depends on what gases are abundant in the area. Typically, green and yellow auroras come from oxygen atoms, while rarer colors, such as violet, come from nitrogen atoms. The best place to see the aurora is in the auroral zone, an area approximately 1,500 miles from the north and south magnetic poles that has the highest intensity of solar electrons in the ionosphere. If you don't frequent the auroral zone, you aren't out of luck, however. Periodic solar storms can cause charged electrons to create auroras in far lower latitudes. This is especially true if the sun happens to be at the end of an 11-year sunspot cycle (the last cycle ended in 2000). Galileo first named this natural wonder after Aurora, the Roman goddess of the dawn. In the Southern Hemisphere, the phenomena is called *aurora australis*.

AVALANCHES

Avalanches are one of the greatest potential dangers to travelers in snow-covered **mountains**. Even small slides can kill. All who travel in avalanche country should know how to judge the safety of a slope, how to travel as safely as possible, and what to do in the event of an avalanche. They should also be carrying the appropriate equipment (as discussed below).

Types of Avalanche

There are two basic types of avalanche. The first type, the loose snow avalanche, begins at a single point and then spreads as it descends. These powder avalanches, in which the snow is airborne, can be incredibly destructive. The second type, the slab avalanche, occurs when a block of snow breaks away and slides as a unit, leaving behind a fracture line known as the *crown wall*. Slab avalanches, which are usually triggered by the victim or victims, are involved in most accidents.

Avalanche Conditions

Where and when avalanches are likely to occur can be predicted, though such forecasting isn't exact. The three main factors involved are the **weather**, the terrain, and the snowpack. All must be taken into account.

Most avalanches occur on slopes of between 25 and 45 degrees. The angle of a slope can be measured with a slope meter or clinometer, or you can also use a pair of ski or **hiking** poles. Stand one pole upright in the snow; then hold the other one at a right angle to the first, with the tip on the snow. Move the tip down the snow until the handle touches the upright pole. If this contact occurs at the top of the handle, the slope is 45 degrees; if halfway down, about 25 degrees.

The angle alone doesn't mean an avalanche is likely, however. The nature of the terrain and the shape of the slope also matter. Smooth, unbroken slopes of large rock slabs or short grass don't hold the snow very well, unlike rough slopes of boulders and bushes. Convex slopes are more dangerous than concave ones because the snow

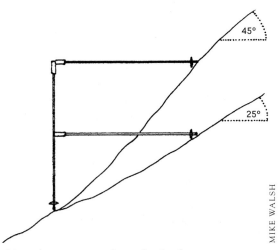

Use poles to measure the angle of a slope.

MIKE WALSH

slab avalanche occurrence

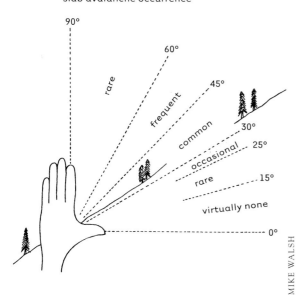

MIKE WALSH

How to estimate the angle of a slope to see the likelihood of an avalanche. Bear in mind that slope angle is just one of a number of important factors to take into account when evaluating avalanche probability.

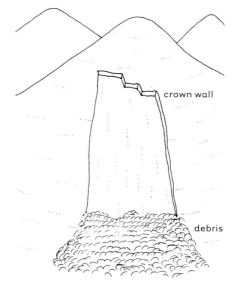

MIKE WALSH

Diagram of a slab avalanche. The crown wall is the line at which the avalanche broke away from the snow above. Avalanche debris often consists of large unstable blocks and should be avoided as it can be hazardous.

is stretched and pulled apart rather than compressed. Gullies are dangerous too, because any slides will be funneled down them, becoming deeper and more powerful than slides on open slopes.

Whatever their angle, underlying terrain, or shape, many slopes are still safe as long as the snow has consolidated and bonded together. Here the weather comes into play. During storms and for twenty-four hours following a storm, especially one that dumps a large quantity of snow, avalanches are likely. When it's very cold, with no thawing of the snowpack, snow can't consolidate and the danger may last for weeks. In spring, heavy **rain** and consistently warm temperatures can destabilize the snowpack, leading to avalanches. Freeze-and-thaw conditions—cold at night, warm during the day—can stabilize the snowpack, however.

Wind direction is also very important. Windblown snow, known as *wind slab*, can be very dangerous. It builds up on lee slopes, so knowing the

direction of the wind during storms that occurred before your trip can help you predict where wind slab is likely to be. On the ground, you can look for **cornices** (see also **snow**). If you see any, there is likely to be wind slab below them.

The pattern of snowfall over the season matters too, because each storm puts down a layer of snow. How well these layers bond can determine whether avalanches are likely.

Testing the Snow

To gain an idea of how safe a slope might be, dig a snow pit to check the consistency of each layer and see whether they slide easily over each other. There are several ways of doing this. Perhaps the simplest is to dig a pit on a slope that has the same angle and aspect as the one you want to cross, making sure that this is in a safe place. With your shovel (see **snow shovels**), dig a pit a few feet wide and either down to the ground or to what seems to be stable, consolidated snow. Level off the back of the pit, and then check the layers of

When you're doing the finger test to check the layers in a snow pit, sudden changes in snow consistency are a sign of instability.

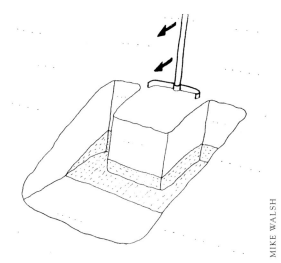

Using a shovel to test snow stability.

snow by gently poking your finger or a thin object, such as a pen, into the snow from top to bottom. Look for sudden changes in consistency, which often indicate instability.

Once you've done the finger test, mark out on the back of the pit a rectangle about as wide and deep as the shovel blade. Dig out the sides of this rectangle to isolate a column of snow; then slide the shovel blade down the back of the column and pull it gently toward you. Keep increasing the pressure until a layer slides off. If this doesn't happen, the snow is stable. However, if a layer of snow breaks away with very little pressure, the snow is unstable. Keep doing this down the back of the column until you reach the bottom of the pit. The snowpack may have more than one unstable layer. This test takes time. While you're traveling across snow, you can occasionally poke the shaft of your **ice ax** or the handle of your ski pole into the snow and see what resistance you find. If the snow suddenly "gives," you may have hit an unstable layer.

Minimizing the Danger

It is impossible to ever say that a snow slope is totally safe. Knowing previous weather patterns and having an up-to-date avalanche forecast are a good start, but even if the latter says the danger is low, it doesn't mean every slope is safe. Conditions can change quickly with variations in temperature or wind direction, never mind from fresh snow. Always make your own observations. Small slides, cornice collapses, or balls of snow rolling down a slope may all indicate avalanche danger. Snow settling under your feet or sounding hollow or cracking suggests wind slab that isn't bonded well to the layer below.

When choosing routes, remember that buttresses and ridges are safer than open slopes and bowls and that gullies can be very dangerous—even crossing their bases can be risky. Wooded slopes are usually safer than open ones, especially if the trees are fairly large. Small trees may suggest that the slope avalanches regularly, preventing consistent growth. Many forested mountainsides have obvious avalanche paths, channels of tree-less ground running down between the trees.

When traveling in avalanche country, always choose the safest route. Learning how to do this comes from experience and careful observation of the terrain. If in doubt, take another route. If you feel there is no alternative to crossing a suspicious slope, cross one person at a time so only one person is ever exposed to the apparent danger. Always aim for rocks, ridges, bare ground, or other safer areas. Cross a slope as high as possible so that, if you trigger an avalanche, most of the snow is below you. Watch each person cross, and keep an eye out for signs of an avalanche starting.

If an Avalanche Strikes

If you're caught in an avalanche, your main aim should be to stay on top of the snow. Initially, ram your poles or ice ax into the snow or grab a rock or tree and try to hang on. If you are swept down, get rid of your poles, ice ax, skis, and **pack,** and try to stay on the surface, making swimming motions or rolling to the side. Keep your mouth closed when under the snow, and keep a hand over your mouth when the fall ends to clear a breathing space. As you come to a halt, push upward and try to get at least an arm out of the snow. If you're buried and unable to move, all you can do is wait. Unless you know searchers are close at hand, there's no point in shouting; it just wastes energy and air.

People buried in an avalanche depend on their companions to find them as quickly as possible. A search should be mounted immediately. Don't go for help unless you're in a large group and can spare a person. There may not be time. However, before beginning a search, check that the slope is safe. The safety of the party comes first: you don't want anyone to be buried in a secondary slide.

Try to keep in sight anyone avalanched, and note the last place they were seen. The initial search should be in a direct line below that point. Start by looking for anything on the surface—items of gear or a hand sticking out of the snow.

Searches need to be organized and systematic. Ideally, everyone should be wearing an avalanche beacon or transceiver—an electronic receiver/transmitter—that is switched to transmit while you are traveling. Beacons should be worn inside clothes so they are unlikely to be ripped off in an avalanche. A beacon search can locate a buried person quite quickly, especially if you are well practiced, as you should be. There are different types of beacons and different ways of searching. Make sure you are familiar with your beacon and the best way to use it.

When you locate a victim with a beacon, avalanche probes can be used to see how far down the person is and to confirm their position. Collapsible probes are available, and some ski poles can be converted to probes. If you don't have a probe, you can use ski poles, skis, or ice axes, although these aren't as effective. When victims are found, use snow shovels to dig them out.

If you don't have an avalanche beacon or you know the victim doesn't have one, you will have to search by probing. This is a slow but necessary process. First probe in the most likely areas: below the point where the victim was last seen and where pieces of gear have been found. Those involved in a probe search should stand shoulder to shoulder, probe directly in front, then move uphill one pace and probe again. If the victim isn't found, the searchers should immediately start probing again adjacent to the first search area.

Once someone has been rescued from an avalanche, make sure she can breathe properly; also keep her warm—otherwise, **hypothermia** is likely to set in.

To learn more about avalanches and avalanche safety, study one of the following books: *Avalanche Safety for Skiers and Climbers*, by Tony Daffern; *The Avalanche Handbook*, by David McClung and Peter Schaerer; and *Snow Sense*, by Jill Fredston and Doug Fesler. Also consider taking an avalanche safety course offered by the American Avalanche Association or the Canadian Avalanche Association.

B

BACKPACKING

Backpacking is walking with everything you need to stay out for more than a day on your back. Backpackers may stay out for a night, a week, or many months. Their loads may weigh 10 pounds or 60 pounds or anywhere in between. To be a competent backpacker requires hiking and camping skills and familiarity with the specific terrain and environment. Backpacking isn't just about equipment, skills, or the **weight** of your load, though. Backpacking is about enjoying nature and experiencing the **wilderness** to the full by living in it night and day. How you do it is up to you.

See also **camping** and **hiking**. For information on equipment, see **packs**.

BAILOUT POINTS

A bailout point is any location on a trip where you have access to outside help. A bailout point can be a ranger station, **fishing** lodge, hunting camp, mine, weather station, or even a road. It can be used to call a doctor, plan an **evacuation**, or simply let someone know you are going to be delayed. Before you begin a **wilderness** outing, it is a good idea to determine all the potential bailout points along your entire route. There is no rule as to how many bailout points you should have on a trip, but it should be obvious that the farther you get from a bailout point, the more

severe the consequences of an accident will become.

Once you have located a potential bailout point, make sure it will be available for your use. For instance, if the bailout is a ranger station, will it be staffed? If it's a fishing camp, will it be open? A locked cabin in the woods doesn't help much when you need to access the outside world. Also find out how the facility might be able to help you. Does it have a radio or phone? Is there fresh **water** available? Does it have access to a road? What about a float plane or a helicopter? This is especially important if you're planning a remote trip where bailout points are few and far between. Calling ahead to bailout points can be a great way to learn about local conditions, such as water or **snow** levels, **fire** bans, and so forth. Be polite, and remember that in most cases it is not the job of these facilities to cater to, or **rescue**, wilderness travelers.

> "I have been on many 40- to 50-day trips where the only bailout points were the beginning and end. Needless to say, precaution was the order of the day!"—AA

To locate bailout points, review your **maps** for any buildings, roads, or other human-made structures along your route. Local officials may be able to provide additional information regarding the status of the facilities, such as whether they are still in use. They may also have suggestions for additional or more convenient bailout points. In the **trip plan** that you leave behind with a friend or family member, include your bailout points and indicate which one you will go to if you run into trouble on any given day. Before the trip, review your bailout points with all members of your party. This will leave you better prepared for an emergency.

BAKING

If you have never melted butter over a steaming slice of freshly baked backcountry bread or watched your pizza dough rise to perfection, then you are in for a treat. Baking in the backcountry is easy, fun, and very satisfying. It also breaks up the monotony of the one-pot meals that are so often the standard. All you need to bake a culinary delight is a good pot or baking device and a few basic ingredients. Breads, biscuits, pizza crusts, cinnamon rolls, doughnuts, and countless other treats can all be made from flour, sugar, and yeast. If that sounds too complicated, you can find many premixed bread and cake mixtures that work almost as well and take less preparation.

The key to good baking lies as much in the process as it does in the ingredients. Without the right technique, you can easily burn one part of the dish while leaving another part uncooked. Start by finding a good baking pan or other baking device. The best baking pans heat up evenly and disperse a constant supply of heat to the **food** inside. To get a golden brown result each time you bake, use the following tips.

- If **cooking** over a fire, build up a pile of smoldering coals (see **fires**) and nestle your pan in its midst. Shovel some coals on to the cover of the pan. If the pan is thin, keep an eye on the food to ensure that it doesn't burn. For this reason, try to find a pan that absorbs heat well without searing the contents. Cast iron works great, although it is very heavy.

- If baking over a stove flame, rotate your pan every so often so the flame heats up more than one part of the pan. This is often called *round-the-clock baking*.
- Build a twiggy fire on the pan lid. This will provide a source of heat that surrounds your food almost entirely.
- If baking over the constant flame of a stove, place a flame disperser, such as a sturdy pot lid, directly over the flame and then put your pan over the disperser. The disperser will absorb the brunt of the heat and disperse it evenly to the pan. This also works great for making golden brown pancakes!
- If you are using an MSR stove or any other stove with a bendable yet sturdy windshield (see **stoves**), you can create a chimney from the windscreen by wrapping the screen around the stove and securing the screen so it doesn't pop open. Your baking pan can then be placed atop the chimney. This helps the contents bake more evenly, but it may lengthen baking times.

> "On a trek in Nepal, I was amazed at the quality and variety of baked goods—everything from savory breads to chocolate cake—produced by the Sherpa cook using heavy-duty aluminum pans over a cast-iron kerosene burner. He did spend hours cooking, mind you."—CT

Baking Devices

The traditional Dutch oven is a hefty cast-iron monster that's fine for horse packers and standing camps but not for self-propelled **wilderness** travel (see **Dutch oven**). However, lightweight versions made from hard anodized aluminum are available. These have a shallow well in the lid so you can light a small fire of twigs on top to ensure more even overall heating. They double as frying pans too. The lightest models weigh around 10 ounces.

Dutch ovens require the use of a fire on the lid. Other lightweight ovens can be used on a camp stove without a fire. The most sophisticated, the **Outback Oven**, involves a fiberglass convection dome that fits over the pot, a foil reflector to direct heat upward, a flame disperser to spread the heat evenly, and even a tiny **thermometer** so you can regulate the heat. This sounds like a lot to carry, yet the total weight is no more than 7 ounces in the lightest version.

Much simpler is the Bakepacker, basically a metal grid that sits in the bottom of a pot, on which you place the goods to be baked in a plastic bag. It's easy to use and lightweight—4 or 9 ounces depending on the size—but won't allow a crust to form.

Simple baked goods can be produced by putting a cake or similar mix in an oven bag, then placing it in boiling water for 10 minutes or so. For **desert** cooking, campers also can make use of solar ovens. With practice, a good cook can produce delicious baked goods with the most basic implements.

The best way to improve your backcountry baking skills is to experiment. Don't plan to do a lot of baking if you are trying to cram a lot of miles into a short trip. Chances are good that, when it comes time to cook, you'll be so tired you'll want to eat something quick and easy. Instead, plan to bake on shorter-distance days, when you will have time to enjoy messing around in the **camp kitchen**. A number of good backcountry cookbooks offer wonderful recipes for trail cooking. One perennial favorite is *The NOLS Cookery*, by Claudia Pearson (see **NOLS**). Find a cookbook you like, and then copy or memorize the recipes of your favorite meals. You'll be sure to impress all who venture into your kitchen.

BANDANNA

The humble bandanna is a very useful item in the **wilderness**. This simple square of **cotton** can be used as a headband, brow wipe, handkerchief, pot holder, dishcloth, flannel, towel, triangular bandage, neck protector, water filter for large particulates, general-purpose mop, shoe wiper, and much more. To keep them relatively clean, bandannas can be easily rinsed out and hung on the back of your **pack** to dry.

> "On hot days, I carry a bandanna attached to my pack's shoulder straps so I can wipe my face with it whenever necessary."—CT

Freshly baked goods, such as this coffee cake, are a special treat in the backcountry.

ANNIE AGGENS

BANNOCK

Spend any time in the North—from Nova Scotia to the Yukon—and you will soon become familiar with a time-honored, trail-honed recipe for bannock. This flour-based bread was a staple among the early explorers of the North. Many a yarn was spun around the campfire while waiting for the bannock to bake. A good bannock recipe was jealously guarded because once it became known it traveled as fast as any river.

A typical bannock recipe called for a mixture of lard, flour, baking powder, and salt—all common ingredients in any voyageur's **food** sack. For every heaping handful of flour, the cook added a pinch of salt, several pinches of baking powder, and a scoop of lard. Just enough water was added to create a stiff dough to be rolled into fist-sized balls and flattened into thin cakes. An experienced outdoorsperson could bake the bannock directly over the smoldering coals of a **fire**, turning it occasionally until it was golden brown and then resting it near the heat (perhaps propped up on a stick) until it had risen sufficiently. Although less exciting, most people today cook their bannock in a greased frying pan (preferably cast iron), which bakes the bannock evenly and thoroughly.

Bannock is still very much a part of traveling in the North. Variations to the traditional recipes can be found in cookbooks and on many websites. One popular alternate is to wrap the bannock dough around the end of a stick and roast it like a marshmallow until golden brown. Others call for the addition of berries, nuts, honey, cornmeal, or oatmeal. Adding diced cheese and lots of garlic to the dough will produce a cheesy delight while **baking**. Bannock has remained a favorite trail food because of its practicality and versatility—so be sure to experiment. Author Sigurd Olson, who celebrates life in the North in his *Listening Point, The Lonely Land,* and *Reflections from the North,* summed up the romantic ideal of bannock best: "Store bread is for city folk, say old-timers, bannock is for the bush."

BEAR BAGGING

Protecting your **food** supplies from **bears** is essential in many areas, especially grizzly country and places where black bears associate humans with food. There are two basic ways to do this: hanging your food (bear bagging) or using a **bear-resistant container**.

The traditional method of bear bagging still works well in many places, as long as it is done properly. However, it does require practice and a little effort. In some areas, such as **Yosemite** National Park in California, bears are likely to get any food that isn't hung perfectly.

For bear bagging you need at least 50 feet of nylon cord and one or two tough stuff sacks for your food. A small stuff sack for holding a rock can be useful too.

Some **camping** areas provide poles or cables for hanging your food. Some even have pulley systems to haul your food up. Usually, though, you will have to find a suitable branch. Figures for how high above the ground food should be hung, how far below a branch, and how far from the trunk of the tree vary, but 12 feet above the ground, 6 feet below the branch, and 10 feet from the trunk of the tree should be ample.

The simplest way to hang food is to tie a stuff sack with a rock in it to the end of your cord, throw it over your selected branch, haul up the food bag, and then tie off the line as high as you can reach around the trunk of the tree. This will only work in areas where bears don't seek food in campsites, because they quickly learn that breaking a cord will produce a bag of food.

Where no suitable branches can be found, suspend food bags between two trees about 25 feet apart. To do this, throw one end of the line over a branch and tie it to the tree trunk. Next, tie the food bag to the center of the line. Finally, throw the other end of the line over a branch on the second tree, haul up the food bag until it is halfway between the trees and 12 feet off the ground, and tie off the line around the trunk. Again, this method only works where bears don't raid campsites for food.

The most secure way of hanging food—though even this won't always work against Yosemite bears— is counterbalancing. This is not easy. To do it, throw the line over a branch about 20 feet up and then tie a food bag to the end of the line. Next, haul the bag up to the branch and tie a second food bag (or bag of rocks, if you haven't enough food) that weighs the same to the other end of the line. Then chuck the second bag

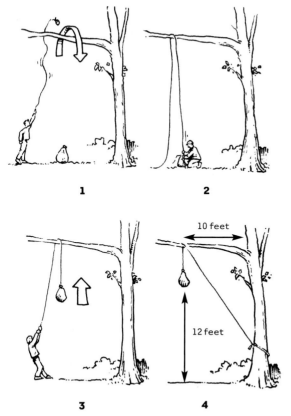

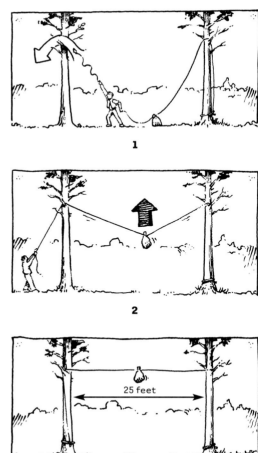

Hanging food from a long branch to protect it from bears. 1. Put a small rock in a small stuff sack. Tie the end of your line to the sack and toss it over a branch about 20 feet high, keeping hold of the other end of the rope. If you can't reach the rock, shake the line in a whipping motion to jerk the line over the branch, and slowly lower the rock. 2. Grab the end of the line and remove the rock. 3. Attach your food sack and haul it up. 4. Wrap the end of the rope around the tree trunk and tie it off.

into the air so that both bags end up 12 feet or more above the ground and 10 feet away from the tree trunk. Tie a loop in the line next to one of the food bags. Retrieve the bags by hooking this loop with a long stick.

Hanging food is difficult and time consuming. After spending ages trying to get your line in the right place and freeing it from snags, you might feel like giving up or making do with improperly

Suspending food between two trees in bear country. 1. Attach your food bag to the center of the line and attach a rock to one end of the line. Toss the rock over a branch and tie the end of the rope around the tree trunk. Toss the other end of the rope over a branch of the other tree. 2. Tug on the free end of the rope, raising the food sack slowly. 3. Tie the second rope end around the second tree trunk.

hung food, but persevere. Otherwise, you might lose your food. Another option is to use an Ur-sack (see below) or a bear-resistant container.

Where there are no trees or none big enough to hang food from, you will have to store your food on the ground. If storing your food in an ordinary stuff sack, double-bag food in plastic bags

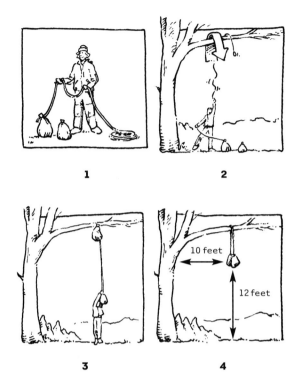

1   **2**

10 feet

12 feet

3   **4**

Counterbalancing in bear country. 1. Start with two stuff sacks of roughly equal weight (if you have to, add stones or gravel to one in order to equalize the weight). Tie one end of your line to one of the sacks. 2. Tie a rock to the other end of the line. Toss the rock over a suitable branch. 3. Haul the first stuff sack up until it's just below the branch. Tie the second stuff sack to the "rock" end of the line (remove the rock) while holding the sack as high as you can. Stuff any spare line into the sack. 4. Throw the second stuff sack up so the two bags are at an equal height. To retrieve, use a trekking pole or stick to haul down one of the bags.

and do not carry smelly foods. You could also submerge food in deep water at the end of a line, hang it down a rock face, or wedge it into a crack in a cliff.

Most bear bagging is done with the food in an ordinary nylon stuff sack. If a bear gets this type of sack, your food is lost. However, one stuff sack, the Ursack, is made from tough Aramid fibers (like those used for bulletproof vests), which bears can't rip or bite into. An Ursack needs to be tied to a tree trunk or a strong branch to stop a bear from running off with it, but it doesn't have to be hung out of reach. Bears can crush the contents of the sack but can't get into it if it's used correctly. Note that in some areas of the High Sierra in California, however, Ursacks do not meet the regulations and bear-resistant containers are mandatory. The big advantages of Ursacks over containers are **weight** and ease of packing. An Ursack with a 600-cubic-inch capacity weighs 5 ounces, whereas a similar-sized container weighs 2.7 pounds. Because an Ursack weighs little more than the ordinary stuff sack it replaces, it doesn't add much to your load. Also, unlike ordinary stuff sacks, Ursacks will also protect your food from other creatures, such as mice (see **mice and other rodents**) and raccoons (although not **wolves**, according to its makers). In most areas, Ursacks could prove the best solution for protecting your food. (For more information on Ursacks, see the resources section.)

When hanging your food, include such items as sunscreen, soap, insect repellent, and anything else that could smell like food to a bear. Always hang or store your food downwind from your site so any curious bears do not have to pass through your campsite to get to it.

> "When camping in the northern Yukon, where the only trees are small spruces, I stored my food on the ground in two separate bags, each placed a hundred yards from camp and a hundred yards from each other. I never lost any food, but this is clearly not that safe a method."—CT

BEARINGS

A bearing is a direction relative to due north and is given in degrees east of north. Bearings are measured with an **orienteering** or protractor **compass**.

See also **navigation**.

BEAR-REPELLENT PEPPER SPRAY

Bear-repellent sprays squirt a mist of very hot ground peppers that irritates the bear and may deter it from attacking you. Evidence suggests that the sprays can work, though they may not do so every time with every bear. They are a final resort but not a substitute for taking all of the other precautions (see **bears**). Sprays weigh from 12 to 16 ounces, and the spray reaches a distance of 18 to 30 feet, depending on the make. That means the bear has to be very, very close to you before it's worth using the spray. And remember that in a crosswind or heavy **rain**, the spray won't reach even close to the maximum distance. Each spray gives one 4- to 10-second burst, and then it's empty. To be of any use, the spray must be easily available. It's no use in your **pack**. Keep it on your belt or on a chest harness. While in camp, sleep with it by your side. When you don't need the spray, keep it well wrapped so that if it goes off by accident it doesn't do any harm. Take time to practice with your spray in advance. You don't want to be trying to work out how to fire one with a grizzly charging you. These sprays work only when sprayed in a bear's face. Spraying it on gear or clothing will not deter bears, and in fact the smell may attract bears.

Note that sprays are illegal on commercial aircraft in either carry-on or checked baggage. If traveling by air, you'll need to buy one at your destination.

BEAR-RESISTANT CONTAINERS

The most dependable way to keep **bears** from getting your **food** is to use a bear-resistant container, often called a *bear can*. These are made from hard plastic or aircraft-grade aluminum. Bears can't get their jaws around the containers, nor can they hook their claws into any part of the surface. The flat lids close with screws that can be easily opened with a coin or multitool. In camp, bear cans are great. They can be used as seats or tables (but don't put hot pots or **stoves** on the plastic ones, as they can melt), and storing them just means leaving them 100 yards from your **tent**.

Now for the disadvantages: they are heavy, bulky, and expensive, and they don't hold much food. The lightest (and most costly) one available holds 650 cubic inches and weighs 1.8 pounds. A more affordable but heavier one of the same size weighs 2.7 pounds. Because they're rigid, they are awkward to fit into a **pack**. Standing them up and packing soft items around them seems to be the best way to pack them. The smaller ones, which measure around 9 by 12 inches, are said to hold six days' worth of food for one person, but to carry this amount you really have to compress the food and squash it in the container. Rebagging everything into plastic bags helps, and don't bother with crushable items like crackers or cookies. Remember, too, that you need room for sunscreen, soap, insect repellent, and any other items that might smell like food to a bear.

Bear cans do make **camping** in bear country easy, and they can help ease worries about bear encounters. In some areas, they are mandatory. Some ranger stations will issue them (for a fee) with your **permit**.

BEARS

Bears are magnificent animals, lords of the **wilderness**. While seeing a bear is a tremendous experience, you need to take precautions to protect yourself and your **food** from bears. Mostly they keep out of the way of human beings but, on occasion, they can be dangerous. In some places, they have become used to human food and will make great efforts to get it. By protecting our food from bears, we also protect the bears, because ones that attack humans or regularly take food are liable to be shot.

Two types of bears can be found in the North American backcountry outside of the arctic coast: the black bear (*Ursus americanus*) and the grizzly or brown bear (*Ursus arctos*). The first is the smaller and more widespread of the two. Both can be dangerous, and neither should be underestimated. However, the grizzly is much the greater

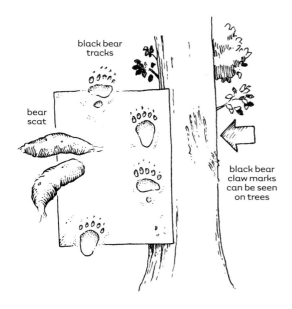

black bear tracks

bear scat

black bear claw marks can be seen on trees

Be alert for signs of bears, which may appear on the ground as prints, droppings, or diggings, and on tree trunks as parallel scratches as high as six feet above the ground.

threat. In the far north, polar bears (*Ursus maritimus*) may be found. These are even more dangerous, and additional precautions are needed in their territory.

Black bears are found in many backcountry areas throughout North America. Grizzlies are found only in small areas in the Northern Rockies in the contiguous 48 states—mainly **Yellowstone** and Glacier National Parks. They are more common in Alaska and western Canada. Despite their name, black bears vary greatly in color, ranging from black through shades of brown to cinnamon. Black bears have longer heads and larger ears than grizzlies, which have flatter foreheads and a prominent shoulder hump. Grizzlies have long, curving claws, black bears fairly short ones, but in either case you probably don't want to be close enough to see them!

Approaching any bear is always unwise. Just because the bear appears to be ignoring you doesn't mean it is unaware of your presence or is not ready to attack if it feels threatened.

Staying Bear Aware

Before any trip into bear country, check the situation and find out what precautions are recommended. Immediately before the trip, get up-to-date information in case any problems have arisen. In grizzly country, **trails** and campsites may be closed if there is bear activity. Find out about food storage requirements too. In some areas, hanging your food, known as ***bear bagging***, is sufficient. In others, **bear-resistant containers** are mandatory.

The first and most important precaution is to be aware of what is going on around you. Look for bear sign: piles of **scat**, scratch marks on trees, mounds of freshly dug earth. If you come upon the carcass of a deer or other animal, be aware of your surroundings and leave the area. A bear might be feeding on it and could be close by. Circle around the carcass or move away quickly, avoiding places where a bear might hide. If you see cubs, move well away, since mother bears are very protective.

A useful tool in bear country is a pair of **binoculars**. You can use them to check that the black lump on the edge of the next thicket of trees really is an old stump and not a bear, or that the animal half hidden in the brush is a deer and not a grizzly. From high points, you can scan meadows and riverbanks to see whether any bears are about. If you spot a bear, either retreat or make a very wide circle around it. If a bear sees you, it will usually move away. Bears don't want confrontations with people any more than people want confrontations with them.

Whether bears will know you're there (and they most often do) depends on the **weather** and the environment. Bears have an excellent sense of smell, so if the **wind** is behind you, they probably know you are there long before you are close to them. However, if the wind is in your face, they won't smell you. Bears can see and hear well too, but good eyesight isn't much use in dense brush, and noisy creeks can drown out sound.

In dense vegetation, especially berry patches, if you can't see far and the wind is in your face, make a noise to alert any bears to your presence. Clapping your hands or calling out loudly should be enough. The little bells some hikers carry are not loud enough to be very effective. However, they are noisy enough to scare away other birds and animals and to irritate other hikers, who might prefer silence and the sounds of nature rather than tinkling metal.

> "I once came upon a hiker sitting having lunch beside a trail in the Canadian Rockies. Every few seconds he gave a loud yell, but not once did he look up. I first saw and heard him when I was several hundred feet away. When I was just a few feet away I greeted him, and he was so startled he nearly fell off the log he was sitting on."—CT

Take care at rest stops in bear country. Ensure that you have a good view so you'll see any bears before they get too close, and don't leave your **pack** if you wander off to look at the view or get some **water**. An opportunistic bear might take the opportunity to grab it.

Handling an Encounter with a Bear

What happens if you encounter a bear at close quarters? More often than not, it will run away before you have time to do anything. Do not run yourself. Not only could the bear catch you easily, but seeing you running could trigger a chase response and you could have a bear, which would have otherwise been harmless, rushing after you.

Instead of running, stay still. Climbing a tree is often advised. That's fine if you're standing next to a tree you can climb fast enough to get out of the bear's reach. Remember, too, that black bears and young grizzlies can climb trees. If you simply stay put, the bear may move away. Even if it charges you, it may back off before touching you. Some experts recommend talking quietly to the bear to show you are not a threat. Don't wave

Possible position for playing dead. This hiker's legs are a little apart to make it more difficult for the bear to roll him over. Keeping your pack on affords some protection to the neck and back.

your arms to scare the bear off: it may see you as a threat and attack.

If a bear does attack you, you have two options: play dead, or fight back. If you have a bear-repellent spray, this is the time to use it. The recommended position for playing dead is to lie face down with your hands wrapped behind your neck and your legs a little apart so the bear can't easily turn you over. Having a pack on will give your internal organs more protection, so don't jettison it. Females with cubs and bears that you come upon suddenly are probably defending themselves if they attack you. In that case, playing dead is probably the best response. However, if you suspect the bear is hunting you, fight back; otherwise, the bear may start eating you. Bears that attack you in camp in the dark are almost certainly predatory. Black bears that attack when they could easily move away, and which haven't been startled, may well be viewing you as food.

> "I once came face to face with a black bear at a bend in a trail in the North Cascades. Before I had time to do more than freeze in fear, the bear was rushing up the mountainside at great speed. Watching it, I realized why one of the things you don't do is run from a bear."—CT

Camping in Bear Country

When **camping** in bear country, choose your site carefully. Many popular places to camp, such as beside water, are popular with bears too. Bears know where people usually camp and may raid those sites regularly. Camp on little-used sites and away from water, and you may never see a bear, even where they commonly visit campsites. Pristine sites where no one has camped before are less likely to be visited by bears. In some places it is appropriate to use such sites, but in many places it isn't. Indeed, in some **national parks**, use of designated backcountry sites is mandatory. If you do use a pristine site, it is imperative that you practice **Leave No Trace** techniques. When choosing a site, avoid beaches and riverbanks, along which bears often walk, and stay away from trails, including animal trails. Open **forest** where you have good visibility is a good place to camp.

When you're using a previously used campsite, the likelihood of a visit by bears is partly determined by the behavior of previous campers. If they have left food scraps behind or allowed bears to get their food, then bears may come back in the hope of more food. When camping, set up your shelter 100 yards or more upwind from where you hang or store your food and from where you cook. Clothes on which you've spilled food should be hung with the food; don't keep the clothes in your shelter. If you leave no food smells to attract bears, they will likely leave you alone. In grizzly country you should always sleep in a **tent** because bears are more likely to attack people sleeping under the stars than those in tents.

"On one 10-day hike in Yosemite National Park, I caught just one glimpse of a black bear and never had bears in camp. One afternoon, my companion and I got talking to another hiker. 'Come and camp with us,' he said. 'We've got a great site by a lake, and there are other good people there too.' What about bears, we asked. 'Oh, they're terrible. In camp every night. But that's always so in Yosemite.' We declined his invitation, camped elsewhere, and had no visits from bears. It doesn't have to be 'always so.' " —CT

"The only time I have had a bear in camp that I'm aware of was at a site in Jasper National Park in the Canadian Rockies. A previous group had left a great deal of trash, much of it food. I arrived at the site late on a rainy day and really didn't want to go any farther. I hung my food carefully and pitched the tent well back in the trees. Nothing happened overnight, but the next morning when I was sitting under a tree eating breakfast, a black bear stuck its head out of some bushes and stared at me. I threw a rock in its direction (not at it—I didn't want to hurt the bear), and the face disappeared. I could hear it moving through the bushes, however. I shouted and chucked a few more rocks but the bear didn't go away, so I packed up and moved on, finishing my breakfast some miles away." —CT

Some people carry **firearms** or **bear-repellent pepper sprays**. Neither is essential, and carrying either of them doesn't mean you can forget other precautions. If you're experienced with firearms, feel confident in their use, *and* have checked with local authorities as to the legality and advisability of carrying one, you might consider carrying a gun in brown or grizzly bear country.

Finally, don't let worries about bears keep you out of the wilderness. If you follow the recommended precautions and stay aware, the chance of having problems with one is slight.

A good book on bears is Dave Smith's *Backcountry Bear Basics*.

BEATER

The term *beater* refers to a flailing wipeout while **skiing**, **rock climbing**, or **hiking**. Short for *eggbeater*, a beater occurs anytime you feel as if you have been tossed around like eggs in a bowl. The term is used in a sentence as follows: "Hey, are you OK? That was a serious beater you took back there!"

BEAUFORT SCALE

Long before the invention of the anemometer, mariners used the condition of the sea to judge the velocity of the **wind**. In 1805, Sir Francis Beaufort, a rear admiral in the British navy, formalized these observations in a scale that has since been called the Beaufort scale. The Beaufort scale translates the speed of the wind into tangible effects that can be expected on land and sea. It helps deduce the wind speed based on your observations. The Beaufort scale is a handy chart to keep with you, especially when paddling international waters; sea conditions around the world are often measured, described, and broadcast in Beaufort nomenclature.

BEE STINGS

See **allergic reactions**.

BELAYING

Good belaying is a skill any climber or mountaineer should be intimately familiar with. It will save the life of your climbing partner if he should fall while on the move. Belaying is the paying out or taking in of the rope that is attached to the climber. If the climber falls suddenly, it is the belayer's responsibility to stop the payout of rope immediately. If the rope is attached to the terrain with adequate protection, stopping the payout of rope will halt the fall of the climber, who can then shake off the shock of falling, get his wits to-

BEAUFORT SCALE

Force	Name	MPH	Effect at Sea	Effect on Land
0	calm	0	calm or glassy, easy paddling	smoke rises vertically
1	light air	1–3	scalelike ripples, easy paddling	smoke drifts
2	light breeze	4–7	small wavelets, requires extra paddling	leaves rustle, wind can be felt on face
3	gentle breeze	8–12	scattered whitecaps, nuisance for beginning paddlers	leaves in constant motion, light flags extend
4	moderate breeze	13–18	small waves, numerous whitecaps, very difficult for beginning paddlers	small branches move, dust and leaves are lifted into air
5	fresh breeze	19–24	moderate waves, many whitecaps, very difficult for intermediate paddlers	small trees move
6	strong breeze	25–31	larger waves, whitecaps everywhere, spray, difficult for advanced paddlers	large tree branches move, hard to set up tent
7	moderate gale	32–38	white foam develops streaks, spray in the air	resistance in walking, tents can blow away, whole trees move
8	fresh gale	39–46	moderate high waves, well-marked foam streaks	twigs and small branches break off trees, walking is very difficult
9	strong gale	47–54	high waves, sea rolls, spray may reduce visibility	slight structural damage to buildings
10	whole gale	55–63	very high waves with overhanging crests, sea churns white	trees are uprooted, moderate structural damage to buildings
11	storm	64–73	extremely high waves, chaotic sea, large vessels may disappear in wave troughs	widespread damage
12	hurricane	74 and above	low visibility, air filled with foam and spray, sea completely white	violent destruction

gether, and start climbing again. A good belay has four components: anchor, friction, position of body and hands, and communication. (See **artificial protection** and **natural protection**.)

Anchor

When a climber falls, the rope acts as a lifeline. But if the rope is not well attached to the rock, or snow, or ice, it won't do the climber any good. Therefore the rope's anchor (or point of attachment) has to be **bomber** (see also **anchors**). In many climbing scenarios there will be two anchors: one that secures the rope to the terrain, and a second that secures the belayer to the terrain. The second anchor, known as a *belay anchor*, will prevent the belayer from being pulled off the ground, or out of position, when the belayer's partner falls. For instance, if a 120-pound woman is belaying a 200-pound man, there is a good chance that she will be pulled off the ground if he falls. To guard against this, she may clip her harness into an anchor that she has built on the ground. Belay anchors aren't as important if the belayer is belaying from the relative safety of the ground, but if the belayer is on a small ledge on the third of five pitches, she should have a rock-solid belay anchor to keep her from being pulled off the ledge.

Friction

Belays work because friction on a rope can cause it to slow down or stop. This friction can be created in a number of ways. Many climbers and mountaineers use belay devices, mechanisms specifically designed to place friction on a rope. There are many different belay devices on the market; a few are shown in the accompanying photograph.

Not all belays require a belay device. A body or hip belay utilizes the friction of a rope wrapped around the belayer's waist. This is a fast, easy belay that can be used for low-angle slopes posing little threat to the climber. Another way to create friction is to use certain hitches. For example, the **Munter hitch** can be tied directly into

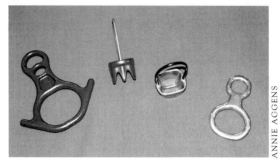

Belay devices use friction to control the speed of the passing rope. A lot of friction makes the rope slide slowly through the device. Less friction allows the rope to slide through more easily. Belay devices can also be used as rappel devices. Common belay devices from left: Black Diamond Super 8, Trango Jaws, Black Diamond ATC, and CMI 8-Ring.

ANNIE AGGENS

a **carabiner** on your harness. It allows you to give or take up slack in a rope, but in so doing it applies enough friction that it can be used in place of a belay device. *When selecting a device for belaying, be sure to read and follow the manufacturer's directions.*

The act of belaying is relatively simple, but it requires complete concentration. A lapse in focus can result in a tragic accident. The illustrations next page show the hand positions for a basic belay. Hand positions are important, and each hand has specific duties while belaying. To help clarify hand positioning, climbers call the hand that holds the portion of rope leading directly to the climber the *guide hand*. The other hand is called the *brake hand*. While the guide hand can be used for swatting flies or zipping up your jacket, the brake hand must remain on the rope at all times. Letting go of the rope with your brake hand, even for a moment, could be a deadly mistake: the rope could slip through your belay device if your partner falls. Even if you could grab hold of the rope after the fact, it would be difficult to regain control. The rule is simple and clear: *the brake hand never leaves the rope.* This makes the task of taking in the rope (or paying it out) a learned skill. Some climbers use slight variations of the basic belay illustrated.

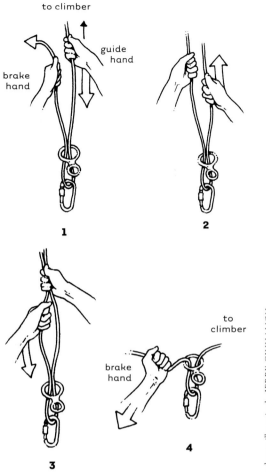

to climber

guide hand

brake hand

1

2

to climber

brake hand

3

4

Based on an illustration by JERRY CINNAMON

Proper hand positions for taking up slack in line during a belay. 1. Slide the rope through the belay device. 2. Hold the brake hand steady and slide the guide hand up the rope. 3. Grasp both lines with your guide hand. Slide the brake hand back toward the belay device. The brake hand should never leave the rope. Repeat steps 1, 2, and 3. 4. To brake a fall, bring the brake hand down to create a sharp bend in the rope against the belay device.

As you learn the different techniques, you'll develop a favorite. In addition, different belay devices require slight variations in your braking position. Learning the correct way to use each belay device is extremely important.

Position

Positioning your body appropriately, so that it is prepared to withstand the forces of a falling climber, is another key component in belaying. Keep these tips in mind when choosing the best belay position.

- Safety—You want to be as protected as possible from rockfall. If your climber is above you, try to find a belay site away from the likely path of a falling rock. If that is not possible, try to belay directly against the rock face.
- Security—Look for a belay site that offers natural security. Examples would be behind a boulder against which you can brace your feet, or sitting on your butt with your heels firmly planted in the snow. In addition, if you are clipped into a belay anchor, try to be taut against it: don't allow much slack in the line connecting you to your anchor. If you are pulled forward by the force of a falling climber, any slack in the line will result in unnecessary shock to the anchor (and your body!).
- Stance—One of the strongest positions for belaying is on your butt with your heels firmly braced against a rock or in the snow. A weak position is standing upright with only two points of contact on the ground. Think about the direction in which a falling climber will pull you, and assume a position that will allow you to strongly resist that force.
- Direction of pull—Position yourself in line with the anchor and the climber. If you are off to one side, a strong pull from the climber could move you significantly, possibly affecting your ability to maintain a strong brake position.

Communication

Belaying is a two-person activity. As such, you need to develop clear and consistent communication skills that work in a variety of settings. Communicating clearly allows you to give slack in the rope when slack is needed and tension when the climber needs a bit more security. In addition, it is the only way to know when you, as the belayer, can finally remove your brake hand from the rope. Think through, in advance, situations where verbal communications become ineffective, such as on windy days or when climbing long pitches. While most climbers use some standard commands (see **climbing communication**), it is a good idea to review communication protocol with each new climbing partner. Depending on where you learned to climb, you may use a different lingo than your partner. Discover these differences on the ground, *before* you climb.

As you progress from **top roping** to **multipitch climbing**, you'll discover there's much more to learn about belay technique. Often, for example, you'll find yourself on small ledges surrounded by piles of rope and webbing. Keeping track of all that rope can become confusing, and you must be certain you're holding the right rope. Belaying the wrong end of a rope or losing track of your anchor can be a deadly error. As with many climbing skills, it's best to learn and practice your belay technique on the ground, where a mistake is simply a learning opportunity. If you're new to climbing, the best way to learn good belaying technique is with a competent friend or **guide**. Many **outdoor schools** offer courses in **rock climbing**, **ice climbing**, or **mountaineering** that teach the skill of belaying.

BENDING THE MAP

Bending the map is the process of convincing yourself that your **map** reflects your surroundings regardless of where you actually are. The process is often accompanied by such thoughts as "So what if it's not the same shape—this *has* to be the right lake," or "Maybe that mountain grew since the map was made." Bending the map usually

> "On a few occasions, I have found myself the victor in a battle against a map, but these instances have all been in extremely remote areas where maps are seldom reviewed or updated."—AA

takes place in the panic-filled moments when you first realize that you may be **lost**. Instead of sitting down and admitting that there could be a problem, many people find a way to make the map justify their progression into the unknown. It's a little like bending the truth when you're recounting the statistics of your last **fishing** trip; it's easy to do, and it makes you look—and feel—a lot better than owning up to the truth.

> "I once paddled eight miles out of my way, all the while thinking to myself, 'This isn't right,' before I stopped and reevaluated. More confused than ever, I was reduced to asking a fisherman where I was (by far the most humiliating thing a competent canoeist can do). He surprised me by telling me I had paddled off my map. No wonder I couldn't find my location! Even after he pointed me in the right direction, it took several stops and a few hikes to nearby hilltops to pinpoint my location. That was the most lost I have ever been. I still can't explain my complete and utter lack of orientation!"—AA

It's hard not to bend the map when you're lost. You may become so desperate to be sure of your surroundings that you will do almost anything to place your finger on the map and confidently proclaim, "We're here!" Even experienced navigators can fall prey to map bending when they are overconfident, desperate, or just plain lazy.

The first step in avoiding bending your map is to develop solid map-reading skills. The second step is to verify your course and position using a **compass** with **bearings** to visual landmarks. The third step is simply to trust the map; if something looks wrong, it probably is. Because maps aren't susceptible to the same fear, stress, and panic that affect people, they are usually much more dependable. In most **wilderness** areas, maps are extremely accurate.

If your surroundings and the map don't match up perfectly, stop and evaluate your position. If you're lost, you may very well be able to retrace your steps. However, if you continue to think that the map will eventually make sense, you could be walking into a disaster. Admitting that you may be lost isn't fun, but if you catch it early, and avoid bending the map, you should be able to up your status to "temporarily misplaced."

BETA

Beta is a climbing term that refers to advance information about a route. When climbing, a person giving you beta might tell you exactly where to place your hand in order to find the best **handhold** or perhaps how to get through the crux of the climb. You may hear a belayer say to a climber, "Can I give you some beta, or do you want to figure it out on your own?"

BIG-WALL CLIMBING

Big-wall climbing generally refers to scaling large vertical walls, such as **Yosemite's** El Capitan. Big-wall climbing necessitates incredible reserves of concentration and strength. Often these routes take several days, requiring the climbers to sleep in hanging **bivouacs**. In this scenario, any items that will be needed over the course of the climb, including **food**, **water**, a **stove**, a **sleeping bag**, and so forth, will be hauled up the route in big bags, called *haul bags*, that are attached to the **rope**.

Climbing a big wall requires considerable planning and preparation. Most big walls are scaled using **aid climbing** techniques. While big-wall climbing falls more under the auspices of extreme **rock climbing** than under general **wilderness** travel, it does require a solid understanding of wilderness travel skills. Often, big-wall climbs are located in remote areas that can have long, difficult approaches.

BINOCULARS

Although usually associated with birders, binoculars are very useful for all outdoors people, whether interested in birds or not. With a pair of binoculars, you can scan the terrain ahead for hazards, check whether that distant, dark object

in a meadow is a boulder or a bear, watch wildlife without causing any disturbance, view details high on cliffs, observe far-off flowers or the tops of trees, work out a route or find a safe-looking **river crossing** from a high point, and much more.

> "Once, on a hike in the Ogilvie Mountains in the Yukon Territory, in a large berry field a quarter mile ahead, I spotted a dark object that appeared to be moving slightly. Through the binoculars, I identified it as a grizzly bear and I changed my route accordingly."—CT

Binoculars come marked with two figures, such as 7x50 or 8x40. The first figure is the magnification; the second is the diameter of the front of the object lens, measured in millimeters, and is called the *aperture*. For easy viewing while holding the binoculars, magnifications from 6x to 8x are best. With anything above 10x, hand shake may make using the binoculars difficult and tiring. Large magnification can also result in a less bright image and a narrower field of view (the area seen through the lens, usually given as the amount of feet that will be in view at 1,000 yards). The aperture tells you how much light the binoculars admit. The larger the figure, the greater the light-gathering power.

However, the relationship between the two figures matters most for how binoculars will perform in dull **weather** or low light. The figure given by dividing the aperture by the magnification is called the *exit pupil*. The bigger this figure, the clearer the image will be in poor light. Thus a pair of 8x30s has an exit pupil of 3.75; a pair of 7x50s, an exit pupil of 7.14. Although the magnification of the latter is slightly less, they will give a much better image in low light.

Unfortunately, large apertures mean bigger, heavier binoculars, so a compromise has to be reached. Keen birders will probably be prepared to carry the **weight** of an 8x40 or 7x50 pair, but others may prefer a pair of mini-binoculars or a monocular with a small aperture, especially on multiday trips. On **backpacking** trips and long day hikes, Chris carries a pair of 8x21s (exit pupil 2.6) that weigh just 5.5 ounces and will fit easily into a shirt or jacket pocket. On short day hikes or when bird watching is his primary aim, Chris carries a pair of hefty 26.5-ounce 8x42s (exit pupil 5.25).

BIVOUAC

A bivouac is an overnight encampment that requires minimal equipment. Bivouacs most frequently occur when poor **weather**, diminishing sunlight, fatigue, or injury forces rock climbers to halt their progress and hole up for the night. Bivouacs—or bivies—are usually endured without the luxury of a **tent**. Unplanned bivouacs are notorious for being miserably uncomfortable and cold. You may hear the term used in a sentence as follows: "We got stuck in a storm and had to bivy on a small rock outcropping—I froze my butt off!"

Because climbers making final ascents are restricted to carrying lightweight backpacks (see **packs**), they usually have to leave their tents behind. To fill the void of shelter, many climbers will carry bivy sacks (also called *bivy bags*). Bivy sacks are extremely lightweight nylon sacks that should offer just enough protection against the elements to keep climbers safe should they unexpectedly need to bivouac. In a pinch, a bivy sack can be improvised using a garbage bag, pack liner, or nylon **tarp**.

Many outdoor enthusiasts will carry a bivy sack even though they aren't going anywhere near a mountain. When used in combination with a sleeping bag, a bivy sack can add warmth and water protection. Many bivy sacks are made with breathable, waterproof materials such as **Gore-Tex**, which makes them great for keeping you dry even if your tent is soaking wet (see also **breathability**).

BLACKFLIES

Forget about the grizzly **bear**, the black widow, and venomous **snakes**. Forget about sounds that go bump in the night. I've spent years in the **wilderness**, and the only thing that scares me

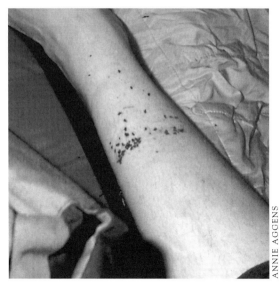

Blackflies are tenacious. Here, about 40 blackflies cling to the sliver of skin exposed where a sock became untucked from the pant. Blackfly bites itch horribly and leave bloody welts.

more than running out of cheese is the collective consciousness of blackflies. These little buggers are more than annoying; they're downright evil. Blackflies crawl all over your body, looking for any point of access to your skin. Got a hole in your shirt? They'll find it. **Socks** that don't cover your ankles? Lost your head net? You're as good as gone.

Blackflies are small, stout-bodied flies with a humpbacked shape. They are found near sources of **water** across North America, from the Arctic in the North to Georgia in the South. Although most common in spring and early summer, they may persist well into July and August. They have an uncanny ability to infiltrate head nets and crawl around inside your nose and ears. Usually, you don't feel the bite of a blackfly. Your only clue that you have been violated is the itching, bloody welts that linger for days.

The best way to fend off blackflies is to wear long-sleeved shirts and pants tucked into your socks. Head nets are a must if blackflies are out in full force. Most bug repellents effectively keep blackflies at bay for a while, but they must be

Blackflies can be a real problem in the wilderness. When they're out in full force, the tundra tarp is a safe haven during breaks and meals.

reapplied frequently. Using the bathroom in blackfly country is a daring feat. Look for windy points or ridges that offer some degree of a breeze. If you are driven to your **tent**, as is often the case, you will notice that the blackflies have a curious tendency to flock to the corners. This is an odd but welcome behavior, as they lose all interest in biting the tent's occupants. Sitting in the corners of the tent, the blackflies become easy targets for retribution. In the subarctic, it is not uncommon to scoop cupfuls of dead blackflies out of a tent at night.

All of this trouble has driven people to create some ingenious pieces of equipment. A favorite is a homemade "bug hut," a mesh bag you can toss over your body so you can go to the bathroom in peace. It can also be used to cover the portion of your body that remains out of water when bathing. Another good invention is the **tundra** tarp, a simple **tarp** with four mesh walls. On a bad blackfly day, the tundra tarp is a little slice of heaven. If you think blackflies go for humans alone, think again. The caribou and **moose** that you see furiously shaking their heads aren't suffering from dementia—just the annoying, persistent blackflies.

BLAZES

See **trail markers**.

BLEEDING

For some people, the mere sight of blood is worse than the accident that caused the bleeding. Somehow it seems that even a small amount of blood looks extreme when it's running down your leg or getting soaked by your favorite **bandanna**. While injuries that result in serious bleeding are uncommon, you should be prepared to deal with such emergencies.

Blood can ooze, flow, or pulsate from an injury. Most common scrapes will cause wounds that ooze, whereas common cuts, such as those acquired while cutting cheese or filleting a fish, usually result in flowing blood. In either case, the bleeding can easily be controlled with direct pressure. Take a good look at the injury, and try to determine the exact source of the bleeding. You may be surprised at the amount of blood small cuts can produce. This is especially true with cuts to the head or face. Once you've located the source of bleeding, apply well-aimed direct pressure to the cut. Placement is important—it does no good to apply direct pressure if you are missing the actual location of the cut. It is best to apply direct pressure with a sterile gauze pad or dressing; however, if none is available, you can use any sort of clean cloth. If the dressing becomes drenched with blood, apply additional dressings on top of the drenched dressing. Do not remove the original dressing, which may disturb the clotting process. Maintain the direct pressure for 5 to 15 minutes. If the injury is to an extremity (an arm or a leg), elevate it above the heart to reduce blood flow to the extremity. However, avoid elevating the extremity if you suspect a **fracture** or other complications, such as an injury to the neck or spine.

If bleeding is severe, you must act fast. *Immediately* apply direct pressure, even if it means placing your hand over the wound, and *then* look for your **first-aid kit**. If the blood is pulsating (look for squirts with every beat of the heart), an artery has been cut. Arterial bleeding is harder to control. Still use well-aimed direct pressure to stop the bleeding, and continue to maintain pressure until the bleeding has stopped. If the wound is large and gaping, you may need to pack it with sterile gauze pads and then apply a snug pressure dressing. Pressure dressings are bandages that maintain pressure over the wound. Usually, they are wrapped around the limb, but it is critical that the dressing is not applied too tightly, which can result in a lack of circulation to the extremity. It is highly likely that the wound may swell in the hours after the injury. Be sure to reassess the bandage every half hour or so to ensure that it isn't too tight. If necessary, you may have to loosen the bandage.

Pressure points and tourniquets can also be used to control bleeding. Pressure points are areas on the body where an artery runs close to the skin. By applying pressure to the artery, you can reduce the blood flow to the injury. Pressure points can be used in conjunction with direct pressure, but they will not stop bleeding on their own. In addition, pressure points can be difficult to locate. Tourniquets should be used only when a limb has been amputated or when bleeding is life threatening and uncontrollable. In most cases, the use of a tourniquet guarantees the limb's eventual amputation. Thus very few cases justify using a tourniquet. Most wounds will develop a clot that, if left undisturbed, will prevent further bleeding. However, any movement of the injured

Control bleeding with well-aimed direct pressure and elevation.

area may cause the bleeding to resume. Therefore, it is often necessary to splint the injury to prevent movement (see **splints**).

Severe bleeding can be difficult to recognize. In some cases, the injured person may be wearing dark or waterproof **clothing** that prevents the blood from being visible. Or the blood may be soaking into the ground or, worse, the bleeding may be internal. When assessing an injured person, always scan the body from head to toe for signs of severe bleeding. This may require you to place your hand underneath the person to feel for blood on the ground or for wet clothing. If the injured person has bruising on the abdomen or groin or has a history of recent injuries to that area, suspect internal bleeding and plan an **evacuation** or **rescue.** Always anticipate **shock,** and be prepared to offer appropriate treatment.

BLISTERS

No matter what outdoor activity you are engaged in, a blister can make you miserable. To understand blisters, rub your hands together firmly for about a minute. They get pretty warm, don't they? The more friction you create (that is, the harder you press your hands together), the hotter your hands get. If you were to do this all day, you'd end up with a blister. Now rub your hands together very gently. You could do this for a long time without getting a blister. The difference? Friction. At points of excessive friction, such as where your heel rubs against your boot or where your palm hits your paddle, blisters are born.

The key to preventing a blister is to take proactive, preventive action against the friction. One good way to do this is to break in your equipment before you rely on it—especially your **boots.** Boots that haven't been broken in will rub in all sorts of strange places. When you break them in, you mold the insides of the boots to the shape of your feet, reducing the areas that rub excessively. Another important step is to keep your gear clean. **Socks** or gloves (see **gloves and mitts**) that have dirt or sand in the weave can wreak havoc on your skin, as can wet clothing.

Often you can tell where a blister will develop because the spot will feel hot and sensitive to pressure. These areas are called *hot spots*. Like your hands rubbing together, these spots eventually will become blisters if you don't take action. At the first sign of tenderness, always stop and reduce the friction on the hot spot. Do this by covering the area with tape, moleskin, or Compeed, products available in drugstores. If the hot spot is on your foot, check to make sure that there are no folds in your socks or debris in your boot. Lay the tape flat across the hot spot. If you cut the covering in an oval shape (rather than a square), it will stick longer. Keep the area covered as long as it stays sensitive to the friction.

If the hot spot develops into a blister, your tactic must change. Now, instead of a flat hot spot, you have a raised blister filled with fluid. To protect the blister from friction, build up a buffer around, but not on top of, the blister. Cut a hole in several layers of moleskin to create a donut shape, and then apply the moleskin so that the blister rests in the center of the hole. If you don't have moleskin, you can build a log cabin around your blister with pieces of tape. Once you have the protection in place, you may need to secure it with a piece of athletic tape. Some people will opt to pop their blisters to reduce friction. If you decide to do this, poke a very small hole in the bottom of the blister to allow it to drain. Keep in

mind that popped blisters can develop into nasty **infections**, so keep an eye on these open wounds for early signs of infection.

> "When I lead backpacking trips, I tell the participants that they shouldn't hesitate to stop if they feel a hot spot. This is especially true during the first few days of the trip, when your feet are getting used to the swing of things."—AA

While blisters can strike anyone, you can do a lot to guard against them. This is a situation where the saying "An ounce of prevention is worth a pound of cure" really is true. Remember, your hands, feet, hips, and other blister-prone areas are your passport to the backcountry. Take care of them, and you'll be OK.

BOMBER

A derivative of ***bombproof***, the term *bomber* refers to something that is really strong. It can be used in a sentence as follows: "My anchor is so bomber it could hold a car!" or "Hey, man, that was a bomber roll you just did!"

BOMBPROOF

The term *bombproof* is used to describe something that has great strength or that is extremely well constructed or organized. For example, it can refer to a **tarp**, a climbing **anchor**, or even a repair job on a backpack or boat. You might hear the term used in a sentence as follows: "We set up a bombproof tarp just before the storm hit, and we never even got wet!" It can also be used as a verb: "Before we left on our day hike, we bombproofed our campsite so nothing would blow away."

BOOTS

Good boots are important for many different outdoor pursuits, from **hiking** and **backpacking** to **mountaineering** and **ski touring**. The same boots won't do for everything, but the key factor is always fit. Badly fitting boots can cause **blisters** and other injuries and can feel uncomfortable enough

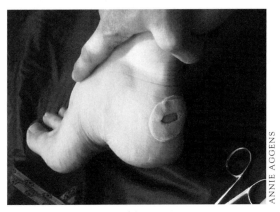

A blister that's been padded donut style. Cut the moleskin in an oval (not a square) for better adhesion.

ANNIE AGGENS

to ruin a day. Because of this, never choose boots on the basis of an advertisement, an endorsement, or even a magazine review. However well designed and well made they may be, the boots won't be suitable for you unless they fit. A pair of inferior boots that fit properly are better than the best-made boots in the world if these are painful to wear.

To ensure you get a good fit, take your time when buying boots and have them fitted by a trained boot fitter, who will examine and measure your feet and recommend the best models. A good fitter may also suggest modifications or additions, such as customized foot beds (foot-shaped inserts that support your feet) or volume adjusters (flat, noncompressible inserts that fit under foot beds and reduce the volume). Once you have a pair of boots that feel OK, test them on an incline board (a sloping ramp on which you can see if your feet move inside the boots) and a rock board or walkway (an area or path covered with stones

and rocks on which you can walk to see if you can feel rocks through the soles). Most good outdoors stores will have these devices. Walk up and down any stairs, and keep the boots on for a while to see if they rub anywhere or whether you feel any pressure points. Only buy when you are sure the boots fit.

Boots vary from light summer hiking models weighing a couple of pounds to monster telemark ski or mountaineering boots, which can top the scales at 8 or 9 pounds. Take care to choose boots suitable for your activities. In particular, don't "overboot." While you may dream of climbing Denali or Everest, if hiking up local mountain

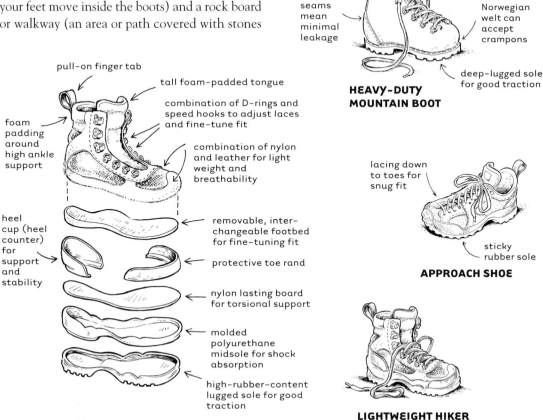

Left: Boot construction. **Right:** Types of boots.

foam padding around high ankle support

pull-on finger tab

tall foam-padded tongue

combination of D-rings and speed hooks to adjust laces and fine-tune fit

combination of nylon and leather for light weight and breathability

heel cup (heel counter) for support and stability

removable, interchangeable footbed for fine-tuning fit

protective toe rand

nylon lasting board for torsional support

molded polyurethane midsole for shock absorption

high-rubber-content lugged sole for good traction

above-the-ankle height for support

fully gusseted tongue keeps water out

minimal seams mean minimal leakage

Norwegian welt can accept crampons

deep-lugged sole for good traction

HEAVY-DUTY MOUNTAIN BOOT

lacing down to toes for snug fit

sticky rubber sole

APPROACH SHOE

LIGHTWEIGHT HIKER
(see details, left)

MIKE CLELLAND

trails is what you actually do, then rigid mountaineering boots aren't suitable. People who take part in more than one activity end up with a whole wardrobe of boots and wear what is appropriate to their chosen activity.

Whatever the activity, the **weight** of your boots matters. You will lift this weight many thousands of times a day (roughly 2,500 times a mile, if your stride is about a yard), so even a slight weight difference can affect how tired your feet and legs will become.

Ask yourself whether boots are even necessary. Would other footwear, such as shoes or even **sandals**, be better? Of course, for **telemark skiing** you need telemark ski boots and for **ice climbing** you need ice climbing boots. But you don't necessarily need hiking boots for hiking.

Whatever boots you have, they'll last longer if looked after properly. With plastic- or nylon-fabric boots, this usually means no more than shaking out dirt and drying them before storage. Leather boots require treating with wax or other dressings. For wet conditions, use a waterproofing wax; for dry and warm conditions, use a leather conditioner or ordinary shoe polish to maintain maximum breathability. The biggest risk to any boots is heat, so don't dry them before a hot **fire** or next to a heater.

BOULDER FIELDS

Boulder fields are found in wild country of every type, from flat **deserts** to steep mountainsides. Boulders vary from small blocks the size of a few bricks to ones the size of cars or even houses. Smaller stones are called *talus*; the very smallest, *scree*. Both talus and scree slopes require different techniques for crossing them.

When crossing boulders, good balance is essential. Even if you're following a trail, it may involve stepping from boulder to boulder. If there's no trail, try to work out a rough route before venturing into the boulders, or at least head for a point, such as a flat area, where you can rest and work out where to go next. When moving, you need to concentrate on your next step, not on

Good balance is essential when crossing boulder fields. Hiking poles can be useful for balance, but make sure they don't get caught between rocks.

which way to go. At the same time, be prepared to vary your route if the going is harder than expected or if the boulders are unstable.

The risks when crossing boulder fields lie in slipping and injuring yourself against a rock or even getting a foot caught between two boulders, either of which may occur if you don't take care or if a boulder shifts under your weight and throws you off balance. In the worst case, a boulder may start to roll downhill and take others with it. Move carefully in boulder fields, and test boulders before fully committing your weight to them.

Some boulder fields are far more stable than others. If the rocks are covered with lichen or have a lot of vegetation growing between them, this suggests that they haven't moved in a while and are probably quite stable, though they still might shift when you stand on them. If you see no plants or lichens and especially if you see any signs of recent rockfall, the boulders may be very unstable.

In addition to testing each boulder before putting your weight on it, step on the uphill side of a boulder or on the side that looks most firmly wedged in place. Sometimes you can see which way a boulder may tip and which part of it is likely to wobble if you stand on it. Leaping from rock to rock or taking long strides isn't a good way to cross boulders, as it will be much harder to recover if one wobbles or falls. Slips become more likely, too. Instead, take short steps and keep your weight over your feet. If a rock does start to move, be prepared to leap quickly out of the way. If a slope seems really unstable, back off and find another route. You don't want to be caught in a rock avalanche.

If the rocks are wet or covered with slimy vegetation or wet moss or lichen, they may be very slippery, requiring great care. It may even be safest to have three points of contact, even if this requires crouching. Dry rocks usually give good grip, sometimes astonishingly so. It is possible to walk up surprisingly steep slabs of rough rock, such as granite. Watch out for the occasional patch of damp moss, however. In deserts, also watch for dry lava beds, which can easily twist an ankle—a serious injury in a waterless terrain.

Tighten your **pack** straps to prevent your pack from swaying and causing you to wobble. If your load is high in the pack and feels unstable, consider repacking it with the heavy items lower down and close to your back.

Hiking poles can be useful if the boulders are fairly stable and not too big. Take care, though—pole tips can get caught between rocks. On large boulders where you may need to use your hands, your poles are best strapped to your pack.

Climbing up boulders is usually easier than descending or traversing them. When climbing, take care not to ascend anything you can't descend, unless you know there are no obstacles farther ahead. When descending, don't lean back into the slope. Although this may feel secure, it actually makes you more likely to slip, because your weight isn't over your feet. In very steep terrain, it is easier to zigzag up or down a slope rather than to ascend or descend directly.

BOULDERING

Bouldering is the simplest form of **rock climbing**. All that's needed to spend hours of happy bouldering is an eager spirit and a nice boulder. Choose a boulder that is stable (you don't want it to roll over!) and free of debris, such as dirt or sand. Also look for a boulder that can offer you a sequence of moves that are challenging or fun. One of the benefits of bouldering is that you can easily repeat a move over and over again until you have it just right. When you're bouldering, it's easy to get absorbed in your climbing and forget that you don't have a **rope** for protection, so be sure to keep an eye on how far you are off the ground. You shouldn't ever get above chest height. It's also smart to have someone spot you in case you fall. If you don't have a partner, consider purchasing a bouldering mat (sometimes called a *crash pad*). These light, foamy mats are good for working on difficult problems close to the ground.

BOWLINE

The bowline is a very popular **knot** in the loop family that is perfect for tying the end of a **rope** around any object. Very strong yet easy to untie, it's often used to create **rock climbing** anchors (see **anchors**) or to tie **painter lines** to canoes. One of the benefits of the bowline is that it is easy

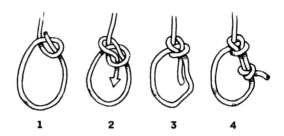

1   **2**   **3**   **4**

Bowline. 1. Create a loop in rope. 2. Wrap the running end (see knots*) through the loop, around the standing end, and then back through the loop. 3. The finished bowline is easy to recognize. 4. A stopper knot can be added for additional security if there's enough tail.*

to recognize when tied correctly. Learn this one, and you will use it a lot!

BRACES

Braces are **canoeing strokes** and **kayaking strokes** that help to stabilize a tipping craft. You may use a brace to stay upright after a particularly large **wave** catches you broadside or after you are struck by an opposing current in the water. There are two basic types of brace: the low brace and the high brace.

In **canoeing**, the low brace is used when the canoe tips to your on-side (the side on which you are paddling). With knuckles facing down, use the back side of your paddle to apply quick pressure against the surface of the water (as if you were slapping it with your paddle). At the same time, use a **hip snap** to roll the boat to an upright position. In **whitewater canoeing**, the low brace is often combined with a reverse **sweep stroke** to make a very powerful turning stroke used by stern paddlers. In kayaking, the low brace is used to stabilize the kayak against small waves or disturbances. Again, with your knuckles facing down, use the back side of the paddle blade to apply pressure against the surface of the water. Avoid letting the paddle become submerged by smartly rolling it out of the water as soon as it hits the surface. Many kayakers combine the low brace with a reverse sweep stroke to create a very strong, stable turning stroke.

The high brace is slightly different. In canoeing, the high brace is used when the canoe is tip-

The low brace is used to keep a canoe or kayak from capsizing. Notice that the knuckles are facing toward the water.

Based on an illustration in ACA, *Canoeing and Kayaking Instruction Manual*

ANNIE AGGENS

Combined with a strong hip snap, the high brace can right a nearly capsized canoe or kayak. Notice that the knuckles are facing toward the sky.

ping to your off-side (the side on which you are not paddling). With knuckles facing up, reach out and plant the paddle in the water. If the boat is tilted dramatically, your paddle may be almost vertical in the water. When paddling tandem, it is common for one paddler to perform a high brace while the other performs a low brace. In kayaking, the high brace can be used against an upset to either side. With knuckles facing up, slap the front face of the paddle (often called the *power face*) against the surface of the water. In combination with a strong hip snap, the kayak can be righted even if almost fully capsized.

When performing a high brace, keep the paddle below and in front of the shoulders, if at all possible. This position protects your shoulders from injury. In kayaking, the high brace is commonly used to prevent capsizing in surf zones (see **surfing**). By planting the paddle and leaning into the face of an approaching wave, the paddler can be driven sideways toward shore. This is called *side surfing*. In both canoeing and kayaking, all braces should be combined with powerful hip snaps.

BREATHABILITY

Breathability refers to the passage of moisture vapor through a fabric. Unfortunately, it's inaccurate and can be misleading because, of course, no fabric actually breathes. The correct though clumsy term is *moisture vapor permeable*, which means that a fabric has gaps between its fibers, through which moisture vapor can pass. This is not the same as ventilation.

Most **clothing** is in fact "breathable," but the term becomes significant in relation to waterproof clothing. Making a fabric waterproof is easy. A solid coating of polyurethane or PVC will do that. However, such a coating won't allow moisture vapor through, so **condensation** will build up inside the garment because your body is always giving off moisture vapor, even if you're not visibly sweating. The more active you are, the more condensation that will appear. Wear sealed rain gear for long when working hard, and you can become quite wet underneath it.

To solve this discomfort, rain gear is made from breathable fabrics that have either microporous holes in them that allow moisture vapor but not liquid moisture through (**Gore-Tex** is the most famous of these) or chains of hydrophilic (water-loving) molecules along which vapor is conducted. To work, these fabrics require pressure to drive the vapor through the material. That pressure is provided by your body in the form of heat and high humidity.

Breathable waterproof fabrics are by no means perfect, and different types vary in how much moisture vapor they will allow through in a given period. None of them will keep you dry inside in all conditions, and they all work best when the **weather** is cool and dry and humidity is low. However, they will keep you drier than nonbreathable fabrics. For improved performance, wear clothing that wicks moisture away from the body underneath rain gear (see **wicking**). In particular, you shouldn't wear **cotton**, especially next to the skin, because it absorbs moisture rather than letting it pass through.

The latest breathable fabrics, such as EPIC by Nextec, have coatings applied to each bundle of fibers but not to the entire surface. This leaves tiny gaps between the fibers through which vapor can escape. Because the fibers are nonabsorbent due to the coating, they repel **rain** and keep the user dry in all but the heaviest downpours.

Many people expect too much from breathable rain gear, due in part to misleading advertising and marketing but also to confusion over the meaning of the term *breathability*. No clothing will ever stop you from giving off moisture vapor (if it did, you would be dead), and no clothing—including nonwaterproof garments—will ever allow all moisture vapor through. Go for a run or hike quickly uphill in an open-mesh base layer or shirt, and see how damp it becomes. It is unrealistic to expect a waterproof garment to keep you drier than a single, thin layer. Breathable garments are worth having. Just be realistic about how they will perform.

See also **waterproofing**.

BRIDGE

To a canoeist, a bridge is not a road that crosses over water. When **portaging** a canoe, a bridge refers to anything that will support the weight of the canoe while you take a break. Unlike when you put a canoe down, a bridge maintains the canoe's upside-down position, with the stern on the ground and the bow resting on a tall object. This makes it very simple to get back into position, remove the canoe from the bridge, and resume the portage.

There are two types of bridges: natural and human. Natural bridges are often found in the crooks of trees or along a large tree branch. If there are no trees around, another person can

Trees make excellent natural bridges.

provide a bridge by supporting the **gunwales** near the bow of the canoe. While human bridges will get tired from supporting the canoe, they can provide a quick, well-deserved rest for your shoulders on a long portage.

You may hear the word *bridge* used as follows: "I wanted to take a break from portaging, but I couldn't find a bridge," or "Can you bridge me?" If you are portaging and people are nearby, you may simply yell "Bridge!" This will let them know that you need a break. They can either then direct you to the best natural bridge or offer to be the bridge themselves.

BUREAU OF LAND MANAGEMENT

The Bureau of Land Management (BLM), part of the U.S. Department of the Interior, administers around 272 million acres of the public domain, mostly in the contiguous western United States and Alaska. Much of this land is little known, yet superb for outdoor recreation. There are many BLM wilderness areas. To find out more, check out Michael Hodgson's *America's Secret Recreation Areas: Your Recreation Guide to the Bureau of Land Management's Wild Lands of the West.*

BURNS

Anyone who has suffered from a burn knows that it is painful. Burns can be caused by the sun, **stoves**, **fires**, and **lightning**. While serious burns are not common backcountry injuries, their side effects can be life threatening. Knowing the basics can help you prevent and treat most burns.

Types of Burns

The most common backcountry burn is sunburn. Sunburns can be painful, but they are generally minor injuries (see **sun protection**). Most sunburns fall under the category of superficial burns (formerly known as *first-degree burns*). Once a blister develops, the burn is considered a partial-thickness burn (formerly known as a *second-degree burn*). Often, partial-thickness burns are caused by accidents with boiling water. For example, many of us are guilty at one point or another of

boiling water on a precariously balanced stove—a disaster waiting to happen. Likewise, careless pouring techniques often result in hot-water burns to the hands and feet. While partial-thickness burns may cause swelling and blistering, they do not seriously affect the tissues, capillaries, or nerves that lie beneath the skin.

Full-thickness burns (formerly known as *third-degree burns*) penetrate the skin and destroy blood vessels and nerves. A full-thickness burn won't swell; it will simply seep. This is because the vessels are no longer intact and are unable to contain any fluid. The skin of a full-thickness burn may appear charred or white. Full-thickness burns can be caused by prolonged exposure to fire or even lightning strikes. With extensive full-thickness burns, **shock** can occur suddenly.

Certain burns are considered higher risk than others. Any burn to the respiratory area can complicate breathing and is therefore considered high risk. A classic example of how this can occur is inhaling embers when blowing into a fire at ground level. Any time facial hair or lips have been singed, you should worry about the state of the respiratory tract. Like any other part of the body, a burned respiratory tract will begin to swell, which may restrict breathing.

Other high-risk burns include partial- or full-thickness burns to the genitals, face, hands, or feet; partial-thickness burns to a large portion of the body (larger than the front side of your torso); electrical burns; chemical burns; burns to children; and burns that are complicating other injuries. A burn that falls under any one of these categories is a cause for **evacuation**.

Treating Burns

The first step in treating a burn is to stop the burning process. This can be accomplished by extinguishing the source of the burn and submerging the affected area in cool **water**. If you aren't near a water source, collect **snow** in a plastic bag or use water from your water bottle. Burns can continue to do damage long after the source of heat is removed. Therefore, keep the area cooled for up to

30 minutes, but watch for signs of **hypothermia**. Burn victims can easily become overcooled.

If the burn is partial thickness, treat the pain by applying cool compresses, such as a wet **bandanna**. Be sure to protect the area against further burning. If the hands are burned, remove any rings or snug bracelets. Partial-thickness burns may produce blisters, which are best kept self contained, especially if they are less than 3 inches in diameter. Keep them covered and clean with a sterile dressing. If they spontaneously open, treat them like any other open wound, washing the area gently with soap and water and applying a sterile dressing. Anticipate and guard against **infections**. A full-thickness burn should be considered a high-risk wound; plan an evacuation to get professional medical care as soon as possible.

People with sustained burns can easily go into shock or become dehydrated (see **dehydration**). Therefore, before you embark on a **wilderness** trip, you should have enough training in **first aid** to know how to handle such a scenario.

Preventing Burns

Most backcountry burns are preventable. By wearing sunscreen and protective **clothing**, you can all but eliminate superficial, or partial-thickness, burns caused by the sun. In addition, wearing sunglasses or goggles can prevent **snow blindness**. A few precautions in and around the **cooking** area can help you avoid common burns from hot water, stoves, and fires. Before you begin cooking, think about your **camp kitchen** site. Is the stove level? Is the **fuel** cap secure? If you are cooking over a fire, is it contained?

Many severe burns are sustained during **tent** fires or other prolonged exposure to flames. Cooking in your tent is inherently dangerous (and, as many people would argue, simply stupid). Most tents are made with flame-resistant material, but this is not a guarantee that your tent won't ignite instantly. If the tent fire is caused by a fuel leak, the fuel can quickly spread over the entire tent floor, coating your **sleeping pad, sleeping bag**, and

anything else in the way, including your hands. Throwing an ignited stove out the tent door and through the vestibule without causing more damage is nearly impossible. It's best to always cook outside your tent, or under a **tarp**, unless conditions simply will not allow it.

The superficial burns caused by a lightning strike may not appear serious. Nonetheless, anyone who has been struck by lightning needs to see a doctor as soon as possible. Minimize your risk of getting struck by lightning by avoiding exposed areas anytime lightning threatens.

BUSHWHACKING

Bushwhacking means struggling through dense vegetation that grabs at your **clothing** and **hat**. It's exhausting, slow, and to be avoided, if at all possible. However, if you hike off trail, you'll probably have to bushwhack eventually. Sometimes unmaintained **trails** can become overgrown and almost vanish in the brush.

Bushwhacking is never easy, but you can mitigate or at least minimize the worst of it.

Be aware of your surroundings while bushwhacking. Stay calm and think. Thrashing desperately through the brush in the vain hope that you can quickly fight your way through it is likely only to leave you frustrated, furious, and possibly **lost**. Whenever possible, keep bushwhacking to a minimum by linking meadows, riverbanks, lakeshores, **boulder fields**, and other brush-free areas. This is worth doing even if it means taking a zigzag course and hiking twice or more the **distance** you would if you tried to take a direct line. Don't expect to make much progress when bushwhacking. Half a mile an hour can be a good speed.

To reduce the damage to your equipment, it's best not to have anything strapped to the outside of your **pack** when bushwhacking. That includes foam **sleeping pads**, which can quickly become tattered and leave behind a trail of nonbiodegradable foam chips. Stuff sacks can prevent this but are also likely to get torn. If at all possible, carry your pad inside your pack—especially self-inflating pads, which are easily punctured.

CHRIS TOWNSEND

Don't expect to move quickly when bushwhacking.

The best clothing for bushwhacking is smooth and closely woven, and has few external features that bushes can hook onto. **Fleece** and **wool** are not good fabrics because they are easily torn and you can end up looking as though you're disguised as a bush. Synthetic windproof clothing is much better. Hats can protect your head and face, but you may have to stop often to retrieve them as bushes whip them away. Gloves (see **gloves and mitts**) can protect your hands too, as long as you don't mind risking tearing them.

> "When I hiked the Arizona Trail, one steep section in the Four Peaks Wilderness was a tangle of spiky shrubs with scarcely a trace of the trail. Fighting my way upward on a very hot day—with thorns tearing my skin and catching on my clothes while sweat dripped into my eyes, blood dripped down my bare legs and arms, and I grew more and more thirsty—was extremely arduous and unpleasant. Luckily, the trail reappeared on the mountain ridge above. That bushwhacking was due to a forest fire, the brush being the first regrowth and the trail having been destroyed by falling trees and washouts."—CT

BUTTERFLY KNOT

The butterfly **knot** creates a loop. Because it can be tied in the center of a **rope**, and because it per-

forms well with a downward direction of pull, the butterfly knot is often used to connect the middle person on a rope team while traversing **glaciers** (see **roping up**). This knot is also handy for suspending a sack of **food** in the middle of a rope between two trees (see **bear bagging**).

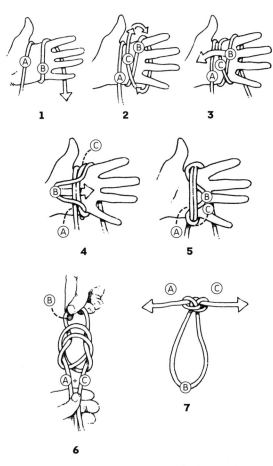

Butterfly knot. 1. Drape a strand of the rope, A, over the palm of your hand. Drape a second strand of the rope, B, over your fingers. 2. Drape a third strand of the rope, C, over the center of your palm, between strands A and B. 3. Pick up strand B and lay it over strands A and C. 4–5. Tuck strand B under strands A and C. 6. Continuing to hold strand B in your right hand, use your left hand to pull on strands A and C. 7. Pull strands A and C in opposite directions to tighten the knot. The butterfly knot is now ready to use.

CACHES

Caching supplies in the **wilderness** means you can stay out longer without having to carry enormous weights. However, placing or arranging caches can require as much or more effort as hiking out to a resupply point (see **resupplying**). In some areas, particularly in Alaska and northern Canada, caching food may be essential for trips longer than a week or so. In some **desert** areas, caching water may be necessary.

> "When I put out water caches on one section of the Arizona Trail, I simply left them in the shade and out of sight of the trail because I was picking them up in the next few days."—CT

You can either place caches yourself or have someone place them for you. Place caches out of sight of **trails** and campsites—both to guard against vandalism or theft and so they aren't an eyesore—and secure them from animals, which in **bear** country means hanging supplies or using a **bear-resistant container**. Caches can be buried, which is a good way to protect them from heat and cold, or hidden in dense brush. In unfrequented areas where animals aren't a problem, caches can simply be left on the ground under a bush or at the base of a tree. In case anyone comes across your supplies, leave a note explaining what they are and when you'll pick them up.

It is, of course, vital that you know exactly where your caches are so you can find them again. Don't rely purely on memory, even if you'll be collecting them fairly soon after placing them. If you arrive from a different direction, in different **weather** conditions, or by a different mode of travel, an area may not look the same as when you placed the cache. Mark the spot on a **map**, and note prominent landmarks or distinctive vegetation. Take a **GPS** reading, if you have a GPS unit, or a **bearing** on a **compass**. Also pace out the distance from the trail or an obvious landmark.

If you're caching supplies on your way into the wilderness and intend to pick them up on your way out, it's easier to find them again, but you should still mark the spot. While you can't take every possibility into account, caches should be left somewhere safe so they don't get washed away by **flash floods**, buried in **snow**, or damaged by hot sunshine. In the remote desert, water caches must not be your only recourse. You must have a backup plan in case the cached water is lost or stolen.

> "On a ski tour in the Canadian Rockies, I once left supplies on a glacier. In this case, we put them on a rise in the ice so we could see them from a distance and so they were unlikely to be buried if it snowed (as it did)."—CT

If someone else is caching food for you, be sure you both agree on the exact spot and have the same markers for finding it. This will be easier if you've both been to the place before.

When you retrieve a cache, take all the packaging away with you, including anything not needed for your journey.

CAIRNS

Cairns are piles of stones used to mark routes or summits. Sometimes they consist of just three stones placed on top of one another, though often they are bigger. Summit cairns may be quite large and in some places are ancient. Cairns may also be found on passes and the top of cliffs. In some areas, they are also known as *ducks*. Keep in mind that cairns built long ago may be inaccurate.

See also **trail markers**.

CAMERAS

See **photography**.

CAMP CHAIRS

The **wilderness** offers an amazing array of seats, such as tree stumps, rocks, grassy banks, and fallen trees. In **snow**, you can even build your own. Some of these natural chairs and stools are very comfortable—soft dry moss, for example, makes a wonderful cushion. Most, however, are quite hard and often wet and cold. The comfort of these natural seats can be easily enhanced with a small piece of closed-cell foam, which adds a little softness and keeps your backside dry and warm. If you don't have any foam, a folded garment or even an empty stuff sack can suffice. A rectangular foam pad can be used as both seat and backrest as long as you have something to lean it against (trying this with a self-inflating **sleeping pad** may risk punctures though).

Your **pack** can act as a backrest, too. If there's no tree or rock to prop it against, a couple of sticks or **trekking poles** can be used. The more rigid the back of your pack, the easier this is. External-frame packs can be propped up with just one stick, but internal-frame packs are more sta-

ble with two. Support frameless packs carefully, or they may give way when you lean against them. However, if you make a tripod with two poles or sticks, frameless packs can also make a good backrest. Packs can even be used as backrests inside a **tent** using short sticks or adjustable poles at their shortest length as supports, as long as you have room to sit up.

The difference a comfortable chair makes is enormous. Rest is important, and being able to lean back and relax is wonderfully refreshing. For those who don't want to rely on finding suitable natural seats, various portable chairs and chair kits are available. Some of these double as sleeping pads, and others turn your sleeping pad into a chair. The first kind are foam or self-inflating pads with buckles and straps that, when fastened, pull the mat into a V shape to provide a seat and a backrest. By adjusting the tension, you can have either a fairly hard upright seat or a soft lounger. Rods in the sides prevent the seat from buckling. With a chair kit, you insert your sleeping pad into a fabric sleeve that has straps and stiff sides to achieve the same sort of seat. Chairs using foam pads are pretty durable and can be used on almost any surface. Chairs made from self-inflating pads aren't that tough, however, and should only be used on smooth ground or a **groundcloth**.

Folding stools and chairs could be carried a short **distance** to a base camp, but these are better suited to roadside campgrounds than to wilderness campsites.

CAMPING

Camping is one of the joys of **wilderness** travel. Staying out overnight far from roads and houses is always a special event. Whether you're sleeping out with just the vast starry sky as a roof or hunkered down in a tent listening to **rain** pattering on the fly sheet and wind rushing through the trees, wilderness camping is a vital part of experiencing nature.

Being wet, cold, and miserable does not enhance appreciation of the wilderness, however, so good skills are essential to comfortable camping. These skills include site selection, setting up shelters (see **tents** and **tarps**), establishing **camp kitchens**, cooking, and coping with stormy **weather**. All of these should be done following **Leave No Trace** principles. Camping has much more impact on the environment than hiking because people are in the same place at least overnight and sometimes for several nights.

Site Selection

Choosing a comfortable campsite is not always easy, especially when you're tired, wet, or cold. Planning in advance where and when you'll camp is always a good idea unless you're in an area where you can camp almost anywhere (see **planning a trip**). The main requirement is somewhere flat, smooth, and big enough for you to lie down and sleep comfortably. Having water not too far away is useful but not essential; water can be carried to a dry camp, if necessary. Shelter from the weather is necessary in some places and at some times of the year. A good view is always welcome but shouldn't override the need for comfort and shelter.

You can't always camp where you want. For example, some **national parks** have designated backcountry sites that campers are required to use. Usually, you have to list the ones you'll use on your **permit**. The regulations in many wilderness areas say that camps should be set up at least 200 feet from any water source and out of sight of trails. It's good to do this whether it's required or not. The edges of streams, **desert** waterholes, and lakes are often vulnerable to damage, and creatures that need the water might be scared away if you camp too close to it.

There are three types of campsites: well used, little used, and pristine. The first are common along popular trails and in popular areas. Although they may be unattractive, with hard bare ground, large **fire** rings, and damaged trees, using them prevents new sites from appearing and becoming overused in turn. If possible, these sites should be tidied up, by packing out or burning garbage and dismantling excess fire rings. At the very least, stick to the already worn areas so you cause no further damage. (See also **Leave No Trace**.)

In some areas, land managers close such sites so they can heal. When this happens, you'll need to go elsewhere. Information about camping restrictions is often posted at trailheads or distributed with permits and other information.

slightly sloping ground allows for better rain runoff

tent on dry ground, far from freshwater source to prevent contamination

When selecting a campsite, look for a place where you can pitch your tent on bare ground or on dry vegetation (such as grass) to minimize the impact. Avoid soft and damp ground and soft, easily crushed plants like flowers and small shrubs.

Contact the local ranger station to find out the situation in advance.

Little-used sites should be used only if you really have no other choice. These sites can still quickly fade back into the wilderness if left alone. This process can be helped by picking up litter, dismantling fire rings, and scattering piles of firewood. Rings or lines of stones that have been used to weigh down tent stakes can be moved to bare ground so vegetation can recover. If you ever have to use rocks on stakes, please return the rocks when you leave.

Rather than cause more damage to a little-used site, it's better to camp in a pristine area, as long as you can do so without leaving any trace. First, seek out durable terrain that won't be easily marked. Good choices are forest duff, mineral soils (sand and gravel), and any bare ground or rock. If you must camp on vegetation, look for dry grass and other hardy plants. Easily crushed soft plants should be avoided, as should damp ground (which doesn't make for a good campsite anyway). In the desert, don't camp on **cryptobiotic soil**, which is necessary for plant and animal life.

A good site is found, not made. You shouldn't need to clear vegetation, rocks, or logs. When walking around the site or going to fetch water, stick to hard ground and try not to create the beginnings of trails. If you have enough water containers, collect all you need in one trip so you don't tramp back and forth to the nearest creek or pool.

Camp kitchens can be set up on flat rocks or bare ground. If **bears** aren't a potential problem, your kitchen can be next to your shelter or even in the porch or under a tarp, if the weather is stormy. That way you don't have to walk back and forth between kitchen and bedroom. (See also **cooking**.)

Pristine sites should be used for only one night. If you want to stay in the area longer, move your camp, unless it's on a really durable surface, such as rock. Before leaving a site, check that nothing has been left behind, including any scraps of litter, and fluff up any flattened vegetation. It should look as though no one has camped there.

Used sites are often found in obvious places—near lakes or riverbanks or in valley bottoms—and may be mentioned in trail guides. They're rarely far from trails and so are easy to locate. By definition, pristine sites are not obvious, so it's best to allow time to find one. Don't wait until just before dark to decide to find a site. In **forests**, you can often wander off the **trail** and simply find a patch of duff to camp on. In flat deserts, you can usually find plenty of bare ground. The problem here can be getting out of sight of the trail.

In steep terrain, where flat ground is rare, don't start long ascents or descents late in the day, unless you know there is a site somewhere on the mountainside. Consulting the **map** can show flat areas where a site may be found. The map won't tell you whether such areas are marshy or covered with dense vegetation or boulders, however, so you can't completely rely on this method. Be prepared to spend a little time searching for a site.

Terraces on a mountainside are often a good place to camp. The views are often better than deep in the valley, and they are warmer too because cold air sinks. Even a few dozen feet can make a difference. Valley bottoms are also more likely to be damp and bug ridden than higher areas.

> "After a day of rain, I once camped on a shingle bank near a river in the Yukon Territory, as it was the only place I could find that wasn't covered by big tussocks and marshy pools. The night was dry, but I still woke to find myself on an island. The river had risen several feet, and what had been an old dried-up channel was now a swirling torrent. I had to make a knee-deep ford to reach the bank."—CT

When you find a prospective site, shrug off your **pack** and lie down on the site to see if the ground is flat. A very slight slope is OK, but anything more and you'll find yourself fighting gravity all night, which doesn't make for a good night's sleep. If you have a choice, sleep where you'll catch the early-morning sun (unless you want to sleep in, of course, or it's summer and you are in the far north, where there are few if any hours of darkness at that time of year).

> "I once spent two nights camped in a small clump of tall trees just on timberline in the Uinta Mountains in Utah. Both nights brought big thunderstorms that echoed and crashed around and around the bowl where we were camped. Huge lightning flashes lit up the mountains as the rain hammered down. It was not a comfortable place to be, until the storms moved on."—CT

A good site is no use if there's no water within a reasonable distance, unless you've carried supplies from the last source. In well-watered country, such as along a river valley or a lakeshore, this isn't a concern, but in many areas, such as the desert, there may be no water for many miles. In such places, an hour or more before you plan on camping, note the time you hike past water. If you then find a good site, you know how far back it is to a water source. Checking the map can often show the whereabouts of water (but keep in mind that some sources may be seasonal). (See **water** for more on locating sources.)

A flat area doesn't on its own guarantee a comfortable camp. For starters, it needs to be big enough for any shelter you intend to pitch. This is where tarps can be useful because they can be adapted to fit the space, which tents can't. Check for objective dangers too. Are there any dead branches above you or dead trees leaning toward your camp (see **widow makers**)? In desert areas, be wary of camping in dry washes in the rainy season (see **flash floods**). Camping next to water when it's raining can be risky too.

In camps above timberline, you face a different storm hazard—**lightning**. In some areas, such as the Colorado Rockies, thunderstorms occur of-ten during the summer. Forest camps are safer at such times. While thunderstorms can be spectacular, camping in one does not lead to a peaceful night.

Rain in itself shouldn't be a problem as long as you have a good, properly pitched shelter. If rain is falling or looks likely, don't camp in hollows, as you may find yourself flooded out. Sometimes, heavy rain can form pools on any flat ground, especially hard-packed dirt that won't absorb much moisture. Pitching your shelter on a slightly sloping raised area can make all the difference.

Wind is much more of a problem than rain. Lying in the dark for hours listening to thrashing nylon just above your head is nerve-racking and exhausting. When the wind is strong, finding a sheltered site is worth the effort, even if it means walking farther than planned. Take care to pitch your shelter carefully, using all stake points and guylines. If biting insects are around, a stiff breeze should keep them away, so a site in the wind may be preferable to a sheltered one.

See also **snow camping**.

CAMP KITCHEN

The kitchen is the focal point of any campsite. This is where everyone gathers and even where solo campers spend most of their time. Traditionally, a **fire** was the heart of the camp, but these days it's more likely to be where you set up your stove.

A kitchen site should be comfortable but, most important, able to stand heavy use. People should be able to walk from their shelters to the kitchen without trampling vegetation or soft ground. And there should be space in the kitchen area for people to stand and sit without causing damage. This means looking for bare ground, especially sand or gravel, or rocky areas with little vegetation. If the site is a pristine one (see Site Selection under **camping**), vary the route between shelters and kitchen so you don't create a trail. If it's a well-used site, stick to the trails and bare areas that already exist so you don't create new paths or do any fresh damage.

Gravel and shingle banks bare of vegetation are good places to set up a kitchen because they won't be damaged. This riverside kitchen is in the Yukon.

In the snow you can dig seats and a table for your camp kitchen. Be sure to fill the area in afterward.

In areas where **bears** may raid campsites, the kitchen should be at least 100 yards downwind from where you sleep.

"When traveling solo in country where bears aren't a problem, I like to site my camp kitchen next to my sleeping bag or in the tent porch. It is especially nice on a chilly morning to have a hot drink and breakfast without having to get out of your warm sleeping bag."—CT

In summer, alterations to kitchen areas are unnecessary and shouldn't be made. If you want a seat, sit on a rock, a fallen tree, or your foam pad. Place the stove on a rock for stability to keep it from scorching any vegetation. Keep the kitchen area clean; spilled food and litter may attract animals. If you do drop or spill anything, pick it up right away. Otherwise, you may forget, and by morning a bear might have found it.

In **snow** you can be much more creative. With **snow shovels**, you can dig out a kitchen table with bench seats around it. Foam pads can be used to sit on and to keep your back warm. If it's stormy, dig the kitchen deep into the snow or build a snow wall on the windward side. Before you leave, fill the kitchen in and flatten the snow so it isn't visible from afar and so other people don't fall into it by accident.

See also **cooking**, **cook kit**, **food**, and **stoves**.

CANDLES

The humble candle has a surprising number of uses in the **wilderness**. The obvious one, of course, is light. A small candle can throw enough light for reading, **cooking**, and general camp life. Candles are vulnerable to **wind**—even a gentle breeze can blow one out—so some form of windbreak is usually needed. A stove windscreen is excellent for this because it also reflects the light. Candles can be placed on the ground but are better on an upturned pot. Make sure they can't land on anything flammable if they fall or are knocked over. Using candles inside a tent is too risky, but with care they're OK in a large porch, as long as

A stove windscreen will keep the breeze off a candle and act as a light reflector. Stand the candle on an upturned pot, a flat stone, or bare soil if possible.

there is space around them and above them. Candles produce a surprising amount of heat and can melt a hole in a fly sheet quite a way above them.

The safest way to use a candle for light is in a candle lantern. These weigh 4 to 5 ounces and protect the candle from wind. Because the lanterns can get hot, keep them away from anything that might melt or burn. Candle lanterns usually need special candles, though some will take ordinary household ones. The candles can last 8 to 10 hours and weigh around 4 ounces.

Because candles give off heat, they can be used for heating as well as lighting a shelter. One candle burning in a porch can make a surprising difference and can help dry out **condensation**. The warmth and flickering light also seem more attractive than the cold light of a flashlight or **headlamp** (see also **lighting**).

Useful for many other purposes besides light and warmth, candles, especially stubs, can be used for starting **fires**. They can also be rubbed on ski bases that stick or ball up with snow. I've occasionally rubbed a ski binding plate with wax to stop it from icing up as well. Rubbing a candle along a leaking **tent** or **tarp** seam can stop the drips, at least temporarily. Candle wax can also be rubbed onto **cotton** clothing (not synthetics—it won't stick) to make the **clothing** waterproof, but it won't let any moisture out and it doesn't last long.

Water can be heated over a candle, although it's a slow process, and the water won't reach a boil. Lanterns that hold three or more candles are better for this because they produce much more heat (keep in mind that the flat lantern tops get too hot to touch).

> "I've melted ice in a small pot over a candle."
> —CT

CANOEING

There are some **wilderness** activities that will always feel like food for the soul. No matter where you go or how long you stay out, they make you feel good. For a lot of people, canoeing is one of those activities. Certainly there is nothing as beautiful as paddling in the mist of the early morning along the shores of a calm lake. Unless, that is, it's bouncing along a lively stream, in perfect sync with your partner on an exciting whitewater run.

The history of canoeing is filled with adventure, exploration, and passion. Every time you pick up a paddle, you have the opportunity to relive some of the historical magic—even if only in your imagination. Canoeing is a popular sport because it is easy, accessible, and cheap. That's not to say it has to remain that way. On the contrary, you can spend several years studying technique and still have more to learn, or you can easily drop three grand getting decked out in the finest equipment. But if you just want to have some fun, it's really simple to find an old canoe and a nearby waterway to explore. Voilà! An adventure awaits.

There are several types of canoeing. Solo canoeing is a one-person activity, while tandem canoeing takes two people. Flat-water canoeing takes place on (you guessed it) flat water, which is usually found on lakes, ponds, or anything that is not moving water. Moving water refers to canoeing on any type of river. When the moving water becomes turbulent, you get exciting whitewater runs. To further complicate this simple sport, you can choose from the following disciplines: **freestyle canoeing**, **whitewater canoeing**, canoe racing, wilderness **canoe tripping**, and **poling**. Needless to say, with this many options there is surely a type of canoeing that will appeal to your sense of adventure.

Many people have been paddling for years with no formal instruction. This is one reason why canoeing is so popular. While it may not be pretty, just about anyone can paddle a canoe. The trick becomes getting the canoe to go where you want it to—and remaining on speaking terms with your paddling partner! The more you learn about proper technique, the easier it becomes to control and maneuver the canoe, even in the most difficult conditions. Instructional courses in any of the above categories can be found across the United States through local paddling organizations. The American Canoe Association is a national organization that has been promoting canoeing as a recreational sport since 1880 (see resources section).

CANOEING STROKES

One of the draws of **canoeing** is that it is a fun and relatively easy sport. Just about anyone can figure out how to make a canoe go forward, turn, or stop. They may be zigzagging across a lake, but at least they're out having fun—or at least trying! If you're willing to invest a little time and work on a few simple canoe strokes, you'll never have to zigzag again. Furthermore, if you've been relegated to paddling in the bow because you don't know how to "steer," you'll find the techniques easy and the view from the stern very pleasant. If you are already an ardent canoeist, you may find yourself able to improve your efficiency with a few simple changes.

There are several different disciplines in canoeing, including **freestyle canoeing**, **whitewater canoeing**, canoe racing, wilderness **canoe tripping**, and **poling**. You'll discover that each style of paddling employs certain techniques that won't be used in others. Conversely, just because a stroke is known as a "freestyle" maneuver doesn't mean you can't use it bouncing down your favorite whitewater run.

All canoeing strokes are divided into three categories: propulsion strokes, correction strokes, and **braces**. Propulsion strokes propel you through the water. Common propulsion strokes are the forward stroke and the backstroke. Correction strokes are used to turn, or correct, the position of the canoe. The J stroke and **sweep stroke** are typical correction strokes. Braces are paddle maneuvers that help to keep your canoe from tipping over, even when it appears to be a lost cause. While many of these strokes can be learned in a day, a dedicated paddler will spend years refining technique and picking up new tricks. Under-

standing the principles behind the basic strokes will take you a long way toward developing excellent technique.

All strokes begin when you plant the paddle in the water. This step is often referred to as the *catch*. Next comes the *propulsion*, or the way the paddle moves through the water during the stroke. Finally, the *recovery* is the act of returning the paddle to the catch position. In addition to learning the different steps to each stroke, you'll soon discover that the position of your body will have a significant impact on the amount of power your stroke generates. In particular, it is important to incorporate upper-body **torso rotation** into every stroke you learn.

The forward stoke is the most commonly used propulsion stroke. Executing a good forward

The correct way to hold a canoe paddle is with one hand on the grip and the other hand on the lower portion of the shaft, above the throat.

stroke starts by holding the paddle correctly. To paddle on your right side, place your left hand on the grip of the paddle and your right hand on the lower portion of the shaft. (Reverse the order to paddle on the left.) Start by planting the paddle in the water at arm's distance from your body. If you rotate your right shoulder toward the bow of the canoe to accomplish this task, you'll wind up your torso and position yourself for a strong propulsion phase. After the catch, unwind your torso by bringing the paddle back to your hip (but not much past it). During the propulsion, your paddle should remain vertical in the water and parallel to the centerline of your canoe.

According to the American Canoe Association, computer analysis of Olympic paddlers shows that 75 percent of the power in their forward strokes occurs within the first 5 to 7 inches of the catch. Using a shorter forward stroke quickens your pace and adds power to your stroke. This is a change for canoeists who have traditionally relied on longer forward strokes. While the power of a short, well-executed forward stroke is undeniable, its style may not be for everyone. Nonetheless, it is a good technique should you ever need additional horsepower.

The simplest description of the backstroke is that it's the forward stroke in reverse order. More advanced adaptations of the backstroke can give the canoeist additional power. While not as frequently used, the backstroke can be an extremely important tool when you need to back up quickly. In addition, the backstroke is often used to ferry across a river in strong current (see **ferrying**).

The J stroke is a combination of a forward stroke and a corrective maneuver that resembles the shape of the letter J. It is an efficient way to prevent having to switch paddling sides regularly. When paddling tandem, the stern paddler uses this stroke. Even on a calm day, you may find that you need to use the J stroke every other stroke to keep a straight course. This is how it works. At the tail end of your forward stroke (by your hip), rotate your lower wrist (the one on the shaft) toward the canoe. This turns the blade so it's paral-

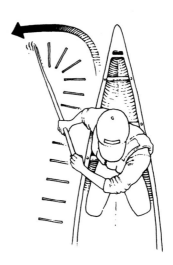

The J stroke is a common stroke for stern paddlers. Rotating your wrists toward the canoe at the end of your forward stroke allows you to apply outward force on your paddle, which corrects the course of the canoe.

lel with the canoe. Next, apply outward pressure to the paddle blade, forcing it away from the canoe. Some people opt to pry the paddle off the **gunwale** for this step. If you were to stop the stroke at this point, it would resemble an L. Instead, transition directly into your recovery (this gives the stroke its J look). Two other common correction strokes are the **sweep stroke** and the **draw stroke**.

If you're serious about making your canoeing strokes as efficient as possible, consider having someone videotape your maneuvers. Videotapes provide an unbiased view of how you paddle. Also consider getting tips from an experienced instructor. Most instructors are trained to diagnose your strokes and help you optimize your efforts. The investment in some personal one-on-one time with an instructor can be well worth your time and money.

CANOE SELECTION

Shopping for a canoe is a little like shopping for a car. There are a lot of options on the market, and you have to decide which features you want.

Like kayaks, canoes are built for specific jobs, such as paddling whitewater (see **whitewater canoeing**), **wilderness** tripping, or simply going out for an afternoon of **fishing**. Therefore, how you intend to use the canoe makes a big difference in what model you purchase. Unfortunately, it's hard to find one type of canoe that can do everything. If, like a lot of people, you can only afford one canoe, you'll just have to decide which features are the most important to you. Are you going on a long expedition or are you planning a simple lazy afternoon paddle? Will you be paddling solo or tandem? In addition, you'll want to consider factors such as width, length, material, and cost.

Here are a few terms and specifications that distinguish one canoe from another.

Length

You should be concerned with two different lengths: overall length and the length of the portion of the canoe that actually sits in the water, or the *waterline length*. Overall length has more to do with whether or not the canoe will fit in your garage. Waterline length is important because it affects the speed of the canoe. In general, longer canoes will go a bit faster and will be easier to track. (Tracking is how well the canoe goes straight.) A shorter canoe will be a bit slower, but it will offer more maneuverability.

Width

Width, or beam, affects the stability and storage capacity of your canoe. Again, it can be measured in a couple of places: at the **gunwales** (pronounced *gunnels*) and at the waterline. Wider canoes tend to be more stable than narrow canoes. As such, they are often the choice for entry-level paddlers or paddlers who need a stable platform for fishing, hunting, or **photography**. In addition, they're a good choice if you have rambunctious children or pets. A boat that is too wide can be difficult to paddle, and a boat that is too narrow may feel uncomfortable or tippy, so try them out before you buy.

Hull Shape

There are several hull designs. The most common are called the *shallow arch* and the *shallow V*. The shallow arch is a design much like a U: the bottom of the canoe is relatively flat. This provides a certain degree of primary stability, the feeling that the canoe is stable when it is sitting still. V-shaped hulls (as in the shallow V) tend to provide secondary stability. Canoes with secondary stability may feel tippy at first, but an experienced paddler can lean a canoe with secondary stability way over on its side without tipping over. Many solo, freestyle, and whitewater paddlers look for this quality.

Rocker

Like the bottom of a rocking horse, the term *rocker* refers to the curvature of the boat from bow to stern. A boat with a lot of rocker will have a shorter length at the waterline than a boat with no rocker. Therefore, boats with a lot of rocker are generally used in situations where turning fast is important, such as in whitewater.

Depth

A canoe with a shallow depth can be a wet ride in **waves**. While you will stay drier with a deeper canoe, you may get blown more by the **wind**. If you are planning a trip where you'll need to carry lots of gear, a deeper boat will give you more capacity.

Capacity

Capacity (or payload) refers to how much gear a canoe will hold, measured in pounds. The length, width, and depth of the canoe affect its overall capacity. High-capacity canoes are great for carrying everything you own, but they can feel awkward when not fully loaded.

Hull Material

Most of today's canoes are manufactured of plastic, composite materials (such as Kevlar and carbon), or wood. Manufacturers use many different

There are many options when looking for a canoe. In this photo, the canoe on the left has attractive wood trim and comfortable cane seats. The center canoe has a lot of rocker and is outfitted with flotation for whitewater. The canoe at right is aluminum, which is an inexpensive material.

types of plastics, but some, such as Royalex, are definitely stronger than others. The main benefit of plastic is that it is very durable. Another reason so many plastic canoes are on the market is that they are very easy to mold and produce in mass quantities. However, plastic canoes can be heavy, and they absorb a lot of your energy before it can be transferred to the water. Nonetheless, plastic boats are a durable, cheap alternative to composites. Plastic is virtually the only material used for whitewater canoes.

Composite materials, including fiberglass, Kevlar, and carbon, are much stiffer than plastic and are extremely light for their strength. Because they are stiff, they absorb far less energy than their plastic equivalents. In addition, the stiff materials allow manufacturers to create fine entry lines and sharp edges. Fine lines help the boat move efficiently through the water. The first time you pick up a 17-foot Kevlar canoe with one arm, you may be sold. Your shoulders may also thank you after that mile-long portage (see **portaging**). Be prepared to pay for the luxury, however. These nice composites can get pricey!

Wood and wood-canvas canoes are both beautiful to watch and magical to paddle. They require a certain dedication to maintain, but they more than make up for any inconveniences

with the sheer pleasure of paddling. If you anticipate any abuse of your canoe, however, go with a more durable option. Nowadays, wood and wood-canvas canoes are more like family heirlooms than the workhorses they once were.

Weight

Weight is not just an issue on portages! More and more people are realizing that if their canoe is a pain to get on their car's roof rack, they simply won't take it paddling. If you need to haul your canoe around by yourself, or if you want to keep your back in good shape, consider a lighter canoe. Yes, you will lose some durability, but for many paddlers the benefits of a light canoe outweigh the drawbacks.

Take a few other details into consideration when looking for a canoe. If you will be paddling in whitewater, ask whether the canoe comes outfitted with a saddle or thigh straps. Also find out if it has attachment points for the **flotation**. If you're looking for more information than the sales clerk can offer, try locating the buying guides from a paddlesport magazine, such as *Paddler* or *Canoe and Kayak* (see resources). These magazines generally publish annual buying guides and reviews of canoes that can help you make the right selection.

CANOE TRIPPING

Canoe tripping is a wonderful way to access the heart of the **wilderness**. Whether it's on a lazy river float or a remote wilderness expedition, canoe tripping is an efficient, fun, relaxing, relatively inexpensive, and personally rewarding way to travel.

If you think you're the type of canoeist who would enjoy wilderness canoe tripping, you must learn some special skills. Along with becoming a competent paddler, you must know how to navigate and live comfortably in the backcountry. In addition, you must be prepared to handle a myriad of emergencies, as you may be several days and many miles from help.

ANNIE AGGENS

Canoe tripping is a great way to discover the wilderness. It took 25 days to paddle to this set of rapids on the Kazan River, Nunavut. Not all canoe trips have challenging whitewater like this: more often than not, paddlers prefer the calmer waters of lakes and gently flowing rivers.

Whether you are a seasoned canoe tripper or thinking about trying it for the first time, these general tips will help you plan a trip and enjoy your experience (see also **planning a trip**).

- Read canoeing magazines to learn about interesting destinations.
- Plan a route that satisfies your need to escape, but not one that is beyond your capabilities (see **route selection**).
- Find out as much information about your route as possible.
- Think about the **goals and expectations** you have for the trip, and choose companions who share the same vision.
- Pack **clothing** that you can be comfortable in no matter how wet you become. Use waterproof bags (also known as *dry bags*) or line your stuff sacks with garbage bags to keep your clothing and **sleeping bag** dry.
- Remember that canoes allow you to travel in style, without as many concerns about weight. Don't forget your comfortable **camp chair**, your favorite **fishing** rod, and the **Dutch oven**!

If you're planning a long trip to a remote area, also consider these tips.

- Try to locate the log of someone who has previously traveled the route. Having a log will give you important information concerning your route, such as which side of the river offers the best portage or where archaeological sites can be found.
- Choose **bailout points** where you can access help if necessary. Sometimes bailout points are few and far between (if you have any at all). Try to make contact with your bailout points before you leave to determine if anyone will be at the site and what facilities they offer (for example, a phone or a float plane). Fishing lodges can often be used as bailout points.
- Consider **resupplying** to extend your trip or to help keep your weight down.
- Take a whitewater safety course, and practice different **rescue** techniques before you leave. If you have an emergency on the water, you want to be confident that you will react promptly and correctly. It also helps to know that other people on your trip will react in the same manner.
- **Maps** are usually very reliable, but keep in mind that your map might be based on surveys from a year with significantly different water levels. This may make your map appear way off, with water where there should be land and vice versa. In reality, water levels (which often fluctuate) change the appearance of many features, including rapids. If you hear rapids but you don't see them on the map, go with your gut. Always scout before you paddle (see **scouting rapids**)!
- Research the history of your route. Many modern canoe routes have exciting, adventurous histories. Taking a book along that recounts an earlier adventure can add special meaning to your trip and make for great tales around the campfire.
- Check out the status of the wildlife in the area by contacting a local natural resources officer. If necessary, ask for advice on the best way to protect yourself from threatening **wild animals**.
- Build your way up to a long trip. Before you take off for 70 days, try going out for 35 days; before you go out for 35 days, try staying out for 14. You want to make sure that you'll enjoy a long trip before you commit yourself to one.

Long trips are often the opportunity of a lifetime. If you think you'd like to plan an **expedition,** give yourself at least a year to hammer out all the details, including finding the right companions, acquiring **permits**, organizing **transportation** and resupply, and poring over maps for the best route. Remember that remote canoe trips often venture hundreds of miles from civilization and that the margin for error is very small. If you decide to participate in such a trip, make sure all your outdoor skills are rock solid and choose your companions thoughtfully.

Shorter trips can be organized in a fraction of the time. If you'd prefer to have someone else deal with the details, consider hiring an outfitter to pack you out. Outfitters can provide everything from the permits, maps, and shuttles to all the gear and **food**. This makes your transportation much easier to organize and lets you maximize your relaxation.

CANYONEERING

Canyoneering is an old sport that in recent years has attracted a growing number of enthusiasts. By combining **hiking**, **rappelling**, wading, swimming, **rock climbing**, and **orienteering**, a canyoneer is able to explore remote canyons the world over. While canyon country is peaceful and calming, canyoneering requires you to be alert, quick acting, and extremely competent. Like many other adventure sports, canyoneering has a host of risks that accompanies its rewards.

The biggest risks in canyoneering come from **flash floods**, which can trap canyoneers deep within canyon walls with no easy way out—a fatal situation. To prevent this, enthusiasts of the sport study local **weather** patterns before they depart. They also research the watershed (the land that drains into the canyon) to determine its ability, or inability, to retain water. Next, they review canyon **maps** and look for potential **bailout points** along their route. Once they're confident of the weather forecast for the entire watershed and satisfied that their route offers adequate foul-weather options, they head

out to the rim of the canyon and descend into its depths.

This is where the fun begins. As a canyoneer, you'll find yourself squeezing through slot canyons and crawling behind waterfalls, swimming across frigid pools, and scaling tall walls. To be successful, you'll need a complete repertoire of outdoor skills.

Canyons are undeniably powerful, yet they are also extremely fragile. Some soils that take decades to grow just a fraction of an inch can be killed by a single footstep. Unintentional scratches and scars left on canyon walls become permanent eyesores. With the sport becoming increasingly popular, the need to preserve the natural qualities of the canyons is paramount. The good news is that many canyoneers are as passionate about preserving canyons as they are

When canyoneering, beware of changing weather. A sudden rainstorm could create enough runoff to turn this beautiful Utah canyon into a sieve.

ANNIE AGGENS

about exploring them. By using **Leave No Trace** techniques that have been adapted to the unique **desert** environment of most canyons, you can explore canyons while preserving them for future generations. One way to do this is to travel below the watercourse—that portion of the canyon that lies beneath the high-water mark—whenever possible. The watercourse is usually free of plant life because floods regularly flush it out. By staying in this area, you minimize erosion and avoid destroying the delicate life that survives above.

Canyoneering is a sport with little room for error. As such, the best way to try it is with a professional **guide** or an experienced friend. The American Canyoneering Association offers comprehensive technical canyoneering courses for the novice or the seasoned canyoneer. As a popular organization for canyoneering enthusiasts, the ACA is a good source for gear, books, on-line forums, and certification programs (see resources section).

Wherever there are canyons, you will find canyoneers. In many tourism destinations, canyoneering tours have become a viable business. If you decide to take a tour, make sure you choose a company with a good reputation and experienced guides. Be sure to inquire about the level of fitness needed to complete the descent. If you are acrophobic, inquire about heights and ledges. If you are claustrophobic, ask whether they plan to take you into any tight spaces. Take the safety issues seriously. For example, find out the weather forecast yourself. If the possibility of a storm exists, or if it's the rainy (monsoon) season, consider another activity. While many qualified guides don't have ACA certification, it is one tool that you can use to assess their experience. In Europe, ask for a guide with a certification from the Commission Europeenne de Canyon (CEC).

CARABINERS

Carabiners (or *biners*) are metal devices generally used to clip a **rope** into protection and **anchor** systems. Biners have countless practical uses in

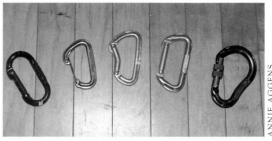

The carabiner type you use depends on how you will use it. For example, climbers concerned about weight often prefer wire-gate biners because they're lightweight. Ice climbers like them, too, because they tend not to freeze up. Bent-gate biners are often the choice of lead climbers because the angle of the gate makes it easy to clip into slings and quickdraws. From left: oval, wire gate, bent gate, D, locking pear.

the backcountry. Most people associate carabiners with the different disciplines of climbing, but they also have a place in **caving**, whitewater paddling, **rescue**, and any other activity that employs **ropes**. You may use a carabiner as a part of a **rappelling** anchor system or as a gadget to hang your camera from your backpack's sternum strap.

Biners are developed to hold weight along their long axis, or spine. The weakest portion of a biner is at its gate. A biner can be nonlocking, locking, or self-locking. A locking biner can be locked in the "closed" position to combat against the off-chance that its gate will accidentally open. Locking biners are generally stronger, heavier, and more expensive. In a pinch, you can get benefits similar to a locking biner from two nonlocking biners that are placed in an opposite and opposed position.

The type of carabiner that you buy will depend on how you intend to use it. Each of the following questions can help you narrow your selection. Will you be climbing? If so, will you be using a belay device? Will you need to create a multibiner brake? Is weight an issue? What about versatility? Your basic choices for carabiner styles are oval, D, offset D, and pear shaped. Variations on these designs are made for added strength, reduced weight, and ease of use. Often, variations also exist in the shape of the gate or spine of one style of biner. Each style of carabiner has a different feel, so after asking yourself the above questions, pick up each style and get a sense for how it feels in your hand. Most carabiners are made of aluminum alloy. However, many rescuers, cavers, and top-rope climbers use steel biners because they are very strong and resistant to abrasion (though much heavier).

When purchasing biners, always pay a little extra for a quality product. Buy carabiners made by well-known and well-respected manufacturers. Compare the open-gate strengths of different biners that you are considering. Avoid cheap or old biners. Never climb on a biner unless it was made for climbing. The kind that you find in the check-out line at the hardware store are good only for "around-camp" uses, such as hanging your candle lantern from the ceiling of your tent.

THE CASCADES

Stretching over 700 miles from Mount Lassen in northern California through Oregon and Washington to the Fraser River in southwest British Columbia, the Cascades are the major mountain range of the North American Pacific Northwest. The range is 30 to 80 miles wide, broken only by the deep Columbia River valley on the Oregon–Washington border. Most of the range rises to 7,000 to 9,000 feet and is heavily wooded, but the dominant features are the line of huge stratovolcanoes, most rising to more than 10,000 feet high and covered with **glaciers**. These volcanoes include the Three Sisters, Glacier Peak, and Mounts Shasta, Hood, Jefferson, St. Helens, Adams, Baker, and Rainier—the last is the highest in the range, at 14,410 feet. Although some are extinct, many of these volcanoes are only dormant; periodic eruptions do occur, the most recent being those of Mount St. Helens in 1980 and 1981.

The Cascade Range is named for the many waterfalls tumbling down the walls of the Columbia River Gorge, but the name is also appropriate because the range lies in the track of storm systems from the Pacific Ocean and therefore experiences plentiful rainfall in summer and running water everywhere. Winter brings heavy snowfalls, and **snow** lies for up to nine months of the year at higher levels. This moisture leads to rich vegetation and huge trees, especially on the western side of the range.

Steep, rugged mountains, the Cascades are a major destination for climbers. Few of the higher peaks can be climbed without **mountaineering** skills. For hikers, the range offers more than 20,000 miles of **trails**, including the **Pacific Crest Trail**, which runs for some 1,300 miles from northern California to the Canadian border, and tl.e 93-mile Wonderland Trail, which circles Mount Rainier. Much of the range is protected in a series of **national parks** and **wilderness** areas, including Crater Lake National Park, the Three Sisters Wilderness, the Mount Hood Wilderness, Mount Rainier National Park, the Glacier Peak Wilderness, and North Cascades National Park.

CATHOLE

A cathole is a small hole that is dug into the ground to bury human waste. When left on the ground, human waste can get washed into the local water supply and can contaminate the surrounding area. In addition, animals attracted to the waste can acquire and transmit diseases that are carried in fecal matter. The best way to dispose of your human waste is to bury it in a cathole that is at least 6 to 8 inches deep, often the depth of your trowel. The organic matter in the ground will help decompose the waste. In addition, at that depth, the waste should go undetected by most critters. The cathole should be at least 70 adult paces away from any source of water. Any **toilet paper** or nonhuman waste (such as tampons) should be packed out, *not* buried in the cathole.

See also **Leave No Trace** and **sanitation**.

CAVING

Caving, or spelunking, is the sport of exploring caves. Caves offer the adventurer a pristine, remote environment unlike any other. If you were ever

Battery-operated headlamps are a popular light source among cavers. Every caver should carry a minimum of three sources of light. Wind Cave, South Dakota.

jealous of the adventurous forays of Tom Sawyer, caving may be your sport. Caves are usually formed when water erodes through layers of limestone. As the water trickles through the highly soluble limestone, it creates passageways deep beneath the earth's surface. Over thousands of years, these passageways progressively erode and eventually become large enough for a person to navigate.

Caving involves a lot more than crawling on your hands and knees with a flashlight. It can be a difficult sport and is not for everyone. As a caver, you can easily find yourself slithering on your stomach through tight passages that can be as narrow as 1 foot! Your field of vision is limited to the scope of your lamp, and the thought that you probably have hundreds of tons of earth above you may fleetingly enter your mind. Needless to say, this is not a sport for claustrophobics. To protect yourself, your group, and the cave, most cavers follow some rules of thumb.

- Never cave alone. The minimum group size should be three people.
- If one person needs to turn back, everyone should turn back.
- Leave a **trip plan** with someone reliable that includes your route and the amount of time you plan to be gone. Remember that time is deceptive in caves, because there is no sunlight. It's easy to lose track of time and stay longer than intended.
- Always carry three sources of light (see **light-**

ing). Battery-operated **headlamps**, flashlights, and **candles** are among the options.
- Ask for help if you need it; caution is the order of the day. If you want someone to spot you over a ledge or assist you across a bridge, just ask. Small accidents can easily become major **rescues**, and falls are the most common accident!
- Cavers carry all their supplies (spare lighting, **food**) in a small, portable **pack**, often the size of a **fanny pack**. Be vigilant about not losing your pack. Without it, you're bound to find trouble!
- Every so often, turn around to get a different perspective on your surroundings. This is what the cave will look like on your way back!
- Be polite to the landowners. If the cave is on private property (as most are), ask for permission to enter and always respect the owner's requests.
- Cave diving is extremely dangerous. Only cavers who are trained in this specialized discipline should attempt a cave dive.

One of the best parts of caving is discovering the beautiful and delicate formations, or speleothems, that dot many caves. These incredible structures are generally composed of calcium carbonate, a by-product of the erosive genesis of the cave. While most people are familiar with the sand castle–like stalactites (the ones that hang down from the ceiling) and stalagmites (the ones that grow up from the ground), a multitude of lesser known formations also await the caver. Their unique names often reflect their appearances: soda straw, bacon, pearls, popcorn, and draperies, just to name a few.

The best way to try caving is with an experienced **guide** or friend. Many **national parks** offer wild cave tours that give the general public a sense of the life down under. Some of these tours can be quite rigorous, so be prepared. Another option is to hook up with the local grotto, or club, of the National Speleological Society. The NSS is the largest caving organization in the United States, with over 12,000 members and 200 grottos across the country. They offer courses, tours, and lots of information on caving (see resources section).

ANNIE AGGENS

Caving Equipment

Basic Equipment
clothing
helmet
knee pads
caver's pack
light
backup lights
knife
emergency gear (including a space blanket
or trash bag, small **first-aid kit**, and
spare lights)
water
food

Advanced Gear
ascending device
carabiner
rappelling device
harness
rope

CELESTIAL NAVIGATION

Celestial navigation is the art of using celestial bodies, such as the sun, moon, planets, and stars, to plot your position and set a course for travel. Over the centuries, mariners, explorers, and clock makers alike struggled to perfect this noble science. The challenge was not determining one's **latitude**, as this could be accomplished with relative ease; the problem was finding **longitude**. Without longitude, navigators could never know exactly where they were. Thousands of sailors lost their lives because of this gap in the puzzle. So desperate were the great navies of the world that in 1714 England's Parliament offered the reward of a king's ransom to the person who could solve this great mystery. Finally, with the invention of the chronometer by John Harrison, a humble British clock maker, mariners were able to calculate longitude in addition to latitude.

Celestial navigation uses a finely crafted instrument called a *sextant* to measure the angle between the horizon and a celestial body. Combining this information with other data found in the annually published *Nautical Almanac*, you can calculate your position in relationship to that same celestial body. Finally, a purpose for calculus! Knowing your position relative to a celestial body, in turn, allows you to calculate your exact position on the planet. Sound confusing? Think about it this way: Imagine that you are near the Eiffel Tower, but you don't know exactly where you are. From a book you are able to determine the exact height of the tower. This means that by measuring the angle between the horizon and the top of the tower, you can calculate your exact distance from its base. Let's say you come up with 35 feet. You could be anywhere that is 35 feet from the base of the tower: draw a circle connecting all the points that are 35 feet from the tower, and you will be somewhere on that circle. Now repeat the same process with the nearby office building, and again with the radio tower. That will put you on another two separate circles. Wherever these three circles intersect will be your exact location. Celestial navigation uses the same process but on a grand, earthly scale. In reality, it's not quite that simple, but you get the picture.

While celestial navigation is not a lost art, it is unfortunately in its old age. Most wilderness travelers prefer to use their handy **GPS** instead of

The basis of celestial navigation is using a sextant to measure the angle between a celestial body and the horizon.

ANNIE AGGENS

hauling around a fragile sextant and ripped-out pages of the current *Nautical Almanac*. The exception to this rule is mariners who like to use a sextant as a backup to their modern navigation systems or who simply prefer the old-school rules of **navigation**. Nonetheless, while it may not be practical to navigate by sextant on your backcountry trip, it sure is fun! If you decide to take up celestial navigation, look for a class with a knowledgeable instructor and plan to spend a lot of time practicing your technique. Many organizations offer instruction in basic and advanced celestial navigation. Check with local marine shops to find a course near you. If you'd prefer to read about the subject first, there are plenty of good books on the subject, including *Celestial Navigation by H.O. 249*, by John E. Milligan; and *A Star to Steer Her By*, by Edward J. Bergin.

If all you want out of the sky is to be able to look up and navigate without complicating calculations, all is not lost. On any starry night in the Northern Hemisphere, you should be able to locate Polaris, the North Star. By facing Polaris, your cardinal directions will be easy to find. North will be straight ahead of you, east will be 90 degrees to your right, west will be 90 degrees to your left, and south will be behind you. Having a basic familiarity with the constellations can make any backcountry trip more fun. Knowing their names and their mythological histories can make good tales for around the campfire. Better yet, there's nothing like lying down under the blanket of a million glistening stars to lull you to sleep. Also see **nature's compass**.

CELL PHONES

Cell phones, one of several **communication devices** available, are often carried as a safety item. While useful, a cell phone isn't a substitute for good **wilderness** skills. There is no coverage in many areas, especially remote ones, and even where there is you may not be able to get a signal in deep canyons or below **mountains** or cliffs. Often, to get a signal you have to climb up high, such as to a summit. Batteries can run low, especially in cold **weather**. Even if you do manage to make a call, it could be many hours before assistance can reach you, during which time you need to be able to keep yourself warm and dry.

If you do have a cell phone, it should be used only in a real emergency, which means one where you can't get yourself out of trouble. Too often, unskilled travelers call for help because they rely on their phone rather than learning how to live in the wilderness.

Cell phones are controversial in the backcountry. Many people go to the wilderness in part to escape from phones and other aspects of modern civilization. If you carry a phone, it is best to use it only away from others so you don't disturb them. Be sure to keep it switched off unless you are making a call. A ringing phone is not something people usually want to hear in the wild (see also **noise**).

CHECKLIST

Any wilderness trip requires carrying a host of items. If you assemble your gear from memory, it's easy to forget some small but vital item. Always work from a checklist that contains every item that you might want to carry. For each trip, make a list of those items you require and then check them off *as you pack them*. This last is important. Don't check something off because you've remembered where it is in the closet, or it will likely still be there when you reach the trailhead. Put everything on the checklist, including items you'll be wearing and items that won't be in your **pack**. People have forgotten their **boots** on more than one occasion because they didn't do this.

If you note the **weight** of each item on the checklist, you can work out how much basic weight you have for a trip. Then, if it's too much (as it usually is), you can work out what to leave behind or whether you have a lighter substitute for something.

After a trip, make notes on your checklist about items that need replacing or repairing; this will act as a reminder before your next trip.

See also **planning a trip**.

CLIMBING COMMUNICATION

To help ensure the safety of any climber, communication between the climber and the belayer (see **belaying**) must be concise and unmistakable. The following communication commands have become the standard choice for most climbers.

"Belay on" — A call by the belayer to notify the climber that she is being belayed. If the climber hasn't heard this command, she can ask "On belay?"

"Climbing" — A call by the climber to notify the belayer that she has begun or resumed climbing.

"Climb" — Also "Climb on." This reaffirms to the climber that the belayer is ready.

"Slack" — A request from the climber for additional rope. Often used when the climber needs to down climb or traverse a section of the route.

"Up rope" — A request from the climber for the belayer to take up the slack in the rope. This may occur if the climber is climbing faster than the belayer can take in the rope.

"Watch me" — A call from the climber signifying that she may be making a difficult move and that the belayer should be prepared for a fall.

"Tension" — A request from the climber to tighten the belay. This may be used before the climber is lowered down from a top-roped climb (see **top roping**).

"Falling!" — Notifies the belayer that the climber is about to, or has already begun to, fall off the rock. This may give the belayer a moment to prepare for the force of the fall (although he should always be prepared for this possibility).

"Feet 'two-zero'" — A call from the belayer notifying the climber of how much rope is left. Starting with the word *feet* gets the climber's attention before the more important information —the actual number of feet left— is yelled. Yelling the numbers individually ("two-zero," as opposed to "twenty") helps to clarify the number. This is especially important on long pitches or windy days.

"ROCK!" — A command signifying that an object (any object) has been knocked loose and is on its way down. This can be hollered by anyone.

"That's me" — Also "zero." A command the climber uses to notify the belayer that she has taken in all the available excess rope and that the belayer is now pulling on the climber.

"Off belay" — Said by the climber to notify the belayer that she is either on the ground or safely secured to another **anchor** and no longer needs a belay.

"Belay off" — Said by the belayer to notify the climber that the belay is broken down and the rope is now free of the belayer.

"ROPE!" — Hollered anytime someone is **throwing a climbing rope** over the edge of a cliff. This notifies anyone below to prepare for a quickly descending rope and anything else it may knock free.

While the majority of the commands are widely used, some regional differences exist. It is always smart to discuss with any new climbing partners the best way to communicate. If you are in an area with a lot of climbers, it also helps to precede your command with your partner's name.

Many climbers use nonverbal signals, such as tugs on the rope for long pitches or other special circumstances that make verbal communication difficult. Every tug represents one syllable in a climbing command. Therefore, you would interpret one tug as "slack" and therefore pay out a little rope. Two tugs would be interpreted as either "Up rope" or "Tension." In either case, you would tighten the belay. While this system can work, it has obvious problems. For instance, it can be difficult to distinguish an intentional tug from a jerky climbing maneuver. Needless to say, if you intend to use this system, be sure to review it with your partner before you get on the rock!

CLIMBING EQUIPMENT
See **rock climbing**.

CLIMBING ETHICS
One of the reasons **rock climbing** is so popular is because you can push your limits and escape boundaries. Climbing offers people an elemental freedom that they find wholesome and addictive. While most people would agree that climbing has no hard-and-fast rules, most climbers feel dedicated to upholding a certain ethic that reflects the true spirit of the sport.

Climbing ethics are different from climbing style. Climbing style refers to the way you decide to get to the top of your route. Were you **free climbing**, or did you "accidentally" step on an old bolt to get past the crux? Did you rappel down and place protection before making your first ascent? Did you hang on the **rope** to think out your next move? All of these questions are related to your style of climbing. While certain styles are more admired than others, style really has to do with how you want to climb. If getting to the top is all that is important to you, your style might be a far cry from the purist who is more concerned with fluid rock-climbing technique.

While climbing style is mostly about you and your personal choices, climbing ethics is about how you relate to your surroundings, including other climbers, park officials, landowners, and even the rock itself. Indeed, respecting the rock and your fellow climbers is the foundation of today's climbing ethic. Most climbers would agree that the following behavior represents ethical climbing.

- Climb the rock as is. Altering the rock in any way, such as breaking off a flake to create a **handhold**, is unacceptable. If you can't climb the route as is, choose an easier route.
- Do not alter a first ascent. In other words, if someone established a route as a free climb, don't go in and bolt the crux to make it easier. Likewise, replacing a damaged bolt on a bolted route is acceptable, and prudent, but don't add an additional bolt to change the skill level.
- Climb as cleanly as possible. This simply means not leaving any protection behind. Bolts and permanently stuck pros (protection) can damage the rock and become eyesores.
- Respect other climbers. Move with great caution anytime there may be others below you.
- Don't put yourself, or other people, in harm's way. Choose a route appropriate for your skill level, and arrive competent and prepared.
- When climbing in a new area, first familiarize yourself with local practices. These often are discussed in guidebooks. You also can inquire at a climbing shop or simply observe the other climbers.

You may not be commended for abiding by climbing ethics, but if you disregard them, be prepared to stand the heat. Climbers have no problem voicing their disapproval over apparent lack of respect for rock, established routes, safety, and access. While some climbing ethics have been and will continue to be debated, ethical climbing is no fad. Most climbers enthusiastically embrace the ethics that protect the natural aesthetics of the rock and promote responsible climbing.

CLIMBING RATINGS
Just as rivers are classified to rate the difficulty of their rapids, so too are **rock climbing** routes rated. The modern climbing rating system in the United

States was born in the late 1930s when the **Sierra Club** began categorizing their alpine ascents. This system, which is still in use today, divides routes into classes that describe the level of difficulty and necessary equipment as follows.

Class 1—Walking or hiking on relatively flat ground. No special equipment needed.

Class 2—Some scrambling. Hands may be needed. Proper shoes are important.

Class 3—Simple climbing or exposed scrambling. You may want a **rope**.

Class 4—Difficult and exposed scrambling or exposed but easy climbing. A fall could be fatal. A rope should be used for protection from exposure.

Class 5—Technical **free climbing** requiring ropes and **anchors** for protection.

Class 6—**Aid climbing** that relies on **artificial protection** for advancement and support.

This system, as organized, was functional but did not address the huge spectrum of difficulty that can be found within class 5, or technical, rock climbing. In response, the **Yosemite Decimal System** (YDS) was introduced. The YDS adds a decimal after the number 5 to further denote the level of difficulty of a class 5 route. A climb that is rated 5.3 (said *five-three*), for instance, is much easier than a climb that is rated 5.9. In fact, for a long time, 5.9 was the most difficult rating a climb could receive. As climbers began to push the envelope, the need to expand the YDS became obvious, and the ratings 5.10 through 5.14 were introduced. In addition, each of the ratings from 5.10 up can be further appraised by placing a letter (a through d) after the decimal. A climb rated 5.11d is significantly harder than a 5.11a climb.

The YDS classification system generally rates the crux (the hardest part) of a climb. If you are on a route that is generally 5.6 but the crux is 5.7, the climb will likely receive the 5.7 rating. If the climb is nothing but sustained 5.7 moves, it might get a 5.8 rating. Confused? Don't worry, you'll get used to it. The YDS rates only for technical difficulty. It does not give the climber-to-be any information on the availability of protection, the length of the climb, or its aesthetic value. To fill these voids, guidebooks often provide additional ratings.

The system that divides routes into grades is an example of a further rating. This system uses Roman numerals to grade climbs based on the amount of time a competent party can expect to spend on the route. The grading system is as follows.

Grade I—Short climb, 1 or 2 pitches, 1 to 2 hours

Grade II—Relatively short climb, 2 to 4 pitches, 2 to 4 hours

Grade III—Short day of climbing, 3 to 7 pitches, 4 to 8 hours

Grade IV—Long day of climbing, 6 to 12 pitches, 8 to 12 hours

Grade V—One or two days of climbing, roughly 10 to 18 pitches

Grade VI—Multiple days of climbing, 15+ pitches

This grading system does not reflect the technical difficulty. You can have a grade I climb that is rated 5.12c or a grade II climb where the crux is a 5.6 move. It is rare, however, to find a grade V or VI that is less than a 5.8 climb.

Another description some guidebooks use is the seriousness rating, which indicates how difficult it is to place protection. This system reflects Hollywood's motion picture rating. A climb rated PG-13, for example, has adequate protection. R-rated climbs may have infrequent or inadequate protection placement, and X climbs are regarded as very exposed and extremely difficult to protect.

Aid climbing has its own system of classification. You would think that, like free climbing, aid climbing would simply add a decimal after the 6. That, however, would be too easy. Instead, aid climbs are rated A0 to A5, with A0 being much easier than A5.

Not to be outdone, **ice climbing** also has its very own rating system. Ice climbs are rated numerically, grades 1 to 7. Grade 1 is a low-angle slope that requires nothing more than **crampons**. Grade 7 is a vertical wall of ice whose quality is questionable, with poor protection placement.

As with most classification systems, there's a lot of latitude in rating a climbing route. Because there is no team of "rating judges" to ensure that the rating system is consistent, you will find that a 5.8 climb in one area might resemble another area's 5.9 climb. In addition, a 5.6 climb could easily have the difficulty of a 5.8 climb if you have poor **weather** conditions, an injured hand, or another hindering factor.

The rating of any climb should be taken with a grain of salt. That said, the rating should be close enough to the real level of difficulty to give you an idea of whether it is suitable for you. Because routes can be difficult to judge from the ground, knowing the rating of a climb in advance is a smart safety precaution. Be aware if you travel outside the United States that the rating systems in other parts of the world are very different. If you plan to climb abroad, familiarize yourself with the local rating system before you find yourself stuck in the middle of a route that's way beyond your skills.

CLIMBING SKINS

Climbing skins are strips of fabric with a brushed back that are attached to touring or mountaineering skis so they grip the snow when you are climbing. They're called *skins* because in the past they were made from animal skin. Today, they're usually made from nylon or mohair. Most skins have glue on one side to stick them to the skis, plus clips that fit over the ski tips. Some have tail clips as well. Skins come in different widths and lengths to fit different sizes of skis.

See also **ski touring** and **ski mountaineering.**

CLOTHING

The purpose of clothing in the outdoors is to keep you as comfortable as possible whatever the **weather.** That means cool in the heat, warm in the cold, and dry in the wet, whether you are moving or at rest. Clothing also needs to be as light as possible, low in bulk, quick drying, easy to care for, and durable.

Heat Loss

Clothing should provide a balance between heat production and heat loss so you don't feel uncomfortably warm or cold. Because activity generates heat, you'll need less clothing when moving than when staying still. How much clothing you wear depends on the temperature, the **wind**, and whether or not it's raining or snowing.

Heat is lost in four ways: convection, conduction, perspiration, and radiation. Clothing has to cope with all of them.

The most important method of heat loss is by convection, the transfer of heat from the body to the air, which happens whenever the air is cooler than the body. The bigger the difference in temperature between body and air, the warmer the clothing needed. Not surprisingly, heat loss due to convection speeds up when it's windy. Windproof clothing is needed to prevent this in cold weather, and loose clothing is useful to promote convection in hot climates.

Conduction is the movement of heat from one surface to another. It occurs with all materials, but some conduct heat more rapidly than others. Air is a poor conductor and thus a good insulator. Clothing made from materials that trap air in its fibers, such as fleece, wool, down, and synthetics (for example, Polarguard), is best for keeping you warm. Water conducts heat well, which is why clothing is much less efficient when wet and why you need waterproof clothing in the **rain.**

Because your body always produces perspiration, in the form of vapor if not visible sweat, clothing also needs to transmit moisture, a feature known, inaccurately, as **breathability.** If not, you will get wet from condensation and trapped moisture. To turn body moisture to vapor, a process called *evaporation*, heat is needed. When you're working hard, you can produce up to a quart of

wool hat

polypropylene undershirt

wind- and water-proof outer layer

hot beverage

fleece top

windpants

gaiters

articulated knees

socks

boots

Hats and gloves are easy to don and shed as needed. Hats especially make a huge difference to how warm you feel. Keep one handy so you can put it on as soon as you feel chilled.

moisture an hour in the form of sweat. This needs to be transported quickly through your clothing to prevent heat loss. Ventilation—as well as "breathable" clothing—is important for this. Of course, in hot weather when you want to lose heat, evaporation can help cool you down. Wearing wet clothes then can be a benefit.

The final form of heat loss is by radiation, the direct transfer of heat between two objects without the intervening space being heated. Clothing cuts out most heat loss by radiation, so this is not a big concern.

Layering

No one layer of clothing can keep you comfortable in all weather conditions regardless of whether you are moving or at rest. Over the course of a day, you might go from a cool start in still air to a warmer but breezy midday to an afternoon of showers. Even if the weather is stable, you'll probably need extra clothing at rest stops.

Several layers of thin clothing enable you to adjust clothing to suit the conditions. While most layers are worn on the torso, layering is also appropriate for the legs, hands, and head in cool or wet weather.

Different layers serve different purposes. The next-to-the skin, or base, layer should wick moisture away quickly (see **wicking**). Midlayers provide insulation to keep you warm and may also be wind resistant. The outer layer should keep out wind and rain. How many layers are needed depends on the weather expected. In hot weather, a thin base layer may be enough while **hiking**, with a light insulating layer carried for rest stops and in camp and a light rain jacket in case of rain. In **desert** areas, a windproof layer can replace the rainwear. In most places, more than this will be required, with a standard outfit consisting of base layer, lightweight to medium-weight midlayer, and outer layer with another midlayer carried for camp and rest stops and in case of colder-than-expected weather.

Base Layer

Base layers may be made of synthetics, such as polyester or polypropylene, or natural materials, such as wool and silk. All of these will wick moisture away from your skin reasonably quickly. None, however, will stay bone dry when you are exercising hard, although they will either dry quite rapidly or, in the case of wool, feel quite warm when damp. Base layers come in different weights. The lightest and thinnest wick moisture fastest and dry quickest, making them suitable for warm-weather and aerobic pursuits, such as **trail running** and **cross-country skiing**. Thicker ones are better for activities where you'll be stationary for periods of time, such as climbing, and for cold weather.

Avoid **cotton** for base layers except in warm weather, because it absorbs large amounts of water and takes ages to dry, requiring much body heat. That's why it feels cold against the skin. This may be pleasant in the heat but can leave you shivering and even at risk of **hypothermia** in the cold.

A base layer should fit fairly closely for maximum efficiency but should not feel restrictive. Zipped-neck tops are useful for both extra insulation and ventilation. Button shirts with collars are also available. For leg wear, look for a snug waist that won't sag.

Midlayer

The choice here is vast. A simple wool sweater or shirt is adequate, but many high-tech garments also are available.

The most popular fabric is **fleece**, also known as *microfleece* or *pile*, a furry or brushed form of polyester that is warm for the weight, dries quickly, wicks moisture fast, and is very durable. Fleece comes in many different weights. The thinnest is fine for summer; the thickest will be too warm to move in except in the depths of winter. Standard fleece isn't windproof, which can be a bonus because it means moisture passes through it very quickly. Windproof fleece, in which a thin windproof membrane is inserted between two layers of fleece, keeps out the wind but doesn't "breathe" as well as nonwindproof fleece.

Synthetic insulation, such as Primaloft and Polarguard, is used to make lightweight filled garments that are windproof, warm, and breathable. The thinner ones are an alternative to windproof fleece; the heavier ones, an alternative to down. These garments are quite rain resistant and dry fairly fast.

The warmest midlayers are filled with goose or duck **down**. Indeed, these are so warm that they are worn only when moving in the very coldest weather. They're great for camp wear, though, or for cold belays. Down's big disadvantage is that it's cold when wet and takes a long time to dry. As a result, many down jackets have waterproof or water-resistant shells.

The garments known as **soft shells**—thin, synthetic, windproof garments that may or may not have thin wicking linings—are usually worn as an outer layer, but they can also serve as a midlayer or even a base layer. Thus they can be worn next to the skin, over a thin base layer, or even over fleece. Some of them are rain resistant, so a rain jacket isn't needed except in the heaviest, most prolonged downpour. Windproof fleece garments also are often referred to as soft shells.

Outer Layer

This is your protection against rain and snow. As well as keeping out storms, it needs to allow at least some body moisture out so you don't get too damp inside. To do this efficiently, both fabric and design are important. Moisture vapor permeable (MVP) or breathable fabrics are best, but don't expect miracles from them. Work hard, and **condensation** will still appear inside. Even the best can't pass moisture vapor at anything like the rate you give it off. With the most aerobic activities—**mountain biking**, cross-country skiing, trail running—you can expect to get damp in any rain gear. No MVP fabrics work as well in the rain or in high humidity as they do in cool, dry conditions.

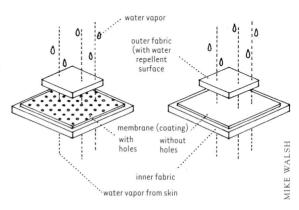

Breathable materials are either coated or laminated. Microporous fabric (left) allows water vapor to pass through microscopic holes in the membrane. In hydrophilic fabric (right), a nonporous membrane absorbs water vapor and then allows it to evaporate.

Three-layer laminate

The membrane is laminated with both the inner and the outer fabrics.

Two-layer laminates
Outer laminate

The waterproof membrane is laminated to the back of the outer fabric.

Drop liner

The membrane is laminated with an interlining material.

Lining laminate
(Laminated to drop liner: LTD)

The membrane is laminated with the inner lining.

MIKE WALSH

Each method of laminating waterproof fabrics has advantages and disadvantages. Three-layer laminates are the most durable, but the fabric is slightly stiffer than with other methods. Two-layer, lining, and drop liner laminates are soft and comfortable, but the membrane is vulnerable to abrasion. Drop liners in particular are unsuitable for use with a heavy pack because the fragile membrane can rub on both the outer shell and the inner lining. Lining laminates are the most breathable, but few garments have this construction.

MVP fabrics vary a great deal in how quickly they let moisture vapor through. With some, condensation starts to appear after only a short brisk walk, while others may keep you dry for a few hours.

A good fabric on its own isn't enough. The garments must also be watertight by design. This means tape-sealed seams, flaps over zippers, and

a good hood large enough to fit over a **hat** or a helmet, if necessary. The best hoods also move with the head so they don't impede vision. For windy areas, stiffened brims are useful too.

However good the fabric, ventilation is the best way to get rid of moisture vapor. This means closing the jacket and wearing the hood only when absolutely necessary. Wearing a waterproof hat instead of a hood allows for ventilation at the neck and can keep you much drier. Many jackets come with underarm, or "pit," zippers. These can be useful for venting moisture vapor, though some are difficult to use and feel quite bulky. Mesh-lined chest pockets can also be used as vents and are easier to use than pit zippers.

Rain jackets come in many different weights and designs. A fully specified, reinforced jacket may be needed for **mountaineering**, when it will be worn all the time, while an ultralight, very basic jacket should be fine for warm-weather hiking.

Rain pants are awkward items disliked by many. In many areas, they aren't really needed, at least in summer. In cold rain, they can be essential. The best have adjustable waistbands and long lower leg zips so they can be pulled on and off over footwear. For skiing and mountaineering, ones with full-length zippers are useful because they can be taken off and put on when you're wearing skis or **crampons**.

All rain gear is given a water-repellency treatment that makes rain bead and run down the outside. In time, this treatment will probably wear off. When this happens, dark damp patches appear on the garment where rain is soaking in. The garment isn't leaking; the rain still won't go through the waterproof coating or membrane. However, the garment may feel as if it's leaking; more condensation gathers inside because moisture vapor can't easily pass through the wet outer fabric.

The water repellency can be restored by heat—ironing or tumble drying—which melts the treatment and spreads it over the fabric. When heat no longer renews the water repellency, you can resort to sprays or wash-in treat-

Key Features of Rain Gear

- waterproof-breathable fabric that allows body moisture out
- taped seams (the fewer the better)
- adjustable hood with a peak that protects but also allows side-to-side vision
- adjustable cuffs
- full-length front zipper with a storm flap
- zippered chest pockets (big enough for maps)
- low weight and bulk

adjustable hood

minimal seams (all sealed)

pit zips

front pockets positioned out of the way of pack harness system

adjustable cuffs

full-length zipper with a storm flap

MIKE CLELLAND

ments. Check the garment's care label for which type to use. Eventually the waterproof membrane or coating will leak—when it does, it's time to replace the garment.

Leg Wear

In most conditions, your legs require much less protection than your torso. Shorts or thin, light long pants are often fine. Some long pants have zip-off legs, which can be very useful if weight is a consideration. For colder weather, carry long base-layer pants. Thicker pants will keep you warmer; in really cold weather, fleece pants are very warm.

For hiking, **ski touring**, and other activities where abrasion isn't a major factor, light synthetic or cotton-synthetic-blend pants will be adequate. The best fabrics, such as Supplex nylon, are windproof, breathable, and quick drying. For **rock climbing** and mountaineering, tougher fabrics (such as those from Schoeller), perhaps with reinforcements at the knees, seat, and ankles, will last longer.

See also **fabric, gaiters, gloves and mitts, Gore-Tex, heat regulation, insulation, sun protection, vapor barriers,** and **wool.**

CLOUDS

The next time you're outside, look up into the sky. Do you know what kind of cloud is overhead? Can you use the height and shape of the cloud to gauge incoming **weather**? Clouds are invaluable tools in predicting weather. Their clues can be subtle or abrupt, and knowing how to interpret what you see will give you advanced warning if the weather should turn sour. While at home, you may listen to complex weather reports that take advantage of intricate Doppler radar readings. On the **trail**, however, you have to rely on your own eyes to do the detective work.

Knowing the exact name for a cloud is less important than being able to recognize the weather it may bring. However, if you are carrying a weather **field guide**, you may enjoy matching up each cloud's name to its corresponding description. The name of any given cloud is simply a combination of terms. For example, the prefixes *cirro-* and *alto-* refer to the height of the cloud; *cirro-* denotes clouds whose bases are at least 20,000 feet high, and *alto-* signifies clouds whose bases are 6,000 to 20,000 feet high. The terms *cirrus, stratus,* and *cumulus* refer to the shape of the cloud. Cirrus means thin and wispy, stratus means

Ten Different Cloud Types and What They Mean

Cirrus clouds are high, white or light gray clouds that appear thin and wispy. Cirrus clouds should tell you that moisture is in the upper atmosphere and that it may be coming your way. If you see lots of cirrus clouds in the afternoon, you may have overcast skies or **rain** the following morning.

Cirrostratus clouds are high, white or light gray clouds that veil the sky in a featureless sheet. Cirrostratus can be thin or thick. They are often seen in combination with a halo around the sun or moon. These flat clouds represent moisture in the air. Keep an eye out for further cloud coverage, as cirrostratus can be a sign of approaching poor weather.

Cirrocumulus clouds are high, white or gray rippled clouds that are thin but somewhat puffy. These clouds are often found in combination with other clouds. Although uncommon, cirrocumulus clouds can signify approaching showers or thunderstorms.

Altocumulus clouds are small, puffy, white clouds that dot a portion of the sky or, in some cases, the whole sky. These clouds are generally benign, although if they continue to develop, they may signify rain to come.

Altostratus clouds are medium-high clouds that cover the sky like a sheet. They are usually gray to dark gray. Altostratus clouds are layered and often have little definition. They signify lots of moisture in the air that could turn to rain.

Stratus clouds are similar to altostratus clouds but lower. Stratus clouds make for an overcast, gray sky with little variation. Their bases can be as low as a few hundred feet above the trees. They represent saturated air near the ground. Stratus clouds are common in coastal areas and some valleys. Often, they will burn off during the day; however, if they persist they may produce drizzling rain.

Nimbostratus clouds are low-lying clouds that produce precipitation. They are usually dark gray or dark blue. Their base is fuzzy because of falling precipitation. If this cloud is over your head, you are probably already wet. Nimbostratus can quickly turn into thunderstorms. Be prepared for high **wind**. If you are on the water, paddle to shore and wait out the weather. If you are on a ridge, descend to lower ground.

(continued next page)

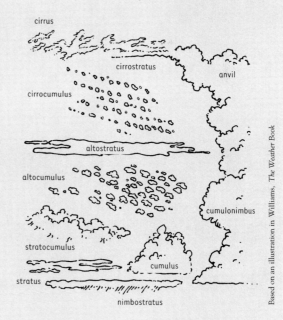

cirrus

cirrostratus

anvil

cirrocumulus

altostratus

altocumulus

cumulonimbus

stratocumulus

cumulus

stratus

nimbostratus

Based on an illustration in Williams, *The Weather Book*

Common cloud formations.

layered, and cumulus means billowing. The term *nimbus* simply refers to a cloud that is producing precipitation.

CLOVE HITCH

The clove hitch is one of those **knots** that get better with age; the longer you know it, the more uses you will find for it. The clove hitch is perfect for securing a **rope** snugly around a circular object, such as a pole or a **pack** frame. Unlike some other hitches and knots, the clove hitch is incredibly easy to adjust.

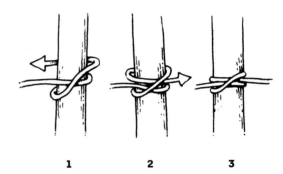

1   **2**   **3**

Clove hitch. 1. Wrap the rope around an object. 2. Wrap the running end (see knots*) around the object a second time and pass it under the first wrap. 3. Pull both ends of the rope taut to secure the hitch.*

COASTAL CURRENTS

There are all sorts of currents along the shores of coastal areas. If you happen to be paddling or swimming when you encounter such a current, it can be alarming and also very dangerous.

One of the more common currents is called a *rip current*. A rip current can occur anytime surf is pushing water up and onto a beach. Looking for a way to return to sea, the water that has piled up on the shore will form a return current that runs away from shore and out to open water. This current usually doesn't exceed 2 or 3 knots, but that's faster than most people can swim, and it can be a nuisance for paddlers. Although rip currents are often called *rip tides*, they have nothing to do with the **tide**. Therefore, paddlers and swimmers in big bodies of freshwater, such as the **Great Lakes** along the U.S.–Canada border, may experience rip currents.

If you find yourself being carried out on a rip current, avoid the temptation to swim directly back to shore, fighting the full strength of the flow. Because rip currents are relatively narrow, you should be able to get out of the current without much trouble. Swim parallel to shore until the current vanishes. Only then should you turn and swim back toward the beach. Often, the main rip current will be fed by smaller, feeder currents.

These run parallel to the shore in the shallow water just off the beach. While they generally pose no threat, they can become frustrating, because they often turn your kayak while you are launching or landing. They can also snatch your paddle if you don't keep a hand on it.

Tidal currents are found only in coastal waters. The current created by an incoming tide is called a *flood current*, while the current created by an outgoing tide is called an *ebb current*. Depending on your location, these currents can be as strong as 15 knots—a lot faster than a sea kayaker can paddle! These currents can resemble the strong currents found in rivers, and experience in river paddling can come in handy when negotiating them. Just as there are tide tables that can help you determine the rise and fall of the tides at your particular location, there are tables to help you assess the tidal currents. These tables give the direction and strength of the current and the times of day that the current will peak and slack. Also try to get information from other paddlers who have been in the area. These tables are not made with kayakers in mind, so the places you find most tempting to paddle may very well not be covered.

Tidal currents follow a few general rules that can help you predict their character. For instance, anywhere there is a narrow passage, such as between an island and land or at the narrow entrance to a bay, expect to find strong tidal currents. Sometimes the currents are strong enough to create **eddies** and whirlpools behind obstructions in the water. Currents tend to be stronger in deep water and less strong in shallow water: if you find yourself paddling against the current, it may be smart to stick closer to shore. Likewise, if you are going with the current, you may get a little boost from heading toward deeper water.

If a **wind** is blowing in the opposite direction of the current, expect to find steep, choppy **waves**. Also expect difficult waves anywhere a river drains into the sea, especially when a river's current drains directly into an incoming tide. The waves in such a location can become frighteningly steep and violent, so much so that they have

been given a name—*clapotis*. Avoid these areas when possible.

A similar phenomenon, called *tide rips* (not to be confused with the poorly named *rip tides*), occurs anytime a strong current encounters an abrupt change in its course. This can be from a significantly uneven sea floor, a landmass jutting into the water, or even an opposing current. Some tide rips are marked on **nautical charts**, while others aren't. Try to identify potential trouble spots before you reach them, possibly by gathering information from local sources. Tide rips can be quite violent and can easily upset a kayak.

COILING A ROPE

For a quick and easy way to carry your **rope**, you should learn to coil it. Coiling a rope keeps it manageable and generally free of the messy knots that can result from poor packing. The two most widely used coils are the mountaineer's coil and the butterfly coil (not to be confused with the **butterfly knot**).

The mountaineer's coil is convenient for carrying a rope over a **pack**. The easiest way to create a mountaineer's coil is to form a series of arm-length loops that drape over your hand. Another option is to wrap the rope around your knees while you're sitting in a diamond position (knees apart, heels together). While this can take some time and does not always produce the best coil, it is a lot easier for people with small hands. When you get toward the end of the rope, tightly wrap the remaining rope around the portion of the loops that is in your hand, and secure the tail.

The butterfly coil is much faster than the mountaineer's coil. It is also an easier coil if your rope is twisted from a belay device. Start the butterfly coil by locating the two ends of your rope and giving yourself several arm lengths from each end of the rope to set aside. Then begin to coil the rope by creating loops on either side of the palm of your hand. The loops should be consistent and uniform. When you run out of rope, take the few arm lengths of rope that you set aside and firmly wrap them around the entire rope several

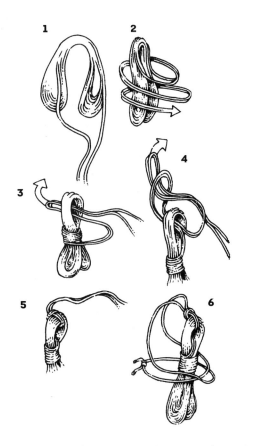

Butterfly coil. Hold both ends of the rope together and measure out several arm lengths of rope, letting them fall to the ground. 1. Drape the remainder of the rope back and forth across your hand. 2. When all the rope is draped across your hand, take the ends of the rope (earlier set aside) and wrap them around the coils several times. 3. Take a bight (see knots) from the remaining ends of the rope and pass it through the loop where you have been holding the rope. 4. Now take the ends of the rope and pass them through this bight. 5. Tug on the ends of the rope to tighten until the rope is secure. 6. If the ends of the rope are long enough, you can carry the butterfly coil backpack style.

times. When you have several feet left, secure the ends. If you aren't wearing a backpack, the butterfly coil can be comfortably secured to your body for easy transport.

Uncoiling a rope also deserves some attention. If you simply grab the ends of the rope and pull,

a massive knot will develop. Uncoil the rope by removing one loop at a time. Your goal should be a pile of rope without kinks and knots. The process of preparing a rope so that it feeds out easily and free of tangles is called *stacking the rope.* If you don't stack the rope prior to a climb, the climber may be in the middle of a difficult move when all of a sudden a knot reaches your belay device—a bad situation. Instead, stack each rope after it is uncoiled. You may also find it convenient to stack the rope prior to creating a mountaineer's or butterfly coil.

COLD-WATER SURVIVAL

Immersion in cold water is a life-threatening situation. Cold water robs you of body heat 25 times faster than cold air does. Some experts estimate that in more than half of all deaths attributed to drowning, victims actually die from the effects of hypothermia rather than from water filling their lungs. Hypothermia is a medical condition induced by a dangerous loss of body heat. In cold water, hypothermia can develop in minutes, causing motor skills, such as the use of your fingers, to become ineffective and severely impairing your **judgment.** As your core temperature drops, you eventually lose consciousness and die.

What should you do? Start by always wearing a **PFD,** or personal flotation device, when you are boating. Wearing a PFD can double your survival time in cold water by allowing you to concentrate on tasks other than staying afloat. Always check the **weather** before heading out to paddle on any body of water. Know the water temperature, and dress appropriately with a wet suit or dry suit. Cold water is considered to be anything below 70°F. Many waterways—be they mountain lakes, the **Great Lakes,** or oceans—are well below 70°F year-round, so don't think you are immune because it is summer. Paddlers should leave a **float plan** with a trusted friend so rescuers will know where to look if they don't return.

If you fall into cold water, expect to become shaken and disoriented. You may even have a hard time catching your breath. Once you do, try not to panic: surviving cold water depends on how clearly you can think. Avoid swimming, unless there is a nearby boat or floating object that you are sure you can get to. Distances in water can be deceptive, so make sure the object is close. The U.S. Coast Guard has a saying called the Rule of 50s. It simply states that an average adult has a 50-50 chance of surviving a 50-yard swim in 50-degree water. That can put things into perspective! If you are able to reach an object, climb onto it while you still have the physical ability to do so. If your boat capsizes and you can't right it, haul your body out of the water and onto the hull as much as you can. Every little bit helps.

If there is nothing to climb on, assume the heat escape lessening posture, or HELP position (see the accompanying illustration). This position will help prevent heat from escaping your body and can increase your survival time by 50 percent. Huddle together with anyone else who has fallen in the water, in order to conserve heat. Make sure that your head and neck are as much out of the water as possible. If you have a **hat**, wear it. Try to keep your legs and armpits closed, because these areas lose heat quickly. Attempt to call for help with a radio or **signaling** device while you can still use your fingers. Try to have a positive outlook. Strange as it may sound, it will increase your chance of survival.

A rescued person who has been in cold water requires special treatment. Often, the person's vital signs, such as pulse and respiration, will be almost undetectable. Some people have survived complete submersion in cold water for 45 minutes. Therefore, if someone looks unresponsive or dead, continue treatment, giving **CPR,** if necessary, and treating for hypothermia. (For details on treating a hypothermia victim, see **hypothermia**.) A person who has had severe hypothermia or who has been submerged in cold water for a long time needs to see a doctor. Plan an **evacuation** or **rescue**, if necessary.

COLD-WEATHER INJURIES

Our adventures often take us into environments in which the unprotected human body was not meant to survive. Modern-day **clothing** and equipment is excellent at protecting us against severe cold, but gear can do the job only to a certain extent. If you can't keep yourself adequately fed, hydrated, and insulated, you'll increase your likelihood of receiving cold-weather injuries.

Such injuries are caused by a lack of blood circulation. Hands and feet are often at risk, as are commonly exposed places such as nose, ears, and cheeks. Lack of circulation is often the result of mild or severe **hypothermia**. In such a state, the body shuts off circulation to extremities in an attempt to keep vital organs warm. Poor circulation can also be caused by wearing restrictive clothing, such as tight boots, or smoking.

The most common cold-weather injury is **frostbite**. It can occur anytime the temperature is below freezing (32°F). Frostbite, simply put, is the freezing of the body's tissues. If frostbite is detected early, its effects will be superficial. This stage is often referred to as *frostnip*. Recognizing frostnip is important because it can quickly progress into severe frostbite, a condition that leads to the death of the tissue. Typical signs of frostnip include numbness and white or waxy-looking skin. Often, a person will not recognize that he is experiencing frostnip. This is especially true with the nose, cheekbones, and ears, since a person can't see his own facial features without a mirror. Keep an eye on one another in severe

HELP   huddle

The HELP position (heat escape lessening posture, left) and the huddle position (right) can extend your survival time in cold water.

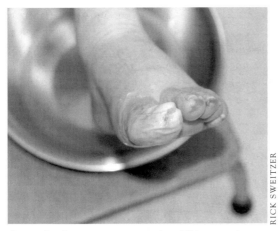

RICK SWEITZER

Severe frostbite requires evacuation. This person's toes were frostbitten while on an expedition to the North Pole. Rewarming was delayed until the person could get to a medical facility.

conditions, and be alert for patches of skin that look significantly paler than the surrounding skin.

Frostnip is generally easy to treat in the field with simple rewarming. Often, the quickest way to do this is with skin-to-skin contact. Frost-nipped facial features can be treated by simply placing a warm hand on the affected area, but make sure that the hand isn't exposed to the cold for too long. People with frostnipped fingers can often rewarm them in their armpits, and frostnipped feet can be placed against the warm stomach of another person. You also will need to find the cause of the frostnip. Is the person hypothermic? Is his boot laced too tightly? Is there a hole in his glove? This may require you to stop what you are doing, but you must identify and fix the problem before resuming your activity.

Serious frostbite results from a failure to recognize and treat frostnip. It is characterized by the rigidity of the skin, which is a result of tissues that have actually frozen solid. These tissues are either dead or well on their way. Rewarming severe frostbite is a difficult process that requires professional medical care. Therefore, if faced with this injury, you'll need to plan an **evacuation** of the person. By no means should the area be rewarmed

and then exposed to cold temperatures again. It is better to insulate the area so it doesn't freeze more, *or thaw out*, while the evacuation is in progress. Healing of severe frostbite can take up to several months and requires close medical attention. The affected area will blister and swell during the process. In worst-case scenarios, severely frostbitten areas spontaneously fall off or need to be amputated.

Another type of cold injury is immersion foot, also known as *trench foot*. Immersion foot is caused by prolonged exposure to cold, wet conditions (like those found in wartime trenches). Like frostbite, immersion foot is caused by a lack of circulation in the feet or sometimes in the hands. Over the course of several days or weeks of inadequate blood flow, damage occurs to the tissues and nerves. Signs of immersion foot include pain and swelling. It can also produce an uncontrollable itchy or tingling sensation that can drive a person nuts. Immersion foot is best prevented by removing cold and wet boots and socks (or gloves) and allowing your feet (or hands) to become warm and dry. Change socks throughout the day, or if appropriate, wear rubber boots that will keep your feet dry. It is easy to delay getting out of your wet boots until long after you have set up camp, but make a point to change into dry shoes and socks as soon as possible—especially if the wet items are particularly cold.

COMBAT ROLL

Combat roll is the term for successfully **rolling a kayak** in rough water conditions. Ideally, everyone who can roll a kayak should be able to perform a combat roll. After all, the main reason you learn the roll is to rescue yourself when you capsize, and you are most likely to capsize in rough conditions. Most people learn to roll a kayak in a swimming pool or a calm lake. This is an ideal learning environment but a far cry from the rough **waves** of a turbulent river or sea. Only when you are able to execute a roll in "combat" conditions can you be sure you really know the skill.

COMMUNICATION DEVICES

The issue of whether to take communication devices into the backcountry is hotly debated, but even people who disagree with radio or phone use in the **wilderness** don't deny that they can be invaluable in emergency situations. If you need outside help during a **rescue** or an **evacuation**, a radio or phone can cut hours or possibly days off the time it would have taken help to arrive if someone first had to hike or ski back to a communication point. If the whole party is incapacitated or if you are a solo traveler, a radio or phone may be the only way to call for help.

A problem arises when people start relying on communication devices instead of self-sufficiency and good **judgment**. Any communication device has its limitations. Annie has had radios fail inexplicably, batteries lose power after only one use, and antennae break in half. Terrain also limits reliability. A signal may be hard to acquire in **forests**, valleys, or mountains, and poor **weather** can interfere with signals. There is simply no substitute for being personally prepared to handle an emergency.

When looking for a communication device, keep in mind your intended use. If you simply want a way to keep in touch with a companion over a short distance, you may opt for a family radio service (FRS) radio, such as Motorola's Talkabout. This type of radio is small, lightweight, and relatively inexpensive. According to Federal Communications Commission (FCC) regulations, it can have a range of only 2 miles, but you might find the actual range to be much less (as short as several hundred yards) depending on the terrain. Anyone can use a FRS radio. It has 14 channels and 38 subchannels, so it shouldn't be hard to find an open channel on which you can communicate.

If you're looking for a longer range, you can use a general mobile radio service (GMRS) instrument. These radios are similar to the FRS radios, but they have a range of about 5 miles. GMRS radios require an FCC license, but the licenses are easy to acquire, and only one person per family needs one. A number of companies manufacture FRS and GMRS radios; as with any communication device, look into their battery life and features (such as water resistance) before you buy.

> "While on a canoe expedition in the Canadian Arctic, I saw in the distance a solo canoeist who was paddling at a feverish pace. Time went by, and the distance between us was still at least a mile. This person was paddling hard! After a few hours, we finally met up along the shore. His name was Dan, and he had started 20 days earlier. According to the trip plan he had left with authorities, he should have already arrived at his destination. In fact, if he didn't arrive by the following morning, he had advised them to begin searching. We were easily 4 days from civilization, and there was no way he would make it. He had been paddling at a crazy pace for a few days trying to make up for a prolonged weather delay, and he was exhausted. Luckily, we were carrying a satellite phone for emergencies, and we let him use it to call the authorities. Needless to say, he was incredibly relieved."—AA

If you want a device that can call for outside help, your practical options are limited. If you aren't too far from a populated area, your **cell phone** may work. Placing a call from high ground often helps when signals are weak or nonexistent. Ham radio operators, who must be licensed by the FCC, can carry handheld versions into the wilderness. They can call out if they happen to be within range of a receiver. Ham radio signals can be patched into the phone system.

If you are paddling in coastal waters or on the **Great Lakes** along the U.S.–Canada border, you should carry a VHF (very high frequency) radio, the standard in marine communication. In the United States, channel 16 is the emergency

ANNIE AGGENS

Satellite phones can be used from almost any location to get medical advice or to advise authorities or friends of a delayed return. Like many other electronic devices, sat phones are becoming smaller and cheaper.

channel monitored by the coast guard and most large vessels. In addition to carrying emergency calls, VHF radios will often broadcast regional weather and local marine forecasts, complete with **wind** direction and wave height. In the remote regions of Canada, many bush pilots transmit on VHF radios. If you are **planning a trip** to one of the northern territories, it is worthwhile to investigate VHF rental prices and what frequency you should monitor on the radio.

Also used in Canada and the United States are personal locator beacons, or **PLBs**. While technically not a communication device (they cannot transmit messages), these emergency beacons can be switched on if a life-or-death **evacuation** is required.

In recent years the price of satellite phones has dropped significantly, as have their size and

weight. It is now common for expeditions to carry a satellite phone, which many organizations rent by the week or month in conjunction with a per-minute rate. Before you invest in a satellite phone, however, make sure that its coverage indeed includes your destination. Some companies have limited coverage in certain countries and above certain **latitudes**. Also consider purchasing an extra battery or a solar battery recharger.

After all this talk about high-tech communication, don't forget good old-fashioned **signaling** techniques. Signaling is an important skill as preparation in the event you urgently need to get someone's attention.

COMPASS

A compass is an essential aid to **navigation**. On clear **trails**, you may rarely, if ever, need one, although it's still a wise precaution to carry one. For cross-country and **snow** travel, a compass is likely to be indispensable.

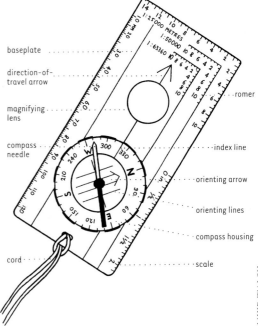

baseplate

direction-of-travel arrow

magnifying lens

compass needle

cord

romer

index line

orienting arrow

orienting lines

compass housing

scale

MIKE WALSH

The main features of an orienteering compass. The compass housing is a rotating ring called the azimuth. *By turning the azimuth you can take accurate bearings from a map or from the landscape.*

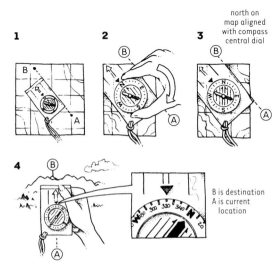

Taking a bearing on a feature. The far summit has a bearing of 043 from the hiker. If she loses sight of this summit on her hike, she can still follow this direction of travel (43°) and reach it as long as there are no obstacles in the way.

The heart of a compass is a magnetic needle that points north. It helps to know where north is, but that isn't enough for accurate navigation: you need to know which direction in relation to north your destination is. This can be measured with an **orienteering** or protractor compass, which has a flat baseplate and a movable transparent dial (azimuth). The dial is filled with a damping fluid and contains the magnetic needle.

Taking a map bearing. See text for a description of steps.

The points of the compass and the degrees of a circle are marked on the edge of the dial, and the base of the dial has an orienting arrow pointing to north. The baseplate has a central direction-of-travel arrow and several other lines running parallel to its sides. It may also have a small magnifying glass for reading details on a **map** and scales on the edges for measuring distances and taking grid references on a map.

With an orienteering compass, you can take a **bearing** on a point you want to get to even if you can't see it. If you can see your destination—for example, a mountaintop—point the direction-of-travel arrow at it and then turn the dial until the magnetic end of the needle (usually marked in red) aligns with north on the compass housing. You have now set a bearing and, by keeping the magnetic needle lined up with north and following the direction-of-travel arrow, you can walk to your destination even if you can't see it.

Of course, if you pick a destination some distance away, obstacles are likely to appear in your path; in this case, it's best to pick a visible object, such as a rock or distinctive tree, that lies on your route, walk to that, and then find another object to walk to. These objects are called *checkpoints*. If you have to go around an obstacle, it doesn't matter as long as you can still see your checkpoint. In dense mist or featureless terrain, you can always send another person ahead and use him as a checkpoint.

When you can't see your destination and you're not sure in which direction it lies, you can take a bearing off the map. Place the compass on the map and line up the lower edge of the baseplate with your present position and your destination (see illustration, step 1). Turn the dial until the orienting arrow is pointing to north on the map, normally the top (steps 2 and 3). Now take the compass off the map, and turn it until the magnetic needle is aligned with north (step 4). The direction-of-travel arrow now points to your destination. The bearing is the number of degrees marked on the compass housing above the direction-of-travel arrow.

Magnetic Declination

There is, unfortunately, a problem with taking bearings from the map. The compass needle points to magnetic north, while the top of the map is true north; these two aren't the same. The difference is called the *magnetic declination*. Magnetic north lies in northern Canada to the west of Baffin Island. Depending on whether you are west or east of a line running south from magnetic north, true north is to the east or west. In some areas, true north and magnetic north do coincide.

Topographic maps usually show the magnetic variation for the area they cover, in a *declination diagram* somewhere in the margins. If you are west of magnetic north, in the **Rocky Mountains** or **Sierra Nevada** of the western United States, for example, you must subtract the magnetic declination when you take a map bearing. In the eastern United States, you must add the magnetic declination.

Topographic maps also indicate the annual change of the variation. Magnetic north isn't static; it moves around, though fairly slowly and in a predictable pattern. This means that the magnetic variation changes too, often by several degrees a year. Variation also occurs when traveling from one **latitude** to another.

Magnetic variation matters only when you need to take a fairly precise bearing off the map. However, don't ignore it when taking a map bearing, or you could quickly find yourself way off course.

Aiming Off

However carefully you take a bearing, it won't be completely accurate. That's just not possible with a handheld compass and a topo map. The greatest accuracy comes with compasses with sighting mirrors; however, these are heavier, more expensive, and more difficult to use than simpler models, and they're unnecessary for most uses.

Any inaccuracy is magnified the farther you travel. One way to compensate for this is to take bearings to places not very far away. Sometimes this isn't possible, however, such as when in a dense forest and trying to reach a bridge over a river several miles away with no distinctive landmarks en route. Taking a bearing on the bridge is risky. What happens if you reach the river but can't see the bridge? Which way do you turn? It's better to take a bearing on the river to one side or the other of the bridge. Then you will know whether to turn left or right if you can't see the bridge when you reach the river. This is called *aiming off* and—apart from travel bearings—is the most useful compass technique for most wilderness travel.

Electronic Compasses

Electronic digital compasses are often built into **altimeters** or **GPS** receivers or are available as stand-alone devices. Although they seem attractive, they can be hard to use and they have limitations that don't apply to mechanical compasses. The first problem with many of them is that for accuracy you have to hold the device absolutely horizontal and ensure that a bubble is in the center of a small spirit level. This can be difficult in calm, warm weather, and in a storm it's practically impossible. If you try placing the device on the ground, you quickly learn how little truly flat ground there is.

Electronic compasses also have to be regularly calibrated or autodeviated, which involves slowly turning the device through 360 degrees while it is kept completely level. Again, keeping it level is the problem.

The biggest drawback of all is that taking bearings off a map with an electronic compass is impossible. However, with electronic compasses built into GPS units, the destination can be entered into the GPS as a waypoint and then the bearing acquired and transferred to the electronic compass.

The electronic compass on a GPS unit offers one big advantage over a standard compass. Because the electronic compass can point to the destination (waypoint) rather than along an unchanging bearing, if you have to go around an obstacle it will still point in the direction of where you want to be (as long as the GPS is switched on). It also has an advantage over a GPS reading of your position, because the electronic compass will point you the right way even when you are stationary, while the GPS will give this information only if you keep moving and take successive readings.

> "When I use a GPS with a built-in electronic compass, I still prefer to transfer the bearing to a standard compass that doesn't need to be held level and use that while walking. Overall, electronic compasses have too many disadvantages to replace standard ones. I wouldn't choose a GPS or an altimeter because it has an electronic compass, either, but I do think that it makes more sense to have one in a GPS rather than in an altimeter."—CT

CONDENSATION

Condensation can be a big problem in the wilderness. It occurs when moisture vapor comes into contact with an impermeable layer of fabric. Unable to escape, the vapor condenses into water droplets on the fabric. Condensation occurs inside rain gear, waterproof **bivouac** bags and **sleeping bag** covers, **tarps**, and **tents**. It's unavoidable, but the effects can be reduced if you use your gear carefully.

Ventilation is the best way to minimize condensation. A flow of cool, dry air can transport away the warm, moisture-laden air from inside a shelter or a rain jacket. Condensation is less likely in a tarp than a tent because at least one side is usually open to the air. It helps to have the edges several inches above the ground too. Even so, in still air, condensation can occur.

If condensation can occur in a tarp with three sides open to the air and the fourth side open above the ground, preventing it in the enclosed confines of a tent is impossible. Good ventilation can still reduce it, however. Whenever possible, leave the doors open or at least partly unzipped

from the top (warm air rises, so it needs a high exit point). Many tents have vents for this purpose. Cool air entering at the lower edges of the tent pushes the warm air up and out of the vents or open door zipper. This is called the *chimney effect*.

Most moisture vapor comes from your body; even when asleep, you're producing it in the form of invisible perspiration. You can't do anything about this. However, you can try to keep other dampness out of your shelter. **Cooking** in the tent porch or under a tarp can result in copious condensation, so do this only if absolutely necessary (and, of course, if you aren't in **bear** country). If you want to sit in your shelter while you cook to keep out of the **wind** or **rain**, place the **stove** outside or, in a tent porch, in an open doorway so the steam goes outside and blows away. Keep wet **packs**, **clothing**, and footwear outside too. If these are in the tent gently steaming away, condensation will be worse.

Of course, in a storm you may have to close yourself into a tent or stake a tarp out as a low-profile, enclosed shelter to keep the rain or **snow** out and then put up with any resulting condensation. Any wind will remove some condensation, but you may still find that the inside of your shelter becomes quite damp. When this happens, all you can do is avoid touching the walls or pushing the inner tent against the wet fly, especially with your sleeping bag. Mop up drips with a **bandanna** or dishcloth. In below-freezing temperatures, the inner tent may become so cold that moisture vapor condenses on it and then freezes rather than passing through. As the tent warms in the morning, from sunlight or just warmth from the inhabitants as they start to move about, this frozen condensation can start to melt and fall from the walls until it seems as though it is snowing lightly inside the tent.

Good ventilation will minimize condensation in clothing too. However, ventilation and keeping out the rain don't go together, and it's much better to be warm and damp from condensation than cold and wet from rain. The quality of your rain gear makes a difference, but condensation

"At one camp in the northern Rockies, I pitched a tarp as a lean-to to keep dew off my sleeping bag. It was a calm night, but early in the morning a breeze picked up and gently shook the tarp, causing drips of condensation to fall on my face and wake me up."—CT

will appear in even the most expensive, high-tech garment if you wear it long enough while exercising. There's little you can do about this except to open any vents and zippers whenever possible and only wear rain gear when you have to. The chimney effect works in clothing too, so the neck is an important ventilation point. Putting up a hood effectively seals this vent, so it's best to do so only when you have to. A **hat** allows warm air to escape and so is a better choice than a hood. Pack hip belts prevent cool air from entering at the hem of the garment, so unfastening your hip belt for a while can make a big difference in how much condensation appears.

See also **heat regulation** and **vapor barriers**.

CONTINENTAL DIVIDE TRAIL

The Continental Divide Trail (CDT) follows the watershed of the United States from Canada to Mexico down the length of the **Rocky Mountains**. Water on the east side of the Divide eventually runs into the Atlantic Ocean; water on the west runs into the Pacific. It's one of the three great north–south **trails** in the United States, along with the **Appalachian Trail** and the **Pacific Crest Trail**. Like the other two, it's designated a National Scenic Trail and forms part of the **Triple Crown**, awarded by the American Long Distance Hiking Association–West to hikers who have completed all three trails. At 3,100 miles, the CDT is the longest of the three trails and is by far the hardest to hike; it goes through some remote and rugged country and is not yet complete, although it is possible to hike the whole route. The newest of the Triple Crown trails, the CDT was first conceived of in the 1960s.

The CDT is a magnificent trail, taking in a great sweep of the American West, from the dark, remote forests and steep mountains of the northern Rockies through the volcanic **Yellowstone** country and the desert heat of Wyoming to reach its highest point in the rolling Colorado Rockies before finishing through the multicolored **desert** mesas of New Mexico.

With a difference of nearly 20 degrees in **latitude** between the northern and southern end of the trail, the CDT covers a huge range of climates and ecosystems. At the northern end, timberline is around 8,500 feet, while in New Mexico, it's at 11,500 feet. Most of the trail is above 6,000 feet, with its highest section in Colorado, where it lies above 10,000 feet for many miles. The lowest point, 4,000 feet, is at the Canadian border.

Much of the trail lies in designated wilderness areas and **national parks**, including Glacier, Yellowstone, and Rocky Mountain National Parks, but it also passes through ranch lands, logging and mining areas, and American Indian reservations. Not surprisingly, many historical relics and references line the trail, from the tracks of westernbound wagon trains on the Oregon Trail in Wyoming to Anasazi ruins and Mogollon cliff dwellings in New Mexico. **Lewis and Clark** crossed the northern Continental Divide in 1805 on their pioneering expedition across the U.S. continent to the Pacific Ocean. The southern Divide was reached much earlier, with the Spanish leaving inscriptions in the soft sandstone of El Morro—Inscription Rock—in New Mexico in the 1500s.

A thru-hike of the CDT is a serious undertaking; the trail is only 70 percent complete, and the distance is such that hikers will almost certainly encounter **snow** somewhere (see **thru-hiking**). Those starting in the north may have to deal with it in Glacier National Park and possibly again in southern Colorado. Those heading north from Mexico will probably find snow in the San Juan Mountains in southern Colorado and again in the northern Rockies near the end of the trail. Heading south means starting in steep mountains with a lot of ascending and descending, while north-bound walkers have easy, flat terrain in the beginning. However, the New Mexico section can be hiked late in the year, unlike the northern Rockies, so south is most likely the easiest direction to head.

For more information, contact the Continental Divide Trail Society or the Continental Divide Trail Alliance (see resources section).

CONTINGENCY PLANS

A contingency plan is a plan for the unexpected. For example, it may direct you in the event your pick-up plane doesn't show, your food runs out, or you become separated from your party. If someone becomes lost, a contingency plan provides guidance for the lost person as well as for the group. It instructs the lost person to either stay put or possibly travel back to the last-known location or camp. It provides crucial information, such as how long the group will look for the person before summoning outside help. By following the contingency plan, both the lost party and the searchers share a common understanding of what is going on and what should happen.

When preparing a contingency plan, think about what could go wrong on your trip and figure out (in advance) how you will deal with such an emergency. Where will you go? Who will you contact? Your contingency plan should include a list of all your **bailout points**. Once you have assembled the plan, spend some time reviewing it with your party before you head into the **wilderness**.

CONTOURS

Contour lines are imaginary lines linking points of the same elevation, thus showing the relief (the actual three-dimensional shape) of an area on a flat surface. When you learn to read contours, a topographic **map** will spring to life and become a wonderful tool for envisioning the nature of the terrain. The shapes formed by contours represent the actual shapes of the land, the shapes of **mountains**, ridges, and valleys. With practice, you can visualize the terrain by studying contours.

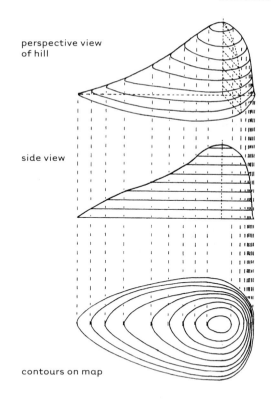

perspective view of hill

side view

contours on map

MIKE WALSH

Each contour line joins points of the same elevation and thus shows three-dimensional relief on a flat map.

This can be fun in itself, but it's also very useful for planning routes (see **route selection**) or working out how steeply a trail climbs or descends.

Contour lines are drawn on maps at regular intervals, usually between 15 and 500 feet, depending on the scale of the map. The contours on U.S. Geological Survey (USGS) 1:24,000 maps (on which 1 inch on the map equals 24,000 inches on the ground, which is roughly 2½ inches per mile on the map), the standard for **wilderness** travel, are at 40-foot intervals. The elevation is usually marked on every fifth contour line, which may be thicker than the others.

Contour lines that are wide apart indicate gentle terrain, while closely packed lines mean steep slopes. Note, though, that sheer drops less than the contour interval may not show up on the map. An arrowhead of contour lines could indicate a valley or the spur of a mountain. Read the elevation figures on the contour lines to see whether the center of the arrowhead is lower (a valley) or higher (a spur) than the edges. (If there's a river marked running down the center of the arrowhead, it's a valley.)

COOKING

Eating well is an important part of any **wilderness** adventure. Good food enhances morale and keeps you fit and healthy. There are several methods of cooking in the wilderness, from one-pot meals to **baking** and grilling. Which you employ depends on whether you want to spend the minimum amount of time cooking or lots of time producing gourmet meals.

The most common form of wilderness cooking is boiling and simmering. Dump some dried food into a pot of **water**, put a lid on the pot, bring the water to a boil (stirring occasionally), and then simmer until done. This is simple, although you can burn food badly if you don't stir it enough or if it doesn't have enough water. It's also possible to end up with food that is crunchy rather than chewy if there is insufficient water or if the food isn't simmered long enough.

You may need to simmer the food for longer than the food packet instructs, especially at high altitude. The boiling point of water drops by roughly 10°F for every 5,000-foot rise in elevation, and cooking times double. For example, on top of Mount Whitney in California, at almost 15,000 feet, a pot of dried beans takes about seven times as long to cook as at sea level. Thus it makes sense to have precooked or partially cooked food for high-altitude cooking. Many packet foods require only the addition of boiling water, at least at sea level. At high altitudes, it's worth simmering them a few minutes to account for the lower water temperature. Food prepared in the packet, such as many specialist **backpacking** foods, are best emptied into a pot so they can be heated longer.

Packet foods come with precise instructions as to the amount of water needed; regard these as guidelines rather than rules. You don't need a measuring cup. Using more water than directed is often a good idea in the wild, where it's always a risk to not consume enough liquid. Put in roughly the suggested amount of water, and then add more if the meal seems to need it. Cooking times aren't absolute either. Longer is often better; packagers like to emphasize how quickly their meals cook, but the food may actually taste better and be more digestible if cooked longer.

Simmering times can be reduced by presoaking food. This can be started during the day by adding water to food in a watertight container. Doing this will allow you to eat sooner, and you'll also save **fuel**. In camp, you can bring water to a boil, add the food, and then turn off the heat. Keep the lid on, and the food will continue to cook. In cool weather, the pot can be wrapped in **clothing** or a **sleeping bag** to keep it warm, but be sure to check that the pot isn't hot enough to do any damage. If you do this regularly, consider making an insulating jacket for your pot from closed-cell foam and **duct tape**.

The reputations of some camp cooks are based on their careful use of condiments and seasonings. Adding herbs, spices, or other seasonings can greatly improve the taste of boiled food. Vary amounts and varieties, and the same basic ingredients can taste different every night.

> "The first camp cooking I ever did as a young boy was to wrap dough around a green stick and then cook it in the flames of a campfire."—CT

Many outdoors people like to fry food; anglers find it a tasty way to cook trout. However, frying is messy and requires a fairly heavy pan and some sort of fat to prevent burning the food.

Freshly baked goods are great to have in the wilds, but baking is a fairly lengthy process best suited to those who enjoy it and aren't in a hurry. You also need a baking device (see **baking**). If you have a campfire, you can bake goods by wrapping them in foil and putting them in hot coals. You don't have much heat control, of course, but this works with potatoes and fresh fish. You can also put a pot of food in the coals.

If you have a campfire, you can also grill food, either on a lightweight grill or by skewering it on a stick and holding it in the heat. Food can be boiled in a pot placed on a lightweight grill over a campfire; the pot can even be hung from a tripod of sticks, if it has a bail handle (a half-circle handle, as on a bucket). Keeping a lid on the pot is important to keep out ashes. While boiling is easy, simmering isn't, so don't cook foods over a campfire that need to be simmered.

When cooking, try to avoid spilling food, and clean up spills as soon as possible. This is not just to keep your kitchen tidy and ensure you don't leave any litter but also to avoid attracting animals, whether **insects** or **bears**. Once you've finished cooking, put cold water into any empty pots to make washing up much easier.

See also **camp kitchen, cook kit, fires, food,** and **stoves**.

COOK KIT

A battered, blackened pot can bring back fond memories of nights in the **wilderness**. Indeed, if the pot is dented and scratched, traces of the spicy chili you ate while watching that sunset last summer may still be there. A well-used pot can become an old friend, a reminder of trips long past. Generally, though, most people do not give pots and pans and the rest of their cook kit much thought. Yet there are big differences in both **weight** and performance between various items. What should be in a cook kit depends on how important weight is (ultralight hikers can get by with a pot and a spoon) and what sort of cooking you do.

Pots and Pans
Materials
Five types of material are used for pots and pans: aluminum, stainless steel, titanium, aluminum and stainless combined, and nonstick aluminum. All have advantages and disadvantages.

A nonstick pot with a lid and grip. This is a GSI Bugaboo Teflon 1-quart pot. To avoid scratching the nonstick surface, use wooden or plastic utensils.

Aluminum alone is the lightest and heats up evenly and quickly, so boiling times are fast. It's also cheaper than other materials. The downside is that aluminum, a soft metal, is easily dented and scratched, which eventually makes it hard to clean. It also can corrode and may taint some foods with a slight metallic taste. Hardened aluminum pots are much tougher but weigh and cost more than standard aluminum ones.

Stainless steel is very tough and hard to dent or scratch, so it lasts a long time and is easy to clean. It does not corrode or taint food. However, it's significantly heavier than aluminum and doesn't conduct heat as well, which means slower boiling times and a greater chance of hot spots and burned food. Steel is also more expensive than aluminum.

Titanium is close to the ideal material: it's lightweight (45 percent lighter than steel), tough, corrosion resistant, hard to dent or scratch, and easy to clean. It doesn't impart flavors to foods, although it can stain slightly, and it conducts heat better than stainless steel. Unfortunately, it is very expensive.

A combination of aluminum and stainless steel is an interesting and effective way of overcoming the disadvantages of both. Aluminum on the outside conducts heat quickly, while a stainless steel lining makes for easy cleaning and no scratches. The weight is less than steel alone, although more than aluminum. The cost, however, is on the high side.

Use of a nonstick coating is another way to improve aluminum. The coating makes pans easy to clean and minimizes the chances of burned food sticking badly. However, the coating is easily scratched, so only plastic or wooden utensils should be used. Once scratched, nonstick coatings can be hard to clean. Nonstick pans are low in weight and price and therefore worth considering if you're prepared to look after them.

How Many?

For most wilderness travel, you don't need a lot of pots and pans. They just add weight and bulk to the load. With single-burner **stoves**, one-pot meals make sense, so one pan is all you need, with a lid to speed up boiling times. A second pan can be useful for making sauces or for boiling water for drinks while the other pan has dried food soaking in it or is waiting to be washed up. When you're going solo, a small pan can double as a mug.

Those who like fried food will want a frying pan. The problem here is that it's difficult to prevent food from burning in thin, lightweight pans, while thicker ones are heavy—12 ounces for a small one. Pot lids can be used for occasional frying if they are free of central knobs and are thick enough. Washing greasy pans in the wild can be difficult.

Designs

Pots that are slightly wider than deep are best. They balance better than tall pans on small stoves, and **water** heats quicker in them than on wider, shallower pans with a greater surface area. Rounded edges make cleaning easier and transfer heat better. Unlike kettles, pans need lids to accelerate boiling, and in very cold or windy **weather** you might need a lid to bring the water to a boil. Some lids can be used as plates, which is useful for groups. Solo campers can eat straight from the pan. When weight really matters, use a piece of heavy-duty baking foil instead of a lid.

Some pans come with foldaway handles, while others need a separate pot grip. Both work well, but attached handles can get hot, especially if they're made of aluminum. With pot grips, check how well they work. Some are flimsy and insecure, particularly with large pans.

If you cook over a campfire, a pot with a bail (a half-circle handle, as on a bucket) can be useful so you can hang it from a tripod of sticks over the flames. Bails stay fairly cool as long as they're in the upright position. Especially with campfires, attached handles aren't as good as pot grips because the handles usually overheat. If a handle does get hot, use a **bandanna** or cotton glove to protect your hand. Don't use anything made from synthetic fabric; it may melt.

If you carry more than one pot, check that the pots nest inside each other to save space. They don't have to be part of the same set to do so.

Lightweight tea kettles and coffeepots are sometimes carried by those who frequently make hot drinks. The smallest kettles will fit inside a small pot, though a standard pot serves just as well as a kettle.

You can see your reflection in most pans because they have a nice shiny surface. Unfortunately, this surface also reflects heat, which is not ideal for quick **cooking** or conserving **fuel**. Matte black pans are much better, but few pans come with this finish. When pans get blackened or sooty, that's good: clean them just enough to keep them from dirtying other items. Indeed, it could be worthwhile to paint your pans with black stove paint.

Size and Weight

A solo traveler can make do with a pot capacity of a quart or less. For two travelers, a 2-quart pot is better, while for groups of three and four, you need 2.5- to 3-quart sizes.

A quart pot with lid can weigh between 3 and 12 ounces, depending on the material. The weight may not matter on some trips but could be significant on others. Larger pans are relatively lighter for the capacity. A typical 1.5- and 2.5-

quart stainless steel pot set weighs 26 ounces, for a weight of more than 6 ounces per quart. A typical aluminum 5-quart pot weighs 20 ounces or less, for a weight of no more than 4 ounces per quart.

> "When cooking for 10, I've found a 5-quart pot just big enough for rice and pasta, as long as the sauce was cooked separately."—CT

Mugs and Cups

Soloists can drink out of their pots. Or you can carry a metal mug that doubles as a smaller pot (or vice versa). Stainless steel or titanium is best for this because aluminum burns the lips.

The standard mug is the now-ubiquitous insulated travel mug with lid. These are great in cold weather because the contents stay hot far longer than in uncovered plastic or metal mugs. You can get double-walled stainless steel mugs that keep drinks warm, but they are heavy. The lightest mugs are simple plastic ones, though they are easily cracked. Lexan plastic ones are much tougher but weigh and cost more.

Plates and Bowls

Plastic plates and bowls are lightweight and reasonably tough, although they can crack if treated roughly. Deep ones are best, as these can be used for soups as well as other foods. Suitable ones can be found in the kitchen departments of big stores; you can even use old margarine tubs. Metal plates are much tougher than plastic but also heavier, and in cold weather can steal the heat from your dinner. You can eat from your mug, although a mug generally holds less than a bowl and you can't have a hot drink at the same time. Solo travelers can eat out of the pot and not bother with a bowl.

Cutlery

For most camp cooking and eating, you only need a spoon. This can be a Lexan plastic or titanium one, if you want to save fractions of an ounce.

Otherwise, a soup spoon from the cutlery drawer at home will do fine. Avoid ordinary plastic spoons because they break easily. You don't need a fork, though some people like to carry one; it could be useful for eating fried or grilled food. If you need a blade, use your backcountry knife (see **knives**). A separate kitchen knife isn't necessary.

Other Utensils

Many other items could be part of a backcountry cook kit. A plastic spatula helps with cooking and serving fried food. If you're cooking for more than one or two people, a large plastic or wooden spoon is useful for stirring large pots of food and for serving it. Those who go in for more sophisticated cooking may want to have a small whisk or grater. And if you really want to cook beans at

---

Cook Kit List

This is everything you might carry—not everything you should carry! It includes items discussed elsewhere, such as stoves and water containers.

one or two nesting pots with lids
frying pan (could be a pot lid)
tea kettle or coffeepot
pot grip, if required
mug or cup (one per person)
bowl or plate (one per person)
plastic or wooden serving spoon
plastic spatula
spoon (one per person)
knife
baking device
stove and **fuel**
grill for **fire**
water containers
whisk
grater
pressure cooker
matches or lighter (or both)

altitude, a pressure cooker will save lots of time but will also add a lot of weight to your load.

Portable Fire

Finally, don't forget matches and lighters. Without the means to light your stove or start a fire, your cook kit is useless.

CORNICES

Cornices are those beautiful waves of **snow** that curve over steep drops, sometimes appearing to defy gravity. Formed by the wind slowly building up the snow out from an edge, cornices are found on the lee side, that is, away from the prevailing wind (see **leeward**), and thus most face the same way in any one region.

Magnificent to look at, cornices are also potentially deadly. Collapsing cornices can trigger **avalanches**, so spending any time directly below one is unwise unless the snow is very stable. The biggest danger is in inadvertently walking or ski-ing *over* a cornice, because it can be impossible to see from the windward side. Here the snow slope often looks smooth and unbroken, with no hint that it juts out into space. Always stay well back from any snow-covered edge where there might be a cornice. Often, you can get a view of at least part of the ridge or cliff as it curves around a bowl. If you can see a cornice, assume there's one along the whole ridge or cliff. If you can't see one, do not assume there aren't any.

Cornices break not in a vertical line directly above the cliff edge but farther back from the edge. Often cracks form where the cornice is starting to sag. Keep well away from these. Sometimes narrow ridges have cornices on both sides and possible collapse lines that overlap, meaning that there is no safe route across.

COTTON

Cotton is wonderful stuff. Tough, comfortable, easy to care for—everyone wears cotton clothing, from blue jeans to dress shirts. However, except in hot **weather**, it isn't the best stuff to wear in the **wilderness**, especially next to the skin. In the heat, cotton clothing helps keep you cool because it absorbs sweat and then takes a while to dry, using body heat to do so. However, this same process makes cotton unpleasant and even dangerous to wear next to the skin in cool weather. Because it soaks up moisture and takes ages to dry, it leaves you feeling chilled (see **condensation**). Cotton garments worn over a wicking base layer (see **clothing**) aren't as bad, although they are heavier for the warmth provided than ones made from other fabrics. They still need to be kept dry, and they don't insulate well when damp—and not at all if sodden.

Cotton shell clothing is uncommon nowadays. The quality name here is Ventile, made from heavy, tightly woven long-staple cotton. A double Ventile jacket is close to being waterproof while still breathable (see **breathability**). When wet, such a jacket more than doubles in weight and becomes so stiff that it will stand up by itself. Ventile is windproof and comfortable, however,

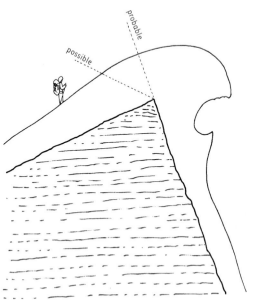

Cornice fracture lines. Cornices may collapse farther back from the edge than you think. So always stay well away from steep, snow-covered drop-offs and ridge crests, and never cross any cracks you see in the snow.

MIKE WALSH

and is often used in dry, cold places, such as Antarctica.

Cotton is often blended with polyester or nylon (as in 65-35 cloth) to make a quicker-drying fabric that still has cotton's comfortable feel. However, modern advances in synthetics mean that these fabrics are slowly disappearing because they no longer have any advantages.

COULOIRS

A *couloir* is a narrow gully on a steep mountainside. These natural breaks often offer the easiest routes for mountaineers and exciting descent routes for skiers because they are usually less steep than the surrounding slopes. However, couloirs are potentially dangerous places because they are usually **avalanche** chutes and are often topped by large **cornices.** Rockfall also may occur when the sun softens the **snow** and **ice.** And while some couloirs are open and straightforward, with unbroken snow and ice slopes leading to the top, others are twisting and complex, with vertical sections of rock or ice and loose, steep sections.

COYOTES

A sudden burst of weird noise—yips, yaps, howls—breaks the silence of a dark **forest** night. The coyotes are calling, a wonderful, wild, eerie, spine-tingling sound. These wild, omnivorous dogs—*Canis latrans*—are found throughout Central and North America from Costa Rica to Alaska. Of all the big predators, they are the most successful, despite decades of persecution, and have spread from their original home in the western United States to the whole of North America in a surprisingly short time. In 1913 the naturalist Ernest Thompson Seton wrote: "Draw a line around the region that is, or was, known as the Wild West. . . . You have exactly outlined the kingdom of the coyote. . . . He never frequented the region known as Eastern America." Coyotes now, of course, are found in the East, and they are found in all habitats too, from city suburbs to remote **wilderness** and from **deserts** to alpine mountains.

Spend time in the backcountry, and you'll likely see a coyote. Sometimes, it will be only a brief glimpse of a doglike shape trotting across the trail or through the bushes. At other times, one may sit in full view watching you or may even approach you. If the latter happens, it's probably a coyote that has been fed by people or has grown used to scavenging scraps from campsites or lunch spots. Coyotes aren't usually dangerous, but there have been a few cases, mostly in small towns, when the ones used to getting food have bitten people, usually children. They have also been known to kill pets for food.

> "On a backcountry ski trip in the High Sierra in California, my group was once approached by a coyote that was clearly hoping for a handout. It didn't get one."—CT

Coyotes are often mistaken for **wolves,** perhaps due to wishful thinking, because the latter are more romantic as well as far less common. Coyotes are smaller than wolves—roughly two-thirds their size—and have a face more like a fox's. Their tails also droop low when they run, while a wolf holds its tail straight out. They vary in color but are mostly gray above, sometimes with black streaks, and buff brown below, with pale bellies. Their tracks and scat look very much like a domestic dog's.

> "Once I spotted a coyote in a meadow and sat and watched it while it hunted for mice, which it caught by suddenly leaping straight up in the air and descending with its front paws on the rodent."—CT

Coyotes may be seen at any time of the day or night and in almost any habitat. They feed on carrion and small animals, such as rabbits and mice, but occasionally hunt in groups and kill deer and larger prey. In the **desert,** they turn to seeds and bean pods when meat is scarce.

The coyote is important in Native American folklore, in which the character Coyote features in a cycle of tales in a variety of roles, including creator and the outrageous mythic figure of the trickster. Imbued with magical powers, Coyote brings fire and light to humanity and can transform animals and objects. As trickster, he constantly tries to satisfy his hunger and greed, usually without success despite his cleverness.

CPR

Cardiopulmonary resuscitation (CPR) is a rescue technique performed on an individual whose heart has stopped beating, a condition commonly known as *cardiac arrest*. While heart disease is the leading cause of cardiac arrest in adults, it can also be brought on by trauma, severe **hypothermia**, **lightning** strikes, and near drowning. CPR combines rescue breathing and chest compressions to circulate blood to the brain and other vital organs. CPR is highly successful in areas that have access to 911 emergency calling because of prompt, professional medical attention. While the remote setting of most **wilderness** excursions makes a quick **rescue** difficult, CPR should be initiated anyway. If the cardiac arrest was brought on by a lightning strike or a near-drowning accident, CPR is often effective. However, if a spontaneous heartbeat does not resume after persistent CPR, it is likely that the patient will not survive the lengthy duration of a rescue. To learn CPR, contact your local chapter of the American Red Cross or the American Heart Association (see resources section). Courses are also offered at hospitals and some fire departments.

CRAMPONS

No rubber boot soles, however deep the tread, will grip on **ice** and hard-packed **snow**. Instead, they'll skid across it as if on a skating rink. Crampons are metal spikes attached to the boot soles, making the difference between safe **hiking** and climbing and sliding about dangerously. As important for hikers as an **ice ax**, crampons are essential for mountaineers.

Styles

The various types of crampons are differentiated by the degree of bend along their length. There are three basic types: rigid, articulated, and flexible. The first are designed for **ice climbing** and should be used only with rigid climbing **boots** because they are likely to break or fall off if used with flexible hiking boots. So-called articulated crampons ("hinged" is a better description) are the most versatile; they can be used for serious **mountaineering** yet still fit fairly stiff hiking boots. Flexible crampons are designed to fit flexible hiking boots and are the best choice if you aren't planning to do any climbing. Crampons may have 8, 9, 10, or 12 points; the number doesn't matter for hiking, but climbers will want as many points as possible, especially front points that can be used for climbing vertical ice.

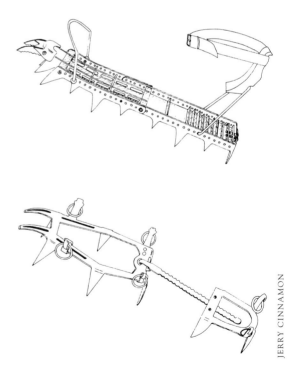

Rigid (top) and flexible (bottom) crampons.

JERRY CINNAMON

Instep crampons, which have four to six points and fit only under the instep, are OK for gentle terrain and short periods, but for anything else full-length crampons are much better and safer.

Materials

Most crampons are made from hardened steel, which is durable, stays sharp a long time, and is easily sharpened. However, it's also relatively heavy. The lightest crampons are made from alloy, which doesn't stay sharp very long and is harder to sharpen. In fact, it's impossible to get the same edge on alloy as on steel. The durability of alloy isn't as good either. However, it is much lighter and is therefore suitable if weight is important and the crampons won't be used very often or for technical climbing.

Fastening Systems

How crampons attach to boots is important. Some methods are easier than others, especially with cold fingers. Difficult strap systems mean that you won't bother to put the crampons on when you should or that you don't attach them properly, both of which can be dangerous.

The easiest fastening system is the step-in system, which has a wire bail at the front and a heel lever at the back. These require boots with a pronounced lip at the heel and toe, such as welt-sewn leather hiking boots with external stitched seams, many **telemark skiing** boots, and modern plastic climbing boots. To minimize the chance of the front bail coming off, these crampons often have a strap linking the toe and heel pieces.

The next easiest system has flexible plastic cradles at the front and back that wrap around the boot when tensioned with a strap that runs from the heel to the front cradle and then back to a buckle at the back. This will fit most boots and is probably the best system for hikers.

The remaining systems use sets of straps, with many variations of strapping methods. A common, relatively easy to use one has an O-ring linked by straps to the front of the crampons and

a long strap at the heel that runs through this ring and then back to the heel. There are also mixtures of systems with O-rings and straps at the front and with heel levers or cradles at the back.

Whichever fastening system you have, practice until you can attach the crampons quickly. When you have to put them on with cold fingers in a blizzard, you don't want to be working out what goes where.

Fit

Crampons must fit your boots properly, or they may fall off, which is always inconvenient and may be dangerous. To check the fit, attach the crampon to the boot but don't fasten the straps; then pick up the boot and shake it. A properly fitted crampon won't fall off.

Basic Use

Walking in crampons isn't difficult, but it requires a little practice because you need to keep your legs well apart. It's easy to trip over your crampons and fall flat on your face or to catch a side point in your **gaiters** or pants and rip them or even gash your leg. For maximum security on slopes, you need to put your foot down flat (flat-footing) so that all the points are in contact with the snow or ice. If your crampons have front points, you can kick them into the snow and balance on them.

Carrying Systems

Crampons aren't easy to pack. Rubber spike protectors are available, but they are prone to tangling and can be hard to sort out with cold fingers. You can use tough Cordura or PVC bags, which can be carried inside a **rucksack** without danger to other gear. Most **packs** come with straps or patches for carrying crampons on the outside, the best place if you are likely to need them often.

See also **ice climbing** and **mountaineering**.

CRATERING

The greatest fear of many rock climbers is falling from great heights all the way to the ground, a disaster not so affectionately called *cratering*. You might hear the term used in a sentence as follows: "Did you hear what happened to Joe? He was 15 feet off the ground when he cratered." Cratering can be prevented by a combination of good **rock climbing** techniques, adequate protection placement (see **artificial protection**), and attentive **belaying**.

CREVASSE

A crevasse is a large crack that forms in a glacier as it moves. Such cracks pose major threats to mountaineers because they can be hundreds of feet deep and may be obstructed from view by surface **snow**. Crevasses form when one part of a glacier moves faster than another part. For example, if the slope of a glacier suddenly increases, the portion of the glacier that is on the steep slope

Crevasses pose a major hazard on glaciers. This crevasse in British Columbia is exposed, but many are hidden beneath a layer of snow. These climbers are roped together to prevent any one climber from falling deep into a crevasse (see roping up*).*

ANNIE AGGENS

will descend more quickly than the rest of the glacier, causing it to break away from the upper portions, at least at the surface. This type of crevasse, a crescentric crevasse, is usually found perpendicular to the angle of the slope.

Another type of crevasse can be found near the edges of the glacier. This type, a marginal crevasse, is formed when the sides of a glacier encounter increased friction from the mountain. This causes the sides to move slower than the middle of the glacier. The faster-moving midsection will create fractures as it breaks away from the slower-moving sides.

Because you can't see all the geographical features of the mountain that lie beneath the **ice**, you can never predict the locations of all the crevasses. Furthermore, as snowfall accumulates, many crevasses become concealed. This is when things become tricky. Climbers are continually on the lookout for depressions in the snow, however slight, that may suggest a crevasse below. To help them locate crevasses, climbers will probe the snow ahead with their **ice axes**, ski poles, or specially designed probe poles. They are feeling for changes in the snow's resistance to the probing object. If, for instance, your ice ax encounters a lack of resistance when you drive it into the snow, you may be on the edge of a crevasse.

When you encounter a crevasse, you need to determine its path. Do this by continuing to probe, keeping in mind that most crevasses run perpendicular to the angle of the slope. Usually, you can walk along the side of the crevasse until it ends. Once you think you have discovered the end, give the crevasse a wide berth, because it may be a false ending.

Occasionally, you will encounter a crevasse that has a snow bridge to the other side. While some bridges may be strong enough to hold your weight, others may not. In addition, a simple change in the temperature or intensity of the sun can compromise the integrity of the bridge. Crossing a snow bridge should be considered a major risk, and anyone who chooses to do so should be belayed (see **belaying**).

If you are traveling solo and fall through a crevasse, it will be nearly impossible for you to get out. **Crevasse rescues** are difficult enough when you have several experienced people who can respond quickly. For this reason, you should never travel on a glacier alone. Furthermore, when you are with a group, you should always travel using a **rope** to connect each member of the team. This rope will become a lifeline if one member of the party falls into a crevasse. Without it, she will simply disappear into the depths of the crevasse. Called *roping up*, this process requires that all team members have solid **self-arrest** skills.

Traveling on a glacier is risky business requiring constant focus and significant technical skill. Before you take one step on a glacier, you should be able to identify the multiple hazards that exist (crevasses are just one). Furthermore, you should be prepared to perform a crevasse rescue, if necessary. The best way to learn about glacier travel is from a competent and experienced **guide** or instructor. Many **outdoor schools** offer courses in **mountaineering** that provide practical glacier experience under the supervision of trained professionals.

See also **avalanches**, **glaciers**, and **glacier travel**.

CREVASSE RESCUE

Crevasse rescues are a critical component of safe **glacier travel**. In the event that a climber on your team falls into a **crevasse**, you must be able to arrest his fall immediately and help him escape as soon as possible. A crevasse is a cold and unforgiving place. As a rescuer, you will need to act fast to prevent the fallen climber from developing **hypothermia** and to treat any injuries he may have sustained during the fall.

While it is possible for any climber on a roped team to fall into a crevasse, it is the lead climber who tests the route. Therefore, if he incorrectly evaluates the integrity of the **snow**, he may be the first (and hopefully the only) climber to fall into the crevasse. If this is the case, the other climbers should immediately drop into **self-arrest** positions. Because self-arrest is such an important

skill, you should practice it repeatedly until it is second nature. When the fall has been arrested, and if the climber closest to the crevasse can maintain the arrest without slipping, the third climber should quickly build a solid **snow anchor** (or, if conditions necessitate, an ice anchor). If possible, the snow anchor should be built in between the crevasse and the climber maintaining the self-arrest. If there are more than three climbers in the party, additional people can be used to back up the self-arrest.

Once the snow anchor is built, it can be attached to the main **rope** (the one going to the fallen climber) with a **prusik hitch**. The load can then be slowly transferred from the self-arrest to the anchor. During this process, at least one person should be ready to reengage the self-arrest should the anchor fail.

After the fallen climber's weight is on the snow anchor, you can devise a plan to get the person out of the crevasse. If the climber is conscious, he can ascend the rope using prusik **slings** or mechanical ascenders. If the climber is unable to do this, the rescuers will have to hoist the climber out of the crevasse. This can be accomplished by pulling on the rope or using the **z-drag**, a hauling system that provides a mechanical advantage. Getting a person out of a crevasse can take time. If at all possible, the person in the crevasse should be engaged in this process by ascending the rope. Not only does this make less work for the rescuers, but it also keeps the fallen climber moving and generating heat.

Crevasse rescue is a complicated, technical subject with a number of variables. For example, what happens if the middle climber on a rope team of three climbers falls into the crevasse? Who builds the anchor? Who holds the self-arrest? As a climber traveling on a **glacier,** you must be prepared for every eventuality. Have the appropriate rescue gear accessible and know how to use it. Spend time practicing the various techniques over and over again until you can do them from memory when the light is fading and you are tired, hungry, and cold.

Based on an illustration in Graydon and Hanson, Mountaineering

Crevasse rescues must be performed quickly to prevent hypothermia. Here the climber's fall into the crevasses was halted by his companion's self-arrest (see self-arrest). A second companion has built a snow anchor to hold the climber in place to relieve the self-arrest (A). An ax has been placed under the rope, parallel to the edge of the crevasse, to prevent the rope from slicing through the edge (B). Finally, a companion is belayed to the crevasse edge to check on the climber (C). At this point the climber can ascend the rope, or a haul system such as the z-drag can be employed to hoist the climber out of the crevasse.

Several books offer extensive information on crevasse rescue. *Mountaineering*, edited by Don Graydon and Kurt Hanson, is a popular text. Another popular book is *Glacier Travel and Crevasse Rescue*, by Andy Selters. However, reading alone will not prepare you for the rigors of glacier travel. Practical experience is critical. Many **outdoor schools** provide excellent training in crevasse rescues and other important **mountaineering** techniques. Making arrangements to learn these skills from a competent and experienced instructor will pay off every time you head out for another adventure on the ice.

CROSS-COUNTRY SKIING

See **ski touring**.

CRYPTOBIOTIC SOIL

See **deserts**.

CRYPTOSPORIDIUM

Like *Giardia*, *Cryptosporidium* is a single-celled animal, a protozoan. If ingested, it causes a digestive upset called *cryptosporidiasis*, the main symptom of which is diarrhea. There is no treatment for this illness, but healthy adults recover in two to four days. Once you've had it, you build up immunity. It's only a potential problem for the very young, the very old, or those with an immunodeficiency.

Cryptosporidium can be found in both backcountry water and contaminated food. To avoid spreading it in food, washing your hands thoroughly before handling food or cooking utensils is as important as, if not more so than, treating water. Chemicals such as iodine and chlorine do not kill *Cryptosporidium*, although chlorine dioxide drops are claimed to be effective. Boiling does kill *Cryptosporidium*, and filtering can remove it.

See also **sanitation** and **water**.

DEAD RECKONING

Dead reckoning is a technique for traveling in a straight line using a compass bearing. To use dead reckoning successfully, you have to judge **distance** accurately and be able to follow a **bearing** closely. Even so, the technique isn't all that accurate: the farther you travel, the less accurate it gets, so it's best used for short distances. It could be used in conditions of poor visibility, such as mist, or when there are no distinctive landmarks between you and your destination, as in the **desert**, on arctic tundra, on large **ice** sheets, or on a large body of water.

> "I've crossed snow-covered plateaus and large ice caps using dead reckoning and have come out roughly where I wanted to be. However, it's not a very accurate technique and should really be used only when there's no other option. It's just not possible to follow a compass bearing or estimate distance traveled absolutely accurately."—CT

To use dead reckoning, take a bearing on your destination and then calculate the distance to it from the **map**. Estimate the time it will take to travel that distance and set off, keeping a close eye on the compass and your watch. Counting paces is a good way for hikers to estimate very

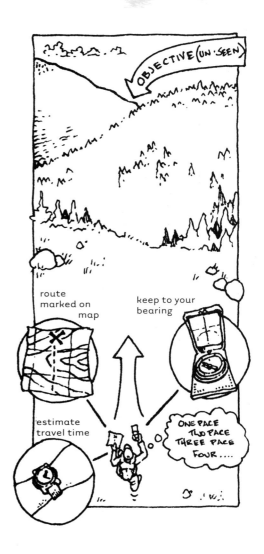

OBJECTIVE (UN-SEEN)

route marked on map

keep to your bearing

estimate travel time

ONE PACE
TWO PACE
THREE PACE
FOUR....

short distances, especially if you know how long your stride is. For longer distances, knowing the speed at which you walk or ski or paddle is crucial, as only the elapsed time will tell you when you should be approaching your destination.

To check how you're going, you can travel for a set time and then mark on your map where you think you are on the line between your start point and your destination. When you really need to stick close to your bearing and there is nothing visible to walk toward, one person can travel ahead and become a marker. The navigator with the compass stands still while the person goes to the edge of visibility. The navigator then waves her left or right until she is in line with the bearing. Then the navigator travels up to her, and the process is repeated. This is a slow process, but if there are hidden dangers on either side, such as cliffs, it is also a safe one.

DEET

DEET is the well-known ingredient in most insect repellents. It's short for N, N-diethyl-meta-toluamide and was developed by the U.S. Army in 1946 and registered for public use in 1957. It repels all biting **insects**, including mosquitoes, no-see-ums, and **ticks**. DEET can be applied to skin or **clothing**.

DEET is a potent chemical that can melt plastic, as you'll find if it gets on your camera or plastic knife handle. The Environmental Protection Agency, which reregistered DEET in 1998, classifies it as "slightly toxic" and says that it's not a health concern as long as consumers "follow label directions and take proper precautions," although it "may cause skin reactions in rare cases."

The advised precautions are as follows.

• DEET should not be applied over cuts, wounds, or irritated skin.
• Only just enough DEET to cover clothing or skin should be used—don't lather it on.
• DEET shouldn't be used under clothing.
• Treated skin should be washed when the repellent is no longer needed.

• Treated clothing should be washed before being worn again.
• Sprays should be applied to the hands and then rubbed on the face, rather than applied to the face directly.
• Sprays should not be used in enclosed areas.
• DEET can be used on children but shouldn't be applied to hands or near the eyes or mouths of young children because it can irritate the eyes and be toxic if swallowed.
• Young children should not apply DEET themselves.

Some people find that the smell of DEET makes them feel unwell or even nauseated. This can occur even if the DEET is on someone else. It's especially bad in enclosed spaces, such as **tents**. Such people need to use a non-DEET repellent, and it's best if their traveling partners do so too.

DEHYDRATION

Dehydration is arguably the most common ailment for backcountry travelers. It causes people to become irritable, have headaches, feel nauseated, and lose their appetites. As a guide, the first question Annie asks when someone complains about not feeling well is, "how much **water** have you had today?" A majority of the time, water is the only cure necessary to get the person back on track.

Dehydration is caused by a lack of water in your body. This can be the result of not drinking enough liquids or of more serious conditions, such as persistent diarrhea or vomiting. Organically, most of your body is composed of water. Every organ, cell, and tissue requires water to stay alive and healthy. If you don't give your body the necessary amount of fluids, things go awry. Your water-depleted brain will ache, and you will feel tired and maybe even sick to your stomach. You may eat, but your body won't metabolize the food. Your blood volume will decrease, making you more susceptible to **hypothermia** and **cold-weather injuries**, such as **frostbite**. You'll become constipated, and infrequent urination will heighten the risk of a urinary tract infection. Eventually, if dehydration is left untreated, all body functions will fail, ultimately leading to death.

As miserable as dehydration sounds, it is amazing how many people bring it upon themselves by not drinking enough water. Your body constantly loses fluid through urination, perspiration, and even breathing. To keep your body hydrated, you need to continually replace the fluids that are lost—and the harder you work, the more fluid you need to replace. In addition, certain dry environments, such as deserts, demand more fluids. Likewise, higher altitudes and cold temperatures drain your body of fluids faster than average altitudes or temperatures.

To avoid dehydration, drink 3 to 4 quarts of water each day while on the trail. Don't drink it all at once, because your body can process only about a quart every half hour. Spread your fluid intake over the course of the day, rather than attempting to replenish water already lost. Avoid waiting until you're thirsty to drink: by the time you have a dry mouth or crave water, you are already low on fluids. Don't count caffeinated beverages, such as coffee, tea, or soda, toward your daily intake. Caffeine is a diuretic and will increase your fluid loss, as will **alcohol**. Take note of your urine's color and the frequency of your trips into the bushes. A well-hydrated person's urine will be "clear and copious," not deep yellow. In addition to drinking water you must also eat. Your body acquires vital salt (lost in sweat) from food. If you drink lots of water but don't eat anything, your body will deteriorate as much as if you didn't drink any water at all.

If someone in your group is suffering from dehydration, have him drink water immediately. Encourage him to drink small amounts frequently. Chugging a lot of water when dehydrated causes you to vomit, which in turn increases your dehydration. Also encourage him to eat. Just about any food will have enough salt to assist in recovery. **Gorp**, crackers, or an energy bar all work fine. If the person's dehydration is caused by vomiting

or diarrhea, treat the cause of the problem in addition to the dehydration. It is important that the person is able to retain fluids. If you cannot control the vomiting or diarrhea, do not hesitate to evacuate the person to the nearest medical facility (see **evacuation**).

Dehydration can cause poor **judgment** and increase the likelihood of accidents. It is also a leading cause of heat-related illnesses, including heat exhaustion and heat stroke. Drinking adequate amounts of water is probably the easiest, and cheapest, way to ensure a great trip—so drink up!

DENTAL EMERGENCIES

Dental emergencies such as loose fillings, broken teeth, or gum infections can make life miserable on the trail. Dental problems can lead to more serious issues if they affect your ability to eat, drink, or sleep.

One of the best ways to prevent dental emergencies is to have regular checkups. Not your style? Then at least consider visiting your dentist before a major trip. It's no fun to have your friends play dentist with candle wax and the stove repair kit. Nonetheless, this may happen. To prepare yourself for a dental emergency, consider carrying dental wax and a commercial filling-replacement material, such as Cavit. In addition, an oral pain reliever (applied like paint) can provide a certain degree of comfort. Cavit, dental wax, and small dental **first-aid kits** are available at large drugstores or grocery store pharmacies. An alternative to Cavit is a denture adhesive, such as Fixodent. While not as permanent, this adhesive works in a pinch to replace lost fillings.

If you have a tooth knocked out, it might reattach itself if you quickly return it to its socket. First rinse it thoroughly in purified water but avoid touching its roots. If your mouth is bleeding, spit out as much blood as possible (swallowing the blood may make you vomit). If your tooth was simply chipped, you may only need to cover the tip with wax. This protects exposed nerves and also prevents excess rubbing against other parts of your mouth.

"The first time I had a dental emergency in the backcountry, I was on a skiing trip in Wyoming's Wind River Range. A bite into a frozen Snickers bar caused one end of a metal retainer to spring out of position and stab me in the back of my tongue. Ouch! The problem was that the rest of the retainer was still cemented to my teeth. After an hour of manipulating the retainer with tools borrowed from the stove repair kit, we were able to cut it in half and remove it from my tongue, much to my satisfaction. However, the remaining half, which was still cemented to my teeth, was in bad shape. Its sharp edges rubbed against my tongue, and my gum line was all scratched up. Because we had no dental wax in the first-aid kit, I melted candle wax for the remaining 11 days and tried to get it to stick to my teeth (not an easy task). In addition, chewing my food became a tedious chore, and I had to avoid hot drinks. Not the best way to spend a vacation!"—AA

Many dental emergencies result in pain that makes it advisable for the sufferer to leave the backcountry. If this is the case or if you suspect that the dental injury or illness is getting worse, evacuate the person to the closest medical facility (see **evacuation**).

DESERTS

Desert: the word conjures up heat, thirst, sand, and mirages—a harsh, threatening environment unfit for humans. Deserts are all this but can also be hauntingly beautiful, fascinating places full of unusual animals and strange plants. Deserts aren't all the same either; they can be hot or cold, sandy or rocky, and flat or mountainous. They are, however, always arid, though it can **rain** and even **snow** at times.

Deserts cover a vast part of western North America, from Oregon and Idaho to Mexico. Scientists don't agree on the exact extent, but estimates range from 500,000 to 750,000 total square miles. The North American desert is made up of four deserts—the Great Basin, Mojave, Sonoran, and Chihuahuan—though the boundaries between these are not distinct. There are also huge areas of arid grasslands and semidesert that aren't included in these regions, although they are deserts as far as the **wilderness** traveler is concerned.

The Great Basin is the largest, coldest, and highest desert in the United States. It's a harsh, rocky, mountainous desert that covers around 190,000 square miles, including much of Utah and Nevada and parts of Oregon, Idaho, Wyoming, Colorado, and Arizona, bounded by the great mountain ranges of the **Sierra Nevada** and the **Cascades** in the west and the **Rocky Mountains** in the east. The Colorado Plateau, that wonderful region of canyon, desert, forest, and mountain, is thought by some experts to be part of the Great Basin. The elevation of the Great Basin is mostly above 4,000 feet, and the typical vegetation consists of sagebrush.

The largest desert in North America is the Chihuahuan Desert. It covers over 200,000 square miles, most of it in Mexico, with some in Arizona, Texas, and New Mexico. Summers there are very hot, but winters are cool. There is a wide variety of vegetation, and shrubs, especially yuccas, are more common than cacti.

The Sonoran Desert is typified by the giant saguaro cactus, with its massive, distinctive, armlike limbs. Covering 120,000 square miles of southern Arizona and southeastern California, the Sonoran is the hottest North American desert. It is also the most densely vegetated of all North American deserts due to the relatively high amount of rainfall it receives. As well as saguaro, it has many other cacti, especially cholla and prickly pear, plus a host of shrubs.

The Mojave Desert lies between the Sonoran and the Great Basin Deserts and covers 25,000 square miles, mostly in southeastern California but also in parts of Nevada, Arizona, and Utah. It includes Death Valley, the lowest point in North America. The most distinctive vegetation in the Mojave is the Joshua tree, a giant yucca found nowhere else.

Deserts offer much to the wilderness lover; activities include **hiking**, **rock climbing**, **canyoneering**, and **canoeing** and rafting down desert rivers. The **Pacific Crest Trail** and the **Continental Divide Trail** both run through deserts at their southern ends, while the Arizona Trail is in desert much of the way. Then there is the Desert Trail, a developing route that will eventually run from Mexico to Canada through California, Nevada, Oregon, Idaho, and Montana. Sections of this route are already worked out, including a 175-mile portion that runs the length of Death Valley.

The concerns in deserts are heat, **water**, and **navigation**. Keeping reasonably cool and well hydrated is crucial to enjoyable and safe desert travel. This means careful planning, especially with regard to water. "Think water" is a good mantra for desert travel. You always need to know where the next water is and to carry enough to get you to the next source. Before any desert venture, get up-to-date information on the location and reliability of water sources. Don't rely on **maps** or guidebooks because sources may be seasonal and can dry up or vanish.

Although springs, creeks, and pools are found in deserts, sources are often human made in the form of cattle troughs, dirt tanks (hollows scooped out of the ground to trap water), and windmills. Look for these on maps, but again don't assume they will have water. Even local information can be inaccurate, imprecise, or out-of-date. If you hear the words *might, maybe, should,* or *once,* assume the speaker hasn't been to the source recently, and make sure you have alternate plans if it's dry. In some places, caching water may be necessary (see **caches**). Since it takes about a week to acclimatize to hot weather, don't try to do too much at first—and do drink plenty.

It's best to avoid the hottest part of the day and hottest time of year, if possible. **Winter** is a good time to travel in low deserts; spring and autumn are the best times for high deserts. Summer is for masochists. Wear loose, cool **clothing** and a sun **hat**. An **umbrella** can make a good sunshade. In addition to exhausting and dehydrating you, the sun can burn you. Use ample sunscreen on exposed skin. (See also **heat regulation** and **sun protection.**)

As well as protecting yourself, you should protect the desert. That hard, stony land may look tough, but much of it isn't. Desert soils are especially fragile because they are so dry. In particular, avoid the unusual raised black material known as *cryptobiotic soil,* which is, in fact, a delicate community of mosses, algae, and fungi. Other plants can be easily damaged too, so walk around rather than over them. Where possible, stay on **trails** or surfaces such as rock or sand.

Of course, many desert plants have protective spines and spikes, and you quickly learn to avoid them. It's best to assume that any plant will stab or scratch you until you know otherwise. Some desert creatures can harm you too, so watch out for rattlesnakes (see **snakes**) and scorpions (see **spiders and scorpions**).

DISTANCE

How far? How fast? These are common questions you may encounter when you return from a **wilderness** trip. Knowing the answers is an easy way to quantify an experience. Long-distance hikers are impressive because of the sheer mileage walked, even though most would say it is the experience along the way, not the overall distance, that matters. Distance in itself does not have a value. A 5-mile hike can be as exciting, intense, or memorable as a 50-mile one.

The importance of distance is a personal matter. Trail runners travel far at a relatively fast speed. **Trail running** is enjoyable, a way of flowing through the landscape and of seeing plenty of country. Others prefer to move more slowly, at walking pace, still covering the miles but taking longer to do it. Still others are happy with much lower mileage, as they like to stop and smell the flowers or fish in the creeks or take leisurely lunch breaks. It's all valid; it's all part of the wilderness experience.

Having some idea of how far and fast you want to travel is advisable, of course, because distance plays a key part in **planning a trip**. How far can you go in the time you have? How far do you want to go? Trail runners will plan on much longer distances than will photographers or bird watchers.

The distance you travel will be determined as much by the total time you spend actually moving as it is by your rate of speed. Hike for eight hours at 2 miles an hour, and you will have covered 16 miles. But that means eight hours of actual hiking; rest stops and other breaks don't count. Sometimes people are surprised that they haven't traveled very far, although they have been out all day. Simple answer: for much of the time, they weren't moving down the trail. They were looking at the view, taking pictures, or picking huckleberries.

On any journey, you need to have a rough idea of how fast you usually travel and how much time you want to spend in actual travel. Six hours a day at 2 miles an hour for two days? Plan a route of 24 miles maximum. That way you aren't faced with a desperate march back to the trailhead when you discover it's still 10 miles away and you have only a few hours of daylight left.

Terrain comes into consideration too. Ascent slows you down, so it needs to be accounted for. A useful formula developed in 1892 by W. Naismith, a leading Scottish mountaineer, is to allow half an hour for every 1,000 feet of ascent plus an hour for every 3 miles. Using that, a 12-mile hike with 3,000 feet of ascent will take five and a half hours, not including stops. This is for **trails** or easy cross-country hiking. Once you get into difficult terrain—**scree**, boulders, dense brush—the time may double or even quadruple. **River crossings**, route finding, and **navigation** problems can take up time too. While a formula like Naismith's can be useful, working out one based on your own rate of travel is much better. If you keep records, it's easy to do.

The amount of ascent is also important because it increases the mileage you cover. **Map** miles are flat miles, so in the mountains you always hike farther than the distance measured on the map. The steeper the angle of the ascent or descent, the longer it will be. For example, if you walk a map mile up or down a 10-degree slope, you'll actually travel an extra 80 feet; on a 20-degree slope, it'll be 340 feet extra. Over a day, that can quickly add up. Switchbacking up a slope adds distance too and is very difficult to measure on a map because each **switchback** is actually very small. Some trail guides take this into account, but many don't. Compare several trail guides, and you are likely to find slightly different distances for the same route. Check the distances on signs along the route and you'll find that they probably differ from the distances in the trail guide.

> "From my records, I know that when walking 8 to 10 hours a day, including stops, with a full pack on trails in mountainous terrain, I average around 2 miles an hour. That drops to 1 to 1.5 miles for rugged cross-country hiking. Using this, I plan on 15- to 18-mile days on trails and 10- to 12-mile days when going cross-country. On terrain with little ascent, I up the daily estimate to 20 to 25 miles."—CT

It is still worthwhile to work out the rough distances, unless you have a good trail guide that does it for you. The most accurate method is probably with a map measurer, a mechanical device with a little wheel that you run along the route on the map. Some map measurers are digital and give you a reading (remember to set the scale); others have a range of scales marked on them against which to read the distance. A cruder method is to lay a piece of fine string or thread along the route and then measure it.

All of the above becomes irrelevant if you own a **GPS** receiver. Enter in each point along the route where you change direction, and the GPS will give you the distance between them plus a total. When you're hiking, you can leave the unit on and it will record how far you walk (at least until the batteries die; remember to carry spares). This distance will almost certainly be slightly longer than the one worked out at home, because the GPS records the route exactly as you walk it, including all small deviations from the straight-line route.

DIVORCE BOAT

A good way to test the strength of any relationship is to take a double sea kayak out for a spin. For many couples, the level of communication and cooperation required to negotiate a double sea kayak successfully is more than they can handle. What started as a relaxing excursion ends up landing the paddlers-to-be in therapy. It starts off with clanging paddles shortly followed by directional commands, such as "Honey, go right!—Now go left!—I said *left*, honey!—Left, dammit, *LEFT!*" Soon awkward silences fill the air, accentuated by occasional huffs and puffs.

> "As a sea kayaking guide, all too often I recognize the red flags before the tension becomes palpable."—AA

While sea kayaking has the added challenge of having to paddle in sync, any tandem paddling sport requires frequent communication and cooperation and can therefore be lethal to a relationship. If you're looking to celebrate your love on any kind of a paddling adventure, consider the risks. Paddling a tandem sea kayak can be fast and a load of fun, but they don't call it the divorce boat for nothing!

DOGSLEDDING

There's something about a traditional sport such as dogsledding that evokes feelings of adventure, challenge, and passion. It's almost as if you could ride a **sled** straight into the pages of a Jack London story. The simplicity of dogsledding creates the feeling of stepping back in time. After all, there's no motor or high-tech gear—just dogs, a sled, and the **wilderness**. But to say that dogsledding is a simple sport would hide the incredible

amount of skill, patience, and persistence required to excel at it.

From afar, an observer might think that the dogs do all the hard work and the musher (the person running the dogs) just rides along. In reality, the job of the musher is strenuous, difficult, and messy. But ask any musher if it's worth it, and you'll get a hearty yes!

Any kind of dog can pull a sled, although some breeds are obviously more built for it than others. The Alaskan husky, for example, is bred to pull sleds. Strangely, many of the dogs that look too small or wiry to pull a sled end up having the best endurance. By comparing them to people who run marathons, this concept begins to make more sense. The person who crosses the marathon finish line first is usually a big bundle of energy in a very small package. Bigger dogs are usually used for bigger jobs—like heavy sleds. They can haul a lot of weight but generally don't have as much endurance.

Dog teams range in size from 2 dogs up to 20 dogs. A team of 20 dogs would be considered pretty darn big, and you'd better be prepared to hold on tight! Every team has a lead dog trained to respond to the commands of the musher. "Gee" means "go right," and "Haw" means "go left." There are also commands for "stop," "go," and "pass on by."

Most mushers in the United States hitch the lead dog in front, followed by a pair of point dogs (sometimes called *swing dogs*), hitched side by side, which help the lead dog change the course of the sled. All the dogs behind the lead dog are hitched two abreast. Wheel dogs are those directly in front of the sled. They do the bulk of direct hauling. In the Arctic, the musher uses a *fan hitch* system, which allows each dog to be on its own tag-line running directly back to the sled. In this system, no dog is ever hitched up to another dog. The fan hitch allows the dogs to spread out (hence the name). This is convenient in the Arctic, where there are no trees. The arctic musher will sometimes use a whip to direct the dogs (don't worry; the musher whips the air next

ANNIE AGGENS

The lead dog in a dog team sets the pace and follows directional commands. The wheel dogs, directly in front of the sled, haul the sled.

to the dogs, not the dogs themselves). The dogs hear the whip off to their side and have been trained to head in the opposite direction.

Mushing developed as a mode of transportation for the Inuit of the far north. If you visit the hamlets of the Arctic today, you are likely to see a sled outside most homes (although snowmobiles are quickly replacing dogs). Outside the Arctic, most mushers race their teams or head out for recreational purposes. In sprint races, mushers compete for the fastest time. Sleds are stripped down to the bare minimum, and the dogs run like hell, flying around corners at Mach 10. Distance racers also compete for the best time but often over the course of several days. The best-known endurance race is Alaska's Iditarod. In races such as this, the mushers are required to make rest stops at designated checkpoints. While the dogs rest, the mushers stay busy keeping the dogs happy and healthy.

If you'd like to try mushing without having to buy, train, and feed your own team of dogs, try joining a dogsledding trip. Many outfitters have dogsledding excursions throughout Canada and the United States (OK, maybe not Florida). Be prepared to have a great time. But if you have a dog, don't get any wild thoughts: most attempts to make a four-legged friend suddenly pull its owner around the yard are unsuccessful and result in

shoes disappearing at an alarming rate. Instead, stick to guided services until you know what you're doing (see **guides**).

DOWN

Down is the underplumage of waterfowl. It's very soft and, unlike feathers, doesn't have a stalk. It's made of clusters of thin filaments that trap air and provide excellent insulation. Indeed, weight for weight, nothing is as warm as down. Down also compresses well and has a low bulk when packed. At the same time, it expands rapidly when uncompressed. Down also allows moisture vapor to pass through it and is very comfortable.

These qualities make down ideal for **sleeping bags** and cold-weather **clothing**. It really has only two disadvantages. One is cost—down products are quite expensive. However, as they will long outlast any synthetic, they aren't that costly over time. The other disadvantage is that if down gets soaked, it takes ages to dry and doesn't provide any insulation in the meantime—this is the most frequent reason for not using down. However, it isn't difficult to keep down dry. Carry it in a waterproof sack inside a **pack**, and it should be fine. Down clothing is usually too warm to wear in above-freezing temperatures, so if it's raining you can leave it in the pack. Many down products now come with water-repellent or even waterproof shells. While it wouldn't be wise to use them in the **rain**, these shells will keep out drips and spills and protect against humidity.

The quality of down affects its performance and warmth-to-weight ratio. All down has a small percentage of feathers in it because removing them all would result in an exorbitantly expensive product. This amount is usually from 5 to 15 percent but can be as much as 25 percent. Down that contains more than 25 percent feathers is not top quality.

The other important factor is fill power, which is a measure of how many cubic inches an ounce of down will fill. This matters because thickness is warmth, so the greater volume a given amount of down will fill the warmer it is. Fill power starts at

550 cubic inches per ounce (called 550 fill) and goes up to a very rare 800 fill, in increments of 25 or 50 cubic inches.

Down products are tough and long lasting as long as they are cared for properly. The key here is to keep down dry. If it gets damp, air it as soon as possible. Down sleeping bags pick up body moisture during the night, so airing them every day is a good idea. At home, store down items out of their stuff sacks and in a cool, dry, and airy place. A large cotton or mesh bag is OK (many sleeping bags are supplied with these), or you can hang them in the closet.

> "I use down bags everywhere, including in very wet climates like the Scottish Highlands, and I've never had problems with getting them wet. Down clothing I only use in dry areas or when the temperature's below freezing. For normally damp places, synthetics or fleece are probably better."—CT

Eventually, down will require cleaning. When it no longer keeps you as warm as it did and areas feel thin, with the down in hard clumps, it's time to wash it. If just the shell is dirty, wipe it clean rather than wash the whole item, because down loses a bit of its insulation every time it's washed.

Washing down at home takes a long time and requires great care. Once wet, a down item becomes very heavy because it absorbs masses of water. Don't lift it when sodden because the internal baffles that hold the down in place may tear. Instead, wash the item in a bathtub and press as much water out as you can before removing it. Don't use standard detergent, which can strip the natural oils that keep the down supple and may also reduce the water repellency of the shell. Instead, use one of the special down soaps available from outdoor suppliers. Dry the item in a tumble dryer set on low heat. The action of the dryer helps keep the down from drying in clumps.

If this all sounds like too much work, you can have a specialist company wash your down item for you. The manufacturer or your local outdoor store should be able to recommend one. Don't have it dry-cleaned, because the solvents used are harsh and can remove the natural oils. They're also not good to inhale. If you ignore this advice, air any dry-cleaned down item well before using it.

DRAW STROKE

There are times when paddling a canoe or kayak that you will want to go sideways, as often occurs when you are **rafting up** with other paddlers for a snack or a look at the map. You may also need to move sideways quickly to a capsized canoe or kayak to execute a **T-rescue**. The draw stroke, which moves you and your boat sideways, is an important stroke to know.

In a canoe, the draw stroke is commonly used to make quick corrections in the direction of travel, as when you're paddling down a lively stream and you see a rock directly in your path. A quick draw stroke by the bow paddler swings the canoe around either side of the rock. Draw strokes performed simultaneously by bow and stern paddlers provide one of the fastest ways to change a canoe's direction.

To perform the draw stroke in a canoe, simply turn your torso until your shoulders are parallel

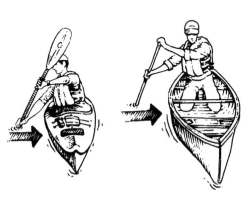

Based on an illustration in *The British Canoe Union Handbook*

The draw stroke moves a canoe or kayak laterally in the water. To perform the draw stroke, rotate your shoulders so they're parallel with the side of the boat. To protect your shoulders, don't raise your top hand higher than your head. This is especially important to remember when kayaking.

with the **gunwales**. Next, place your paddle in the water an arm's length away so the blade is parallel to your boat. Now pull the canoe toward your paddle. During this process, keep the paddle vertical in the water with the blade fully submersed and parallel to the canoe's hull. You may need to apply slight outward force with your top hand while pulling in with your bottom hand. Once the canoe nears the paddle, turn the paddle blade 90 degrees by rolling your bottom wrist forward (as if you were decelerating a motorcycle). This allows you to slice the paddle blade through the water and back to the beginning position. Repeat the stroke as necessary. Be careful not to let the canoe run over your paddle. When this happens, the canoe can abruptly capsize.

Once you are comfortable with the draw stroke, practice the crossbow draw stroke. It is performed by bringing your paddle across the bow to your off-side (the side on which you aren't paddling). Without changing your hand position, follow the directions for the regular draw stroke above. This requires a lot of **torso rotation**. The crossbow draw stroke is for bow paddlers or solo canoeists. It should **not** be used in the stern where it would be difficult and ineffective. (For stern corrective strokes, see **canoeing strokes**.)

The kayaking draw stroke is very similar (see **kayaking strokes**). Be careful that your top hand does not end up way over your head, as this can result in a serious shoulder injury. Instead, keep your upper arm across your chest, as if you were reading the time from your wristwatch.

DUCT TAPE

Duct tape is amazing stuff. This simple sticky tape has inspired websites and books, and you can buy clothes made from it. People have even been married wearing it. As far as the **wilderness** is concerned, it's a very popular **repair** item. Some people take pride in using it, as can be seen by their

> "I have a plastic camera tripod with a broken joint held together with duct tape. I've been waiting for it to fail for over a decade."—CT

duct tape–spattered down jackets. Outdoor magazines have even done comparative tests on different brands of duct tape.

> "I was first introduced to duct tape many years ago when I was given some to reattach a hip belt that had ripped off an external pack frame. I was very dubious as to whether it was adequate, but it held for a couple of weeks of hiking. Much more recently, I used duct tape to attach some pieces of closed-cell foam to an inadequate pack hip belt."—CT

Duct tape is strong and very sticky, so it can be used to repair almost anything. It's commonly used to repair tears in everything from **tents** to clothes to self-inflating **sleeping pads**. It can also patch damaged canoes and hold together broken ski poles (with a splint) and split ski tips. Some people use duct tape to cover **blisters** because it sticks to skin well and the shiny surface doesn't snag on socks. It can be used to hold dressings and bandages in place too. Always carry some in your **repair kit**.

> "As far as I'm concerned, if a duct tape patch works, why remove it?"—CT

Duct tape is great if you're going to leave it in place. However, if you're using it only as a temporary repair, be prepared to deal with the glue residue, which can be hard to remove. A solvent is the best bet, though you might not want to put solvent on some items of gear.

Traditionally, duct tape is silver. If you'd rather use something less conspicuous than silver or use something the same color as your gear, other colors (even camouflage) are available.

DUMPING

Dumping has several meanings in outdoor and wilderness contexts. In **canoeing** and kayaking, a dump often refers to tipping over or capsizing (as in "I dumped as soon as I hit that last wave"). In meteorology, dumping means that it's either raining or snowing very hard ("Did you hear the rain last night? It dumped on us!"). When referring to personal hygiene, dumping is going to the bathroom for a #2 (no example needed).

DUTCH OVEN

If you have yet to sample the gastronomic delights that emerge from a Dutch oven, you have something to look forward to! Dutch ovens can be used over a **fire** for heating pea soup, making a hot casserole, or frying fresh lake trout. But their real beauty comes when they are resting in a bed of hot coals **baking** a loaf of garlic bread or melting the cheese on a perfectly made pizza.

Dutch ovens are sturdy, round baking kettles with an equally sturdy flat lid. They are built to absorb and distribute the heat of hot campfire coals to the food inside. This practical design makes the Dutch oven a true working oven capable of withstanding and maintaining temperatures over 400°F without burning the culinary goodies inside.

Most Dutch ovens are cast iron, although some are aluminum. Cast-iron Dutch ovens are the preferred choice when **weight** is not an issue, because they disperse and maintain heat extremely well. Aluminum Dutch ovens, while lighter in weight, are more prone to burning the food. Still, an aluminum Dutch oven may be the best choice if you want the benefits of a Dutch oven but are traveling by foot or ski and have to carry all your gear.

The key to successful Dutch oven cooking is having a good bed of hot coals. Create a nest the size of your Dutch oven in the smoldering coals of the fire, then place the oven in the coals, covering it with the remaining hot coals. To avoid burning the bottom of your food, about two-thirds of the heat should come from the top of the Dutch oven. This means that you'll have to shovel more hot coals on the lid than are underneath the oven. A traditional Dutch oven has a rim around the edge of the lid that keeps the hot coals from sliding off. Some Dutch oven enthusiasts opt to use charcoal briquettes instead of fire coals. The benefit of charcoal is that you don't need to build a campfire, but the downside is that charcoal is yet another item to carry.

Like any piece of quality equipment, a Dutch oven (especially one made of cast iron) requires some maintenance. A cast-iron Dutch oven has to be seasoned before cooking in it. Seasoning any cast-iron pot is like waterproofing a good pair of boots with oil. The more oil that is absorbed by the pot, the easier it will be to use and clean over time. You can tell a well-seasoned cast-iron Dutch oven by its black appearance. The black comes from years of carbon buildup in the pores of the cast iron. While it may look dirty, you don't want to scrub the black off. On the contrary, Dutch oven owners work hard to maintain the black seasoning because it gives the oven a nonstick coating. To preserve the seasoning, owners use only plastic or wooden utensils and staunchly avoid soap or abrasive materials while washing.

> "I once learned the hard way not to use soap or abrasives on a Dutch oven after spending over an hour scrubbing a friend's Dutch oven until it sparkled, much to the mortification of its owner."—AA

Most outdoor stores and some hardware stores carry cast-iron Dutch ovens. Aluminum Dutch ovens are harder to find. Before you buy, consider how many people you will be feeding. An 8-inch or 10-inch Dutch oven is a good size for two or three people. Any more people than that, and you'll want to go with a bigger Dutch oven, but remember—they get heavier as they get bigger!

EDDIES

Eddies are small pockets of a river that have a reversed current, meaning the water flows upstream. Eddies are caused when water flows around an object that is at or near the surface of the water. Because the water cannot flow through the object, it needs to diverge around it. This causes a lack of water immediately downstream of the object. As the diverged current meets up again below the object, it rushes back toward the object in an attempt to fill the void. Sometimes the reversed current is undetectable, and the eddy appears to be a calm pool. Other times, the reversed current is very strong and requires constant attention from the paddler. Most eddies are welcome rest stops for paddlers who want to take a break from downriver travel by turning their boats into the eddy and facing upstream while stopped. In addition, they are often used for **scouting rapids** if you are unable to get to shore.

While eddies are usually found downstream of rocks, they are also formed downstream of bridge pilings, islands, bends in the river, and outcroppings of bedrock. The character of an eddy is largely based on the shape of the rock or other object, but the strength of its reversed current is based on the force of the downriver current. Therefore, if the river is fast and the current is strong, you can expect the eddy to be the same. Because the eddy has a circular flow, extremely strong eddies often resemble big whirlpools and can be quite turbulent.

The water in the eddy is separated from the downstream current by the eddyline (see **eddylines** for information on navigating across one). While most eddies are created by objects above

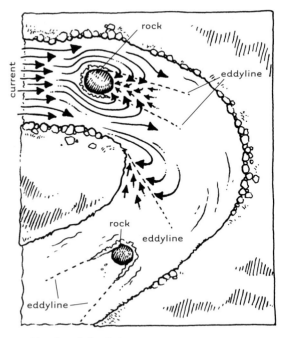

Eddies form behind obstructions in moving water or where rivers bend. The arrows show the way the water flows in an eddy. The dotted lines show the locations of the eddylines, also known as eddy fences.

the surface of the water, objects below the water surface can create a reverse flow as well. These hazards are identifiable because the water beyond the object is aerated and frothy. They are generally referred to as **holes** or **hydraulics**, and unlike eddies, they are not good places to take a break.

EDDYLINES

An eddyline forms the transition between the downstream current of the river and the upstream current inside an **eddy**. Eddylines are at their strongest near the top of the eddy, just below the rock or other object forming the eddy. If the current differential between the eddy and the downstream current is strong, the eddyline will be very powerful. In addition, there will likely be whirlpools that form within the line. This is generally not a problem if the eddyline is narrow and you can punch through it quickly. If it is a wide eddyline, you may find it difficult to navigate.

Another feature common to strong eddylines is a change in the level of the water, often referred to as a *fence*. This is created when water piles up on the upstream side of the rock or other object forming the eddy. This piled-up water wraps around the side of the rock before eventually dissipating back to the standard water level of the river. The difference in water level can go undetected, or it can be severe and quite restrictive (hence the word *fence*). Paddlers who find themselves in an eddy that is lower than the surrounding water may find it difficult to exit.

When **scouting rapids**, judge the strength of an eddyline before deciding to take refuge in the eddy. Some eddylines are hazardous and should be avoided. This is particularly true when the eddyline has noticeable whirlpools or fences.

EDIBLE PLANTS

After you've been eating dehydrated meals for days, there is no better treat than a fresh salad picked right off the mountainside or a cup of tea brewed fresh from the **forest** floor. Need to spice up your pancakes? How about some fresh berries! Nature's grocery store is filled with delectable

ANNIE AGGENS

Learning to recognize edible plants can help supplement mealtime. Several of these dwarf Labrador tea leaves were picked just after the photo was taken. When brewed with hot water, they make a wonderful tea.

items if you know where to look and how to identify them. Don't worry if you haven't been raised as a gatherer; there are numerous **field guides** to edible plants that make finding wild food both

> "Now that I can identify a handful of leafy edible plants in the western United States, I always make sure to take some oil and vinegar for an easy dressing when I head to the mountains."—AA

rewarding and fun. Choose a guide that is easy to use and that offers clear and thorough identification procedures as well as suggestions for the best way to prepare the food. Some plants can be poisonous to ingest or may cause topical irritation, so identifying them correctly is important (see **poisonous plants**). For example, never eat any kind of mushroom unless you're an expert. Living off the land—even if it is only for an appetizer—can be exciting and nutritious.

ENERGY BARS

You can't buy outdoor gear, gas, groceries, or many other items without encountering energy bars at the checkout. They're generally marketed for short-burst, highly aerobic activities or as snack substitutes for lunch.

The energy in these bars is provided by calories, energy units contained in all food. A plate of vegetables containing 400 calories provides the same energy as a 400-calorie energy bar. The difference is that the bar is light, compact, and portable. Of course, a candy bar is as well, and some candy bars have as many calories as energy bars.

Where the calories come from is significant though. In candy bars, it's usually from vegetable fat and from simple carbohydrates in the form of sugar. Some energy bars aren't much different, but the best ones have high levels of complex carbohydrates, which release their calories more slowly and don't cause energy "spikes" and slumps; they also have lower levels of simple sugars and fats. Some contain vitamins and minerals.

For **wilderness** use, the advantage of energy bars lies in the high calories and low **weight**. On long journeys, bars with vitamins and minerals are good too because these may otherwise be lacking in a lightweight backcountry diet. However, many energy bars need to be eaten with plenty of water and can turn solid in the cold. These are not good choices for **desert** travel or anywhere else water is in short supply, while in cold weather they need to be carried inside your clothing to keep them soft enough to eat without breaking your teeth.

Whether energy bars are better than fruit and grain bars is questionable; they certainly don't provide any more energy. They are not appropriate as the main part of your diet.

See also **food.**

ESKIMO ROLL
See **rolling a kayak.**

ESTIMATING DISTANCES
See **distance.**

EVACUATION
When it's not possible or practical to bring medical care to an injured individual, it may be necessary to get the person out of the backcountry and to medical care. This is called an *evacuation*. Evacuations are almost always logistical puzzles, requiring considerable planning and lots of hard work. Add to the scenario the stress of injury or illness, and you begin to see evacuations as they really are—not a whole lot of fun.

"Once, while leading a backpacking trip in the Canadian Rockies, I dealt with an unusual situation. A sixteen-year-old girl twisted her ankle on the second-to-last day, and I suspected that it might be broken. We were only 15 miles from the trailhead, but she was unable to walk. Fifteen miles is an awfully long way to carry a person, regardless of how you do it. Even with seven other trip participants, we quickly ruled out carrying her out as an option. For a brief moment, we considered using an old wheelbarrow that we came across, but the wheel kept getting stuck in the mud. Luckily, we ran into a college geology class that was expecting a helicopter supply drop. After some negotiation, I was able to coordinate a fly-out. The injured girl and I flew to the trailhead and got a ride to the local emergency room, where she was X-rayed and fitted with a cast up to the knee. The rest of the group (including the co-leader) hiked out and met us at the trailhead the following evening. We were saved by an unlikely chance encounter—helicopters usually don't present themselves exactly when and where you need them!"—AA

If the injury is minor and the person is able to walk or hobble out, consider yourself lucky. Wait until the person is feeling up to the task, and divide his gear among the rest of the group. Adopting a slow pace and allowing plenty of time for rest will make the trip easier, as will a healthy dose of moral support.

Any injury or illness that prevents a person from walking makes the evacuation significantly more difficult. There are many ways to carry a person, but all of them are arduous. If access to care is more than a mile away, chances are you will have to get assistance from another party or

piggy-back
—only when conscious

fore-
and-aft
carry

firefighter's carry

four-handed seat (when victim can use arms); each helper grips his own left wrist with his right hand, helpers link up; patient sits on helper hands as shown

Evacuation is hard work. These carries work well for short distances—a few hundred yards at most—but if you're farther than that from help you'll need to send for assistance. Carrying someone to a safe or comfortable place is feasible; carrying them all the way out of the wilderness is not.

send a runner for outside help. If you think you can handle the evacuation alone—and the injury is not life threatening—take some time to experiment with various carrying techniques. For example, a piggyback carry can be improved by wearing an emptied internal frame **pack** upside down. This creates a seat for the person to sit in. A **rope** coiled mountaineer style can be split and worn over the shoulders of the rescuer to create a piggyback seat (see **coiling a rope**).

A litter can be created out of emptied frame packs, canoe or kayak paddles, or long branches lashed together. Even on a good trail, it may take 5 to 10 people to carry a litter half a mile. An awkward carrying method or too few rescuers can result in additional injury, either to the person being carried or to one of the rescuers. If carrying the person 20 feet on a good **trail** is difficult, how will you manage when the trail gets tricky and you have a mile left to go? It may be better to stay put and send a runner for help.

When sending a runner for help, choose someone competent with **navigation** and **wilderness** travel. Spend time reviewing the route with the runner, and make sure she is prepared with all the necessary **food** and equipment for the journey. If possible, send a minimum of two runners. They should carry a detailed description of the injured person's medical condition, medical history, and precise location. A copy of this information also should be kept back at camp with the injured person. Give advance thought to what assistance you will request. Will you ask for additional people? A horse? A helicopter? Do you need a paramedic? What about oxygen or an IV? In addition, make sure the runners carry the appropriate emergency contact information. Finding out who to contact in the event of an emergency should be a part of your pretrip preparation. Once the runners find help, they need to be sure all the information is transferred to the correct **rescue** agency. It is likely they will be asked to accompany the rescue party.

If the injury is life threatening, the speed of the evacuation becomes critical. At such a time, it's hard not to take additional risks, such as traveling over rough terrain in fading light, but the rescue party must take every precaution, even if it means stopping for a while or traveling slow.

If a walk-out evacuation is impossible and no runners can be sent for help, you will have to signal for attention. **Signaling** is most effective if you are prepared with signaling devices, such as a signal mirror, flares, or smoke cartridges (be aware of your surroundings, however; you don't want to start a wildfire). Under these circumstances, your only help may come when someone reports you overdue or missing. This is why it's so important to file your trip itinerary with a trusted friend or local authority (see **trip plan**).

Any emergency triggers a rush of adrenaline that surges through your body. If the emergency is medical, the natural response to act quickly can overshadow the importance of making a good plan. If you run into an emergency that requires an evacuation, remember the acronym STOP (Stop, Think, Organize, Plan). A poorly thought-out evacuation can lead to additional injuries, lost runners, or rescue personal who come unprepared to handle the true nature of the emergency. A well-planned evacuation can run smoothly, regardless of how many different parties are involved.

EXPEDITIONS

Expedition: the word alone is enough to stir the blood. It stimulates visions of skiers crossing the polar sea or mountaineers departing from a base camp. Bestow the title "expedition" on your trip and you give it an illustrious flavor. Indeed, going on an "expedition" has different implications than going on a "trip." Most people associate the word *expedition* with extremely long and arduous journeys that require extensive training and intense logistical preparation. However, there is no rule to use when classifying a trip. For instance, many modern adventurers participate in "expedition cruises." What would Ernest Shackleton or Thor Heyerdahl have thought of that?! Despite its trendy use, most serious backcountry travelers reserve the term *expedition* for trips that are exceptionally long, technical, scientific, and, in some cases, expensive. In the end, however, how you classify your trip is all a matter of personal choice.

FABRIC

See **breathability**, **clothing**, **cotton**, **Gore-Tex**, **waterproofing**, and **wool**.

FANNY PACKS

Fanny packs are popular with trail runners because a **pack** that sits on the hips and the lumbar region without covering the back is very stable. Also, you can swivel the pack round to the front without having to take it off when you need something from it. Finally, you don't get a sweaty back.

> "I often carry a fanny pack containing an ultralight rain jacket, gloves, a hat, a compact camera, and mini-binoculars on one- to two-hour hikes in cool or stormy weather."—CT

The drawback of fanny packs is their limited capacity: there's only so much you can carry around your waist. The largest fanny packs run to 1,200 cubic inches, and these need to be packed carefully so they don't bounce when you move. To solve this problem, some fanny packs now come with shoulder straps. Called *lumbar packs*, these have capacities running to 2,000 cubic inches. Both fanny and lumbar packs often have water bottle holders that add greatly to the capacity. Some even come with built-in water bladders and drinking tubes.

Some fastpackers manage to cram everything they need for overnight and two-night trips into a fanny pack (see **fastpacking**). Less speedy travelers may find them useful too. For short day hikes, a fanny pack may be all you need. For **backpacking**, you can wear a fanny pack around the front for quick access to small items often needed along the way, such as a trail guide, a **map**, a **compass**, snacks, a **hat**, **gloves**, a compact camera, and mini-**binoculars**. The same pack can then be used for short forays away from camp. Some backpacks have lids that can be converted into fanny packs, either with a built-in hip belt or by using the one from the pack.

See also **trail running**.

FASTPACKING

Fastpacking (also known as *speed hiking* and *power hiking*) bridges the gap between **backpacking** and **trail running**. It's about covering as many miles as possible each day so you can see more country and get deeper into the **wilderness**, especially when time is limited. Fastpackers always travel ultralight. "Fast and light" could be their slogan. They cover more distance both by moving faster than more heavily burdened hikers and by **hiking** for more hours each day, which is easier to do with a light **pack**. Fastpackers may run at times too, but running isn't the aim.

See also **distance**, **trail running**, and **ultralight hiking**.

FERRYING

Ferrying is a technique used by paddlers to move a boat directly across a current without being pushed downstream. It is commonly used in whitewater paddling to get to the opposite side of the river for a better or safer run or an easier portage route.

Visualize the ferry technique like this: You are on one side of a river, and you want to swim to an object at the same location on the opposite side, but the current is strong. If you dive in and swim straight across, the current will push you downriver while you are swimming and you'll miss your target. To avoid being pushed downriver, you swim directly into the current, but now you are going nowhere. Finally, you decide to swim at an angle—almost as if you were heading to a point on the opposite bank *upriver* of the object you are actually trying to hit. That's it! When you swim at just the right angle to the current, you manage to slide directly across to the other side. That's a ferry.

There are two types of ferries: the forward ferry, in which you paddle forward, and the back ferry, in which you paddle backward. Deciding which to use depends largely on circumstance and ability. Let's start with the forward ferry.

The process of leaving the protection of a riverbank or an **eddy** and entering the current can be tricky. If the angle of the boat in the current is too wide, the bow will be pushed downriver and the boat will inadvertently spin around. Instead, keep the angle of the boat fairly tight toward upriver as you paddle forward until the whole boat is in the current. A tighter, narrow angle is easier to control. Remember to lean downriver: one false lean upriver, and the edge of your boat can get caught in the current, flipping you over.

Once the entire boat is in the current, open

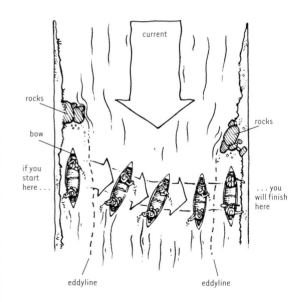

It takes practice to find the correct angle for ferrying. Here, the bow paddler, who is paddling on the right side, is supplying the majority of propulsion with a forward stroke. The stern paddler, who is paddling on the left, corrects the angle with a J stroke or pry stroke.

the angle slowly in the direction that you want to ferry and continue to paddle forward. In a tandem canoe, the bow paddler is primarily responsible for forward momentum, while the stern paddler is responsible for keeping the angle. Finding the perfect angle is the key to a good ferry. Too little angle, and you will wear yourself out against the current. Too much angle, and your bow will be pushed downriver.

With the correct angle and the right speed, your boat will gracefully glide sideways. Finding the right speed and angle is a combination of judging current strength and having a good amount of on-water practice. This is time well spent, as a solid ferry can literally save your life. There is also something very Zen-like about finding the equilibrium among the current, the angle, and your forward speed. Slipping across a choppy river with a solid ferry feels effortless and magical.

The back ferry is identical to the forward ferry in all but one way. Instead of facing upriver and paddling forward, the boat is facing downriver and you are backpaddling. Confused? Imagine yourself as a swimmer. Let's say you want to face downriver instead of upriver. Simple: you do a backstroke instead of a crawl. Everything else is the same. You use the same angle and the same momentum; you just switch your stroke. This might sound easier than it is, particularly for tandem canoeists. A canoe back ferry requires the bow paddler to maintain the angle, while the stern paddler provides momentum. Trying to maintain an angle while paddling backward doesn't come naturally, so practice this maneuver thoroughly before relying on it.

One last note: if one end, or side, of the boat is significantly heavier than the other, ferrying can become more difficult. It's a good idea to **trim** the boat well before attempting any significant ferry.

FIELD GUIDES

One of the benefits of traveling in the **wilderness** is the opportunity to learn about the natural world. Whether you are interested in plants, animals, minerals, the **weather**, the stars, or any number of other topics, there is sure to be a field guide to explain what you see. Field guides are just what they sound like: compact guides you can easily carry into the field. Using a field guide, you will be able to identify a subject by its appearance and then read all about its life span, mating habits, migratory patterns, and so forth. While field guides can be heavy, they more than make up for their weight with the value they add to your trip.

When choosing a field guide, be sure it's well

> "Since I discovered the Audubon Society's *Field Guide to North American Weather*, I don't go on a trip without packing it along. Even though it's worn, tattered, and waterlogged, I pull it out at least twice a day to identify different cloud formations."—AA

organized and easy to use. Color pictures make it easier to identify your subject, but they also drive up the cost and weight of the book. If your subject

is broad, such as flowers or trees, look for a field guide that focuses on your region (for example, **Rocky Mountain** wildflowers). Nationally popular field guides, such as the Audubon Society's field guides and the Peterson Field Guide series, are very thorough and user friendly, but locally published field guides may be more helpful for specific locations.

FIELD REPAIRS
See **repairs**.

FIGURE-EIGHT KNOTS

Figure-eight knots are a series of **knots** that take on the shape of a figure eight. They are most commonly used in **rock climbing, mountaineering, caving**, and other sports that require you to belay or rappel (see **belaying** and **rappelling**). The two most important figure-eight knots to know (of a total of four) are the figure eight on a bight and the figure-eight follow-through (also known as the *figure-eight rethreaded*). (See the accompanying illustration for instructions on tying both.)

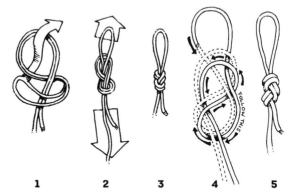

Figure-eight knot on a bight: 1. Take a bight of rope and bend it into a figure eight. 2. Tug the loop and the ends of the rope in opposite directions. 3. A finished figure-eight knot on a bight.

Figure-eight follow-through: 4. Make a figure-eight knot (follow steps 1–3 only with one strand of rope); using the running end (see knots), follow the dotted lines (which mimic the figure eight). 5. Tug the loop and the end of the rope in opposite directions. The figure-eight bend is not shown.

FIREARMS

There is little use for firearms in the backcountry, and most **wilderness** travelers do not carry them. Carrying a firearm into the backcountry can create at least as many hazards as it is supposed to protect against. Whether or not you carry a firearm is a personal choice, except when regulations prohibit them. But unless you're on a hunting trip or are carrying a weapon that has been recommended to you by an authority, leave your firearm behind.

If you are concerned about **wild animals**, contact the Forest Service, Department of Natural Resources, Park Service, or other agency for help in determining the best ways to protect yourself. Unwanted encounters with animals can be prevented almost entirely by taking a few simple steps such as being aware of your surroundings and keeping a clean kitchen (see **bears**). There are several types of wild animal deterrents that are safer and easier to use than a firearm such as various noisemakers and pepper sprays. Most animals are terrified of humans and work hard to keep their distance. For self-defense against people, it's prudent to be trail-smart in your interactions with others, especially if you are alone or near unsettled areas or borders where smuggling or other illegal activities may be expected (see **safety**).

"Several years ago, while paddling on Hudson Bay, I ran into a polar bear while waiting to paddle the high tide. While the incident was uneventful, I felt very much like live bait (and was even referred to as such by the local officials who heard of the encounter). Now when I travel to the area, I carry a marine-grade shotgun as a precaution. My decision to carry a firearm was well thought out and involved several conversations with local wildlife officials and polar bear experts."—AA

If you decide you must have a firearm, or if you are hunting, research the most appropriate make and model and the best ammunition. Get a license, take a course in firearm safety, and learn how to take apart and clean your weapon. If you're using a firearm for self-defense, there is not much point in having it unless it's easily accessible and you're absolutely confident you can shoot it on target. Consider in advance how and where you'll store the weapon and the ammunition. Discuss with other party members the safety issues of having a firearm, and establish some safety guidelines that everyone will follow. If you plan to travel outside the United States, or if you're taking public transportation or a chartered bus to your destination, check with officials regarding firearm regulations prior to your departure.

DIRK JENSEN

Cleaning a firearm involves taking it apart and inspecting each piece for adequate lubrication and removing unwanted moisture.

FIRES

The campfire is a symbol of **wilderness** travel—the flickering orange flames flaring up in the dark, shadowed forest, providing warmth and protection, a feeling of security, of home. To many people, no backcountry camp is complete without a campfire.

However, fires leave scars, especially if built in the wrong place or in the wrong way. Old fire pits can take decades to disappear. Too many meadows and clearings are disfigured by fire rings and blackened ground. Too many trees have had their lower branches broken off and burned. Because of this, campfires are banned or restricted in many areas.

Then there are the dangers of **forest fires**. Walk for mile after mile through a graveyard of dead trees, their blackened skeletons still standing, and you realize how devastating a forest fire can be. Take great care when you light a campfire, and observe all restrictions. If fires are banned for a period due to a high-fire risk, it's for a sensible reason, not just a bureaucratic whim.

In some places, whether permitted or not, fires shouldn't be built because of the damage they can do. At timberline, tree growth is very slow, and the nutrients from fallen twigs and branches are needed to replenish the thin soil. Burning this wood can damage the subalpine forest.

With the availability of efficient backpacking **stoves,** fires are no longer needed for cooking, and the quality of modern **tents, sleeping bags,** and **clothing** means that fires aren't required for warmth. A fire still satisfies a deeper, less utilitarian need, however. There is a magic in the flames and the glowing coals that can't be found in a camp stove and a reassurance in the heat given off that not even the warmest jacket can provide. This elemental feeling goes back to the dawn of humanity, to the discovery of fire, to the knowledge that fire gave warmth and light and safety from **wild animals**. We may take these for granted in our electric civilization, but once back in the wilderness our subconscious still knows the importance and value of fire.

Nonetheless, it is best for the environment to use a stove for **cooking** and to use clothing and a sleeping bag for warmth. Fires should be regarded as an occasional luxury, not as a normal part of **camping**. (See also **camp kitchen**.)

Minimum-Impact Fires

Being able to light a fire is still important, however. A fire can be useful for **signaling** in an emergency and for providing warmth if your equipment proves inadequate or becomes soaked. You need practice to become proficient at lighting fires, especially in wet, cold, or windy conditions.

In some places, you can still light fires without causing damage, as long as you take some care. Use existing fire rings so you won't cause damage elsewhere. First check for availability of dead wood for fuel. Often, well-used fire rings mark an area where there has been high impact. If there's little dead wood close by, it would be better not to have a fire.

In pristine areas, ensure that no trace of your fire will be left when you leave. This means never lighting fires in meadows or other vegetated areas. The best sites are shingle (large gravel) and sand below the high-water levels on coasts and rivers. Tides and floods will then wash away all traces of your fire, although you should still try not to leave any when you're done. Because people gather around a fire, the area surrounding it should be immune to trampling; rock or sand is best. Soft vegetation is worst.

Away from water, fires should be lit only on mineral soil. The three minimum-impact methods are

- fire pans
- mound fires
- pit fires

Fire pans have the least impact because the fire is lit in a portable shallow metal container.

Lightweight fire pans are available for hikers, or you can use anything suitable, such as a garbage can lid. The pan shouldn't be used on top of vegetation because the heat may damage the growth. In addition, it's best to support the pan on rocks so the base isn't in contact with the ground. To use the pan, cover the bottom with sand or gravel, then build the fire on top of it.

> "I once spent two days walking through a burned area in the Four Peaks Wilderness in the Mazatzal Mountains in Arizona. That fire, which burned 60,000 acres, was started by a campfire that got out of control."—CT

For a mound fire, build the fire on top of a pile of mineral soil at least 6 to 8 inches deep. This can be gathered and heaped onto a **groundcloth** or **tarp** and then the fire can be lit on top of it. Make sure there is no organic matter below the mound. Use a toilet trowel to dig the soil, and find something to put it in for transporting to the fire site—a large stuff sack or garbage bag will do. If you regularly use mound fires, you could carry a fire blanket to place under the mound. When searching for suitable mineral soil, look for areas that are often disturbed so that moving the soil won't have much additional impact. Dry washes and streambeds can be good sources, as can ground ripped up by the roots of large fallen trees.

For a pit fire, dig a shallow pit in the soil and light the fire in that. Be sure there is no organic matter below the pit. The former practice of removing vegetation and organic soil and replacing it when the fire is out has been shown to be damaging. Pit fires should be built only on mineral soil. Even sparse vegetation and forest duff can be damaged by pit fires, and fire may spread in duff.

Whatever the type of fire, only build it if safe to do so. Check that there is nothing flammable near the fire. It's all too easy for a burning twig to set fire to dry grass, which in turn ignites a dead bush, and then—well, you can imagine the scenario. In strong **winds**, fires shouldn't be lit:

there's too great a chance that a spark will ignite vegetation. In any situation, don't build a fire ring. It doesn't really contain a fire, and it will blacken the rocks.

To leave no trace, all wood should be burned to ash. For the fire, collect small pieces of wood that can be broken by hand. Never break wood off trees for your fire. If there's not enough on the ground, don't have a fire. Spread out and collect wood from a wide area, rather than taking everything within a short distance.

Building and Lighting the Fire

The secret of lighting a fire is to use dry tinder and then start small and build slowly, allowing plenty of air to reach the flames. You don't want a large fire anyway; sitting close to a small one keeps you just as warm as standing back from a large one, and it's much easier to cook over a small fire.

The shape of a fire doesn't matter, although you can find descriptions of all types. Start with a tiny pyramid, regardless of what shape you end up with. Crumpled bits of paper—scraps saved from food packets or pages from the book you're reading—can be used as tinder, or you can search out tiny twigs, dry moss, small pine cones, and dry leaves. Slicing the end of a twig into wafer-thin slivers (known as a *feather stick*) also makes for good tinder. If you have a candle stub or a solid-fuel tablet, place it at the heart of the tinder pile.

Dry tinder isn't usually hard to find. If it starts to **rain**, it's worth gathering some immediately and carrying it with you in a waterproof bag. In wet and cold places, highly flammable tinder can be prepared at home and carried with you. Apart from candles and solid-fuel tablets, which you may carry anyway, strips of cardboard, cotton balls or cotton cord (not nylon), and compressed lumps of paper can be soaked in melted paraffin. An old trick is to fill a cardboard egg box with wax and then tear off sections as needed. This is more effective if the egg box is also filled with flammable material, such as lint from a dryer, bits of charcoal, or cotton balls (make sure they are 100 percent cotton). Waxed paper, such as that often used for milk cartons, also makes good tinder. Wax-coated tinder is waterproof and will burn for some time, often long enough to ignite damp kindling. Very fine steel wool can also be used as tinder. Amazingly, it burns easily. A piece of steel wool placed across the positive and negative ends of two batteries should ignite. It burns very quickly, so have some tinder close to hand.

Starting a fire is easiest with matches or a lighter. Wooden matches are far better than book matches, which tend to disintegrate quickly and don't burn for long when lit. It's worth carrying two or three boxes in different places, so if one box gets soaked you still have some dry ones. Pack them inside a waterproof plastic bag, or transfer them into a plastic or metal match safe or a waterproof container, such as a film canister, along with a strip of sandpaper or the striker off the side of the box. Ordinary matches can be waterproofed by covering the heads with melted wax. These can be hard to light, however. Water- and wind-resistant matches are available commercially. A container of these is worth carrying as an emergency item, with ordinary matches or a lighter for everyday use.

The traditional means of lighting a fire is with a flint and steel; kits for doing this can be found in outdoor stores. Magnesium fire-starting bars are also available. In both cases, shaving fine threads off the metal produces sparks. Highly flammable tinder, such as charred cloth, also is needed. Wood-on-wood friction can also start a fire, but this requires much practice and experience as well as the right wood. It's not a good method for starting a fire in wet or very cold conditions.

Once you have some tinder loosely piled up, surround it with a pyramid of small twigs. Light the tinder, and wait for the kindling to catch. Once it does, slowly add larger pieces of wood. Be cautious, though. It's easy to smother a new fire. When the fire is lit, make sure it stays in place. Break all fuel small enough that it doesn't project beyond the fire area. If you're **cooking** over the fire, it's best to position your pans over hot coals rather than flames. Using a grill with

sprinkle water on the ashes

stir the coals with a stick and sprinkle again until no more steam rises

feel the ashes to be sure they're cool

scatter the ashes over an unvegetated area

A properly doused campfire leaves no ashes at the site.

short legs prevents the ground or any rocks from being damaged by the hot pans. It also makes spills less likely.

After the Fire

A fire is only truly out when the ashes are cool enough to handle. Once the ashes are cool, scatter them widely, preferably on bare ground. Return mineral soil to where you found it, and redistribute any unused firewood around the forest. On pristine sites, there should be no trace of a fire when you leave. On popular sites, any fire rings should be empty, with no garbage or half-burned wood. There should be only one ring per site, so dismantle any additional fire rings so they won't be used again.

See also **Leave No Trace**.

FIRST AID

First aid is a topic that can easily fill an entire book on its own. Indeed, there are many excellent first-aid books on the market that deal with backcountry traveling. Every **wilderness** traveler should, at a minimum, be familiar with basic first aid. What you really need is a solid understanding of the human body and education in prolonged patient care. In the event of an emergency, there is no substitute for prior training. With so many organizations providing first-aid training, and wilderness first aid in particular, you no longer have any excuses for being unprepared. The information here will simply touch on a few topics relating to wilderness first aid, such as how to receive training and the types of injuries and illness that are common to wilderness travel. Additionally, see the following first-aid topics scattered throughout this book: **allergic reactions, bleeding, blisters, burns, cold-weather injuries, CPR, dehydration, evacuation, first-aid kits, fractures, hypothermia, infections, lacerations, puncture wounds, shock, splints,** and **sprains and strains**.

Wilderness First-Aid Training

There is a big difference between regular (or urban) first aid and wilderness first aid. Urban first aid will teach you to recognize an emergency situation and then dial 911 to get help. In the wilderness, you don't have the luxury of calling for help. Even with all of the available **communication devices,** you cannot rely on outside help. Radios can break, batteries die, and signals vanish, even on satellite phones. Even if you contact help, it could take days to execute a rescue.

Having proper training in wilderness first aid should be a prerequisite to any trip. What's considered "proper?" Many organizations teach basic wilderness first-aid courses. These are usually 16 to 20 hours long and provide a solid introduction to the subject. More advanced courses, such as the Wilderness First Responder or Wilderness Emergency Medical Technician certifications, are good for serious backcountry travelers. These courses are lengthy and can be quite expensive, but they are well worth the time, energy, and money. Various outdoor clubs and organizations across the country sponsor wilderness first-aid courses. Generally, these sponsors will hire an organization—such as Wilderness Medical Associ-

ates, Wilderness Medical Institute, or Solo Inc. (see resources section)—to teach the course. These educational companies make it their business to stay on the forefront of wilderness medicine. Their curriculums are researched by both medical and backcountry experts, making the skills you learn practical and effective. If you're looking for a certification, make sure the company certifying you is recognized in the industry before you take the course.

Common Injuries

The wilderness is an unpredictable place; as a backcountry traveler, you need to be prepared to deal with a wide array of scenarios. Having said that, there are certain injuries that seem to occur more frequently than others. By the nature of what people do in wilderness areas, musculoskeletal injuries are common. Whether you sprain an ankle on a hike or pull your groin showing off your new **rock climbing** maneuvers, musculoskeletal injuries usually require you to stop what you're doing. If the injury is serious, such as a fracture or dislocation, an evacuation may be in order. Other common injuries, such as cuts and scrapes, can be expected when traveling in areas of dense brush or fallen trees. Deep cuts also result from accidents with **knives,** much to the embarrassment of the knife handler (the ol' cutting-a-bagel-in-the-hand scenario). Burns often result from hot-water accidents, such as knocking over the stove just as the water boils. Exposure to sun also causes burns, even on sun-smart people. These injuries are usually easy to treat but require careful attention.

In addition to dealing with injuries, be prepared to provide assistance and comfort to people who fall prey to an illness. The most common gastrointestinal illnesses are often caused by lax hygiene. These illnesses usually involve lots of toilet paper and frequent mad dashes into the woods. Diarrhea can spread though a group like wildfire and cause a lot of discomfort (see **sanitation**). On the flip side, folks who are either dehydrated or reluctant to take care of business in the

First-aid knowledge is a must for any backcountry trip. Here a blister is being treated with moleskin and tape.

outdoors may experience constipation. Simple gas, or a woman's menstrual cycle, can cause a person to double over in pain. Dehydration can cause a myriad of problems.

Being prepared for these medical problems, and the countless others that exist, requires advance preparation. By becoming adequately trained and carrying a proper first-aid kit, you'll be able to assess and treat the majority of medical emergencies that you encounter on the trail.

FIRST-AID KITS

Different people carry different types of first-aid kits in the **wilderness**. The climber, concerned with every ounce of weight, will bring a far different first-aid kit (at least on the climb) than the canoeist, who has fewer restrictions on space and weight. In addition, some people prefer to be extra prepared, while others get by with the minimum necessities. It's true that many items in a first-aid kit can be improvised with items found in your **pack**. Other items, such as sterile dressings, would be hard to replace. When creating a first-aid kit, consider the following.

• *Know the contents.* Becoming familiar with the contents of your first-aid kit is critical. It does you no good to have something in your kit that you don't know how to use. It is also pointless to dis-

cover after the fact that you actually *had* the diarrhea medication in your kit—you just didn't know it was there! This is especially true for commercially prepackaged first-aid kits.

• *Bring a book.* Find a book on **first-aid** that is complete and easy to read. One favorite is the *Outward Bound Wilderness First-Aid Handbook*. Whichever book you choose, don't be afraid to refer to it—even doctors use reference guides.

• *Know your medical histories.* Take time to review the medical histories of the people you are

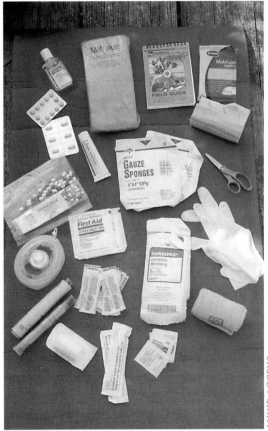

The contents of a typical first-aid kit: a protective mask, gloves, a first-aid guide, an assortment of dressings and bandages, small scissors, and various medications (including epinephrine if you require it). Alcohol prep pads or an iodine solution are good for cleaning skin. Sam Splints are bulky but can be useful. If you're hiking, bring plenty of moleskin or Compeed for blisters.

traveling with before building your first-aid kit. Are they allergic to latex or bandage adhesive? What about aspirin and other common medications that contain aspirin? Do they need to travel with epinephrine (see **allergic reactions**)? It's a good idea to have people fill out a simple medical form that you keep with the first-aid kit, even on personal trips.

• *Have items appropriate to your level of training.* This may seem like a no-brainer, but needing to be medically self-sufficient and having a medical degree are two different things. Don't carry items that are beyond your scope of training.

• *Pack it well.* If sterile dressings get soaked in swamp water or if your prescription medication dissolves, neither will work too well. Pack your kit in a waterproof container, and make sure it is accessible. Some people organize the contents into color-coded plastic bags, keeping all the trauma bandages in one bag, the medications in another, and the commonly used items, such as moleskin, tape, and Band-Aids, in yet another. This way, when they go into their kit, they can quickly grab only what is needed, without having to unpack the whole thing.

Many people like to divide their first-aid kit into two mini-kits: one for everyday items such as moleskin, tape or ibuprofen, and another for emergency items such as trauma bandages and epinephrine. This way the critical items won't get misplaced in daily packing and repacking. Also, a mini-kit of regularly used items can be kept more accessible than a bigger, all-in-one kit.

FISHERMAN'S KNOT

The fisherman's knot, also called the *fisherman's bend*, is a good **knot** for connecting two ends of rope. The single fisherman's knot is easy to learn and is a good stepping-stone to the double fisherman's bend, which is really the stronger of the two. The double fisherman's knot is often tied in accessory cord to make a prusik sling (see **prusik hitch**). Watch out, though! This knot is hard to untie once it has been under a heavy load.

Single Fisherman's Knot

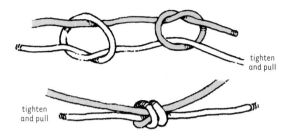

tighten and pull

tighten and pull

Double Fisherman's Knot

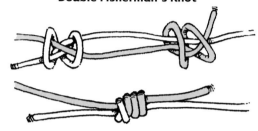

Single and double fisherman's knot. To tie the single knot: 1. With two ropes, tie the end of the first rope in an overhand knot around the second rope. Tie the end of the second rope in an overhand knot around the first rope. 2. Tighten and pull. The double knot is more complicated: follow the illustration closely to ensure a well-tied knot. Note that the tails on a correctly tied double fisherman's knot are on the opposite sides of the knot.

FISHING

Not all people are anglers, but for those who enjoy fishing, there's no better place than the **wilderness** to land the perfect fish.

The two main categories of fishing are freshwater and saltwater fishing. These can be broken down into subcategories both by the type of bait used (natural bait or artificial lures, including flies) and by the type of equipment used (reels, rods, poles, and tackle). Regardless of what type of fishing you prefer, your goal remains the same: to convince the fish that the bait you are using is worth biting and, this accomplished, to keep the fish on the hook until you are able to remove it from the water.

This simple act requires some knowledge and skill. The serious angler is an outdoor detective who, by observing a series of small clues—including the **weather**, time of day, **wind** speed and direction, shoreline habitat, direction of current, and local **insect** population—solves the mystery of the best time and place to position the bait.

If this sounds complicated, don't be deterred. For those of us who don't have the knack for interpolating clues, a class in fly-fishing or an afternoon out with a local **guide** can take you a long way toward learning what you need to know. If you like to read, there are more books on all aspects of fishing than there are old fishing tales. In addition, regional guides or maps specific to your lake or river can help you identify the hot spots.

For best results, research the area in which you'll be traveling before you depart. Identify the types of fish that you most likely will be fishing for, and learn about their habitat, behavior, and diets. If you're unfamiliar with fishing, ask for assistance in selecting equipment appropriate for your needs. Many manufacturers make lightweight rods specifically designed for backpackers or other adventurers who need to keep their eye on size and **weight**. Calling ahead to your destination can be a great way to learn what bait to bring and where to go. A local resource can also tell you the most convenient way to purchase your fishing license.

Fishing licenses are required in all 50 states and most countries, although young people commonly are exempt. Department of Natural Resources officials can require a license from anyone who is simply carrying a fishing rod or tackle, so if you don't have a license, don't carry the equipment. Licenses are valid for periods ranging from one day to all season and can usually be purchased wherever bait is sold. When you buy your license, also pick up information on the local fishing regulations. Often, there are rules outlining which fish can be kept and which must be released. If you keep your fish, it is best to clean them away from and downwind of your campsite—especially if you're in **bear** territory.

To clean a fish of its entrails, make a shallow incision with a sharp **knife** from the anus to just below the lower jaw. Next, cut the membrane that connects the entrails to the jaw. Get a good hold of the fish, and lift the membrane and the attached entrails up and out of the fish. Remove any remaining blood or debris. To fillet a fish, lay the fish on its side and slide your sharp fillet knife into the flesh just behind the gills. Once you hit the backbone, angle the knife toward the tail and smoothly slide the knife toward the tail, making sure not to cut into the backbone. Once you reach the tail, flip the fish over and repeat on the other side. When both sides are completed, cut the fillets entirely from the fish. If any bones remain in the fillet, they should be easy to extract.

There are many delicious recipes for **cooking** fish on the trail. Plan ahead and bring extra ingredients and spices for your angling buffets. Never plan to catch fish as your main source of food, however. Fish have an annoying habit of skipping town when they are most needed.

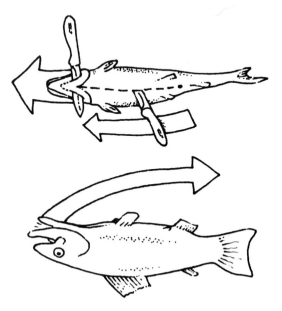

To clean a fish, make a shallow incision on the belly from the anus to the mouth. Cut the membrane connecting the entrails to the jaw and remove the membrane and the entrails.

Instead, plan on supplementing your existing menu with fresh fish from time to time.

Here are some general fishing tips.

- Fish are easily spooked. Avoid making loud noises or sudden movements in the water.
- Replace old or damaged line regularly (don't leave old line behind in the wilderness).
- In lakes, look for fallen trees, lily pads, or overgrowth that provides natural protection and ample food. In rivers, fish often feed on the stirred-up nutrients at the bottom of rapids or in **eddies**.

And here are some tips for practicing catch and release.

- To preserve the fish's health, always wet your hands before touching it.
- Land the fish as quickly as possible to reduce the stress on the fish.
- Use forceps (or pliers) to remove the fly or hook from the fish.
- When returning the fish to the water, cradle it in your palms beneath the surface until it swims away on its own power.

FIXED PROTECTION

Fixed protection (or "pro") is a climbing term for permanent **artificial protection**. Examples of fixed pro include bolts and pitons (pins). While fixed pro was a staple in early climbing, the trend since the 1970s has been to execute clean climbs, which is a climb that does not damage or scar the rock and that leaves no protection behind. While some climbers use pitons on big walls, they are all but gone in **free climbing**. Bolts, on the other hand, have made a comeback (along with increasingly easy-to-use bolt drills) with the popularity of **sport climbing**. Sport climbs are entirely bolted routes that allow the climber to carry minimal gear.

Opinions about the ethics of bolting previously "free" routes vary. Some people argue that bolts are overused, while others point out that bolted routes have led to increased access. Re-

gardless of your opinion on the use of fixed pros, you will likely encounter a fixed pro at some point in your climbing career. The question you'll be faced with is whether or not you should rely on the piece. When placed correctly, bolts and pitons are very strong and, for the most part, multidirectional. Over time, however, these pieces become damaged by the elements, other climbers, and old age. In addition, the person who placed the pro may not have known much about fixed protection. To be safe, avoid using a fixed pro whose history you know nothing about. However, if you find yourself in a pinch and you want to use a fixed pro with an unknown history, look for the following red flags.

- Unstable rock, or rock that is flaking or exfoliating, can cause a bolt or piton to fall out. Check that the rock is stable.
- Rust or small cracks in the pro are a definite sign to leave it alone. While you will probably not be able to see the bulk of the bolt or piton, you can examine its head and its hanger (the eye into which you clip your **carabiner**).

ANNIE AGGENS

Fixed protection such as this bolt should be closely evaluated before use. Check for rust, instability, and the overall quality of the placement before relying on any fixed pro.

- Is the piece placed only halfway in the rock? This is a sign that the piece was improperly placed or is possibly falling out. Look for a pro whose hanger is flush with the rock.
- Is the piece easy to move? Push on it with your hand, or attach a runner and give it a yank. If it moves at all, don't use it. Never hit the pro with a hammer to test it, as this will damage its overall integrity.

Another form of fixed pro is a regular artificial piece of protection, such as a stopper, that got left behind because it was impossible to retrieve. Before you rely on this kind of "fixed" pro, check it out for the same red flags listed above. In addition to the effects of time and the elements, this piece has probably been heavily poked and prodded in an attempt to remove it. These attempts at retrieval may have damaged its integrity. Also see **rock climbing**, **artificial protection**, **natural protection**, and **anchors**.

FLARES
See **signaling**.

FLASH FLOODS
Flash floods are among the most dangerous weather-related hazards in the backcountry. In a matter of seconds and with little or no warning, a flash flood can turn a dry riverbed into a raging torrent of water. To make matters worse, the water surging toward you may be carrying tree trunks, cars, boulders, propane canisters, and anything else it has picked up along the way.

Flash floods occur when more **rain** is falling than can be absorbed by the land—a particular danger in **desert** country. The immediate runoff is diverted into channels, such as valleys, creek beds, and rivers. The steeper the terrain, the faster the effect. Mountainous regions and canyons are particularly susceptible to devastating flash floods. One flash flood in a Colorado canyon killed 139 people in a matter of two hours. During a holiday weekend, a wall of water 19 feet high descended on the unsuspecting vacationers.

Water takes the path of least resistance on its course. Often, you can identify the path of flash floods by the lack of vegetation along the bottom of a canyon or valley. If your route calls for travel in such a location, make sure you camp in an area that is higher than the apparent path of water. Never spend the night on the sandy bottom of a tight canyon or along the dry riverbed of a valley floor. If you must set up camp in a constricted area, look for the highest ground possible—regardless of the **weather**.

"Once, while I was climbing with friends in Wyoming, a sudden and unexpected rainstorm turned our gully into a class II rapid. When we were finally able to reach our camp, the entire kitchen had been washed away. We were lucky that lost gear was our only casualty!"—AA

The key to surviving a flash flood is twofold. First, learn to recognize high-risk areas, and avoid them in questionable weather—especially during the rainy (monsoon) season. The weather can be fine where you are, but if it is raining anywhere upstream, you may be in trouble too. Know the weather forecast for your entire region before you head out. If you are unable to obtain a forecast, minimize your exposure to high-risk areas. Second, learn to identify the warning signs of flash floods, and never hesitate to take action. If you notice an increase in water levels or a change in water color, immediately move to higher ground. Sounds, such as the roar of thunder in the distance, also can be a good signal to take action. If you hear the ominous sound of water rushing toward you, it may be too late, but get to ground as high as possible. Survivors of severe flash floods have reported that the sound of the approaching flood was like the roar of jet engines.

With any of these signs, don't wait around to make sure your assessment was right. Move to higher ground immediately. Never try to outrun a flash flood, because it will always win. Survivors

ANNIE AGGENS

A flash flood turned this ravine into a raging river.

commonly say that the water was deeper and faster than they ever thought possible. Drop your **pack** if it prevents you from reaching safety quickly. If on a bend, try to scramble up the inside curve. By the nature of river dynamics, water will run the fastest and deepest around the outside curve. Even if you are perched precariously above the water, wait until the flood has subsided before leaving high ground.

Waterways in flood stages (including small creeks) are notoriously dangerous. Never try to cross one that is more than knee deep (even that height is risky). Water moving at only 4 miles an hour (a good walking pace) will exert a force of 66 pounds of pressure on every square foot of your body. That's enough pressure to swipe you easily off your feet. At just 8 miles an hour, the force jumps to 264 pounds of pressure. In addition, floating debris can bombard or even crush you. If you are swept into the water, assume a defensive swimming position by lying on your back with

your feet pointing downstream. Try to reach a safe shore as quickly as possible.

Flash floods can wipe out roads and create dangerous mudslides. Don't think that just because you are driving in your car, you are safe. Many people drive into flooded areas because they think their car will protect them. It only takes 18 to 24 inches of water to float most cars, so don't let your desire to start your adventure push you to drive where you shouldn't. If your car does get stuck in rising water, get out and seek higher ground. You are much safer on your own than in your car. If you see a river or creek swollen by flash flood, don't go near its banks—even for a quick look. Erosion can cause significant chunks of land to fall into the water and be swept away. Instead, retreat to high ground.

Rain isn't the only cause of flash floods. Broken dams, be they human made or natural, can cause catastrophic floods. While the runoff from melting **snow** is usually less abrupt, it too can cause flooding. By studying the watershed of your destination, you should be able to determine the likelihood of a flash flood so that you can adequately protect yourself.

FLEECE

Fleece actually describes two things: (1) a soft synthetic fabric that is very warm and comfortable, and (2) the wool coat of a sheep or other animal. That's why synthetic fleece is called *fleece* (sometimes *microfleece*); it's a substitute for **wool** —and a good one too. It's fast drying, almost nonabsorbent, easy to care for, hard wearing, and long lasting.

Synthetic fleece is usually made from polyester, although acrylic and nylon are sometimes used and some fleece is a combination of different fibers. Whatever the fabric, it is knitted into a flat material that is brushed, cut, and otherwise manipulated to produce different types of fleece. Some fleece is fairly smooth and dense, while other fleece is fluffy with an open structure. The latter is warmer but less wind resistant. No fleece is fully windproof. So-called windproof fleece has an ultrathin layer of windproof material bonded between two layers of fleece or between fleece and a thin wicking inner layer.

The thickness of fleece determines the warmth. Thicker fleece isn't necessarily the heaviest fleece, however; loosely knitted fleece with a raised fluffy surface can be quite thick while also being very light. Some fleece has Lycra added to it to make it very stretchy. This can be worn close to the skin without restricting movement.

Fleece is used for all items of clothing, from **socks** to **hats**. Fleece **sleeping bag** liners are also available and can be used on their own in warm weather.

FLOAT PLAN

Anytime you are heading out on the water, whether it's for a two-week trip or a three-hour paddle, you should leave a float plan with a trusted friend or local authority. A float plan gives detailed information about your trip. In the event of an emergency, the float plan will aid **search and rescue** crews in locating you quickly.

When preparing a float plan, make sure to include the following information.

- Your name and the names of all group members
- Type of boats you are paddling, with their approximate lengths and colors
- Camping gear that you have with you (this should include a list of your **signaling** and **communication devices**)
- Approximate skill levels and health information of all group members
- Launching site (if you drove, include the license plate number of your car)

A Sample Float Plan

Float plan for: Annie Aggens
Date: June 12, 2003
Other paddlers: Dirk Jensen, Caroline Bone
Boats: One 17-foot single kayak (orange), one 20-foot tandem kayak (yellow)
Gear: 2 bilge pumps, 2 float bags, 1 spare paddle, extra layers of clothing, some food, and water. We're wearing wet suits, and we all have lights on our kayaks.
Communication/signaling devices: A VHF radio, flares, water dye, whistles
Skill level: Advanced, confident with rolls and rescues
Health: All healthy, but Caroline is recovering from the flu
Starting point: Otter Point public access (my car should be parked near there, license #3G8 2213)
Destination: Ford Bay public access (alternative landing—Red Beach)
Route description: Paddle east from Otter Point to lighthouse on Round Island

(2 nm), continue SE to the sea caves off Red Point (4 nm) and explore caves. Continue SE to Red Beach, where we'll take a break and evaluate the conditions of the crossing to Ford Point. If conditions allow, make the crossing to Ford Point (4 nm) and head south to the Ford Bay public access (3 nm).
Total distance: 13 nautical miles
Speed of travel: 2 knots
Tidal schedule/Currents: High approx. 10:32 A.M., low approx. 4:40 P.M., high approx. 11 P.M. Flood heading SE at approx. 2 knots, ebb NW at same.
ETD: 9 A.M. ETA: 5 P.M.
Proposed search time: 7 P.M.
Search number: Ford Point Coast Guard Station, 341-555-8472
Hazards: Possible rough crossing from Red Beach to Ford Point, lower than normal energy level for Caroline
Maps: Round Island and Ford Bay nautical charts (1 set)

• Destination (if you will be gone for several days, include your proposed campsites and alternate campsites)

• Route description and distances (include points of interest that you are likely to check out as well as any foul-weather alternatives for your route)

• Approximate speed of travel

• Tidal schedule as well as the direction and speed of any current

• Estimated time of departure

• Estimated time of return

• Time that a search should begin if you haven't returned

• Contact information for whoever would conduct the search (coast guard, sheriff, etc.)

• **Open-water hazards** that you may encounter along your route

• List of the specific maps or charts you are carrying

Creating a float plan should be a regular part of your paddling routine. In addition to providing a safety net, creating a float plan is a great way to review your route and become familiar with the challenges it may present. Be sure to leave it with someone who will remember to call the authorities if you don't return. Also, remember to check in with that person immediately upon your return. It would be awful if a search for your kayak was being conducted while you were at home watching a movie!

FLOTATION

When canoes or kayaks fill with water they quickly become impossible to control. The simple tasks of turning, going forward, or stopping seem all but impossible. For this reason, canoes and kayaks that are likely to see a lot of wave action (such as sea kayaks, or canoes and kayaks designed for whitewater) should be used in conjunction with flotation. Flotation more often than not comes in the form of air bags that you blow up and insert into the empty spaces inside the hull. If there is no space for the water to go,

the canoe or kayak will stay much drier. The drier the boat, the higher it will ride in the water, and the easier it will be to control.

Most sea kayaks come with waterproof bulkheads, that do the same job as flotation. Usually they have two bulkheads (one located in front of the paddler and one behind the paddler), that separate the cockpit (where the paddler sits) from the rest of the kayak. This way, if the sea kayak tips over and takes on water, it will only fill up the cockpit. The bow and stern compartments created by the bulkheads are called *hatches* and can be easily accessed by hatch openings on the deck. This is how you pack your gear. Hatch openings usually come with one or two waterproof covers to ensure that water doesn't get in through the hatch. For the most part, this construction negates the need for floatation bags, although some paddlers still use them if they have empty hatches. You can buy flotation at most paddlesport shops or on-line.

See also **canoeing**, **sea kayaking**, **whitewater canoeing**, and **waves**.

FOG

Fog can appear at any elevation and anywhere there is enough moisture. On coasts, it can sweep in from the sea, thick and gray. Sometimes in **forests**, you can wake to fog sliding through the ghostly trees. Fog is most common above timberline, when low clouds cover the summits.

"I once had a long ski down a large, fog-shrouded frozen lake. I knew that two-thirds of the way down the lake I needed to turn into a side bay. With too little visibility to see the bay and a need to stay out in the middle of the lake to avoid any weak areas where streams ran into it, I skied on a compass bearing and time. Once I'd skied for several hours and knew I should be level with the bay, I turned off and there it was. Without timing my progress, I would have been very lucky to find it."—CT

Morning fog can occur after a cold, clear night. As the air cools, it may reach a point where the moisture vapor in it condenses and forms fog. This usually dissipates, or "burns off," as the sun rises and heats the air, causing the moisture droplets to evaporate. Fog will also disperse if a wind picks up, scattering the moisture.

"I can remember waking to a dense fog at a camp in the Canadian Rockies. The whole world was dull and gloomy. But as I walked down to the nearby lake, there were flickers of pale gold on the edge of the fog as the sun began to penetrate it. Then, although there was no wind, the fog started to move, swirling in white tendrils above the water. Shafts of brilliant gold light cut through it, slicing across the surface of the water so it glowed silver and blue. Soon the fog was gone, leaving a pleasant forest pool that, for a few minutes, had been intensely, magically beautiful."—CT

Fog can make **navigation** very difficult because visibility may be reduced to 50 yards or even less. On clear **trails** you shouldn't have any problem, but when going cross-country, good **map** and **compass** work is needed to stay on course. Timing your progress is a good idea because traveling in a featureless gray fog can destroy any sense of time. Was it 10 minutes or an hour ago that you last checked the map? Go slowly anyway, and be prepared to retreat if you get onto unexpectedly dangerous ground. Fog on water or ice causes navigation problems too.

While watching fog sweep down and cover the peak you are heading for can be dispiriting and frustrating, the opposite, when the fog clears and breaks, is uplifting and often amazingly beautiful. Sitting on a pass or summit as the fog starts to dissolve, shapes start to form, the gray light brightens, and colors start to appear in the monochrome world is a wonderful experience. Suddenly, instead of a wet gray wall that moves with you, always staying the same distance away, the world expands and explodes into light and space and color. Instead of 50 yards, you can see many miles. Instead of a pool of dull light, you can see mountains, valleys, forests, and rivers.

Morning fog can also be spectacular when it dissipates. And then there are times when you can climb through fog into bright sunshine and into a world where only the peaks are visible above a blanket of cotton wool clouds. Cloud inversions like this are glorious and give a real feeling of being in a different world far above the gray dampness of the valleys.

Walking in fog can be claustrophobic and tedious, however. Keeping in mind how wonderful it will be when the fog clears is one way to cope with this hardship.

FOOD

There are many approaches, from gourmet to minimalist, to eating in the **wilderness.** What is undisputed is that the right food can make a big difference to a backcountry trip. The right food consists of food that provides enough energy in the right form at the right time and that is portable, easy to prepare, and tasty. Travelers differ, however, in their definitions of portability, ease, and taste. What is portable to a canoeist will probably seem far too heavy to an ultralight hiker. Some people enjoy **baking** in camp, while others say any cooking is too much of a chore. And when it comes to taste, some people can't live without fresh vegetables or meat, while others happily subsist on granola and cookies.

On short trips of a few days, you can get away with a poor diet that doesn't provide good nutrition or enough calories, although it's not a good idea. On longer excursions, nutritional deficiencies will begin to cause problems that can hurt the trip.

To Cook or Not to Cook

Hot food is not essential. No more energy comes from a hot meal than from a cold one. If you don't cook, you don't need a **stove** or a **cook kit**, which saves weight, and you'll have more time to do other things.

> "I traveled part of the Arizona Trail with a hiker who ate granola for breakfast and lunch and pasta meals soaked in cold water for dinner. He was quite happy with this diet."—CT

For some of us though, hot food has a psychological value. Even in warm weather, a hot drink helps some people wake up in the morning, and others find a hot meal very sustaining in the evening. In cold and wet weather, hot food and drink can help warm you.

Nutrition

Any food will keep you going if it has enough calories, but the number of calories alone isn't enough: how they're provided also matters. The best sources of calories are complex carbohydrates, found in grains, legumes, and vegetables, because these release their energy slowly and regularly. Complex carbohydrates keep you going hour after hour without slumps. Simple carbohydrates are basically sugar in all its forms. They give you a quick burst of energy, but this is often followed by a crash that leaves you feeling exhausted. To avoid these lows, it's best to eat simple carbohydrates in conjunction with complex ones.

Carbohydrates aren't enough on their own for more than a couple of days. You also need proteins and fats. Protein renews muscle and tissue, but you don't need a lot and your body can only use small amounts at a time for muscle regeneration. Ultimately, regular small portions of protein are best. Protein is found in meat, eggs, and dairy products as well as in grains (such as rice) and legumes (such as beans), although the grains and legumes need to be eaten together to give complete protein.

Fat is needed by the body but, because it releases its energy slowly and isn't as easy to digest as carbohydrates and protein, it isn't a good food to eat in any quantity when you're active. The evening meal is the best time to eat fat. The slow release of energy during the night can then help keep you warm. Fat is found in meat, oils, and dairy products. Many processed foods, such as cookies and chocolate, are usually high in fat too. In temperate climates, you don't need much fat. Indeed, some people find fat unpalatable in the heat. However, when it's cold, you should eat more fat because it provides more than twice as much energy for the weight as protein and carbohydrates do.

Overall, a carbohydrate-rich diet—60 to 70 percent carbohydrates with the rest split equally between protein and fat—seems the best for wilderness travel.

Food also provides vitamins and minerals, although dried food is often deficient in these. For short trips, this isn't a problem; on long trips, bring food that does contain them or else take a daily supplement.

Energy

Calories are energy, so for wilderness travel, foods high in calories are a good choice. Otherwise, you end up carrying more **weight** than necessary. How many calories you need depends on a number of factors, including your gender, age, metabolism, weight, activity, and weather. The amount needed could vary from as little as 2,500 for a small person in hot weather to 7,500 for a big person in extreme cold. In more useful food terms, most people need 1.5 to 2.5 pounds of food a day.

> "I find 2 pounds per day to be about right for me, so rather than count calories when packing food for a trip, I just weigh it."—CT

Most dried and compact food is high in calories, though it's always worth checking the labels when purchasing new items. Two pounds of dried food generally works out to be 3,500 to 4,000 calories.

Weight

For short trips (one to two days), the weight of food doesn't really matter, unless you're aiming for high-mileage days. Fresh fruit and vegetables, bread, and canned food are all worth considering.

For longer trips, food weight becomes significant. That's where dried food comes in. At 2 pounds a day, a week's food weighs 14 pounds, a significant amount and the most that many people would want to carry.

Breakfast

Breakfast is perhaps the most varied meal in the backcountry. Some people like to make hotcakes, hot oatmeal, or even bacon and eggs, while others are happy with a handful of granola and a mug of water. Granola or muesli with reconstituted dried milk is a good compromise if you want to feel you've eaten properly but don't want to spend much time preparing food. Pour hot **water** on it if the **weather** is really cold or wet and you fancy something hot.

Lunch

An old backpacking saying is that lunch starts right after breakfast and ends just before dinner. The principle behind this saying is a good one. Continuous exertion requires a constant energy supply, so "little and often" is the best way to eat. Regular snacks will keep you going much better than a big meal in the middle of the day.

Trail mix (also known as *gorp*—good old raisins and peanuts) is the staple snack food. It can be bought already prepared, or you can make your own from anything you fancy. Nuts, seeds, and dried fruit are the standard ingredients, along with M&Ms. Granola can be added too, as can chocolate or carob chips. The mix can be sweet or savory, and even hot and spicy if you add a touch of cayenne pepper or chili powder. The great advantage of trail mix is that no preparation is required and you can snack on it anytime. In stormy weather, you can carry a bag in a pocket so you can eat without having to stop.

Most wilderness travelers also carry bars of various sorts. These can range from **energy bars** to candy bars and fruit and grain bars. The good varieties are light—3.5 ounces a bar—but pack an energy punch of over 400 calories.

For something more like a meal than a snack, crackers and flat breads (such as tortillas) along with cheese, salami, or a spread of some sort are a good choice.

Dinner

Dehydrated meals are the standard for wilderness travel. They are lightweight, quick cooking (some require only the addition of hot water), and low in bulk for carrying. They range from supermarket macaroni and cheese and other pasta meals to specialist backpacking meals from an outdoor store. Health food stores carry many suitable meals too.

Some of these meals are quite tasty, but some are bland. It's often recommended that you try meals before taking them into the backcountry. This is fine in theory, but in practice what tastes good under the stars at the end of a long day may not taste the same at home. Instead, just take one of any new meal, so if you don't like it you only have to eat it once. It's also worth carrying a spice and herb kit to add flavor to meals or even

CHRIS TOWNSEND

Food for a 9-day backpacking trip, with dinners on the right. Some of this food has been repackaged from cardboard boxes into zippered food-storage bags; the rest doesn't need to be repackaged.

disguise their taste, if necessary. This can contain anything you like, but something hot—such as cayenne pepper, chili powder, or curry powder—is always a good idea.

Home Dehydrating

Many people like to dry their own food, and there are several dehydrators available on the market. Almost anything can be dried, from complete meals to sauces to individual items, though some foods taste better and reconstitute better than others. Dehydrating takes time, but you do end up with exactly what you want.

Menu Planning

For solo hikers, planning food is easy because you know what you like and quickly learn how much to take. Planning for groups requires more thought, and it's best to work from a list so you get the right amounts of each item. How much oatmeal is needed for four people for three days? Or how much pasta? With a list, you can also check things off to ensure nothing is forgotten. After the trip, you can make notes on how it all worked out. What did you have too much of? What could you have used more of?

Packing

Most food can be repacked into plastic bags to save space and weight. If you need the cooking instructions, tear these off the packaging and put them in the plastic bag too. Each day's food can be packed into a larger plastic bag, and then the whole lot can be carried in a stuff sack. Carry a few spare plastic bags just in case any tear. Double-bagging messy foods, such as sugar and dried milk, is a good idea.

Storage in Camp

How you store food in camp depends on whether animals are likely to raid it and what the weather is like. In stormy weather, store food next to your sleeping bag so that you can cook and eat without having to get up. However, this is a terrible idea in **bear** country (see **bear bagging** and **bear-**

resistant containers). Where critters smaller than bears are the potential problem, sleeping with your food can be the best way to protect it. It can also be a good way to ensure that you get little sleep, because mice might become your new best friends. If this happens, hang your food bag from a low branch.

FOOTHOLDS

Foothold is a climbing term that denotes a fixture on rock onto which a climber can place her foot. When taking advantage of a foothold, you will generally choose from one of three foot-placement techniques: edging, smearing, and jamming. Edging is most commonly used on small ledges by placing the edge of your foot along the ledge. Generally, climbers will use the inside edge of

Wedging your foot into a crack, also called jamming, makes a great foothold.

their foot, but this is by no means a rule. Smearing is achieved by placing the ball of your foot against the rock and dropping your heel. A good smear relies heavily on the weight of your body pushing down on your foot. Jamming is a solid way to wedge your foot into a crack. You may discover that a foothold is good for only one type of placement; as your skill develops, you'll be able to predict which maneuver to use in a particular situation.

FORAGING

See **survival**.

FOREST FIRES

Every year forest fires burn thousands of acres of pristine **wilderness**. While **lightning** causes many of these fires, an increasing number are ignited by careless individuals. Irresponsible use of campfires and thoughtless disposal of matches and cigarettes can cause whole **forests** to burn to the ground.

Anytime you are planning a wilderness trip, check with local officials regarding the fire hazard. If it is moderate or high, there may be a fire ban. During fire bans, you are required to carry a **stove** and **fuel** for **cooking**. Even if there is no fire ban, you should consider cooking over a stove and limiting your use of campfires to special occasions. When you do build a fire, always keep it small and contained (see **fires**). Before turning in at night, the fire should be completely extinguished. A fully extinguished fire has no hot coals or smoke. In fact, you should be able to place your hand against the ashes without feeling any heat (be careful!). When using a stove, place the stove on a durable fireproof surface, such as rock or dirt. Ensure that no grasses or twigs ignite when you light the stove. If you smoke, always pack out your matches and cigarette butts. Never toss them on the ground.

Forest fires can be ferocious, traveling quickly and indiscriminately. If you are camping and you suspect that a forest fire has ignited, take the following action.

- If a fire is in the vicinity, immediately evacuate the area.
- If you are on a forested mountain, head downhill. Fires travel several times faster when ascending a slope. In addition, moving to lower ground usually puts you in an area with more moisture.
- Avoid steep slopes, chutes, and narrow valleys. These areas often act as chimneys for fire and smoke.
- Stick to clearings, if at all possible. If you are **canoeing** or kayaking, paddle to open water.
- If a wall of fire separates you from safety, you can attempt to run through it. However, this is risky and could result in serious injury or death. If you decide to make a run for it, cover your body with dry **cotton** or **wool** clothing and secure your hair under a nonsynthetic hat.
- If you become trapped, move to the most open area you can find. Clear the ground around you of anything flammable. Remove all synthetic clothing, including your backpack and any jewelry. Synthetic clothing can easily melt onto your body and cause serious burns. If you have dry cotton or wool clothing, put it on. Avoid putting on wet clothing, because the moisture will turn to steam and scald you.
- Lie down with your face against the ground. Place a dry **bandanna** over your mouth to filter out the smoke. Wait for the fire to pass.

Avoid forest fires by becoming fire smart. Check with local officials to gauge the threat of fire, and keep tabs on the **weather**. If it has been hot and dry for days, the threat of a fire increases. Know your route, and identify potential escape routes. File a **trip plan** with a local official. If a fire breaks out in your vicinity, the officials will know where to look for you. Finally, review what to do in the event of a fire, so all members of your group know how to act accordingly.

FORESTS

A forest is a place of wonder and beauty, a magnificent example of life at its most complex and interdependent. Forests are found all over the world outside of polar and **desert** regions. They are an essential part of the **wilderness,** although in many areas they have been reduced dramatically in size.

There are two basic types of forest: coniferous and broad-leaved. (Broad-leaved forests are sometimes called *deciduous*, as if all broad-leaved trees lose their leaves in the fall; however, this isn't accurate, because some conifers, such as larches, are deciduous, while broad-leaved trees in the tropics retain their leaves year-round.) A great sweep of conifers, the taiga or boreal forest, encircles the world in the subpolar regions. This northern forest is found in much of Canada and the northern United States. As you travel south, broad-leaved trees become dominant, at least at low elevations.

Elevation makes a difference in the type of trees found because of the way climate changes with altitude. A rise in elevation is equivalent to

Coniferous old-growth forest in the North Cascades in Washington State.

a change in latitude. For example, conifers that grow at sea level in Canada can be found at 11,000 feet in Arizona. Similarly, timberline can be just a few thousand feet in the far north but 12,000 feet in the southern United States.

To add a further complication, the direction that a site faces also influences the type of trees. Cool, shaded, north-facing valleys may contain trees that only grow much higher up on south- and west-facing slopes.

Hike regularly in forests, and you can quickly learn about the various vegetation zones and see which trees occur in which places and at what heights. Note which plants and animals live there. At first glance, a forest can seem simply a block of dark trees that cut out the view and the sunlight. Look closely and you will discover an intricate world of light and shade, color and texture, life and death. Every kind of tree is different, and each has its own characteristics—from soaring, massive conifers to delicate rowans and birches.

Some forests can be almost impossible to get through without a **trail** because of their tangle of fallen trees and clinging bushes. Fighting through a rain forest in the **Cascades** of the western United States or a black spruce forest in northern Alaska or Canada can reduce your progress to almost literally a crawl. By following natural breaks in the trees, you can often find a roundabout way that will eventually lead you where you want to go. It may triple or quadruple your intended distance, but that's better than fighting the forest. Look for creeks and meadows, because staying out of the trees can make hiking much easier.

In most areas, following trails is the best way to travel in forests. The United States and Canada have thousands of miles of forest trails. The **Appalachian Trail**, in the eastern United States, is in forest for much of its 2,100 miles, with forests reaching up to many of the summits. In most other areas, only the lower flanks of mountains are forested, with the summits rising far above the trees. In hot, dry areas, such as the North American Southwest, trees are found on summits and in sheltered canyons, washes, and arroyos, but not on the lower flanks of the mountains. Here you climb from open **desert** through increasingly taller trees to the full subalpine forest of the summits.

Any forest can feel mysterious, secretive, and even threatening. What lies behind that tree? What's that rustling in the bushes? It isn't surprising that forests play a large part in myth and folklore. At the same time, a forest can feel protective, welcoming, sheltering. Run down from a high mountain pass with thunder and **lightning** at your heels, and the dark enveloping cover of the trees will bring relief and security. A forest can be a shady retreat from the hard sunshine or cold **wind** of the open desert or bare mountain. Forests are often a soothing mix of leaves, branches, and bark, with shafts of sunlight slipping through the dark foliage to brighten a patch of flowers. Walking in a forest can be easy after the rigors of rocks and **snow** and **ice**.

FOREST SERVICE

For **wilderness** lovers, the USDA (U.S. Department of Agriculture) Forest Service is a significant organization because it manages 191 million acres of land. In total, this is an area the size of Texas. Established in 1905, the Forest Service has to balance many conflicting activities under the doctrine of multiple use. While it was originally established to provide water and timber rather than to preserve lands, the movement to protect areas and keep them roadless began early.

A key figure in this movement was Aldo Leopold, author of the seminal environmental book *A Sand County Almanac*. Leopold, who worked for the Forest Service in New Mexico at the time, campaigned for wilderness preservation in the late 1910s and 1920s. In 1924, 574,000 acres of the Gila National Forest came under protection in the Gila Primitive Area. Leopold's work was taken up in the 1930s by Robert Marshall, a prodigious hiker and principal founder of the Wilderness Society, who also worked for the Forest Service and for whom the Bob Marshall

Wilderness in the **Rocky Mountains** in Montana is named.

The number of conserved areas in national forest grew slowly after Marshall's death in 1939, at the early age of 38, until the passing of the **Wilderness Act** in 1964. This far-sighted act has led to the creation of many designated wilderness areas, many of them on Forest Service land and including the entire forest wilderness preserved up to that time. There are many de facto wilderness areas in national forests as well as designated ones. These are prime areas for backcountry activities.

The Forest Service oversees 155 national forests and over 600 ranger districts. The district ranger's office is the place to contact to find out information about **trails**, campgrounds, and wilderness areas. The Forest Service produces **maps** of all national forests as well as special maps of wilderness areas.

FRACTURES

When traveling in the backcountry, accidents can, and do, happen. Fractures, or broken bones, result from excessive force being applied to a bone. This can happen when you trip on your bootlaces, swim through rapids, or fall on blunt objects, such as rocks or tree stumps. Fractures

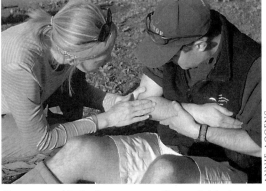

Fractures in the backcountry usually aren't life threatening, but they can be difficult to diagnose. Check for immediate swelling, deformity, or loss of circulation. If you're not certain as to the extent of the injury, treat it as a fracture by immobilizing the area with a splint.

generally fall into two categories: open (or *compound*) and closed (or *simple*).

Open fractures penetrate the skin. Because there will probably be an open wound or a portion of bone protruding from the injury, you will most likely be able to tell that a fracture has occurred. Closed fractures occur beneath the skin. If there is no deformity, it may be difficult to diagnose the injury as a fracture as opposed to a sprain or a strain (see **sprains and strains**). Without an X-ray, you'll have to rely on your own detective skills in determining if a fracture exists. Asking these questions can help.

- Did the injury start swelling immediately after the accident?
- Is the person unable to use the injured body part? (Can he stand? Can he move his wrist?)
- How did the accident happen? Was there a significant cause for the injury?
- Is there an obvious deformity?
- Is there a grinding sound coming from the injured bone when it's moved?
- Did the injured person hear a cracking sound during the accident?
- Is there a loss of circulation to the extremity?

If the answer is yes to any or all of these questions, or if you are in doubt, you need to treat the injury as a fracture.

With any fracture, immediate treatment is necessary. Start by attending to any life-threatening emergencies, such as **bleeding** or **hypothermia**. Don't get so absorbed by a gory fracture that you forget to cover the more important ABCs of basic **first aid**. Many fractures can be splinted in the position in which they are discovered. Bones will sometimes slide back into their normal position after a traumatic fracture. For bones that remain deformed, evaluate your options. If the deformed bone is preventing blood circulation to an extremity, it may be necessary provide some traction so that circulation can resume. A good wilderness first-aid course can teach you this skill. If the bone is not restricting circulation, and if it

does not hamper further treatment (such as an **evacuation**), it is best to bandage and splint the fracture as is (see **splints**).

Splinting the fracture provides stability and prevents further damage. When splinting, use any material that is appropriate. Now is a good time to be a creative thinker. Sticks, paddles, skis, and frame **packs** are just a few options for providing structure. **Sleeping bags**, **PFDs**, spare clothing, and Ensolite **sleeping pads** can create padding. The golden rule for splinting a broken bone is to also splint the joint above and below the bone (see **splints**). Don't splint the injury too tightly! You want to ensure blood circulates to the extremity. A number of different pain medications, ranging from prescription drugs to over-the-counter relievers, can be given. Be sure to ask about any **allergic reactions** before providing medication.

> "Once, while leading a trip in the Canadian Rockies, one of the participants on my trip fell and broke her arm just as we were crossing a peak. A storm was rapidly approaching. Amid the flurry of treating her swelling arm and descending to avoid lightning, I was thankful that I knew how to treat fractures."—AA

Of all the medical emergencies that can occur in the backcountry, fractures usually are not life threatening (although accompanying injuries may be). Therefore, take the time to assess the situation as best you can and come up with the best solution. Always have a good **first-aid kit** and medical training before you head into the **wilderness**, so that you know what to do in the event of an emergency.

FREE CLIMBING

The term *free climbing* refers to the style in which a route has been climbed. The word *free* in *free climbing* simply means that the climber had no assistance when ascending a route (i.e., no mechanical ascending devices, etc.). A free climber relies on his own strength, endurance, and agility to make it to the top. This is not to be confused with soloing or free soloing (see **solo climbing**) in which the climber uses no protection and no rope. Free climbers use a rope and will often place **artificial protection** along their route to guard against a fall. They do not, however, step on the artificial pros to gain good footing. Rather, the climber uses only natural **footholds**, and **hand-holds**, balance, and other skills that promote fluid **rock climbing**. You might use the term in a sentence as follows: "That route was first climbed by a well-known **aid climber**, but some of today's climbers are so good they climb it free."

FREE HEELERS

"Free heelers," "pinheads," or "trad daddys" are skiers who use **telemark skiing** or backcountry skiing bindings on their skis. Because these bindings allow you to lift your heel (as you do when you walk or **cross-country ski**), they are the obvious choice for backcountry skiers who will be traveling long distances over mixed terrain. People who telemark ski tend to be strong advocates of the sport. It isn't uncommon to hear a telemark enthusiast attempt to convert other skiers with the old adage "Free your heels, free your mind!"

FREESTYLE CANOEING

Freestyle canoeing is the art of making your canoe gracefully play on the water using a combination of fine-tuned strokes. While freestyle canoeing is not a **wilderness** sport per se, many freestyle paddlers transfer their skills to other **canoeing** disciplines. Likewise, many solo paddlers and whitewater canoeists borrow techniques that have been developed and refined by the freestyle crowd.

While most freestylers paddle solo canoes, many others practice tandem freestyle. This provides the additional challenges and rewards that come from having to communicate with a partner as well as anticipate, and complement, her paddle stroke with yours.

You may see a freestyle canoeist out for an evening paddle on a calm lake or perhaps on a tiny river making even the sharpest bend look like a piece of cake. Because freestyle paddlers are able to maneuver their canoes with such precision and tranquility, they are often rewarded with first-class observations of wildlife and countless other unique interactions with their natural surroundings.

FROSTBITE

Frostbite is a painful condition that can be very serious. It occurs when parts of the body are so cold that the skin and flesh start to freeze. Extremities are the most at risk, particularly exposed ones (such as the nose and ears) but also the fingers and the toes. Inadequate **insulation** is the cause. Toes are especially vulnerable when **mountaineering** or **ski touring** because you can easily not realize that frostbite is setting in. The first signs of frostbite are a colorless, dull, waxy appearance to the skin and, perhaps, a painful tingling sensation.

> "I was leading a party along a mountain ridge in zero-degree weather when I noticed that one of the group had a large, pale patch on her nose. She admitted she couldn't feel it at all and donned a thick balaclava that could be pulled up over her nose. Half an hour later, the color had returned and she was fine."—CT

Superficial frostbite, known as *frostnip*, can be dealt with by warming the affected area. Deep frostbite, however, requires medical attention, and the sufferer will have to be evacuated or, if there is no other choice, will have to walk or ski out (see **evacuation**). Thawing out rapidly in a warm bath with a carefully regulated temperature is the recommended treatment, but obviously the victim has to get to the bath first.

With care and the correct equipment, frostbite shouldn't be a problem. On below-freezing

The extremities (nose, ears, cheeks, fingers, toes) and exposed skin are the most likely places to suffer frostbite.

days, especially when it's windy, watch one another's faces for signs of frostbite. The dull, white appearance is quite distinctive, and you may spot it before the sufferer realizes it's happening. If frostnip occurs, warm the affected area immediately. Usually, this just means covering it up and protecting it from the wind.

What you shouldn't do is follow any of the old remedies that still appear occasionally, such as rubbing the frozen area or, even worse, applying snow to it. These are likely to cause damage.

If any part of your body starts to feel cold, do something about it at once. Don't wait. If the area goes numb, don't think that means that's OK. It's more likely to mean you have frostbite. One way to return warm blood and heat to an area is to move it rapidly. If your hands are cold, windmill your arms until you feel the warmth returning. Stamp and shake cold feet, and wiggle your toes. The returning blood may give you the "hot aches," but it's better to put up with the pain than risk frostbite. Put on extra **clothing**, making sure it doesn't constrict

any cold areas. An extra pair of **socks** crammed into your **boots** won't help. Putting on warm layers on the body may help, however, because if your torso is warm, the blood supply to the extremities is more likely to be maintained. If your socks or gloves are damp, replace them with dry ones. Dry clothing is always warmer. **Food** and drink, especially if hot, will help too. Just holding a hot mug can warm cold fingers.

If you can't keep moving to stay warm or if you're already in camp, you can warm cold extremities on one another's bodies. Feet and hands can be placed on a warm stomach or under armpits. Breath is warm and can be blown onto cold areas, especially the face.

Once frostbite has set in, the area should be warmed only if the sufferer can be kept warm. Otherwise, it is better to leave the frostbite alone until you are out of the **wilderness**. In particular, if someone's feet are frozen, do not rewarm them before the person walks out, because damage is likely if the feet freeze again. It is better to walk out on frozen feet.

See also **cold-weather injuries** and **hypothermia**.

FUEL

Food is fuel for humans and wood is fuel for fires, but here let's consider fuel for camping **stoves**. The choices are solid fuel, alcohol, white gas/automotive fuel, kerosene, and butane/propane. Each has advantages and disadvantages.

Solid Fuel

Solid-fuel tablets are made from compressed inflammable chemicals. Common names are hexamine and trioxane. They are lightweight, compact, easy to carry because they're solid instead of liquid, and simple to use. However, you can't control the flame, and heat output is low compared with pressurized fuels. If all you want to do is heat water, solid fuel is fine. For real cooking, however, other fuels are better. Because of its low weight, solid fuel is popular with ultralight backpackers and long-distance hikers.

Alcohol

Alcohol suitable for stoves is found under the names denatured alcohol, rubbing alcohol, methanol, ethanol, and others. Unlike petroleum fuels, it doesn't need pressurizing and is burned as a liquid. It isn't a hot fuel, although it will burn more strongly in a draft—some alcohol stoves have holes in the windscreen that can be turned into the wind for a hotter flame. Alcohol is a fairly safe fuel because it doesn't flare and it can't explode, making it a good choice for cooking in tent vestibules. The flame is invisible in sunlight though, so it can be hard to tell if the fuel is still lit. Alcohol is clean and will evaporate quickly if spilled.

Alcohol is popular with ultralight backpackers and long-distance hikers because it's easily obtained and the stoves are very lightweight.

White Gas

White gas is like automotive gas without the additives. It burns hot and is very efficient. However, it is highly volatile, and great care is needed in its use. It has to be pressurized before use, either by heating or pumping or both, so that it burns as a gas rather than a liquid. When being lit, it can flare up.

White gas designed for stoves, such as that from Coleman and MSR, is clean and doesn't block fuel lines. Automotive gas can be used, but it's much dirtier, blocking fuel lines and emitting fumes you don't want to breathe.

White gas is a good fuel for melting **snow**, because of the heat output, and for long trips away from civilization, because you need to carry less of it than other fuels (except kerosene).

Kerosene

Kerosene is harder to light than white gas, which makes it somewhat safer, but it burns just as hot when lit. Like white gas, it needs to be pressurized so it will burn as a gas, not a liquid. Some form of wick is needed to light raw paraffin, or solid fuel or alcohol can be used to preheat it. If spilled, kerosene leaves a dirty, greasy stain.

Kerosene is a good fuel for melting snow and for **expeditions**, especially overseas ones, because it's easy to find in many countries. Jet fuel is a form of kerosene; it may be available at airports. A clean version of kerosene is sometimes sold as lamp oil.

Butane and Propane

Butane and propane are both types of liquefied petroleum gas that come in pressurized metal canisters. Butane is really only suitable for warm weather use because it doesn't vaporize properly in temperatures below 40°F and may not light at all below freezing. At high altitudes, this isn't such a problem, due to the lower air pressure. At elevations of 10,000 feet or more, butane is said to work down to 14°F.

Propane is a more volatile fuel and so requires thicker-walled, heavier canisters. This means it's not so good for wilderness travel. However, mix a small amount of propane with butane and you have a fuel that will work better at low temperatures and that can still be contained in lightweight canisters. Butane/propane in 80:20 and 70:30 mixes is now standard in camping stove canisters, although pure butane ones can still be found. A variant of butane called *isobutane* is sometimes used in the mix. This is said to increase cold-weather performance.

Although the mix works better in the cold, it's still not as good as other fuels. The more volatile propane tends to burn off first, so when a canister is more than two-thirds empty the heat output drops. Also, if you need to burn the fuel for a long time, such as when melting snow or **cooking** for a large group, the power falls away no matter how full the canister is, because the pressure drops. Butane/propane is best used for short periods.

Fuel Planning

The amount of fuel needed for a trip depends on the number of people, the type of cooking that will be done, and the temperatures expected. For basic cooking—hot drinks and perhaps hot cereal at breakfast and a quick-cook dried meal and hot drinks in the evening—a quart of white gas or kerosene can last one person up to 10 days.

"For winter trips with a group, I plan on a quarter pint (4 fl. oz.) per person per day. With alcohol, half as much again is needed. With canisters, a 9-fluid-ounce one lasts me four days."—CT

Carrying Fuel

Liquid fuels—white gas, kerosene, alcohol—need to be carried in a fuel bottle designed for the pur-pose with a lid that seals tight. You don't want the bottles to spill in your pack. For maximum safety, carry fuel bottles in an outside pocket. If carried inside the pack, keep them away from food.

Air Transportation

Do not fly with fuel, either in carry-on or checked luggage. It's illegal and dangerous. In-stead, buy fuel at your destination. Just the smell of fuel may result in the confiscation of fuel bot-tles and stoves, so air these thoroughly before traveling by air. Fuel bottles can be washed out with scented soap, if necessary. Some airlines won't allow you to carry liquid-fuel bottles even when empty. Check in advance to avoid disap-pointment.

G

GAITERS

Gaiters—coverings that fit around the lower leg and over the top of boots—are one of those love-hate items of gear. Some people dislike them so much they never use them, while others wear them year-round. The advantage of gaiters is that they keep **snow**, mud, grit, dust, twigs, and more out of your **boots**. The disadvantages are that they can be awkward to put on and take off, are prone to breaking, and can be hot to wear.

Gaiters vary from short anklets that just cover the top of the boots to knee-high super gaiters, which cover the whole upper boot and much of the sole. Most are knee high but cover only the top of the boot, being held in place by a front hook that clips onto the laces and an underfoot strap or cord. Simple tube gaiters have to be slid on over your foot before you put your boots on. They have no zippers to jam or break, but you can't easily ventilate them, and taking them off means removing your boots too. Most gaiters have zippers or Velcro flaps (or both) at the rear, side, or front. The easiest to use are at the front. With these, you can also adjust your bootlaces without having to take the gaiters off. Side fastenings are OK, but rear ones are awkward to use. Zippers are prone to jamming with mud or ice and can break. Velcro flaps are easier to use and more durable but can still fail to work if they ice up.

Super gaiters have tough stretch rubber at the base that fits around the edge of the boots and under the instep. This provides an excellent seal, but the instep rubber can tear if the gaiters are used on rocks and stones. It is replaceable, but that's not much use in the middle of a trip. Super gaiters are great for wearing on snow, making them excellent for **ski touring** and **mountaineering**. Standard gaiters have cords or straps underfoot. Again, these can break or tear, but they are easy to replace with any handy bit of cord or webbing.

Gaiters can be made out of waterproof fabric, waterproof-breathable fabric, or breathable non-waterproof fabric (see **breathability**). The last kind works well for anklets whose sole purpose is to keep dirt out of your shoes. Waterproof-breathable gaiters are best for all-around use because they'll keep your socks and lower pant legs dry. Some **condensation** may occur when you're working hard, but undoing the zips can help reduce this. Nonbreathable gaiters result in copious condensation. Their only advantage is their low cost. Some gaiters are insulated with closed-cell foam or fills, such as Polarguard and Primaloft. These are very warm and designed for subzero weather. They might be great on Denali or ski trips to the North Pole, but they're too hot for most uses.

Gaiters are virtually essential in deep snow, unless you like wet socks and boots and cold feet.

GIARDIA

A microscopic, single-celled creature, *Giardia lamblia* can cause the unpleasant intestinal disorder called *giardiasis* if ingested. Sufferers feel unwell and have diarrhea, bloated stomachs, and foul-smelling feces. The ailment should clear up in 7 to 10 days if you're healthy but also can be treated with certain antibiotics, particularly metronidazole (sold under the trade name Flagyl). For many people, *Giardia* doesn't cause any symptoms. Also, once you do catch giardiasis, you'll probably become immune to future exposures.

Giardia has become a bogey word for **wilderness** travelers, and there's a tendency to assume that any stomach upset or bout of diarrhea is giardiasis, even though many other possible causes exist. There is also a fear of water in the wilderness, perhaps due to all the warnings about not drinking it without boiling, filtering, or chemically treating it. Although *Giardia* can get into water in the form of cysts excreted in the feces of animals and humans, it's probably not as common as you would think from all the warnings.

Giardiasis can also be caught from dirty hands, food, cutlery, and cooking utensils. Washing your hands thoroughly after going to the toilet and washing mugs and bowls regularly are important. Sharing unclean items or eating food that has been handled with unwashed hands can spread giardiasis (see also **sanitation**).

Giardia can be killed or removed from water by boiling, filtering, or treating with chemical purifiers. See **water** for more on treatment.

To find out if you have giardiasis, you need to visit a doctor and have a stool sample taken. If you have diarrhea, drink plenty of water whatever the cause, because diarrhea dehydrates you (see **dehydration**).

GILA MONSTER

Most lizards are interesting, entertaining, and harmless. The Gila monster is a different matter,

however; it's one of the only two venomous lizards in the world (the other is the closely related Mexican beaded lizard). The Gila monster is a big lizard, reaching 18 to 24 inches long and with a bulky body and a fat tail. The head is huge and has strong, wide jaws that grip firmly and are very hard to shake off. The legs are short, and the feet have curved claws. The skin is covered with small scales colored black and orange or pink, which give a mottled effect.

Gila monsters are found in the **deserts** of the North American Southwest. In the heat of the summer, they are nocturnal, and on the coldest days they are dormant. On warm winter days and in spring and autumn, they are out during the day.

Their bite is painful but not fatal unless other complicating factors arise. The victim may feel sick and faint and, in serious cases, suffer from fever and even paralysis. The wound bleeds, sometimes profusely. Because neurotoxin venom continues to enter the wound as long as the lizard goes on biting, the lizard needs to be pried off the victim as quickly as possible. Be sure to seek medical help.

Being bitten is very unlikely, however, as long as you leave Gila monsters alone and observe them only from a distance. Handling or trying to trap them is dangerous (and illegal!), and they can move surprisingly quickly for such a cumbersome-looking creature.

WWW.CLIPART.COM

The bite of the gila monster is painful but not life threatening. Gila monsters are harmless unless threatened.

GIRTH HITCH

Even if you don't think you know the girth hitch, there's a good chance that you have already used it at some point in your life. This simple hitch is commonly used to create **anchors** for **rock climbing**, **mountaineering**, or **caving**. Experiment with this hitch, and you will think of countless other uses for it. (See also **knots.**)

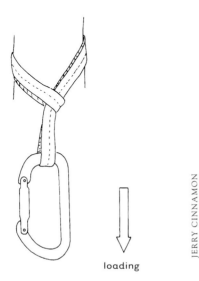

loading

The girth hitch can be created with any loop of rope or webbing. Simply wrap the two strands of the loop around an object, then pass one end of the loop through the other end.

GLACIERS

Glaciers are large rivers of solid **ice** that flow through mountainous regions. Their sheer weight and immense power slowly erode the sides of **mountains** and sculpt the landscape. Glaciers currently cover about 10 percent of the earth's land surface.

Glaciers are formed over many years when the accumulation of **snow** in a certain area is greater than the amount that melts off. As the area receives more and more snowfall, the lower, older portions of the snowfield are severely compressed. Eventually, most of the snow is compacted into ice. When the total depth of the ice reaches roughly 50 feet, the immense weight of the ice causes the mass to creep with gravity. This is when it technically becomes a glacier.

Glaciers continue to grow by accumulating more snow because the upper portion of the glacier usually is above the snowline (called the *accumulation zone*). The other end of the glacier, often called the *snout* or *terminus*, may be lower in elevation and will be exposed to melting and evaporation. This is called the *ablation zone*. If the accumulation zone is amassing more snow than is melting in the ablation zone, the glacier will appear to grow, or advance. If the glacier is melting faster than it accumulates snow, it will appear to shrink, or retreat. Usually, this process is extremely slow and most noticeable over long periods of time. However, there are exceptions to this rule. An example would be the Hubbard Glacier in Alaska, which, in 1986, advanced more than 15 feet per day!

At times it can be hard to tell whether a mass of white snow is a snowfield or a glacier. Most glaciers are marked on **maps** as such, but you can also look for such typical characteristics of glaciers as moraines and **crevasses**. Moraines are piles of rock and rubble that have been pushed together by the force of the glacier. They can be found at the sides of glaciers (lateral moraines), in the middle of glaciers (medial moraines), and at their snouts (terminal moraines). Crevasses are cracks that develop in the glacier as it moves. Some crevasses can be very deep, and falling into one can be a fatal accident. Therefore, mountaineers use great caution to identify crevasses that may be hidden beneath recent snowfall. If a climber falls into a crevasse, his partners must act fast and perform a **crevasse rescue** to get the climber out as soon as possible. A climber should never travel on a glacier alone.

Because of the risks associated with traveling on a glacier, many climbers prefer to travel in groups of at least three. In addition, climbers often connect themselves to the same **rope** while they travel, a system called *roping up* (see **glacier travel**).

JERRY CINNAMON

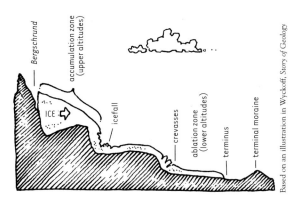

Based on an illustration in Wyckoff, Story of Geology

Glacier anatomy. Certain features make glacier travel difficult and dangerous: climbers will often negotiate their way around wide crevasses or up a steep icefall only to discover a deep gap between the head of the glacier and the mountain, called a Bergschrund.

GLACIER TRAVEL

Traveling on a glacier can be exciting and awe inspiring. While it may appear easy, the first time you try it you'll quickly realize that it's a demanding endeavor that requires distinct skill, preparation, and focus. In addition, before attempting glacier travel, you will need to acquaint yourself with an assortment of specialized equipment.

For a mountaineer traveling on a glacier, the **ice ax** is indispensable. It can be used for balance, as a probe to check for **crevasses**, and as a brake during a **self-arrest**. In addition, it can be used to belay your partner and build **snow anchors**. Another necessity is a pair of **crampons**, which attach to the soles of your boots, usually with straps made out of neoprene-coated nylon (which doesn't freeze as easily as regular nylon). Crampons made for glacier travel or **ice climbing** generally have 12 metal spikes that grip the ice, much like a football player's cleats grip artificial turf. Both crampons and ice axes become effective when they dig into the snow or ice. If the ice is extremely hard, however, it is possible that neither will perform well.

When climbers travel on a glacier, they "rope up" (see **roping up**). This simply means that they connect themselves to a common rope, generally in groups of three to four climbers per rope. The purpose of the rope is to prevent a climber from falling to his death if he should fall into a crevasse. The system only works if the other climbers are able to stop the fall with self-arrests. Therefore, as soon as someone falls into a crevasse, all the other team members immediately drop into self-arrest positions. To prevent everyone from falling into the same crevasse, climbers will spread themselves out single file, maintaining approximately 25 feet of rope between each person.

Traveling effectively as a rope team takes some getting used to. If the rope between climbers happens to be slack when a climber falls into a crevasse, there will be no resistance to the fall. Therefore, you want to keep the rope as spread out as possible, though not prohibitively taut. This requires the lead climber to set a steady, even pace that's neither too fast or too slow but just right for the whole team. It also demands that each climber keep track of his own pace to match the leader's pace. If you climb faster than the established pace, you will allow slack to develop in the line. If you travel slower than the established pace, the rope will begin to tug on the climber directly ahead of you.

Keeping the line extended is difficult when the lead climber is rounding the end of a crevasse or switching directions for some other reason. When this happens, you may need to alter your route just to keep the rope extended between you and the person in front of you. At water breaks, the urge to huddle together for conversation or warmth can be strong. Unless you are certain you're on stable ground, resist this temptation in favor of keeping the rope extended at all times. Imagine the horror if you gathered to share a snack and all fell through the same crevasse!

Because most climbers wear heavy backpacks, the likelihood that they will spin upside down if they fall into a crevasse is high. To guard against this, each climber should wear a body harness or a seat-chest harness combination. Under no circumstances should you ever tie the rope directly

ANNIE AGGENS

Glacier travel requires certain precautions, such as roping up. When taking breaks, stay spread out, as shown here, to reduce the possibility of the whole climbing party falling through a hidden crevasse.

around your waist; a fall in this position could easily cause serious injury or even suffocation. In addition to a harness, each climber should wear a helmet and carry a mechanical ascender or two prusik **slings** that are kept easily accessible. Prusik slings are simply 10- to 15-foot lengths of accessory cord with which you can tie a **prusik hitch** around the rope. If you fall through a crevasse, you can use the prusik hitches to ascend the rope and escape the crevasse.

If it seems to you that traveling on a glacier is one big exercise in avoiding crevasses, you're beginning to get the picture. Crevasses pose a major threat, and climbers are vigilant about evading them. If you can get a good look at the glacier from above, you might be able to see many of the

crevasses. If you don't have this opportunity, try to avoid areas where crevasses tend to form, such as on steep slopes and near outcroppings of rock. If you must cross a high-risk zone, keep the rope perpendicular to the likely path of the crevasse (crevasses tend to run at right angles to the fall line of the slope). At times the leader may need to travel parallel to a crevasse in order to get around it. In this case, the other climbers should alter their routes so that the rope remains both extended and perpendicular to the crevasse.

If you are new to glacier travel, find a competent **guide** or experienced friend who can help you learn the necessary skills. Reading a book about glaciers is not enough. As with most outdoor pursuits, you could spend years practicing your glacier travel techniques and still have more to learn. No two glaciers are alike, and no two days will present the same combinations of **weather**, energy, terrain, and group dynamics. Many **outdoor schools** offer courses in all aspects of **mountaineering**, including glacier travel. If you take the time to learn proper technique and exercise good **judgment**, you will be able to enjoy the majesty of glaciers for many years to come.

GLISSADING

Glissading is a technique used to descend the snowy slopes of a mountain rapidly. While sitting on your butt, crouching on your feet, or standing upright, glissading allows you to slide down the mountain using the spike of your **ice ax** as a brake and rudder. No special footwear is needed, although you should take **crampons** off if you're wearing them.

Glissading can be a lot of fun, but it has certain risks. As your momentum builds, it is easy to lose control. This is particularly dangerous if the slope is steep or has a poor run-out. (*Run-out* refers to the path of the slope in its transition to flat ground. Poor run-out would be a slope that ends in a boulder field or one that suddenly drops to a frigid lake.) Choose a route that has minimal rocks. Maintain control by shifting your weight, applying pressure to the edges and heels

ANNIE AGGENS

Glissading is a lot of fun but requires practice. Use an ice ax as a rudder to help guide your descent. Slide on your boots, applying pressure to their edges and heels as needed. A moderate slope, such as this one, is a great place to learn this skill.

of your boots, and digging the spike of your ice ax into the **snow**. Are conditions ripe for an **avalanche**? Be sure to evaluate the slope and snow conditions before you begin your descent. In addition, the first person down a route should stop frequently to scout for potential hazards.

Having a reliable **self-arrest** is a prerequisite to glissading. If you lose control, a good self-arrest can easily save your life. For this reason, you should hold your ice ax using the self-arrest grip and be prepared to self-arrest at any time. Before you rely on your glissading skills to make a rapid descent, spend time practicing the various techniques, including the transition to a self-arrest, on a moderate slope with a safe run-out.

GLOVES AND MITTS

Keeping your hands warm is important but not always easy. It can be particularly hard to warm hands up again once they're cold.

Thick, bulky mitts are the best way to keep hands warm in extreme cold. Unfortunately, it's hard to do anything with your hands while wearing these. A layer system is more versatile because you can wear just the thin inner layer when you need good dexterity and when it isn't too cold.

Inner or liner gloves may be synthetic or silk—both work. Liner gloves aren't very warm,

but they allow you to use your hands for such tasks as tying a bootlace or undoing a cordlock, tasks that are almost impossible with thicker gloves. They may be all you need when it's not too cold. These gloves aren't windproof, so for areas where winds are likely, such as above timberline, windproof **fleece** gloves are an alternative. These are slightly thicker and a little warmer than synthetic liner gloves but still allow reasonable dexterity. The best have protective reinforcements over the palms and fingers. Ones without these reinforcements don't last long. For wet areas, fully waterproof but still breathable liner gloves are available. Some people just wear thin rubber gloves.

If you're going to light campfires or handle hot **cooking** pots, avoid synthetic gloves because they can melt and leave nasty burns on your hands. Instead, use gloves of **cotton**, wool, or silk.

For cold conditions, wear thicker mitts or gloves over the liner gloves. These may be made from wool or fleece. Again, reinforcements on the fingers and palm will prolong their life.

The final layer is a windproof-waterproof-breathable shell for use in storms. This needs to be big enough to fit comfortably over the other two layers. In wet or windy weather that isn't too cold, you can, of course, wear the shells over just the liners.

Some gloves combine shells and insulation. These are less bulky than two layers, but you can't wear the two layers separately. Also, if they get wet, they take longer—sometimes much longer—to dry because you can't separate them.

Gloves always allow better dexterity than mitts but aren't as warm because the fingers aren't together. People who suffer from cold hands are better off with mitts for the middle and outer layers.

In addition to fitting well over each other, gloves and mitts need to form a good seal with your jacket cuffs. A gap here can allow **rain** or **snow** to trickle into your gloves. If you have elasticized jacket cuffs that are hard to get over gloves, then use gloves with wide wrists that can be pulled over the cuffs. Gauntlet-style gloves that cover the forearms are also good for climbing, skiing, and **hiking** with **trekking poles** because they prevent rain and snow from being blown into your jacket sleeves. Of course, when you're hiking without poles, rain could run down your sleeves into the gloves, so ones that fit inside your jacket cuffs are better in that situation.

Gloves and mitts can easily be lost, usually when they're whipped away by the wind after you've taken them off. Always carry a spare pair. It's also worth attaching loops to your gloves so you can dangle them from your jacket cuffs when you take them off rather than tucking them under your arm or putting them down. If you're going to leave them off for a while, put them inside your jacket: this keeps them not only safe but also warm, and it helps them dry out if they're damp.

If you lose your gloves or the weather turns colder than expected and your gloves aren't warm enough, **socks** can be used as emergency mitts. Also, plastic bags worn next to the skin or over liner gloves will act as **vapor barriers** and keep your hands warmer.

GOALS AND EXPECTATIONS

People head into the **wilderness** for a reason. Your last trip may have been about escaping the hectic demands of urban life and relaxing for a while, or maybe it was about bagging as many peaks as you could in a week. Both are valid reasons for hitting the trail, but the two trips would end up being dramatically different. Your personal goals should determine a great deal about the character of your trip. For instance, if you want to spend a lot of time fishing, or shooting photos, you're better off with a low-mileage route, or a route with several layover days. If you want to cover as many miles as possible, you might decide to go with people who like long days and have good physical stamina. There are many factors to consider, and your decisions will influence not only your route but also the make-up of your group, your menu, the length of your trip, and the equipment that you take.

Here's an example: A friend of yours just planned a whitewater kayaking trip. He wanted it to be an exciting trip with a few good thrills, but the main purpose was to relax. Basically, he wanted to be with old friends with whom he could reconnect. So he set off planning. A trip with a few good thrills meant he needed to invite only skilled paddlers who could handle the rigors of the river with ease. At the same time, he wanted to relax a lot, with relatively low daily mileage. This meant he had to find a river where the rapids weren't very far apart. He wanted first-class cuisine, including steaks, fresh vegetables, ice-cold beverages, and no lack of snacks. This meant that he needed a cooler, which meant he also needed a support raft. OK, so now he needed a friend who could paddle an oar rig! Not all trips need to be this complicated, but you can begin to see how your goals and expectations affect the entire planning process and all aspects of your trip.

"A friend recently got back from a fishing trip to the Boundary Waters Canoe Area in Minnesota. He and a buddy have an annual outing up there, but this year they invited a few friends from work. They had fun, but it was a much different trip. Some of his friends brought a boom box. They woke up every morning and turned on the news. At night they jammed to their favorite tunes. At times it was fun, but he would have preferred no music and a crowd that appreciated the silent quality of the wilderness. Next year he plans to communicate early on with the group about goals and expectations to make sure that everyone's on the same page."—AA

Discussing goals and expectations is a prerequisite for any trip. There are many ways to enjoy the wilderness, and you want to be with people who share your same values, particularly in regard to respecting one another and the environment.

A difference in traveling styles can lead to significant problems if it isn't resolved early.

See also **group travel** and **planning a trip**.

GORE-TEX

Gore-Tex hit the market in 1976. Until then, shell fabrics were either waterproof or moisture vapor permeable ("breathable") but not both. Wearing a rain jacket meant you would be soaked in **condensation** very quickly. Gore-Tex was the first waterproof fabric to allow significant vapor to escape, and it revolutionized outdoor clothing. Condensation still appears, of course, but while Gore-Tex may not be perfect it's far better than what went before.

Many people use the term Gore-Tex to refer to any waterproof-breathable fabric, but this is incorrect. It's the trademarked name of a specific fabric, although different versions of it now exist. Gore-Tex is actually a very thin membrane made from expanded polytetrafluoroethylene. This membrane is microporous, that is, full of microscopic holes. These holes are big enough to allow water vapor through but far too small for liquid water to penetrate; hence, the membrane is waterproof-breathable. On its own the membrane is fragile, so it has to be laminated to other fabrics before it can be used. The most durable method is to laminate the membrane between two layers of fabric. This is called a *three-layer laminate*, though the finished garment has only one layer. Confusingly, with two-layer laminates, the finished garment does have two layers, because the membrane is laminated to the outer layer and there is a separate, free-hanging lining.

The Gore-Tex membrane can be laminated to different weights of nylon and polyester. The heavier ones are more durable but make for heavier and bulkier garments.

Standard Gore-Tex has been joined by two variations, XCR (Extended Comfort Range) and Paclite. Gore-Tex XCR is said to be 25 percent more breathable than standard Gore-Tex, while Paclite is 15 percent lighter in weight.

Many alternatives to Gore-Tex now exist, some of which work very well.

GORP

Gorp, also known as *squirrel food*, *trail mix*, and *trail crumbs*, is said to stand for "good old raisins and peanuts," although some may describe it as "God-awful raisins and peanuts." It's been a staple snack food for hikers and mountaineers for many decades. You can make your own, adding nuts, seeds, dried fruit, candies, or anything else you fancy, or you can choose from a wide selection of prepackaged varieties. Whatever you call it, it's great trail food.

Gorp is now also the name of a website about the outdoors (see resources section).

GPS

GPS stands for global positioning system, a network of 24 satellites (with 4 more as backups) 12,000 miles up in space that each orbit the earth twice a day and send out continuous radio signals giving their position and the time. Lock into those signals with a GPS receiver, and you can pinpoint your position anywhere on earth.

How this works is complicated, to say the least, but here's a highly simplified description. First, to find your position accurately, you need to have contact with at least four satellites (called *3-D mode*). Your GPS receiver calculates your position by triangulation, using the distance between it and the satellites. If there is only a signal from one satellite, then you can be anywhere on the circumference of a circle centered on the satellite, a circle whose radius is the distance between the receiver and the satellite, which will be at least 12,000 miles. Add a signal from a second satellite, and you are at one of the two points where the two circles intersect. A third signal leaves only one place you can be—where the three circles intersect. And the fourth satellite? It's needed because your receiver's quartz clock is not as accurate as the atomic clocks of the satellites and the time between the two clocks has to be synchronized because the distance between them is measured by the time it takes for the signal to travel between them. Because the signal travels at the speed of light (186,000 miles per second), the time measured is only a tiny fraction of a second, so both clocks have to be very accurate. However, atomic clocks cost tens of thousands of dollars, so putting them in GPS receivers isn't feasible. Instead, the receiver uses a reading from a fourth satellite. If the clocks aren't synchronized, the fourth circle won't cross at the exact point where the other three circles cross. The GPS receiver recognizes this as an error and corrects its time so that the circles do cross at the same point. This, by the way, makes the clock in your GPS very accurate.

If a GPS can get only three signals (called *2-D mode*), it can still give a position by using elevation instead of the fourth satellite. This is only accurate enough at sea level, however, so 2-D mode shouldn't be used anywhere but on the ocean.

GPS receivers can be accurate to just a few feet in 3-D mode. They're certainly as accurate as you're likely to be with a **map** and **compass**, as long as they can acquire signals from at least four satellites. Most of the time this isn't a problem, but it can become one in dense **forests**, in narrow canyons, and below cliffs, because the signals can't travel through these barriers. If you can't get a signal, head for an open area with fewer obstructions and try again. It's also possible, especially in really remote areas, that there might not be enough satellites in direct line-of-sight to give an accurate position fix. Because of these potential problems, you should always use a GPS with a map and compass rather than rely on the GPS alone.

GPS receivers give positions in **latitude** and **longitude** or in Universal Transverse Mercator (**UTM**). Both are marked on the margins of U.S. Geological Survey maps, and grids can be drawn between the points to enable you to plot a precise position. To use the grid readings given by a GPS receiver, you need to be able to work out grid references accurately. Latitude and longitude and UTM are used the world over, so once you're

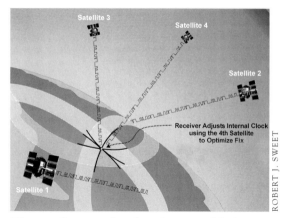

Three satellites provide a three-dimensional fix for GPS; the fourth satellite allows the GPS receiver to refine its clock for a more accurate position.

familiar with them you can use maps with them anywhere. With practice, you can enter into your GPS the grid references for places you want to go and then use the unit to guide you there. It won't matter how many changes of direction obstacles force you to take; each time you look at the GPS, it will point toward your objective.

GPS receivers also need to be set for the correct map datum (a fixed point around which a map is drawn). In the United States and Canada, this point is the North American Datum of 1927 (NAD 27), though this is due to be replaced by NAD 83, which is consistent with World Geodetic System 1984 (WGS 84)—the current world system. Your map should tell you which datum it uses. There are hundreds of map datums; if you travel abroad, you will need to change the datum for different countries. Plans are afoot to have just one datum for the whole world, because this will make electronic **navigation** much easier and less prone to error by using the wrong datum.

If you use a GPS independently of a map, datum and grids become irrelevant. You can take a position fix at the trailhead and other fixes at points on your journey where you change direction. These are called *waypoints*. This way you can use the GPS to retrace your route simply by going back to each waypoint in turn. You can also mark the positions of anywhere interesting

—a good fishing pool or a spectacular viewpoint—on the GPS so you can find them easily at a later date.

GPS receivers have many more functions than just giving your position and storing routes. A receiver can tell you how far it is to your destination, the speed at which you are traveling, the time it will take to get there, the estimated time of arrival, and the time the sun will rise and set. Many receivers also will record logs of your journey that you can download to a computer afterward. Receivers also give the altitude, though not with enough accuracy to be useful. Indeed, it could be dangerous to rely on the altitude reading of a GPS. Because of this, some come with electronic **altimeters** that don't rely on the GPS readings. Otherwise, it's best to ignore the GPS altitude and use a separate altimeter.

GPS receivers usually require two to six AA batteries. If you keep your receiver switched on all day, carry a few sets of spare batteries. In hot weather, batteries can last a long time, but in the cold, standard alkaline ones fade quickly. Lithium batteries are better. If you use the GPS only to get an occasional position fix, the batteries will last days or even weeks.

A GPS unit isn't a navigational requirement like a map and compass are, but it can make navigation much easier, particularly for cross-country travel in featureless areas, such as **deserts**, arctic **tundra**, and ice fields. One can also be useful when mist obscures landmarks or when darkness falls before you reach your destination.

GRAND CANYON

The Grand Canyon, located in the southwestern United States, is one of the most magnificent places on the planet, a stupendous example of the forces of nature. Edward Abbey called it "a national and international treasure" (see **Abbey, Edward**). Words cannot give an adequate impression of it. Even photographs cannot really show its scale, let alone its emotional impact. John Muir, a master of natural description, wrote that "it is impossible to conceive what the canyon is,

or what impression it makes, from descriptions or pictures, however good," although he made a good attempt (see **Muir, John**).

Statistics can't show how overwhelming, beautiful, or colorful the canyon is, but they can give some idea of the scale. Put simply, it's huge: roughly 280 miles long by 4 to 16 miles wide and 3,500 to 6,000 feet deep. Inside that massive slash in the earth's crust are 5,000-foot-high mountains that don't reach as high as the canyon's rims, which range from 6,000 to 7,500 feet in elevation on the South Rim and 7,500 to 8,500 feet on the North Rim. The rims are forested, but the bottom of the canyon is **desert**.

The magnificence of the canyon may seem obvious to us now, but it wasn't always so. "After entering it there is nothing to do but leave. Ours has been the first and will doubtless be the last party of whites to visit this profitless locality," wrote Lieutenant Joseph Ives in 1858.

Most people, however, are more likely to agree with Theodore Roosevelt, who in 1903 said, "Do nothing to mar its grandeur for the ages have been at work upon it and man cannot improve it." Five years later, he created Grand Canyon National Monument. It became a **national park** in 1919.

For **wilderness** lovers, the real canyon begins when you leave the few maintained **trails** and the developed rims and head into the wild country beyond. Hikers, rafters, and rock climbers all come to the canyon. Indeed, the numbers who wish to visit this "profitless locality" are such that **permits** are required for overnight stays, and it can take a very long time to secure a place on a raft trip.

The canyon is not a place for the inexperienced. The steep terrain, heat, and lack of water make it challenging and potentially dangerous. **Flash floods** have killed more than a few experienced hikers. Exploring away from the maintained, ranger-patrolled trails requires good route-finding skills, knowledge of where to find **water**, and a good head for heights. If you have these, the rewards are immeasurable, for this is a very special place.

Unsurprisingly, the canyon has inspired some great writing. Edward Abbey wrote about it often, in such essays as "Havasu" from *Desert Solitaire* and "In the Canyon" from *Down the River*. Colin Fletcher described the first end-to-end hike of the national park in *The Man Who Walked Through Time*, one of the best hiking stories ever. John Wesley Powell, who led the first boat trip through the "Great Unknown," as he called it, in 1869, wrote a gripping account of the trip in *The Exploration of the Colorado River and Its Canyons*, while a more modern though no less exciting account can be found in Colin Fletcher's *River: One Man's Journey Down the Colorado*.

GREAT LAKES

The Great Lakes, located along the U.S.–Canadian border, consist of Lake Superior, Lake Michigan, Lake Erie, Lake Huron, and Lake Ontario. Together these lakes contain 18 percent of the world's supply of freshwater. In fact, only within the polar icecaps is there more freshwater in one location.

The Great Lakes basin offers countless forests, trails, and waterways to tempt the outdoor enthusiast. Lake Superior, the largest and deepest of the Great Lakes, presents unbeatable **sea kayaking** opportunities in the Apostle Islands (Wisconsin) and at Pictured Rocks (Upper Michigan). Likewise, Lake Huron, and Georgian Bay in particular, is known for its paddling. Among the many hiking trails is the Superior Hiking Trail, which offers **backpacking** along the shore of Lake Superior for more than 200 miles. In other areas, you will find sand dunes, including the world's largest freshwater sand dunes on the shores of Lake Michigan. Isle Royale, the least-visited U.S. **national park,** lies in the heart of Lake Superior and is accessible only by ferry or floatplane. Most people take to the island's miles of hiking trails for a week or two of backpacking. Those who bring their canoes or kayaks are doubly rewarded with scenic paddling.

With four solid seasons, the Great Lakes region offers many wilderness adventures year-round. During the summer, **canoeing**, sea kayaking, and backpacking are the favorites. Come winter, **cross-country skiing**, **snowshoeing**, and **dogsledding** take over. With increased popularity has come the need for **permits** and reservations in many of the area's state and national parks. Plan in advance if you want to access the most popular destinations.

GROUNDCLOTH

A simple groundcloth can be a surprisingly useful **wilderness** tool. Used under a **tarp** or when sleeping under the stars, it keeps your **sleeping bag** and **sleeping pad** dry if the ground is damp. You can also place other items on it to keep them dry and clean as well as organized and in one spot. A groundcloth makes a waterproof seat at stops, either spread out so you can lie down or folded up to give a bit more padding.

A groundcloth can also be used as a windbreak or a sunshade at rest stops and in camp and even as a small tarp to keep off **rain**. The latter is useful in **bear** country because you can cook under it when it's raining rather than in or by your tent.

You can also line a leaking **pack** with a groundcloth to keep the contents dry or wrap **clothing** or a **sleeping bag** in it. In a pinch, one can even be wrapped around the body and head as a crude poncho.

Groundcloths come in a variety of sizes. It's easy to cut one down to size to save weight, perhaps tapering it toward one end. **Tent** makers also sell groundcloths, often called *footprints*, shaped to fit under their tents. With one of these, you can use just the fly and the groundcloth to save weight. Most groundcloths are nylon, but other options do exist. Some people make their own from Tyvek, a polyethylene wrapping material. Ones with a reflective silver coating on one side, usually sold as All Weather or Sportsman's Blankets, are particularly useful as sunshades. Plastic, such as Visqueen, is lightweight but tears more readily than other materials and, because it's cheap, is often regarded as disposable and likely to be left behind in the wilderness.

Modern tents have such good floors that separate groundcloths aren't needed. If you use a groundcloth under a tent, make sure it's folded under at the edges and tucked in so that rain can't run between it and the tent floor.

GROUP TRAVEL

Traveling in a group can be a lot of fun, and it adds an element of **safety** to a backcountry trip. In addition, having other people around to share an experience can make it more meaningful and memorable.

When organizing a trip, determine the size of your group early on. This will affect important logistics, such as **permits**, reservations, **transportation**, gear selection, and **food** supply. Many people agree that a minimum party size for **wilderness** travel should be four, a good number in the event of an injury or illness that requires sending a runner or two for help. As your group size diminishes, so too do many of your options in case of an emergency.

On the other hand, having a large group presents its own problems, including environmental and visual impacts. Despite their best intentions, large groups are often loud (see **noise**). Many wilderness areas limit the size of groups, so check with local officials before moving ahead with plans. If you decide to travel with a large group (eight or more people), consider traveling in two separate parties during the day to minimize impact on the land, especially if you are traveling off trail. (If you do break into smaller parties, see that each has its own **first-aid kit**, **repair kit**, trowel, and other important items.) Unless you'll be camping at a designated site, consider spreading yourselves out at night. This enhances the feeling of being in the wilderness and reduces the group's visual and environmental impact. You may find it quicker to break into **cooking** groups and cook several smaller meals instead of one big one. This also reduces the need for the entire group to arrive at a consensus on what to eat.

Choosing the right companions for your wilderness venture is one of the most important steps in **planning a trip**. Pick people you get along with, who have similar styles of traveling, and who possess an appropriate level of experience. There's nothing like discovering too late that you have a complainer in the group or someone who is always the expert. If you don't personally know someone who wishes to join you, get to know the person a little before extending an invitation.

"On a recent trip, I was in charge of organizing the transportation of the boats, finding a good grill, ordering the tarp, making the sprayskirts, and packing out the food. Other people were in charge of such items as compiling a first-aid kit, menu planning, securing a large enough roof rack, finding a satellite phone, and applying for the appropriate permits. In addition, we selected one person to be the official accountant of our trip. This person managed all the receipts and ensured that we all ended up pitching in the same amount of money."—AA

More trips have fallen apart because of lack of group cohesion than anything else, so invest time together to discuss **goals and expectations** as well as concerns. It is common for disagreements to arise within a group on such issues as route se-

Travel in small groups often fosters lifelong friendships.

lection and meal preparation. Discuss the best ways to communicate and to deal with disagreements. If no leader has been designated, consider appointing one. Choose a person who has good **judgment** and who can facilitate discussions and conflicts as well as emergencies. Once people have agreed to join, consider having them contribute a monetary deposit. This is more crucial on long trips and **expeditions**, where commitment is important. If the trip is anything more than a short getaway, consider splitting up tasks among the party members.

If you are thinking of joining an organized commercial tour, ask the company about the typical makeup of its groups. Are they mostly couples? Singles? Elderly people? Will there be children? What is the typical size? Knowing these answers will help you select a group experience that fits your personal goals and expectations.

GUIDES

Sometimes the best way to experience the backcountry is with a skilled and experienced guide, a person with technical expertise, an intimate knowledge of the area, and good **judgment**. It is a guide's job to be prepared for almost any eventuality, be it foul **weather**, injury, or broken gear. A guide can also provide instruction and help you develop your skills. If you want to head into the **wilderness** but don't feel as prepared as you should be, consider hiring a guide.

Just about every wilderness activity has its own community of guides and guiding services. A guide may be self-employed or may work for an outfitter, an adventure travel company, or an **outdoor school**. If you don't mind traveling with other people, you'll find that joining an organized group trip is often the most cost-effective option for securing the benefits of guide service. Organized trips range from luxury tours, where the guides do all the cooking and camp work, to more hands-on trips, which require you to participate in all aspects of the experience, pleasant or not. Before you sign up for an organized group trip,

carefully assess whether it's likely to meet your **goals and expectations**. If you are looking for a more personal experience, you can hire a guide to accompany your own party.

To find a guide or guided trips, you can contact a professional association specific to your outdoor activity. Many mountain guides are trained, certified, and registered with the American Mountain Guide Association (AMGA). Other such organizations include the American Canoe Association, the Professional Paddlesports Association, the British Canoe Union, the National Speleological Society, and the American Canyoneering Association (see resources section). Another option is to contact an outdoor shop near your destination and ask for recommendations. You can also search the Internet by destination and activity (for example, Boundary Waters canoeing). Outdoor magazines such as *Outside*, *Backpacker*, and *Rock and Ice* carry many ads at the back of the publication for guides, outfitters, and adventure travel.

In the United States, just about anyone can print up a business card and declare himself a guide. Attempts are being made to standardize the guiding industry, and a number of professional organizations have developed examinations to evaluate the skills and judgment of potential guides. Because this is a growing trend, and because not all outdoor activities have guide certification programs, you may well encounter a guide who is fully qualified but is not certified by a professional organization. Certified or not, you should interview any potential guide or guide service to evaluate the level of experience and professionalism. Consider asking the following questions, and don't be shy: reputable guides will be happy to tell about their qualifications.

- What are your credentials?
- Are you certified to guide? If so, by whom?
- How long have you been guiding?
- What is your safety record? Have you ever had any accidents?
- Are you insured?

- What is your medical training?
- What is your client-to-guide ratio?
- Do you have references I can contact?

Hiring a guide or joining a group trip offers a margin of safety over traveling alone. It does not, however, give you license to be irresponsible or unprepared. Many people look to guides as superhumans who are infallible. On the contrary, guides have limitations like everyone else. It is your responsibility to learn about risks of your activity and prepare accordingly.

GUNWALE GRABBER

When a canoe becomes unstable, whether from **wind**, **waves**, or a sudden shift of weight, your immediate response makes the difference between remaining upright and flipping over. A skilled paddler in this situation will quickly respond with a **brace** to prevent the canoe from capsizing. A less experienced paddler often panics and, thinking it will somehow rectify the predicament, drops his paddle and grabs the **gunwales**. This response is akin to jumping in the water, as it inevitably results in an upset. Experienced canoeists often refer to the people who make this blunder as gunwale grabbers. These people are infamous for pulling their trademark move at the worst possi-

RICK SWEITZER

A classic example of gunwale grabbing—the bow paddler, gripped with fear, has dropped his paddle and taken hold of the gunwales. Experienced paddlers respond with a brace or other maneuver to help steady the canoe.

ble moment, much to the shock and horror of their paddling partners. While gunwale grabbing can be expected from neophyte paddlers, observing a more experienced paddler grab the gunwales definitely warrants extensive harassment.

GUNWALES

Gunwales (pronounced *gunnels*) are the strips of wood, plastic, or aluminum that create a rim along the top of a canoe hull. They run from the bow of a canoe to the stern.

HANDHOLDS

The climbing term *handhold* refers to a feature on rock that a climber can use with her hand for balance or to aid in upward movement. Handholds come in an assortment of shapes and sizes. Sometimes the best way to grab a handhold isn't the first that comes to mind. When you discover a handhold, experiment to find the right type of grip. It may be that you have to grab the underside of it and pull up (an undercling), or you may be lucky and find a good knob that you can wrap your entire hand around (a jug). If you are climbing a crack, you'll probably want to use a hand jam. Depending on the crack, you'll be able to jam either a finger or two or maybe even your

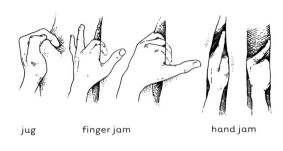

jug   finger jam   hand jam

Once you've found a handhold, experiment to find the strongest position. When climbing, you'll be lucky if you find a jug, also known as a "hallelujah!" hold. Other holds include the finger jam and hand jam.

whole hand into the crack. When you jam your hand in a crack, experiment with thumb-up versus thumb-down positions. Surprisingly, the position of your thumb makes a big difference in the way your hand fills a space.

HANG DOGGING

Hang dogging is a climbing term that refers to hanging on the rope, either while taking a break or while reviewing the route. It is often shortened to "dogging" to describe a person who climbs a certain sequence and then gets lowered so he can repeat the process and master the move. For example, a climber may "dog" the sequence of moves on a route several times before he climbs it clean.

HATS

Hats keep your head warm in the cold and cool in the sun and are a vital piece of equipment.

Hats for the Cold

A warm hat is crucial in cold weather. Just putting on a hat can make a huge difference in how warm you feel. This is because the blood supply to your brain has to be constant regardless of the temperature; unlike in the hands and feet, where the capillaries will shut down to save heat, a lot of heat is lost from an uncovered head.

What sort of hat should you wear? That's a personal choice, as long as the one you choose is warm enough. Hats come in all shapes and sizes and may be made from **fleece**, knitted acrylic or polyester, **wool**, silk, or a **wicking** base-layer material such as polypropylene. All of these will keep your head warm. Thicker ones are warmer than thin ones, and hats that can be pulled down over your ears work well in extreme cold.

In terms of design, simple watch or stocking caps are fine for most uses. Balaclavas that can be pulled down to cover the ears and neck are good in extreme conditions. Billed caps with ear flaps are nice too, especially in storms, when the bill protects the face. Neck gaiters can be worn with a billed cap to give the same protection as a balaclava but without the restricted feeling. A neck gaiter can also be rolled up and worn as a hat.

Most hats aren't windproof, which means you wear a hood over them in cold, strong winds. If you don't like wearing a hood, wear a windproof fleece hat or a hat with a waterproof-breathable shell (see **breathability**). These are great for winter wear but can be too warm at other times.

Hats for the Heat

A hat is also important for keeping the sun off, whether in the open **desert** or high on a **glacier**. Wearing a hat helps keep you cool and also prevents sunburn, especially if it shades the ears and neck as well as the face. There are two basic styles of sun hats: hats with wide brims and baseball-style caps with large bills. The latter may come with a neck flap, which is often detachable. If not, a **bandanna** makes a nice temporary neck flap.

Sun hats are an area of clothing where cotton **does** make sense. Soak a cotton hat in a creek or pool, and the slowly evaporating moisture will keep you cool for quite a while. In the heat, you don't want a hat that dries quickly.

See also **sun protection**.

HEADLAMPS

See **lighting**.

HEALTH

Staying healthy on a wilderness trip is important. First, you need to ensure you're healthy before setting out. If you have any doubts, check with a doctor. A minor problem at home could turn into a major emergency in the wilderness. If you have a long trip to a remote region planned, especially abroad, consider getting a full medical checkup.

If you have an ongoing condition that needs medication, be sure to take enough with you and keep it well protected against heat, cold, **rain**, dust, and jostling. Keep it easily accessible though, or you might forget to use it.

Health can be a big concern on ventures abroad. Many countries have health hazards not found in North America. Some trips require vaccinations, which may need to be done well in advance, so check on what you'll need at least six months before the trip. The Centers for Disease Control and Prevention (CDC) publishes an annual list of the vaccinations needed for every country as well as any other required or recommended precautions. Your local health department should have a copy, or you can contact the CDC directly (see resources section). Carry your vaccination records with you because you may have to show them on entry into some countries.

Also research the health hazards of any country and what medications, **first-aid** items, or other supplies you should carry. For example, in malaria-prone countries mosquito repellents and netting are essential. General items that are worth carrying are broad-range antibiotics, prescription painkillers, and disposable syringes. Keep prescription and over-the-counter medications in their original containers in case an official asks what they are.

HEAT REGULATION

When traveling in the backcountry, maintaining an appropriate body temperature is crucial. Most people are familiar with the threat of getting too cold, but in many areas the risks of getting too hot are of greater concern.

Your body can deal with a limited amount of heat on its own. But at some point you need to take deliberate action to help your body maintain a healthy temperature. Your normal body temperature probably hovers somewhere around 98.6°F. As your body heats up, your brain tells your blood vessels to dilate, allowing the blood to flow closer to the surface of your skin. This is why you often appear flushed after exercising. Having the blood flow close to the surface allows it to dispense much of the heat to the skin, where it is easily dispersed by the wind and surrounding air. Your brain also tells your heart to pump faster, allowing more blood to reach the surface. In addition, your body begins to sweat. The sweat by itself does not cool you, but evaporation of the sweat does. Each sweat droplet is filled with heat that the body is trying to expel. With evaporation, the heat is carried away and the body continues to cool down. If any part of this process can't take place, the body becomes unable to deal effectively with the heat.

Staying hydrated is absolutely critical to dealing with heat. This often means drinking a gallon of **water** a day. If your body has no water to create sweat, it cannot keep your core temperature from rising. Without water, things go downhill fast (see **dehydration**). By the time you are thirsty, you are already somewhat dehydrated, so don't wait to take a drink.

If you feel uncomfortably hot, stop your activity and rest in any available shade. At this point, your body is like a car overheating: you need to pull over, add water, and cool down. If there is no **wind**, fan yourself or have someone fan you. Place a wet **bandanna** around your neck, wrists, or groin to cool the area: these are the places where your blood flows closest to the skin and will offer the best results. You will probably be sweating, and your skin will be flushed—a sign that your body is experiencing heat exhaustion and is working hard to cool itself. If this is the case, don't overload your body with too many other tasks, such as trying to climb a mountain. Instead, relax, cool off, and enjoy the view. Recovery can take a full 12 hours.

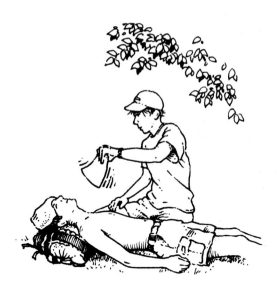

Fanning a person and allowing water to evaporate from the skin will help lower body temperature. Take advantage of any available shade.

If you notice that someone has stopped sweating or is pale, irrational in behavior, confused, or unresponsive, she could be in serious, life-threatening trouble. These signs suggest that the person's body has become overheated to the point of shutting down. She is experiencing heat stroke. She will not be able to think for herself, and she must be cooled off immediately. The best method is to sprinkle or swab her in cool water. If there is no water source around, use the water from your water bottles. Fan her like there's no tomorrow. Fanning will increase the rate of evaporation, promoting a reduction in body temperature. Heat stroke can come on quickly and can be fatal. If you are near help, send a runner, but don't let the knowledge that help may be on the way prevent you from taking immediate action to cool the person down.

Heat emergencies are largely preventable. Begin by researching the environment you will be traveling in. Is it very hot? Is it also humid? What are the average temperatures at the time you will be visiting? Is water readily accessible? Once you know what you're facing, you can plan to bring

clothing designed to keep you cool and protect you from the sun. You can also decide the best way to carry your water and how many containers to bring.

If the weather is extremely hot or humid (or both), plan most of your activities for morning or evening. Opt for a long lunch so you're not exerting yourself in the hottest hours of the day. Keep an eye on your own well-being and those of your companions. Heat injuries can occur almost anywhere, even on a paddling trip when the water is cool. By being aware of your temperature, drinking lots of water, and restricting activity to the coolest hours of the day, you should be able to enjoy yourself safely in the heat.

HIKING

Hiking is the simplest and most essential form of **wilderness** travel, one that requires in itself no equipment whatsoever. A hike can last a few hours, a few days, or a few months. All you need is a modicum of fitness, the ability to put one foot in front of the other, and the desire to explore the backcountry, following **trails** into the unknown.

Of course, once a hike extends beyond a short time in easy terrain in good weather, you will need some equipment for comfort and safety. Staying out overnight requires shelter, hiking for many days requires **food** supplies, and hiking in wet or cold weather requires adequate **clothing**. For hiking away from well-marked, signed trails, you'll also need **navigation** skills.

Hiking can be an end in itself. Most journeys into the wilderness are made on foot. Simply walking through the wild can be relaxing, refreshing, energizing, inspiring, and exciting—a way to renew oneself and shed the strains and stresses of urban life.

Hiking is essential to other outdoor activities too, even if it isn't the main aim. Mountaineers hike to the start of their ascents, and often large parts of the climb are no more than uphill hiking. Skiers may need to hike to the snow, and even through the snow if it's easier than skiing. Even canoeists may have to carry their boats to the water or portage them around rapids or waterfalls (see **portaging**). And those who want to watch birds or study flowers will also need to hike.

Hiking for long in the wilderness requires fitness. The ability to hike long **distances** over many days opens up the backcountry for you. As well as being enjoyable and invigorating, this ability can also be useful for safety because it means you can hike *out* of the wilderness, if necessary.

No equipment, however expensive, will improve your hiking. Only practice (by hiking) can do this. But every walk you take, however short, will help make those wilderness hikes a little bit easier.

HIP SNAP

Hip snap is a paddling term that refers to the ability to make a canoe or kayak snap from one edge, or **gunwale**, to the other using your hips, thighs, and knees. This is an important skill when you are performing **braces** or are **rolling a kayak**. Hula dancers would be naturals at hip snaps because they have the whole hip thing down to an art. It is the same motion (only with a little more punch) that can save you when your canoe or kayak is about to capsize (or, in the case of a kayak, already has).

Solid hip snaps come with practice. A great way to practice hip snaps is to lean your boat over to one side until you are about to tip over and then rescue yourself by quickly snapping your hips. Soon you'll discover that the hip snap can be improved by incorporating the power of your thighs and knees. Practicing hip snaps is a wet process. If you have a friend willing to help, you can use your friend's hands for stability as you lean the canoe or kayak onto its edge. When your ear is near the water, use your hips and knees to roll the boat back to its upright position. If you're alone, you can practice in very shallow water or along the side of a pool or dock. When you think you've got a good hip snap, take to the deeper water and test yourself. If you can develop a powerful hip snap, you are well on your way to performing reliable **braces** and rolls.

HOLES

Hole is a whitewater term that describes a potentially dangerous **moving-water hazard**. See also **hydraulics**.

HORSEPACKING

If you're looking for a new way to explore the **wilderness**, consider going by horseback. Horsepacking is a traditional mode of mountain travel and a great way for families and nonhikers to access the backcountry. Even hikers who traditionally view horsepacking as the "easy option" can appreciate its finer points (as long as they can get used to sore butts instead of sore hips).

In recent years, horsepackers have made great improvements in practicing **Leave No Trace** techniques to preserve the environment. For example, many horsepackers have adopted the lightweight practices of backpackers to minimize the number of horses needed to support a trip. Instead of huge canvas **tents**, they bring nylon versions at a fraction of the **weight**. Instead of big **cooking** stations, they travel with smaller pack **stoves**. Still, there is no doubt that horses have more environmental impact than humans do. To minimize their presence, horsepackers let their horses graze over a large area and limit the number of participants on each trip, thus requiring fewer horses.

If you like the sound of horsepacking but don't consider yourself an equestrian, fear not. Horse-packing isn't quite the same as riding wildly across the range. Chances are that you'll move along at a relaxed, steady pace that allows you to take pictures and soak up your surroundings. Even-tempered, sure-footed horses are the norm.

If you decide to travel by foot on your next wilderness trip, you may still want to consider setting up your resupply with a local horsepacker. Getting resupplied in the field, instead of hiking out, allows you to stay in a wilderness frame of mind and gives you more time to explore the backcountry (see **resupplying**).

Horsepacking is a great way for people of all abilities to experience the backcountry.

RICK SWEITZER

HYDRAULICS

Hydraulics (also called *holes* or *keepers*) are **moving-water hazards** formed when water rushes over a rock or ledge and into a riverbed that is flat or slightly depressed. Water pouring over a rock or ledge will hit the riverbed, rise to the surface, and flow back toward the rock or ledge. This creates a reverse current; the water actually flows upstream. Hydraulics can be dangerous because they can trap a paddler or swimmer in the upstream current. In addition, the recirculating water in a hydraulic is often extremely aerated, making it difficult for even buoyant objects to stay afloat.

water pouring over submerged rock

the edges of the hydraulic provide the best exit

recirculating aerated water

ANNIE AGGENS

Big hydraulics, such as this can be very dangerous. To escape a hydraulic, go to its edges and try to get flushed out.

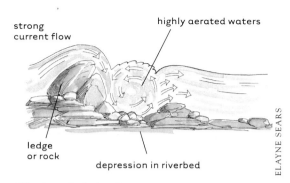

strong current flow

highly aerated waters

ledge or rock

depression in riverbed

ELAYNE SEARS

Side view of a hydraulic.

Some hydraulics are more dangerous than others. Hydraulics wider than 4 feet should be considered very hazardous and difficult to escape. Hydraulics that have a smooth, uniform backflow are the most dangerous, especially when they stretch across a river. Low-head dams are a good example of this type of deadly hydraulic. Natural ledges can also create uniform drops. Hydraulics that have breaks in the backflow, where water is able to escape downriver, are the least dangerous, although they may still be strong enough to trap a paddler or swimmer.

If you become trapped in a hydraulic, try to get to either of its edges, which provide the best escape route. If the hydraulic is wide, this may be difficult. In this scenario, try to find any break in the uniformity of the backflow where water is flowing downstream. Sometimes just changing your shape will be enough to get you flushed out (for example, curling into a ball or spreading out your arms). As a last-ditch effort, you can try to dive down to the bottom of the river, although this is difficult with a **PFD**. Sometimes a downriver current exists near the bottom of the river at the base of the hole. If you can't dive, repeat one of the above maneuvers. Whatever you do, *do not take off your PFD!* By the time you get flushed out of the hole, you will be exhausted and you'll need the PFD to stay afloat.

HYPERTHERMIA
See **heat regulation**.

HYPOTHERMIA
Hypothermia is a condition brought on by a dangerous drop in body temperature. Left untreated, it can lead to death. Hypothermia is caused when the body loses more heat than it generates. Surprisingly, hypothermia can occur in mild temperatures as well as in extreme cold. People can become hypothermic in temperatures as warm as 70°F if they can't generate their own heat. The body's normal temperature is a balmy 98.6°F. All it takes is a drop to 95°F for many people to show the first signs of hypothermia.

Hypothermia can be divided into two stages: mild and severe. Almost everyone has experienced the beginning stages of mild hypothermia: a feeling of being chilled, shivering, and numbness in the fingers and toes. Mild hypothermia, in its early stages, is easy to reverse. If the situation is not reversed, however, the person will begin to lose the ability to think or speak clearly and to perform common tasks. The body may begin to shiver violently as muscles involuntarily contract in an attempt to generate heat. This affliction is often called the "umbles" because the person begins to mumble, stumble, and fumble. At this stage, the hypothermia is becoming dangerous, and immediate action must be taken to increase the person's body temperature. If the person continues to lose heat, she will slide into severe hypothermia.

Severe hypothermia is usually marked by irrational behavior, such as taking off one's clothing or becoming combative. If the person can stand at all, she will most likely need assistance doing so. At this point, her body has ceased shivering, and she may be unresponsive or barely responsive. She may even appear dead.

A person with mild hypothermia will most likely have a temperature above 90°F. Once the person's temperature drops below 90°, she will show signs of severe hypothermia. Unfortunately, severe hypothermia is extremely difficult to treat in the field because it leaves the body in grave condition. Blood vessels don't behave normally, breathing is irregular, and the heart becomes extremely irritable—to the point where attempts at warming or even normal movement of the patient's body can cause the heart to stop beating normally (a state known as *ventricular fibrillation*).

A person with severe hypothermia needs to be evacuated immediately and with great care. Even the slightest jostling can cause the heart to fail. Prevent further temperature loss by insulating the person from the environment as best you can. Create a cocoon out of Ensolite pads and sleeping bags and tuck the person inside. A lot of heat can be lost into the ground, so be sure to insulate the patient from the ground as well as from the air. Place bottles of hot water (that have been wrapped in several socks) in the groin and under the arms of the patient. Monitor her closely and avoid moving her unnecessarily.

The best way to treat hypothermia is to prevent it. If you're prepared with adequate **clothing**, equipment, and **food**, you should have no problem avoiding this dangerous condition. However, should you discover a companion in mild hypothermia, take the following steps.

• Remove the person from the cold environment. This may mean pulling her out of the water or **wind**, removing wet clothing, and erecting a **tent** or **tarp** to protect her from the elements.
• Give the person extra layers to wear, but make sure that any wet clothing is removed first, especially if it is **cotton**. Top off the layers with a good wind shell to prevent too much heat from escaping from the body.
• Get her moving. Heat is generated when the muscles are put to work. This is especially true with the long muscles of the legs. It is not enough for the person to stand in place swinging her arms. She should be doing leg squats at the very least. A person who is in poor physical condition will have limitations. Have them engage in physical activity appropriate to their level of fitness.
• Give her food. Calories that burn quickly, such as candy bars, hot cocoa, or Jell-O, are much better than nuts or cheeses, which take hours to burn.
• Give her **water**. Water is the catalyst that makes it possible for the body to burn food.
• Keep her warm. The best warming comes from within the body. External sources of heat, such as hot water bottles or heat packets, help prevent further cooling, but they rarely generate the heat needed to rewarm the patient.

Heat is lost through radiation (heat rising off the body and clothes), evaporation of sweat, conduction (sitting or standing on a cold surface), convection (carried by the wind), and respiration (breathing). To keep warm, you must trap heat before it can escape. Wear a protective wind layer over your **insulation** to guard against convection and help minimize the heat lost to radiation. Insulate yourself from cold surfaces by sitting or sleeping on foam pads. Drink plenty of water and eat sufficient amounts of food. Remember, food is the fuel for your body's furnace. In extreme conditions, it is not uncommon to eat 5,000 calories of food every day! Above all else, monitor yourself and your friends for the first signs of hypothermia. Be proactive about staying well fed, hydrated, active, and warm.

ICE

Traveling over an ice-covered body of water can be a quick and easy way to cover miles, but there is always a degree of risk. There's no simple way to judge the strength of the ice and whether it will safely support your weight. The strength of the ice can vary from extremely solid to downright weak and deadly in a matter of a few yards. But thousands of outdoor enthusiasts venture onto frozen waterways every year without incident, and it's a liberating feeling to ski out of a forest and onto the open expanse of a frozen lake. If your wilderness travels lead you to a point where you have to decide between crossing ice or sticking to land, remember the following tips.

• Try to wait until the ice is at least 4 inches thick before you walk on it. This is a conservative thickness, and many people will venture out on 2 inches, but it's good to give yourself a margin of safety in the wilderness. With a dog team, look for a thickness of 6 to 8 inches.
• If you are with a group, spread yourselves out to disperse your weight.
• On lakes, shallow areas generally freeze first. If the lake is spring fed, it will take longer to freeze, and it will break up earlier. The area directly surrounding the spring may never freeze over completely.

• Like spring-fed lakes, chains of lakes (or flowages) are usually the last to freeze and the first to thaw. Portions of these lakes may never freeze.
• Rivers often remain open despite cold temperatures. Even if there is ice coverage, be extremely wary. Breaking through the ice on a river is more dangerous than on a lake because you may be swept away or pulled beneath the ice.
• Big lakes are easy to identify beneath snow and ice, but a heavy snowfall may disguise a smaller body of water. Use your **map** and keep an eye on your location. A wide clearing that cuts through a forest may look like a **trail**, but it might be a river that you should avoid. Also be suspicious of unusual depressions in the snow as well as sounds of rushing water.

If you must cross ice you consider marginal, disperse your weight as much as possible. If you have skis, wear them. Avoid using your poles, unless it is to test the ice ahead of you. Have an ice awl (or ideally, two awls), at the ready. You can buy small ice awls or make a pair from wooden-handled screwdrivers, which float. If you break through the ice, act quickly. Face the direction from which you came and try to kick your way onto the ice. If the ice breaks, be persistent and continue your efforts in the same direction. Use your ice awls to help you get a grip on the ice, al-

Never rush to assist someone who has fallen through ice. Instead, use an object (branch, ski, or pole) to reach to them, or throw them a rope.

lowing you to pull yourself out of the water. Once you get out, avoid the urge to stand up and run. Instead, roll your way to safety or slide across the ice on your belly, dispersing your weight as evenly as possible. If you are unable to get out of the water, use **cold-water survival** techniques to improve your chances.

If you're traveling with someone who falls through the ice, try to reach him by throwing a **rope** or extending an object (such as a ski, ski pole, or branch) to him. Whatever you do, don't run to where he fell in, or you'll be in twice the trouble!

A person who has been submerged in cold water needs immediate treatment. If he doesn't already have hypothermia, he is probably well on

his way. Care for him by removing all his wet clothes, cutting them off if necessary. Be gentle. A person who has been in cold water for a prolonged period may have a very fragile heart. Get him out of the cold as soon as possible and into a **tent** and **sleeping bag**. Warm the person carefully by placing heat packs or bottles of hot water under his arms and in his groin—but avoid burning him in the process. Warm his body core first, not his extremities. If he is alert, give him some food with fast-burning calories, such as a sugary drink mix. (For more details on treatment, see **hypothermia**.)

ICE AX

For **snow** and **ice** travel, an ice ax is essential. Ice axes began with the first recreational mountaineers in the Alps in the nineteenth century as long "alpenstocks." These heavy wooden implements are long gone, and there are now two basic types of ice ax: those designed for **ice climbing** and those designed for general **mountaineering**, including hiking above the snowline and **ski touring**. The first are specialist tools with reverse curved picks and twisted shafts to prevent your knuckles from hitting the ice. The latter are standard ice axes, with a straight shaft with a spike at one end and a pick and adze at the other. The more curved the pick, the more suitable the ax is for more difficult climbing.

Mountaineering axes range from ultralight ones designed for occasional use to ones suitable for easy snow and ice climbs. Which is best depends on your aims. If you'll only need an ax from time to time and basically hope it will spend most of its time on your **pack**, the lighter version is better. If you have ambitions to climb mountaineering routes, a more technical, heavier ax is called for.

Far more important than the model of ice ax you choose is knowing how to use it. If you've never used an ax before, the best way to learn is in an instructional course or from an experienced friend. Teaching yourself is difficult and can be dangerous. Once you do know how to use an ax

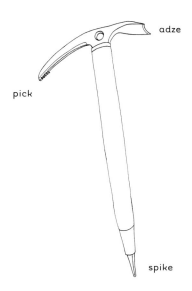

adze

pick

spike

MIKE WALSH

Always carry an ice ax and crampons if you're likely to encounter steep, snowy areas, or ice. Make sure you know how to use them properly, and practice safety techniques regularly. This ice ax is suitable for mountaineering and ski touring.

for **self-arrest**, an important safety function, practice regularly. If you slip, you'll need to be able to react automatically.

Designs and Materials

An ice ax should have a gently curved pick with a few teeth at the end for stopping falls on hard snow. Steeply curved picks are better for technical climbing but don't work very well for self-arrest. The adze is far less important and the design doesn't really matter, but do keep in mind that wide adzes are better for digging **snow shelters** if you don't have a **snow shovel**.

Steel is the standard material for ax heads because it's strong and easily sharpened. However, it's also quite heavy, so the lightest axes have alloy heads. These aren't as strong as steel, and they blunt much more easily. They're fine for hikers and skiers who have no climbing ambitions and who don't use an ax often, and they're especially useful for backpackers with heavy loads.

Shafts are usually made from aluminum alloy

because it's strong and light. However, it's also cold to hold and slippery when wet. A rubber handgrip or synthetic coating overcomes this.

Weight

There is no need for an ice ax to weigh more than 1.5 pounds; many weigh less. A heavy ax is more tiring to use and to carry on your pack. If **weight** is important, consider one of the ultralight axes, which weigh less than a pound.

Length

How long an ax should be is a matter of debate. Hikers often prefer longer axes than climbers do. Shorter axes are easier to use in ascending very steep slopes and on technical climbs. Very long axes can be unwieldy and hard to use in self-arrest if you start to slide down a snow slope. However, they are better for descending steep slopes because you can reach farther down the slope either to cut steps or to plunge the ax into the snow for security. Also, shorter axes can be awkward on moderate slopes because you may have to crouch to keep the ax in contact with the snow. Long axes are better for self-belays too, in which you shove the ax shaft into the snow to prevent a slip. This is perhaps the most important use of the ax in general mountaineering.

CHRIS TOWNSEND

Use an ice ax for support and self-belay when kicking steps up a snow slope. Note the use of the wrist loop. If the snow is firm, kick hard to make large, supportive steps, and take a step only after thrusting your ax handle into the snow so you can hang onto it if you slip.

CHRIS TOWNSEND

If you carry an ice ax on the back of your pack, make sure the ax doesn't endanger other people when you take off or put on your pack. If you're likely to need the ax, slide it between the pack and your shoulders, with the head resting on the top of a shoulder strap, so you can access it without removing the pack.

A good compromise is an ax that reaches to the ankle when held at the side, which means one in the 25- to 30-inch range for most people.

Wrist Loops (Wrist Leash)

Wrist loops are fitted to many axes. If one isn't provided, it's easy enough to thread a sling through the hole in the ax head. There are arguments for and against wrist loops. Using one means you're unlikely to lose the ax if you drop it. On short sections of rock scrambling, the ax can be dangled from your wrist. On the other hand, you have the danger of the ax injuring you if you drop it in a fall and it lashes about while

still attached to your wrist. Wrist loops are also awkward to switch from hand to hand when changing direction while zigzagging up a slope. While you're learning to use the ax, however, a wrist loop will probably be useful.

Carrying an Ice Ax

Packs usually have ice ax straps on the back. Using these is fine when the ax isn't likely to be needed. In between bouts of using the ax, however, it's better to slide it between your back and the pack so the ax head rests on the top of the shoulder straps. Then it is easily accessible without taking your pack off.

ICEBERGS

Icebergs are incredible formations of **ice** that have calved (broken) off a **glacier** and are floating in the sea. As amazing as icebergs look above water, their actual size is even more tremendous. It is estimated that only one-tenth of an iceberg is visible from above the waterline. Therefore, if an iceberg looks the size of a minivan, its actual size is probably more along the lines of a big house.

If you're paddling near one of these giants, use extreme caution. As icebergs melt and transform into new shapes, their center of gravity changes, causing them to roll. Even if you aren't actually hit by a rolling iceberg, you can easily be caught in the ensuing forceful wave and capsized.

To enjoy these beauties from a sea kayak, plan to keep a distance of at least 10 times the diameter of the viewable portion of the iceberg. Also beware that pieces of icebergs that have broken off (called *bergy-bits*) have the same tendency to roll over and should be considered suspect.

ICE CLIMBING

Ice climbing is not merely **rock climbing** on ice. There are similarities between the two disciplines, but there are significant differences in equipment, stability of the terrain, and techniques.

While the rock climber usually dons minimal clothing, the ice climber has to bundle up for frigid temperatures. In addition to **hats**, gloves, and layers of insulating **clothing**, ice climbers need stiff mountaineering **boots**, **crampons**, **ice axes**, and a full rack of assorted climbing gear.

> "A friend of mine once explained ice climbing to a nonclimber as the best way to get cold, tired, and wet. Indeed, I couldn't agree more."—AA

Unlike rock, the stability of **snow** and **ice** can change by the hour. What is as solid as concrete in the morning can morph under the afternoon sun into a wet, heavy mess. While subtle differences between types of ice go undetected by most people, the ice climber has specific names for each variation: Styrofoam, chandelier, cauliflower, plastic, verglas, and more. Each type of ice requires a slightly different technique. Take a good swing at plastic ice and your pick should slide right in, but do the same on verglas and it's likely to bounce out. Good ice climbers quickly determine the type of ice and adjust their technique to work with whatever they have encountered.

Ice climbing does share a few basic techniques with rock climbing. Two common rules are to keep your weight over your feet and to use your legs more than your arms. Ice climbing also involves mastering the art of efficiency so that you know exactly where to plant the ax in order to take advantage of the best ice. If your swing hits its target, you only have to swing once. Being efficient includes the ability to place ice protection (such as ice screws) with either hand. It also means being able to keep yourself warm during long belays and to stay focused on the task at hand even after a long day of climbing.

There's a saying in ice climbing that the best protection is to not fall in the first place. Ice climbing protection is notoriously dicey, and even a short fall can result in serious injury: crampons that snag on the ice can break your ankles, and as for ice axes, well—let your imagination run wild. If you aren't on vertical ice (a lot of ice

Based on an illustration in Raleigh, *Ice*

Ice climbing requires complete efficiency. Note the climber's feet: the left foot is "front pointing" (the front points of the crampons dig into the ice—commonly used on vertical ascents) and the right foot is "flat footing" (all crampon points dig into the ice—used on moderate slopes). A combination of the two techniques can be used on very steep slopes, as here.

climbing is on moderate or steep slopes), a fall still can have serious consequences, even if you have a well-practiced **self-arrest**.

The best way to learn ice climbing is with an experienced **guide** or friend or through an **outdoor school**. Courses in ice climbing offer invaluable practice in a supervised environment. A number of books provide details on the subject, including *Ice World: Techniques and Experiences of Modern Ice Climbing*, by Jeff Lowe; *Climbing on Ice*, by Yvonne Chouinard; *Mountaineering*, edited by Don Graydon and Kurt Hanson; *Ice: Tools and Technique*, by Duane Raleigh; *How to Ice Climb*, by Craig Lubben; *The Complete Climber's Handbook*, revised edition, by Jerry Cinnamon.

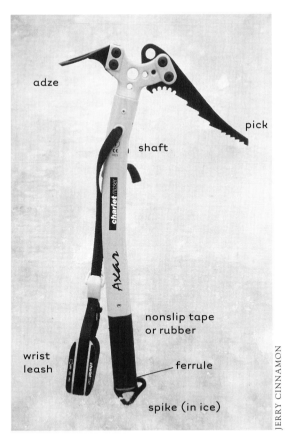

adze

pick

shaft

nonslip tape
or rubber

wrist
leash

ferrule

spike (in ice)

JERRY CINNAMON

Classic ice axes usually have a one-piece head (see ice ax), but technical ice axes, like the one shown here, are modular. This lets you switch picks to better accommodate changing ice conditions. You can also easily replace a pick or adze if it breaks on a swing.

INFECTIONS

Many backcountry injuries affect the skin and the soft tissues beneath. These injuries often are accompanied by a break in the skin, creating a wound. This may be from a cut, a scrape, or possibly a popped **blister**. Wounds act as open houses for infection. It's like saying to a crowd of bacteria, "Hey guys! Come check this place out! If you like it, make yourself at home." Infections can enter the bloodstream and affect your entire body. Whatever the cause of the wound, and no matter how small it is, you need to treat it as a possible site for infection.

To prevent the bacteria from thriving, elimi-

nate any environment that might foster bacterial growth so that your body can take over the natural healing process. Begin treating a wound as soon as you discover it. Once the **bleeding** has stopped, flush the wound with clean water. A good way to create water pressure is to squeeze water through a pencil-point-sized hole in a plastic bag. Flush the wound until you no longer see any dirt or other debris. This may take some time, but don't stop until you're convinced the wound is clean. You can also wash the area around the wound with soap and water or an antiseptic like a diluted iodine solution (such as Betadine).

Next, cover the wound with clean dressings. If possible, avoid closing wounds with sutures or butterfly bandages. Wounds that have been closed in the backcountry can develop serious infections. Instead, if the wound looks big enough for stitches, arrange an **evacuation** to get the person to a medical center.

Once the wound is cleansed and dressed, avoid overusing the affected area. This is no problem if you scraped your pinky finger while climbing, but it can become an issue if you have a big cut on the ball of your foot or another heavily used area. If the wound is big or in a difficult location, you may need to **splint** the area to allow healing to begin. Monitor the wound until it has healed completely. This will likely include removing the dressings and recleaning the area. Some redness and swelling is common with wounds, but if these symptoms persist for several days, or if they get worse, the wound is likely infected.

An infected wound means that bacteria have made their way past the body's natural defenses. The body will continue to fight, but if it is unable to stop the growth of the bacteria, the infection will become systemic, affecting the major systems of the body. The person will probably develop a fever and feel achy from swollen joints. As soon as you realize you have a wound that is not healing, begin plans to evacuate the person.

Flush wounds extensively to prevent infections. Cut a small hole in a plastic bag to create a strong stream of cleansing water.

Some wounds are more prone to infection than others. These include **puncture wounds** and complex injuries, such as broken bones (see **fractures**) or damaged joints. These wounds are particularly difficult to clean and should be considered high risk. Other factors that affect the healing process are moist and particularly dirty conditions. Keep wounds as dry and clean as possible. When it comes to infections, prevention is the best cure. In the backcountry, cuts, scrapes, and blisters aren't always avoidable, but with the proper care, infections usually are.

INSECTS

Insects are found just about everywhere. Over 800,000 species have been identified, and scientists estimate there could be as many as 10 million. Lucky for us, only a very small number of these are likely to have an adverse effect on **wilderness** travelers. Most are never seen or felt. Many—butterflies and dragonflies, for example —are interesting and attractive and add to the enjoyment of a wilderness trip. If you really don't like insects, though, stick to going out in **winter**.

The bugs that cause concern are those that bite and sting. The biters are various flies—mosquitoes, **blackflies**, no-see-ums (midges), horseflies, and deerflies—and some ants. The stingers are wasps (yellow jackets) and bees. (Note that

ticks, spiders, and scorpions aren't insects but arachnids.)

Bites

In North America, biting insects are irritating but generally don't pose a health threat, because they don't normally spread disease. The exceptions are mosquitoes that spread the West Nile virus, which is now found in much of the United States.

Bites can itch, but if you scratch them, they can turn into open sores. It's best to leave them alone, no matter how distressing they are. People's reactions to insect bites vary enormously. If you suffer badly, antihistamine lotions are available that can ease the itching and swelling.

Mosquitoes can be swatted fairly easily but often come in such numbers that you can't kill many of them. Walking is one way to escape them, as is heading for open, windy areas.

No-see-ums also come in swarms and are so small that they get into **clothing**, and even through it if it's open weave. Clouds of them buzzing around your head can be maddening. However, walking briskly will leave them behind. Also, no-see-ums don't appear in dry, sunny weather or in any wind above a very light breeze. They are worst in calm, humid **weather**.

Horseflies are large, cumbersome insects with a painful bite. They will follow you for miles, which can be very irritating. Swatting them is easy, but you have to hit them hard or they'll

quickly recover and come after you again. People who react badly to horsefly bites must be treated with an antihistamine.

Blackflies, found near water sources across North America, are the most insidious biting flies. They don't make any noise, and they like to bite around the hairline and behind the ears. Often, the first sign of a bite is a trickle of blood running down your neck.

Stings

Stings from bees (see **bee stings**), wasps, and fire ants are much more painful than bites but also far less common. They can be fatal, however, for the small number of people who have a severe **allergic reaction** to them. Anyone who has had a bad reaction to an insect sting should carry epinephrine (adrenaline) and, if stung, inject it as soon as any symptoms appear.

For most people, a sting will result in a sharp pain followed by swelling and reddening of the area. If the site swells severely, future stings could be worse, so be sure to carry epinephrine on future outings.

Venom extractors are available that can be used to extract poison from stings.

Repellents and Insecticides

Insect repellents will stop insects from biting you as long as they're applied properly and regularly. The standard is **DEET**, a chemical. For those who don't like applying chemicals to their skin, various natural repellents made from plant oils are available. Citronella is the best known of these. Others include eucalyptus, lemon leaves, peppermint, lavender, cedar oil, canola, rosemary, lemongrass, geranium, and pennyroyal. These repellents generally don't last as long as DEET, so they need to be applied more frequently.

Just because repellents are designated "natural" doesn't mean they're safe regardless of how you use them. It's still best to look for repellents approved by the U.S. Environmental Protection Agency and to follow the instructions. Do not put repellents on cuts and sores or get them in your eyes or mouth.

Repellents can be applied to clothing as well as skin, especially around cuffs and hems. Repellents on hats can help keep insects away from your face.

Repellents don't kill insects; they just stop them from biting by creating a vapor zone above the skin that confuses the insects so they can't find the food source that initially attracted them (you).

More effective than repellents on clothing is permethrin, a plant extract derived from chrysanthemums. This is an insecticide that kills insects that land on anything treated with it. It can be applied to **clothing**, netting, **tents**, and **sleeping bags** and will last for a couple of weeks or more depending on how much is put on. It's not worth putting permethrin on the skin, where it lasts only around 15 minutes.

In camp you can burn mosquito coils (usually a form of permethrin) or citronella-scented candles to keep insects away. When they're out, burn the coil in the tent porch or under a tarp to concentrate it.

Netting and Clothing

You can minimize the use of repellents with the right clothing and some insect netting. To stop insects from biting, clothing needs to be either quite thick or tightly woven. The latter is more practical in warm weather when insects are out. Mosquitoes can bite through base layers and thin **fleece** but not through pants and jackets made from synthetic windproof fabrics. Midges can't bite through any clothing, but they can easily creep in through the smallest gap. Mosquitoes will enter at the wrist and ankle cuffs and the neck, so clothing needs to fasten tightly at these points. A hood that can be tightened around the face helps keep them off your ears and neck.

The best clothing for keeping insects out, then, is lightweight windproof pants that can be closed at the ankles and a hooded jacket that can

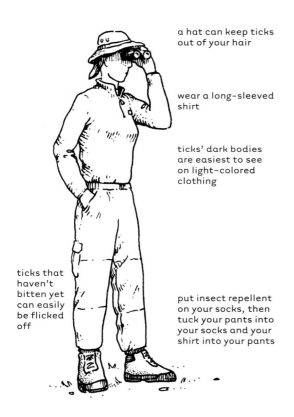

a hat can keep ticks out of your hair

wear a long-sleeved shirt

ticks' dark bodies are easiest to see on light-colored clothing

ticks that haven't bitten yet can easily be flicked off

put insect repellent on your socks, then tuck your pants into your socks and your shirt into your pants

Protect yourself from ticks and biting insects by dressing appropriately. Apply repellent to all bare skin.

be closed at the wrists. Such garments are breathable and cool enough to be worn in all but the hottest weather. Light colors are good too, not only because they are cooler but also because insects are apparently more attracted to dark ones.

To supplement the clothing and repellents when insects are really bad, head nets are a boon; these will keep the insects from buzzing close to your face. Head nets need to be draped over a broad-brimmed or billed hat so they hang away from your face. Some hats come with a roll-up head net built in. You can also get gloves made of netting, and even netting jackets, which are cooler than regular jackets but of no use for anything but fending off bugs. I've found netting to be the best protection against blackflies, since repellents need to be reapplied frequently.

Netting doors on tents are essential in warm weather if you don't want to get very hot and sticky inside (with netting, you just get slightly hot and sticky). You can also get netting canopies to hang inside tarps and **bivouac** bags with netting hoods. Any netting will be more effective if treated with permethrin. Note that if no-see-ums are the problem, the netting needs to have very small holes. No-see-ums can fly through some mosquito nets.

Avoidance

Whenever possible, avoid insect gathering places rather than use repellents. Insects like humid, still places, so heading uphill is always a good idea. A camp on a breezy knoll can be insect free, while one only a few hundred feet lower in the shelter of a thicket may be swarming with mosquitoes. Similarly, a hike along a windy ridge top may be quite pleasant, while the **trail** in the swampy valley below is thick with flies. If you are traveling through insect country, look for windy, dry spots when you want to stop.

INSULATING YOURSELF

Because we are warm-blooded creatures, we need insulation outside of the tropics, at least at night and often during the day. How much we need depends on the temperature. Often just a fraction of an inch is enough on a summer evening. In the depths of **winter**, however, several inches might be required.

As far as pure insulation goes, almost any dry material that can be wrapped around you or into which you can burrow will do. Wood shavings, leaves, and sand could all be used. Newspapers provide good insulation when tucked into clothing, as tramps found out long ago. Paper isn't very practical in the **wilderness** though. In addition to being warm, wilderness insulation needs to be lightweight, compressible, durable, and easy to care for. For wilderness use, this means **wool**, **fleece**, synthetic fills such as Polarguard and Primaloft, and that ultimate insulation, duck and goose **down**. If it resists water and **wind**, all the better, although other items—rain jackets, **tents**, **tarps**—can be used for this.

The best insulating materials trap air in their fibers. Air is a poor conductor of heat. Fluffy fabrics are warmer than smooth ones. They trap more air. Of course, if you flatten the fluffed-up fibers, they lose most of their insulation value. That's why you need a **sleeping pad** under your sleeping bag. The warmest pads—self-inflating ones—work by trapping the air inside so it can't escape when you put weight on it. Closed-cell foam pads are warm because they're thick. If your insulation proves inadequate, improvise. Don all your spare clothing. Even a thin windproof top adds some warmth. Wrap your sleeping bag or a tarp or tent around your shoulders or, if you don't have warm enough pants, around your legs. If you're in your sleeping bag, spread your rain jacket over it—it will make a difference—and put on a **hat**. If cold is seeping through your sleeping pad, put clothing or your **rucksack** on top of it.

See also **clothing** and **sleeping bags**.

J

JOHN MUIR TRAIL

Named for the great conservationist, the John Muir Trail runs for 212 miles from **Yosemite** Valley to the summit of 14,494-foot Mount Whitney, the highest peak in the 48 contiguous states. It's a spectacular **wilderness** trail running through the dramatic, beautiful, incomparable High Sierra of California, with its granite domes, splintered ridges, pristine conifer **forests**, timberline lakes, and rushing creeks. Following the crest of the **Sierra Nevada** Range, it runs through the Inyo and Sierra National Forests and Sequoia and Kings Canyon and Yosemite National Parks; it also runs through the John Muir Wilderness. About half of the trail was incorporated into the much longer **Pacific Crest Trail**.

The idea for a trail following the crest of the High Sierra was conceived by **Sierra Club** member Theodore S. Solomons in 1892. Originally to be called the High Sierra Trail, it was renamed in honor of John Muir (see **Muir, John**) after his death in 1914. Although construction began a year later, the trail wasn't completed until 1938.

The trail is well built and maintained, but it's not an easy hike. Much of it is above 10,000 feet, with a lot of ascent and descent as it climbs over a succession of high passes. There are few opportunities to resupply, so many days' worth of food has to be carried. For one 140-mile stretch, the trail crosses no roads.

The John Muir Trail is popular, so apply well in advance for **permits** from the appropriate national park or ranger station.

JUDGMENT

Having good judgment is perhaps more valuable than any individual backcountry skill. It minimizes your exposure to risk and helps you respond

"Once, while mountaineering, my friends and I spent way too long on a summit, enjoying beautiful, sunny weather and a spectacular view. An hour or so later, while we were descending, the snow had become so soft that rocks were dislodging all around us. After one particularly close call, we realized the seriousness of our mistake. Later that night, we all talked about what we could learn from the experience. For me, the experience reinforced something that I already knew but was becoming complacent about: by the time you summit, the climb is only halfway completed. The descent is just as hazardous (if not more so) than the ascent. That experience, and more importantly my group's evaluation of the experience, has helped me to avoid similar hazards on countless occasions."—AA appropriately to serious situations. Without such judgment, you'll regularly get yourself into trouble.

Good judgment involves appraising or evaluating something correctly. In **wilderness** terms, it means knowing how to evaluate hazards as well as your own abilities or those of your group. It entails reviewing all options for responding to a given circumstance and choosing the one most appropriate for the situation.

Good judgment comes with lots of experience and thoughtful reflection. For instance, if you ignore a hot spot on the first day of a hiking trip and it turns into a **blister**, you might never ignore a hot spot again. Then again, if you throw away that learning opportunity, you might get blisters all the time! Without reflecting on your experiences and learning from them as much as you can, you won't develop your judgment. Practiced backcountry travelers are continually developing and refining their judgment, no matter how experienced they are.

Sometimes the best learning opportunities come after a bad experience. While making mistakes and getting into serious situations can be embarrassing and humiliating, don't rush the process of putting mistakes behind you. Learn what you can to develop your judgment and become a better backcountry traveler.

KAYAKING STROKES

Kayaking strokes are easy to learn. Even if it's your first time kayaking, you can probably pick up the basics in a matter of minutes. There are only so many strokes, and it doesn't take long to become familiar with them.

Sound too easy? Here's the catch: being familiar with a stroke and being able to perform it flawlessly, perhaps in adverse conditions, are two different things. Expert paddlers spend years refining their technique to make their strokes as efficient and effective as possible. It all starts, however, with the basics.

While **sea kayaking** and river kayaking have many differences, their respective strokes are similar. Most paddle strokes can be organized into three categories: propulsion strokes, turning or corrective strokes, and braces. Propulsion strokes and turning strokes are discussed here (see **braces** for an explanation of that technique).

Propulsion Strokes

Propulsion strokes are used to provide forward or backward momentum. They include the forward stroke, the reverse stroke, and a handful of adaptations of these two strokes. The forward stroke can be as simple as putting the paddle in the water by your toes and bringing it back to your hips. That's it! Repeat this movement on alternating sides. The reverse stroke is just the oppo-

site: start with the paddle at your hips, push it to your toes, and repeat the same process on the opposite side. If you need to stop, simply put one side of the paddle in the water at your hips; then do the same on the other side. Alternate sides repeatedly until you come to a full stop (it shouldn't take very long). Avoid placing weight on the paddle while you're stopping, as this can make you feel unstable.

Perhaps most important is learning to tap into the strength of your torso muscles while paddling. Good **torso rotation** will make your forward and reverse strokes—and any other kayaking stroke—more powerful. Another key to these strokes is the position of your paddle. When sea kayaking, the paddle should be inserted into the water at a relatively low angle. This helps you conserve energy, allowing you to paddle great distances. To

This is the correct angle for a forward stroke. For additional power, place the paddle so it's more vertical in the water.

gauge the angle of your paddle, keep an eye on the position of your hands. If either hand ever goes above your shoulders during your stroke, the opposite end of the paddle is probably too deep in the water. To correct this problem, drop your hands closer to your waist. If you need more power, such as when you are paddling a sea kayak through surf or paddling a river kayak in whitewater, you'll want to be more aggressive by placing the paddle so it's more vertical in the water.

Turning Strokes

Although the forward stroke provides forward momentum, it doesn't mean that you will go in a straight line. Many beginning paddlers complain that their forward stroke isn't working because their kayak just goes in circles. That's OK. It isn't the job of the forward stroke to keep you going perfectly straight. That's the responsibility of the turning, or corrective, strokes. Turning strokes are used to correct the position of your boat when it gets blown, pushed, or somehow carried off course. These strokes are also used to change direction. The most common turning strokes are the sweep stroke, the bow and stern rudders, and the draw stroke. (For instructions on performing the sweep stroke, see **sweep stroke**.)

Both the bow rudder stroke and the stern rudder stroke are used to control the direction of the kayak. As you might expect, the stern rudder is used at the stern of the kayak, and the bow rudder is used at the bow. To execute a stern rudder, simply place one end of the paddle in the water alongside the stern. If the kayak is moving forward, this friction will cause the kayak to turn toward the paddle. This simple stroke is one of the easiest ways to turn the kayak, although it reduces forward momentum. Once you've mastered this stroke, experiment by slightly pushing the submerged paddle away from the kayak or pulling it toward the kayak. These two slight variations on the basic stroke give additional control.

The bow rudder is a little trickier, but it can produce powerful results. Start by bringing one

end of the paddle up to the bow and placing it in the water so that the paddle is parallel to the kayak. This will require you to place your off-side forearm (the side you're not paddling on) across your chest or head. You don't want your off-side forearm to be above your head, which sets you up for a shoulder injury. Rotate the paddle so the blade is angled slightly away from the kayak (cock your wrist slightly). Holding your paddle in this position will turn the boat toward the paddle as long as you have forward momentum. This stroke can easily be transferred into a forward stroke to create a powerful turning combination. It is frequently used to enter and exit **eddies** in whitewater situations (see **reading rapids**).

Use the draw stroke to move your kayak sideways. Start by turning your torso so your shoulders are both facing the same side of the kayak. Place your paddle vertically in the water at almost an arm's length away so the blade is parallel to the boat. Now pull the kayak toward your paddle. Repeat the process by carefully removing the paddle from the water (this takes practice). Once again, the power needed for this stroke comes primarily from torso rotation.

Techniques of Practicing

- Practice with an instructor who can point out what you're doing well in addition to areas you need to improve.
- Try to have someone videotape your strokes. It is much easier to evaluate yourself when you can actually see yourself paddling.
- Try paddling a short distance with your arms completely straight and locked— even on the recovery. Paddling with locked arms for a short distance will force you to rely on your torso for power, allowing you to feel the strength it provides.
- Exaggerate your torso rotation until it becomes second nature.

ANNIE AGGENS

The bow rudder stroke—executed by placing your paddle toward the bow of your kayak, at a slight angle to your boat—is very effective for turning a sea kayak.

Paddlers have created variations and adaptations of these strokes to meet specific needs. However, learning these basics will allow you to progress, refining each stroke until you are a proficient paddler.

KAYAK SELECTION

Choosing a kayak is an exercise in compromise. A kayak that has lots of **rocker** might turn easily, but it will be difficult to paddle straight over longer distances. A kayak made of Kevlar may be very light and responsive, but it will be prone to damage if it hits ice or lands on a rugged beach. This doesn't mean you have to compromise your fun on the water, but you should understand some of the differences in hull type and materials before shopping for a kayak.

When you decide to buy a kayak, be honest with yourself about how you're most likely to use the boat. Will you be paddling in the local reservoir, or along the coast of Greenland? Is your idea of fun bobbing down a class II riffle with the kids, or banging down a steep creek in the Smokies? Buy a boat that will perform at your highest ability level, yet will allow for skill improvement. Making a large investment in a kayak and equipment only to find that it will not perform adequately for you the following season is not going to encourage your development as a paddler.

An absolute must is paddling the boat before you buy it. Every boat has its quirks, and the manufacturer's specifications won't tell if your butt will fit in the seat. Overall comfort is essential to your enjoyment. This includes the mold of the seat, the position of the thigh braces, and the backrest. If you find a model that sounds perfect on paper but is uncomfortable once you're in it, you probably won't have much fun paddling. A good paddling shop will be happy to arrange for you to try out one or several boats. And while you're at the shop, ask about used or demo kayaks for sale. Demos are often available at the end of each season for a discounted price.

As you consider buying a kayak, ask at least one other paddler about her boat. Ask what she likes or dislikes about the boat. What would she get next time and why? Where does she paddle? She may let you take her kayak for a spin, which is especially valuable if that brand or model is not available for demo at the paddling shop.

Now let's get down to brass tacks. The terminology you will encounter while shopping for a kayak is straightforward.

Length

There are two different lengths to be concerned with: overall length and length at the waterline. Overall length has more to do with whether or not the kayak will fit in your garage (always a good thing to check). The length at the waterline (the length of the portion of kayak that sits in the water) is important because it will affect the speed of the kayak. In general, a kayak that is longer at the waterline will be faster and easier to track. Tracking refers to the kayak's tendency to go straight. A shorter kayak will be easier to turn, but it will also be slower.

Width

Width, or beam, affects both the stability and the storage capacity of your kayak. It is measured at the widest part of the kayak. Wider kayaks tend to be more stable than narrow kayaks. As such, they are often the choice for entry-level paddlers.

Hull Shape

The hull shape (or cross-sectional hull shape) affects the latitudinal stability of the kayak (how much it tips from side to side). Some hull designs give a kayak good primary stability—the feeling that the kayak is stable when it is upright. It's what most entry-level paddlers look for to build their confidence. Secondary stability refers to the stability of the kayak when it's not upright. Experienced paddlers who often lean the kayak onto its side while performing advanced edging techniques appreciate kayaks with secondary stability.

Chine

Chine is the transition between the side and bottom of the kayak. It may be sharp or rounded. A hard-chined kayak (one with a clear distinction between the side and bottom of the kayak) will tend to have better primary stability, but it can easily get pushed around in the **waves**. A rounded, or softer, chine will often have less primary stability, but will react better in waves.

Rocker

Rocker refers to the curvature of the kayak from bow to stern: think of the bottom runner on a rocking chair. A kayak with a lot of rocker means that the bow and stern appear raised out of the water. This gives the kayak a shorter length at the waterline and makes it easier to maneuver. Look for a kayak with some rocker if you think you'll need to make quick moves, such as in whitewater.

Depth

It's no fun to get into a kayak only to have to curl your toes because they just won't fit inside! This can happen in kayaks that don't have much depth (especially if you have big feet). If you're a larger person, you'll find that more depth adds to your comfort. The best way to check this is to simply sit in the kayak with your feet on the footpegs. If you will be paddling with shoes on, wear them when you demo the kayak.

Volume

Volume is essentially the total interior space of a kayak, measured in cubic feet. The length, width, and depth of a kayak's design all affect its total volume. High-volume kayaks are great for carrying everything you own, but they may feel awkward when not fully loaded.

Hull Material

Today's kayaks are generally manufactured from plastic, composites (such as fiberglass or Kevlar), or wood.

Most entry-level kayaks are made from polyethylene plastic, a relatively strong plastic that is soft enough to mold easily and so can be mass produced. The downside of soft plastics is that they're heavy, so they absorb a lot of the paddler's energy before it can be transferred to the water. Nonetheless, plastic boats are durable and a comparatively cheap alternative to composites. Plastic is virtually the only material used for whitewater kayaks

Generally reserved for sea kayaks, composite materials are much stiffer than plastic and are relatively light for their strength. Because they're stiff, they absorb far less energy than their plastic counterparts. In addition, the stiff materials allow manufacturers to create fine lines and sharp edges. Fine lines help the kayak move efficiently through the water. If you're not in a position to buy a composite boat, don't paddle one: they feel so good that you may lose sight of your financial constraints.

Wooden kayaks are both beautiful to watch and magical to paddle. They require a certain dedication to maintain, but most paddlers would consider the maintenance a small additional price for such an elegant craft.

Two other kayak constructions are skin-on-frame and folding kayaks. Skin-on-frame kayaks, like those traditionally made in Greenland and the Arctic, are exciting to paddle and fun to build. Most plans call for the use of canvas or nylon for a covering instead of animal skin. These kayaks tend to flex with the waves, absorbing

ANNIE AGGENS

*There are so many different kayak models on the mar-
ket that it can take time to find the right one for you.
Attending a kayak symposium—as shown here—will
allow you to look at a variety of kayaks before deciding
which to buy.*

much of the pounding shock a rigid boat endures.
Folding kayaks are built on the same principles
as skin kayaks, substituting modern synthetic materials for traditional organic materials. But, as
the name implies, folding boats fold. This is a
great boon for the kayaker who wants to take a
kayak on a plane, as most folding boats can be
checked as luggage.

Weight

More and more kayakers are realizing that if their
boat is a pain to move around when it's out of the
water, they're less likely to go paddling. This isn't
such an issue with short whitewater boats, but it
certainly can be a factor if you have a 15-foot sea
kayak. Check the weight and try to find a kayak
that you can manage. If a heavy boat suits the
kind of kayaking you will be doing, because of
rocky shorelines and the like where you paddle, a
set of collapsible wheels can help ease the load
when moving your kayak.

Many sea kayaks come with options. Once you
find a model you like, check to see if you can order the features you want. Options include **rudders**, **skegs**, **compasses**, bilge pumps, and the
number of hatches. Also look at the shape of the

cockpit: there are different cockpit styles and
most paddlers find one more easy to enter (and
exit) than another.

For more information on a specific kayak
model, look for the annual review and buyer's
guide issue of a paddlesport magazine such as *Sea
Kayaker* or *Canoe and Kayak* (see resources
section).

KEEPERS

Keepers are particularly nasty **holes** or **hydraulics**
that can trap a paddler. As you become familiar
with **moving-water hazards**, you will be able to
distinguish those holes that offer fun **surfing** opportunities from the holes that are keepers.
Avoid the keepers, and you'll live a long, happy
life filled with many years of great paddling.

KNIFE SHARPENING

Consider this proverb: "A dull knife is a dangerous knife." Without a doubt, dull **knives** require
more force and command less respect than sharp
knives—a bad combination. If you have ever
tried to cut something with a dull knife, you
know the mess it can make. You may also be familiar with the ominous feeling associated with
putting an inordinate amount of pressure on the
blade. If you carry a knife with you on the **trail**
(and you should), you should know how to
sharpen it.

Sharpening a knife is a simple process that
takes minimal time. While there are several different methods of sharpening knives, the easiest
and most practical on the trail is to use a sharpening stone. Sharpening stones come in various
sizes and can be purchased at most hardware
stores. Many stones are pocket sized and also fit
well in a tackle box or **repair kit**.

To use a sharpening stone, lay it flat on an
even surface and apply some oil to the stone.
Cooking oil is fine; water will work in a pinch.
Clean your knife of the food residue that tends
to collect on the blade. Hold the stone with one
hand and the knife with the other. Place the
knife's cutting edge at a shallow angle to the

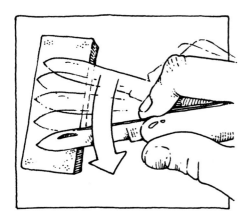

A sharpening stone is the easiest way to sharpen knives in the field. Apply oil to the stone and push the blade across the stone at a shallow angle, using even strokes. Repeat as necessary. Lift the blade off the stone and place it back at the top of the stone between strokes rather than dragging it up along the surface.

stone, and push it across the stone in a smooth, even motion as though you were carefully whittling the stone. Do not apply so much pressure that the blade bends or catches on the stone. When you reach the end of the stone, pick up the knife and repeat the process several times. Do not drag the blade back across the stone. When you finish one side of the blade, turn the knife over and sharpen the other side, making sure to use the same number of strokes. You will have to adjust the blade slightly to sharpen the tip. Continue to sharpen the blade until the knife can effortlessly slice a piece of paper with merely the weight of the knife.

With sharpening stones that have a coarse side and a smooth side, do the initial, rough sharpening on the coarse side of the stone, and use the smooth side for finishing touches.

KNIVES

Most people have a favorite knife they like to take on backcountry excursions. A good backcountry knife is one that is versatile. Like most items that you pack for your trip, it should be able to perform a variety of tasks.

Most blades can be categorized into two basic styles: fixed-blade knives or folding knives. Fixed-blade knives, also called *sheathed knives*, are easy to use because they require no opening or closing. They're also easy to clean and have no moving parts to jam or fail. Because they don't fold, however, they can be burdensome. Nonetheless, many people like fixed-blade knives for their traditional qualities. Almost all fillet, skinning, and boning knives have fixed blades.

Folding knives are more popular for recreational outdoor use. Folding knives have either a locking blade or a nonlocking blade. Locking blades will lock into place when they are opened, a nice safety feature. Folding blades have a pivot point, which can get clogged with food, dirt, or other grit. They require more maintenance and cleaning than fixed-blade knives. Unlike fixed-blade knives, they require no sheath, one less thing that can get lost. Most pocketknives and multitools are folding knives.

"My favorite knife is a Gerber folding knife that has a 3.75-inch-long stainless steel blade and a soft rubber grip that's easy to hold even when wet. It weighs only 5 ounces. It is easy to open and close, and small enough to stash easily in the top of my day pack or in the breast pocket of my jacket. It cuts cheese and spreads peanut butter without getting too messy. It's strong enough to strip the bark off of wet wood when I am trying to start a fire in the rain, and once I have the fire going, it will clean the fish that I intend to cook."—AA

To choose the best knife, think about what you will use it for. Do you need a multitool? If so, what features will you likely use? While it is important to have a multipurpose knife, some activities require specialized knives. For example, filleting a fish is best accomplished by using a fillet knife (see **fishing**). Whether or not you decide to carry the extra weight of a fillet knife in addition to your regular knife depends on how badly you want a nice fillet!

> "When I am on a paddling trip, I carry three knives: my multipurpose knife, a fillet knife, and a river knife that's always attached to my PFD. On backpacking trips, I simply carry my multipurpose knife."—AA

Regardless of which type of knife you carry, remember the following useful tips.

• Select a knife with a good grip. Some knives have beautiful wood or ivory handles that become impossible to use if your hand is wet or sweaty. Make sure the knife you select is easy and secure to hold.
• Always keep your knife sharp. Sharp knives are easier and safer to use than dull knives. Sharpen your knife before each trip into the backcountry. For longer trips, you can buy an inexpensive sharpening tool or honing stone at any hardware store. (See **knife sharpening**.)
• Dry your knife before you close it or return it to its sheath. A wet knife may develop rust, especially if it has been exposed to salt water. Returning a dry knife to a wet sheath will also rust it, so keep your sheath as dry as possible.
• Avoid burying the entire blade in food (particularly with folding blades): food can get in the folding mechanism and cause it to jam. It can also get into the grains of wood handles. Peanut butter is the biggest culprit.
• Wipe your knife clean, and periodically oil (cooking oil is fine) moving parts. If the knife has difficult-to-remove grime, immerse it in a pot of boiling water for a few minutes.
• Never use your knife as a screwdriver unless it is designed as such, and never use it as a lever to pry something open. If you do, don't be surprised if the blade breaks.
• Before you buy a particular knife, consider how easy it is to open or to remove from its

ANNIE AGGENS

Popular trail knives. From left: Leatherman Wave, Buck NXT, Gerber EX Out, CRKT Mt. Shasta, and Swiss Army Climber.

sheath. Can you do this with one hand? Can you do it wearing gloves?

Anytime you use a knife, you must also use common sense. Cutting a piece of cheese in the palm of your hand is a sure way to end up hiking out for stitches. Likewise, cutting your thumb while closing a folding blade isn't that hard to do if you aren't paying attention.

KNOTS

There's nothing quite like knowing the perfect knot for any given situation. Want to tie your boats to shore? Fix your rain **tarp**? Hang a hammock? No problem! Need to hang a bear bag? Make a harness from webbing? Piece of cake. All it takes to become a knot virtuoso is a basic understanding of knots, a piece of **rope**, and practice, practice, practice.

Almost all knots can be broken down into one of three families: loops, bends, and hitches. A loop is a knot that, when tied, leaves a loop in the rope. You might tie a loop around a tree or a boulder. The most popular loop is probably the **bowline**. Bends are knots that tie together the ends of rope. That makes it easy to remember—bends tie ends! Bends are convenient if you need to tie two pieces of rope together to make one longer piece. A well-known bend is the fisherman's bend (see **fisherman's knot**). Hitches are really relatives of knots. In fact, if you take away the thing that a hitch is tied around (the tree, the tent pole, and so forth), the hitch doesn't exist—it can be pulled into a straight piece of rope. A common hitch is the **clove hitch**. To be fluent in knots, you should know several members of each of these families. This way, you can select the best knot for your situation. The following knots are described elsewhere in this book: **bowline**, **overhand**, **figure eights**, **fisherman's knot**, **butterfly knot**, **clove hitch**, **girth hitch**, **trucker's hitch**, **prusik hitch**, **Munter hitch**, and the **water knot**.

Before you begin practicing your knots, learn the basic knot nomenclature. If you have a pile of rope lying on the ground and you pick up one end and begin to tie a knot with it, you will be holding the *running end* (also known as the *working end*) of the rope. The running end is the end of rope that gets the most action. It is wound, twisted, and fed through loops to create a knot. The other end of the rope is the *standing end*. The standing end may be in a pile on the ground, or it might be in your other hand. Knowing which end is the standing end and which is the running end helps clarify the directions of knot tying. A *bight* of rope is a piece of rope that's doubled over. To envision a bight, imagine holding a 2-foot piece of rope in the middle, half the rope falling on either side of your fingers. What you have in your hand is a bight. A *loop* is a circle created by laying a section of rope back on itself. Now that you know these terms, you're set to go!

While most knots are very strong when tied correctly, a knot actually creates the weakest spot in a rope. Some knots can weaken a rope's strength by as much as 40 percent; other knots,

Knot terminology.

as little as 25 percent. Regardless of the knot's strength, you will want to ensure that all knots are *dressed*, or *clean*. This means that there are no unintended twists or crosses in the rope. A knot that's tied correctly but isn't dressed is incomplete. Remember, when tying a knot you should always leave extra rope for the *tail*, the end of the rope coming out of the knot. It should be long enough to tie a quick overhand knot as a backup.

Again, the only way to become proficient at tying knots is to practice regularly. One way to get lots of practice is to get a good knot book and two or three sections of rope in different colors, and then put them all next to the toilet. Why read a magazine when you could be learning the fisherman's knot or the butterfly knot?

LACERATIONS

Lacerations are cuts that penetrate the skin. They're often sustained by accidentally slicing yourself with a knife or sharp object. Most lacerations are easy to treat in the field. After controlling the **bleeding**, irrigate the wound with clean **water** and cover it with a sterile dressing. Monitor the wound for signs of **infection**. Deep lacerations may require stitches: in such cases, evacuate the person as soon as possible to a medical facility. See also **first aid**.

LANDING IN CURRENT

Many people have met their fate (or come close) by not knowing the correct method of landing their canoe or kayak in moving water. Thinking that they can simply plant the bow of their boat on shore, they are surprised and unprepared when they end up heading downstream—backward. Always exercise caution when landing a canoe in current, especially above rapids, falls, or other **moving-water hazards**. The upstream end of the canoe (usually the stern) should be pulled into shore first. This may require you to back-paddle into position. If the downstream end of the canoe hits shore first, the current will catch the back end and swing it around in a fast, and sometimes violent, motion. Instead, practice maneuvering into shore stern first (or bow first, if you are facing upstream). Once the upstream paddler has

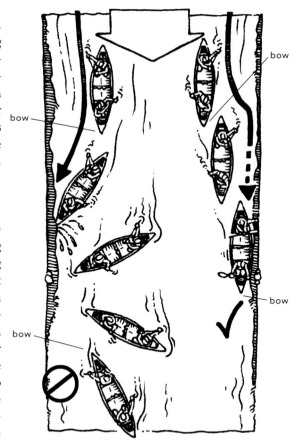

The upstream end of a canoe should always land first when landing in current (right). If the downstream end touches land first (left), the canoe is likely to swing around and continue downstream backward.

reached shore, he can climb out and steady the boat while the downstream paddler gets out. As the person who is maintaining the boat's position in the current, the upstream paddler should always be the first person out of the boat and the last one in.

When landing a kayak in current, apply the same principles. The upstream end of the kayak should always approach shore first.

When paddling in technical waterways, always scout ahead to make sure there is a spot to land your canoe or kayak. Never wait until the last moment to land upstream of a rapids or falls; an unexpected upset could spell tragedy.

See also **canoeing**, **canoeing strokes**, and **kayaking strokes**.

LATITUDE

The latitude of a location denotes its distance (either north or south) from the equator. Lines of latitude run parallel to one another from the equator, at 0 degrees latitude, to the poles, at 90 degrees North latitude and 90 degrees South latitude. Each degree of latitude is 60 nautical miles (a nautical mile is a little longer than a statute mile). Therefore, at 3 degrees North latitude, you are approximately 180 nautical miles north of the equator. Because it would be hard to identify a precise location within one whole degree of latitude (you'd be searching over 60 nautical miles), each degree of latitude is divided into smaller units called *minutes*. There are 60 minutes in every degree, with each minute equal to 1 nautical mile. To get even more precise, each minute of latitude is divided into 60 seconds. Each second is roughly equivalent to 100 feet.

Knowing your latitude won't do you much good unless you know your **longitude** as well, which gives you your location east and west. Using both longitude and latitude, you can pinpoint your location anywhere on earth.

Latitude is almost always given in degrees, minutes, and seconds. For example, the latitude 41 degrees, 11 minutes, and 20 seconds North would be written 41°11′20″ N. Latitude can be found along the right and left margins of most maps.

LAYOVER DAY

See **rest days**.

LEAVE NO TRACE

Leave No Trace is a national and international program that helps people understand and minimize their impact on their surrounding environments. Developed by the National Outdoor Leadership School (**NOLS**) and an assortment of national land management agencies, Leave No Trace has become the standard code of ethics for minimum-impact **camping**. The following seven principles are the foundation of Leave No Trace.

- Plan ahead and prepare.
- Travel and camp on durable surfaces.
- Dispose of waste properly.
- Leave what you find.
- Minimize campfire impacts.
- Respect wildlife.
- Be considerate of other visitors.

While these principles remain constant regardless of where you travel, research has shown that certain geographical regions require special consideration. In response, Leave No Trace has developed adapted guidelines for various regions in the United States. Leave No Trace also has created activity-specific guidelines for rock climbers, mountain bikers, sea kayakers, and equestrians. Although the guidelines vary slightly to accommodate the ecological needs of each region, the seven principles remain the same.

Plan Ahead and Prepare

Plan ahead by thinking about what kind of experience you want. Consider going with a group of six or fewer, which will reduce your impact on the land. Think about your capabilities, the terrain on which you'll be traveling, and the equipment you'll need. Plan a menu that allows you to carry the right amount of **food** while minimizing the amount of food packaging. Take water containers to minimize the number of trips you need to make to your **water** source from camp. By planning ahead, you'll be able to evaluate in advance your high-impact activities and thus mitigate them. (See also **planning a trip**.)

Travel and Camp on Durable Surfaces

If each person in the wilderness were to create his own **trail**, there would be nothing but trails. Use existing trails, and avoid taking shortcuts that connect two paths (such as on **switchbacks**). When encountering a muddy or wet section of trail, walk right through the mud rather than walking around it. Going around it will eventually *increase* the extent of the mud, affect trail vegetation, and create visual impact. If your route calls for traveling off trail, avoid creating new paths by having everyone in your group take a slightly different route. Try to stay away from delicate meadows and fragile terrain. Camp on surfaces that will survive your visit, such as rock, sand, or pine needles. If at all possible, stay at least 200 feet (that's 70 adult steps) from water (in the **desert**, camp at least a quarter mile away from waterholes so as not to scare off wildlife), meadows, or other trails. In **bear** country, separate your **cooking** and sleeping areas by at least 100 feet, and hang your food at least 12 feet off the ground and 6 feet away from the tree trunk when possible (see **bear bagging**). Avoid staying at one site for a lengthy period. If you are traveling on a waterway, choose your launching, landing, and camping sites for their durability. Choose sites that are below the high-water mark—but only if you are confident that the water won't rise and whisk your gear away!

Dispose of Waste Properly

Waste comes in many forms, such as orange peels, dishwater, candy wrappers and, of course, human excrement. Disposing of waste properly is critical for the safety of the food chain and for the aes-

thetic value of the **wilderness**. Any solid waste, with the exception of human waste (and sometimes even that!), should be packed into garbage bags and carried out. Dishwater should be strained of solid particles and scattered at least 200 feet away from any water source or campsite—preferably on a durable surface. Dispose of water used to wash your hands or face in the same manner.

As for human waste, if there is a pit toilet in the area, use it, even though it may stink. If no facilities exist, you'll have to find a natural alternative. To urinate, choose a spot far from where people may congregate or travel. For a bowel movement, dig a **cathole** at least 6 to 8 inches deep (that's often the depth of your trowel) and aim well. Choose a spot at least 200 feet away from water sources and campsites, and ensure that you are not in a depression or other area where water will collect and stagnate. If you're traveling with a group, this may be your only chance to be alone, so find a pleasant spot with a good view and take your time. If you use toilet paper, pack it out. Bury natural **toilet paper** (you can experiment to find the best) along with your deposit. Once you've covered your cathole, scatter some debris over the site to return it to a natural appearance. Certain areas, such as some heavily traveled rivers in the western United States, may require that you pack out your waste, including fecal matter. Several types of "portable johns" are on the market for this purpose.

Leave What You Find

The saying popularized by Terry and Renny Russell in *On the Loose*, "Take only photographs and leave only footprints," still rings true. Avoid making any alterations to your campsite, such as digging trenches or creating fire rings where none exist. If you see something beautiful or historical, leave it for the next person to see too. Don't pick flowers and berries in a fragile landscape, such as an alpine meadow, or anywhere they are scarce. Natural and cultural artifacts are important clues to the history of a nation's past and should be left undisturbed (in the U.S., they are also protected under several acts of Congress).

Minimize Campfire Impacts

While campfires and wilderness trips have gone hand in hand for a long time, consider minimizing your use of them. **Fires** often cause damaging scars and may be hazardous in certain situations. Always check on fire regulations with local officials before heading out, and carry a camp **stove** as an alternative for cooking. If you decide it's responsible and appropriate to have a fire, make it small and safe. Use only small pieces of wood that are dead and lying on the ground. Avoid gathering all your wood from one spot. Rather, widen your search area so you don't create a noticeable absence of wood in any given area. Use a fire ring if it exists, but don't create your own. Instead, build your fire either in a fire pan or on a mound of mineral soil or sand. Return the soil or sand to its original location after the fire is extinguished. (See also **fires**.)

Respect Wildlife

Admire all wildlife from afar. Remember that even your indirect actions, such as leaving trash behind or being loud, can have a severe and negative impact on wildlife. Respecting wildlife not only protects them but also you. Angry, threatened, or injured wildlife can become aggressive and dangerous. When you respect **wild animals**, you'll be able to coexist with them and enjoy their presence.

Be Considerate of Other Visitors

Nobody likes going to the wilderness to hear loud music or to see partially biodegraded toilet paper. As a backcountry traveler, you have a responsibility not only to the land but to the other users as well. Think about your actions, and remember to be pleasant to those people you pass. Consider distancing yourself from other travelers to allow each of you the privacy you came for. Bear in mind that sounds travel far in quiet places. (See also **noise**.)

Leave No Trace is a nonprofit organization that is, in part, member supported. Contact Leave No Trace to learn more about the Leave No Trace principles and how they can be used in your area (see resources section).

LEEWARD

The downwind or leeward side of an object or landmass is protected from the **wind**. Leeward is the opposite of **windward**. It can be used in a sentence as follows: "We set up the **tent** on the leeward side of the ridge to shelter us from the blowing wind." Often, it is easier to travel on the leeward side of an object, such as a ridge or an island. However, if you're traveling in a mountainous region in the winter or spring, be cautious when traveling on leeward slopes. They can accumulate significant **snow** in a short period of time and thus may be more likely to **avalanche**. **Cornices** develop on the leeward side of ridges. Windward slopes may offer a harder and safer snowpack for traveling in these conditions.

When cooking, wind can reduce the efficiency of your stove. By locating your kitchen on the leeward side of an object, such as a large rock, you can cook meals faster and conserve fuel.

LEWIS AND CLARK EXPEDITION

One of the great **wilderness** journeys in the history of modern America took place between May 1804 and September 1806. In those 28 months Meriwether Lewis and William Clark led an expedition conceived by President Thomas Jefferson and funded by the U.S. Congress to explore the 1803 acquisition of the United States, the Louisiana Purchase, bought from France at a cost of $15 million. The main aim was to follow the Missouri River upstream and search for a viable water route to the Pacific, but the expedition also planned to study the natural history of the region as well. Guided by local Native Americans, to whom this land was home, Lewis and Clark traversed some 8,000 miles of wilderness previously unknown to Europeans. A significant and constant guide on the two-year trek was the 16-year-old Sacagawea, who was pregnant when she joined the expedition and whose son was born during the journey.

Setting off from St. Louis, Lewis and Clark traveled by boat up the Missouri to the **Rocky Mountains**. There they took to horses and foot travel, crossing the Continental Divide at Lemhi Pass in the Bitterroot Range and then **canoeing** down the Clearwater and Snake Rivers to the Columbia. They followed the Columbia to the Pacific, reaching the ocean on December 3, 1805 ("Great joy in the camp" wrote Clark, "we are in view of the Ocean"). Over the next nine months they retraced their route back to St. Louis.

Although they failed to find a water route to the Pacific, Lewis and Clark's expedition was a great achievement, an arduous venture into unknown territory whose scope is impossible to imagine now. They were the first Europeans to see vast areas of country and encounter the wildlife of the Rockies and the coastal ranges, bringing and sending back a great wealth of knowledge. Many of the specimens are still held in the Smithsonian Institution in Washington, D.C.

LIGHTERS

The common lighter is an invaluable gadget to carry in the wilderness. Unlike matches, lighters can self-ignite—a handy feature when there isn't anything to strike a match against. Some lighters are sold as waterproof and windproof, but it's difficult to find a lighter that lives up to this claim.

Most lighters stop working when they get wet. After they dry out again, however, they should work fine. If the **wind** allows, you can keep a lighter lit for a long time, but eventually the lighter becomes too hot to handle. If you don't have small children around, look for a lighter without the child-safety feature—these are much easier to use. Finally, always take a handful of matches in a plastic bag as a backup to your lighters. If all your lighters get wet, or if you run out of lighter fluid, you may need the matches to start a **fire** or **stove**.

LIGHTING

There is a certain moment in the life of every outdoor enthusiast when he is incredibly thankful to have a good source of light. Luckily, the days of bulky lights with inefficient batteries are behind us. Today's lights are lighter, brighter, and longer lasting than previous generations. Popular backcountry light sources are the flashlight, **headlamp**, and **candle** lantern.

> "My 'certain moment' came one night while I was descending from a longer-than-expected multi-pitch climb in Wyoming. As the light began to fade, we realized we still had several hundred feet to negotiate on our descent. With a cloudy sky to hide the moon, the darkness enveloped us. By the time we reached the ground, I could barely see my hand in front of my face. Without my trusty headlamp, I can only imagine how complicated the process of building anchors and rappelling would have become."—AA

Unless you don't like wearing an elastic band around your head, headlamps are the way to go. In the past few years, headlamps have evolved into lightweight, comfortable, and powerful sources of light. Depending on the intensity of light you want to project, you can get a headlamp with an LED (light-emitting diode), halogen bulb, or incandescent bulb. The longest-lasting light source is the LED, which is also highly energy efficient. LEDs can last up to 100,000 hours and can run for 150 hours on just three AAA alkaline batteries. Unlike bulbs, however, the LED light cannot be focused into a beam, and the light it emits isn't nearly as bright as what a bulb can produce. However, the glow can span up to 30 feet on a fully charged battery. This is more than enough for regular camp chores or reading a book, but not the best choice for activities that require a far-reaching light, such as mountain biking at night.

For a light that can cast a long-distance beam, select a halogen bulb. With a fully charged battery, a halogen light can span 300 feet with an obnoxiously bright light. The downside to halogen is that it uses a lot of energy. Compared to a regular incandescent bulb, which will last up to 12 hours on a few AA batteries, the halogen bulb of the same wattage will only last 4.5 hours. Still, it is the bulb of choice for many cavers and mountaineers who need a lot of bang for their buck.

Incandescent bulbs are the same bulbs you probably still use throughout your home. They fall somewhere in between LED and halogen in terms of both energy efficiency and intensity. A standard incandescent bulb of about 6 watts can cast a beam of light 60 feet with a full battery.

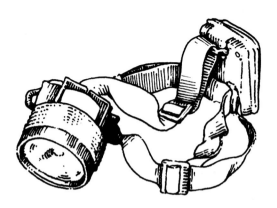

Headlamps keep your hands free and can be more convenient than flashlights. Rear battery compartments are rarely used these days on many lightweight LED headlamps.

While alkaline batteries certainly do the job, lithium batteries run for much longer and in much colder temperatures. However, compared with alkaline batteries, lithium batteries are much more expensive and they can be hard to find.

If you need a waterproof light, shop around for the one best suited to your needs. Some headlamps (and flashlights) are waterproof to a depth of 2,000 feet.

If you just want enough light to read, play cards, or write in your journal, consider a candle lantern, which can burn up to 9 hours with one candle. They radiate a comforting glow and can even warm the air inside a **tent** or **snow shelter**. Various models of candle lanterns are on the market, but most collapse to around 5 inches long and weigh about 7 ounces.

To light a large area, nothing is more traditional than a **fire**. Fires provide the added bonus of warmth, but they require a lot of maintenance. Many areas may restrict fires, or you may simply not be in a suitable location for a fire. If this is the case, you may opt for a lantern. Lanterns can run on white gas, kerosene, alcohol, or propane. While they're very effective, they tend to be bulky and require you to carry additional **fuel**. For these reasons, they are best used at base camps or car camping sites.

LIGHTNING

OK, so the chances of getting struck by lightning are not very high—about 1 in 280,000. But then again, if you're reading this book, you probably spend a lot of time outdoors, which increases your risk. You might also travel to exposed areas, such as mountain ridges or open bodies of water. Hmm . . . now the odds are increasing!

If you've spent a lot of time in the **wilderness**, you probably have had more than a few experiences with lightning. Although a very real threat in the backcountry, lightning injuries are also very preventable. Knowing when and how to prepare for lightning significantly increases your chances of surviving potential strikes.

First of all, what is lightning? Lightning occurs

when electricity travels between positively and negatively charged particles within a cloud and on the ground. When a connection is made between these particles, an electrical charge one third the speed of light, and as strong as millions of volts, flashes before our eyes. So strong is the intensity of the bolt that at certain points along its path, lightning is hotter than the surface of the sun. The air directly around the bolt expands and contracts, creating the sound waves we interpret as thunder. Lightning usually comes from cumulonimbus **clouds**—these are the ones that build up tall in the sky. They are easy to see if you have a clear view of the horizon, but if your view is obstructed by trees or nearby mountains, these storm clouds can appear quickly and unexpectedly.

As soon as you spot a cumulonimbus cloud, start monitoring its progress. A storm doesn't have to be on top of you to be lethal. Lightning strikes can occur several miles away from what appears to be the actual storm. If you see lightning, begin listening for thunder. To gauge the distance of a strike from your location, simply count the number of seconds between the flash of the lightning and the crack of the thunder, and then divide by five. Because sound travels at roughly a fifth of a mile per second, you can easily calculate the lightning's distance. For example, at 10 seconds, the strike is 2 miles away; at 25 seconds, the strike is 5 miles away.

To be safe, start planning an escape as soon as you can discern there may be a storm. If you count 15 seconds or less between lightning and thunder, it's really time to act! Increase your safety by staying away from high or exposed areas, such as mountain ridges, open fields, or lakes. Do not take cover under a large tree or in a shallow cave. If you're above treeline, head to a low point or close to—but not next to—a large boulder or cliff. If you're in a forest, stay closer to the smaller trees and brush. If you're on a lake, paddle toward shore. There is a "cone of safety" extending around an object that provides some protection. Imagine the object lying on the ground from its present base. To be in the cone of safety, stand

inside the distance between the base of the object and its tip, but far enough away from the actual object that lightning doesn't jump from the object to you (see the accompanying illustration). Lightning has been known to jump 15 feet!

In all cases, try to avoid contact with any metal. Take off your frame **pack**, put down your **trekking poles**, and so forth. You may even want to remove your **knife** from your belt. Squat on your feet, keeping your hands off the ground. Try to put a dry insulator, such as a camp chair or an Ensolite sleeping pad, under your feet. If you are in a group, spread yourselves out (preferably in a straight line) at least 20 feet apart. Don't resume activity until the threat of lightning has subsided.

If lightning strikes someone, their chances for survival are relatively good. Often, a strike will affect the electrical systems in the brain and heart. The shock may cause the heart to stop, but it can resume spontaneously. The brain, on the other hand, might not be sending the signal to breathe. For this reason, you may have to provide rescue breathing techniques immediately or start **CPR**.

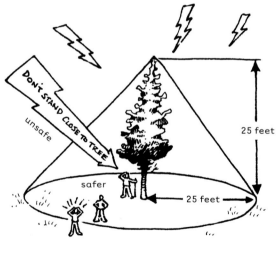

The cone of safety helps identify the safest place to stand during a lightning storm when trees are nearby. It's very dangerous to stand under or next to trees. Standing in clearings will also increase your risk of being struck by lightning.

The patient may also have **burns**, which will require treatment, or other injuries sustained from the force of the shock. Be sure to check the patient thoroughly, and plan an **evacuation** as soon as possible. The effects of a lightning strike can be complicated and long lasting, and this person must see a doctor as soon as possible.

> "I was once in a lightning storm when a bolt struck a tree 12 feet from my body! I didn't hear it or see it coming. One instant I was counting how long it had been since the last flash, and the next I was sitting next to a 6-foot chunk of tree stabbed into the ground! Luckily, I avoided any possible ground current because I had been insulated from the ground by my foam camp chair."—AA

LINING

Imagine that you are paddling a canoe down a river and you encounter a big set of rapids. After scouting the rapids, you determine that shooting them is not an option. Most people will automatically prepare to portage (see **portaging**), but there may be a more practical solution: guiding your canoe down a set of rapids from the relative safety of shore, a procedure known as *lining*. Technically, you can also line kayaks and even rafts, but as it mostly pertains to canoes, that's what we'll discuss.

To do this, two **ropes** (known as *painter lines*) are secured to the boat, one to the bow and one to the stern. The other ends lie in the skillful hands of the paddlers. With one person controlling the bow line and the other handling the stern line, the partners maneuver the canoe around rocks, in and out of **eddies**, and over ledges. Lining requires both a keen understanding of currents and the ability to think fast and act quickly—all the while hopping from one slippery rock to the next. It also requires plenty of practice and lots of communication with your paddling partner. Lining is one of those skills that, when performed perfectly, looks and feels like art.

Lining a set of rapids is not all that different from shooting the rapids. It is a good idea to scout your route and anticipate which maneuvers you will need to employ (see **scouting rapids**). You must also understand how canoes and currents interact. For the best results, tie two ropes (each at least 20 feet long) as close to the bottom of the canoe as possible, one each at the bow and at the stern. You may have to outfit your canoe with tie-in points near the waterline. Another option is to create a harness for your canoe with tie-in points along the keel line. Books written specifically about **canoeing** can teach you how to make these preparations. It is possible to line a canoe with your lines attached directly to the bow and stern plates, although this is the least preferred method.

Begin lining by pushing your canoe into the current with the stern upstream of the bow. As you maneuver it along the shoreline, you'll quickly realize that anytime the canoe isn't parallel with the current, the force against the hull can become overwhelming. When lining, it's the responsibility of the upstream person (usually the stern person) to control the angle of the canoe in the current; the more experienced liner should take this position.

The bow person works with the stern person to maintain the canoe's parallel position by giving and taking slack in the line. As you negotiate obstacles such as rocks, adjust the direction and angle of the canoe. The stern person can usually control this either by drawing the stern closer to shore or by letting it out gently into the current. The bow person quickly follows by adjusting the line so the bow is, once again, directly downstream from the stern.

Beware of letting the stern get too far into the current; it's easy for the force of the current to overwhelm the person at the stern. If a strong current catches the stern of the canoe, it may be necessary to let go of the rope to avoid being pulled into the current. In this scenario, the canoe will quickly swing around so the bow is now upriver of the stern. If you need to let go of the

Paddlers will sometimes line their canoes around obstacles in a river instead of paddling. Lining is accomplished with painter lines attached to the bow and stern. When lining, keep the canoe parallel to the current.

RICK SWEITZER

stern line, first warn your partner, who will soon feel the weight of the canoe on the bow line.

Ideally you should be able to line a set of rapids without ever getting wet. Whether or not you're able to do this depends on your skill and the makeup of the rapids. If you keep your canoe close to shore, you should be able to give it a shove if it gets lodged on a rock, but be careful. Remember, the reason you're lining is because the rapids are too complicated to shoot! Don't compromise your safety by getting in water deeper than your knees. Also beware of becoming tangled in your line. Feet, wrists, and fingers can easily fall prey to a messy wad of excess line.

The benefits of lining are many—no unloading and reloading the canoe, no heavy packs to haul, no sore shoulders. The drawbacks are that it requires a lot of skill and **judgment**. It is *not* always the easiest or safest solution. The combination of slippery rocks and fast-moving feet can lead to some bad spills. Still, lining can be fun. Like a game of chess, it is a process of calculating your moves and anticipating the river's reaction. It gets easier with practice and offers a great alternative to the average portage.

LLAMAS

If you are investigating having your next backcountry trip supported or resupplied, don't be surprised if a llama is recommended as your pack animal. While the use of llamas as pack animals is fairly recent in the United States and Europe, they have been used for over 4,000 years in the remote and rugged Andean Mountains of South America. Llamas are naturals at carrying loads through the backcountry. A healthy male can carry between 80 and 100 pounds and travel up to 20 miles a day (females are usually reserved for breeding). Llamas are known for their surefootedness and low maintenance. A member of the camel family, they can travel long distances without water. With padded feet (instead of hooves), they have a minimal impact on the land. They are safe to handle and have a gentle demeanor. While their amiable nature makes them easy to work with, you still don't want to tick off a llama. A llama that feels threatened is likely to douse the offender in a shower of foul-smelling spit.

LONG-DISTANCE HIKING

On a long-distance hike, you stay out for weeks, maybe even months, at a time, moving on every day and **camping** each night. It's not only longer than a shorter hike but also qualitatively different. A hike of a few days or a week or two is a break from life's normal routines, a release from the confines of work and home. But a long-distance hike becomes your life; it becomes what you do.

The reasons for long-distance hiking are many. One desire is to achieve a goal, for example, to hike one of the **long-distance trails**, such as the **Appalachian Trail** in the eastern United States or the **Pacific Crest Trail** in the western United States. Achieving that goal—reaching the end of the trail—yields a feeling of satisfaction and success. But many, probably most, long-distance hikers come to realize that what really matters is the journey itself, the process of moving through the **wilderness** and living with nature day after day. The deepest insights and self-knowledge come along the way, not with the apparent triumph of the finish. Indeed, many long-distance hikers approach the end of a hike with sadness because their great adventure is ending. The finish is simply a place from which they can look back at the journey and see it as a whole, as a complete experience.

> "When you're out long enough, so that both the start and the finish of your hike are far away in distance and time, walking in the wilderness becomes the norm. For me, this means that I feel much more part of the wilderness, much more in tune with nature, than on a short hike. Because of this, I think that time is as, if not more, significant than distance."—CT

Long-distance hiking does involve a challenge, which some people relish. Often, people will make the challenge tougher by trying to hike a trail quickly or in **winter** or by trying to complete more than one trail in a short period of time. For most people, though, the challenge of hiking long distance over many months is quite enough in itself.

Challenges other than completing the distance are also involved in long-distance hiking. Hikers have to contend with the **weather** and the terrain, in the knowledge that they won't be home in a few days. As well as good hiking and camping skills, mental discipline and a strong will are required to get you through day after day of **rain** or mile after mile of rugged terrain. Once you've completed a long-distance trail, your **backpacking** techniques will be finely honed and you'll be mentally prepared for anything.

One of the joys of long-distance hiking is that after a week or two, camping and hiking become so normal that they require little conscious thought and you can devote yourself to being in the wilderness. Fitness—mental as well as physical—improves too, and concerns about aching muscles and tiredness fade along with those about equipment, campsites, **water**, and more. At the same time, alertness grows; you notice small details of the wilderness, such as patterns on stones shining in a pool, the movement of small creatures, and the play of sunlight in a **forest** glade. The landscape flows past with a satisfying completeness. The different ecosystems and life zones gently merge and separate, at once different and part of the same wholeness. Although a long-distance hike may pass through widely varying places, at walking speed you have time to see how they fit together, how they are part of a greater unity.

See also **trekking**.

> "The final result of long-distance hiking is a feeling of being at home in the wilderness, of hiking every day as natural and right. I never feel quite so complete, quite so relaxed, quite such well-being as when I'm on a long-distance hike."—CT

LONG-DISTANCE TRAILS

Long-distance trails are found the world over. The United States probably has more long-distance wilderness trails than anywhere else however, including the big three south–north National Scenic Trails, the **Appalachian Trail**, the **Pacific Crest Trail**, and the **Continental Divide Trail**, plus other famous though less lengthy trails, such as the **Long Trail** in Vermont and the **John Muir Trail** in California. There are cross-state trails, such as the 471-mile Colorado Trail, the 780-mile Arizona Trail, and the 1,300-mile Florida National Scenic Trail, the last a good choice for hikers who don't like hills. Some trails cross a particular region, such as the not-yet-completed Pacific Northwest Trail, running 1,100 miles through Montana, Idaho, and Washington, and the huge North Country Scenic Trail, which, when finished, will run about 4,200 miles through seven states, from the Adirondack Mountains in New York State to the Missouri River in North Dakota.

Another new and exciting-sounding trail is the Desert Trail, which is planned to run from Mexico to Canada through the **deserts** of California, Nevada, Oregon, Idaho, and Montana. Parts of the trail already exist, including 656 miles in California, which includes 175 miles through Death Valley. The Desert Trail is a little different from other long-distance trails in that it will be a trail corridor rather than a constructed trail (rather than an actual trail, there is instead an area through which the hiker passes, either cross-country or on a trail, with options as to the exact route).

The longest U.S. trail is the 6,356-mile American Discovery Trail, which runs from the Atlantic Ocean to the Pacific Ocean through 15 states, 14 **national parks**, and 16 national forests. It includes urban and cultivated areas, but there is much wilderness along the way.

Canada also has many long wilderness trails, some in very remote areas, such as the Canol Heritage Trail, which runs for 222 miles over the Mackenzie Mountains from the Northwest Territories to the Yukon Territory. This may not be as long as some other trails, but it's more challenging than most because there are several major river crossings, and all supplies must be carried for the whole hike.

The first long-distance trail in Canada was the 500-mile Bruce Trail, which follows the forested Niagara Escarpment through the province of Ontario. The western end of the Bruce Trail can be linked to the planned Voyageur Trail, which will run 700 miles from Lake Huron along the north shore of Lake Superior.

Perhaps the most spectacular wilderness trail in Canada is the Great Divide Trail, an unofficial route that runs 900 miles through the magnificent Canadian Rockies from the U.S. border to Kakwa Lake Provincial Park.

See also **planning a trip**.

LONGITUDE

Longitude is a navigational term that denotes your location either east or west of the prime meridian, an imaginary line that runs through Greenwich, England.

To understand longitude, imagine the earth as an orange. A peeled orange reveals lines that run from top to bottom. At the midsection of the orange, these lines are fairly evenly spaced out, while at the ends of the orange all the lines come together. Lines of **latitude** (also called *meridians*) are much the same way. At the equator, the meridians are evenly spaced, at about 60 nautical miles apart. As soon as you leave the equator, the meridians begin to converge until they are all touching at the North and South Poles.

There are 360 degrees of longitude on the earth, just as there are 360 degrees in a circle. Degrees of longitude are numbered 001° to 180° and designated as east or west, depending on which side of the prime meridian they lie. Each degree marks one line of longitude (one line on the orange). Therefore, if you know your longitude, you can locate your east-west position on a map. Longitude is generally given in degrees, minutes, and seconds. For example, the longitude 120 degrees, 39 minutes, and 32 seconds West would be written 120°39′32″ W.

Knowing your longitude does you little good without also knowing your **latitude,** which is your position either north or south of the equator. Together, latitude and longitude can pinpoint any location on earth. Longitude is marked along the top and bottom margins of most maps.

LONG TRAIL

The 265-mile Long Trail, which runs through the Green Mountains in Vermont, in the northeastern United States, is the original **long-distance trail**. In 1910, school headmaster James P. Taylor came up with the visionary idea of a series of connecting trails running through Vermont from Massachusetts to Canada to create a long, continuous trail. He founded the Green Mountain

Club with the objective of establishing the trail. The southern section is now also part of the **Appalachian Trail**.

Completed in 1930, the Long Trail runs through the East Coast's native **forest** with a lot of ascent and descent as it follows the crest of the mountains. There are shelters roughly a day's walk apart, but these can be crowded, so carrying a **tent** or **tarp** is a good idea. High summer through fall is the best time to hike the trail. **Blackflies** are a problem in early summer.

For more information, check out the Long Trail website (see resources section).

LOST

Being lost is usually at least as much a state of mind as a physical reality. If you find yourself disoriented or unsure of your whereabouts, stop and think. You should at least be able to work out which direction to head in to get out of the **wilderness** or to reach somewhere you recognize.

> "I once spent a week hiking through a remote region of the Canadian Rockies, unsure of exactly where I was. I knew that as long as I headed north, I would reach an east-west—running road though—so I wasn't lost.
>
> At times, not being sure of where you are can be liberating, or at least it is for me. Not being sure what lies ahead, over the next rise, or around the next bend can be exciting and stimulating. Being lost can be an opportunity for exploration."—CT

Stop and think. That is the first and most important action to take. Don't panic! Panic and fear can send you tearing around in circles, desperate to find out where you are; in the process, you really may become lost. Don't abandon your gear. People have done just that in order to travel faster, leading to a far more serious situation when they became cold or wet and had no shelter or extra **clothing**.

If you think you're lost, remember the acronym STOP: Stop, Think, Organize, and Plan. Determine the last point at which you're certain you were on track. Backtrack to that spot only if you're confident that doing so won't confuse you more. Otherwise, *stay put.* How long is it since you knew where you were? That gives you an approximate distance to that spot. If it's less than an hour, you can't be more than a few miles out of your way. Which direction have you come from? Can you retrace your steps? Look at your **map**. In which direction should the **trail** or a recognizable feature, such as a lake or a cliff, lie? Can you identify any visible landmarks on the map?

If you really can't work out how to get back on route, head for a major objective, such as a large lake or a road.

There are many reasons why people get lost. Some of the more common are described below. See also **navigation** and **signaling**.

Poor Navigation Skills

Many people get lost because they fail to read their map correctly. Get a good grip on map reading, including orienting the map to your surroundings and understanding the topography. A person who can't read a map shouldn't be in the wilderness. This goes for using a **compass** as well. Don't assume that skills you learned ages ago are still sharp. Being confident with a map and compass takes training and practice.

Traveling in Difficult Terrain

You may need to plan extra time for navigating if you're traveling in difficult terrain. Examples are **hiking** through dense brush where visibility is limited, and paddling on a large lake with several islands. In such situations, you may need to stop more frequently to assess your position. If necessary, hike to a high point to get a big picture of your surroundings.

Poor Weather

If you have reason to believe that poor weather is on the way, locate your position on a map and then decide if it is really necessary or smart to continue. If bad **weather** sets in, you may just have to hunker down in your **tent** until it passes. Traveling in dense **fog** or a whiteout can render visual landmarks useless. Relying on a compass **bearing** works if you had the chance to take one, but one false reading can lead you miles astray. Be sure your skills are top-notch before attempting to travel by compass alone.

Poor Communication

Poor communication often involves relying on verbal directions instead of using a map. When you hear someone say, "Yeah, I've been there a lot—just go up the trail to this one bent tree, you'll know it when you see it," *beware*. Navigating on the basis of someone else's memory (or even your own) is a good way to get lost. You're far better off relying on a map. Poor communication can also result when a group splits up. If your group decides to split up temporarily, first identify an easy-to-find meeting location, as well as the routes you plan to follow. Choose an appropriate hour to meet (and be explicit, specifying A.M. or P.M.), and discuss contingency plans in case one party doesn't show up.

Impaired Judgment

Don't think you're safe from impaired **judgment** just because you don't do drugs. Heat, **hypothermia**, exhaustion, **dehydration**, and even fear can impair your judgment. While dangerous, impaired judgment can usually be prevented. Don't drink alcohol or use drugs that cause drowsiness or other altered states. Take care of yourself by monitoring your body temperature and staying hydrated (see **heat regulation**). If you're unable to continue without risking your safety, or without certain knowledge of where you are, stop and reassess your situation.

It can be hard to keep your cool when you realize you're lost, but it's essential that you try. First, avoid panic. The frantic feeling that accompanies the realization that you aren't where you should be often leads to poor decisions that compound the problem, such as hastening your pace.

If you're separated from the other members of a group, they will begin to look for you when they notice you're gone. Help them by creating visual signals that mark your location (see **signaling**). Create clues for rescuers by wandering out a short distance and building arrows with twigs, pointing to your location. If possible, relax and make yourself comfortable. Conserve your energy by eating, drinking, and staying warm. Whatever you do, don't waste your time traveling at night. Not only is it difficult to navigate at night, but it's also a prime time for accidents to occur.

If you're traveling solo, try to determine your location by reaching an elevated point and assessing the big picture. Find significant landmarks, such as bodies of water and drastic elevation changes, and try to locate them on your map. Don't rush this process! It's all too easy to make the map look like whatever you want when you are under stress (see **bending the map**). Instead, take your time. When you come up with a theory about your location, try to prove yourself *wrong*. Before you begin to travel again, find some landmarks you can use to double-check your location. For example, say to yourself, "If I am where I think I am, then in a quarter mile I should cross a stream. From the stream I should go downhill about 80 feet, and then enter a meadow . . ." Test your theory against your actual surroundings.

When planning your trip, be specific about identifying the challenges of the route and how you'll deal with them. Ensure that every member of your group is comfortable with the terrain and the required map and compass skills. If they aren't, travel strictly as a group or consider an easier route. Decide in advance what to do if someone should get lost, and develop a contingency plan for such an event.

MAPS

Maps are wonderful, exciting, inspiring creations. Look at any map with much wild country on it, and possibilities and adventures spring out. What's that trail like? How beautiful is that alpine lake? What's the best route up that peak? Where are the **water** sources and campsites?

You have to be able to read a map, of course. Otherwise, it's just so much colored ink and confusing lines and symbols thrown on a piece of paper.

The first step in map reading is to learn to distinguish between planimetric and topographic maps. Planimetric maps, as the name suggests, are plans. Features are shown and perhaps the elevation of some individual points is noted, but a planimetric map (such as a typical state highway map) tells you little about the shape or character of the terrain. Everything looks flat.

Topographic (topo) maps, however, show the topography—that is, the actual shape of the land—by means of contour lines. These lines make patterns on the maps that represent the shape of hills and valleys. Understand them, and you can visualize what the terrain will be like, see which slopes look good to climb or ski and which look too steep, and which valleys are wide with gentle passes at their heads and which are box canyons. Topo maps are the standard maps for wilderness travel. Planimetric maps can be useful though, especially for showing roads and towns and other features. U.S. Geological Survey (USGS) maps are topo maps; Forest Service ones are mostly planimetric.

The scale of a map is very important. It tells you how much real **distance** a distance on the map represents. Maps are often referred to as large scale or small scale. This can be confusing because a large-scale map covers a smaller area than a small-scale one. The larger the scale, the more detail a map shows, because a given distance on the map represents a shorter actual distance than on a small-scale map. For example, on a 1:24,000 map, 1 unit on the map equals 24,000 units on the ground, while on a 1:250,000 map, 1 unit on the map equals 250,000 units on the ground. This means that roughly 2.5 inches on the 1:24,000 map represents 1 mile on the ground, while 1 inch on the 1:250,000 map represents 4 miles on the ground.

For wilderness travel, maps with a scale larger than 1:100,000 are best because you need as much detail as possible for accurate navigation. However, smaller-scale maps can be useful for planning because they give a good overview of an area.

USGS topo maps have a scale of 1:24,000. This gives great detail, but a single sheet doesn't cover a large area. There are many non-USGS topo maps, especially for popular areas. These come in various scales, including 1:30,000; 1:40,460; 1:48,000; 1:50,000; 1:62,500; 1:63,360; and more. All are fine for **wilderness** use. Just know which scale you're using, especially when you change maps.

Most maps have a key showing what the various symbols stand for, although many of these are obvious. Maps should also indicate the date of publication and the datum (needed for calibrating GPS units). Older maps are likely to be out of date regarding such information as roads and other developments. However, they may be all you can get for some remote areas that are rarely resurveyed. This is where small-scale planimetric maps can help because they're usually updated more often, especially with human-made features.

Maps are all you need for most navigation, though you should always carry a compass. By relating features you see to the map, you can follow your progress and always know where you are. If this is difficult, try orienting the map, which means turning the map until north on the map is facing north on the ground. Then, for example, a feature northwest of you will now be northwest of where you are on the map too. A line from your position on the map (use the edge of your compass for this) should point at the feature both on the map and on the ground.

See also **bearings**, **compass**, **contour lines**, and **navigation**.

Protecting Maps

Some maps, such as those from Trails Illustrated, are printed on tough waterproof and tearproof plastic. Most maps are still made of paper, however, and therefore vulnerable to rain. Soggy paper maps tear easily and details may be rubbed off the surface, so protecting your map from rain and damp is essential. This can be done in two ways: by storing the map in a waterproof case or by coating the map with a waterproof treatment. A "case" may be no more than a simple plastic bag. Better is a tough purpose-made map case such as that from Ortlieb. A good map case can be sealed

against the weather and folded for carrying in a garment pocket.

Alternatively you can treat paper maps with a product like Map Life or Nikwax Map Proof to make them waterproof and more durable. If you print your own maps from CD-ROMs or websites, waterproof inkjet paper is available (for example Adventure Paper from Fresh Tracks Map Store and Waterproof Paper from Kapco Graphics Products).

Finding Maps

Outdoor stores are a good source of local maps. For further afield, websites such as Map Link, Fresh Tracks Map Store, and the USGS are very useful. Maps can also be downloaded or purchased on CD-ROM from companies such as TopoZone and Topo USA. (See resources section.)

MAYTAGGED

The term *maytagged* refers to what happens to a whitewater paddler who gets stuck in the vicious recirculating water of a **hole** or **hydraulic**. Like a loose piece of laundry in a washing machine, the paddler will go around and around under the water until either he extricates himself or the hole spits him out.

MICE AND OTHER RODENTS

Mice and other small rodents can be a problem when camping because they quickly learn that

> "I was once asleep in a tent with the door open when I was woken abruptly by a sharp pain in my head. I looked up to see a small mouse tugging on a hair. Presumably, it looked like good nesting material."—CT

human food is very tasty. Sometimes it isn't even the food they're after. They've also been known to rummage through camping items for nesting material.

Even if mice can't get your food, they can be a nuisance. To protect food against rodents, people used to make various contraptions out of soft metal and wire mesh. A better bet are the Ursack stuff sacks, which are made from the same Aramid

> "Sleeping under the stars at one site in the Grand Canyon, I was constantly awakened by mice running over my sleeping bag and scrabbling in my pack (it's best to leave packs open, so mice can get in and out without having to bite holes in the fabric). In the end, I pitched the tent just to get away from the mice. They didn't get my food, however, which was in a stuff sack hung from a tree branch. On other occasions, when sleeping in a trail shelter or where there was nowhere to hang my food, mice have bitten holes in the stuff sacks and taken some food."—CT

fabric as bulletproof vests and are designed to withstand animals biting into them (see **bear bagging**). Or you could place a metal or plastic disk (such as a bottle top or can lid) or container on the line suspending the stuff sack to stop mice from running down the cord.

Losing food or being kept awake were the two biggest problems posed by small rodents until the mid-1990s, which brought the first hantavirus outbreaks. This virus, which can cause a serious fatal illness, is spread by rodents, especially deer mice, which are found in most parts of the United States. It's extremely rare, however. Only two hikers, one on the **Appalachian Trail** in the eastern United States and one in the **Sierra Nevada** in the western United States, are known to have caught it.

People catch hantavirus by inhaling it. Mice carry the virus and leave it in their droppings, urine, and bedding. So anywhere mice live may harbor the virus. Disturb the floor of a trail shelter, a common habitat for mice, and the dust that

drifts up may contain the virus. Sleep on ground where mice live, and you could inhale it.

To minimize contact with mice, it's best to sleep in a **tent** or on a **groundcloth** rather than directly on the ground. In shelters, try not to kick up dust or disturb mice droppings—much easier said than done, of course. Certainly avoid touching mice feces. Avoid shacks and derelict buildings completely. Mice also attract rattlesnakes. On the **Appalachian Trail**, where mice-infested shelters are common, some hikers have taken to carrying and setting mousetraps.

MINIMUM-IMPACT CAMPING
See **Leave No Trace**.

MOOSE
Moose are the largest members of the deer family and the second-largest native land animal in North America. Only the bison is bigger. Bull moose can weigh up to 1,800 pounds and reach 10 feet in height. The huge, flat antlers can have a spread of over 6 feet. Simply put, moose are huge. With their humped backs and heavy bodies atop long spindly legs, they look awkward and ungainly, but they can run fast—up to 35 miles an hour—and their long legs are useful for wading through deep **snow** and water. They swim well too and can dive in search of water plants. Moose have large split hooves, which leave tracks 5 to 6 inches long.

Moose are creatures of the cold, snowy northern coniferous **forest** and are found in the **Rocky Mountains** south to Colorado, in much of Canada and Alaska, and in northern New England. Outside North America, they occur in northern Europe and Asia. Moose spend much time in water and are usually found in swamps and near lakes and streams, especially where willows—one of their favorite foods—grow. (*Moose* is an Algonquin word meaning "twig eater.") In addition to willows, they eat other small shrubs and trees, such as poplar and aspen, as well as water plants.

Moose are usually quiet and shy, keeping well away from people. However, in early fall, which is the rutting season, bull moose become very ex-

> "Walking through light forest near a timberline lake, I caught a glimpse of something moving slowly out on the water, something very big. I looked more closely. A huge bull moose with a massive rack of antlers was standing in the shallow lake. Dropping my pack, I crept to the edge of the water, binoculars and camera in hand. Two moose cows were also out in the lake, one of them vigorously plunging its head into the water and emerging draped in dripping green water weeds. For more than an hour, I lay on the ground, watching these ungainly yet magnificent animals. The bull barely moved at all during this time, but the cows were quite active, one of them eventually swimming to shore and trotting off into the forest. Beyond the moose lay the dark forest with deep red cliffs rising above it, a perfect wilderness scene."—CT

cited, noisy, and aggressive. Attacks on people by rutting moose have occurred, resulting in death in some cases, so it's wise to give bull moose a wide berth. Cow moose with young calves can also be aggressive because they are very protective of their offspring, so it's best to stay well away from them too.

MOUNTAIN BIKES

Thinking of hitting the backcountry **trails** on your favorite pedal-powered two-wheeler? If your only bike is the trusty Schwinn Varsity sitting in your garage, plan to leave it behind. While road bikes (such as your average 10-speed bicycle) are built for efficiency on paved roads, mountain bikes are designed to withstand the rigors of serious off-road riding.

The main differences between mountain bikes (sometimes called *ATBs*, or *all-terrain bicycles*)

and road bikes are the specially designed tires, braking systems, handlebars, and gears used in mountain bikes. The wide, knobby tires of a mountain bike provide more traction than the narrow tires of road bikes and are more capable of surviving a mile of sharp gravel or an encounter with a big rock than a thin road tire is. A mountain bike's special cantilever brakes increase braking power—a feature you'll appreciate your first time down a steep, unforgiving slope. The mountain bike's wide, flat handlebars offer better leverage than the curved handlebars of road bikes. This comes in handy when climbing a steep ascent. Also handy in ascents are the 15 to 25 different gears offered by most mountain bikes, a feature made possible by an additional chain ring on the cranks. Finally, the beefy frames of mountain bikes are designed to sustain significantly more abuse than their road-riding cousins.

For a fast way to determine if a mountain bike is the right size for you, straddle the top tube (the tube running between the seat and the handlebars). Lift up on the handlebars until the top tube reaches your crotch; then lower it back down until the front tire is on the ground again. That distance (from the top tube's resting position to resting against your crotch) should be only 2 to 4 inches. If the top tube is lifted more than that, the frame is probably too small. On the contrary, a top tube that rides just beneath your crotch is a painful accident waiting to happen. Better to go with a slightly smaller frame. Next, hop on the saddle and place your feet on the pedals. Rotate your feet until the pedals are at 12:00 and 6:00. In this position, your leg on the lower pedal should be almost fully extended, *almost* being the key word. If the leg is straight enough to lock, lower the seat. If your legs can't extend properly, you will have no leverage with which to pedal. If this is the case, go ahead and raise the seat until your legs are almost straight. While in the seated position, grab the handlebars. Is this a comfortable reach? If not, consider a different frame.

When you have found a bike you really like (you should test-ride a few before you buy), don't leave the shop without a good helmet. This is one sport where a solid helmet is a necessity.

See also **mountain biking**.

MOUNTAIN BIKING

Mountain biking is fun, healthy, and invigorating, and it usually doesn't require lengthy preparation. For some enthusiasts, all it takes is an hour's ride on a good **trail** to satisfy their sense of adventure. But if you want to explore the uneven routes of the backcountry, you'll need to be sure you have the right equipment and good technique.

In selecting a bike, choose one that fits your body (see **mountain bikes**) and is designed for off-road use. Also look into accessories, such as a helmet, gloves, water bottles or hydration packs, an air pump, and a small **repair kit** with a spare tube and a few tools.

Riding over potholes and branches or up and down steep terrain is no simple task. The following tips and a good attitude should help you stay upright, comfortable, and safe.

Descents

Riding downhill is a lot of fun, but good brakes are essential to maintain control. Avoid building up a lot of speed and then slamming on the brakes or using only one brake. Instead, use your brakes frequently, squeezing both with the same amount of pressure. This is important. Because each brake handle controls only one tire, squeezing one without the other could lead to an accident. If you squeeze the front brake too hard, you might flip over your handlebars. If you squeeze the back brake too hard, you're likely to skid.

Keep your weight centered on the bike by raising your body off the seat and onto your feet. If the slope is steep, it helps to shift your weight toward the rear of the bike. You'll be using your knees and elbows as shock absorbers as you bounce down the hill, so try to keep them somewhat loose and flexible, not locked. To increase the lateral stability of the bike, pinch your seat with your thighs. This gives you more points of contact with the bike, which increases your over-all control. Avoid a white-knuckle grip on the handlebars by keeping a loose hold, though not so loose that the handlebars bounce out of your hands. Use your feet to keep your cranks (the arms attached to your pedals) horizontal to the ground (in the 3 o'clock and 9 o'clock position). In this position, your feet are less likely to hit rocks on the trail. Finally, keep tabs on your speed. You'll want to slow down in advance of tight corners, such as **switchbacks**. Think ahead and use your brakes earlier than you would on pavement.

Ascents

Steep ascents may look daunting, but they can be negotiated by keeping up a high cadence (the number of times your feet make a rotation). This requires that you look ahead and choose the right gear before pedaling becomes too difficult. If it becomes hard to pedal, you should have already shifted into a lower gear. While it's tempting to stand up, it's likely that the shift in weight will cause your back tire to spin out, which will make you lose momentum. Instead, remain seated to increase the traction of your back tire. Keep looking ahead and pick out a good line—one that is free of loose debris, branches, or holes.

If you encounter sand, **snow**, or mud, maintain a high cadence. This may mean that you need to downshift—that's fine. Forward momentum is the key to making it through the tough spots. Keep looking ahead, and avoid making abrupt changes in direction. Stay seated to maintain traction. If the mud, sand, or snow is really thick, consider getting off and walking or carrying your bike across. While not ideal, walking or carrying your bike is often the fastest and sometimes the safest option.

Mountain bikers often share trails and backcountry byways with hikers and horsepackers. Most mountain bikers work hard to promote responsible use of backcountry trails. In addition to standard **Leave No Trace** techniques (which include staying on trails and not littering), avoid locking your brakes, because it causes unnecessary damage to the ground. Announce your presence when you're passing other bikers and hikers (a simple "on your left" will do). If you encounter an approaching group (whether hikers, bikers, or horsepackers), stop and pull over to the side of the trail, allowing the other party plenty of room to pass. Livestock are easily spooked, so avoid sudden movements or loud behavior around them.

These basic tips will get you going, but you'll discover that some trails require more advanced skill. When that time comes, get some hands-on instruction from an experienced friend or mountain biking guide (see **guides**). For a good read, check out *Mountain Bike! A Manual of Beginning to Advanced Technique*, by William Nealy; *Mountain Biking*, by Bill Strickland; or *Mountain Bike Technique*, by Steve Jones.

MOUNTAINEERING

Mountaineering is the art and science of climbing **mountains**. No easy task, mountaineering requires that you be fit, smart, experienced, and adventurous. From afar, mountaineering appears glamorous—standing atop high peaks with 360-degree vistas. Indeed, climbing mountains is exciting and rewarding. At the same time, it's one of the most demanding outdoor pursuits. The mountaineer will be exposed to a myriad of challenges: blizzards, **avalanches**, high **wind**, long and difficult approaches, physical discomfort, pain, and often failure. Then why do people do it?

"Because it is there." This was the simple answer that George Mallory blurted out when an annoying reporter pushed him on why he intended to climb Mount Everest. Yet, for an unprepared statement, his short answer seems to pinpoint the thoughts of mountaineers the world over. Why climb mountains? Because they will challenge you like nothing else, their beauty will envelop you, and their demands will haunt you. Like a love affair, you will be seduced to return time and time again. Why climb mountains? The answer is simple—because they are there, and because we can.

The history of mountaineering is filled with exceptional and sometimes tragic accounts of people who push the upper limits. Luckily, the sport has come a long way since the early days of climbing with cotton **ropes** and tweed jackets. Today's mountaineer has the benefit of finely engineered equipment and laboratory-tested clothing. Nonetheless, the act of climbing has changed little, and if you don't have proper skills, you could put yourself in grave danger.

Mountaineering requires you to be proficient at many disciplines, including **rock climbing**, **ice climbing**, **glacier travel**, **camping** and **cooking** at altitude, **first aid**, **rescue**, **navigation**, and general **wilderness** travel. To venture into the mountains without an understanding of these topics is a recipe for disaster. Because not everyone possesses the skills needed to ascend beautiful and lofty peaks, some adventurers choose to travel with a **guide**. Guides can offer the technical know-how and familiarity with a mountain that novices lack. While guides can offer you support and guidance, it is not their role to physically take you to the top. In fact, before you head out on a mountain, you should have, at the very minimum, a working knowledge of the systems and skills that you will employ.

If you're looking to gain those skills, consider taking a course in mountaineering. Several **outdoor schools** offer instruction in mountaineering for all levels of experience. To find one, contact the American Mountain Guide Association (AMGA; see resources section). While there are many excellent guides who are not AMGA certified, AMGA's certification is becoming the U.S. standard. In Europe and Canada, ask for guides certified by the IFMGA (International Federation of Mountain Guides Associations).

As you develop a broad repertoire of skills, you'll be able to explore the wild, remote landscapes of the world. But defying gravity on the world's tallest peaks is not a requirement. In fact, many mountaineers never climb above 15,000 feet. There are plenty of peaks that offer a good challenge without supplemental oxygen! While

RICK SWEITZER

Mountaineering demands that you be adept at many skills, including recognizing mountain hazards. A misstep onto a protruding cornice—this one in the Swiss Alps—could be disastrous (see cornices*).*

the height of the mountain can certainly add risks (see **altitude sickness**), it is the route of the ascent that determines its level of challenge. In fact, there are often several routes up the same mountain; some are walk-ups, while others are daunting endeavors.

Be aware that mountaineering can easily become a full-time avocation. If you are into mountaineering (or want to be) and you're looking for an outlet for your mountain-bred energy, look for a local mountaineering club near you. These clubs can provide camaraderie, outings, instruction, and guest speakers to share tales from around the globe. To find a local club, ask at your local outdoor shop or search on-line. Some universities sponsor mountaineering activities

through their outdoor clubs. If you're more interested in books, you have an assortment to choose from. An old favorite is *Mountaineering: The Freedom of the Hills*, edited by Don Graydon and Kurt Hanson.

MOUNTAIN LION

The largest wild cat in North America, the mountain lion, also known as the *cougar*, *panther*, or *puma*, is found throughout the western United States and Canada and in some areas in the eastern United States, mostly in **forests**, though also in **deserts** that contain plenty of brush. Mountain lions are sandy brown in color and can grow to 8 feet long with a black-tipped tail 2 to 3 feet long. Despite their name, they are more closely related to leopards than to lions.

Mountain lions are solitary and secretive and so are rarely seen. However, you may see their tracks, which are like those of a domestic cat but far larger, with the forefoot print up to 4 inches wide. The tracks are usually in a straight line.

Mountain lions mostly eat deer but will also hunt other animals, including, very rarely, humans. Although attacks on people have increased since the mid-1980s, they're still rare, averaging about 14 a year, with less than one a year being fatal. Statistics vary on attack numbers, but all sources show that the risk is low. Between 1890 and 2002, 17 people were killed by mountain lions in the United States and Canada according to one source, with 9 of these deaths occurring since 1990. Detailed research by Kathy Etling (*Cougar Attacks: Encounters of the Worst Kind*) came up with 284 attacks in total, including 42 fatalities, between 1800 and 2001. To put this in perspective, less than one person a year is killed by a mountain lion, but on average twelve people a year are killed by domestic dogs and around 800,000 need medical attention for dog bites. You are also far more likely to be struck by **lightning** than attacked by a mountain lion. Most **wilderness** travelers never even see a lion.

For a number of reasons, attacks are increasing, albeit slowly and from a very low base. One reason is an overall increase in the number of mountain lions, since they are no longer exterminated as vermin and not hunted at all in many areas. As the numbers increase, more territory is needed, so mountain lions spread into new areas. Given that the human population is growing and that people are moving into mountain lion territory, the chance of encounters is bound to increase.

Mountain lions usually attack from behind and aim for the neck, so if you see one approaching, *don't run*—the lion is likely to classify you as prey and chase you. Instead, stand your ground, act aggressively, shout, wave a stick, or pick up a rock. Chances are the lion will back off. Most known attacks are on people out alone, so traveling in groups is a good defense. In particular, don't let children wander off alone in mountain lion country; lions seem to be particularly interested in children, possibly because they appear to be easy prey due to their size. Dogs may attract lions, so it's best to leave them at home when going into lion country.

MOUNTAINS

Mountains are magnificent, the glorious results of the twisting and cracking of the skin of the earth, further sculptured by the forces of **ice** and **weather**. Just the names of the big mountain ranges—the **Rocky Mountains**, the Alps, the Himalaya, the Andes—are enough to bring a shiver of delight, a quickening of the blood, a stimulation of the senses, and a desire for adventure and exploration.

Everyone knows what a mountain is, and yet actually defining one is difficult. Aesthetically speaking, it can be said that a mountain is a complex landform containing at least some of the following: cliffs, ravines, ridges, spurs, bowls, **glaciers**, icecaps, snowfields, and waterfalls. By contrast, a hill is simpler, a rounded mound with few, if any, features. In this way of thinking, then, a hill can be higher than a mountain.

The classic mountains are alpine mountains, those great white snow spires and domes covered with glaciers and cliffs. Alpine country is some of the most spectacular on earth and a magnet for **wilderness** lovers. All of the highest mountain ranges are alpine, from the original Alps in western Europe to the Andes, Himalaya, Alaskan mountains, and Rockies. The **Cascades** are alpine too, especially the great stratovolcanoes, like Glacier Peak and Mounts Hood, Adams, Rainier, and Baker, along with the tangle of peaks that make up the North Cascades. Technical **mountaineering** skills are required to ascend most alpine mountains.

Similar in form to alpine mountains but drier and with little or no permanent ice or snow are ranges like the Sierra Nevada. Some people describe these as alpine, but overall they have more in common with **desert** mountains found elsewhere in the southwestern United States. These peaks are often easier to climb than alpine ones, though scrambling and even **rock climbing** may be needed.

The lower slopes of many mountains are clad in **forests**, and in some areas the forests reach right to the summits. These forest mountains are wetter and warmer than other mountains. They tend to be more rounded too, in danger even of being thought mere hills. The Appalachians in the eastern United States are classic forest mountains. The terrain, although rugged in places, allows **trails**, including the **Appalachian Trail** and the **Long Trail**, to be built along the crests of the mountains.

MOVING-WATER HAZARDS

The moving waters of a river can provide a great deal of fun. On the flip side, river currents can sometimes be a pain. When currents combine with other river features to create hazards, you may need to carry your canoe or kayak around the dangerous areas. To enjoy the benefits of moving water, you should be aware of these hazards and how to identify them.

Strainers

A strainer can be any object in a river that allows water but not solid objects to pass. Strainers usually take the form of downed trees, fences, or any type of debris that acts as a sieve. Strainers are dangerous because, once you hit one, it becomes very difficult to remain above the surface of the water. If you get sucked below the surface, chances are you'll get stuck in the strainer, unable to push your way through it. In addition, it will be virtually impossible to get back to the surface, even for a breath of air. If you can't avoid a strainer, try to get on top of it (a tricky endeavor). Build enough momentum to force yourself over the strainer or, at the very least, onto it. If you can swim or climb your way onto a strainer, you'll have a much greater chance of surviving this dangerous encounter.

See also **strainers**.

Entrapments

An entrapment is a situation in which you are stuck in the river in a dangerous position. For instance, your foot might become wedged between rocks in the riverbed. Unable to move, you might be overwhelmed by the current and forced beneath the surface.

Another form of entrapment is being caught between your boat and a rock after a capsize leaves you swimming. If you are downstream of your boat, you could become pinned to a rock by the great force of the current holding the boat against you.

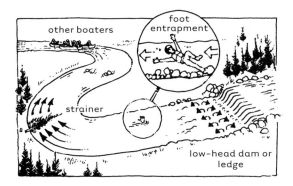

Rivers have many hazards, including dams and ledges, possible entrapments, strainers, and even other boaters.

There's also a danger of becoming caught when a boat is badly damaged. For instance, if the nose of the kayak hits a rock or gets wedged in the bottom of the river after going over a steep drop, it could possibly bend or fold. If you're still in the kayak at the time, you could become trapped.

Most entrapments are avoidable. To avoid foot entrapment, never stand up in a current deeper than your knees. If you have been swimming and are unsure of the depth, don't put your feet down until you can feel the river bottom with your hands. If you must wade into the current, gently feel around with your feet for cracks and potential entrapments before committing your weight to an area.

To avoid being pinned between a rock and a boat, always swim upstream of any object, including your canoe or kayak. This should be the first thing you think of when you capsize: *get upstream of the boat*.

It helps to paddle boats that have adequate **flotation**. Flotation in your canoe or kayak reduces the amount of water that can enter the boat, making it much more buoyant and unlikely to wrap around an object. It also helps to use boats that have some form of internal structure. **Scouting rapids** and being familiar with how to handle drops and tight turns are also important.

Hydraulics
See **hydraulics**.

Undercut Rocks
Boulders, cliffs, and steep banks will often be eroded below the waterline. This could spell trouble if you capsize and find yourself being pushed toward such a feature. The current may be strong enough to hold you against the undercut portion for a long time.

Because you can't know for certain that an object will be undercut, you will have to make an educated guess. Look for areas where the water seems to slam into a rock or boulder. On corners, the current is strongest on the outside bend; this is where you should suspect undercut rocks. If the current is strong, be particularly careful. A strong current will cause erosion faster than a weaker current.

Low-Head Dams and Ledges

Low-head dams often look innocent, sort of like cute little waterfalls. Don't be fooled, however: they are anything but friendly. These drops, with their uniform overflow, create powerful hydraulics that can recirculate boats and swimmers for hours. They are deadly. Ledges can also create dangerous hydraulics. Beware on both the upstream and downstream sides of these hazards. Several paddlers have met their doom by getting too close to such obstructions on the downstream side. There's no surfing these bad boys! Simply stay away.

Floods

A flood can raise the water level dangerously in a matter of minutes, creating rapids out of otherwise calm waters. It can also carry hazardous debris, including downed trees, shopping carts, cars—you name it! Flood danger doesn't come simply because it's raining where you are: rains upstream of you can pose the greater threat. Avoid rivers in flood stage. If you are on a river when it floods, watch out for new rapids and flood debris. If possible, head to shore.

See also **flash floods**.

Other Boaters

Being on the water with other boaters is smart, but running into them isn't. When paddling in moving water, give the boat ahead of you plenty of space. If it becomes stuck or if the paddler decides to play in a hole, you'll need enough time to slow down to avoid a collision. In general, downstream boats have the right of way. Use river signals to tell other boaters when a route is clear and when they should stop and wait (see **paddle signals**).

Bridges

Treat bridges and other human-made obstructions with the same caution you use in approaching rocks and strainers. Be on the lookout for such objects, even if they aren't marked on your maps.

These hazards are not reasons for staying away from moving water. After all, if traveling on a river was dangerous all the time, it wouldn't be such a popular pastime. But being able to recognize hazards is critical to having a safe and enjoyable trip.

MUIR, JOHN

John Muir was one of the most significant **wilderness** thinkers and explorers. His work to preserve **Yosemite** in California marks a key period in the history of wilderness conservation, and his writings remain relevant and inspirational.

Born in Scotland in 1838, Muir immigrated with his family to Wisconsin when he was 11 years old. In 1867 he hiked south to Florida (described in his *A Thousand-Mile Walk to the Gulf*). Then, in 1868, he went to California and visited the **Sierra Nevada**—his "Range of Light"—for the first time, working there in 1869 as a shepherd (also read *My First Summer in the Sierra*). During this work, he saw the damage that overgrazing by these "hooved locusts," as he called them, was doing to the beautiful Sierra meadows. By 1872 he was writing articles for magazines, calling for the preservation of Yosemite and the wilderness. As a result of his efforts, in 1890 Yosemite National Park was created. In 1892 he and a group of friends formed the **Sierra Club**. Muir's first book, *The Mountains of California*, was published in 1894. He died in 1914.

Muir was an excellent field naturalist as well as a conservationist. Through his studies, he determined that the spectacular rock formations of Yosemite and the High Sierra were formed by **glaciers**. He also relished the wilderness, making many solo first ascents, **hiking** untold miles, and **camping** out regularly. Today major sections of the High Sierra are preserved in his name as the John Muir Wilderness, through which the **John Muir Trail** runs.

The influence Muir had and still has cannot be overstated. Roderick Nash notes in his important work *Wilderness and the American Mind* that "as a publicizer of the American wilderness, Muir had no equal."

MULTI-PITCH CLIMBING

Multi-pitch climbing is climbing a rock face that is made up of several pitches. A pitch is the distance that connects two belays. In other words, if a route is extremely long, you won't be able to climb it with one length of **rope**. Instead, you'll need to climb the distance of your rope (or thereabouts), build a new **anchor**, and repeat the process.

A multi-pitch climb begins on the ground with a minimum of two people: a climber and a belayer. Together you work as a team to ascend the route. Before you begin, establish the exact communication commands that you'll use during the climb (see **climbing communication**). In addition, before every new pitch, you should check each other's knots and harnesses. By double-checking each other, you ensure that the knots have been tied and dressed correctly (see **knots**), that the harness buckles are double-backed, and that any **carabiners** are locked.

If you're the first to climb, you will be lead climbing. This means that, as you ascend, you will place pieces of protection along your route. The protection can be either natural (see **natural protection**) or artificial (see **artificial protection**). The purpose of the protection is to prevent you from falling completely off the rock should you miss a move. Because your belayer is able to stop the payout of the rope, you should fall only twice the distance to your last piece of protection.

As lead climber, you will stop and build a new anchor when you run out of either rope or pieces

ANNIE AGGENS

Lead climbing requires excellent protection placement and fluid movement. Here, a lead climber pauses to insert a piece of artificial protection in the rock face.

of protection. You may also see a spot that would make a great ledge for **belaying** and not want to pass it up. Whatever the reason for stopping, at some point you will cease ascending and build a new anchor out of the cracks or boulders that surround you, using whatever pieces of protection you have left. When the anchor is complete, you will clip yourself to the anchor and yell "Off belay" to your belayer. This signals that you're secured to a new anchor and do not require further belay.

At this point, you will prepare to belay your partner. When you are organized and ready, you will yell "On belay!" This means that you are actively belaying your partner. Meanwhile, your partner is now preparing to climb. When he is ready, he will notify you by yelling "Climbing!" and proceed up the same route. Following a lead climber is often referred to as seconding. As the second climber passes the protection that you placed, he will pause and "clean" the route by removing the piece of protection and carefully clipping it to his harness. This is usually a simple process, but every so often a piece of protection

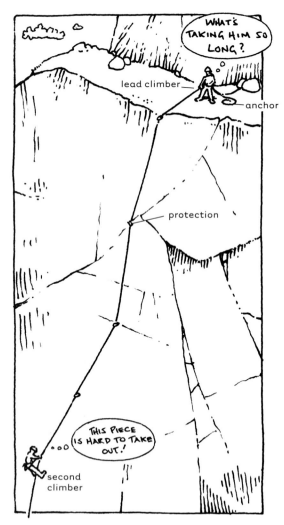

Following, or seconding, involves removing, or "cleaning," the protection placed by the lead climber.

will become so jammed that it's impossible to remove. Because leaving gear behind is less than ideal, the person cleaning the route is often left debating how long he should work to free a piece. Eventually, he will finish his task of cleaning the route and arrive alongside you at the top of the pitch. You will continue to belay the second climber until he's clipped either into the anchor that you built or into one of his own.

If the anchor you built is multidirectional, the second climber may just take a quick break and continue on by leading the next pitch. This eliminates the need for you to switch spots on the rope, which can become difficult and confusing on a small ledge. If the second climber is not experienced with leading, he will reorganize the rope and get himself into position to belay you once again as you lead climb the next pitch.

This process of lead climbing and seconding is repeated the whole way up the route. Some routes consist of only 2 pitches and require very little time. Others have more than 20 pitches and require several days to ascend. It is obvious that multi-pitch climbs are a commitment in more ways than one. As such, they're reserved for climbers who are competent at an assortment of skills, including climbing technique, placing protection, building anchors, and belaying. Furthermore, you need to come prepared with the right type of equipment for any given route. If you would like to participate on a multi-pitch climb but don't have the necessary experience, consider taking a climbing course from an **outdoor school** or hiring a local climbing **guide**.

MUNTER HITCH

The Munter hitch is unique in that it can be used in place of a braking device for **belaying** as well as for **rappelling**. When tied directly to a **carabiner**, the Munter hitch can rotate on the axis of the biner. This allows you to take **rope** in as well as feed it out. At any time, the Munter hitch can provide the necessary friction to stop a descent

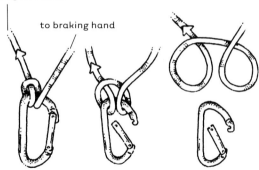

to guide hand

to braking hand

The Munter hitch can be used in place of a belay device. Because the Munter hitch can reverse itself, it works for taking rope in and feeding it out. The strongest braking position for a Munter hitch is with the braking hand close to the guide hand—this is different from many belay devices.

simply by placing your brake hand into a braking position. While the Munter hitch enables a simple belay or rappel brake, it tends to kink your rope more than other devices. Nonetheless, it is often used by mountaineers and is a good alternative if you misplace your favorite belay or rappel device.

N

NATIONAL PARKS

North America is blessed with countless destinations for just about any type of backcountry experience. In the United States, many people take advantage of the 384 "units" that comprise the National Park System. Among these units are 57 national parks. The other 327 sites include national monuments, seashores, lakeshores, recreation areas, battlefields, memorials, and preserves. In all, the NPS (National Park Service) covers more than 83 million acres in 49 states, the District of Columbia, American Samoa, Guam, Puerto Rico, Saipan, and the Virgin Islands (Delaware is the only state without an NPS site).

Organizing a trip to a national park will most likely land you in a beautiful locale. Because most national parks were designated as such for their scenic and historic attributes, you will have no problem finding the picture-perfect spot to pitch your **tent**. The only problem is that you may not be alone. In 2002, the NPS welcomed 277.3 million visitors to their parks. While many of these visitors never leave their RVs, backcountry travel is becoming more and more popular. Take, for example, **Yosemite** National Park in California. In 2002 more than 125,000 backcountry visitors registered to explore the **wilderness** areas of this national treasure. As crowded as it may seem at the start, the masses can usually be lost within a day or two of most trailheads. As

you explore the interior of a national park, you'll discover natural wonders that 99 percent of the park's visitors will never see—and they're usually well worth the trek!

The best way to plan a camping trip to a national park is to contact the park directly. To find contact information for each park, visit the NPS website (see resources section). If you're planning to stay in a park campground or lodge, find out whether it's on the National Park Reservation Service. If so, you can make your reservations through this service (see resources section). Most national park campgrounds are usually booked to capacity months in advance during the high season, so plan early. If you're planning a backcountry trip, make sure to inquire about backcountry **permits**. Some parks issue only a limited number of permits each day, while others have few restrictions. In any case, it is important to know early in your planning the issues regarding backcountry travel. Often, the park officials will be your best source of information regarding routes, local wildlife, **water** sources, and so forth.

If your travels call for visits to several national parks, consider buying a National Park Pass for a yearly fee, which allows you to enter all of the national parks without having to pay the regular entrance fee (which can be fairly steep!). If you are looking for an alternative to the national parks, try visiting a national monument, seashore, or

The 10 Most Popular National Parks in 2002

1. Great Smoky Mountains (North Carolina and Tennessee)
2. Grand Canyon (Arizona)
3. Olympic (Washington)
4. Yosemite (California)
5. Rocky Mountain (Colorado)
6. Cuyahoga Valley (Ohio)
7. Yellowstone (Wyoming, Montana, and Idaho)
8. Grand Teton (Wyoming)
9. Acadia (Maine)
10. Zion (Utah)

Source: National Park Service

10 Least-Visited National Parks in 2002

1. American Samoa
2. Kobuk Valley (Alaska)
3. Lake Clark (Alaska)
4. Gates of the Arctic (Alaska)
5. Isle Royale (Michigan)
6. North Cascades (Washington)
7. Wrangell–St. Elias (Alaska)
8. Katmai (Alaska)
9. Dry Tortugas (Florida)
10. Great Basin (Nevada)

Source: National Park Service

lakeshore. Often overlooked by the masses of tourists, these areas offer exceptional beauty and solitude.

NATURAL HISTORY

Natural history is the study of nature in all its aspects. All **wilderness** travelers are students of natural history, whether they intend to be or not. The movement of **clouds**, the patterns of river water, and the nature of terrain are all part of natural history. Learning about the habits of **bears** or **mice** so you can protect your food from them, studying **glacier** formations so you can avoid **crevasses**, and knowing which rocks give good grip and which are greasy when wet all come under the heading of natural history. It covers everything from birds and flowers to geology and land formations.

> "Binoculars are a great help for discovering nature, and not just for birds and animals. I was once puzzled by what looked like a line of trees on a high desert ridge. Surely there shouldn't be trees in such a dry, exposed place? Through my binoculars, I saw they were saguaro cacti, which can grow to 40 feet high and can look like small trees at a distance."—CT

Every wilderness traveler picks up some natural history knowledge, but enjoyment of the wilderness can be greatly enhanced the more you understand nature and how it works. There are **field guides** to every aspect of natural history, including many excellent single-volume, general guides, for example: *Handbook of the Canadian Rockies*, by Ben Gadd; the Audubon Society's *Field Guide to the Southwestern States*; *Sierra Nevada Natural History*, by Tracy Storer and Robert Usinger; and *Sierra Club Naturalist's Guide to the Sierra Nevada*, by Stephen Whitney. These are worth carrying when weight isn't an issue. Even when weight does figure in, there are tiny booklets, such as the Nature Study Guild Finder series, which weigh less than 2 ounces each.

The best aid to learning about nature is a curious mind. Ask questions, and you will begin to learn the answers. A notebook helps with this so you can jot down ideas, thoughts and, especially, rough descriptions of birds and animals. Take the time to photograph plants. The aim here isn't to take a wonderful picture but to capture an image that enables you to identify the plant later.

Assuage your curiosity in the wilderness by reading about the natural history of an area before going there so you'll better understand what you're seeing when you get there.

NATURAL PROTECTION

Natural protection is a **rock climbing** term that refers to using natural objects, such as trees or boulders, as anchors from which you can either hang your **rope** or belay (see **belaying**). The benefits of natural protection over **artificial protection** are many. Not only is good natural protection typically strong, but it also makes for fast and simple anchors requiring little gear. Like any other type of protection, you must know how to evaluate natural objects for their strength, stability, and direction of pull (see **anchors**).

Trees

Finding a sturdy tree near the edge of your climb is very lucky. Trees provide incredible strength, and they are easy to **sling** as an anchor. In addition, trees are great for multidirectional pulls. The problem comes when the tree isn't perfect and you question its ability to bear significant weight. Perhaps the tree is old, diseased, or simply very small. What then? To judge whether a tree should be used for protection, ask yourself the following questions.

- Is the tree alive? Only use a tree that is alive and healthy. If a tree is dead or diseased, if it has no leaves, or if it has flaking bark or brittle branches and roots, do not use it.
- How large is the tree? Height matters less than diameter: look for a tree at least 6 inches in diameter.
- What is the condition of the root system? Is the tree firmly rooted in deep soil or simply clinging to the cliff through sheer perseverance? Any tree that has shallow roots or is rooted in sand, gravel, or **scree** should be avoided.

Test a tree by giving it a good shove. While this will not simulate the force generated by a falling climber, it will give you some sense of its strength. If you decide to use the tree, sling the

Trees used for anchors should be healthy and with trunks at least 6 inches in diameter.

tree as low as possible to avoid unnecessary torque on the trunk.

Boulders

When evaluating a boulder, the first thing you'll notice is its size. For the most part, the larger and heavier the boulder is, the less likely it is to move. Therefore, the bigger the boulder, the better. There are some exceptions to this rule. First, if the boulder is too big you may not have enough webbing to sling it. Second, a big, heavy boulder that is teetering on a small pebble is a recipe for disaster. The only thing worse than having your anchor fail is having it fail and then having a 2,000-pound rock fall on top of you.

Whenever you choose a boulder for protection, consider its purchase on the ground and surrounding rocks. How likely is it that this rock can budge? Is it crumbly? If so, what could happen if a part of the rock crumbles away? If a shift in the boulder's center of gravity could dislodge it, consider it questionable. If the boulder is lying on gravel or sand, also question its stability. Boulders don't always offer multidirectional protection, so make sure you check that the direction of pull on the boulder will only increase its stability.

Chockstones

In earlier days, adventurous climbers would wedge stones into the constrictions of cracks and run their ropes behind the stones. Their hopes were that, if they should fall, the stones would stay wedged in the crack and keep their rope attached to the cliff. This was often their only form of protection. In fact, on their approach to the climbs, the climbers would choose a variety of stones in different shapes and sizes and haul them up the climb. Fortunately, the modern climber has more options available.

Nonetheless, natural chockstones that are found already in place during a climb can still be used as effective protection, if necessary. Evaluate a chockstone for its structural integrity. Will it crack, flake, or crumble? If so, disregard it. Also look at the chockstone's position in the crack. The crack should be constricting so that a downward (or outward) direction of pull only wedges the stone further into the crack. In addition, the stone should have good surface contact with the sides of the crack. If the stone is merely resting on a crystal or small protrusion, don't rely on it, because the protrusion could easily break off.

Knobs and Horns

Knobs, horns, and other protrusions from the rock can be used for protection, but it's often difficult to assess their security. Be aware that these protrusions can easily break off the rock, causing a major hazard for the climber and anyone below. Check the knob, horn, or flake for signs that it is cracking or becoming loose. Try to determine the extent of its connection to the main wall, and also consider the direction of pull. If the protrusion is rounded or shallow, it may be easy for the sling to slide off.

Anytime you're using natural protection to build an anchor, you should be redundant. In other words, using a big tree for protection is OK, but it is much better to use a tree plus a boulder, or two trees. Doubling up can save your life if you incorrectly evaluate the integrity of any one object.

Never assume that natural protection will be available or suitable for your use. If you're climbing in a new area, bring a full assortment of artificial protection to complement any natural protection that you may find. If you frequently visit a favorite climb that uses natural protection, reevaluate the protection each time you use it. Trees may become diseased, struck by **lightning**, or otherwise damaged between your visits. Likewise, boulders can crack or move with changes in the seasons.

THE NATURE CONSERVANCY

The Nature Conservancy is a nonprofit organization whose mission is to preserve the plants, animals, and natural communities that represent life on earth by protecting the lands and waters they need to survive. Founded in 1951, the Nature Conservancy has acquired more than 92 million acres worldwide through gifts, purchases, exchanges, and easements. It offers Adopt-an-Acre programs that combine the efforts of thousands of individuals to purchase endangered rain forests and other significant ecosystems worldwide. To learn more about the Nature Conservancy and to get involved with conservation efforts near your hometown, visit their website (see resources section).

NATURE'S COMPASS

Having a good sense of direction is a practical quality when traveling in the **wilderness**. If you're lucky, you might have the innate ability to determine north from south or east from west. But what happens if you aren't blessed with an internal **compass** or, worse, if you lose your compass and are unable to determine the cardinal directions?

Fortunately, nature has provided a few natural clues for determining direction. You may remember hearing that moss grows on only one side of a tree or that leaves always face south, but many of these tales are filled with inconsistencies. For instance, moss can grow on all sides of a tree, and simply too many variables exist to generalize the growth patterns of leaves. There are, however, a few fairly reliable tactics you can use to determine the cardinal directions with nothing more than the sky overhead.

The earth's relationship to the sun allows for several natural compass techniques. The easiest requires a sunny day and knowledge of the local time. If you're wearing an analog **watch**, orient it so the hour hand points in the direction of the sun. (If you have only a digital watch, use a stick to draw the time on the ground, clock style, with the hour hand pointing toward the sun.) Next, note the direction of 12:00. There will be two points on the edge of the watch face that lie exactly halfway between the hour hand and 12:00; one will lie clockwise on the arc, the other will lie counterclockwise. If you connect these points with a line you have found your north–south axis. One end of the axis bisects the shorter arc on the watch face; point in that direction. If it is between 6 A.M. and 6 P.M., the direction you're pointing will be approximate south. If it is between 6 P.M. and 6 A.M., the direction you're pointing will be approximate north. If you are in daylight saving time, substitute 1:00 for 12:00. If you're in the Southern Hemisphere, line the sun up with 12:00 (instead of the hour hand). Bisect the shortest distance between 12:00 and the hour hand to discover approximate north.

Another technique provides a relatively accurate east–west line over the course of several hours. Find a straight stick about 3 feet long, and place it vertically into flat ground. Find the tip of the stick's shadow and mark it with a small stone. Next, take a string and run it from the stone to the base of the stick. Holding one end of the string at the base of the stick, use the other end (at the stone) as a guide to create a perfect circle in the ground around the stick. The stone should lie on that circle.

As time passes from morning to afternoon, the length of the stick's shadow will shorten and then grow long again. When the shadow becomes long enough again to touch the circle, mark the spot with another stone. Draw a straight line from the first stone to the second stone. This is your approximate east–west axis, with the first stone on the west end of the line and the second stone on the east end of the line. To determine north and south, stand on the line with your left shoulder

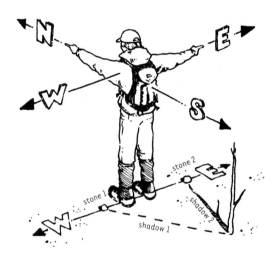

A relative east–west line can be determined by tracking a stick's shadow over the course of several hours. An upright stick casts a long shadow in the morning and a second long shadow in the afternoon. Mark the tip of the morning shadow with a stone and measure its length. When the afternoon shadow reaches the same length, mark it with another stone. Draw a line on the ground connecting the two stones. The line will run approximately east–west.

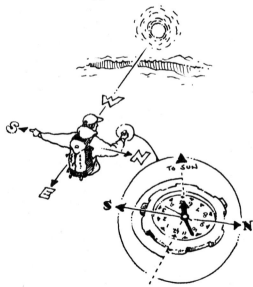

By pointing the hour hand of an accurate analog watch toward the sun you can determine an approximate north–south axis.

pointing west and your right shoulder pointing east. North will be straight ahead of you, and south will be behind you.

If sunlight eludes you all day but you are blessed with a clear night sky, the stars themselves make an excellent compass. Anytime you look to the sky in the Northern Hemisphere, you should be able to identify the North Star. Contrary to popular belief, the North Star is not the

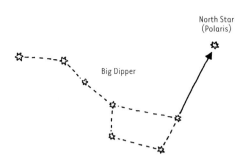

When you are facing the North Star—found in the Northern Hemisphere by following the front two stars of the Big Dipper—north will be directly in front and south behind you.

brightest star in the sky (a distinction held by Sirius). Rather, the North Star can be found by locating the two stars that create the farthest right edge of the Big Dipper. Follow an imaginary line through the two stars toward the top of the sky, and you will find the North Star. When you're facing the North Star, north will be directly in front of you, south behind you, east to your right, and west to your left.

While these natural compass techniques are fun to use and good to know in an emergency, the best **navigation** trick is to keep close tabs on your **map** and compass and to be familiar with your route. There simply is no substitute for good navigation skills. Likewise, a good **contingency plan** is a real comfort if you become **lost** on your trip.

NAUTICAL CHARTS

Nautical charts are **maps** of open or coastal waters. They provide crucial information, such as

the depth of the water, the direction and speed of **coastal currents**, and the location of tidal flats. In addition, they mark lighthouses, buoys, and even the occasional shipwreck. Nautical charts are as important to the coastal paddler as topographical maps are to the backpacker. Without a nautical chart, the paddler will be unable to predict the behavior of **waves** or the composition of a shoreline.

Like any other type of map, nautical charts have several different scales. For the purposes of paddling, you'll want the largest scale possible (the most detailed chart). This will allow you to explore the nooks and crannies of the shoreline—something you can only do in a sea kayak. It is obvious from the size of most nautical charts that they aren't made for paddlers: by the time you fold your chart into a size suitable for your map case, it's as thick as a club sandwich. If possible, use a large map case and try to avoid having to open and refold the map while on the water.

Reading a chart takes practice. Unlike topo maps, many nautical charts don't display land-based elevation changes. This means you have to rely on other clues to help you navigate. To use your **compass** with a nautical chart, you need to be familiar with compass roses and have some understanding of deviation. In addition, there are a host of symbols that take some getting used to. A description of nautical charts and how to use

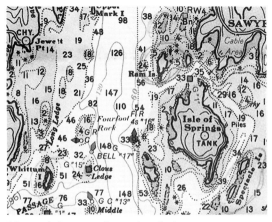

Nautical charts are the sea kayaker's topo maps.

them is in David Burch's *The Fundamentals of Kayak Navigation*. You may also find *How to Read a Nautical Chart*, by Nigel Calder, helpful. To find the nearest authorized dealer of nautical charts, check out the National Oceanic and Atmospheric Administration website (see resources section). Authorized dealers also carry chart surveys, which help you determine the exact chart you need for your destination.

NAVIGATION

Navigation is an essential **wilderness** skill. Learn to navigate, and the freedom of the backcountry is yours. Without navigational expertise, you have to stick to well-marked **trails**, and even then you are at risk of going astray if you wander off the trail or take a wrong turn.

There are two aspects to navigation: (1) planning and following a route using a trail guide or a **map** and **compass** or **GPS**, and (2) route finding on the ground. The latter is normally only necessary when going cross-country or when **snow** covers the trails.

> "I regularly use two natural phenomena for backup navigation. These are the sun and the wind. I note where they are in relation to my route, so I'll notice if their position changes and realize I've veered off course. When doing this, it's important to check the wind direction, just in case it has changed, and keep track of the time, so you know where the sun should be."—CT

Good navigation starts before the actual trip with the planning of your route. For any plans more complex than following a trail, go over your route just before you set out and check your progress regularly. Look at the route at rest stops and in camp in order to stay familiar with it. That way, you know how far it is to the next **water** source or proposed campsite.

While on the move, keep your navigational tools handy so you can consult them whenever you need to. If your map and compass are buried in your pack, it's all too easy to make guesses instead of stopping to get them out. If your guess is wrong, it could take far longer to correct the error than stopping to find the map. When in a group, it's best to still keep an eye on the navigation, even if someone else is leading. The leader could make a mistake, or you could become separated from the rest of the group. If you think the leader has gone wrong, say so.

Following a good trail is easy and usually requires only an occasional glance at your map or trail guide at trail junctions or prominent features so you don't take a wrong turn and so you know where you are. Trails are usually signed with blazes on trees or by **cairns** or ducks (small piles of stones) in open areas (see **trail markers**). As long as you see these occasionally and the trail is clear on the ground, you should have no problems. Take care at junctions though, particularly unsigned ones, because you could wander off on an old, unused trail or even an animal track. If what should be a good trail becomes indistinct and hard to follow and there are no waymarks, turn back to the last junction. Note the time at any junction so you'll know how long it will take to get back to it if you need to.

It's also easy to take the wrong trail at an unmarked junction, especially if it isn't marked on the map or described in the trail guide. Seeing two or three trails on the ground where there's only one on the map can be confusing. Some of these may be trail relocations, or they could be new trails. Either way, the map or guide is out of date. The first thing to do is check for blazes or waymarks. If one trail has these but not the others, it's probably the right one. Of course, if all the trails are blazed, this won't help.

Rather than guess, use your map and compass to find out which trail goes the right way. The easiest way to do this is to look for obvious features—such as creeks, lakes, or cliffs—that the correct trail passes, take a **bearing** on them, and then follow the trail nearest to that bearing. In open country, you may be able to see the feature, in which case you simply take the trail heading toward it. If you note the time and the distance on the map to the feature, you should know roughly how long it will take to get there. If you see no sign of the feature even after it should have appeared, turn back and take the next most likely trail. Notice too the line a trail takes, and compare it with the trail on the map. If the trail is descending or following a valley bottom and the map shows the trail climbing, you're probably on the wrong trail. Note the compass direction too, and check it every so often to make sure the trail hasn't changed direction, something that's easy not to notice. If an unexpected feature does appear, try to locate it on the map.

With a GPS, you can plot in the coordinates of a point farther ahead on the trail and the place where you are and then take the trail that lies on the route the GPS gives between the two points.

Occasionally a perfectly good, well-signed trail may suddenly disappear into brush or **avalanche** debris or blowdowns. Chances are it will reappear on the far side. However, it may not cross the obstruction in a straight line. If safe and easy to do so, you can cross to the far side and begin searching along the edges for the trail. More often though, you'll need to follow the edges around the obstacle. While you do this, keep an eye out for signs of the trail, such as an artificial-

Plan your route carefully when going cross-country in steep, rugged terrain. Take care not to get into a difficult situation it's hard to retreat from, and be prepared to backtrack and find another route if necessary.

looking straight line through the trees or cut branches and logs. Spending time searching for the trail is normally far better than heading off cross-country and hoping you'll come across it.

Even if you take the wrong trail for miles, it only means it will take a while to retrace your steps. Once you go cross-country, however, everything changes. First, any planning you've done will give you only a direction to head, not the detail of the actual route. The details usually have to be worked out as you travel. Your plan may be to hike up a particular valley and then cross the pass at its head. The route you take up the valley will depend on the nature of the terrain and the vegetation, because trying to follow a direct line will likely result in a slow, frustrating journey. It's always easiest to take the line of least resistance, even if this doubles or triples the distance hiked. Perhaps the valley bottom is choked with brush or the **forest** there is dense. In that case, the mountainside above the trees may make for easier walking, enabling you to contour around (follow a line of the same approximate elevation) to the pass. If you stay in the valley, look for meadows, creek banks, animal trails, and open forest, and be prepared to zigzag all over the place in order to link these. A good route finder will seek out such easy terrain while always keeping an eye on the compass to avoid getting completely turned around. When going cross-country, you should always be thinking about the best route and constantly making small adjustments to your route.

If you can survey the terrain from a high point, use this as an opportunity to plan out the next part of the route. Scan the land ahead with **binoculars**, if you have them, looking for the best route. Think about the topography and the type of vegetation too. Once you understand the nature of the land, it is much easier to tell where the best **hiking** is likely to be.

Sometimes when going cross-country, you'll need to retrace your steps because of an insurmountable obstacle. To make this easier, frequently turn around and look back to see where you've come from. That way, the land will look

CHRIS TOWNSEND

at least a little familiar if you have to find your way back.

You can, of course, navigate by natural phenomena. The primary way of doing this includes using the stars in **celestial navigation**. (See also **nature's compass**.)

NIGHT TRAVEL

The world changes when darkness falls, becoming mysterious and secretive, sometimes disturbing, and even frightening. The darkness isn't totally impenetrable though. Once your eyes adjust to low light levels, you begin to see shadowy shapes and vague outlines, some recognizable, some unclear. To move confidently in the dark, you have to learn to see in monochrome. All color leeches from the world at night; everything mutes to a shade of gray. Only the sky, if clear, is sharper and more distinct than in daytime, alive with stars and, when it's visible, the pale orb of the moon.

> "Bad weather can make night hiking even more eerie. I once followed a narrow, rocky trail along the side of a mountain lake on a stormy night with mist drifting over the water and all around me. If I used my headlamp, the beam just bounced back off the wet fog, so I had to hike by what little light there was. Below me, the water shimmered and shivered, apparently floating in the air. The trail rose and fell, but I could never tell how far below me the water lay. Rocks loomed up out of the darkness, insubstantial and hazy. The wet, silver thread of the trail wound through dark vegetation, an unreal, magical-seeming thread leading on into the dark heart of the mountains. It was easy that night to believe in the supernatural, and it would have been simple to conjure spirits and beings out of the swirling pale mist."—CT

With your sight limited, your other senses are enhanced. Hearing becomes acute, and you hear every twig snap, every leaf rustle. Your sense of smell is sharpened too, and the land gives off many complex scents.

It's preferable to use artificial light as little as possible when traveling at night. This is most easily done when there is a bright moon but can be done in open areas without a moon, as long as the sky isn't covered with low, dark clouds. Once you switch on a flashlight or headlamp though, your vision is limited to its cone of pale light, unless you cover it with a red lens or cloth (a red **bandanna** is good for this).

Snow makes night travel easier too, and snow and moon together are excellent. Skiing through forests at night under a full moon with the black, frosty sky glittering with stars is a wonderful experience. By visually connecting patches of pale moonlight between the black shadows of the trees, you can ski quite quickly, but beware of skiing into those shadows because the visible world suddenly ceases when you do and you can see nothing.

Once your eyes adjust to the dimness of nighttime, you can learn to distinguish between different shades and different shapes. Pale gray lumps may mean rocks; darker gray, the **trail** or forest floor. Silvery lines and patches mark water. Avoid total blackness: it could be a hole in the ground or a big rock. If you have to go into one of these black holes, prod it with a ski or **trekking pole** first.

Don't expect to move as fast at night as during the day. Greater care and concentration are required, and the occasional stumble is inevitable. A slow pace means you're less likely to end up on your face or flat on your back. Following a trail is more difficult at night too. Indeed, to some extent, going cross-country is easier because you're not trying to stay on one thin line of dirt that disappears into blackness every so often.

Few people choose to travel at night, although it's interesting to do so, particularly when the moon is full. Also, the experience prepares you for when you have no choice. For example, a lack of **water** or decent campsite may mean you prolong your day and push on into the dark. In many areas, this is fairly safe as long as you're careful. However, don't hike at night in **bear** country unless you're in a large group, or on steep mountainsides at any time.

> "On the Pacific Crest Trail, I hiked at night a few times in the Mojave Desert along with three other thru-hikers. However, after we were startled by a rattlesnake, which eventually turned out to be between one hiker's legs, we stuck to hiking in daylight. On another night hike, in the Grand Canyon, I followed a narrow trail around the back wall of a huge rock amphitheater, all the time aware that on one side the ground fell away steeply into nothingness. On the rim of the Grand Canyon, I had the most wonderful and awesome night hike ever, with a brilliant starry sky and the canyon a great, black, bottomless cleft stretching out into the distance with just the tops of the cliffs visible."—CT

Hikers sometimes choose night hiking in the desert as a way to escape the heat of the day. However, one problem with this is rattlesnakes, which are hard to distinguish from sticks and which like to lie across warm trails and tracks at night (see **snakes**). The best ways to avoid them are to use a headlamp, stay on the trail, tamp the ground ahead of you with a hiking staff, and be alert.

NOISE

Many people go to the **wilderness** for peace and quiet, for an escape from the constant, draining noise of urban living. The silence of a star-filled **desert** night or a placid lake deep in the **forest** can refresh and heal. Of course, the wilds are not always, or even often, quiet. The rush of a mountain creek, the roar of wind in the treetops, the songs of birds, the unearthly wailing of coyotes or bugling of elk—the wilderness has many noises. Thunderstorms can be deafening, while many campers have been woken at daybreak by the harsh cries of jays. All these noises are a natural part of the wilderness, part of the world travelers come to enjoy.

Totally different are the noises of human machinery and even, if raucous and prolonged, human voices. The sound of a motor can totally shatter feelings of solitude, quiet, and connection with nature. Of course, motorized vehicles aren't allowed in wilderness areas, and most wilderness lovers will head for areas where encounters with motors shouldn't occur. There are other sources of noise however, especially radios. All of us have heard music blaring across the landscape, totally dominating a wild area. Listening to music in the wilderness is fine as long as you use headphones. If you like to make your own music with whistle, flute, harmonica, or other portable instrument, camp well away from others and play your instrument quietly, please.

Groups should be careful about keeping the noise down too. People often don't realize how far sounds carry when it is quiet and still. It's easy for laughter and shouting to disturb others. Youth groups are often exuberant and excitable and can easily become very noisy. Those in charge of such groups should try to keep the noise level low, especially at night, and should set up camp far from others, which means staying away from popular sites.

Overall, not being noisy in the wilderness is simply being courteous and thinking of others so you don't disturb them.

NOLS

The National Outdoor Leadership School (NOLS) is the leading **outdoor school** in the United States. NOLS trains over 3,500 students a year in the skills, **judgment**, and leadership techniques necessary to travel safely in the **wilderness**. Courses range from **mountaineering** and **rock climbing** to **sea kayaking**, **whitewater canoeing**, and **horsepacking**. In addition, they offer a wide variety of specialty courses, including those designed for people over 25 years of age and courses created especially for outdoor educators. As the largest wilderness **permit** holder in the United States, NOLS organizes over 300 **expeditions** annually, most 30 days long. It also has played a critical role in developing **Leave No Trace**, a program that has become the standard minimum-impact camping ethic. NOLS also offers courses abroad and has branches on four continents. To find out more about NOLS, visit their website (see resources section).

NORDIC SKIING

See **ski touring**.

NORTHERN LIGHTS

See **aurora borealis**.

OPEN-WATER HAZARDS

For some people, paddling on a big lake or exploring a coastal region is the perfect way to escape the stresses of a hectic life. Large bodies of water can be peaceful and invigorating. They can also be as wild, unpredictable, and dangerous as any other aspect of the wilderness. Whether you are on an expedition in the Arctic or simply out for an afternoon paddle in an urban area, it's important to bear in mind the hazards associated with paddling in open water.

One of the largest impacts on the character of open water is **weather**. Weather patterns, both local and distant, create conditions that can be either relaxing and fun or terrifying and deadly. Wind, air and water temperature, **fog**, and **lightning** are among the hazards that must be considered. The best preparation for weather-related hazards is to monitor the weather with all available resources, including radios, instruments, and observation.

Wind

Wind can be a paddler's friend or foe. A nice tailwind can create perfect conditions for sailing your canoe or kayak, but with a little more strength the wind can create challenging obstacles. Being **windbound** for a day or two is often a safe, relaxing alternative to paddling in strong wind. On big bodies of water, wind blowing onshore makes cer-

Wind is a major factor when paddling. This windstorm came suddenly, with little warning. Seemingly small waves were actually quite large, and the wind was blowing ferociously. Even a few feet from shore, the waves could have capsized a canoe, or even a kayak.

tain hazards, such as waves and surf, easy to identify from the shore. However, wind blowing offshore can be deceptive. From the shore, the water may look surprisingly calm and inviting, but an offshore wind can rapidly blow a paddler out to open water and more dangerous conditions. Strong winds can appear to come out of nowhere, so it's best to err on the conservative side when paddling on large bodies of water. (See also **wind**.)

Waves

Strong winds generate waves that can compromise the stability of any boat and create conditions ripe for capsizing. This is particularly true if the waves start to crest or if you enter a surf zone. Big waves might be just what you're looking for if you are out to practice your rescue skills and you are prepared with rescue equipment and experienced partners; more often than not, however, a capsize in rough conditions creates a worst-case scenario. In a canoe or a kayak, even waves of 1 to 2 feet can seem pretty big. Your head is only a couple of feet above the water; when waves build to 3 feet or higher, you'll occasionally lose sight of shore and other paddlers. In this situation, you must have solid paddling skills, an action plan that includes possible landing sites, and practiced group communication. (See also **waves**.)

Temperature

When considering an open-water excursion, find out the temperature of both the air and the water. Most people take extra precaution when the air temperature is cold by wearing multiple layers and bringing extra **clothing**. The greater hazard, however, often lies in the temperature of the *water*. If it is 70°F and sunny outside but you're paddling in

When the water—or air—is cold, dress defensively. A wet suit (left) or dry suit (right) are good options. Under the wet suit, the paddler is wearing a thermal top. Hats and gloves help contain heat. Neoprene booties or rubber boots do a good job of protecting your feet.

40°F water, it does you no good to be in a T-shirt and shorts when your boat tips over. Capsizing in water that cold will lead to loss of consciousness in a matter of minutes unless you are prepared with the right apparel (see **cold-water survival**). Even water temperatures in the mid-60s can quickly lead to **hypothermia** (remember that your body temperature is a whopping 98°F!).

The best rule of thumb is to dress for the water temperature, not the air temperature. This often means wearing a wet suit or dry suit even on warm days. Always keep aware of how hot or how cold you are. It's possible to get heat exhaustion on the water. Much more likely, however, is getting too cold. If it's a nasty day out and you need to make some miles on the water, plan ahead by eating lots of fatty food and having extra clothing layers easily accessible.

Fog

All bodies of water are susceptible to fog. Fog occurs when the temperature of the air near the surface reaches its saturation, or dew, point. If you have warm, humid air passing over a cold body of water, beware of approaching fog. Fog can obstruct your view of just about anything, including fellow paddlers, your destination, the shore, and approaching vessels.

Because fog can occur quickly and unexpectedly, you should always carry a **compass** and know the **bearing** to your destination. When paddling in a group, stick close enough together that you can communicate in the event of a dense fog. In heavily traveled waters, be familiar with the shipping lanes so you can avoid them. Many paddlers carry foghorns to make their presence known. Small radar reflectors will make you appear as an object on a ship's radar screen. The best way to be prepared in fog is to have a plan of action, including practiced **navigation** skills and good group communication. (See also **fog**.)

Lightning

If you find yourself on open water during a storm, lightning can be a serious hazard. The best course of action is to head toward shore as fast as possible. But if the only landing is a rocky shore with huge surf, you'll have to weigh the options. If getting to shore is a reasonable option, choose an area that offers more protection than you had on the water. If you're using a sail, disassemble it and remove the mast. (See also **lightning**.)

Non-Weather-Related Hazards

The following hazards can be found in all weather conditions.

Submerged Objects

Shoals, outcroppings of rock, and even shipwrecks can create obstacles for the paddler in open water. In calm conditions, it's usually easy to identify these objects—they may even be marked on your **map**—and exploring them can be a lot of fun. In rougher seas, such features can be tough to identify amid the confusion of whitecaps and swirling water. Look for unusual breaks in the patterns of the waves, and avoid areas with spray shooting into the air. Pay attention to changes in the color of the water, which may signify something just below the surface. It is often easier to identify submerged objects from a distance, because you can compare the pattern of a suspect area to that of the surrounding water.

Other Boats

Other kayaks and canoes aren't usually a concern, but bigger boats are. There are rules of the road for boating just as there are for driving, and you need to know them. But keep in mind that the driver of an approaching boat may not be familiar with the rules or with who has the right of way. He may even be drunk or not paying attention.

The safest tactic is to be acutely aware of your surroundings and your escape routes. Do what you can to make you and your boat visible, including use of bright colors, multiple boats, paddles in the air, and lights at night. Remember that you are a small object and close to the water. If you think a boat doesn't see you, get out of the way quickly.

ORIENTEERING

Orienteering is an organized sporting event that combines cross-country travel (usually on foot, although ski, canoe, horse, and mountain bike orienteering events are also held) with map and compass skills. Orienteering usually takes place in forests but sometimes in open terrain. It began in Sweden in 1918 and gradually spread to other countries, although a world championship wasn't held until 1966, and the United States didn't have a National Orienteering Federation until 1971; Orienteering Canada was founded in 1968.

In an orienteering event, participants copy the position of points they must go to (known as *controls*) onto their maps and then set off at intervals to find each control in turn and punch or stamp a card there to show they've visited it. Controls are marked by orange and white flags but can't usually be seen until you're almost on top of them. Participants can take any route they like; one of the skills lies in picking a good route, which is often not the most direct one. The winner of a competition is the one who completes the course (visits every control) in the shortest time. Those seeking a fast time run, but some people are quite happy to walk the course.

Orienteering can be done with ordinary maps, but in most events special 1:15,000 or even 1:10,000 topographic maps are used. These show far more features—such as boulders and ditches—than standard topos and are ideal for the micro-navigation needed to locate a control hidden in a clump of bushes.

Orienteering is an excellent way to learn and improve your **navigation** skills.

OUTBACK OVEN

The Outback Oven is a lightweight contraption that allows backcountry travelers to bake over their camp **stoves**. It consists of a nonstick frying pan and lid, a flame disperser (to buffer the frying pan from the direct flame), a flexible fiberglass dome-shaped cover (that encompasses the frying pan and traps heat), and a thermometer to indicate the approximate temperature inside. With a little practice the Outback Oven can make some wonderful baked foods, like pizza or fresh bread. The Outback Oven comes in three sizes and weighs as little as 7 ounces.

While the Outback Oven is fun, it is extra weight and is more a specialty item than a necessity. In other words, you don't need one to become a regular backcountry chef. There are many ways to bake in your **camp kitchen**, and some of them require nothing more than your standard **cook kit**. See also **baking** and **fires**.

OUTDOOR SCHOOLS

Thinking of paddling whitewater? Want to become a mountaineer? Interested in learning survival techniques? If you want to learn a new set of skills but are unsure of where to find instruction, consider taking a course from an outdoor school. There are hundreds of outdoor schools, centers, and institutes worldwide that specialize in everything from whitewater kayaking to fly-fishing to **search and rescue**. A quick search on the Internet for "outdoor schools" will turn up a multitude of options. Among them are such schools as the National Outdoor Leadership School (**NOLS**) and **Outward Bound** (see resources section). If you can't find what you are looking for on-line, flip through advertisements in the back of outdoor magazines.

Most schools offer an assortment of courses that range in length and intensity, and some offer transferable college credit. Check out the school's mission or core curriculum to ensure that it matches your **goals and expectations**. Finally, check into the school's reputation. Ask the school for references, and ask about the qualifications of its staff and about the instructor-to-student ratio.

OUTWARD BOUND

The Outward Bound schools (there are 50 internationally) are outdoor schools that offer challenging wilderness courses ranging from sailing to **rock climbing**. Students of all ages can regis-

ter for courses that are as short as a few weeks or as long as several months. Outward Bound was created in Great Britain during World War II as a way to teach young men endurance. In 1963 it was brought to the United States, where it grew exponentially. The core principles of Outward Bound are challenge and adventure, character development, learning through experience, compassion and service, and social and environmental responsibility. To find out more about Outward Bound, visit their website (see resources section).

OVERHAND KNOT

The overhand knot is the simple knot you use every day to tie your shoes. While the overhand knot has many purposes, the overhand on a bight—a quick and easy way to create a loop in a rope—is the variation that is tied most often (see **knots**). While not as strong as the **bowline**, the overhand on a bight is fast and can be tied in the middle of the rope.

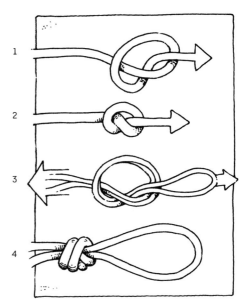

The overhand knot makes a great stopper knot, which is used to prevent rope from slipping through an object. 1. Create a loop and feed the running end (see knots) through the loop. 2. Tighten by pulling both ends. 3–4. The overhand on a bight is one of the fastest ways to tie a loop.

P

PACE

The right pace is often all that separates novices from experienced walkers. Different for every hiker, it's the one you can comfortably maintain hour after hour. Good hikers also know when and how to vary their pace to take into account changes in the terrain, especially rough ground and steep slopes.

The classic mistake inexperienced hikers make is to set off at too rapid a pace, charging up the trail as fast as they can. Later in the day, as in the fable of the tortoise and the hare, experienced hikers—going the steady pace they have held since starting out—pass the inexperienced hikers.

Hiking at the right pace is the least tiring way to walk. However, in a group some compromise has to be made. If it's safe, the group can spread out, with individuals setting their own pace. Ensure that everyone is familiar with the route and that you have prearranged meeting places (see also **contingency plans**). When you must stay close together, the slowest person should set the pace. Otherwise, he may fall behind the group or become exhausted. Even if he manages to keep up, which is unlikely because it's difficult to maintain a faster than normal pace for long, he won't be having much fun.

PACIFIC CREST TRAIL

The Pacific Crest Trail (PCT) is one of the three great south–north **trails** in the United States and the second trail to be designated a National Scenic Trail. Along with the **Appalachian Trail** (the first National Scenic Trail) and the **Continental Divide Trail**, it makes up the **Triple Crown**, a distinction awarded by the American Long Distance Hiking Association–West to hikers who complete all three.

The PCT runs for some 2,650 miles from Mexico to Canada through the deserts and transverse ranges of southern California, the **Sierra Nevada** in central and northern California, and the **Cascades** in Oregon and Washington.

The first idea for a "trail winding down the heights of our western mountains" came from Catherine Montgomery in 1926, according to Joseph T. Hazard in his 1945 book *Pacific Crest Trails*. Montgomery relayed the idea to the Mount Baker Club in Bellingham, Washington, which set about with other mountain clubs to promote it. In 1928 the Forest Service of Washington and Oregon began to build the Cascade Crest Trail from Canada to Oregon, followed by the Oregon Skyline Trail through Oregon to California. Both these trails were incorporated into the PCT; signs for them can still be seen along the trail.

Montgomery's original idea for a Mexico-to-Canada trail was forgotten, however. Then, in

1932, Clinton C. Clarke, the chair of the Mountain League of Los Angeles County in California, proposed a wilderness trail from Mexico to Canada to the **Forest Service** and National Park Service. Clarke then founded the Pacific Crest Trail System Conference, which he chaired for the next 25 years, in order to see his vision become reality. In 1935 Clarke published a guidebook to the PCT, and over the summers of 1935 to 1938, Warren L. Rogers, secretary of the PCT Conference, explored the proposed route with relay teams of boys. However, even though it incorporated such existing trails as the Desert Crest, **John Muir**, Tahoe-Yosemite, Lava Crest, Oregon Skyline, and Cascade Crest Trails, the PCT wasn't officially completed until 1993.

The PCT is an extremely varied trail, with terrain ranging from hot **deserts**, such as the Mojave with its strange Joshua trees, to the high, rocky, often snowbound passes of the Sierra Nevada and the long line of huge stratovolcanoes strung out along the northern 1,000 miles of the trail from Mount Shasta to Glacier Peak. Eighty percent of the PCT is on public land, and it runs through 25 national forests and 7 **national parks**, including Sequoia and Kings Canyon, **Yosemite**, Rainier, and the North Cascades.

Thru-hiking the PCT is a major challenge because some of the terrain is quite remote; there are long distances between supply points in places, so a choice must be made between heavy loads and high mileage. The large, total distance means that **snow** is likely to be encountered somewhere along the way too, usually in the High Sierra for northbound hikers. In the desert areas, **water** is scarce and must be carried. Storms are likely in the mountain areas, especially the North Cascades. All this means that PCT hikers need a full range of backpacking skills.

South to north is the easiest way to hike the PCT; the first 500 miles are in the deserts and transverse ranges of southern California, which can be hiked in April or May without too many problems with snow. Depending on how much snow has fallen and how quickly it has melted, the High Sierra might be either almost snow free or completely snowbound in June when thru-hikers arrive. Usually, there is still snow above timberline at that time of year, requiring an **ice ax**. Once through the Sierra, you should encounter little snow as long as you reach Canada by mid- to late September. A hike of five to five and a half months assumes an average of 15 to 20 miles per day. Do more than this, and you can start later and finish sooner and not encounter much, if any, snow. But you do have the pressure of maintaining that high daily mileage.

Heading southbound means starting in the tough, steep terrain of the North Cascades, which are usually snowbound until July. Once through these mountains, you'll then need a big push to get through the High Sierra before the first snows of the next winter. Whichever way you go, this is one of the great hikes of the world and likely to offer an unforgettable experience.

PACKING A CANOE

Canoe tripping is unique from other forms of **wilderness** travel because weight is not much of an issue. Items you wouldn't even consider for a **backpacking** trip—such as a cast-iron **Dutch oven**, a big roomy **tent**, bulky **food**, and multiple **fishing** rods—suddenly become an option. Some canoes have a weight capacity of over 1,000 pounds (see **canoe selection**); that's a lot of gear and food, maybe too much! The trick quickly becomes getting all of your gear packed into your canoe so that you aren't lopsided, bow heavy, or susceptible to the whims of a gusty **wind**. While it's tempting to fill the canoe to its **gunwales**, exhibiting some self-restraint while packing will serve you well.

Once you have amassed all your personal and group gear, you can begin to stow it in your **packs**. Canoe packs are larger than backpacks, and they usually don't have a frame. It is easy to dump items into a pack and have everything fit, but for the sake of comfort and convenience, it's best to develop a system. For instance, it is not a bad idea to spread your food out among several packs. This way if one pack becomes soaked, you'll still have food that's not waterlogged. It's also smart to line your canoe packs with a plastic pack liner or some other type of water-resistant bag. Get in the habit of packing items in the same pack day after day. By repeatedly using the same pack for the same equipment, you'll discover the best way to stow it. Further, if you always pack items in the same place, you'll be able to find them in a hurry.

> "Canoeing allows you to bring a lot of stuff, but sometimes it can become excessive. On every trip, I have to eliminate a dozen or so items. They may be small, such as an extra book, or big, such as my ultra-deluxe sleeping pad. Once I have pared down my items, I go through them again."—AA

When packing your packs, leave accessible any items that you'll want during the course of the day, such as **rain** gear, **photography** equipment, **first-aid kits**, **throw bags**, and fishing rods. "Accessible" means that these items are easy to get to, not loose in the bottom of the canoe. Pack your canoe so that you have minimal loose gear. Items that aren't secured can quickly disappear in gusty wind or during portages (see **portaging**). Furthermore, if your canoe ever capsizes, you'll be grateful to have only a few packs to pluck out of the water instead of twenty miscellaneous items, many of which may sink.

If you're traveling with more than one canoe, it's worth creating a packing strategy. For instance, try to make sure each canoe has at least one food pack and one equipment pack. This means that, in the event of an emergency, each canoe will have a tent, some food, a **sleeping bag**, **clothing**, and, if necessary, a **stove**. This is especially important if there is a chance that a canoe might capsize or become separated from the group. Furthermore, if you have more than one **communication device**, make sure they are carried in different canoes. This way, if one canoe dumps in a set of rapids and

takes off downstream, you haven't lost your only means of communication.

To prevent gear from getting washed out of a capsized canoe, most **wilderness** travelers use a tie-in system to secure their gear. This can be as simple as strapping each pack in with one of its buckles, or it can be more complex. However, if you decide to tie in your gear, you must ensure this is done each time you load the canoe: it does no good to have a tie-in system that you forget to use.

Load the canoe when it's floating on water, if possible. This provides critical support for the

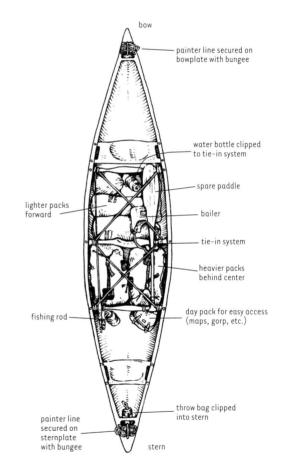

Keep in mind balance and accessibility when packing a canoe. Keep the area under the seat empty so you can quickly shift to paddling on your knees for stability. Tie down large gear.

hull. Start by loading the big packs. Attempt to keep the canoe evenly balanced. The balance of a canoe is also known as its *trim*. If the packs are not of equal weight, it is usually best to put the heavier packs toward the stern. This is especially true if you anticipate hitting some waves over the course of the day. If the stern paddler is significantly heavier than the bow paddler, however, you may choose to place the heavier pack toward the bow to even things out.

After the bigger packs are loaded, start filling the open spaces with your smaller packs and extra gear, such as fishing rods, your spare paddle, and the first-aid kit. When you're finished, float the canoe (if it isn't already in the water) to ensure it isn't lopsided. Fix a lopsided canoe before embarking: not only is a badly trimmed canoe ridiculously frustrating to paddle, but it can become hazardous in **waves**. If you've checked the trim and all looks good, you are set to go. Occasionally, you may need to adjust packs over the course of the day. This is especially true after portages and changes in paddling partners.

PACKING A SEA KAYAK

"There's no way it's all going to fit!" Ahhh . . . the common cry from beaches across the country as paddlers size up their pile of gear next to the small hatches in their sea kayaks. As a paddler, you may know the feeling all too well—performing a last-minute triage of your accessories to determine which "essentials" you need to leave behind. The good news is that, with a few smart packing techniques, you can usually bring along more stuff than you could possibly need.

The key to packing a sea kayak is to make use of every single inch of space and distribute the **weight** evenly. Utilize the entire hatch by shoving pliable objects, such as **tarps** or **tents**, all the way to the ends of the kayak. This may mean taking the tent out of its bag and packing it loose. You may also need to attach a piece of cord to the tent that trails back to the hatch opening to help you unpack. Let no space go unoccupied. Fill pots and pans with **food** items. Large pots fit well over

the ends of **sleeping bag** stuff sacks. Place heavy items along the keel line and close to the cockpit, with the heaviest items in the aft hatch, just behind the cockpit. Pack your **fuel** apart from your **food**, and ensure that all the fuel containers are well sealed. Set aside anything that you want accessible during the day and pack it last, just below the hatch cover.

Before paddling away, and if conditions allow, float the kayak to ensure it's well balanced. If you can tell that the day is going to be windy, think

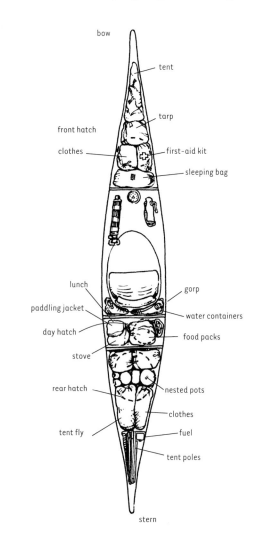

Make use of all available space when packing a kayak.

about your weight placement. If there's too much weight in the bow, you'll plow into waves and have a wet ride. Rather, keep the bow light enough that you can ride up and over the waves, but not so light that you'll have trouble with crosswinds.

By taking a look at the hatch openings, you'll quickly realize that small objects fit and large ones don't. Keep this in mind when packing your **clothing**. Pack it in multiple small bags. As for your sleeping bag, try to buy one that easily condenses into a size that fits into your hatch opening—and keep in mind that hatch openings can be as small as 8 inches. If your sleeping bag isn't that small, pack it loosely into a larger bag, which ensures that it is pliable enough to stuff into the kayak.

Emergency gear, such as flares and a VHF radio, should be on your body at all times. The last thing you want to do in an open-water emergency is have to open up a hatch to get to your **signaling** or **communication devices**. Keep the hatches closed and free of water. This helps you stay buoyant and keeps your gear from floating away. As for storing items on your deck, try to avoid it if possible. Large items make you top-heavy and can create problems in **wind** and surf. If your deck has bungee cords or webbing, place there only those items that you wouldn't mind losing, as they have a nasty habit of disappearing in the waves. The only items that will stay on your deck are those that are tied on or clipped in.

Items to Keep Accessible

- Rain gear
- Extra layers
- Camera and film
- Snacks and water
- Sunscreen
- Maps
- Toilet paper and trowel

A salesperson might tell you that your hatches are waterproof. Don't believe it. They are water resistant, but items in the hatches can easily get wet. For this reason, many people pack their gear into dry bags. Most dry bags are stiff and hard to pack, although some nylon versions are much easier. To avoid this problem, simply line regular stuff sacks with heavyweight garbage bags for protection against water. As with any waterproof bag, you have to ensure that it gets properly sealed, but you'll find that it does the job just fine and it's a lot cheaper. Make sure that your hatch covers are closed properly and secured before you depart. If you only have a few items to place in the hatches, secure the items so they don't shift should you need to edge your kayak or execute a roll.

PACKS

A pack is essential for land-based wilderness activities. The choices can be bewildering, with myriad sizes, shapes, and styles available. Specifications and construction can be confusing too. Do you need all those straps and adjustments or that complicated frame? That depends on your chosen activity and, in particular, on how much you'll carry in the pack.

Day Packs

For summer day hikes, any small pack is adequate. One with a capacity between 1,500 and 2,500 cubic inches should hold all you need. The simplest packs are nylon or polyester bags with padded shoulder straps and perhaps a webbing waist strap. These are very light, 16 ounces or less, but need to be packed carefully to be comfortable. Sliding a piece of foam, which can be used as a cushion for sitting at rest stops, down the back of the pack will greatly improve the comfort. Outside pockets, whether zipped fabric or open-topped mesh, are useful for carrying often-needed or wet items but aren't essential. Many day packs come with padded backs, and some have internal frames and padded hip belts. These make a pack comfortable but add some **weight** and aren't really necessary in a small pack. Also, whereas a simple pack will fit almost anyone, one with a frame and a padded belt has to fit properly to be comfortable, which means it needs to be available in different back lengths.

Day packs for **mountaineering, ski touring,** and **snow** hiking (often called *alpine packs*) have to carry bigger loads than summer ones and need external attachments for hardware, such as **ice axes, crampons,** snowshoes, and skis. Packs in the 2,000- to 3,500-cubic-inch range are usually adequate. Hip belts (which may not be padded) are standard, in part for stability because they help stop the pack from bouncing up and down. Back padding is standard too, and many packs have internal frames. These packs might have to handle 30 pounds or more, so they need more complex constructions than summer day packs. How many external straps you need depends on what you plan to carry. A set of ice ax loops is the minimum. Side straps are useful not just for attaching gear but also because you can tighten them when the pack isn't full, in order to keep the contents from moving around inside and perhaps throwing you off balance.

Backpacks

The larger day packs, especially ones designed for snow use, can be used for **backpacking** if your load is light and compact or if you're out for only one or two nights. True backpacks start at around 3,000 cubic inches and go up to 7,500-cubic-inch monsters. The first are great for ultralight hiking; the second, for expeditions to very remote areas. Something in between the two is usually fine for most people and most uses.

> "I use a 7,200-cubic-inch pack for ski tours of longer than a week without resupply and a 3,000-cubic-inch pack for summer overnights."—CT

Soft packs with foam padding in the back but no frame will support loads up to 30 to 35 pounds if they are packed properly. For bigger loads, you need some type of frame to help transfer the weight to your hips, which are far better at supporting heavy loads than the shoulders, and to hold the load steady and keep it from sagging.

External Frame

Traditional backpacks have an external, ladder-shaped metal or plastic frame, a design first introduced in the early 1950s. This is a strong, functional design good for carrying heavy loads on **trails** and relatively even terrain. Items can be lashed to the frame above and below the actual pack bag, so capacities can be enormous. The rigidity of the frame keeps the weight transferred to the hips, and the height of the frame keeps the load up high and close to your center of gravity, so you can walk upright. However, these advantages mean that external frames aren't very stable on rough terrain. Because the frame is rigid, it doesn't move with you and can sway from side to side; because the weight is up high, the pack can feel top-heavy. The best externals overcome this to some extent with carefully shaped curved frames and some of the harness features of internal-frame packs.

Internal Frame

External-frame packs aren't ideal for mountaineering, although they have been to the summit of Mount Everest and other major peaks. On the other hand, soft alpine packs aren't comfortable with heavy loads. To resolve this dilemma, the internal-frame pack was developed in the 1960s. The first internal frames consisted of two parallel, malleable alloy bars fitted into the back of the pack, a frame still found in many packs. However, many internal frames now consist of a flexible sheet of synthetic material in the back of the pack with perhaps one or two frame bars in it or flexible rods running around the edge. The best internal frames can carry very heavy loads as well as an external frame does, as long as they are fitted properly. Because the frames are malleable, they can be bent to fit the back closely, leading to a body-hugging pack that moves with you for good

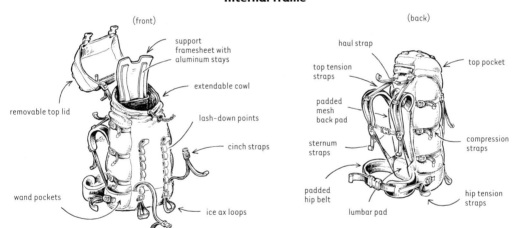

External frame

(front)

stuff sack/ sleeping pad

lash strap

lash-down points

aluminum frame

cinch straps

external pockets

area for sleep bag stuff sack

lumbar pad

sleeping bag stuff sack

(back)

area for stuff sack

aluminum frame

sternum strap

back pad

lumbar pad

padded hip belt

area for stuff sack attachment

Internal frame

(front)

support framesheet with aluminum stays

extendable cowl

removable top lid

lash-down points

cinch straps

wand pockets

ice ax loops

(back)

haul strap

top pocket

top tension straps

padded mesh back pad

compression straps

sternum straps

padded hip belt

hip tension straps

lumbar pad

MIKE CLELLAND

External-frame versus internal-frame backpacks.

balance. For cross-country **hiking**, mountaineering, and ski touring, internal frames are the best choice. Many hikers like them for trail use too.

Ultralight Packs

Over the decades, packs have become heavier and heavier as thicker fabrics, more complex harness systems, and an increasing number of accessories have been added. By the 1990s, the pack was often the heaviest single part of your load. In the same decade, a reaction set in against this weight, and much simpler ultralight packs began to be developed, especially for backpacking, **fastpacking**, **trail running**, **ultralight hiking**, and other activities that don't require very heavy loads or extremely durable packs.

Simple in design, ultralight packs are made from lighter materials than standard models. Developments in fabrics mean they're still surprisingly tough, however, and they are often used by long-distance hikers. The most basic are simple bags with shoulder straps and a few external mesh pockets. These can weigh as little as 15 ounces for a pack with a capacity of 3,000 cubic inches. They aren't comfortable with loads much over 20 pounds, however.

Add a shaped back with some padding in it and a hip belt, and you can have a pack with a capacity of more than 3,600 cubic inches that weighs 20 ounces and will comfortably carry 30 pounds. Add a frame sheet and some padding to the hip belt, and the pack will weigh more like 40 to 50 ounces but should carry 40-plus pounds comfortably—and it's still half the weight of a standard pack. If you aren't going to drag your pack up granite chimneys or carry 70 pounds of winter mountaineering gear, ultralight packs make sense.

Overall, a pack shouldn't weigh more than 10 percent of your total load. For example, if you're only carrying 30 pounds, your pack should weigh no more than 3 pounds.

The Hip Belt

For loads much over 20 pounds, it is far more comfortable and efficient to carry the weight on your hips rather than on your shoulders. Weight on your shoulders causes you to lean forward and makes your back and shoulders ache. Transferring the weight to your hips takes the pressure off your back and shoulders, allowing you to stand upright. The difference in comfort between carrying weight on your shoulders and carrying it on your hips makes the hip belt the most important part of a pack harness. Complex frames and fancy curved shoulder straps are all so much extra weight if the hip belt isn't adequate and doesn't fit well.

Unpadded belts can be adequate for loads up to 30 to 35 pounds if the pack back is shaped carefully so the weight is directed to your hips. For heavier loads, you need a padded belt, and the heavier the load, the more padded and stiff the belt should be. For loads up to 40 pounds, light padding and no stiffening should be fine. Above 40 pounds, thicker padding and some stiffening to

prevent the belt from twisting are needed. Above 60 pounds requires a massive belt with rigid stiffening and at least half an inch of thick, soft padding. With a good, properly fitting hip belt, you should be able to carry virtually all the weight, however heavy, on your hips.

Fitting the Pack

To be comfortable, a pack must fit properly. The key to this is matching the length of the pack to the length of your back. With simple packs without hip belts or frames, this isn't crucial—although a short pack sitting between your shoulders like a basketball doesn't feel good, so even here you might want to check the back length.

With packs with hip belts, the fit becomes much more important. The belt should fit across the hips with the top of the belt about an inch above the hipbones, so the weight is carried on the widest part of the hips. Too short a distance between the shoulder straps and the hip belt, and the belt will ride too high and won't carry much weight without hurting your stomach. Too long a distance, and the hip belt will hang too low. If you tighten it up, it will restrict leg movement.

On a pack without top tension straps, the shoulder straps should join the pack at a point level with your shoulders when the hip belt is in the right position. If the pack has top tension straps, which should rise off the shoulder straps and run up to the top of the pack at an angle of between 20 and 45 degrees, the shoulder straps should curl over your shoulders and attach to the pack an inch or two below them. The purpose of the top tension, or load lifter, straps is to stabilize the top of the pack so it doesn't sway; they also lift the top of the shoulder straps off the sensitive nerves on the top of the shoulders. You should be able to just slip a finger under the top of the shoulder straps when the top tension straps are tightened up.

Many packs have adjustable harnesses so you can vary the position of the shoulder straps and sometimes the hip belt. There are various ways of doing this, but none can make a frame or back that is the wrong size for you fit properly. Adjustable backs are for fine-tuning the fit.

When trying on packs, always do so with the weight you expect to carry in them. Any pack can be comfortable filled with foam or bubble wrap. Walk around with the loaded pack on to see if it rubs anywhere or feels uncomfortable. A pack that fits well feels snug and comfortable and moves with you. Any discomfort in the store will be magnified in the **wilderness**.

While using the pack, you can tinker with the various straps to adjust it for different types of terrain. If a pack feels uncomfortable at any time, minor adjustments of the straps can make a big difference. Slackening the top tension and shoulder straps puts virtually all the weight on the hips but reduces stability, which is fine on a flat trail or gentle slope. For more stability when descending, especially on skis or if the terrain is rough, tighten the top tension and shoulder straps so the pack hugs the body closely. This puts some weight on the shoulders but minimizes swaying.

Many hip belts have side stabilizer straps running from the sides of the belt to the sides of the pack. These need to be loosened every time you don the pack, or they will distort the shape of the hip belt. On easy terrain, you can leave them slack, which allows your hips to move more freely, but on rough and steep terrain, they should be tightened so the base of the pack doesn't sway.

Pack Bags

Pack bags, the part of a pack that holds your gear, come in many types, from simple single-compartment ones with few or no pockets to twin-compartment, multipocketed ones with a plethora of straps and attachment points both inside and out. While complex designs make organizing your gear easier (as long as you can remember what went where), they are also heavier than simple ones. Compartments make the most sense on the biggest packs, in which gear at or near the bottom otherwise can be hard to reach.

A pack bag is the right size if it will hold all your gear and **food** except for hardware, such as

ice axes and perhaps foam pads. With external-frame packs, you can strap items above and below the pack bag without affecting the fit. With an internal-frame or soft pack, however, too much gear on the outside affects the balance and comfort. Gear on the outside is vulnerable to damage anyway, so it's best to have a pack that will hold everything inside.

Many packs can be expanded to hold more gear. This is why you sometimes see volumes listed as "3,500 + 1,200 cubic inches" or something similar. It's best to view such a pack as a 3,500-cubic-inch one, not a 4,700-cubic-inch one, because if you use the extension the pack will be unstable and probably uncomfortable. Extensions are useful for the occasional day you have extra food or gear, but not for regular use.

Pockets are great for small items. With mesh pockets, you can stick wet items inside and the items can drain and dry without wetting anything else. Mesh pockets are also lighter than solid fabric ones, and you can see what's in them. Of course, they aren't waterproof, but you can't trust a standard zipped pocket to keep the **rain** out anyway. Open-topped lower side pockets can be used for water bottles so you can get at them without taking off the pack. If you prefer **water** bladders, many packs come with an internal pocket designed to hold a bladder, with an exit hole near the top of the pack for the drinking tube.

Top lids protect the contents and usually have pockets in them. They aren't essential, though, and doing without one saves weight. Many ultralight packs come with roll tops rather than lids.

The standard material for pack bags is textured nylon, such as Cordura, which is tough but also heavy. It's fine for mountaineering packs but is overkill for hiking packs. Nylon pack cloth is lighter and tough enough for most uses. Ultralight packs are often made from ripstop nylon in which the ripstop threads are Spectra, an extremely tough polyethylene material. Spectra is white and can't be dyed, so these packs have a distinct grid pattern on them. Pure Spectra packs, which are solid white, are available, but they're expensive.

Packing a Backpack

The best-fitting pack can still be uncomfortable if it isn't packed properly. The main concern here is to keep heavy items close to your back. If they're away from your back, the pack will pull you backward and you'll have to lean forward to compensate. This means that if your pack has a rear pocket, it should only be used for light items. For hiking on trails and easy ground, having the weight high up also helps you maintain an upright stance. On rough ground and when skiing or climbing, however, carrying your weight high can make the pack top-heavy and unstable, so pack dense, heavy items in the middle of the pack. The pack needs to be balanced from side to side too. If you put full water and **fuel** bottles on one side of the pack and soft **clothing** on the other, the pack will pull to one side.

A frameless pack needs to be packed carefully so that hard items don't poke you in the back and so that the pack doesn't buckle in the middle. Slide a folded foam pad down the back of the pack for extra cushioning and stiffening, or let the pad unroll inside the pack and pack your gear inside it. As well as packing for comfort and stability, you need easy access to items you're likely to want during the day.

Putting on a Pack

One advantage of light packs is that you can swing them on and off your back without thought. Once the weight gets above 25 pounds, however, a little more care is required; in this case, it can help to lift the pack onto your hip and then onto your back. Once above 40 pounds, this move becomes essential, and it's best to lift the pack onto your thigh rather than your hip and then shift it slowly onto your back. With really heavy loads—above 50 pounds—finding a platform to rest the pack on helps greatly.

The Pack off the Back

A pack, even a frameless one, makes a good backrest. You can just lean it against a tree or rock for

"There are many ways of packing, but here is what I do with the pack I mostly use, which has a single compartment, side and front mesh pockets, and a lid with large pocket. First, I stuff my sleeping bag into the bottom of the pack (inside a large stuff sack and a pack liner, if rain is possible) followed by spare clothes I don't think I'll need during the day. Tent poles, if carried, are then slid down the inside of the pack. If I have a self-inflating pad, it's folded up and packed in the back of the pack, where it's protected from damage. A foam pad goes inside if there's room or else is strapped on the outside when everything else is packed. Cookware, stove, butane/propane canisters (if carried), and empty water containers go on top of the sleeping bag and clothing. Food goes in next, packed into two or more stuff sacks or heavy-duty plastic bags, as these are easier to pack than one large bag. To keep food, which is a heavy item, close to my back, I put my tent or tarp in front of it, along with spare footwear, if carried. At the top of the pack goes rain gear, a stuff sack containing any paperbacks and spare maps I have with me, and my warm top. The lid pocket holds hats, gloves, notebook and pen, insect repellent, sunscreen, camera lenses, camera film and accessories, first-aid/repair kit, stakes, headlamp, toilet paper and trowel, and any other small items. (When I use a pack with no lid, these items go into a stuff sack carried at the top of the pack.)

"The side pockets hold full water bottles, lunch and snack food, and liquid fuels, such as white gas or alcohol (in a different pocket than the food). In the rear pocket goes the tarp or tent fly sheet, if wet, or any damp clothing. This leaves map, compass, and mini-binoculars, which I carry in my shirt or jacket pockets."—CT

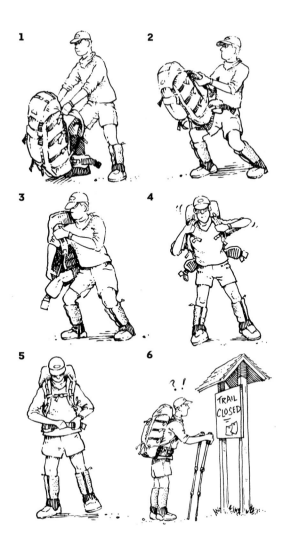

Putting on your backpack. 1. Using both hands and with the harness system facing you, pick up the pack by the shoulder straps. 2. Lift the pack onto one bent leg (here, right leg). 3. Twist your torso slightly and slip your right arm through the right shoulder strap. 4. Swing the pack onto your back. 5. Slacken the hip tension straps on the hipbelt if needed. Bend forward slightly and pull in your stomach muscles as you cinch the hipbelt to tighten it securely. Retighten the hip tension straps. 6. You're ready for the trail!

extra padding or prop it up with sticks or trekking poles. One stick is enough with an external-frame pack, but for internal frames and soft packs, you'll

need two. You also have to get the angles just right, or the pack is liable to collapse.

In camp, if little animals are a potential problem, it's best to leave the pack open, including all of the pockets, so creatures can explore it without having to chew their way in.

PADDLE SIGNALS

Paddle signals are an important form of communication between members of any paddling group. They can relay vital messages from one paddler to another despite the distance between them and the loud roar of rapids or ocean surf. The universal signals used by most paddlers are shown next page.

Knowing these paddle signals is key to communicating with other paddlers, but don't assume that all paddlers know them. It is always a good idea to review the signals with new paddling partners. You may also add some personal signals to the collection.

Signals can also be made with whistles. Whistles can be good for getting attention over short distances, but even the loudest storm whistles are hard to hear over a longer distance.

PAINTER LINES

Painter lines are lengths of rope attached to the bow and stern of a canoe. The term *painter line* is left over from the days when canoes were regularly hung from the rafters of garages to paint their hulls. When the lines were left attached to the canoe, they proved very useful. Painter lines are individually referred to as *bow* and *stern lines*.

Many people use painter lines to secure their canoes to shore when they take a break from paddling. In wilderness **canoe tripping**, painter lines are used for **lining** stretches of river that are too difficult to paddle. When they aren't being used, painter lines are often stashed under bungee cords attached to the bow and stern plates of the canoe.

Painter lines can be any length; however, if you plan to use them for lining, you'll want at least 20 feet. Some paddlers prefer as much as 50 feet, but a painter line more than 30 feet long can

"All clear"

"Go ahead"

"Run river center"

Paddle straight up, with the blade in the air (hold the blade flat to optimize its visibility). Or, arms together pointing straight up in the air. This signal is often used by sea kayakers for "come here."

"Stop"

"Don't go"

"Wait for further instructions"

Paddle held horizontal in the air parallel to the water. Or, arms held out to either side parallel to the water.

Paddle signals are the best way to communicate over distances of water. The most commonly used signals are shown here.

"Emergency"

"Send assistance quickly"

Paddle up in the air, waving the blade from side to side. Or, wave your helmet or PFD over your head.

"Go right"

Paddle or arms overhead pointing to the signal recipients' left.

"Go left"

Paddle or arms overhead pointing to the signal recipients' right.

"A couple years ago, I was leading a group of paddlers in northern Canada. We had stopped to scout a set of rapids that was approximately a quarter-mile long. It looked relatively easy, and we chose a route along 'river right' that looked good. Our system was to let the lead boat go first and have the rest of the boats wait until the all-clear signal was given. In the lead boat, I enjoyed the fun ride bobbing up and down over waves and small drops. About midway through the set, we passed a huge ledge smack in the middle of the river. While scouting we had noticed that something was there, but being next to it was a different matter entirely. This was a gnarly, boat-eating hydraulic that we hadn't been prepared for. Good thing we ran river right—but to be safe we should have been even farther to the right!

"When we got to the end, we pulled over. Instead of giving the signal to go ahead, I gave the signal to stop. This was unusual for our group. I could almost hear the others commenting on how easy the run had looked, questioning the delay. After walking partway up the bank, I met up with one of the party and explained the unexpected hazard. The rest of the group shot the set far river right, and we continued on our way."—AA be too difficult to handle, messy, and even dangerous. Choose a line made of a buoyant material, such as polypropylene. The rope construction is less important, but kernmantle-style ropes hold their knots well and remain flexible (see **rope**). Brightly colored lines are also useful because they stand out against the darkness of the water. This isn't so critical if all you need out of your painter is to tie the canoe to a tree, but if you're lining a turbulent set of rapids, it's important to be able to identify your line easily.

PEAK BAGGING

There are many reasons for exploring the **wilderness**. Climbing mountains is one reason that attracts many people. To stand high above the world and look down at the flatlands below or over **mountains** rippling into the distance is awe-inspiring and glorious. The challenge and beauty of the ascent, whether it's a hike or a difficult technical climb, is wonderful too, combining physical effort with wilderness skills.

> "I've climbed the Scottish Munros twice, the first time over a number of years and the second in one continuous walk, on which I also climbed all the subsidiary summits, making a total of 517 summits. This has given me a knowledge of the Scottish hills in all weathers that I would probably not have otherwise and a wealth of mountain days to relish and look back upon."—CT

Some people like to climb the same mountains by different routes, getting to know them well; others like to climb peaks by difficult routes, reveling in the technical intricacies of the ascent. Peak baggers like to climb a specific set of peaks, usually by the easiest route, and often tick them off on a list. There are many such lists, both in the United States and worldwide, along with clubs that keep track of those people who complete all the peaks and then issue them certificates and awards. Some people try to complete lists in the fastest possible time, in continuous journeys, or in the **winter** to make the challenge more exciting or fulfilling.

Aficionados of peak bagging debate enthusiastically what constitutes a separate mountain and which peaks should be on each list. New maps might give revised heights for peaks too, so the numbers on lists vary over time. Some lists are suitable for mountain hikers, with few if any peaks requiring any technical climbing skills, while others are for experienced mountaineers only.

In the United States, the Highpointers Club is for those climbing the highest point in each of the 50 states (see resources section). You can also set out to climb the 91 peaks over 14,000 feet in the United States—54 in Colorado, 21 in Alaska, 15 in California, and 1 in Washington State. Just climbing the Colorado 54 is a goal for some people. In the **Sierra Nevada** in California, you can climb the 247 Sierra peaks. There are many lists of peaks for the eastern United States, including the Northeast 111, which covers 115 4,000-foot peaks in the Northeast (originally 111 peaks, hence the name). There are many more such lists, including those covering lower peaks, such as the Colorado 13,000ers, and the New England 100 Highest Peaks under 4,000 feet.

Abroad, there are many lists too, with the ultimate being the 14 8,000-meter peaks, all of which lie in the Himalaya and Karakorum mountain ranges in Central Asia, and the Seven Summits, the highest points on each of the seven continents. These are challenges for experienced high-altitude mountaineers with both time and money. In Europe, climbers can ascend the 61 4,000-meter Alpine Peaks, while walkers can head for the 284 3,000-foot summits in Scotland, called *Munros* after the mountaineer who first listed them.

Peak bagging can be seen as mere list ticking, and it's often decried by nonparticipants. However, it can be a very satisfying way to explore the wilderness. Having a goal gets you out when the weather's bad or when you're feeling lazy, often resulting in fine days you otherwise would have missed, and increasing your experience of dealing with storms. Visiting many different summits also means you visit a wide variety of landscapes and gain great experience in mountain travel.

PEE BOTTLES

Just as they sound, pee bottles are bottles you take with you to bed so you don't have to leave the comfort of your **tent** during the night to answer the call of nature. Pee bottles are convenient in cold or buggy conditions, when leaving your tent (or even your **sleeping bag**) becomes a major hassle.

If you have never used a pee bottle, don't assume that it will work on the first try. Some men develop "stage fright," and women have to contend with aim. Make sure to practice in advance of your first attempt so you don't end up with a wet and smelly sleeping bag. When selecting a pee bottle, choose a sturdy bottle with a screw-on lid (you don't want it to break or leak!). Women should consider bottles with wide mouths, such as a standard wide-mouthed Nalgene bottle. Women can also purchase funnel-like urinary aide devices such as the Lady J and the Freshette. Make sure to label your pee bottle with red tape, skull and crossbones, "Don't drink!" written large, or some other noticeable markings so no one can confuse it with your water bottle.

PEMMICAN

With an increasing number of energy-boosting snacks available to outdoor enthusiasts, it may seem that the sports bar is a recent invention. These lightweight, calorie-packed snacks are the perfect mini-meal for any outdoor adventure. But to claim them as an invention of the last decades of the twentieth century would be a mistake. The real ancestor of the **energy bar** is pemmican.

Pemmican is a high-fat concoction of meat and animal fat that is pressed into easy-to-store, thin, rectangular blocks. For the indigenous people of the United States and the early Canada fur traders, pemmican was a staple. Not only could it

Pemmican

3 ounces ground meat (ground beef is fine)
3.5 ounces lard, beef tallow, or vegetable shortening (although vegetable shortening will not set up quite as firm)

Cook the meat, drain off the fat, and dry it in an oven or a food dehydrator. Once the meat is completely dry, crush it into a powder. Heat the lard to a smooth consistency, and mix it into the meat. Pour the mixture into a lined or greased baking pan, and let it harden. The pemmican can be wrapped in plastic wrap in individual pieces or as a whole and stored in the freezer.

For variations, consider adding dried, ground berries or dried, finely diced onions.

last several years in almost any environment, hot or cold, but pemmican was also very nutritious for its weight. Small pieces could be broken off the larger block for fast, easy meals that required no **water**. The smaller pieces could be stashed in a pocket or hoarded in a secret **cache** for use at a later date without worrying about spoilage.

Most pemmican was originally made from buffalo meat, although moose meat and caribou meat were also used. Once dried, the meat was crushed into a flaky powder and then mixed with melted animal fat. The mixture was pressed into several inch-thick blocks about the size of a briefcase, each weighing about 90 pounds. Easily transported, the blocks were stored by the dozens at forts and settlements along established trade routes.

The traditional taste of pemmican would not have won awards. Indeed, tastiness was a mere luxury for most pemmican eaters. Berries were sometimes added to the mixture of meat and animal fat to give the pemmican a sweeter taste. For a change of pace, and if conditions allowed, pemmican could be added to a pot of hot water along with a few other ingredients to create a warm soupy mixture called *rubbaboo*.

Today, outdoor adventurers have many options for fast and easy food. Still, some people may want to sample the cuisine of the early explorers. For a traditional taste of pemmican, try the accompanying recipe.

PERMITS

A permit hardly seems in accord with the freedom of the **wilderness**, but in many popular backcountry areas one is required. Permits are used by land managers for various reasons, primarily to limit the number of visitors and to monitor visitation and activity. Land managers assess how many people can be in an area in a given time before the impact becomes too great; permits are limited to that number. In places such as the **Grand Canyon** in the U.S. Southwest, where there is little **water** and there are few places suitable for **camping**, you have to apply for permits for the popular areas many months in advance. In other areas, permits are used not to limit numbers but to keep track of users, so you can pick up a permit at the start of your trip. However, it's always best to check well in advance about permit requirements. There's no standard procedure for issuing permits, so make sure you understand the process for each location. If you book permits in advance, that's one less hassle to deal with at the start of your trip. Often, though, you have to pay a registration fee for advance booking, and sometimes you have to pay for a permit as well (see also **planning a trip**).

Some permits allow you to go anywhere in the permit area; others limit you to certain trails and campsites. If your journey will take you through several different permit areas, as can happen in places such as California's **Sierra Nevada**, you can often get one permit from the area where you start that also covers the others. Single permits are available for some long-distance trails too, such as the **John Muir Trail** and the **Pacific Crest Trail**.

Some areas abroad also require permits. Nepal, a major destination for hikers and climbers, charges for both trekking and climbing permits. Again, it's wise to find out well before the start of your trip what permits you'll need. Permits may require photographs, so carry passport photos with you. Take quite a few because each permit-issuing office may require one or two for their files plus the ones stuck on your permit.

PFDS

Personal flotation devices (life jackets) are an important part of any paddling ensemble. Their purpose is to keep your body afloat if you become immersed in water. You should wear your PFD anytime you are on the water, and in some cases when you're just near the water. If you think you don't need to wear your PFD just because you're a good swimmer, think again. Any number of circumstances can make it difficult to stay afloat, including cold water, rough conditions, strong currents, surf, injury, or illness. If you capsize and need to concentrate on staying afloat, you may be unable to perform other critical maneuvers, such as holding onto your paddle and canoe or kayak, finding and using **communication devices**, performing a **T-rescue** or, if you're in a river, getting upstream of your boat. With the advent of com-

> "My favorite PFD is so comfortable that I completely forget I'm wearing it. When the weather turns cold, I put my PFD on before I leave the tent in the morning and take it off only when I'm ready to go to sleep at night."—AA

fortable and convenient PFDs, you no longer have an excuse for not wearing one.

Finding the right PFD is important. The more you like your PFD, the more you'll wear it. In adverse conditions, your PFD becomes an important layer that helps keep you warm and dry. Your goal should be to find one that you'll feel comfortable wearing for long periods of time.

The PFD on the left is too large (notice how it can be pulled over the head). The PFD on the right fits well.

Like many outdoor gear essentials, there isn't one style of PFD that's perfect for all paddling endeavors. Features such as design and buoyancy determine the PFD's limitations. *Buoyancy* is the amount of flotation a PFD provides. For example, an average adult wearing a bathing suit weighs between 10 and 12 pounds in the water. Therefore, to keep his head above the surface, he needs a PFD that will provide flotation for a greater weight than that. The U.S. Coast Guard has set 15.5 pounds as the minimum flotation acceptable for an adult PFD. This is enough flotation to keep a 160-pound person floating at chin level in the water. You may want to float higher than chin level, or you may weigh more than 160 pounds. If this is the case, you can purchase a PFD with more flotation. You may also want to consider more flotation if you'll be paddling in turbulent water, such as whitewater or surf. Keep in mind that the higher-flotation PFDs tend to be bulkier. Still, they may be a better option for your needs.

Once you determine the appropriate amount of flotation, look for a good fit. PFDs that don't fit are more than uncomfortable; they're dangerous. If your PFD is too big, you may slide out of it! If it's too small, it will chafe your skin and restrict your breathing. A PFD should fit snugly, but not too tight. If you feel as if you can't take a deep breath, go with a larger size. Have a friend pull upward on the shoulders. If the PFD rises to your ears or beyond, it's too big. Try to find a PFD that is adjustable. This way you can wear it over many layers or just over your bathing suit. If you're at a store with boats, try sitting in a canoe or kayak and simulating the paddling motion while wearing the PFD. This can be a good way to determine if it will feel comfortable while you are paddling. Often, kayakers prefer a shorter PFD that doesn't interfere with the seat back of the kayak. Canoeists, who don't have this restriction, usually prefer a longer PFD that offers more protection.

Consider all the small safety items you want to carry on your PFD, and choose a model that has appropriate pockets and placements for rescue **knives** and so forth. Carrying a lot of gadgets may be convenient, but it can be a pain while you're in the water or trying to get back in your canoe or kayak. Try to minimize the amount of stuff that you attach to your PFD. If remaining visible in the water is important, choose a brightly colored PFD or one with reflective tape.

Any PFD should be approved by the U.S. Coast Guard (or equivalent in other countries). For more information about PFDs, including the USCG classification of PFDs for various uses, visit the U.S. Coast Guard website (see resources section). Look for the U.S. Coast Guard endorsement on the inside of the PFD or on the tag. Don't rush the process of finding the perfect PFD. Shop around until you find one that is practical and feels comfortable. After all, a PFD will keep you afloat only if you wear it.

PHOTOGRAPHY

Photography is probably the most popular secondary activity for **wilderness** travelers. Most people like to have pictures of their trips. Quick snapshots are OK if all you want is something to jog your memory, but if you want control over the results and higher-quality pictures, you need to know a little about photography. With a fully automatic camera, anyone can take some passable photos just by pointing and shooting, but taking truly good photos requires a little more effort. The quality depends on the photographer, not the equipment. Photography is about seeing and vision, not which camera you use. The best equipment in the world won't make anyone a top photographer, despite what the advertisements say. However, a great photographer can take excellent photographs with a simple, basic camera.

> "Since taking photography seriously, I've become more attuned to slight variations in the light and more prepared to follow the light and to look for dramatic and beautiful scenes."—CT

It is sometimes argued that photography detracts from enjoyment of the wilderness, that a camera forms a barrier between you and nature, distancing you from the landscape. This may be true when you are learning photography and you have to think about the mechanics of equipment, but the opposite is true once you are comfortable with your camera. Take the time to get used to and comfortable with any new camera gear at home before heading into the wild.

Photography can increase your appreciation of the wilderness because it makes you look more closely and more deeply. To capture everything about a trip, don't just photograph the grand and spectacular, but capture people, campsites, signs, **trails**, bridges, and details such as rocks, flowers, and small pools.

Equipment

Reading the lists of equipment that professional photographers take on trips can be daunting, and you might think there's no point trying to take good photographs since you can't afford the great expense of such equipment and couldn't carry it all if you could. However, you don't need all that gear unless you're a professional. It is perfectly possible to take excellent photographs with very basic, lightweight equipment.

Camera Types

A lightweight camera is best for most wilderness lovers; heavy ones too often get left at home. Unless you're taking photographs for publication or for printing at large sizes, professional and semi-pro cameras are too heavy. Indeed, such cameras aren't needed for most professional photography either. The biggest advantage they have over lighter weight cameras is ruggedness. This may seem a major benefit for wilderness use, but if you look after your camera you don't really need the extra durability. A popular option is a lightweight SLR (single lens reflex) camera with a medium-range zoom lens and a total weight of 20 to 30 ounces, less than some professional SLR bodies.

The lightest cameras are compacts with a permanently attached lens (unlike SLRs), which are fine for most uses, especially with print film, the kind most people use. Zoom compacts give you more options with composition, but ones with a fixed lens are lighter in weight and usually take better-quality images (see Lenses below).

> "I have a very good compact camera that has a superb 28mm lens and weighs just 6.7 ounces. I've taken photographs with it that have appeared as double-page spreads in magazines. It makes a great backup for an SLR and is a good camera on its own for ultralight trips."—CT

SLRs and compacts use film. Digital cameras do not, although tiny, reusable storage cards are needed on anything other than short trips. With a digital camera, you can see the picture on an LCD screen after you take it and then delete it if you don't like it. Back home, the images can be viewed on a computer screen, uploaded onto a website, or turned into prints.

While it's a boon not to have to deal with film, which is easily damaged, digital cameras do have drawbacks, although the technology is improving all the time. Consumer models don't give the same quality as film cameras when making large prints, although they're fine for computer and website images and small prints. Top-quality digital cameras are both expensive and heavy.

Practically speaking, digital cameras are heavy

on battery usage. Rechargeable batteries are usually recommended, but they aren't much use if there's nowhere to recharge them. They are susceptible to cold temperatures too. Carrying batteries in a pocket close to your skin can help to keep them working. Put them in the camera only when taking a picture. Even in warm climates, batteries don't last long, so carry plenty of spares if you're out for more than a day and hope to take a lot of shots.

Automatic vs. Manual

If all you want to do is take snapshots, then a fully automatic camera is fine. Good composition and good light will still make for better photographs (see Taking Photographs below), but without manual controls, you won't be able to get the best from some situations.

Cameras with manual override allow you to adjust the exposure to account for changes in the light, which can be important, especially in low light such as at sunset and sunrise. Exposure refers to the amount of light the camera allows in, which is determined by the size of the aperture (the hole in the lens) and the shutter speed (the time the aperture is open). Being able to set the aperture and shutter speed makes a huge difference. Want to record a waterfall as a soft sweep of white water? Set a slow shutter speed. Want to get everything in focus, from the flowers a few yards away to the mountains in the distance? Set a small aperture. With a fully automatic camera, you can't do this. Full manual control gives you the most choices. However, few compacts have this option. Some compacts do allow you to set the aperture (called *aperture priority*), and then they set the shutter speed.

Manual focus, which is virtually nonexistent on newer compacts, is useful too. With it, you can set the lens to get as much as possible in focus rather than just one point. If your camera doesn't have manual focus, you can focus on something about a third of the way into your intended photo, lock the focus (usually by keeping the shutter button partially depressed), recompose the shot, and then take the picture. This should mean everything is in focus.

Lenses

Whatever camera you choose, the lens matters tremendously, and not just in terms of quality. For landscapes, a wide-angle lens is best because it includes more of the scene and captures some of the scale. A 24mm or 28mm wide-angle lens is ideal. However, for portraits and details, you need a longer focal length. The solution is a zoom lens because it is much lighter and more compact than the several fixed-focal-length lenses it replaces. If you carry only one lens, a 24–70mm or 28–80mm zoom are good choices. If weight isn't an issue, you can also carry an 80–200mm, 70–210mm, or 70–300mm zoom lens, which lets you isolate distant details and take some animal photos. If you're really into animal photography, then you'll need a longer lens, at least 400mm and maybe as much as 600mm, so you can get pictures while staying a long way from the subject.

Zoom lenses are also useful because they let you alter the composition without having to change your position. This can be important in the wilderness, where there may be no other safe place from which to take the photo.

These lens choices apply whether you have an SLR, digital, or compact camera. However, the best compacts often only have a fixed lens. Sometimes having just one focal length can be a positive—for example, it can impose a discipline on your photography. You'll have to think hard about what you can do with it.

Filters

Camera shops carry a wide variety of filters, most of which will ruin your photographs unless you're trying to create surreal fantasies. Few filters are actually useful, and even these need to be used carefully.

Purely to protect the lens, skylight or ultraviolet (UV) filters are worth having. UV filters are said to cut out UV light and reduce the blueness sometimes found in high mountain scenes. These filters don't affect the exposure, nor do they alter what the image looks like, so they can easily be used with cameras where you don't look through the lens, including all compacts and most digital cameras.

With most other filters, being able to see and alter the effect they have is essential, which re-

> "I sometimes use a polarizing filter with my compact camera by holding it up to my eye and turning it to get the required effect and then putting it on the prefocused lens in the same position. This is awkward enough that I don't do it often, however."—CT

quires an SLR camera. However, it's possible to use filters with non-SLRs with great care.

A polarizing filter is probably the most useful filter of all. It darkens the sky so it doesn't look washed out, brings out colors, and cuts glare. Some people leave polarizers on their lenses all the time; however, because they work only at a 90-degree angle to the sun and they cut out some light, requiring a slower shutter speed or bigger aperture, it's best to use one only when it will have an effect.

Neutral-density graduated (ND grad) filters are used for scenes with a bright sky and a dark landscape. Film cameras can't handle huge variations in exposure, so you end up with either washed-out skies or land that is too dark. The ND grad filter reduces the light from the sky so that details in both land and sky are recorded. ND grads aren't easy to use and require a tripod (see Supports below) and time, so they're definitely for the more committed photographer.

Film

Most published wilderness photos are taken on film. Of course, you can scan film images, whether slides, prints, or negatives, into your computer and then treat them just the same as images taken with a digital camera. However, while digital im-

ages can be uploaded quickly to the computer, it takes a bit longer to scan film images and make any necessary adjustments.

If you do use film, the type is important. Slide or print? For most uses, prints are probably best: they are easy to show other people and to stick into journals or albums. Enlargements and reprints are fairly inexpensive too. Print film is also more forgiving of exposure errors than slide film, making it the most suitable film for automatic compact cameras. Another advantage of print film is that fast films, 200 or 400ISO, can produce top-quality results. The faster a film, the more quickly it reacts to light, so it doesn't need to be exposed as long as slower film. This means you can use a faster shutter speed, which is useful for avoiding camera shake, especially in low light.

However, if you'd like to see your pictures in print publications or if you want to give slide shows, then slide (transparency) film is best. This is still the choice of most professionals. And you can't choose just any slide film either. Slow film, 100ISO or less, produces the best results. Slide film needs to be exposed more accurately than print film, so you need a camera with exposure control, which means a top-end compact or an SLR.

Supports

In bright sunlight, you can take sharp handheld photos, especially with a wide-angle lens and fast film. In low light, especially with slow film, you may find the shutter speed so slow that it's difficult to avoid camera shake and an unfocused photo. If you use a long telephoto lens, 200mm+, steady handholding becomes extremely difficult, except with very fast film and in very bright light. A good rule of thumb for judging whether you can safely hold your camera by hand is that the shutter speed shouldn't be any lower than the focal length of the lens. Thus, with a 28mm lens, you should be able to take sharp photos at 1/30th of a second, but with a 200mm lens, the slowest shutter speed becomes 1/250th—hence the need for bright light and fast film.

The solution is to use some form of support for

your camera. This can be you. For more stability, sit cross-legged so you can rest your elbows on your knees, or lie down and rest your elbows on the ground. You can also use some of your outdoor equipment. Take off your pack and rest your camera on top of it, or roll up a soft garment and use that as a support on top of a rock or branch.

A monopod makes a great support, especially when photographing moving animals or people. Many **trekking poles** can be quickly converted

> "For support, you can just rest the camera on a rock or the ground, but it's often difficult to get it level doing this. I spent too much time wedging pebbles and twigs under a camera to make it level before I started carrying a camera support."—CT

to monopods by removing the top of the handle to reveal a camera attachment. A monopod can be especially useful for animal photography when you want to stay hidden and don't want to fiddle with a tripod.

When you have time to set it up, a tripod is the most stable camera support. It's excellent for really low light situations, such as before and after sunrise and sunset. Most tripods are far too heavy to lug far into the wilderness, however, although canoeists can carry them. Lightweight tripods that most professional photographers would probably regard as jokes are ideal in the wilderness. They are light enough to carry and adequate for lightweight camera equipment.

Another function of a tripod in landscape photography is that it slows you down. Just setting up a tripod means taking time for your photography instead of just grabbing a quick shot. Slowing down allows you to study the scene, find the best viewpoint, and work out the best composition (see Composition below).

Protection

Whatever camera you use, it must be protected from knocks, water, dust, grit, temperature ex-

tremes, and more. Sand is a particular enemy to cameras in the desert. Carrying a camera in your pack isn't the answer. Instead, carry a padded camera bag on a waist belt, on a chest harness, or slung across your body bandolier style. Paddlers can use float bags.

Taking Photographs

Taking technically adequate photographs isn't difficult with modern camera gear, especially in good light. The camera can sort out the focusing and exposure, so all you have to do is hold it steady when you press the shutter button. However, a sharp, correctly exposed photograph can still be dull and lifeless. While fundamental mechanics are important, photography is about light and composition. Poor composition or flat light can make a photograph of a spectacular scene uninteresting. At the scene, your eye will compensate for flat light to some extent; you can still see the grandeur of a landscape despite the dullness. Record it on film, however, and the dullness might dominate. You need to learn what a scene will look like on film and then decide whether to take a photograph.

Composition

Good composition is vital. When you look through the viewfinder, think about the final result and how to find the best composition. Often, a position lower than eye level will produce a better image. Leaving the trail can often produce a better viewpoint too. Consider what you want in the photo and how the different elements relate to one another. Move around with the camera, looking at different compositions through the viewfinder. If you aren't sure which is best, take them all. If you have a zoom lens, zoom it in and out slowly to see which image looks best.

Think about everything that will appear in the photo. Large, plain areas, such as cloudless skies or, even worse, unbroken foregrounds, can detract from the heart of the image. Landscapes look best if the horizon is a third or less from the top or bottom of the picture. If the sky is featureless, reduce it to the top third of the image or less. If there are interesting clouds but the foreground is plain, the sky could make up two-thirds of the image. A uniform foreground is a common fault, especially when using wide-angle lenses. To avoid this, look for something to break up the foreground, such as a rock, creek, or bush. This will make the image more interesting and give more depth to the picture. A companion can be used for this too, but don't let him stand facing the camera in the center of the picture, looking awkward or posed. If he is stationary, move him to one side and have him look at the view, not the camera. It's usually better, though, to have him walking across the scene or away from or toward the camera, which makes the picture more dynamic.

When photographing a person or an object, such as a rock or a tree, rather than a broad landscape, ensure that the subject is large enough in the frame and not in shade or dull light. Think about the surroundings, and position the subject accordingly. Dead center is not usually a good place for a person or an object, unless she or it fills the whole frame. Again, people look more natural if they're doing something—walking, reading the **map**, looking at the view—instead of staring straight at you.

Light

Landscape photographers often talk of the magic hours of dawn and dusk, and for good reason. At these times, the light is more intense and the colors richer. The low angle of the sun gives good side-lighting and reveals shapes and textures too. When the sun is high in the sky, the light is flatter and less detail and color are visible in the landscape. Photos taken at this time can look washed out or hazy. A polarizing filter can help, but nothing beats the light of the magic hours.

The best times to take landscape photographs during the day are often just before and after a storm, when the sun cuts through the clouds and the light is dramatic, with a bright foreground or horizon set against dark backlit clouds. Pictures of people struggling in strong **winds** or **snow** can

capture some of the feel of what it was like to be there.

While snow can transform a landscape, it can be difficult to photograph because it's so bright that your camera reduces the amount of light it lets in; thus dark objects and people are underexposed, and the snow itself looks gray rather than white. With print film and digital cameras, this isn't a big problem, but it is with slide film, which has to be precisely exposed. One way around this is to let in more light: open the aperture by one to two stops or use a slower shutter speed. If your camera has an exposure compensation dial, you can turn this to plus one and a half or plus two. Or you can meter (take an exposure reading) off a patch of blue sky or gray rock, and use that reading.

Anytime the light is unusual or changing quickly, it's worth taking photos at different settings (called *bracketing*). That way, you're more

> "In dull light, I tend to concentrate on details rather than wide landscapes, because they can still make interesting photographs."—CT

likely to get the results you want. If in doubt, take the photograph.

After your trip take care to store your photos carefully so you can view them in years to come and remember your adventures.

PILLOWS

A pillow is an upwelling of water that signifies a rock lying beneath the surface of the water. It is created when a strong current slams into a rock, causing the water to surge on the upstream side. If you see a pillow with an eddy immediately downstream of it, suspect a rock (see **eddies**). When a rock is so close to the surface that water just skims over the top, it is often referred to as a *sleeper*. Be careful—sleepers can be difficult to identify when the water is turbulent or there is a strong wind.

See also **moving-water hazards**.

PLANNING A TRIP

Planning a wilderness outing can be as simple as deciding Saturday morning to go away for the weekend and hopping in the car with your best friend, a few boxes of mac-n-cheese, and a map to the nearest state park. More often than not, however, trip planning involves more complicated logistics. Take for example a trip that Annie organized to northern Canada. The subarctic is a beautiful but demanding place, and it's not for everyone. Planning such a trip, especially one lasting 45 days, meant she had to choose her companions wisely. Annie knew that she wanted the trip to be somewhere in the Canadian North, but exactly where was eventually determined by the group. This involved a lot of research and time spent calculating distances. Once the location was selected and the dates were set, the group had to work out the logistics of transporting the people and their gear to the drop-off. This required making plane reservations months in advance. A permit also had to be acquired—another step that required several months' notice. Needless to say, it took a great deal of preparation for the trip to come off without a hitch.

Several common components need to be determined during the planning process for any trip. You need a destination and a route. You have to know who you're going with and how long you'll be gone. You must find appropriate equipment and pack enough **food**. You must decide if everyone has adequate skills and **judgment** (and if not, how you will accommodate any such person). Finally, you should have a sense for the type of trip you want. Each of these components demands careful scrutiny. **Goals and expectations, route selection**, and **group travel** are important topics that can be found elsewhere in this book. Read on to learn how to proceed with planning on a timely basis.

Gathering Information

Information is required for any trip away from local areas. You may need to know about **maps,** guidebooks, **permits** and regulations, **weather,** hazards, animal problems, **insect** problems, **water** sources, supply points, campgrounds, access to the start and finish points, public **transportation,** and more.

The best place by far to start a search for information is on the Internet. The only problem with this is the sheer amount of information available. For example, a recent search on

> "When I returned to the North Cascades for the first time in nineteen years, I was delighted to discover via the Internet the Green Trails series of maps, which didn't exist on my previous visit."—CT

Yosemite, in California, and the **Appalachian Trail,** of the eastern United States, got 711,000 and 123,000 results, respectively. Even the remote Richardson Mountains in the far north of Canada's Yukon Territory brought 2,290 results.

Narrowing the terms of the search will reduce the number of results, but even then the numbers are high. Luckily, many search engines will bring up the most useful results first. If not, you just have to scroll down and look for those that seem most likely to have the information you need. Government agencies (such as the National Park Service, Bureau of Land Management, and Forest Service in the United States) have excellent websites with all the information you need about permits and regulations and much more, so you could try these first (see resources section). Often you can book permits online.

While websites may have most of the information you need, you'll still probably need to purchase maps and perhaps guidebooks. What the Internet can do is tell you what's available and where to get it. With maps and guidebooks, always check the date of publication to see how up-to-date the information is likely to be with regard to trails and other developments.

There's still no substitute for direct contact with rangers and other local officials. They should be able to give you current information about **bear** problems, river levels, **trail** relocations, snowfall or snowmelt, and similar topics. Local outdoor equipment stores can often provide information too.

When asking questions, it's best to gauge how likely the answer is to be correct. Has the person actually seen the water source, or is it a case of "the friend of someone I know was there a week or two back and said . . . "? Has the person crossed that **glacier**, or does he just *think* the **crevasses** look small from below? People are usually very willing to help, but they don't always have the actual information you require.

For trips outside North America, much more information is needed and can be harder to find. Allow plenty of time. If you have to write for material, it could take weeks or even months before you receive a reply. You need to find out about visas and permits and any regulations affecting your type of trip. Check out travel and medical insurance, and don't forget to apply for a passport if you don't already have one (and if you do have one, check that it isn't out of date). It's best to order foreign currency well in advance.

Equipment

Develop an initial equipment list by writing down everything you think you will need. Don't forget

> "To organize my information, I like to list all the questions I have and then check them off as I find the answers. That way, I don't forget something important and only realize it at the last minute."—CT

small items such as extra cord, matches, and needle and thread. Decide who, among your group, can supply each of the various items. If the trip is long and the gear is bound to endure a lot of wear, consider offering the owner some sort of compensation. If the trip requires new gear and it is purchased by the group, decide *before the trip* how the equipment will be dispersed at the end.

If you don't know what gear you need, seek the advice of someone familiar with your destination. When buying equipment go for quality. Cheap gear is usually just that—cheap and unreliable. Research a product in outdoor magazines or online before making a purchase. Learn how to use the product correctly before you rely on it. As your planning continues, you might discover that you need additional items. Finally, make a list of all the gear you will actually be taking, a step that will save you time in planning your next trip.

Food

Before you plan your menu you'll need to know the duration of the trip and how many people will be going. Consider having everyone fill out a quick menu questionnaire describing their dietary preferences and food allergies. These can be compiled and given to one or two people, who can then create the trip menu.

There are two basic ways to pack food: by weight or by meal. Packing by weight means bringing a certain number of pounds of each type of food. When mealtime comes you can shuffle through your food bag and mix something together. Packing by meal means that your food bag is organized by meals—in other words, all the ingredients for Monday's dinner are packed together, as are Tuesday's, Wednesday's, and so forth. There are merits to both systems. Packing by weight is much faster and allows you more flexibility on the trail. Packing by meal is convenient at mealtimes and is often the choice for people who prefer prepackaged backcountry foods.

Whichever system you use, keep your eye on the nutritional value of the food as well as the variety. Never underestimate the value of a well-planned menu; it is an insurance policy of sorts. A well-fed person is generally more positive and far happier than someone who is hungry or unhappy with the choice of foods. (For more information on planning a menu see **food**.)

Timeline

Collecting information and developing group consensus takes time. A timeline checklist can help any individual or group stay on track and prevent missing key preparations when planning a trip. A typical timeline looks like this:

Seven Months Out

The decision has been made to plan a trip.
1. Start organizing a group.
2. Research possible destinations.
3. Think about transportation options.
4. Set some goals for the trip. What do you want this trip to be about? Relaxation? Fishing? Hiking as many miles as you can?

Five Months Out

The destination has been picked.
1. Finalize the group; consider having people commit to the trip with payment of a deposit.
2. Finalize exact dates.
3. Divide tasks among the group.
4. File for permits.
5. Make tentative transportation arrangements.
6. Discuss group goals and expectations.
7. Develop equipment lists.

Three Months Out

Things are beginning to come together.
1. Organize resupplies (see **resupplying**).
2. Finalize transportation arrangements.
3. Get your gear together. Does any of it need repair?
4. Finalize the menu and order hard-to-find supplies.
5. Touch base with trip mates.
6. Develop contingency plans.
7. Are you physically prepared? If not, start working out!
8. Consider going to your doctor for a physical.
9. Have everyone fill out medical histories. Do you need any special first-aid supplies?
10. Does anyone need a refresher course in first aid? How about a shakedown trip of some sort?

A Few Weeks Out

The departure date is approaching.
1. Reconfirm transportation.
2. Pack food (if you haven't already).
3. Make a **trip plan**.
4. Get together personal clothing and gear.
5. Ensure that boots are broken in (if you're hiking).
6. Arrange personal details for your absence from home (who will pay your bills, feed your pets, take in the mail, watch your house).

Before You Leave

It's time to go!
1. Give someone your trip plan.
2. Check with authorities about fire bans, water levels, snow conditions, etc.
3. Take a group "before" picture.
4. Get on your way to adventure!

Planning a trip can be an exciting part of the journey. Not only does it help you prepare mentally, it's also satisfying as it all comes together. Take time to think through all aspects of your trip, keeping in mind that no detail is too small if a perfect trip is the goal.

PLBS

PLBs, or personal locator beacons, are pocket-sized emergency beacons that allow you to summon outside rescue assistance in dire emergency situations. Weighing in at just over a pound, PLBs are small enough and light enough to be kept on your person—a good place to carry one if there's a chance you could lose your kayak in a set of rapids or your **pack** in a **flash flood**. Once switched on, the PLB transmits a one-way signal that will be picked up by satellite within the hour. Using Doppler Shift technology, the satellite determines the source of the signal to within 3 miles (and often more precisely). A PLB alert is automatically routed to the U.S. Air Force, which then notifies a local **search-and-rescue** organization of the emergency. The search-and-rescue organization then picks up a homing signal transmitted by the PLB (assuming they have the technology) and locates the person in distress.

Once you purchase a PLB, you must register it with the National Oceanic and Atmospheric Administration (NOAA; see the resources section for contact information). Registering allows NOAA to document information about the owner, information that becomes vital in the event of a search and rescue. For instance, if you were to switch on your PLB, you are sure to get a call ascertaining, for example, whether you had mistakenly turned it on while showing it off to your friends (a mistake that at the present time does not result in a fine). Armed with the name of the person they're looking for, search-and-rescue personnel are able to interview friends and family to learn important information, such as what gear the person in distress may be carrying, their itinerary, how much outdoor experience they have, and how they may react in emergencies.

The PLB is the land version of the EPIRB (emergency position-indicating radio beacon), which is designed for use by ships at sea. For several years, the PLB has been available outside the United States, but the Federal Communications Commission (FCC) prohibited its sale (or use) in the United States. This ban forced **expeditions** that wanted to carry emergency beacons to use EPIRBs for remote journeys despite the fact that the FCC strictly prohibited EPIRB use for land-based operations. Now that the PLB is legal in the United States, it will likely become the next "must-have" item for serious outdoor enthusiasts.

The legalization of PLBs is not a license to be careless in the wilderness. It does not lessen the consequences of making poor decisions, and it is not a free ticket home if you decide to take unnecessary or stupid risks. Any electronic communication or signaling device can unexpectedly fail or become lost. Likewise, once a search and rescue is commenced, a host of people may be risking their lives to save yours. Needless to say, PLBs

or any other emergency signals should be used sparingly and wisely. Despite the fact that rescue technology continues to improve, the law of the land remains the same: If you go into the wilderness, you should be prepared to handle any emergency that arises on your own.

For more information visit the NOAA satellites website (see resources section). See also **communication devices** and **signaling**.

POISONOUS AND STINGING PLANTS

Many plants will scratch or cut you if you brush against them, which can be painful and unpleasant. Spend an hour picking cactus spines out of your skin and you'll be more careful in the future. None of the cacti is poisonous though. The few plants that are can be a real problem, especially if you're sensitive to them.

The worst and most notorious offenders are poison oak and poison ivy, both members of the *Rhus* genus. They are found throughout the contiguous 48 U.S. states and southern Canada, mostly in low-elevation woods. Both are small, vinelike bushes with long, thin branches that often reach out across trails. The easiest way to

Poison oak.

CORBIS IMAGES

Poison ivy.

ALAN CVANCARA

identify them is by the leaves, which grow in clusters of three. These leaves are red when new, turn shiny green in summer, and become red and orange in the fall.

The sap of poison oak and ivy contains urushiol, an oily chemical that can cause Rhus-dermatitis, which results in severe itching, a rash, a burning sensation, and small blisters that may take 7 to 10 days to clear if not treated. The sap comes from bruised plants. Poison oak and ivy are delicate plants and are easily damaged, especially in the spring and early summer when the leaves are tender. Present all year round, urushiol is contained in every part of the plant. It's also present in dead plants. Just brushing against a bruised plant can transfer the sap to your clothes or skin. The sap is potent, so only a tiny amount can cause problems.

Rinsing the affected area with cold water as soon as possible is the best way to remove at least some of the oil. Whether to use soap or not is a difficult question. Apparently, soap will help remove urushiol, but it will also slough off any protective layers of your skin, making absorption of the poison more likely. Soap or detergent is more effective to wash urushiol from **clothing** and footwear. If you are affected by poison oak or ivy, use calamine lotion and cool compresses to help ease the itching. If a large area of your body is affected or you're particularly sensitive to urushiol, seek medical attention.

Avoiding contact with poison oak, sumac, and ivy is the best policy. Keep an eye out for it anywhere there is brush along the **trail**. Wearing long pants and a long-sleeved shirt can help too.

Of less concern, though painful if you come into contact with them, are stinging nettle and devil's club. The first are widespread throughout North America. Stinging nettle can grow to 9 feet high, though most are no more than 3 feet. The leaves are covered in small poison-containing spines that stick in the skin, causing a burning sensation and intense itching. A small rash of white spots appears. The itching usually wears off in an hour, although it can last for 24 hours. The poison is formic acid, which an alkaline such as baking soda can neutralize. The large leaves of the dock plant, which often grows near nettles, can also help if rubbed on the affected area.

Devil's club is a large shrub, 3 to 6 feet tall with big leaves, found on western-facing mountain slopes in the northwestern United States, western Canada, and Michigan and Ontario. The stalks are covered with long, razor-sharp spines. They were once thought to be poisonous, probably because they break off in the skin and the wound can become infected, but apparently this is not so.

Stinging nettle.

CORBIS IMAGES

Devil's club.

POLING

Poling is the traditional art of guiding your canoe across water using a pole instead of a paddle. This skill has been kept alive through small communities of enthusiasts across the United States. In recent years, poling has become a fully competitive sport—albeit one that is not well known. Poling gives a canoeist the ability to travel upstream, even when the current is strong and rapids are present. All it takes to pole a lightly loaded canoe is 6 inches of water. This makes it possible to travel rivers with extremely low water (a prospect that usually makes most canoeists cringe). Even when the water gets deep, a good poler can maneuver in and out of **eddies** and take advantage of the natural features of the river. When traveling downstream, a pole can slow or even stop the momentum of the canoe, a technique called *snubbing*.

Poling is a skill best learned through hands-on experience. Start on flat water by standing just behind the stern thwart of a canoe. Make sure you have a good stance. Take your pole and plunge it into the water just behind your feet. As you push against the pole, walk your hands toward the top of the pole in a hand-over-hand fashion. When your hands get to the top of the pole, lower your center of gravity and give a final push off the bottom of the lake or river. Quickly pull the pole out of the water and repeat the process. This is the traditional method of poling; however, there are several different techniques. One popular style is to pole on both sides of the boat. Another is to make short, quick jabs against the bottom of the river or lake. This technique is often used when poling up a lively stream.

No special canoe is needed for poling, but you do need a pole. Poles should be 10 to 12 feet long and made either of wood (spruce or tamarack is nice) or aluminum. If desired, a metal or leather shoe can be attached to the end of the pole to prevent it from splitting and to help it grip rocks along the way.

Poling a canoe requires as little as 6 inches of water.

A pole can be outfitted with a metal shoe to prevent it from splitting on rocky bottoms.

The American Canoe Association holds poling events across the country (most are in the Northeast). To find the nearest poling event, check out the ACA website (see resources section). If you're looking for a good book about poling, try *The Basic Essentials of Canoe Poling*, by Harry Rock.

PORTAGING

Ah, the portage—the bane of the canoe trip for some people, and for others a welcome opportunity to get out and stretch their legs. Like them or not, portages will always be a part of **canoe tripping**, and a reality on some kayaking trips as well. Portaging is the act of carrying your gear and boat over land, either to connect lakes or to avoid heavy rapids. Portaging is so linked with canoeing that old stories about fur traders competing to carry the heaviest load are still told today. Some people take their time on portages, stopping to lie in the sun or prepare a meal. Others have speed as their ultimate goal and analyze the process of portaging until they determine the most efficient method. Wherever you fall in this continuum, there are a few basic rules of thumb that can help any portage run smoothly.

• *Pack your packs carefully.* There's nothing more painful than hauling around a 60-pound canoe pack with a corner of the grill stabbing into your back. When you pack, ensure that the back of your pack is flat and, if possible, padded, perhaps with the **tarp.** (See **packing a canoe.**)
• *Be organized.* Minimize what you have to carry by packing loose items, such as drying clothes, **map** cases, and **fishing** equipment, into packs before the portage. Stuff them into the tops of the packs, where they're easily accessible, but make sure they won't fall out.
• *Know your route.* If the portage is longer than a simple carry, you may want to scout it to ensure the route is clear. In areas that aren't heavily traveled, **trails** often seem to peter out among the paths of roaming **moose** and caribou—that is, if there are trails at all! If there aren't, take a **bear-**ing on your **compass** from your map and follow the path of least resistance. If you're with a group, stay close together unless the route is clear and obvious. If the portage is long (over a mile), consider dividing it into segments and moving your entire spread of gear one segment at a time. This keeps people, and important items such as the **first-aid kit,** closer together.
• *Devise a system.* If efficiency is important to you, come up with a system. If you take the canoes over first, people who carry the packs can simply reload the boats at the end of the portage. This might not be that big of a deal if you're out for a weekend trip and your packs are light, but on longer **expeditions** packs can get extremely heavy, often requiring multiple people just to lift them off the ground. Consider ways to reduce the number of times you need to move heavy packs.
• *Watch your footing.* Often, portages take you over wet or mossy rocks that are slicker than wet fish. Take care to ensure that you don't slip and fall. Carrying a heavy load over rocky terrain is an invitation for a twisted ankle or worse, but sometimes it can't be avoided. Watch out for swampy areas too. Taking a step into knee-deep muck will halt your forward momentum before you realize it. It can also take the boot right off your foot.
• *Choose good yoke pads.* Finding perfect yoke pads is a personal pursuit. Simple screw-on pads are comfortable and easy to make (see **yoke pads**). When choosing your yoke pads, remember that you may not always be portaging on flat ground. Find a **yoke** and yoke pads that allow the canoe to angle both up and down and still feel comfortable and secure.
• *Consider the time of day,* **weather** *conditions, and energy level of the group.* This should be done before starting a portage. If necessary, eat a snack before you begin. On long portages, fill your water bottle at the start, because purification can take a while. By the time your **water** is drinkable, you'll probably be eager to quench your thirst.

In well-traveled areas, portages are usually marked on the map. If you're crossing a large lake, a compass bearing can help you identify the correct destination. If you decide to use a compass, it is a good idea to "aim off" by a few degrees. This way, when you reach the opposite shore, you'll know exactly which direction to turn to find your target. If a portage is not marked on the map, go to the area that makes the most sense, often the shortest distance to the next lake or the route with the least elevation. Avoid areas marked on your map as **swamps**. Some portages are marked with signs or blaze marks (see **trail markers**). Others can be found by looking for the erosion on the shore or for campsites that often develop at the portage sites.

If you're new to a route, get as much information about your portages as possible before you head out (see **planning a trip**). One way to do this is to follow the logs of earlier paddlers, a tactic

> "I once looked for a portage trail for over an hour, scouring the same shore again and again and scouting countless caribou trails. After breaking for lunch, I read a passage from a journal dating back to 1933—and there it was! Exact directions to its hidden location in a small bay covered with reeds. Virtually nothing had changed in the 65 years since the journal was written. In fact, the author had even commented on how long it had taken him to find the trail."—AA

especially helpful in extremely remote country. If you come across hard-to-find portages, avoid marking their location with trail blazes. Trying to find your way in the wilderness is part of the adventure that lures us back time and time again.

A special note should be made for paddlers who are traveling on rivers with significant whitewater. Portages can be incorrectly marked on maps and should therefore be taken with a grain of salt. Combine the information on the map with other clues you have amassed, such as advice from previous paddlers and the appearance of the actual terrain, before deciding what side of the

RICK SWEITZER

Portaging is easier when gear is organized and compact.

river to head for. Avoid ferries across long and hazardous stretches of river whenever possible (see **ferrying**).

PRUSIK HITCH

The prusik hitch, also known as the *prusik knot*, can be used for ascending a **rope**, creating an emergency brake for **rappelling**, or connecting sections of a pulley system, such as a **z-drag**. Even if you don't think you'll ever use a prusik hitch, learn it anyway: you're sure to find a way to use it at some point in your outdoor career.

The prusik hitch is best used with ropes of different diameters. A piece of accessory cord with the ends tied together in a double **fisherman's knot** makes a good **sling**, often called a *prusik sling*, for the prusik hitch because it will likely be a smaller diameter than your other rope. Take your prusik sling and wrap it around your rope (as shown). When the prusik hitch is under tension,

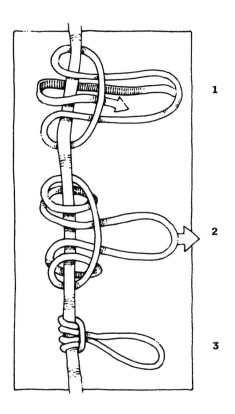

The prusik hitch can be used in ascending ropes or as an emergency brake for rappelling. 1. Wrap a loop of accessory cord or webbing around a rope. (It's best if the diameter of the line is thinner than the line to which it is tied.) 2. Add two or three more wraps to increase friction. The more wraps, the greater the friction. 3. Dress the knot (see knots) so all the wraps lie flat against the rope.

it bites into the rope onto which it is tied, locking into position. To unlock the hitch, remove the tension by loosening, or opening, the hitch. When the hitch is in the open position, it slides freely along the rope, although sometimes it requires a little assistance. If you're using the prusik hitch as an emergency brake for rappelling, make sure you don't grab the hitch during an uncontrolled descent. If you hold the hitch, you may inadvertently keep it in the open position, preventing it from locking into position.

PUNCTURE WOUNDS

Puncture wounds occur when an object, such as a twig or nail, penetrates the skin and disturbs the deeper tissues. Puncture wounds can cause more problems than you might expect. While the injury may not appear to be severe, the potential for **infection** is very high. Therefore, all puncture wounds should be thoroughly cleansed and kept protected while they heal (see **first aid**). If natural healing does not occur, arrange an **evacuation** of the person for medical treatment.

If the object piercing the skin isn't easily removable, bandage the area with the impaled object in place, securing it well enough so it doesn't get jostled during transport, which can cause additional tissue damage. Evacuate the person to a medical facility as soon as possible.

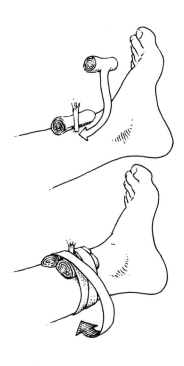

Puncture wounds become infected easily.

Based on an illustration by ALLAN PARKER

R

RAFTING UP

Rafting up is the joining of several canoes or kayaks on the water, with the paddlers either holding onto each other's boats or with the boats connected in some other fashion. Rafting up provides more stability than one canoe or kayak on its own, offering a way to come together for a snack or to review the map without having to head to shore. Rafting up also provides a platform from which you can hoist a makeshift sail and take advantage of a following **wind**.

A few products on the market let you clamp your canoes together quickly and easily. Unless you plan to raft up frequently or for extended periods of time, however, it makes more sense to devise your own system, such as laying a branch (or paddle) across the boats and securing it with a rope. These systems can be extremely difficult to untie and may need to be cut, so don't use your emergency **rope** or even your favorite **bandanna**.

RAIN

Pouring down from a dull gray, featureless sky, the **mountains** hidden in blankets of dense **cloud**, rain drenches the landscape. The earth becomes damp, then saturated; pools form in hollows, and creeks burst with floodwater. Sodden vegetation soaks clothing and bodies. Dampness pervades everything. The world is wet.

Wet **weather**, especially prolonged wet weather, can be hard to endure. A sudden downpour or an afternoon cloudburst can drench you, but the return of sun and warmth soon warms and dries you. Steady rain that falls hour after hour and day after day slowly seeps in everywhere until nothing is dry. Coping with such conditions means keeping your gear as dry as possible and also keeping your morale high. It's all too easy to fall into a negative frame of mind.

Protecting Gear

If your gear gets wet, life quickly becomes miserable. Damp **clothing** cools you and feels unpleasant. Wet matches and **lighters** won't strike. **Stoves** fizzle and go out. Powdered foods, such as dried milk, sugar, and instant potatoes, turn to wet, sticky lumps. **GPS** receivers and **headlamps** can stop working. **Maps** and trail guides turn to soggy pulp. Wet **sleeping bags** feel cold, leaving you shivering through the night.

To prevent these hardships, all water-sensitive gear should be packed in waterproof bags. Crucial items, such as sleeping bags, can be double-bagged. Plastic bags are ideal for most items, and waterproof stuff sacks are useful too. (Note that not all stuff sacks are waterproof.) Sack liners made from heavy-duty plastic or waterproofed nylon are available, or you can use a large trash bag. In wet weather, you should keep items you may need during the day, especially rain clothing, easily accessible at the top of your **pack** or in external pockets. Your **tent** or other shelter should be handy too, so you can set up camp before unpacking anything else.

> "Rather than one large sack liner, I use two and also pack items inside smaller bags. My sleeping bag goes inside a waterproof stuff sack inside a sack liner. Carried like this, my down bag has stayed dry through days of rain. Wet items, such as the tent or tarp or damp clothing, go in outside pockets—mesh ones are particularly good for this—or else at the top of the pack outside of any sack liners."—CT

A pack cover can be useful too, but you do have to remove it to get at items inside the pack. The cover is also vulnerable to snagging on vegetation because the fabric is much less durable than that of the pack itself. A cover can't be used if you have items, such as an **ice ax** or **trekking poles**, attached to the outside of your pack. Even if you use a pack cover, be sure you also have waterproof liners or bags.

Keeping Dry

Although rain usually feels cold on bare skin, the actual temperature may not be that cold. You can work up a fair amount of warmth inside rain gear. Many people bundle up in the rain and then overheat, which results in **condensation** that dampens inner clothing. Once they stop moving, this damp clothing chills them. To avoid this, it's best to wear only the amount of clothing that keeps you just warm enough when you're moving, but no more. Of course, if you start to feel cold, stop and put on some more clothes, preferably in the shelter of a rock or tree. A quick, efficient way to control your temperature is with a warm hat, which can be carried in a jacket pocket and put on if you start to cool down. Because so much

heat is lost through the head, this can make a big difference in how warm you feel.

When you stop for a rest, put on warm clothing immediately, before you cool down, because it's much harder to get warm than to stay warm. In areas where a lot of rain is likely, you can carry a synthetic-filled jacket, which you can pull on over your rain jacket so you don't lose heat or get your inner layers wet by having to remove the rain jacket. The synthetic jacket can be kept on when you start hiking again and removed when you start to feel hot. Such synthetic jackets are windproof, water resistant, and quick drying.

Avoiding condensation can be a problem. If the rain lasts for many hours and you have to keep your rain jacket fully closed, some dampness inside is inevitable no matter how "breathable" your garment (see **breathability**). Open vents whenever possible to help reduce condensation. The neck is a crucial area here because warm, moist air rises. Many people like to wear a waterproof **hat** and leave the jacket hood down in all but the windiest conditions because this allows some of that moist air to escape. A hat with a broad brim also keeps rain off your face and stops it from dripping down your neck.

In **forests** and anywhere that isn't too exposed to **wind**, an **umbrella** gives the best rain protection. You won't have to wear a rain jacket at all, so condensation isn't a problem. You can shelter under the umbrella when you stop, and use it to cover your pack as you are getting things out.

Rain that starts hard and fast will send you scrambling to get into your rain gear before you get soaked. Much more insidious is rain that starts gently, with just a few sprinkles, followed by a light drizzle that slowly becomes heavier and heavier until it's raining hard. Initially, it's tempting not to bother with rain gear in the hope that the rain won't amount to much. Sometimes this is the case. Often it isn't, however, and you finally realize you are getting wet and need to don your rain gear. Wearing rain gear over wet clothing increases the likelihood of condensation and will leave you feeling chilly and damp.

It's better to put on rain clothing when the first drops fall and then have to take it off when the sun comes out five minutes later, than to wait until you get wet to put it on. If your rain gear is handy, rather than deep in your pack, you'll be more likely to put it on sooner. If you're in a hot climate, such as the jungle or **desert**, you might be better off without wearing your rain gear during a monsoon downpour because the rain will wash off dirt and sweat; in rain gear you'll just get soaked with sweat.

A rain jacket is far more useful than rain pants, although in cool, wet areas you should carry both. Because rain pants can feel restrictive and hot, sometimes it's best to wear them only if it's cold and windy as well as wet. In warm weather, wear shorts in the rain. Otherwise, you can wear windproof, synthetic long pants, which dry quickly and are reasonably comfortable when wet. If it looks as if you might need to wear rain pants all day, wearing them over wicking long underwear or lightweight **fleece** is comfortable because these stay drier next to your skin than other fabrics.

Keeping your feet dry in prolonged rain is difficult, if not impossible. Boots treated with waterproofing wax or boots with waterproof-breathable membranes help, but eventually water will get in at the ankle, even if you're wearing **gaiters**. Waterproof-breathable **socks** can keep your feet dry when your **boots** are soaked. They'll probably keep your feet dry longer than anything else, as long as you don't get water down the top of them.

> "Except in cold weather, I just accept that if it's raining for long, my feet are going to get wet. Once they're wet, I can at least stop bothering trying to keep them dry by dodging puddles and rock hopping across creeks."—CT

Trying to keep your feet dry can lead to trail erosion. Too often hikers go around wet sections of a trail, breaking down the edges and widening it. The widened section then gets wet too, so hikers spread even farther out. This can lead to a wide, muddy swath or a series of eroded **trails**. To avoid this destruction, splash through the water on the main trail and accept wet feet (see also **Leave No Trace**).

Rest stops should be fairly short in wet weather, unless you find good shelter or erect your own. Otherwise, you can get quite cold (see **hypothermia**). Don't neglect to eat, though. **Food**, especially if it's high in carbohydrates, provides warmth and energy. Easy-to-eat snacks that require no preparation, such as trail mix, energy bars, and granola bars, are best in the rain. These can even be eaten while **hiking** if there's no shelter and you don't want to stop. You need to drink occasionally too, though not as much or as often as in dry weather.

For a long stop, perhaps while you wait to see if the rain will cease before climbing to a high pass or a summit, you can pitch your shelter, put on dry, warm clothing, even get in your sleeping bag, and light your stove for some hot food and drink. And if the rain continues and your shelter is comfortable, you might well decide to spend the night there.

Creeks and Rivers

Creeks can rise rapidly in heavy rain, turning from shallow streams to impassable raging torrents. It may be necessary to change your route or to even retreat. On day hikes or side trips away from camp, be careful not to be cut off by rising creeks. Trails near creeks and rivers can flood if the rain is heavy enough. (See **river crossings** and **flash floods**.)

Camping in the Rain

Typically, temporary stopping places to get out of the rain don't make good campsites. In the rain, finding a good—which in this case means well drained—site can take time, but it's always worth the effort.

Hard-packed, well-used campsites often flood in heavy rain because the ground is too compacted to absorb much water. Forest duff and mineral soils are both good ground surfaces because these are porous and will soak up much rain. They may be damp, but they are unlikely to flood. Any hollow, whatever the ground type, and even very

---

"On one fall trip, my partner and I camped on a raised grassy site in a wide valley some distance from a small river. The second day, the weather was wet and windy so we day hiked (or rather sloshed) up the valley to a wide side stream that would have been difficult to ford. Turning back, we retraced our steps in now torrential rain. The mountain-sides were white with fresh foaming rivulets that hadn't been there a few hours earlier. Back at camp, we found water seeping under the groundcloth and the tent thrashing in the wind.

"Rather than be flooded out, we decided to abandon the trip and hike out. The trail was muddy and covered with pools, and water was spreading out across the riverside meadows. At one point, steep, craggy slopes closed in and the valley narrowed, squeezing the trail in close to the river—except there wasn't a trail, just water spreading everywhere. Abandoning the line of the trail, we waded through knee-deep water to the edge of the valley, where we could climb above the water a little way and traverse the slopes above the now 2-foot-deep fast-flowing water that covered the trail. Eventually we were able to regain the trail at a point where the river crashed down into a narrow gorge. If the water had been much deeper, we would have been trapped and would have had to spend another night."—CT

---

slight dips in otherwise flat ground, may turn into a pool. Raised ground, even if it's only a few inches higher than the surrounding terrain, can mean the difference between staying dry and get-

ting wet. Camping on a slight slope so water can run off will help.

Once you have found a reasonably dry site, make camp carefully so nothing gets wet. If possible, find somewhere sheltered to put your pack while you pitch your shelter. Try to leave your pack standing up, either leaning against a rock or tree or propped up with a hiking pole, so water can't soak into the side lying on the ground and so rain strikes the lid rather the back or sides. If your shelter is a tent, it helps to have one that pitches the rainfly first or as a unit with the inner tent; if it pitches inner-tent first, you need to be fast in the rain.

After erecting the shelter, place your pack inside, either in the porch of a tent or anywhere under a **tarp**. Don't get in yourself, though, unless your water containers are already full. Once inside, you won't want to come out again, so it's best to fill the containers first. When you do get in, remove wet clothing carefully so it doesn't soak anything else. In a tent, this means crouching in the porch. It's easier under a tarp because there's plenty of room and no inner tent to keep dry. Next, get into some warm, dry clothing even if you don't feel cold. Otherwise, you might be surprised at how quickly you cool down.

Once under cover, stay there; cook in the tent porch or at the edge of the tarp, and lie in your sleeping bag and watch the rain fall outside. The only problem could be **condensation**. If condensation does form, wipe it away with a **bandanna** or soft cloth.

In country where **bears** may raid campsites, do not cook where you sleep. This may mean **cooking** in the rain occasionally. This is not something you want to do night after night, however, so in areas where both bears and rain are likely, carry a small tarp to use as a cook shelter. Pitch this 100 yards or more from your sleeping shelter.

Drying Out

If it rains heavily all day or for days on end, you will gradually become damper and damper however good your gear. In addition to condensation, rain will eventually trickle in at the neck and wrists and wick up from the hem of your jacket. When humidity is high, moisture soaks in everywhere. Eventually all your clothes will feel damp and your feet will be soaked. As long as you aren't cold as well, your alternatives are to put up with the rain or to hike out. Keeping your sleeping bag as dry as possible is crucial; a warm night's sleep is rejuvenating and can prepare you to face another rainy day.

Anytime the rain does clear, stop and spread out your gear to dry and air out. It might be raining again in a few hours.

RAPPELLING

Rappelling is the process of lowering oneself down a steep slope or vertical wall by sliding down a **rope**. Despite its glamorous looks, most climbers avoid rappelling when at all possible. In fact, it's one of the more dangerous activities in climbing because it has absolutely no margin for error. Rappelling forces that you unconditionally place all your weight on the rope and **anchor** system—situations climbers generally try to avoid. In addition, it's highly likely that you could be descending after a full day of climbing and that you may be tired, hungry, dehydrated, or for some other reason unfocused when you set up your anchor and prepare your rope. Despite its risks, rappelling is necessary and common in **rock climbing**, **mountaineering**, and even **caving**. Rappelling has several components: choosing a site, building an anchor, throwing your rope, descending and, finally, retrieving your rope.

Choosing a Site

If you're rappelling down a climb you've just completed, it may be easiest to descend along that same route. Use your previous belay ledges if they were good. You may also be able to use the same anchors if they were multidirectional. If you need to locate a new rappel site, look for a spot that offers good anchor options that are close to the

rappel. Try to find a route that is free of loose boulders, rocks, and unstable snow.

Building an Anchor

Prepare to rappel by building a **bomber** anchor (see **anchors**). If any part of your anchor is questionable, back it up with additional protection (see **artificial protection**). Keep in mind that it may be impossible to retrieve your anchor. This may leave you debating whether you should accept some loss of gear or rappel with an inadequate anchor. If at all possible, accept the loss of gear. However, if you have to descend multiple pitches, remember to ration your gear so you don't end up on the last pitch with no anchor-building equipment.

Furthermore, if you know in advance that you'll be leaving equipment behind, purchase webbing in colors that will blend in with the environment, thus reducing the visual impact of your visit. In frequently traveled areas, you may encounter rappel anchors from a previous climber. Before you trust such an anchor with your life, evaluate its integrity and inspect it for environmental damage. If it looks as if marmots have been gnawing on the webbing or if the anchor has been abused (look for partially burned or welded webbing), you may want to reinforce the anchor with new webbing or add a new **carabiner**.

Throwing Your Rope

Once your anchor is prepared, find the center of your rope and use at least one locking carabiner to clip it to the anchor. If the rappel is longer than your rope allows, you may need to tie two ropes together. If this is the case, tie the ropes together using a figure-eight bend (see **figure-eight knots**), making sure to tie off the tails with a simple **overhand knot**. Clip the connected ropes to the anchor, and remember which side of the anchor the knot is on. This will be important information when you retrieve the rope. Before you toss the rope over the edge, find the ends and tie into each a large figure-eight knot. The figure-eight knots will act as stopper knots to prevent you from inadvertently rappelling off the end of your rope. Now coil the rope, shout "Rope!" and throw it over the edge (see **throwing a climbing rope**).

Descending

To descend the rope, you need to apply friction. If you're descending a low-angle slope, you can easily create friction by wrapping the rope around your body. This is known as a *body rappel*, and while it is a quick and easy technique, it is much too uncomfortable to rappel any great distance. Most climbers use lightweight, compact rappel devices that can be clipped to their harnesses with a carabiner. These accomplish the same task of creating friction and controlling descent. Often, rappelling devices and belaying devices are interchangeable (see **belaying**). A good example of this is Black Diamond's ATC. Whichever rappelling device you choose, it should be clipped into your whole harness (not just the belay loop) with a locking biner. Ensure that any loose clothing is neatly tucked into your harness and that long hair (including a long beard) is contained. Loose clothes, hair, and jewelry can easily get caught in the rappel device and cause a complicated and painful descent. Always get hands-on training from an expert before attempting to rappel.

Once you have double-checked your anchor and harness, and your partner has double-checked it again, you're ready to descend. Stand facing your anchor with your feet about shoulder-width apart. Place your guide hand on the rope that leads to the anchor, just above your rappel device. With your brake hand, securely hold the loose end of the rope below your rappel device, next to your hip (make sure to double-check the braking position for your particular rappel device). The brake hand is responsible for controlling the speed of your descent and, if necessary, stopping the descent. Therefore, it should never let go of the rope. How fast or slow you go will depend on how much friction there is on your rope. With a lot of friction on the rope, you will go slow; less

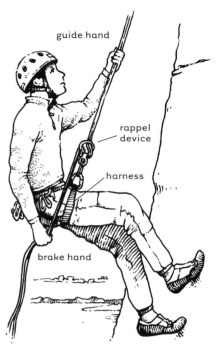

guide hand

rappel device

harness

brake hand

feet are shoulder-width apart

This climber is in the correct rappel position. His guide hand is above his rappel device, his brake hand is on the rope below his rappel device, and his feet are stabilizing his body.

friction, and you'll speed up. You can get an idea of how much friction a rappel device will apply by counting how many times the rope bends around the device. More bends equal more friction and, thus, slower descents.

As you begin to walk backward, lean against the rope. This is the moment of truth, and it can be hair-raising, especially when you are rappelling on a less-than-ideal anchor. When you encounter the edge, keep your feet in place and continue to lower the rest of your body. Stop when you're able to hold your body away from the rock with your feet. As you let rope slide through the rappel device, walk your feet down the wall (or slope) deliberately, keeping an eye out for loose rocks and other debris. Never bounce your way down a rappel. While it looks good in the movies, bouncing down a rappel puts tremendous strain on your rope and anchor. Instead, lower yourself in a slow, controlled fashion. If you need to stop midrappel, you can wrap the free end of the rope around your thigh several times, creating a brake. This technique, known as a *leg wrap*, will allow you to use both hands for a task.

Retrieving Your Rope

When you reach the bottom of the pitch, secure yourself to an anchor before you unclip yourself from your rappel. Obviously, you don't need to do this if you rappel all the way to the ground, in which case you can simply walk away from the rope. A shout of "Off rappel!" signals that you're finished with the rappel. If you can move to a position that is safe from falling debris, do so. A shout of "All clear!" lets the next person know that you're in a safe position. When the last person has descended the rope, retrieve your rope (see **retrieving a rappel rope**).

There are a few safety techniques you can use to back up a person who is rappelling. These are particularly good for first-time rappellers and people who are sick, injured, or scared. If you have an extra rope, consider **belaying** the rappeller. This may seem redundant, but it allows the person to get a feel for rappelling with the safety of a belay. If you need to slow or stop a person who is rappelling and you are beneath him at the bottom of the rappel, you can add a great deal of friction to his rappel device by pulling the rappel rope taught. This is a handy maneuver if the person rappelling cannot remain in control.

While there are other methods to ensure safety on a rappel, the best way is to practice the technique on a low-angle slope. Practicing will allow you to work out the kinks, literally, and it is a relatively low-risk environment.

READING RAPIDS

To the inexperienced observer, a set of rapids looks like a mass of erratic white foam, splashing water, and confused waves. But to the trained eye, reading a river is similar to solving a dynamic puzzle. Each wave is a clue to the size and depth of the object beneath, and every change in the direction of current tells a story. You can always pick paddlers out of a crowd, because when they're near rapids, they can't help but study the water, looking for the best run.

Imagine looking at a river. What do you see? Is it calm, or are there rapids? Are there rocks? Are there many waves? What do the waves look like? Are the banks straight, or do they turn? All of these observations are clues to what is going on in the river and to help you decide if (and how) you should shoot the rapids.

Reading rapids involves locating rocks. If you know where the rocks are, you can plan your route around them. To identify the rocks and other hazards, look for disturbances in the water. These disturbances can take the form of **waves**, changes in the direction of current, changes in the color of the water, and water that looks suspiciously calm. All are signs that something is going on beneath the surface.

When water runs over a rock, it typically generates a wave immediately downstream of the rock. Any increase in the strength and flow of the current may also increase the size of the wave. Another way to identify rocks is to look for V-shaped patterns in the water. When moving water hits a rock, it is diverted to either side, which can make the rock appear to be at the apex of a V. These Vs are known as *upstream* Vs because their apex is pointing upstream. Paddlers should avoid upstream Vs and instead aim for downstream Vs, identified by the apex of the V pointing downstream and formed when a chute of water flows between two rocks. Downstream Vs generally signify a clear passage. Running a set of rapids is often the process of moving from one downstream V to another. Because they aren't always conveniently placed one after the other, getting from one to the next can be a challenge, however.

A wave formed by an underwater rock is a type of stationary, or standing, wave. **Standing waves**, however, don't always signify a rock. Some standing waves are clear of rocks and offer great rides through the whitewater! When fast-moving water suddenly hits slow or still water, such as at the end of rapids, the fast-moving water piles up into a series of waves that eventually peter out. These are known as *haystacks* or *wave trains*. Wave trains can also be found at the end of a constriction in the river. These waves generally signify deep water that is navigable as long as the waves aren't too big. Paddling through a wave train can be a fun yet bumpy and often very wet ride. Once the bow of your canoe or kayak passes the crest of one wave, it will slam into the trough of the

next. If you're in an open boat, there's a good chance you'll be **swamped**. If the waves are big, it's best to avoid them or just skirt their sides.

The calm pools found behind protruding rocks and shorelines are **eddies**. Eddies can offer a break from downriver travel, but be cautious as you turn into them. When reading the river, identify the various eddies and remember that the water in an eddy is flowing in a direction opposite to the river's current. Sometimes you want to avoid eddies so you don't get caught up in their reversed currents.

In order to read rapids effectively you must be intimately familiar with the **moving-water hazards** of rivers, including **hydraulics**, undercut rocks, **strainers**, and strong **eddylines**. With practice you should be able to identify such hazards without much effort. Always **scout rapids** before you shoot them. Keep in mind that as water levels fluctuate the dynamics of rapids will change. If you have the opportunity, try to visit the same set of rapids in low and high water. Some obstacles will become much more significant, while others will get washed out. For this reason, always stop and scout, even if you have paddled the river many times before.

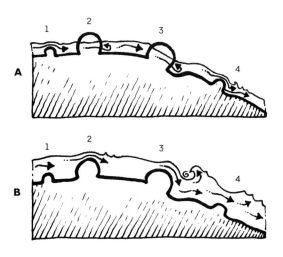

Low and high water levels help illustrate the challenges of reading rapids. **(A)** *Low water exposes more rocks, often creating more technical whitewater. 1. A pillow is created as water runs over a rock. 2. An eddy forms behind a protruding rock. 3. Another eddy forms behind a rock. Notice the depression immediately after the rock: this will cause a hydraulic to form in higher water. 4. A pillow forms over a submerged rock, followed by small standing waves. In low water, the waves are small ripples.* **(B)** *At higher water levels, the dynamics of the river change. 1. The original pillow is washed out; you won't even be able to detect the rock deep beneath the surface. 2. Now slightly submerged, a pillow will form over this rock. The eddy has been washed out. 3. Water pouring over this rock will hit the depressed riverbed and create a hydraulic. 4. The small standing waves have significantly increased in size.*

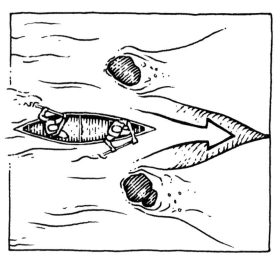

Water flowing between two rocks will create a V downstream that signifies a clear passage.

REPAIR KIT

On any trip there's a chance some item of gear will need repairing. Problems don't occur very often, but when they do, a repair kit will prove useful. What your kit should contain depends on your activity, what gear you have, and how long you'll be gone. Skiing, **canoeing**, and **rock climbing** trips all require some specialist items, such as ski binding and **crampon** spares. Some items, such as self-inflating pads, and **stoves** using liquid **fuel**, often have specific repair or maintenance kits.

> "My repair kit for hiking doesn't weigh more than 4 ounces. For ski touring, this goes up to about a pound, although this is shared among the group. Not everyone needs to carry a repair kit. Do make sure, though, that a group kit covers everyone's potential needs. You don't want to discover miles from the trailhead that you don't have the right bits for a broken binding."—CT

Remember, don't carry too much. It's easy to put together a comprehensive repair kit that weighs several pounds, but in the field, all you want to do is patch gear so it works. Longer-lasting **repairs** can be done at home or by a specialist. Below is a list of general useful items for your repair kit and recommendations for use.

• Sticky-backed ripstop nylon. This is a frequently used item for repairing tears in **clothing**, **sleeping bags**, and **tents**. Carry several small 9- by 3-inch rectangles. When applying a patch, make sure the item is dry and press firmly; then smooth out any wrinkles. Round off the edges of the patch so there are no corners to catch and lift off.
• **Duct tape**. This strong, sticky tape can be used for broken **pack** frames, broken poles (tent, **hiking**, or ski), split ski tips, and just about anything else.
• Adhesive. Seam sealant (see **seam sealing**) or quick-setting epoxy is useful for many repairs.

Running some around the edge of a patch secures it more firmly and makes it less likely to come off. Items under tension, such as ski tips, can be glued back together and then bound with tape until the adhesive has dried. Adhesive can also be used to cover **boots** and other footwear seams if these start to come apart. (If your footwear has many seams, coat the stitching with seam sealant in advance as a preventive measure.) You can seal leaking seams in shelters as well, but wait until the glue dries before using the shelter (so you won't inhale its fumes). Adhesive isn't needed often, so don't carry more than a very small tube.
• Needles and thread. A few needles and some lengths of tough synthetic thread (not **cotton**, which rots and breaks) come in handy for repairing tears in clothing and other items and for sewing on buttons. Include at least one heavy-duty sewing needle in case you need to sew through pack fabric or other tough material. (Not all repairs can be done with sticky tape.) A sewing awl makes this type of repair easier, but it isn't essential (see **Speedy Stitcher**). Needles also have other uses, such as bursting blisters. Very thin needles can be used to unblock stove jets.
• Nylon cord. This essential, all-purpose item has uses far beyond repairs, from **bear bagging** to hanging a clothesline. Nylon cord can be used to replace broken shoelaces, tent guylines, **gaiter** instep straps, and **hat** neck cords. It can also be used to bind broken items, such as pack frames, back together. Parachute cord is strong and light and comes in convenient 50-foot hanks, but any light cord will do. When cut, the ends need sealing with a match or lighter to stop them from unraveling.
• Multitool or Swiss army knife. This is an essential part of a repair kit but is usually carried separately (see **knives**). Scissors and a sharp blade are its most important features.

REPAIRS

Major repairs are best done at home or in a specialist repair shop. Some repairs can't be done in the **wilderness**, anyway. If you check your gear regularly before, during, and after a trip, you should be able to catch most potential problems before they become serious and sort them out at home.

Occasionally, items will fail or get damaged out in the wilderness, making at least a temporary repair necessary. Having a few repair items (see **repair kit**) makes this easier, but with a little imagination you can always improvise. Band-Aids may look odd stuck to a **down** jacket, but they do keep the fill from escaping. A twist tie from a plastic bag can be used as a zipper pull, pushed through a button and **fabric** to hold them together, or used to replace a broken snap. If you need cord, remove some from the neck of a stuff sack.

Mending

Mending rips, tears, and split seams in **clothing**, sleeping bags, and shelters is easy. You either sew the edges together or stick on a piece of **duct tape** or sticky-backed nylon (or both). With down-filled items, either use a patch or seal any stitching with adhesive. Otherwise, down will work its way out of the stitch holes. Sealing stitch holes is necessary in waterproof items too. Before applying a patch, clean the area well; dirt may prevent the patch from sticking properly. Alcohol swabs, which you should have in your **first-aid kit**, are good for this. Sealing the edges of a patch with adhesive will help it stay in place.

Zippers

Zippers are a common component in tents, sleeping bags, packs, clothing, and more. Quality zippers are tough, but they can break if mistreated. Open and close zippers smoothly and don't yank them hard if they stick, and they'll last longer. If fabric gets caught in the zipper, ease it out by gently pulling on each side, not by jerking the zipper up and down. Keeping zippers clean prolongs their life because dirt can jam them.

It's often the slider that fails on a zipper: you run the slider along the zipper to close it only to have it slowly open up again. Often, just running

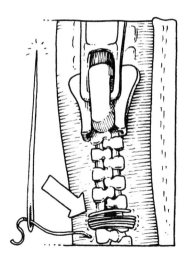

If your zipper loses some teeth, put a few stitches through the gap where they broke off and sew the two sides of the zipper together.

the slider back over the zipper closes it, but sometimes it just keeps opening up. This can be solved by squeezing the two sides of the slider together so it grips the teeth or coils more firmly. This is a delicate operation, though, one best done with pliers.

Where zipper teeth break off, the zipper won't close beyond that point and the slider will probably come off. You can't replace the teeth—the long-term solution is to replace the whole zipper—but you can put a few stitches through the gap where the teeth broke off and sew the two sides of the zipper together. This stops the slider from coming off, though you'll just have to manage with a shortened zipper. Broken coil zippers can be stitched at the break point too, again leaving you with a short but still functional zipper. The stops at the end of a zipper may also break off. Again, stitches can replace them.

Slider pulls often break off. A slider pull can be replaced with a twist tie, bit of cord, strong thread, or thin wire, such as a paper clip.

Packs

Packs are crucial items that get hard use. Pack problems include broken frames, ripped-out hip belts, snapped and torn-out shoulder straps, blown seams, and broken hip-belt buckles.

Plastic buckles are very strong but will break if you stand on them. When this happens, there isn't much you can do unless you're carrying a spare buckle, though you could try taping the broken buckle with duct tape.

Torn seams and broken stitching can be sewn if you have a strong needle. An awl helps too (see **Speedy Stitcher**), or you can use a pebble to push the needle through several layers of fabric.

The clevis pins that hold pack bags, shoulder straps, and hip belts to traditional-style external frames sometimes break or fall out. Bits of wire or even cord will do as temporary replacements, though if you have this type of pack you should carry a few spare pins.

Cracked, bent, or broken frames, whether internal or external, need replacing, but until you can do so, you can hold them together with duct tape, perhaps also using a stick or a piece of tin can as a splint.

Shelters

Rips in **tents** and **tarps** can be repaired with sticky-backed nylon patches and adhesive. The latter will seal leaking seams too, although then you can't use the shelter until it dries. If you don't have any adhesive or if you want to stay under cover—quite likely if it's raining—you can rub the seam with a **candle** or even margarine if you aren't in **bear** country. Seams often leak at stress points, where the inner tent attaches to the fly sheet (rainfly), and at door tie points because there are many stitch holes at these points and they can't be sealed with seam tape. It's worth coating these with adhesive to prevent problems.

Tents usually come with short, rigid pole sleeves for use in repairs. If a pole snaps, just slide the sleeve over the break and tape it in place. If you don't have a sleeve, you could jam a stick into the broken pole or use a half-moon tent peg as a splint. Once you're home, replace the broken pole section.

Webbing stake points and guylines may start to tear out of a tent or tarp. These need to be stitched back into place. Coat the stitching with adhesive to protect and strengthen it and also to prevent water from wicking into the tent.

Eventually, fly sheets and **groundcloths** start to leak. Once the coating has worn off the fly sheet, it's time for a new one, although you can seal small areas with adhesive tape. Spray-on and wash-in **waterproofing** agents will restore some of the water resistance, but it will never be as waterproof again. Leaky groundcloths can be covered with a sheet of plastic or another groundcloth or tent footprint (a groundcloth cut to the shape of the tent floor).

Sleeping Bags

Most **sleeping bag** repairs are simple. Mending or zipper repairs can be dealt with as already discussed. Tears need to be patched very quickly in down bags, or you'll lose masses of fill.

Dampness is the most serious threat to sleeping bags, especially down ones. Whenever possible, air sleeping bags so moisture can evaporate. If you have to pack a damp bag, unpack it as soon as possible, even if it's inside a tent. Your body heat will help dry a bag, so lie in it rather than on it. A really wet bag can be dried near a campfire, although take care not to let sparks melt holes in the shell. Don't let the bag get too hot to touch. Once you're home, air any bag before storing it, even if you think it's dry. There's almost always some retained moisture.

Sleeping Pads

Self-inflating **sleeping pads** are very comfortable but also prone to punctures, and a deflated pad is not good for sleeping. To avoid punctures, carry pads inside your pack or in a durable stuff sack if on the outside. Don't toss them on the ground without first checking for sharp objects.

If you do get a puncture, the first thing to do is find it. This can be difficult because it takes only a pinprick for a pad to deflate slowly, waking you up as you begin to feel the hard, cold ground. Sometimes you can find a leak by squeezing the pad and listening for the hiss of escaping air. If this doesn't work, find a pool, submerge the inflated pad with the valve closed, and look for escaping bubbles.

Once you find the leak, clean and dry the area around it, deflate the pad, and close the valve. If you have a mattress repair kit, press one of the

Find a leak in a self-inflating pad by submerging it in water and looking for air bubbles.

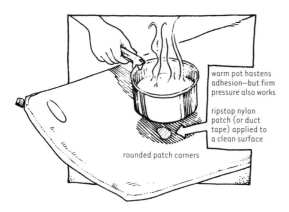

warm pot hastens adhesion—but firm pressure also works

ripstop nylon patch (or duct tape) applied to a clean surface

rounded patch corners

Repair a self-inflating pad with a nylon patch.

patches firmly onto the leak. Then spread adhesive, provided in the repair kit, around the edge of the patch. If you don't have a mattress repair kit, you can use duct tape, although this makes proper patching more difficult later because it leaves a sticky residue.

If you don't want to risk punctures, use a closed-cell foam pad. These are very tough, although they do compress with time and provide less insulation. Torn corners and the odd rip don't affect their performance.

Stoves

Blocked jets are the most common problem with liquid-fuel **stoves**. Dirt in the jet can cause a stove to sputter and flare and possibly go out. Many stoves have built-in cleaning needles, which can be operated by shaking the stove or turning a lever or key. If the stove doesn't have one of these, you need a jet pricker. You could clean the jet while it's in place, but that just pushes the dirt back into the **fuel** line and in time it will probably block the jet again. It's better to remove the jet first and then clean it. If you break, lose, or forget your jet pricker, you can improvise with a fine needle or even a bristle from a toothbrush.

Sometimes, cleaning the jet doesn't improve the stove's performance. Then you have to clean the fuel line or generator, which can be done in many stoves with a built-in wire. With some stoves, the generator can't be cleaned and has to be replaced.

To avoid these problems, use clean fuel, such as branded white gas, and filter all fuel.

For many stoves, maintenance kits are available that contain spare jets, O-rings, pump oil, and other items. They weigh very little and are worth carrying.

Pumps sometimes cease working and won't pressurize the fuel bottle or tank. Usually, this is because the leather cup inside the pump has dried out. Applying pump oil or a substitute, such as lip balm, sunscreen, or even margarine, should solve this.

Footwear

Problems with footwear are fairly rare considering the hard use that boots receive. Most problems are caused by a lack of care. Leather that isn't treated with boot wax at least occasionally can dry out and crack. Drying **boots** too quickly—for example, close to a campfire or in hot sunshine—can have the same effect and can also cause soles to split away from the upper.

Small tears and splits in the upper can be repaired with adhesive. This is more effective if you clean and dry the area around the tear first. Large tears probably mean new footwear, although a shoe repair shop might be able to patch them up.

A separating sole is difficult to repair in the wilderness, but unless you have alternative footwear, you have to do something. Adhesive—preferably contact cement—will stick the sole back to the boot as long as you bind the boot up tightly with duct tape or cord while it dries. This

sort of repair isn't likely to last long, so consider heading for the nearest trailhead.

If the boots have stitching around the welt—a construction still found on some leather **mountaineering** and **Nordic skiing** boots—and the stitches tear, you can sew the boots back together with an awl and a strong needle. However, this takes a very long time. Duct tape, cord, or wire could be used to hold the boots together just long enough for you to hike out. Coating the stitching with seam sealant prevents the stitches from tearing in the first place.

Trekking and Ski Poles

Most **trekking poles** have plastic sections at the tip that are designed to break before the main sections of the pole. If this happens, you can keep using the pole, although you may damage the exposed end. Plastic tips can't be repaired; they have to be replaced.

If one of the main sections of a pole breaks, it can be repaired with a half-moon tent peg or a section of tin can as a splint, bound in place with duct tape. A small stick can be jammed inside as well for added strength.

Equipment repair is a topic big enough for a whole book. For more information, see Annie and Dave Getchell's excellent *The Essential Outdoor Gear Manual*.

RESCUE

A rescue is the act of saving either yourself or someone else from harm. Rescues often go hand in hand with **evacuations** and searches (see **search and rescue**). In well-traveled areas, a rescue may be performed by passing individuals who notice there is trouble or by a local rescue team. In remote regions, rescues become much more difficult. In some instances, they're impossible.

If an emergency arises, first try to deal with it on your own. A self-rescue requires you to be prepared and capable of responding. For instance, if you are going **mountaineering**, you'll need to know how to rescue a person from a **crevasse**. If you're paddling a wild river, be prepared to rescue

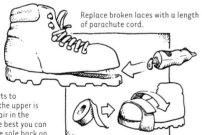

Repair small tears in leather with a urethane adhesive such as Seam Grip. You can use the same stuff to stick patches onto torn fabric footwear. In both cases clean and dry the surface before applying the adhesive.

Replace broken laces with a length of parachute cord.

A sole that starts to separate from the upper is difficult to repair in the field. About the best you can do is to glue the sole back on with contact cement (urethane adhesive will do if it's all you have, but it doesn't hold up very well) and then tape the sole and upper together by wrapping duct tape around the boot. Let the glue dry before using the boot. Don't rely on the boot to get you far, though—just out to the nearest trailhead.

If you have an awl and strong enough thread, you can stitch torn boot seams, but it's a long, tough job. Duct tape makes a quick, temporary repair that again might hold until you get to a trailhead. Coat the seams with urethane adhesive to protect them against damage.

Boot repairs call for duct tape or some type of adhesive.

a person from the middle of a large set of rapids. If the situation is such that you cannot perform such a rescue on your own, get outside assistance.

Outside assistance can be summoned by sending runners to the nearest trailhead or by using a **communication device** (as long as the batteries are charged and the signal can transmit). The decision to summon outside help should not be made lightly. Anytime you ask for outside help, you are, in effect, asking others to risk their own safety in exchange for yours. Help the rescuers as much as possible by providing accurate **map** or **UTM** coordinates for your location and any other information that may prove useful. Be clear about what kind of assistance you require. A rescue can take several hours or even several days to execute. Factors such as the **weather**, the terrain, and the nature of the emergency will influence the response time.

If the rescue calls for a helicopter, you must make special preparations. If possible, prepare a landing site that is at least 100 feet in diameter and offers options for takeoff and landing from any direction. Mark the landing area with brightly colored objects that are well secured and will not blow away or get sucked into the helicopter rotor. Mark the **wind** direction with a well-secured makeshift flag or with smoke. If you're using smoke, build the fire (or place the smoke cartridge) downwind of the landing site so the smoke won't interfere with the pilot's vision. (Be cautious in dry conditions—the rotor downwash can fan flames outward. You don't want to start a forest fire!) If you can't mark the wind direction with smoke, stand with your back to the wind at least 100 feet from the landing, with your arms pointing toward the landing. Never approach the helicopter from an uphill position or from behind the helicopter, because the rear rotors are virtually invisible when in motion. Remember that helicopters can fly only in good weather conditions: poor visibility, strong winds, or high altitude may make a helicopter rescue impossible. Furthermore, helicopter rescues are expensive, potentially hazardous, and disruptive to the **wilderness**. Request a helicopter only in dire situations.

Before you venture into the wilderness, establish a **contingency plan** that includes who to contact in the event of an emergency. You should also file a **trip plan** that states your proposed route and estimated date of return. Should you fail to return, rescue parties will use this plan when organizing their search-and-rescue efforts.

REST DAYS

A rest, or layover day is a day dedicated to recuperating from the rigors of **wilderness** travel. This is accomplished by not moving your camp and instead taking time to relax. Such days can seem either an unnecessary luxury or an integral part of a wilderness trip. Some people want to be active every single day so as not to waste any time. Others regard a day spent lazing around camp as a valuable use of their time. In this respect, it depends on your goals and desires.

On trips of more than a few days, many people need a rest on the third or fourth day, whatever their intentions, because their bodies aren't used to such sustained exercise. Minor illnesses or injuries may make a rest day advisable too. It's best to prepare for this by allowing time in your schedule. If you find you don't need a rest day, you can always explore a side canyon or climb a peak.

> "When I started long-distance hiking, I didn't plan any rest days, not wanting to lose a single day. I soon found this wasn't a good idea, however—I needed the occasional day off. I now plan on a rest day every 7 to 10 days on long trips. This works well for me, but everybody is different. Some people will want more frequent rest days; others, less frequent ones. Even half a day is enough for some people."—CT

Factoring in rest days is wise in many areas because of the **weather**. This is especially so on **winter** or high-altitude trips (see **altitude sickness**).

Spending a day or two trapped in the tent by a storm is slightly less frustrating if you have allowed a few spare days in the schedule.

While the fit and keen may be happy to go for a week or two without a rest day, few will want to go longer than that. Pushing too hard without a rest can result in a gradual slowing down and a growing sense that the trip isn't fun anymore. A day off can be amazingly revitalizing, leaving you full of energy and in a positive frame of mind.

Rest days are days off from your main activity, not necessarily inactive days. If taken at resupply stops, rest days can be busy as you deal with restocking, mail, phone calls, shopping, and information gathering (see **planning a trip** and **resupplying**). Sometimes there's so much to do at a town stop that you *have* to have a day off from your target activity. Rest days in the wilderness are usually more relaxing because there is nothing to do but enjoy where you are. Of course, if it's stormy, you may be trapped in the **tent** all day, so it's best to choose a sheltered spot for a rest day.

RESUPPLYING

How many days you can go without resupplying depends on how you're traveling. Canoes and kayaks can hold many days' worth of supplies, as can **sleds** in winter. For those carrying everything on their backs, however, a week's worth of **food** is probably the most they can carry comfortably. Resupplying a trip can be as easy as coming off the trail for a day to visit the local grocery store. But if your route is in the middle of the wilderness and no town is nearby (or there's no transportation to and from town), you'll need to make special arrangements. Depending on the type of trip, the options for resupplying will vary.

Buying at Supply Points

If you plan to resupply by buying food along the way, you need to know the location of possible supply points (such as a town or a rural general store) and how far it is between them, so you can work out how many days of food you need for each section based on your planned daily mileage. Even if you have a canoe or a sled, there's no point carrying more food than you need.

Supply points that lie very close to the route make resupplying easy. If there are grocery stores in several towns that are convenient to your route, you can simply buy food as needed during the trip. However, it does make you dependent on whatever the store sells, and you might have to compromise on your ideal diet.

> "I always plan on buying some of my supplies along the way, usually snack foods and breakfast cereals because these are generally obtainable everywhere—though I did once have to breakfast on crackers for a few days when a town in the Pyrenees had no cereals at all."—CT

If you plan to restock in this way, it's best to make a shopping list for the next supply point as you go along. This list can include items other than food, such as **candles**, batteries, camera film, sunscreen, and insect repellent. Don't be surprised if you have to carry some items over from list to list, however, due to lack of availability.

Sometimes there will be a possible supply point some miles away from your route, and you'll have to decide whether or not to go there. If you're a week or more from the last supply point and it will be another week before the next one, going off route to resupply might be worth the trouble. For backpackers, this could save having to carry a very heavy load, even if it takes a day to hike out to the supply point and a day to hike back.

For popular areas, information about supply points is found in guidebooks and on websites. For less popular and remote areas, you might have to work a little harder to get resupply information. Contact the local tourist office to ask about the locations of possible supply points and what facilities are available, in particular a grocery store and a post office.

Sending Supply Boxes

Packing and mailing supply boxes to be picked up during the trip ensures you have just the supplies you want, but this requires time and effort well in advance of your departure. In addition to food, supply boxes can hold **maps**, guidebooks, **film**, **first-aid** and toiletry items, spare **socks**, paperback books, plastic bags, and anything else you might need. Dried food can be bought in bulk and then weighed and repacked in the right amounts for each section of the trip. Don't mail fresh or perishable food; it probably won't last.

Pack supplies tightly in sturdy boxes to avoid damage. Keep in mind that the boxes could be stored in a hot area awaiting your pickup. Is the margarine in a sealed container? Could chocolate bars or other items melt?

The standard place to send supply boxes is a post office. In North America, send to yourself c/o General Delivery, town, state, zip (in Europe, c/o Poste Restante). Additionally mark the packages "Hold for Hiker" (or "Skier" or "Canoeist" or whatever is appropriate), along with an expected pickup date and a return address. Mark each box for a particular destination with numbers, using the following system for a shipment of, for example, four boxes: 1 of 4, 2 of 4, 3 of 4, and 4 of 4. This ensures that everyone handling the boxes knows whether they have all been accounted for.

For trips of a month or less, you can mail your boxes in advance. For longer trips, contact the post offices and find out how long they will hold boxes. You may need to have someone at home mail them for you. If you have no one who can mail boxes for you, commercial mail forwarders can handle the chore.

Find out in advance the days and hours of operation for each post office. Carry personal identification when collecting the boxes. Plan to arrive well before the post office closing time. At the same time you pick up the boxes, you can mail home items you're finished with, such as maps of the areas you've already traveled. Pack parcel tape in each supply box so it's handy to reseal the box with items you're sending home.

Many areas may not have conveniently located post offices. Instead, local businesses such as outfitters, fishing lodges, and cafés may hold boxes for a fee. Guidebooks and the local tourist office or ranger station can help you locate these businesses. Using them may save a long diversion to the nearest post office. Many long-distance hiking guides recommend United Parcel Service (UPS) as the best option for sending boxes to these places.

The Running Supply Box

A resupply method that combines supply boxes with buying items along the way is to mail a box ahead to yourself from each supply point. This running supply box can be used for gear that you don't need at the time but may need again later in the trip, such as warm items or spare footwear. The box can also contain items you only need while in a town, such as a set of clean clothes, shampoo, and a towel. Include a roll of parcel tape and labels addressed to all the supply points to make forwarding the box easier.

> "I packed a running supply box on the Arizona Trail, and it worked well. This box contained a slowly diminishing supply of maps, film, and other items I used regularly as well as food. If I found a good store, I bought extra items and put them in the box in case the next supply point wasn't so good. I also put surpluses in it when I had to buy more of something than I needed."—CT

See also **caches**.

Special Delivery

Resupplying often is important if you're trying to avoid heavy loads, especially the case for backpackers. If you don't want to leave the **wilderness**, you may be able to coordinate resupply by pack animals. Horses, donkeys, and **llamas** are all used as pack animals. Under the watchful care of their owner, pack animals can carry your resupply of food many miles into the wilderness, saving you the inconvenience of having to hike out and then hike back in again. Hiring an outfit to resupply you in the field can be costly but well worth it if you have only limited time and you want to spend it all in the backcountry.

Friends and family can resupply you at road crossings, trailheads, or river or coastal take-out sites. You must have clear agreement about the meeting time and place, and a contingency plan in case either of you is late.

If your trip takes you to a highly remote area, you can organize a food drop by plane. Pack your food in animal-proof containers and mark them with your name and the date of the drop. Make sure there is absolutely no confusion about the drop location. Confirm the exact coordinates with the pilot, and mark the site with a big X on your map.

> "I recently went on a trip in northern Canada, and we flew some food up in advance. The trip was in July, but because we were sending fuel in addition to food, we needed to send the supply on a special nonpassenger flight in May!"—AA

Plan to be at the site on the day of the aerial drop. But be ready with contingency plans for foul weather, delayed travel, and in the worst-case scenario, lost food. Resupplying by plane or helicopter is a great expense, but if you're in the middle of nowhere, it may be your only option.

RETRIEVING A CANOE OR KAYAK

One of the dangers of paddling a canoe or kayak in a river is that it may become pinned or in some other way stuck against an object. This generally occurs when a capsized canoe or kayak drifts down a river into a rock, a bridge piling, or even a tree stump. Sometimes the canoe or kayak will bounce off the object and continue downstream, but if it hits the object at the center of the boat, there is a good chance that it will get pinned. This occurs when equal amounts of current hit the bow and stern, forcing the canoe or kayak to become stuck against the rock. Even relatively weak currents can have enough force to wrap the boat around a rock. While both canoes and kayaks can become pinned, the greater hull capacity of a canoe makes for a more difficult retrieval. For the sake of simplicity, the text here refers to all pinned boats as *canoes*. If you are a kayaker, simply substitute the word *kayak* for *canoe*.

If you see a pinned canoe, first *locate the paddler*. The situation is life threatening if the paddler is stuck in the canoe or between it and the rock; if this is the case, you have only a few moments to act. The steps to rescue a pinned paddler can be technical and complex, requiring practice until you can perform them in an instant. Learn about these skills by reading whitewater rescue books, such as *The Whitewater Rescue Manual*, by Charles Walbridge and Wayne Sundmacher, and by taking whitewater rescue courses offered by the American Canoe Association and other instructional organizations (see resources section).

> "I've come across several canoes in the wilderness that had been abandoned by their owners. Finding an old canoe split up in the middle of a set of rapids is always eerie. In addition, they become their own hazards!"—AA

Once you've located the paddler or paddlers and ensured that everyone is safe, your only problem is retrieving the boat. There are a few things to bear in mind about retrieving a stuck canoe. First, don't risk your life to get the boat back. If the canoe is jammed against a rock just upstream of a vicious, house-sized **hole**, you may want to leave it there—at least for now. While abandoning your canoe is not an ideal choice, it may be

RICK SWEITZER

This canoe was lodged on a rock in a relatively shallow river. Before building a complex hauling system, paddlers should try simple maneuvers, such as using a branch as a pry bar, shifting the balance of the boat in the water with a rope, or applying sheer force.

the only one you have at the time. This is another reason to think twice before shooting a set of rapids in the wilderness.

To salvage a pinned canoe, start with the least technical efforts and progress to more complex systems. Frequently, all it takes is a simple shift in the center of gravity to dislodge a pinned canoe. This can be attempted by wading out to the canoe and vigorously rocking it back and forth or up and down (see **river crossings**). The more people available to do this, the better! If that doesn't work, try prying your wading stick (as long as it's not your paddle) against the canoe. Always be prepared for sudden movement or the dislodging of the canoe. Remain upstream of it whenever possible.

If the canoe is still stuck and you have a long **rope** (and you should, for this very reason), tie one end securely to the canoe and the other end to a fixed object on land, such as a tree or boulder. Locate the center of the line, and pull perpendicular to the rope. Called a *vector pull*, this is effective because it applies an exponential amount of pressure on the fixed objects. Remember, all you're trying to do at this point is shift the equilibrium of the canoe. Also try to use the force of the current to help dislodge the canoe whenever possible.

If the canoe is really stuck, you may need to employ a system that utilizes a mechanical advantage, such as a **z-drag**. A z-drag is the same system that is used to haul a fallen mountaineer out of a glacial **crevasse**. By offering a 3:1 mechanical advantage, the z-drag can provide far more strength than a simple vector pull.

Retrieving a pinned canoe involves risk. Wading, standing in cold water, and working with ropes under tension are just a few of the hazards that the rescuer will face. Place your safety and that of everyone else above the need to retrieve the boat. Leaving a pinned canoe can be hard on the spirit, but it doesn't compare to how you would feel if you lost a friend in the retrieval process.

RETRIEVING A RAPPEL ROPE

Retrieving a rappel rope is an important step in any rappel. The last person to rappel should examine the route to ensure that the rope is clear of any cracks, gullies, or potential snags. She should also try to free the **rope** of any kinks. To retrieve a single rope, simply pull on one end until the other end has cleared the **anchor**. If you're using two ropes tied together, make sure you pull on the correct end of the rope. Pulling on the wrong end will cause the knot to get jammed in the anchor. Be aware that the descending rope can cascade on the retriever with force and can also knock loose rocks, snow, or other debris, causing a mini-avalanche of rubble. Wear a helmet and make sure that you're in a position that offers some protection. This will be either away from the rock face or directly against it.

If the rope gets stuck, try to free it by pulling away from the rock face or alongside it. If this doesn't work, try pulling on the opposite end of the rope. Still stuck? Avoid climbing up the rope because it could become dislodged under the weight of your body. If you have a spare rope, extra gear, and experience lead climbing, climb back up to find the jam. If you don't have a spare rope, you're in a bit of a bind. If you have only one end of rope and there is a lot of slack, you can use the slack as protection for lead climbing up to the jam (but only if you're an experienced lead climber).

See also **rappelling**.

RISK ASSESSMENT

The **wilderness** is filled with risks, including **avalanches**, **bears**, **lightning**, falling trees, **flash floods**, hail, blizzards, getting **lost**, falling off cliffs . . . the list could continue for pages. Still, we go into the wilderness despite these risks, or in some cases because of them. There is no denying the thrill of adrenaline shooting through your blood when you encounter a risk and survive to tell the story. But statistics would argue that, if you put yourself in enough risky situations, eventually one or more of them will have injurious results.

To offset the risks, most outdoor enthusiasts regularly assess risk levels, even though they may not realize it. Looking at a windswept lake and deciding to cancel the afternoon paddle, for example, is risk assessment. So is deciding not to get too close to the slippery precipice of a waterfall. While there are some risks that are hard to ignore, such as an approaching storm's booming thunder, other risks, such as aging equipment, are less obvious and easier to overlook. Both of these risks could lead to injury or loss of life, but many more people will assess the threat of a thunderstorm than will assess the threat of using aging equipment.

Recognizing risk in all its various forms is critical. If you are **rock climbing**, a fraying rope might send your internal risk meter into the red zone, but the real danger may not be the rope. The real danger may be the lack of respect that your friend has for his equipment and for safety in general. If you can't identify the risks, how are you going to assess them before it's too late? The answer is simple—you won't. Sooner or later, you will run into trouble. Responsible backcountry users make a commitment to educating themselves about all aspects of wilderness travel. They make a habit of preventing accidents by being attentive and responsive to their surroundings.

They listen to their internal risk meter and grow to trust it. They develop and practice good **judgment**.

The outdoor industry takes assessing and managing wilderness risks seriously. **Outdoor schools** and guiding services invest a lot of time, energy, and money identifying risks and developing risk management plans. A **guide**'s job may look fun and easy, but as a professional risk manager she is hard at work, and underneath her tinted sunglasses she is constantly assessing risks: Is that buildup of cumulus **clouds** heading this way? Has the **wind** picked up? Are there **widow makers** near the campsite? Has Bob really been drinking his **water** or just pretending? The point is, if guides spend this much time assessing risks, shouldn't you too? Many people find themselves in trouble because they're not aware of the risks they're taking (weekend warrior rafters, listen up!). Don't be an accident waiting to happen: invest in learning about your favorite wilderness pastimes to become a safer and smarter backcountry user.

RIVER CROSSINGS

Hiking in the backcountry, you will eventually need to cross a river. If there's no footbridge, you'll have to rely on your own skills to get across. This is arguably one of the greatest hazards of backcountry foot travel. Why? Because rivers are full of slippery rocks, cracks, and holes that can trap your feet. Add cold water and the possibility of getting swept into the current, and you have a potentially dangerous situation. Knowing what to look for and learning a few crossing techniques will help you stay safe.

The best place to cross a river is a shallow location with little current. Anything over shin deep can become challenging, especially in fast current. If this is the case, look for alternatives both upstream and downstream. Check the **map** for locations where the river is separated into smaller branches, such as upstream tributaries. Narrow channels in the river might look like tempting shortcuts, but they tend to be deep and swift. A better location to cross usually can be found where the river widens.

Look for rocks or boulders that can act as stepping-stones or for logs that have fallen across the river. Be aware of **moving-water hazards** that could be a threat to a swimmer. Rapids, falls, and **strainers** don't mix well with hikers. Choose a crossing that has a clear run-out, one with no major hazards downstream. If you don't see a good spot to cross, reroute to a better location. It's much easier to hike a few extra miles than to try to recover all your gear—let alone your friends—from miles of remote river shoreline.

Location isn't the only factor to consider when crossing a river. The temperature of the water, the **weather**, and the capabilities of the group are equally as important as the depth and speed of the river. If the water is coming straight off of a **glacier**, it will be freezing cold. Crossing a cold river increases the threat of **hypothermia**. In addition, your lower extremities can become numb, which makes feeling your way across very difficult. Is it late in the day? In the **mountains**, streams have a tendency to run higher in the afternoon and evening as sun-warmed **snow** melts and adds to the flow. Sometimes it's best to camp and wait until morning to make your crossing. Is the weather threatening? Nearby **rain** can quickly increase the water to dangerous levels. It may be sunny where you are, but if it's raining upstream, beware. **Flash floods** can be a very real threat. Consider also the abilities of your party. Are you tired? Is it the end of a long day? Are you all strong swimmers? Tall, heavy people have a distinct advantage when crossing anything but shallow water.

Once you've found a spot to cross, devise a plan. Do you need to waterproof anything in your pack, such as your **sleeping bag** or spare clothes? Consider removing your **socks** and insoles to keep them dry, but always wear shoes. Scout the river, and choose a **bailout point** that you can swim to in case you lose your footing. Unfasten your hip belt, and loosen your shoulder straps. This will allow you to remove your **pack** quickly should you end up in the water. The key to staying upright is to make slow, calculated moves and maintain your balance. Feel ahead with each foot before committing your weight to a position. As you scan the river bottom, feel for cracks and converging rocks that could trap your foot. Avoid any such area. Feel for flat surfaces, and avoid slippery rocks, if possible. Always move one foot at a time, and communicate your actions to the people crossing with you.

Crossing Techniques

If the river is shallow and calm, you can easily cross without trouble by facing upstream and wading across. If you're in a group, hold one another's hands for support. In stronger currents, use one of the following techniques.

Inline Crossing

This is a good technique for a group of people. Facing upstream, form a line with one person behind the next. Put the strongest person at the upstream end of the line, with a long stick or pole to use for support. Have this person keep an eye out for any approaching debris. Put the weakest

The inline river crossing technique creates an eddy behind each person, so the last person in line has the least current to contend with. This works well when someone in the group is significantly smaller or weaker than the others.

person toward the rear. Place your hands on the shoulders of the person in front of you, and push down for added support. As a group, shuffle into the water, and slowly begin to cross the river. The lead person should move first and find good footing before the rest of the group follows. This technique creates an **eddy** behind the lead person and provides some protection from the current for the rest of the group. Those people farther downstream will feel much less current than those at the front of the line.

The Huddle

This is also a good technique for a group. Form a circle and put your arms around one another, securing your hands on the shoulders of your partners. Push down to add stability. The person in the huddle who is farthest upstream becomes the anchor for the group. The rest of the group slowly rotates around the anchor person until another person is upstream enough to become the new anchor. This technique shares the tiring position of

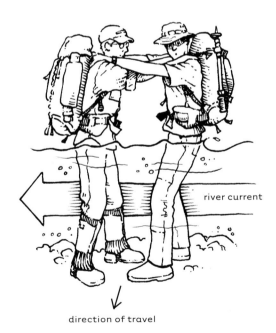

river current

direction of travel

In the two-person river crossing technique, each person moves only one foot at a time, pressing down on the other's shoulders for support.

anchor among the group, though it is not the best choice if the group contains someone who requires a lot of assistance.

Two-Person Crossing

Two people can cross using the inline technique or, as an alternative, have the upstream person turn around and face the downstream person. Grab each other's shoulders and push down. Have the upstream person move and find secure footing before the downstream person. Take turns, communicate clearly, and avoid moving at the same time. With this technique, the bigger person should be in the upstream position, in order to create a bigger eddy for the downstream person.

One-Person Crossing

As a solo crosser, you will be greatly aided by the use of a pole or stick. The pole can be used for stability and also as a probe to check the bottom for holes or cracks. It also provides a critical third point of contact, which increases stability tremendously. By maintaining at least two points of contact at all times, you can shuffle your way across the river.

If You Fall

If you lose your footing and fall into the water, remove your pack as quickly as possible. Get onto your back with your feet at the surface pointing downstream, and swim on your back toward shore. If you're unable to get to shore and you need to swim more aggressively, roll into the crawl position and swim toward your bailout point with your head upstream. If you've missed your bailout, look for a good spot to get out of the water, such as an eddy. Avoid the temptation to stand until you can feel the river bottom with your hands. If you see an unavoidable strainer approaching, roll onto your stomach and swim toward it with your head downstream, aggressively building up enough speed so you can push yourself up and onto the strainer as opposed to getting sucked under it (see **swimming in rivers**).

Additional tips for crossing rivers include the following.

• If possible, have a spotter watch each person who crosses. This can greatly increase the speed of rescuing a person who accidentally falls.
• Avoid crossing at river bends because the water is usually deep and fast on the outside corner.
• Always keep an eye out for approaching debris, such as logs.
• Never tie anyone into a rope when the person is in or near a river.
• Take a break after you cross. Change into dry clothes, warm up, and have a snack.

Remember this rhyme about water levels when assessing the difficulty of your crossing: At ankle height, no problem's in sight. At the shin, trouble can begin. Near the thigh, difficulty's high. Any higher than that, turn around *stat!*

RIVER RATINGS

To gauge the severity of any section of river, the paddling community uses an international scale of river difficulty. While this classification is widely used, it should serve only as a general guideline because regional and personal interpretations of the scale can vary. Like **climbing ratings**, this scale will likely evolve to accommodate technical complexity within one class (the difference between an easy class IV and a hard class IV, for example, is huge). The scale, at present, classifies moving water (water with a current but no rapids) and whitewater (moving water with rapids) as shown in the accompanying table.

INTERNATIONAL SCALE OF RIVER DIFFICULTY

Moving Water

Class A	Flowing under 2 miles per hour (mph)
Class B	2 to 4 mph
Class C	Greater than 4 mph

Whitewater

Class I	Easy: Few or no obstructions—all obvious and easily missed. Fast-moving water with riffles and small waves. Risk to swimmers is slight. Self-rescue is easy.
Class II	Novice: Straightforward rapids with wide clear channels that are obvious without scouting. Occasional maneuvering may be required, but rocks and medium-sized waves are missed easily by trained paddlers. Swimmers are seldom injured, and group assistance, while helpful, is seldom needed.
Class III	Intermediate: Rapids with moderate, irregular waves that may be difficult to avoid and capable of swamping an open canoe. Complex maneuvers in fast current and narrow passages requiring good boat control frequently exist. Large **waves**, **holes**, and **strainers** may be present but are easily avoided. Strong **eddies** and powerful current effects can be found, particularly on large-volume rivers. **Scouting rapids** is advisable for inexperienced parties. Chance of injury while swimming is low, but group assistance may be required to avoid long swims.
Class IV	Advanced: Intense, powerful rapids requiring precise boat handling in turbulent water. Depending on the character of the river, there may be long unavoidable waves and holes or constricted passages demanding fast maneuvers.

International Scale of River Difficulty (continued)

Class IV
(cont.)   A fast, reliable eddy turn may be needed to negotiate the drop, scout the rapids, or rest.

Rapids may require "must" moves above dangerous hazards.

Scouting is necessary the first time.

Risk of injury to swimmers is moderate to high, and water conditions may make rescue difficult.

Group assistance is often essential but requires practiced skills.

A strong Eskimo Roll is highly recommended (see **rolling a kayak**).

Class V   Expert: Extremely long, obstructed, or violent rapids that expose the paddler to above-average risk of injury.

Drops may contain large, unavoidable waves and holes or steep, congested chutes with complex, demanding routes.

Rapids often continue for long distances between pools or eddies, demanding a high level of fitness.

Eddies may be small, turbulent, or difficult to reach.

Several of these factors may be combined at the high end of this class.

Scouting is mandatory.

Rescue is extremely difficult, even for experts.

A very reliable Eskimo Roll and above-average rescue skills are essential.

Class VI   Almost Impossible: Difficulties of class V carried to the limits of navigability.

Nearly impossible and very dangerous.

Risks are high, and rescues may be impossible.

For teams of experts only at favorable water levels, after close study, and with all precautions.

The frequency with which a rapid is run should have no effect on this rating because there are a number of class VI rapids that are regularly attempted.

"ROCK!"

"Rock!" is the universal warning that an object (rock or otherwise) has become dislodged and is falling down a vertical rock face or any other kind of slope. If you hear someone yell "Rock!" take cover as quickly as possible. If you're next to a cliff and have nowhere else to go, stand tight against the rock. Chances are good that the falling object will bounce off the rock and land a few feet away. If you aren't wearing a helmet, cover your head with your arms. If you're climbing when you hear "Rock!" bring yourself close to the rock and hide under your helmet.

Falling rocks and other debris have claimed the lives of many climbers. While some rockfalls are natural and unpredictable, many others are caused by human error. If you're at the top of a **rock climbing** route, be careful in all of your movements. One careless kick of a rock could result in a tragic accident. Ensure the safety of those below you by keeping any loose items, such as water bottles, a safe distance from the edge. If you inadvertently dislodge an object, you can warn those below by loudly yelling "Rock!" regardless of what the object is. Whether you're climbing the local crags or finishing a **wilderness** ascent, keep your eyes peeled for potentially loose objects and your ears tuned for this life-saving call.

ROCK CLIMBING

Traditionally, rock climbing has been one component of **mountaineering**, a necessary skill that was required to ascend the most sought-after mountain peaks. Climbers practiced their techniques on local cliffs so they could progress to more technical mountain terrain. Eventually, these same alpinists began to view rock climbing as an entity of its own. Why leave the crags? Why not progress to more difficult pitches or more fluid movement? Why not aspire to scale even the smoothest vertical walls? The answer came like a calling. Why not!

In the past several decades, rock climbing has transformed from an eclectic subculture to a widely popular sport and a multimillion-dollar industry. In fact, if you're heading out to your local climbing crag for the first time in a long while, bring a good book, as you may have to queue up to get on the best routes. Along with the increased popularity have come improvements in rock climbing equipment and rock climbing technique (see below). Climbs that were once considered impossible are now being scaled by preteens with chalk bags, practicing for the next national competition.

As climbing developed over the years, the following different disciplines emerged: **bouldering, top roping, multi-pitch climbing, sport climbing, big-wall climbing, free climbing, aid climbing,** and **soloing**.

While climbing is a sport with inherent risks, dangers can be minimized through good technique, good **judgment**, and the proper use of modern climbing equipment. Start your learning by surrounding yourself with skilled climbers. Don't be lured into thinking that someone is skilled just because he has a full rack of equipment and lots of stories. You want a mentor with years of competent experience, not just experience. Many climbing schools offer weekend courses or one-on-one lessons. This is a great way to learn solid skills and also meet fellow climbers who are in the market for climbing companions. If you don't know where to find a class, go to your favorite outdoor store and ask the person at the climbing or mountaineering counter. Most likely they will know who in the area offers classes and, better yet, their reputation.

Solid instruction is invaluable, but at some point the best teacher is your own experience—and lots of it. Before you rely on your talents as a climber during a backcountry trip, make sure you've developed a solid repertoire of climbing skills. If the rock type changes from stable to crumbly, or if protection placement is hard to come by, it is important to know how to adapt to ensure the safety of your party. Most important, having a repertoire of climbing skills gives you the freedom to explore more of the **wilderness**—and what could be better than that?

Rock Climbing Equipment

Rock climbing is a good sport for people who love gear. Luckily, the gear that you need to get started is rather basic, albeit pricey. As your skill develops, so too will your collection of climbing gear, until the back of your car resembles a disheveled hardware store. The following subsections will guide you through basic climbing equipment and why (or if) you need it.

Harness

Your harness is a critical piece of equipment because it keeps you attached to the rope. Harnesses come in many styles, but most models for climbing incorporate a waist belt, often called a *swami*, that's connected to two leg loops. This is commonly referred to as a *seat harness*. The waist belt,

gear loops on both sides of the waist belt · waist belt · buckle · belay loop · leg loops

PETZL

Rock climbing harnesses consist of a waist belt attached to leg loops. Most harnesses also have a belay loop on the front and gear loops on the side. Try your harness to make sure it's comfortable and easily adjustable, important when you're adding or removing layers of clothing.

which provides most of the strength, should be padded and comfortable. This is less important if you will be wearing many layers under your harness, as is often the case in the backcountry. When purchasing your harness, spend some time trying on different models. If possible, see how they actually feel under tension. Choose a harness comfortable enough for long belays yet snug enough to keep you secure during a fall. Full-body harnesses are generally recommended for children, for glacier travel, and for climbers whose bellies are larger than their hips.

Shoes

Rock climbing shoes are notoriously uncomfortable. While a tight fit improves your control on the rock, too tight a fit can limit sensitivity. Choosing the right shoe is important. A shoe that doesn't fit well won't do you any good. When buying shoes, get the best pair you can afford. Quality shoes are more versatile, and they will help you perform your best.

Helmet

Helmets are critical because they protect your fragile head from falling objects, such as rocks, **carabiners**, and even water bottles. A mindless onlooker or even your belayer could inadvertently kick an object over the edge of the climb. Without a helmet, you're much more likely to sustain serious injury. Many climbers choose not to wear a helmet because it can be bulky, hot, and distracting. But, like most other climbing equipment, helmets are now better designed and more user friendly. Wearing a helmet, or choosing not to, is a personal choice. Make sure you're educated about the risks of not wearing a helmet before you make your decision. It only takes one rock falling from above to kill you, so choose wisely. Helmets are designed to meet standards dictated by the Union Internationale des Associations d'Alpinisme (UIAA) and the European Committee for Standardization (CE or CEN). Look for their stickers of endorsement when purchasing your helmet.

Rope

See **rope**.

Belay/Rappel Devices

There are an assortment of belay and rappel devices on the market that apply friction to a rope and act as a brake. Read more about them in **belaying** and **rappelling**.

Carabiners

See **carabiners**.

Artificial Protection

See **artificial protection**.

Webbing and Runners

Webbing has so many uses at a climbing site that you can never have too much of it. The webbing most commonly used in climbing is 1-inch tubular webbing. It's used to connect parts of your anchor systems as well as to clip into an anchor or make a runner (also called a *sling*). Runners are lengths of webbing tied into a loop using the **water knot**. The most popular length of runner is 24 inches, although 12-inch lengths are quite handy. Quickdraws are short pieces of webbing with a carabiner on either end. They are commonly used in sport climbing and are found on most climbing racks.

Other Stuff

While the use of chalk can be a point of contention, most climbers use it to help keep their hands dry. Chalk can easily be accessed by attaching a small chalk bag to the back of your harness. Before using chalk at a new site, talk to locals to determine whether it's used there. In the backcountry, chalk leaves a visual impact that can detract from the pristine feeling of the wilderness.

All climbing gear is susceptible to wear and tear and should eventually be retired. Proper maintenance and regular inspection of your gear are important. Never let other people borrow

Basic rock climbing equipment for the backcountry includes a rope, helmet, harness, carabiners, webbing, a belay device, and an assortment of artificial protection.

your gear unless you're certain they'll treat it with the same care that you do. Likewise, don't use gear whose history you aren't familiar with. To learn more about selecting and maintaining climbing gear, check out the book *Gear: Equipment for the Vertical World*, by Clyde Soles.

Rock Climbing Technique

Good movement on the rock is what makes climbing fun and, at times, easy. Knowing the right climbing techniques can be the key to a successful climb. It also makes the climbing look effortless and graceful. Develop a repertoire of movement techniques and you'll get beyond even the hardest parts of your climb. Stuck in a crack? No problem. Sliding down a rock face? Not anymore. Caught under an overhang? Piece of cake. All it takes to move efficiently on rock is an understanding of balance and friction and lots of time to practice.

Balance is key to fluid movement on rock. Without good balance, your body weight can shift into a compromising position and your center of gravity can work against you to pull you off the rock. When your body is well balanced, most of your weight is over your feet. This weight creates friction against the rock and keeps you in place. Sometimes, this seems counterintuitive. Indeed, you may often have to think hard about how to get your weight over your feet. You may have to

drop your shoulders, arch your back, or bring your torso in close to the rock.

Placing your body weight over your feet does much more than provide the necessary friction to maintain a good position, however. It also makes you rely on the strength of your legs rather than your arms, which can tire quickly. To illustrate this point, think about how long you can stand on your legs versus how long you can hang from your arms. The legs are much stronger. As climbers, we need to rely on them as much as possible. This may be refreshing to some people, particularly women, who tend to have weaker upper bodies compared to the strength of their legs.

Relying on arm strength is a common mistake for beginning climbers. In fact, these climbers can often be identified by the way they spend most of their time looking for **handholds** rather than **footholds**. A fun exercise is to find a relatively easy route and try to climb it, first with one hand, and eventually with no hands, save for balancing. This will help you rely on good balance and the strength of your legs. In addition, you'll get pretty good at finding footholds in seemingly difficult surfaces.

When you find a foothold, the next step is to shift your balance so your weight moves over your foot. Remember, it's the friction caused by the weight of the body that makes most footholds stick. Often, people will claim that their foot is sliding when in reality there is just no weight on it. As you experiment with finding footholds and shifting your weight, expect to slide a little. This is all part of the learning process. It can be frustrating, but when you realize how to use your balance fully, it will be a big "aha!"

Another common mistake for beginners is to waste a lot of energy. Be sure to practice conserving energy while on a climb. One way to do this is to rely on your skeletal system as much as possible, particularly when you're resting. Try to straighten your arms and legs whenever possible to minimize the use of your muscles. For example, if you're clinging to the side of a rock face and you're pulling yourself close to the wall with your arms, your muscles won't last very long. Rather, straighten your arms into a locked position and lay back on them. This will transfer the majority of your weight to your skeletal system, allowing you to save the muscles in your arms for the next move. This goes for your legs as well. By locking your knees, you can transfer your weight to your skeletal system, a welcome change.

Another way to conserve energy is to think about your moves before you execute them. If you think several moves ahead, you'll avoid the frustrating scenario of getting into a tricky position and only then thinking about how you will continue. Instead, you can progress gracefully from one move to the next without losing momentum. Thinking ahead will also help you avoid climbing into dead-ends that can require difficult down climbing.

Ascending a rock face is a combination of using footholds, handholds, and an assortment of movement techniques. If you're just starting out, a good rule of thumb is to always have three points of contact with the rock—for instance, both your feet on footholds and at least one hand on a handhold. This will generally give you enough stability to make the next move. As you progress, you may find yourself in situations where you have fewer than three points of contact. As soon as you're comfortable on the rock, begin to experiment with some climbing maneuvers. A brief description of some of the more common maneuvers follows.

• Undercling—Holding onto the underside of a handhold and pulling up by your arms while pushing down with your feet. Often used on overhangs, this one is great for getting a view of what's ahead.
• Mantel—A technique used to bring your body up and onto a ledge. Manteling is similar to how you get out of a swimming pool.
• Stemming—Spreading your legs apart and pushing against two different footholds, or faces, such as in a corner. This technique uses opposing forces to keep you in place. You may have

stemmed up the door frame of the front hallway in your house as a child.
• Lieback—Just as it sounds, you straighten your arms and lie back on your upper skeletal system while at the same time pushing against the rock with your feet.
• Jamming—Used in cracks to wedge various body parts (arms, legs, feet, fingers) into the cracks. Jams can feel very solid when placed correctly.

The final process is connecting these maneuvers into a graceful ascent of a route. Depending on the type of route you're climbing, you may use only one or two techniques or perhaps all of them. For example, if you're climbing a crack, you may use fist jams and toe jams, with an occasional lieback. If you're climbing a chimney, you'll probably do a lot of stemming. By becoming familiar

You can shuffle up the edge of a rock by pulling back with your arms and pushing into the rock with your feet. This position is known as a lieback.

with each of these techniques, you will be able to perform them flawlessly when the time is right.

The best way to become proficient on the rock is to practice, practice, and practice. Incorporating the help of an experienced friend, mentor, or **guide** will give you valuable feedback. Climbing is a big subject with lots of important information. If you're looking for an in-depth book about climbing, check out *The Complete Climber's Handbook*, by Jerry Cinnamon. In addition, several other excellent books about rock climbing have well-illustrated, easy-to-understand sections on movement. To learn more, check out *How to Rock Climb* and *Advanced Rock Climbing*, by John Long, and *Mountaineering: The Freedom of the Hills*, edited by Don Graydon and Kurt Hanson.

ROCKER

Rocker is the curvature of a canoe or kayak from bow to stern. A boat with a lot of rocker will have a raised bow and stern, and its hull will resemble the shape of a banana. If it has little or no rocker, the shape of the hull remains virtually flat all the way from bow to stern. The purpose of rocker is to minimize the length of the boat at the waterline. A short waterline length makes a boat easier to maneuver, whereas a long waterline length helps the boat track (go straight). Because whitewater paddling demands quick turns, whitewater canoes and kayaks have a lot of rocker. Touring canoes and kayaks, which are used to paddle long distances on relatively straight courses, are designed with little rocker.

ROCK GARDEN

A rock garden is a section of river in which there seems to be more rocks than water. Rock gardens are commonly found at the ends of rapids in rivers experiencing a period of low water. Paddling through a rock garden can be a good test of your technical whitewater maneuvering. Because there are so many rocks to avoid, you need to think and act fast. Rock gardens might leave you feeling as if you just got off a bumper car ride and will often wreak havoc on a new canoe or kayak.

Sometimes rock gardens are so extensive they become impenetrable. If this is the case, you may need to portage (see **portaging**). Rock gardens made up of boulder-sized rocks are sometimes called *boulder gardens*.

ROCKY MOUNTAINS

The Rocky Mountains are one of the great **mountain** ranges of the world. Stretching about 3,000 miles from northern British Columbia to New Mexico and up to 300 miles wide in places, the Rockies are not a single range but a tangled mass of a hundred or more different ranges. Experts disagree as to exactly which ranges constitute the Rockies, especially in the far north, but the Liard River in British Columbia marks a clear geological boundary. The Rockies can be roughly split into four major areas: the Canadian Rockies, which geologically include Glacier National Park just south of the international border; the Northern Rockies in Montana and Idaho; the Middle Rockies in Wyoming and northeast Utah; and the Colorado Rockies, which include ranges in southern Wyoming, Utah, and New Mexico as well as in Colorado. Some people also include the Colorado Plateau and Four Corners region in Utah, Colorado, New Mexico, and Arizona.

However you define them, the Rockies are not an unbroken chain of mountains. In Wyoming, the mountains fade away to be replaced by the desert of the Great Divide Basin, which separates the middle and Colorado Rockies.

The Rockies consist of a magnificent mixture of landscapes. The highest peak is 14,433-foot Mount Elbert in Colorado, a state that contains all 54 peaks over 14,000 feet in the Rockies. Peaks over 12,000 feet are found throughout the range: Mount Robson is the highest in the Canadian Rockies at 12,972 feet; Granite Peak in the Absaroka Range in Montana is the highest in the Northern Rockies at 12,799 feet; and Gannett Peak in the Wind River Range in Wyoming is the highest in the Middle Rockies at 13,804 feet.

A key feature of the Rockies is the Continental Divide, the watershed of North America, which runs along most of the Rockies, although it leaves them at each end, in northern British Columbia and New Mexico.

The first people probably arrived in the Rockies before the end of the last ice age, some 11,000 years ago. These first inhabitants were nomadic hunter-gatherers, a lifestyle that was maintained until the westward expansion of European settlers in the nineteenth century. The Rockies were a major barrier to the first European pioneers. They were first seen from the south by the Spanish when Francisco Coronado reached the Rio Grande in what is now New Mexico in 1540. Another two hundred years passed before French fur traders reported the first sighting of the Northern Rockies in 1743. Fifty years after that, the Scottish explorer Alexander Mackenzie became the first European to cross North America when he crossed the Rockies in the north of what is now British Columbia and pushed on to the Pacific. The most famous expedition was that of **Lewis and Clark**, who crossed the northern Rockies and also reached the Pacific in 1804–6. This set the scene for further explorations by men like David Thompson of the Northwest Company and the rise of the "mountain men" and the fur trade. After the fur trade began to decline in the 1840s, miners arrived and settlers began to cross the mountains, initially via South Pass at the southern end of the Wind River Range, heading for potential farmland farther west in Oregon and California. By the end of the nineteenth century, many towns had been established.

Despite all the developments that have appeared, mostly during the late twentieth century, the Rockies are still a wild, spectacular mountain range with vast areas of wilderness and much wildlife, including, in the north, grizzly **bears** and **wolves**. Much of the land is protected in designated wilderness areas and **national parks** in both the United States and Canada, such as **Yellowstone**, Glacier, Rocky Mountain, Jasper, and Banff. They offer myriad opportunities for wilderness adventure and exploration, whether on foot, on skis, or by canoe, kayak, or raft. Thousands of miles of trails lace the mountains, including the 3,100-mile **Continental Divide Trail** in the United States and the 750-mile Great Divide Trail in Canada. In winter, the mountains are covered by deep **snow**, and **snowshoeing, ski touring,** and **mountaineering** are popular activities. Mountain towns, such as Boulder in Colorado and Banff in Alberta, are centers for outdoor activities and great places to gain information and inspiration for **planning a trip.**

ROLLING A KAYAK

Rolling a kayak is the act of bringing an upside-down kayak back to an upright position without exiting the boat. This technique is most frequently used in whitewater kayaking or **sea**

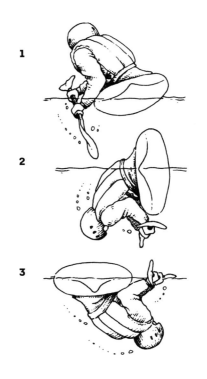

Based on an illustration in ACA, Canoeing and Kayaking Instruction Manual

Rolling a kayak is all about proper technique. Start with the correct setup position (1): head and torso tucked forward, arms stretched over the edge of the kayak. As you tip over, remain in the setup position (2). After an unexpected capsize, you'll need to assume this position before you can initiate your roll (3).

kayaking when a **wave** or strong current upsets the kayak. The first people to roll kayaks were the Inuit who paddled the frigid waters of the high Arctic (hence the maneuver's other name, the Eskimo roll). Arctic waters are very cold, and early Inuit paddlers were generally not good swimmers. Therefore, when a hunter's kayak capsized, there was only one good option: get the kayak back upright and fast!

Being able to roll a kayak remains important today for a couple of reasons. In whitewater, staying in your kayak means you won't have to swim down a potentially long set of rapids. Rapids can be full of **moving-water hazards**, and your best bet is to maneuver around them in your boat. If you tip over and **wet exit**, you expose yourself to substantial risk. Furthermore, in both whitewater kayaking and sea kayaking, a solid roll prevents you from having to perform a self-rescue or an assisted rescue (see **T-rescue**). These rescues take time and energy, and if the water is cold you can easily develop **hypothermia**.

The roll is a relatively easy maneuver, especially once you understand the underlying principles. It may take a long time to learn, but once you get it you will probably conclude, "That felt so easy!" It's true that the roll requires very little strength; what it does require is technique. This is one skill you can't muscle your way through.

There are three steps to rolling a kayak: the setup, the sweep, and the **hip snap**. While all three steps are important, you simply won't come up without a good hip snap. Therefore, it's critical that you practice your hip snap until it is **bomber**. The other two steps (the setup and the sweep) also require practice.

A C-to-C roll is a type of Eskimo roll. To set up for a C-to-C roll, hold your paddle parallel to your kayak using a regular grip. Most right-handed people will set up on the left side of their kayak, while left-handed people will set up on the right side. Let's assume you're right-handed (all you lefties substitute the word *left* for *right* in the following text). Your hands and paddle should be close to the surface of the water, with your fore-

arms touching the deck. You'll want to lean forward and to your side, a position that protects your head from becoming too exposed. It also puts you in a good position to begin your sweep. Now tip yourself over. When you roll over, your body should remain in the setup position. This means that when the boat comes to a rest upside down, your forearms should still be against the hull and your hands and paddle should be at or near the surface of the water. From this position, you can begin your sweep.

The sweep is the portion of the roll that positions your body and paddle for the hip snap. The sweep requires some flexibility and torso strength. From the upside-down setup position (head tucked, forearms resting against the hull of the kayak, hands and paddle at the surface of the water), reach up to the surface and attempt to raise your hands and paddle out of the water. Use those ab and lat muscles! By reaching to the surface, you can keep your back arm (the arm closest to the stern) tucked tight against the kayak while you sweep the forward blade across the surface of the water in an arc out to 90 degrees, perpendicular to your kayak. If you're really flexible, you can keep the paddle out of the water this whole time. If you aren't so flexible, keep the paddle as close to the surface of the water as possible. Try to watch the end of the paddle as you perform your sweep. Watching the paddle blade will place your body in a perfect position to execute your powerful hip snap.

As you initiate your hip snap, your body should rise out of the water in this order: hips, torso, shoulders, and head. Your head is heavy and if you try to lift it out of the water first (as most beginners do), your hip snap won't do you any good. Keep your head in the water until the very last second. When you finally bring your head out of the water, it should be tilted toward your right shoulder. This is one of the most difficult aspects of the roll. If you have a hard time keeping your head down, try pinching a sponge between your ear and shoulder. This forces you to keep your head in the correct position.

1. sweep

2. sweep

3. sweep
and hip
snap
across
water

4. hip snap

Based on an illustration in ACA, Canoeing and Kayaking Instruction Manual

*To roll a kayak, start from the setup position (1).
Reach toward the surface of the water and plane your
paddle across the surface (2). As your paddle sweeps
away from your kayak to 90 degrees (3), initiate your
hip snap. Remember to keep your head down! You
should end up looking at your paddle blade (4).*

Your hip snap can be aided by the tension of your paddle against the water. Note the word *aided* here. If you think you can use your paddle to pull yourself up, you're wrong. Get in the habit of using your paddle for balance and a little assistance. Eventually, you should be able to perform a roll without your paddle (known as a *hand roll*).

Learning to execute a solid roll can be more difficult than it sounds. The best way to learn is under the guidance of a patient instructor, who can verbalize and demonstrate the process.

Furthermore, practicing in a warm pool, as opposed to a murky river or lake, makes the learning process easier and more comfortable. Using nose plugs will help you keep a clear head, literally. Goggles allow you to make sense of the whole process underwater. There are a few instructional videos that walk you through the rolling progression step by step, including one called *Grace under Pressure* and *The Kayak Roll* (see resources section). If possible, have someone videotape you while you practice your roll. Watching yourself roll is a great way to critique your performance.

Looking for some paddling partners? Often local universities will have an open pool night specially designated for kayakers. This is a great place to practice your rolling skills and meet some new paddling buddies.

ROPE

Back in the days of early mountaineers, organic ropes, made of such fibers as **cotton** or manila, were the only option on the market. Mount Everest's George Mallory survived several harrowing falls on such a rope, but nowadays you'd be crazy to even think of using a cotton rope for anything other than hanging your clothes out to dry. Today's ropes are high-tech to say the least. Gone are the days when you can use one all-purpose rope for all your outdoor pursuits. Instead, you may have to choose between three different models for the same activity—each with its own bells and whistles.

When looking for a rope, think about the situations and environments in which the rope will be used. Will it be used in watersports such as **canoeing** and kayaking? Will it hang over a rocky cliff? Will it haul heavy loads? Will you use it for climbing? If so, what type? **Sport climbing**? Traditional **rock climbing**? **Ice climbing**? By reviewing the features of a rope, you can begin to understand how to select a rope for your purpose. Finding the perfect rope is always a game of give and take, but eventually you'll discover which qualities are most important to you.

Construction

The most common type of rope on the market today uses kernmantle construction. Kernmantle ropes have an inner core (the kern) surrounded by a tightly braided sheath (the mantle). The core provides most of the rope's tensile strength, which is the force a rope can withstand in a lengthwise direction before it breaks, such as in a game of tug-of-war. Kernmantle ropes are made to have either a lot of stretch (dynamic) or little stretch (static). By the nature of their design, kernmantle ropes are the strongest on the market and are virtually the only type of rope used in rock climbing and **mountaineering**.

Braided ropes and laid (or twisted) ropes are two other common types of rope construction. Because most ropes used by today's outdoor enthusiast are of kernmantle construction, most of the information provided here will pertain to kernmantle ropes. Be aware, however, that there are many ropes on the market with braided or twisted construction. The strength of these ropes varies significantly. Usually, they're cheaper than kernmantle ropes and appropriate for general purposes, such as hanging food (see **bear bagging**), tying boats to shore, and so forth. While some high-tech versions of these ropes are sold, don't use a braided or laid rope for any type of climbing, mountaineering, or water rescue.

Stretch

As already mentioned, kernmantle ropes can be either dynamic (lots of stretch) or static (little stretch). Most climbers prefer dynamic ropes because they absorb much of the shock generated by a fall. Without the stretch of a dynamic rope, a climber who falls even a short distance could easily be injured. In addition, the force generated by such a fall on a static rope could overload the webbing or protection used in the **anchor**. Therefore, dynamic ropes should be used in any climbing that could result in a fall. While all ropes have some give, static ropes are designed for minimal stretch. Because they don't stretch much, they're

often used to haul heavy loads. They are the preferred type of rope for **rappelling**, ascending, **caving**, and high-angle or water-related **rescues**. Static ropes are much stiffer than dynamic ropes. This makes them more difficult to handle, but they tend to be less susceptible to abrasion and general wear and tear.

Strength

Climbing ropes are rated by their tensile, or breaking, strength and also by the number of falls they can withstand. The breaking strength is measured by gently pulling a rope in opposite directions until it snaps. When this test is administered, the rope is free of any knots or kinks, because they reduce the rope's strength. The test simulates a rope under a constant load. It is therefore more common to review the tensile strength when you're looking for a static rope, because a static rope is the choice for carrying heavy loads. A dynamic rope is designed to withstand a sudden and severe pull (like that of a falling climber) and is therefore rated by the number of falls that the rope can sustain. Generally, the thicker the rope, the greater number of falls it can withstand.

Dynamic ropes also are rated by their impact force and elongation. While these factors are not directly related to the rope's strength, they're still important. The impact force measures the amount of force transferred during a fall through the rope to the climber and anchor system. A lower impact force means that a rope is absorbing more energy, leaving less to be absorbed by the climber and the anchor system. Elongation is the amount of stretch you could expect from your rope if you were to hang a 176-pound weight from it. While this gives you an idea of how much it stretches, hanging a weight off a rope is very different from taking a 10- or 15-foot fall on it. Thinner ropes tend to have more stretch and therefore will have a higher elongation. The standards for these ropes are set by the UIAA (Union Internationale des Associations d'Alpinisme) and the CE (European Committee for Standardization, also called the CEN). Look to ensure that your rope has met or exceeded the UIAA or CE standards (see resources section).

Dry Ropes

When ropes get wet, they weaken and become heavy. Even worse, if it's below freezing, your rope can morph into a useless block of ice. To prevent ropes from absorbing moisture, several companies coat their ropes in a chemical finish that repels water. These "dry" ropes can still absorb water, but at a significantly slower pace. If you know your rope will be getting wet, or if you plan on climbing in cold or icy conditions, consider getting a dry rope. Ropes that are designed to be in the water, such as throw ropes, are generally manufactured with a highly buoyant fiber such as polypropylene. These types of rope are not referred to as *dry* or *nondry*.

Single vs. Double

Most climbing routes are fairly straightforward in terms of going straight up. With such a climb, a single rope is most appropriate. If the route zigzags a lot with significant lateral movement, consider using double-rope technique, which employs two lighter ropes (also known as *half ropes*). These identical ropes are used at the same time. By alternately clipping each rope into every other runner, you in effect give yourself two separate yet redundant rope systems. A single rope is less bulky and weighs less than the two lighter ropes and is more commonly used. Double-rope technique, however, can be the choice for complicated or particularly long routes.

Size and Length

Rope size is determined by its diameter. Most single ropes range from 9.4 to 11 millimeters. Double ropes range from 8 to 9 millimeters. The thinner the rope, the less weight you have to carry, but thicker ropes are usually stronger and can hold more falls. The most popular length for climbing ropes is 200 feet. You can also go shorter (150 feet) or longer (260 feet) depending on your needs. Water-related ropes, such as those used for river rescue, are usually sold by the foot. They can also be purchased in the form of **throw bags** or towlines (see **towing**).

Color

Bright colors make a rope stand out against its environment, which can be especially handy in a rescue scenario. If you're using multiple lines, consider using different colors. This will help you to distinguish between the lines. Many ropes are made using two different color patterns, one for each end of the rope. This helps you easily determine when you have reached the center of the line.

Maintenance

Keeping a climbing rope in top condition ensures it will provide maximum strength when you need it most. It will also increase the life of any rope. Take care of your rope by incorporating the following guidelines into your routine.

• Know the history of your rope. Record its use in a journal, including the number of falls it has sustained. Be wary of lending your rope to other people, because they may not treat it with the same reverence you do.

• Reduce your rope's exposure to unnecessary bouncing or swinging. When rappelling, descend at a slow, steady pace. Fast rappels can cause excessive friction and heat, which can burn the sheath of your rope.

• Avoid running your rope over sharp or abrasive edges. Ropes become much more susceptible to abrasion and cutting when they are under tension.

• Avoid stepping on your rope. One step can grind particles of dirt into the sheath and core. If you're wearing **crampons**, you can easily puncture the core, severely compromising the rope's strength.

• Keep your rope free from dirt and sand. Even little particles can work their way through the sheath and into the core. Long after you think the dirt is gone, these particles will be hard at work degrading the integrity of the rope.

- Minimize your rope's exposure to direct sunlight. The sun's ultraviolet rays damage nylon over time.
- Keep your rope away from all chemicals. Certain chemicals eat away at nylon and can wreak havoc on your rope. Among the top culprits are acids (especially battery acid), alkalis, and any kind of bleach compound. If you're unsure if a chemical has damaged your rope, err on the side of safety and retire it.
- Keep your rope clean. If you need to wash it, do so in cool water with a mild soap. Rinse the rope thoroughly, and then air-dry it away from direct sunlight. Never use a bleaching agent or soap containing bleach.
- Learn how to use your rope correctly. An educated user has a better appreciation for the importance of rope maintenance.

Store your rope in a bag away from heat, chemicals, and sunlight. Coiling the rope for storage is convenient, but it may cause the rope to kink or twist excessively. If the rope is flexible, try stuffing it loosely into a protective bag.

Evaluate your rope frequently for signs it should be retired. Look for abrasion along the sheath, such as fuzziness and fraying at the ends. Feel the sheath for melted nylon, which can result from excessive friction. Look for irregularities in the diameter of the rope, and feel for inconsistencies in the core. These are often indicated by a flat, soft, or lumpy texture. If you discover imperfections, and eventually you will, consider retiring the rope. Remember, this rope may have to save your life—so don't take any chances.

A rope should be retired anytime you discover or suspect damage to the core. Damage to the sheath may be your only indication that the core has been affected, so inspect the sheath carefully. As a rule of thumb, a heavily used rope (one used several times a week) should be retired after a year. Weekend warrior ropes should be retired after two years, and any rope should be retired after four years. A rope's history is much more important than how old it is, however. Knowing your rope's history and inspecting it for damage are the only ways to ensure that you retire it at the appropriate time.

ROPING UP

When mountaineers traverse a **glacier**, they tie into one common **rope**, with each climber spaced approximately 40 feet apart. The purpose of the rope is to catch a climber who unexpectedly falls into a **crevasse**. In this scenario, the other climbers will suddenly feel a significant pull on the rope. This prompts them to drop to the ground in the **self-arrest** position. Under the right conditions, and when performed correctly, the self-arrest will halt an uncontrolled slide down a slope or into a crevasse. Mountaineers will generally climb with two to four climbers per rope team. To be safe, a minimum of two rope teams should travel together at all times. This allows one rope team to assist the other with a **crevasse rescue**, if necessary.

Select the best rope-team position for each climber by evaluating his skill. The goal should be to minimize the overall threat to the party. For example, on the ascent the most experienced climber should take the lead position. This way she can evaluate the conditions and choose the safest route. The least experienced climber should be at the end of the rope team, or in the middle. On the descent, consider putting the least experienced climber at the lead of the rope team (downhill from the other climbers). Since the least experienced climber is more likely to fall, this position will minimize the threat to the rest of the party. If you have a climber who is particularly heavy, consider putting him on the downhill end of the rope team, where a potential fall will be less hazardous to the team.

Climbers on rope teams tie in using various knots depending on their position. Usually climbers on the end of the rope team will tie in with a figure-eight follow through, while climbers in the middle will tie in with a **butterfly knot**. For a good description of roping up (and how to tie in) read *Glacier Travel and Crevasse Rescue*, by Andrew Selters.

ROUTE SELECTION

Planning the route of your **wilderness** trip can be a lot of fun. If you have no idea where to go, start by choosing an environment that you're familiar with. Assess your skills carefully, and avoid a route that exceeds your abilities. Ask friends or local outdoor shops for recommendations, or simply flip through old issues of such magazines as *Outside*, *National Geographic Adventure*, or *Backpacker*. Once you have selected a destination, figure out your **transportation** to and from the trailhead. Will you need a shuttle? What about **resupplying**? Some trailheads offer plenty of places for parking, while others are just off major roads. If you're leaving a car behind, inquire with local officials about potential problems, such as wildfires or theft.

Next, determine which **maps** you need and lay them across the floor. Select the best starting point, and then start linking days together. Look for flat areas that are near water to pitch your tent. Some areas have restrictions on how close to the water you can camp, so make sure to check this out before you begin your trip. Also research the need for **permits** and reservations early. Some backcountry destinations are so popular that there are waiting lists for permits. Other places don't have waiting lists, but the permit application process may take a couple of months. These are exceptions to the rule, but you should be prepared nonetheless. Also keep the following in mind when planning a route.

Paddling Trips

- For beginning paddlers on flat water, 10 miles a day is a healthy distance. On a river, the suggested distances vary depending on the speed of the current. Plan less mileage for the first day because it may take time to get organized.
- Only plan long crossings between landmasses if you're skilled in rescuing a capsized canoe or kayak in big **waves**. Water crossings can be dangerous and should be undertaken only in the most favorable weather conditions.
- Learn the direction of the prevailing winds, and plan for possible **wind** delays.
- Research all rivers to ascertain their level of difficulty. Paddle in water only if you're comfortable performing a rescue in it. Get training in whitewater paddling and basic **rescue** techniques.
- Find out the water levels from local sources, such as paddling shops, before you go. Low water could mean having to walk your boat over stretches of river. If the water is high, anticipate increased speed and difficulty. Never paddle a river in flood stage unless you really know what you're getting into. Rivers in flood stage are unpredictable and hazardous, and they should be treated as such.
- Be aware of local fire regulations, which may require you to carry a **stove**.

Backpacking Trips

- If you're entering a higher elevation, plan a day or two in the beginning of your trip to acclimatize to the altitude (see **altitude sickness**). On this day, you should plan to stay put or at least not travel very far.
- Gains in elevation take a while. Plan at least an additional half hour into your day for every 1,000 feet of elevation gained.
- Plan your route so it follows a **water** source or a series of water sources. If you're planning a trip in the **desert** or a particularly dry area, bring extra water containers.
- Be aware of the treeline and the density of the brush. Camping above treeline necessitates a cooking stove and **fuel**. Traveling above treeline also means more exposed travel. Traveling in dense brush and undergrowth can slow your progress considerably. Try to get an idea of the terrain before you leave. Are there well-marked **trails**, or will you be traveling off trail?
- Be aware of local **fire** hazards and potential bans. Have a backup plan if your route is closed.

RUCKSACK

A rucksack is small to medium-sized pack (up to 3,000 cubic inches), often without a frame. The word comes from the German *Rücken*, meaning "back," and *Sack*, meaning "sack." In some English-speaking countries, such as the United Kingdom, *rucksack* refers to packs of all sizes.

See also **packs**.

RUDDERS

Rudders are devices found on sea kayaks that help maintain the kayak's direction of travel. They're helpful in many situations but are best used in heavy crosswinds and following seas (with waves pushing you from behind).

Rudders are usually made of plastic, aluminum, or steel. They're attached to the stern deck of a kayak and are often deployed from a cleated cord behind the cockpit. Once dropped, the rudder is controlled by the footpegs. Pushing on the right peg cocks the rudder and causes the kayak to veer to the right. Pushing on the left footpeg turns the kayak to the left. It's pretty easy, which is why using the rudder is so alluring.

Contrary to the belief of many recreational sea kayakers, the rudder is not a steering wheel. While it certainly makes turning the boat easy, many kayakers incorrectly rely on their rudders to turn the kayak even in the calmest of conditions, when a simple paddle stroke would do. Rudders and rudder cables can break, and in some instances rudders are actually dangerous to use, so make sure you have a solid repertoire of paddle strokes under your belt before embarking on an outing.

In following seas, the rudder helps prevent broaching. As your kayak's stern is pushed up and out of the water by a following wave, a dropped rudder increases your keel line and prevents you from being pushed around. If the waves are large,

however, and your stern is way out of the water, the rudder may not be long enough to have any effect. Rudders are particularly handy for long kayaks, such as **expedition** touring kayaks or doubles. In a double, the stern paddler generally controls the rudder, although it can also be rigged for use by the bow paddler.

When performing a rescue, remember that the rudder is a heavy piece of metal bobbing around in the water. Getting donked in the head or face by a rudder is painful and can cause serious injury. Also beware of rudders in surf zones, where upsets are common (see **surfing**). Strong surf can break a rudder quickly. It's hard to take the time to raise your rudder when you're in the heat of the action. A deployed rudder will create drag and slow your progress, but it will also save your shoulders and arms from fatigue and repetitive strain. **Sea kayaking** purists scoff at the use of rudders, but when push comes to shove, most people prefer to have a rudder or a **skeg** on their kayak.

A rudder requires maintenance. Sand and small pebbles can prevent you from deploying it just when you need it most. Cleaning and occasionally lubricating all moving parts adds to the dependability and longevity of any rudder.

ANNIE AGGENS

Maneuvered by footpegs in the cockpit, a sea kayak rudder makes turning easy, but don't rely on it too heavily. This rudder is in the deployed (down) position.

SAFETY

The backcountry is filled with risks. Some of them are tangible, such as **avalanches**, **river crossings**, and **lightning**. Others, such as gauging the intentions of potentially threatening strangers, are more difficult to judge. While you are safer in the **mountains** than shopping in New York City, the possibility exists that you could run into a threatening person or group of people.

Keeping yourself safe from humans on the **trail** can be a disturbing topic but is one that you should think about. Consider using these tips to become "trail smart."

• Plan safety into the preparation of your trip. Inquire about the safety of the area just as you would about **water** sources or **permits**. Ask rangers or local officials questions such as "What safety concerns should I know about?" and "Have there been any crimes?"

• From the start, develop an awareness of your surroundings. This will help you observe all the beautiful things about the **wilderness** as well as things that seem out of place. If you encounter suspicious people at the trailhead, go elsewhere or wait for them to leave before you head out.

• Don't be overly friendly. Don't tell people where you are going. Of course, you will encounter people who are just like you—out to enjoy the wilderness—and it's common to talk about your route. Just remember that this information could well serve someone who has bad intentions. Consider offering vague answers, such as "We're heading north" or "We're following the river for a while." Be wary of people who take a keen interest in your plans.

• If you have expensive gear or high-tech camera equipment, don't flaunt it. Also, don't advertise the fact that you are traveling alone or in a very small group.

• Trust your intuition. If something or somebody gives you the heebie-jeebies, listen to your gut and be proactive about getting out of the situation. Don't worry about appearing overly cautious or even rude.

• Consider traveling in a group, which is less likely to be a target of crime.

• Keep your camp low profile. In addition to making you less of a target, it will reduce your visual impact for other backcountry users.

• Know that your risk increases with proximity to urban areas. If you're **planning a trip** to a site within an hour of a major city, you should be more concerned than if you were, say, in the middle of the Brooks Range in Alaska.

• Consider taking a self-defense course. These are great for getting you to think proactively about staying safe. While many courses are geared toward urban environments, the information is transferable.

"One time I was leading a group of girls on a backpacking trip in Montana. We were about 8 miles from a popular trailhead when we ran into three odd-looking men hanging out by the side of the trail. They seemed very out of place. Immediately, I got a pang in my stomach. For some reason, these guys gave me the chills. We were refilling our water bottles at a stream when they started asking us questions about who we were and where we were going. The way they were looking at us wasn't right. Then they asked us if we went swimming a lot and if they could take our pictures. The red flags in my mind were flying high. So many things about the men seemed strange: their gear, their behavior, their hygiene, and their lack of fitness. We hurriedly left and continued down the trail until we found a hidden area where we could rest with our packs off.

"No sooner had we dropped our packs than the guys reappeared out of nowhere. Again, they started talking, asking us questions. After noting our obvious disinterest in conversing with them, they walked a few yards away. They talked in low voices and every so often nodded in our direction. One of them lit up a cigarette and tossed the match into the woods. I desperately wanted to appear calm and capable, strong and in control. We gave one another hand signals to wrap up and put on our packs. As we were getting ready, we were whispering our tactic. I would take the tail; my co-leader would take the lead. If we passed any other groups or individuals, we would warn them of the men or ask for their assistance if we felt we needed it. Instead of staying at a nearby lake as planned, we would hike all the way to the trailhead, where there was a popular campground.

"We hit the trail, blazing past the men. Within minutes, they were on our tails pestering us. We just kept hiking in the waning sunlight. Finally, we reached the trailhead, where we faked them out by pretending to load our van as if we were leaving. When they finally left, we unloaded and went to the campsite, found a spot among some families, and conked out. Sometimes I wonder if they were waiting for us around a bend on the remote and rugged road.

"Is that an unusual event? Yes. Could it happen again? Yes. The fact is that I've had a few weird experiences in the backcountry. While the vast majority of people I have met on the trail have been extremely friendly, there have been a few encounters that I wouldn't care to repeat."—AA

To learn more about self-defense and staying safe, check out the book *Trail Safe: Averting Threatening Human Behavior in the Outdoors*, by Michael Bane.

SANDALS

Often underrated, sandals are versatile in the outdoors. The first sandals designed for active backcountry use, called *sports sandals*, were developed by river runners who wanted footwear that didn't capture debris and take ages to dry. Such sandals needed to grip well on wet rocks, gravel, and sand and be tough enough to last for long river trips.

Hikers often carry sandals for camp wear or **river crossings**, but few hike far in them, even though a well-made pair of sandals is far more comfortable in the heat than any **boot** or shoe. On the other hand, some hikers have completed long-distance trails, such as the **Appalachian Trail**, in sandals. Sandals are cooler and better ventilated than any other footwear. Gone are sweaty **socks** and hot, swollen feet. Instead, your feet stay dry, cool, and fresh. You can walk through puddles and creeks without worry because feet and sandals will dry quickly. Because they're exposed to the air and dry rather than sweaty most of the time, feet toughen up in sandals, rather than becoming soft and **blister** prone, as they can in shoes and boots.

For long hikes on which you'll carry a pack, look for sandals with a tread that grips well, a cushioned sole that protects against hard and hot ground, and straps, especially a heel strap, to hold the feet in place. A slightly raised or curved rim prevents you from stubbing your toes and helps keep your foot from sliding off the sandal. Sports sandals may be made from leather or synthetic fabric.

> "I have been surprised at the wide range of temperatures in which my feet feel comfortable in sandals. I've worn them on cool, rainy days without my feet feeling cold. However, I always carry a pair of wool socks for camp wear and in case my feet feel cold, and a pair of waterproof-breathable socks for cold, wet conditions."—CT

Some people worry about bruised toes or the lack of ankle support, but these are no more likely than in light shoes or soft boots. However, the skin on your feet can dry out and may crack in places if you wear sandals in dry conditions for many days. When this happens, coat the cracks liberally and regularly with sunscreen. It's wise to apply sunscreen to the tops of your feet anyway to prevent sunburn when wearing sandals.

> "I once hiked cross-country through the desert in sandals with a companion wearing running shoes. He had problems with cactus spines piercing the soft soles of his shoes. My sandals were too hard for the spines to penetrate."—CT

The only terrain where sandals aren't ideal is thick, low vegetation because twigs and thorns can hurt your feet. In **deserts**, you need to watch out for cacti too. Sandals are not much worse in this respect than soft shoes and boots, however, and can even be better.

SANITATION

In the **wilderness**, it's important to employ stringent sanitary practices to guard against the possibility of becoming ill. Lack of sanitation causes innumerable problems, including diarrhea, vomiting, fever, loss of energy, and loss of appetite. In addition, when you're sharing a close living space and cooking equipment with others, it's likely that your illness will spread quickly to the other members of your party.

The best way to avoid sanitation problems is to wash your hands and dishes regularly. This may seem like a no-brainer, but a surprising number of people leave their standard sanitation habits at the trailhead when they head out to the wilderness. "I'm on the trail!" they might say. "I'm supposed to be dirty!" OK, so maybe you're not taking showers every day like at home, but being somewhat dirty and being unsanitary are two different things. Tiny amounts of human waste can get stuck in your fingernails, in the cracks of your hands, or simply on your skin. If you happen to dip your hand into a bag of **gorp** or prepare a meal without washing your hands, you're putting the whole group at risk. Drinking **water** or eating **food** that is contaminated with fecal matter can cause serious health risks, including hepatitis. **Cooking** with and eating from dirty cookware and dishes is also a recipe for a bacterial infection.

To stay clear of hygiene-related problems, consider the following tips.

- Always wash your hands after going to the bathroom and before preparing or eating food. If you don't have soap readily available, rub your hands together vigorously in the water. If you don't have water, use hand-sanitizing lotion. Don't forget to wash some distance from your water supply (see **Leave No Trace**).
- Make sure to wash your personal utensils (cup, bowl, spoon, and so forth) after every meal. Hot

When burying human waste, dig the cathole at least 6 inches deep and 70 adult paces from any water source. Always wash your hands after going to the bathroom.

water works best for removing grease and grime. Share the responsibility for cleaning the pots and pans with the other members of the group.

• Every few days, consider sanitizing your utensils by submerging them in boiling water for a few minutes. You may want to do this more often if one member of your party is sick.

• Avoid having everyone reach into one common bag of food for a snack. Instead, suggest they pour the food into their hands, or supply a scooper they can use to scoop out a handful of food. Another option is to prepare individual snack bags each morning before you depart—first washing your hands, of course! This way, each person can snack whenever she becomes hungry.

To prevent contaminating the local water supply, practice Leave No Trace techniques for waste disposal. When going to the bathroom, choose an appropriate location at least 70 adult paces away from any water source or campsite. In addition, avoid depressions in the land where water may collect. Dig a **cathole** at least 6 inches deep, and cover the area so it looks as natural as possible when you leave.

If you're on a long trip, consider how you will wash your body. This is particularly difficult in cold conditions. Maintaining a certain amount of personal hygiene will help you to remain comfortable and healthy, not to mention a little less smelly.

SCAT

From the Greek word *skat*, meaning "excrement," *scat* refers to animal droppings. While scat may seem unpleasant and to be avoided, studying it can tell you a great deal about the animal life of an area. Being able to distinguish the scat of different animals can tell you whether it was a **coyote** or a **moose** that passed by your camp during the night. It is particularly useful to be able to identify bear scat because this shows whether there are **bears** around. The freshness of the scat matters too. Old, dry scat means it has been days since the bear was there. Fresh, steaming scat may mean it was there just a few minutes ago.

Some helpful books for identifying scat are *National Audubon Society Pocket Guide to Familiar Animal Tracks of North America* by John Ferrand, *North Woods Animal Scat Guide, Tracking and the Art of Seeing: How to Read Animal Tracks and Sign* by Paul Rezendes, and *A Field Guide to Animal Tracks* edited by Olaus Murie (see resources section).

SCOUTING RAPIDS

When on a river, scouting rapids ranks at the very top of the "smartest-things-to-do" list. Scouting rapids is the process of evaluating a set of rapids either from the shore or from your boat. Your goals are to determine (1) whether you should shoot, line, or portage the set (see **lining** and **portaging**), and (2) if you are going to shoot the rapids, the best route to take. Before you can scout rapids, you need to know how to read them (see **reading rapids**). Otherwise, you will simply be staring at lots of white splashing water, wondering what to make of it all.

You might think that scouting is a stationary event. On the contrary, a proactive scout can be rewarded with lots of valuable information. Here are a few tips.

• The best place to scout rapids is from the bank of the river. This allows you the freedom to move

ANNIE AGGENS

Scouting a set of rapids can save your life. These paddlers are planning their route past a small hole and a series of standing waves. Scouting from shore offers a better perspective than scouting from your boat.

upstream and downstream and look at a hazard from many angles. This can be especially valuable if you suspect the presence of a ledge, which is much easier to identify from downstream. Utilize the shoreline along the entire length of the rapids, if necessary. Be careful of slippery rocks and logs. A less satisfactory alternative is scouting from your boat, although sometimes this is your only option.

• Crouch every so often to look at the rapids from a few feet above water level. This is how they will look from your boat. Some features might be harder to see from this vantage point, so it's good to be prepared!

• Choose a landmark along the shoreline, such as a specific bush or tree, to help remind you when a hidden hazard is approaching. This can be particularly helpful when the rapids are long and you have a lot to remember.

• Ask yourself if you can perform a **rescue** along your route if it becomes necessary. If the answer is no, then consider an alternate route. This may not be important if you are out for the day and an upset simply results in a swim. If you're on a long trip, however, getting your boat, or a member of your group, stuck in the middle of a big set of rapids that you can't access is a dangerous situation.

• Take into consideration the temperature of the air and water. Be more cautious when conditions are less than ideal.

• Evaluate the physical and mental status of each member of your group. Is it late in the day? Are you tired or cold? Or are you in top form and ready for a big challenge? If you're not at your best, choose the most conservative route, often a portage.

• Finally, be sure to share with other party members the route that you decide to take. Sharing routes often sparks feedback and suggestions from group members. It also comes in handy if there is an unexpected upset, because the person with the **throw bag** or the rescue boat will know where to aim.

SCREE

Slopes of very small stones, known as *scree*, make up some of the most difficult **wilderness** terrain because the stones move underfoot. The word *scree* comes from the Old Norse *skritha*, meaning "landslip" or "glide." Sometimes as you climb or descend scree, the whole slope seems to start moving under you. Indeed, you can run down scree, allowing the stones to move under you. However, this damages the slope and can reduce it to a potentially dangerous ribbon of dirt and bare rock, so it should be avoided. You can't travel on scree without the stones moving; trying to do so is futile. Climbing scree is tedious and slow because you'll slip back with every step. Unless the slope is short, it's best to avoid ascending scree. Sometimes angling upward can seem easier than climbing directly up, although whichever you do will be hard work. It can help to kick the edges or toes of your boots into the slope, but don't lean into the slope or your feet may slip from under you.

When descending scree, be wary if you can't see the bottom of the slope. It could end in a cliff, and if the scree is moving you may not be able to stop. To stay in balance, keep your weight over your feet and place your heels down first. Keep your knees bent so they act as shock absorbers. Let the stones roll under you, and be prepared for random speed changes that may throw you off balance as one foot shoots ahead of the other. If you have a heavy load, go slowly so you're less likely to hurt yourself if you fall.

Scree can damage footwear, especially if you descend fast, and can fill it with small stones. Wearing **gaiters** can prevent this.

If there are other people on a scree slope, be cautious because it's easy to send a stone bounding down the slope. Don't stand directly above or below anyone else. Groups can move in an arrowhead formation or an angled line so that when a stone is dislodged, no one is below. If a stone does start rolling, yell **"Rock!"** to warn anyone below. If you hear someone else yell this, turn your head away from the slope so your **pack** protects your head, or put your hands over your head. *Don't look up:* stones move fast.

SEA KAYAKING

In recent years, sea kayaking has become one of the fastest-growing water sports in the United States—and with good reason. Sea kayaking can be as relaxing or exciting as you decide to make it. You can unwind on a short half-hour paddle along an inland lake, catch a wave as you learn to surf the swells, or plan a full-on expedition to the ends of the earth.

Sea kayaking differs from whitewater kayaking in a few ways. While the goal in whitewater kayaking is to maneuver around rocks and in and out of small **eddies**, sea kayaking seeks to set a relatively straight course and paddle for a long distance. To aid in this endeavor, the equipment is quite different. Perhaps the most noticeable difference is the size of the kayak. While whitewater kayaks can be as short as 5 feet, most sea kayaks are between 12 and 17 feet long, with some surpassing 20 feet. Sea kayaks are also outfitted with hatches (storage compartments) and **rudders** or **skegs** that can help maintain the direction of travel. In addition, sea kayaks are designed as either singles, meaning one person pad-

Sea kayaking allows you to explore wilderness areas inaccessible by foot.

dles the kayak, or doubles, which use two paddlers. Sometimes, doubles are referred to as *tandem kayaks*. While sea kayaking strokes differ somewhat from other **kayaking strokes**, the guiding principles remain the same. In addition to learning kayaking strokes, a sea kayaker needs to learn a variety of **rescue** and **navigation** skills. People often adapt quickly to sea kayaking if they've had previous kayaking experience.

The history of sea kayaking is fascinating. Many people may know that the origins of kayaking come from the Inuit communities of the far north. For most Inuit, kayaks were the only source of water transportation. and they were heavily relied upon for hunting and fishing. While motorboats have generally replaced the kayak for hunting and fishing, many Inuit still kayak and excel at paddling. In Greenland, where the art of kayaking is considered an important part of the traditional culture, an annual competition selects the most competent sea kayaker. After a grueling contest that includes such events as sprinting, harpoon throwing, running over land with the kayak, and rolling (30 different ways!), the winner is presented with the prestigious Golden Harpoon award.

Luckily, you don't have to submit yourself to the same rigors to enjoy this sport. If you'd like to learn how to sea kayak, many organizations offer instruction for entry-level paddlers. Most will follow the guidelines of either the American

Canoe Association or the British Canoe Union. These two agencies govern the certification of instructors and help promote the sport through symposiums and events. Contact either organization for information on upcoming events (see resources section), or ask around at your local paddle shop to find the nearest instructional course.

Sea kayaking allows you to explore some of the world's best coastlines and most remote waterways. If you're **planning a trip** to a wilderness area, be sure to research the route. If you intend to paddle on coastal water, you'll need to learn about the local **tides** and **coastal currents**. The best way to do this is to contact a local paddling shop or club. If there isn't one, try contacting the sheriff's office or the local coast guard. The **open-water hazards** of coastal areas and big lakes can be demanding. Conditions often change quickly from pleasant to ferocious. Always be prepared for the most challenging circumstances. Remember to leave a **float plan** with a local authority, friend, or relative that includes pertinent information, such as where you're going, what gear you have with you, and when you think you'll return.

Sea Kayaking Equipment

Sea kayak
Paddle
PFD
Paddle float
Bilge pump
Nautical charts or **maps**
VHF radio or **weather radio**
Flares or emergency pack (see **signaling**)
Booties
First-aid kit
Kayak repair kit
Food and **water**
Dry suit or wet suit
Helmet (if surfing)
Gloves (see **gloves and mitts**)

If you'd rather have someone else do the planning, you can join one of the many sea kayaking tours that explore exotic and beautiful destinations. Find a tour operator who has experience paddling the area and can offer the type of trip you want. Many tour operators use tandem sea kayaks for their trips, so if paddling a single is important to you, request one before you register.

See also **kayak selection**.

SEAM SEALING

No matter what type of **tent** or fly you use, you'll likely have to seal some of the seams for protection against water. Seam sealing is the process of coating the seams of a tent, **tarp**, or garment with a waterproof gel. Most quality tents come with factory-sealed floor seams, which means the seams have been covered with a clear piece of tape that is then heat-treated onto the material. If you don't see clear tape over the floor seams, seal them yourself. This is easiest to do with the tent set up. Seal any seam that will be exposed to the elements. Pay particular attention to the corners of your tent and to areas that collect and drip water. In addition, seal the seams of your rain fly. Seams that are frequently exposed to water should be sealed on both the inside and outside of the tent.

Purchase seam sealant from any outdoor store or catalog. It usually comes in a small bottle with a spongy applicator that you glide across the seam. It's smart to apply two thin coats of seam sealer. The second coat can be applied when the first becomes tacky. Drying can take several hours, depending on how thickly you've applied the sealant. Seam sealant usually begins to delaminate after one or two well-used seasons, even if the manufacturer claims otherwise. If you need to reapply seam sealant (and eventually you will), use a toothbrush to remove as much of the old sealant as possible. The surface should be clean and dry before you apply more sealant.

A longer-lasting alternative to seam sealant is seam grip, which is a thicker gel that, when dry, becomes rubbery. Seam grip is more expensive

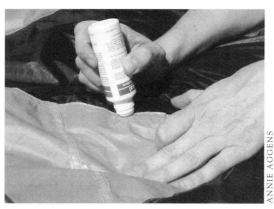

To prevent tent and fly seams from leaking, apply seam sealant in several thin coats, allowing each coat to dry before applying the next.

than seam sealant but will last much longer. It is also handy for repairing small tears in the tent floor or even a tear in a dry bag or a self-inflating sleeping pad.

Whichever type of sealant you use, leave your tent up overnight to ensure adequate drying time. Disassembling your tent and returning it to its stuff sack before the sealant has dried is a sure bet for a sticky mess.

See also **waterproofing**.

SEARCH AND RESCUE

Everyone hopes they'll never have to use their search-and-rescue skills. Nonetheless, it is important to know how to look for a missing person and what you should do if you can't find him. By understanding why people get **lost**, you can try to reduce the possibility that someone in your group will end up missing. However, sometimes even experienced backcountry travelers become disoriented or delayed. If someone does go missing, ask yourself the following questions to determine the most appropriate course of action.

• Is this person able and equipped to handle himself in the backcountry?
• What equipment does he have with him?
• Does he have a **communication device**, such as a **cell phone** or radio?

• Is he in need of medication that he doesn't have?
• Is he mentally stable?
• Has this happened before? If so, where did he go last time?
• Does the group have a **contingency plan** for being separated?

After considering these questions, take a look at the **map** and determine the last point that the lost party was actually seen. This is known as the *PLS*, or "point last seen." Mark this location on your map. Use your knowledge of the lost party and your common sense to determine how he might have become lost or delayed. Was there a particularly tricky section of the route? Was there severe weather that would have prevented him from crossing a section of the route? Is there a reason why he might have diverged from the planned route (such as a **flash flood** or downed trees)? According to the National Association of Search and Rescue (NASAR), approximately 50 percent of backcountry travelers are found within a 3-mile radius of the PLS. Ninety percent are found within a 6-mile radius of the PLS. To give you a visual on what that means for your situation, draw two circles on your map, one at 3 miles from the PLS and one at 6 miles from the PLS. This gives you an idea of how far the lost party may have wandered. Keep in mind that people have a tendency to wander downhill rather than uphill. Now that you have thought through the situation, devise a search plan, which should include the following components.

• Organize a team to quickly search the areas where the lost party is most likely to be located. They should travel fast and light but also be prepared with **food**, **water**, and shelter in case their return becomes delayed.
• Back at camp, use any and all means to draw attention to your site. If the lost party can see you, he will have a better chance of reaching you. Building a **fire** and setting up a colorful **tent** in an exposed area are just a couple ideas.

• Consider the surroundings. Are there specific places in the vicinity that a wandering person would likely pass, such as a bridge or trailhead? If so, leave a visible note or message informing the person what to do. This is called *confining the area*. Leaving notes isn't the only way to confine an area: you can also draw a message in the sand or tie in a tree some object the lost person would recognize. Try to confine the routes that lead out of the 3- and 6-mile circles that you drew on your map. Amazingly, 75 percent of people are found by confinement, not searchers.

• Search for clues of the missing party's location in addition to looking for the missing person. Important clues, such as footprints or broken branches, are often overlooked when you're searching only for a person.

• Avoid searching at night, if at all possible. Night searches can be dangerous and are exhausting. Instead, reserve your strength. Most lost people don't travel at night—neither should you.

• Document your search efforts. This will help you keep track of where you have looked. It also helps professional rescuers should they be needed.

• Preserve any clues of the missing party's whereabouts. This might seem unimportant at the time, but preserving boot tracks and other clues at the scene will greatly aid professional rescuers.

When to Get Outside Help

If you're unable to locate the person within a few hours, consider seeking outside help. You may feel this is premature, but most rescuers are much happier having an early response called off rather than starting a search long after the trail is cold. There are some exceptions for requesting outside help this early. For instance, if the missing person is adequately trained and prepared to be on his own, you may be able to extend your search time to one day. On the other hand, if the missing person is a child, mentally or medically unstable, or unprepared for the elements, a request for outside assistance should be hastened.

If you need outside help, send no fewer than two people out to request assistance. They will be interviewed by the rescue organizers and should be prepared with the answers to the questions you asked yourself earlier. In addition, give the rescue organizer any other information that may prove helpful, such as maps marked with the PLS, the location of your camp, and pertinent medical information concerning the missing person. Keep in mind that from the time you decide to ask for help to the time the professional rescue team actually starts searching may be several hours or even days. This all depends on how quickly you can access help and the amount of time it takes to mobilize the search team.

See also **rescue**.

SELF-ARREST

Self-arrest (also called *ice ax braking*)—stopping a slide on **snow** with your **ice ax**—is an essential skill that could save your life.

Before venturing onto slopes of hard snow or **ice**, you should always be aware of what lies below them. If there is a gentle run-out into a bowl of deep snow, a slide may not result in injury, but if there are cliffs, boulders, or gullies in the way, a slip could lead to a serious accident. It's surprising how quickly you pick up speed during a slide, especially when wearing smooth, synthetic **clothing**. You need to be able to react very quickly, using the pick of the ice ax, backed up by your body weight, as a brake.

The best way to learn self-arrest is at a mountain school or from an independent **mountaineering** instructor. Second best is an experienced friend. Written descriptions are a distant third. Self-arrest should be practiced until it becomes second nature. In a real incident, there isn't time to think about what to do. You need to stop as quickly as possible.

A concave snow slope with a long, safe run-out is the best place for practicing self-arrest. Be sure there are no boulders in the way. Choose a slope that will let you slide—but not very fast. Soft snow is no good for this practice because your body weight will cause you to sink in and stop before you even start to slide. And hard snow or ice is too slippery for your early practices; instead select a slope that offers snow that is just fairly firm. Wear a climbing helmet and warm, waterproof clothing, including gloves (see **gloves and mitts**). You'll be spending much time lying in the snow. Initially it's easiest to practice without a **pack**, but once you've built up some confidence try it with the pack on.

To start, slide down the lower part of the slope without your ax a few times so you feel comfortable with the movement. Try it on your front and back and with your head downhill. Next, lie on

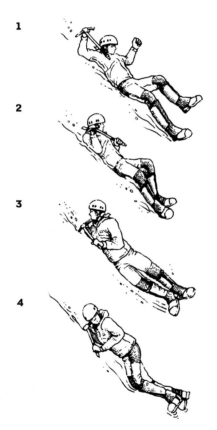

Self-arrest. 1. Sliding out of control. 2. Grasp the ax with one hand over the head with the pick pointing away from you, the other hand around the shaft near the spike. 3. Roll sideways toward the head of the ax, pressing the pick into the snow. 4. The self-arrest position: the adze is tucked in the shoulder and the pick is pressed firmly into the snow by your body.

your back with your feet downhill, and push yourself off down the slope, holding the ax diagonally across your body with your lower hand on the shaft near the spike, your upper hand over the head, and the pick pointing away from you. Once you have started to slide, roll sideways toward the head of the ax and onto the pick, tucking the adze in just above your shoulder so you can use your body weight to push down on the shaft and press the pick into the snow. Keep your elbows close to your body, and turn your face away from the ax head so you don't catch it on the adze. Arching your back exerts extra pressure.

Don't hold the ax at arm's length because this prevents your weight from helping to force the pick into the snow and may lead to the ax being ripped out of your hands. Make sure your lower hand controls the spike, so it doesn't stab you in the thigh; don't roll toward the spike or it may catch in the snow. Pulling up with your lower hand keeps the spike out of the snow and helps you arch your back. With a short ax, you can put your hand over the spike to stop it from sticking into you. Your knees can be used as extra brakes.

Although you may be wearing **crampons** in a real fall, you should never do so when practicing because the crampon points can catch in the snow and flip you over onto your back, injuring your legs in the process. Lift your feet well off the snow when practicing because this is what you should do with crampons on. This also prevents a **boot** catching in the snow and twisting your leg, which can also cause injuries.

Once you're comfortable stopping at slow speeds, slide farther and faster. The idea is always to stop as quickly as possible. That cliff might be very close.

Of course, if you slip, you're unlikely to always fall with your head up the slope, so you should also practice self-arrest when sliding headfirst both on your back and on your front. The self-arrest position here is exactly as described above, but getting into it is harder. When sliding headfirst on your back, grasp the ax with both hands; then place the pick off to the side and roll onto your front while pivoting around it until your feet are downhill and you can stop. If the ax ends up above you, lift the pick out of the snow, pull it into the arrest position, and then press it back into the snow.

Facedown, headfirst slides are harder to stop. Again, with the ax held in both hands, place the pick off to the side and pivot around it to get your legs downhill. This, however, results in the ax being out at arm's length above your head. To stop it from being snatched out of your hands, lift the pick out of the snow so you can pull the ax into position close to your shoulder.

With both headfirst falls, make sure you place the pick to the side on which it lies. Don't bring it across your body because you could stab yourself with it or the spike could catch in the snow. It also takes more time.

Your ax may be in either hand when you fall, so you need to be able to self-arrest on both sides. Once you feel confident with self-arrest, try swapping the ax from hand to hand each time you slide down the slope. If you find it harder on one side than the other, as many people do, practice more on that side.

Although you don't usually slide far in soft snow, you can self-arrest with the adze of your ice ax.

Self-arrest is an emergency procedure, and if you're careful, it shouldn't be necessary at all. On any terrain where a slip is possible, hold the ice ax ready to arrest, which means with the pick facing backward so that when you swing it up to your shoulder it will be pointing away from you and ready for use as a brake.

SELF-RELIANCE

Self-reliance means you can travel into the **wilderness** alone and cope with whatever happens. It also means that when part of a group, you can contribute your skills and confidence rather than depending on others.

Self-reliance lies at the heart of wilderness travel. Without it, you will always be dependent on others; with it, you will be independent. Self-reliance is mostly psychological. Confidence in your equipment and skills helps. Some people feel self-reliant very quickly when they first venture into the backcountry, and others have been brought up to be so and are used to being in the wilderness. Many people, however, need to build their self-reliance over a period of time, becoming more confident as their experience increases.

True self-reliance means knowing your limits and having confidence in your abilities. Being overconfident and overassessing your abilities represents not self-reliance but a lack of self-knowledge and self-respect. Self-respect is an essential part of self-reliance. When you're able to say, "This is where I turn back," without feeling you have in some way failed, you have succeeded.

SHELTER, EMERGENCY

So you lost your **pack**. The canoe tipped over and floated downstream. What now? If you're in the **wilderness** without a shelter, all is not lost. Given the option, many people will sleep out under the stars even when they have shelter available. Still, if conditions require shelter, you can build a makeshift home without too much effort.

Assuming you don't have any gear with you, you should start by looking for a refuge that you

If you need to build an emergency shelter, think creatively and use all available resources. This shelter was constructed by leaning several sturdy sticks against a center branch. The sides were then lined with leaves, branches, grass, and twigs. Build emergency shelters small and low to trap the body's heat.

don't have to build from scratch. Small shelters with low ceilings are best at trapping heat. Shallow caves are nice, but they only exist in certain environments. Upended trees with large root systems can easily be augmented with branches and leaves to trap heat and fend off **rain**. Likewise, evergreen trees with low, sweeping branches are great at keeping you dry. If the tree's branches are long enough, you can fasten them to the ground with rocks, creating a natural tepee. Overturned canoes make natural shelters. Even large cracks in bedrock and the area directly against downed trees can be padded with duff for insulation and then covered with branches for warmth. In hot, arid environments, you will need to protect yourself against the sun. Look for shade from any source, such as a canyon wall or a tree. Restrict your building efforts to the morning and evening hours. In colder climates, if adequate **snow** is on the ground, a **snow shelter** is one of the easiest natural shelters to build.

If you're without gear but still able to hike or

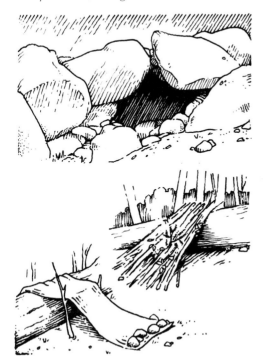

Emergency shelters can be built in caves, large cracks in rocks, or beside downed trees.

paddle out, your shelters need to suffice for only one night each. However, if you're lost, stranded, or injured, your shelter will need to be more durable. Always choose a site that is dry and well drained: there's no sense making a great shelter only to have it become a swamp when it rains. Build your shelter above the high-water mark if you're near a river or ocean. Avoid locations that are buggy or laden with ants, wasps, or termites. Remember that your sanity is a key component to survival! Also avoid locations that are naturally dangerous, including areas prone to **avalanches** or **flash floods**, the bases of tall trees in thunderstorms, and sites under dead branches or severely diseased trees (see **widow makers**). In addition, low-lying valleys and depressions have a tendency to trap cold air at night and should be avoided.

Remember that people may be looking for you. This is especially true if you left a **trip plan** with a trusted friend or local authority. Your natural shelter is probably difficult to see from the air, so create some type of visual signal, such as a big X made out of rocks or sticks (see **signaling**). Don't give up hope. All the ingredients for a wonderful shelter are right around you. All you need to do is think creatively and be resourceful.

SHOCK

Shock is a breakdown in the body's ability to circulate blood. If left untreated, even mild shock leads to death. Among the several types of shock, volume shock—which occurs when the volume of blood in a person's body decreases significantly—is the one most commonly found in the backcountry. Such inadequate blood flow is usually the result of a traumatic accident, severe dehydration, or severe burns.

The physiological effects of shock often make it difficult for shock victims to identify the condition in themselves; in the wilderness, you need to count on your companions to realize you're in shock and to treat you. Symptoms in the early stages may be so subtle as to make shock difficult to detect. The affected person may simply feel nervous or anxious. Others may misinterpret this as the anxiety that often develops after an accident. Normal anxiety gradually subsides, but a shock patient's nervousness and restlessness only increase over time.

As the shock progresses, you may notice an increase in respiration (breathing) and changes in the color and temperature of the person's skin. If blood flow continues to diminish, the body will restrict the flow of blood to only the vital organs, resulting in a loss of color and a drop in temperature in the extremities. The person's pulse will become rapid as the heart attempts to distribute the limited blood supply throughout the body.

If shock becomes severe, the person's behavior will change, possibly becoming lethargic, combative, or unresponsive. While mild shock can be treated in the field, severe shock requires intravenous fluids, advanced medical attention, and oxygen. Because you won't have access to these tools (unless you're on a heavily supported **expedition**), you need to initiate a rapid **rescue** or **evacuation**.

Whenever a person has experienced a traumatic injury, serious **burn**, or prolonged illness, look for signs of shock. This is true even if there is no visible **bleeding**. Treatment begins with identifying why there is such low blood volume. Is it from a broken leg or internal bleeding of some sort? Is there severe **dehydration** from days of persistent diarrhea? Have blood vessels been so severely burned that they are unable to transport blood? Any of these situations must be treated before the signs of shock will subside. If you can't treat the cause yourself, plan for an immediate rescue or evacuation.

In addition to treating the cause of low blood volume, you can minimize the effects of shock by taking these steps.

- Keep the person warm and insulated from the ground. People in shock are unable to generate any heat, so you need to do it for them.
- Calm the person. Speak to her in a reassuring voice, and avoid frightening her with gory descriptions of her condition. If the person is bleed-

ing severely, you may want to limit her ability to see it. Do everything in your power to reassure the person and make her feel comfortable.
- If it does not compromise the injury, have the person lie down and elevate their feet 12 inches to help increase perfusion in the vital organs.
- Only attempt to give the person fluids to drink if she is fully conscious. Oral fluid replacement is slow and may not be as effective as needed. However, if you're waiting for a rescue or treating mild shock in the field, give the person small, frequent amounts of water.

Shock is one of several medical emergencies that can occur in the backcountry. Prepare yourself adequately by getting proper training in wilderness **first aid**. Many organizations offer courses that cover shock and many other medical scenarios. Learning how to respond in a medical emergency can save your life and the lives of your traveling companions.

SIERRA CLUB

Founded in 1892 by John Muir (see **Muir, John**), the club's first president, the Sierra Club has grown from a local organization concerned with the preservation of the **Sierra Nevada** in California to a major national environmental organization whose slogan is "explore, enjoy and protect the planet."

From the beginning, the Sierra Club has always promoted **wilderness** travel and has run regular outings, both locally and internationally. There are many local chapters who run their own outings too.

For more information, visit the Sierra Club's website (see resources section).

SIERRA NEVADA

"The most divinely beautiful of all the mountain-chains I have ever seen." So John Muir (see **Muir, John**) described the Sierra Nevada in California, the **mountain** range that changed his life and led to his becoming one of the founders of **wilderness** preservation.

As well as beautiful and spectacular, the Sierra Nevada is big, the longest unbroken mountain range in the contiguous United States. It stretches some 400 miles from the Mojave Desert in southern California to its northern terminus at the **Cascades** in Oregon. The Sierra Nevada ranges from 60 to 80 miles wide. It's an asymmetric mountain range, a great block of tilted, uplifted granite with wooded foothills dwindling away gradually to the Central Valley in the west and a steep escarpment on the east that drops abruptly to the high **desert** of the Great Basin. This sudden wall of mountains is particularly visible from Owens Valley (California), which runs below the southern Sierra.

The most impressive and popular part of the Sierra Nevada is the High Sierra, which lies south of Sonora Pass and encompasses all of the highest peaks of the range, **Yosemite**, Sequoia, and Kings Canyon National Parks, and many wilderness areas. The High Sierra is about 150 miles long and is made up of a tangle of ice-sculpted golden granite peaks, deep glaciated gorges, many beautiful timberline lakes, tumbling creeks, and magnificent conifer **forests**. The highest peak in the Sierra, as well as the highest in the contiguous United States, is 14,494-foot Mount Whitney. Eleven other peaks are over 14,000 feet, and hundreds of others are over 12,000 feet. Indeed, some of the passes, such as Forester, are over 13,000 feet, and for 90 miles the main crest never drops below 11,000 feet.

The first Europeans to see the Sierra Nevada were Spanish explorers pushing north from Mexico in the 1770s. It was one of these explorers, Father Pedro Font, who called the mountains the "sierra nevada," or "snowy mountains." John Muir reached the area in 1868, a century later, just in time to inspire the preservation of much of the range. He proposed they be called the Range of Light.

The light in the Sierra Nevada is magical and has inspired many artists, most famously the great photographer Ansel Adams. The climate helps too. It is amazingly benign for such a high mountain range. Muir's well-known delight in storms was perhaps due to the fact that they didn't occur very often and were short lived when they did.

Its natural beauty and pleasant weather make the Sierra Nevada a wonderful destination for wilderness lovers. Many activities are possible, but the range is particularly noted for **hiking** and **rock climbing** in summer and **ski touring** in winter and spring. There are thousands of miles of **trails** for the hiker, including the **John Muir Trail** and the Tahoe-Yosemite Trail, while the **Pacific Crest Trail** runs the length of the range. The great rock walls of El Capitan and Half Dome in Yosemite Valley are some of the most famous rock climbing venues in the world, and there are many opportunities for climbs of all grades elsewhere in the Sierra. Skiing opportunities range from easy cross-country skiing in the lower valleys to more strenuous ski tours over the high passes and ski mountaineering ascents and descents of the peaks (see **ski touring**). Whether it's a short hike through the giant sequoias, the biggest trees on earth, or a winter mountain ascent, any visit to the Sierra Nevada is a tremendous experience.

SIGNALING

For thousands of years people have used signaling devices to communicate over distances beyond the reach of the human voice. Signaling devices differ from **communication devices** because they don't provide a means for two-way verbal communication; they simply draw attention or communicate through predetermined code. Signaling devices attract attention through sound (audio signals), visual displays, or electronics. Even in today's electronic world, knowledge of simple signaling can mean the difference between life and death. Signaling devices are primarily used to attract attention in emergency rescue situations, though some backcountry travelers use them to identify a **food** drop, **cache**, or rendezvous location.

Audio Signals

Audio signals, such as whistles, are useful when your voice cannot be heard, such as over the roar of a river. They also allow communication that won't make you hoarse, which may be important if you need to shout. Many people suggest that all backcountry travelers carry a whistle. Indeed, whistles are handy if you're lost and you suspect someone is trying to find you. However, they can be virtually useless in strong wind, because anyone upwind of you won't hear the whistle. Avoid blowing whistles except in an emergency (usually distinguished by three sharp blows), because they disrupt the serenity of the **wilderness** and might unnecessarily alarm other travelers.

Air horns are another type of audio signaling device. People traveling on open water, such as sea kayakers, can use an air horn to signal their presence to larger vessels. Smaller air horns, popular with some paddlers, are easily broken, so pack them carefully.

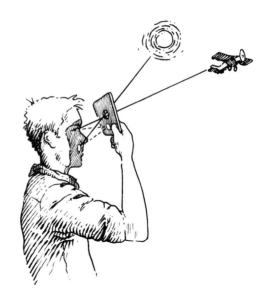

Many signaling mirrors have a small hole that allows you to direct the reflected light to your target. Spot your target through the hole and tilt the mirror until the reflection of sunlight on your face disappears into the hole. In this illustration, the mirror needs to be tilted back a little more for this to happen.

Visual Signals

Visual signals include **fires**, smoke signals, water dyes, brightly colored equipment, flares, and strobe lights. Only flares, strobe lights, and flaming fires are effective visual signals at night.

On open water, flares can be highly visible. There are many different types of flares offering various burn rates, and heights. Be aware that flares have a high "dud" rate, meaning that often nothing happens when you pull the cord or trigger. Therefore, carry multiple flares. Strobe lights are easily seen from a distance, particularly from the air. White strobe lights are the most visible and are usually recognized as a sign of distress.

Fires are especially visible at night if they can be seen from a distance. During the day, fires are less visible unless they produce a lot of smoke. Burning leafy green branches or placing damp wood in the fire are good ways to produce copious amounts of smoke. Another option is commercially produced smoke signal cartridges, which are generally bright orange and can be seen well

from a distance, particularly on clear days. They also indicate the wind direction, which can be important to a rescue helicopter or small plane.

Dye cartridges disperse a dye into the water and are a wise addition if your journey takes you on open water. As the water disperses, the dye leaves a colorful trail leading to your boat. Smoke signals and water dyes are small and easy to pack.

Signaling mirrors work well if used correctly on clear days. To use a signaling mirror, hold it with one hand and place your other hand over the intended target (the plane, the ship, and so forth). Maneuver the mirror until you can reflect light onto the hand covering the target. Now remove your hand and continue to move the mirror slightly back and forth. If you don't have a mirror, try anything that reflects light—your watch face, cooking utensils, a belt buckle, or eyeglasses.

Colorful equipment can be useful but often blends in with the surroundings. Unless you're at sea or on **snow**, white is probably the most visible color. A **tarp** or rain fly usually has the largest

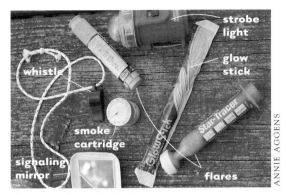

A variety of signaling devices.

surface area and can be spread out to attract attention.

In heavy brush or forest, try tying a rope to a tree branch or bush and tugging the line fiercely. A moving branch or bush is very noticeable from the distance.

Electronic Signals

Electronic signaling devices, such as an EPIRB (emergency position-indicating radio beacon) or PLB (personal locator beacon), emit a radio signal that is picked up by satellite and directed to a rescue resource, such as the army, navy, or coast guard. According to the Federal Communications Commission, EPIRBs are illegal to use except at sea. Still, many expeditions have carried them to extremely remote locations for use in dire emergencies. In recent years, a land version of the EPIRB, known as the PLB, has been gaining in popularity. For more information, see **PLB**.

All wilderness travelers should carry, at the very least, one signaling device. To choose the best device, consider the terrain you'll be traveling in and who you may be trying to signal. Signals in sets of three—that is, three blasts on the whistle, three flashes of your flashlight, and so forth—are generally interpreted as a sign of distress. Read the directions of your device prior to departing. Develop a plan, and a **contingency plan**, for food drops, **resupplying**, pickups, and emergency **evacuations**. Discuss these plans with your compan-

ions and any appropriate parties. If it's at all likely that you could be separated from your gear, carry a signaling device on your person at all times.

SKEGS

Retractable skegs are alternatives to **rudders** on sea kayaks. A deployed skeg is usually within an arm's length aft of the cockpit, and its left-right orientation is fixed, making it look much like the fin on a surfboard. A skeg is deployed from a cable or cord located near the cockpit. In most models, the depth of the skeg can easily be controlled (unlike a rudder).

Because of their midboat placement, skegs are most helpful when deployed to maintain direction in heavy crosswinds and to prevent broaching in large following seas (which is likely to make a rudder pop out of the water). Unlike rudders, they cannot be used to change direction. In fact, a

A skeg in the down (deployed) position on a sea kayak. Most skegs are retractable.

deployed skeg can make turning your kayak more difficult. Like a rudder, the deployed skeg creates drag, reducing your speed. However, unlike a rudder, a skeg won't get in your way during a **rescue**. Pebbles and stones can get caught in the housing making the skeg difficult to deploy. To avoid this, regularly maintain the skeg, its housing, and its cable.

Because skegs don't require movable footpegs, paddlers who prefer fixed footing often choose a kayak with a skeg over one with a rudder.

Skegs are difficult to find on plastic kayaks but are often a standard feature on higher-end fiberglass touring kayaks.

SKIING

The standard image of skiing is of brightly colored hordes sweeping down the manicured slopes of a downhill resort. Backcountry may surround these playgrounds, but they have little to do with **wilderness**.

Another kind of skiing, however, takes place away from the noise and bustle of a ski resort and doesn't require lifts to carry the skier up the slopes. This skiing involves exploring the snowbound wilderness, whether covering long distances, ascending a peak, or enjoying the thrill of a descent. For more information on this type of skiing and its many branches, see **ski touring**.

SKI MOUNTAINEERING

See **ski touring**.

SKI TOURING

Ski touring means traveling the backcountry on skis. This may be with skinny skis in forests and gentle terrain or with ski mountaineering gear in steep mountains. Because people often use the term *ski touring* to describe what they do, it's always wise to find out what they mean. Go to the Alps, and ski touring is often used to refer to alpine ski mountaineering; go to Norway, and it means skiing between backcountry huts on Nordic skis.

Ski touring in the High Sierra.

Nordic Skiing

Nordic skiing is the original form of skiing as it was developed thousands of years ago in the Nordic countries of Norway, Sweden, and Finland. A fragment of a ski between 4,000 and 5,000 years old has been found in Sweden, and ancient cave paintings of skiers have been found in Norway and Russia. The word *ski* itself is Scandinavian, from the Old Norse *skith*, probably meaning "snowshoe."

Nordic skiing began as a means of travel over country that was snow-covered most of the year rather than as a competitive sport or a form of recreation. As a form of travel, Nordic skiing involves skiing uphill, downhill, and on the flat.

Today Nordic skiing encompasses any skiing involving a free heel, including cross-country, backcountry, and telemark skiing and ski jumping. Skiing in which the heel is locked to the ski is known as *alpine skiing*.

As far as the **wilderness** is concerned, when there is snow on the ground, backcountry or Nordic ski touring is the best way to get around everywhere except the steepest slopes. The gear used for this is a compromise between ease of glide on the flats and control on descents. Depending on the type of terrain, it may veer toward light, skinny cross-country skis or heavy-duty, downhill-oriented telemark gear.

Traditional Nordic ski boots are made of leather and are similar to three- or four-season walking **boots**. They need to flex forward fairly

The basic diagonal stride (left), and a more energetic diagonal stride (right).

TOM FROST

easily, but they must be stiff from side to side. If you can twist a boot sole when holding it by the toe and heel, put it back on the shelf because it will be very difficult to turn a ski with it.

The lightest suitable boots have soft uppers but don't give as good control for downhill skiing as stiffer boots. Stiffer, higher boots give better downhill control and are worth having if you will encounter many descents, but they aren't as comfortable on flat terrain. Most have stiffened ankles plus straps and buckles to pull the boot into the foot for better control.

Plastic, which is standard for alpine and telemark ski boots, is making inroads into Nordic touring, especially for mountain tours. Plastic boots have many advantages. They keep your feet warm and dry and don't soak up moisture like

leather. Upkeep is minimal, with no need for boot wax. The inner boots can be used in huts and tents. And, very important on **camping** trips, there's no need to fiddle with frozen laces and then ski in sloppy boots because you can't do them up tightly. However, most plastic boots are too stiff and heavy for touring in all but the steepest mountains.

Nordic skis have double camber, with a stiff midsection that stands off the snow. It's hard to squeeze the bases of Nordic cambered skis together. This camber makes travel on undulating terrain easier and less tiring but doesn't give as good downhill control as softer cambered skis. Double-cambered skis are ideal for covering long distances on undulating terrain and for any tours where long descents aren't the prime aim.

Nordic touring skis should have metal edges for icy terrain and some degree of sidecut (the difference between the width of the middle and tip of the ski), usually 10 to 12 millimeters. Typical dimensions are 63-54-58 millimeters and 68-55-62 millimeters (tip, middle, tail).

Nordic skis may have wax or no-wax bases. The first are smooth and require the application of special waxes before they can be used. Grip or kick wax comes in small tubs and tubes and is rubbed into the base of the skis. Different waxes are needed for different snow temperatures and for newly fallen and old snow. A properly waxed ski grips the snow when weight is applied and glides over the snow when the pressure is released. For touring, three or four wide-range waxes should be adequate. Waxing does require a little practice, and wax works best in temperatures below freezing.

In temperatures around freezing, no-wax (waxless) skis are easier to use because the snow changes rapidly, making waxing difficult. No-wax skis have a pattern cut into the base that acts like wax, gripping the snow when weighted and gliding when pushed forward. When no-wax skis work well they are very efficient, but they don't work well in some conditions, especially very cold snow but also warmer snow. Their big advantage is that you can just head out the door, put them on and ski, without having to stop to apply wax. That said, there are glide waxes for no-wax skis that will help prevent sticking, which can happen in warm, wet snow.

Nordic bindings are lightweight, simple, and easy to use. The choice is between three-pin bindings, in which the pins slot into holes in boot soles, and cable bindings, which wrap around the boot heels. Many cables are available these days, but most are designed for telemark skiing. The lighter ones are good for touring in mountain terrain. Three-pin bindings generally give freer heel movement and are better for long, flat tours.

Systems bindings—such as New Nordic Norm (NNN) and Salomon Nordic System (SNS)—have a bar at the toe of the boot that slots into a groove in the binding. They're usually used for groomed cross-country track skiing, but the heavier-duty models can be used for Nordic touring. If you use these, make sure your boots and bindings are compatible.

Cross-Country Skiing

Despite the name, cross-country skiing means skiing on groomed trails, not across unbroken snow. It involves the lightest ski gear—long skinny skis and soft sneakerlike boots—designed for fast travel on flat and gently undulating terrain. There are two basic techniques: classic, in which the skis are kept parallel in a technique called *diagonal stride*, and *freestyle* (or skating), in which the skier "skates" on the skis. For classic skiing, tracks are cut into the trail; for skating, a smooth, wide trail is needed.

Cross-country skiing is regarded as the most efficient aerobic sport and therefore a great way to get and stay fit. Although it may take you through beautiful scenery and into wild country, the need for machine-groomed trails means it isn't a wilderness pursuit.

Telemark Skiing

Telemark skiing is named after one type of turn rather than a broader style of skiing, such as alpine. Some people are surprised to learn that telemark skiing isn't new. The turn was the first modern turn devised, way back in 1869 when Sondre Norheim, a Norwegian farmer, won a skiing competition in Christiania (now called Oslo), Norway. Norheim developed what soon became called the *telemark turn* (after the county in Norway he was from) to give stability when landing after a ski jump and to control speed when skiing downhill.

During the late nineteenth century, recreational and competitive skiing grew in popularity in the Alps. There the terrain was steeper and the runs were narrower than in Norway, so shorter skis were developed and different techniques used, mainly the parallel turn, leading to a split between alpine skiing, with its locked-down heel, and the free-heel Nordic skiing.

For resort skiing and ski mountaineering in the Alps, alpine skiing became the norm, leaving the telemark turn, which can't be done on alpine gear, to ski tourers in the undulating terrain of Scandinavia. As Nordic skis became narrower and lighter, the telemark turn was used less and less.

All this changed in Colorado in the 1970s. Skiers who wanted to venture into the mountains on skis found that Nordic skis were great for skiing in along the valleys but very difficult for skiing downhill, while alpine skis were very slow and cumbersome on the approaches but gave good control on descents. Looking for a compromise, they rediscovered the telemark turn, which could be done on Nordic skis.

Since then, telemark skiing has become increasingly popular—indeed, it's almost a cult with some people—and telemark gear has developed until, ironically, the heaviest telemark equipment is heavier than alpine touring gear and is no more suitable for long valley approaches. This gear often never leaves ski resorts and is rarely seen in the backcountry. However, light telemark gear, which is really just heavy-duty Nordic touring gear, still exists and is suitable for touring in all but the steepest terrain.

Plastic telemark boots look much like alpine boots, with the same clips and straps. The crucial difference is that telemark boots aren't locked down at the heel for descents, and they flex across the forefoot to enable telemark turns to be made. This difference means that however alpine the boots may look, telemark skiing is still part of Nordic skiing.

Telemark bindings have to allow the boot to lift off the ski at the heel and flex forward at the front. They range from light cable and three-pin bindings that can also be used for Nordic touring to heavier step-in release bindings that are more suitable for ski mountaineering with wide skis and the heaviest boots.

Telemark skis are similar in dimensions to alpine skis but are usually softer flexing, although some skiers use alpine skis for telemarking. The difference between some telemark and alpine skis lies only in the names and graphics anyway. The lightest telemark skis, which can also be used for alpine touring, are no heavier than Nordic touring skis, though quite a bit wider and with an alpine camber, which means they don't stand off the snow in the center the way Nordic skis do. Sidecut—the difference in width between the tip and the middle of a ski—is important for easy turning; most telemark skis have 20 to 30 millimeters of sidecut.

What, then, is this turn that has attracted such attention and devotion (and opprobrium— just listen to some alpine skiers)? It basically involves extending one ski forward and bending both knees into a distinctive, almost genuflecting position. This makes for a long platform with good fore and aft stability—hence its use by ski jumpers. To turn the skis, apply pressure to the edges and steer the skis round a turn. When done properly it can feel wonderful, as if soaring down the slopes, and it looks quite elegant.

Modern telemark gear, with plastic boots and wide alpine-cambered skis, has led to a change in technique, placing more emphasis on weighting the rear ski, which can be more difficult in stiff plastic boots, and tighter turns more appropriate

The telemark turn is a basic backcountry skiing move.

to narrow trails at ski resorts. These turns, in which the telemark position is held only briefly, look more like alpine turns. However, in the backcountry, the old long-radius, sweeping telemark turn, which is most easily done in soft snow, is still a delight and well worth learning.

Ski Mountaineering

Ski mountaineering involves travel in mountains where both mountaineering and skiing skills are required. Thus ski mountaineers usually carry an **ice ax**, **crampons**, **rope**, and other climbing gear. Ski mountaineering involves both climbing and descending mountains on skis and also crossing the mountains by high passes, such as in the Haute Route in the Alps, probably the most famous ski mountaineering route.

Alpine touring gear is the norm for ski mountaineering, although heavier telemark gear is increasingly used. Alpine touring or ski mountaineering boots have a rigid sole that can be locked down at the heel for descents and released at the heel for ascents, and which can also be used for climbing with crampons. Bindings always have a release mechanism in case of falls. The boots are made of plastic and have several fastening clips and removable inners that can be used as hut or camp boots.

Alpine skis are wide and have an alpine camber—there is little rise in the midsection when the skis are unweighted. This makes them easy to turn. **Climbing skins** are used for grip on ascents. Also for easy turning, alpine mountaineering skis also have plenty of sidecut—the difference in width between the middle and the tip. Typical dimensions range from 96-67-86 millimeters to 115-82-105 millimeters (tip, middle, tail).

The basic skiing skills needed for ski mountaineering are the same as for downhill skiing at a resort, although skiing in the variable snow found in the mountains is more difficult. However, good mountaineering skills are more important than skiing techniques. In particular, ski mountaineers need to understand and be prepared for avalanches by carrying avalanche beacons and **snow shovels** (see **avalanches**).

SLACKPACKING

Slackpacking originally meant taking time over a long-distance hike; it was coined by some **Appalachian Trail** thru-hikers who wanted to complete the trail but were happy to do so slowly (see **thru-hiking**). This form of slackpacking is for hikers who like to follow whims and diversions, do low-mileage days, and spend time following up anything that takes their interest, from flowers to clouds.

Slackpacking has also come to mean hiking with a backup vehicle and support team who carry gear and food or even your whole pack for you and meet you at road crossings. There are now commercial services that will do this for you on some **trails**.

SLEDS

Dragging a sled (sometimes known as a *sledge*) across a frozen landscape sounds arduous and forbidding, reminiscent of the labors of Shackleton and Scott and other early polar explorers. However, when the choice is between carrying a load on your back or pulling it on a sled, the latter has many advantages, especially if the load is very heavy. Hundreds of pounds can be hauled on a sled, if necessary.

Sleds aren't suitable for all types of terrain, however. In particular, they aren't recommended for steep slopes because dragging them uphill is hard work. On flat and gently sloping or undulating **snow**, however, they work well. Soft, deep snow isn't ideal for sleds either, and it may be necessary to make a track before the sled can be moved.

A good sled should have a deep shell with a cover to protect the contents and narrow runners underneath for glide. The shafts that connect the sled to the user should be rigid so the sled can't catch up with you and take your legs from under you when going downhill. Many sleds also have a chest harness to spread the load. For carrying, the shafts usually fold up so they can be packed inside the sled. The shafts attach to a padded hip belt. Empty sleds can be fastened to the back of a **pack**. Although not comfortable, it's a good way to transport them across snow-free areas.

A sled can be as short as 2 to 3 feet, weigh 10 pounds or less, and carry up to 90 pounds. A typical one has a fiberglass shell, polyethylene runners, aluminum shafts, a proofed nylon cover, and a padded waist harness. That's big enough for most purposes unless you're setting out on a self-supported polar **expedition**.

Ski touring with a sled.

Expedition-specific sleds are expensive, heavy, and worth having only if they'll be regularly used. For occasional use, a simple plastic child's sled will work with some modifications, in particular the addition of hauling shafts. If the sled will only be used on the flat or uphill, rope can be used. However, if any downhill is likely, you'll need more rigid shafts. Slipping PVC pipe over the rope provides the rigidity needed.

Pulling a sled takes the weight off your back, leaving you more comfortable and more stable. If you have a lot of gear, you can carry a pack as well, perhaps putting it in the sled when the **food** supplies start to dwindle and you have more room.

SLEEPING BAGS

Having the right sleeping bag can make the difference between a comfortable, refreshing night and a miserable, shivering one that leaves you wanting to go home the next day rather than continue with your trip. Your sleeping bag is an important item of gear.

All sleeping bags work by trapping warm air in their filling. The more warm air a bag traps, the greater its ability to insulate you from the cold. Generally, the thickness of a bag—known as the *loft*—is the primary indication of how warm it will be: a thicker bag will trap more warm air than a thinner one.

However, you can't say with certainty that a sleeping bag of a certain thickness will keep you warm at a certain temperature. There are many other variables involved, including the following.

- the design of the bag (a close-fitting one will be warmer than a roomy one)
- what insulation you have under the bag (all bags compress under you)
- what clothes you're wearing
- whether you're in a **tent** or under the stars (a tent can add many degrees of warmth)
- whether you're well fed (**food** provides heat)
- how tired you are (it's harder to get warm when you're fatigued)

- how humid it is (humidity makes bags damp and reduces loft as well as increasing heat loss by conduction)
- whether you're a warm or a cold sleeper

Consider sleeping bag ratings as rough guides, not as absolutes, since there's no standard rating system. Some makers give comfort ranges and extreme temperatures, those at which you will survive but won't feel very warm. Be wary of descriptions such as "three seasons." Three seasons where? Arizona? Alabama? Alaska? Also, even in the same area, temperatures can vary enormously between early and late spring and early and late fall. Temperature ratings are a better guide than season ratings. Many bags have upper comfort ratings too. These may seem irrelevant, but they give an indication of the temperature range the bag will be comfortable in. They're certainly far more useful than descriptions like "four season," as no bag can be used comfortably over four seasons. If it's warm enough in the middle of winter, it'll be too hot in summer.

Such features as zippers, shoulder baffles, zip-out side panels, zip-off top panels, and waterproof-breathable shells add weight. The lightest bags have only hoods and foot boxes. See the Size and Design section below.

With down bags, models with 12 to 20 ounces of down fill and rated between 20°F and 30°F will likely weigh between 1.25 and 2.5 pounds. Down bags rated to 0°F with 24 to 32 ounces of down weigh between 3 and 3.5 pounds. Synthetics are heavier, weighing 2+ pounds for 30°F bags and 3.5 to 5 pounds for 0°F bags. See the Fill section opposite.

Size and Design

Body-hugging sleeping bags are the warmest but not necessarily the most comfortable unless, like a few, they have stretch seams. If a bag is roomy, it won't be as warm because you have to heat up all the dead air space. A close-fitting bag that is comfortable will be warmest. This is why bags are tapered: you don't need as much space around your legs as you need around your torso. To keep the feet warm, you need a shaped foot box that has room for your feet to move and plenty of fill. You also need a hood, because a lot of heat can be lost from an unprotected head. Many bags also have a shoulder baffle, which can be pulled around the shoulders to cut out drafts.

The standard mummy shape is efficient, but it must fit properly. Too long or too wide a bag won't be as warm as a smaller one and will weigh more and take up more room in your **pack**. Too small a bag is even worse, though, because it will be uncomfortable and the fill will compress where you press against it, leading to cold spots. Because of this, bags are available in different lengths; women's bags are also available, which have a different shape from men's and a different distribution of fill.

To overcome the somewhat restricted feel of a mummy bag, some designers have added extra side panels that can be zipped open to create a roomier bag when you don't need maximum heat.

Most bags come with full-length side zippers with filled baffles behind them to stop heat loss. Zippers make getting in and out of the bag easier and allow for ventilation, but they add a little weight. To save weight, some bags come with half-zippers and some with no zippers at all.

Fill

The biggest difference between sleeping bags lies in the fill. There are two basic choices: synthetic fills and down from geese and ducks.

Synthetic Fills

Synthetic fills are made from tangles of very fine polyester and other synthetic fibers designed to mimic down. Weight for weight, they're still not as warm as down, but the best are pretty good. Synthetic fills dry more quickly than down and retain some of their loft when wet. They aren't warm when soaked, however, despite what is often claimed, but they're better in situations where your sleeping bag is likely to get damp.

Synthetic fills come in two forms: short fibers and continuous filaments. Primaloft is a top-quality name in short fibers; Polarguard is a top-rated continuous filament. There are many short-fiber synthetics but few with continuous filaments. Low-cost synthetics are bulky, heavy, and not very warm, and they don't last long. They may be fine for occasional **camping** but not for prolonged wilderness use.

Compared with down, even the best synthetics don't last as long, aren't as comfortable over a wide range of temperatures, weigh more, and are much more bulky.

Synthetic bags slowly lose their loft, and therefore warmth, even when not in use, because the fibers lose their elasticity and compact together. Cram a synthetic bag into a stuff sack, crushing the fibers together, and the loft will decline much more quickly. Synthetic bags should always be kept loosely stored. When you do need to put one in a stuff sack, use as large a sack as possible. The compression stuff sacks supplied with many synthetic bags in order to reduce the bulk are an excellent way to wreck your bag and shouldn't be used. Indeed, it's best to carry a synthetic bag at the top of your pack so other items don't crush it. Use the bag to fill out the space at the top of your pack, allowing it room to expand.

After four or five years, even a top-quality synthetic bag will have lost some loft. It may look exactly the same as when it was new, but it won't keep you as warm.

Down

Down is the fluffy underplumage of ducks and geese and is made up of clusters of ultrathin filaments. Down plumules are not feathers; there are no stalks. However, down sleeping bags usually contain 5 to 15 percent feathers, because separating all the feathers from the down is extremely difficult.

Down is the lightest, warmest, most comfortable, and longest-lasting fill. It also packs up much smaller than synthetic fills and isn't damaged by being stuffed into a small space. Down shapes itself around your body for a snug, warm fit, unlike synthetics, which tend to stand away from the body, leaving cold spots. Down is also comfortable over a wider range of temperatures.

The only problem with down—a problem often exaggerated—is its poor performance when wet. It won't keep you warm when very wet, and it takes ages to dry. However, it isn't that easy to get a down bag wet unless you dunk it in a river or sleep out in the **rain**. This is especially so with modern shell materials, which resist moisture and dry fast. To keep your bag dry, carry it in a waterproof stuff sack inside the pack and sleep in a tent or under a tarp in wet weather. Air the bag whenever possible to remove any moisture buildup.

> "I've used down sleeping bags on many long hikes, including in very wet areas, such as the Scottish Highlands and the mountains of Norway, and have never had one get more than slightly damp."—CT

Not all down is the same. In fact, there are several different grades, described by such numbers as 550, 650, and 775. Each number is the total cubic inches that an ounce of a particular grade of down will fill, and represents the down's *fill power*. The higher the fill power, the warmer the bag for the weight. So, a 750-fill bag will have a higher loft than a 550-fill bag containing the same weight of down.

Down is sometimes described as goose down or duck down. Although many people believe goose down is better than duck down, fill power is the real measure of quality.

See also **down**.

Construction

Various methods are used to hold the fill in place in a sleeping bag. The type of construction affects the warmth and weight of a bag. The simplest, lightest construction is to place the fill into channels running across the bag and then stitch the inner and outer shells together along the edges of the channels. This straight-through or sewn-through stitching is suitable only for warm-weather bags because heat can escape through the stitch lines. It's used for both down- and synthetic-filled bags.

More complex constructions are needed to avoid heat loss through the seams. With down bags, these take the form of internal walls, or baffles, that create chambers inside the bag in which the down can expand. These walls may create boxes (hence the term *box-wall construction*) or lie at an angle (*slant-wall construction*). All except the lightest down bags have wall construction.

Synthetic bags either have double construction, in which two or three sewn-through layers are used with the seams offset, or shingle construction, in which overlapping sloping layers of fill are sewn to the inner and outer shells. Shingle construction is lighter than double construction because less fabric is involved; it's also said to be warmer because the fill can expand more freely.

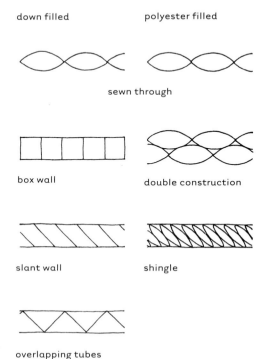

down filled   polyester filled

sewn through

box wall   double construction

slant wall   shingle

overlapping tubes

MIKE WALSH

Terms used in sleeping bag construction.

Most bags have a top and bottom separated by side baffles that prevent the fill from shifting from one side to the other. Some down bags have no baffles here so you can shift the down from the bottom to the top for more warmth and vice versa for less warmth. However if you sleep on your side or turn over during the night so the bottom of the bag is on the top, a lack of side baffles could be a disadvantage.

Some bags have filled side compartments to create more room inside. This is particularly useful in cold-weather bags because the fill at the sides is less likely to be compressed, leading to cold spots. Alternatively, bags may have the side seams at ground level so the upper section is bigger and has more fill.

Because the fill under you is crushed and therefore has less insulating value, some bags have more fill in the top than the bottom. This is helpful unless you tend to turn over with the bag during the night. A few ultralight bags take this to the logical limit and have no fill on the bottom at all, just a sleeve for inserting a **sleeping pad**. Other bags have extra top sections that can be added or removed according to the temperature.

When selecting a sleeping bag, make sure that any baffle construction is compatible with your sleeping habits.

Shell Fabrics

As well as keeping you warm, a sleeping bag needs to allow body moisture through to the outside or you will get very damp. Thus shell fabrics need to be breathable (see **breathability**). They should be hard wearing, quick drying, and lightweight too. For down bags, they must be downproof to stop tendrils of down from working through the fabric and escaping. Most shells are made from nylon or polyester. The best of these synthetics are soft and comfortable and feel good next to the skin. They shed moisture too, helping to keep your bag dry. Some, such as Dryloft, have a waterproof membrane or coating that will keep out water; however, the bags aren't fully waterproof,

because the seams will still leak. Dryloft and similar shells aren't needed for most camping, but if you **bivouac** or use **snow shelters** they can be useful. They're also good choices for those nervous about getting a down bag wet.

Care

Airing bags to rid them of any moisture is the main care required in the wilderness. Also keep them away from sharp objects, **fire**, and sparks or hot objects because shells can tear or melt. Patch holes or cuts with sticky-backed ripstop nylon or **duct tape** (see **repairs**).

At home, ensure that bags are dry before storing them. Keep them uncompressed by hanging them in a closet or storing them in one of the breathable bags often provided by makers.

Eventually, any bag will need cleaning. Wearing clothes in the bag or using a liner can delay this for a while but not indefinitely. Sponging off stains helps too, as does turning the bag inside out and airing it well after every trip. Don't clean a bag, especially a down bag, until it really needs it, because some of the loft will be lost. However, if the bag is no longer keeping you as warm as it once did, cleaning may restore some of the performance.

Bags shouldn't be dry-cleaned because the solvents used may damage the shell or the fill. Also, any solvents left in the bag may give off fumes that make you ill.

It's best to wash bags by hand in a large tub or bath, but they can also be machine washed. Home machines are often too small, so you may need to use a large commercial one. Use soap—there are special soaps available for down—instead of detergent, and run a gentle cycle with cold water. Rinsing out all the soap is important, so soak them a lot in clean water in a tub or wash them a second time without soap in a machine.

Once clean, bags can be tumble dried on a low-heat setting. You will need a large commercial dryer, and it can take a long time. Check the bag periodically since too much heat can damage both the shell and the fill.

If all this seems too much trouble, specialist companies will clean your bag for you. Check with the bag makers or the store you bought the bag from for recommendations.

SLEEPING PADS

Sleeping bags don't insulate against cold ground, nor do they protect against hard ground, because the fill is compressed beneath you. For insulation, you need a sleeping pad. In warm weather, you can get by without a pad, perhaps by putting **clothing** and even your **pack** under you, though you won't be very comfortable. Most of the time though, you'll need a pad to keep warm.

There are two main types of portable sleeping pad: closed-cell foam and self-inflating. The first are long slabs of noncompressible foam. They are warm, quite light, inexpensive, and durable, but they're not very soft and they're bulky when packed. Self-inflating pads consist of open-cell foam inside a waterproof nylon shell. When you open the valve, air is sucked inside and the foam expands (often a few puffs of breath are required too). By regulating the amount of air, you can decide how soft or hard you want the pad to be. Self-inflating pads are comfortable and warm, and they pack smaller than closed-cell foam. However, they weigh and cost more and need to be protected from sharp objects. They aren't so comfortable or warm when they deflate in the middle of the night, so carry a **repair kit** with nylon patches and adhesive or use **duct tape** (see also **repairs**).

Both types of pad come in different lengths and widths. They vary in thickness too, with the thicker ones being warmer and providing more protection against stones and lumps. A three-quarter-length, thin closed-cell foam pad adequate for summer can weigh as little as 4 ounces, while a thicker one suitable for colder conditions will weigh about 10 ounces. The lightest three-quarter-length self-inflating pads weigh 14 ounces.

If you're tall, you'll probably want a full-length pad, but many people can get by with a three-quarter-length one, using clothing or a pack under their head and feet.

Closed-cell pads can be unrolled inside your pack, if there's room, and other gear packed inside them, although they're usually strapped to the outside of the pack. Self-inflating pads are best carried inside the pack—small ones can be folded into squares—to protect them from damage.

Alternatives to the standard designs are **down-** and synthetic-filled pads and thick open-cell foam inside a nylon cover. These all sound very comfortable, but they're heavier and bulkier than standard pads.

Self-inflating pads should be stored flat with the valve open.

SLINGS

Slings are lengths of webbing (or sometimes rope) that are tied or sewn together to create a loop. They are commonly used in **rock climbing**, **mountaineering**, or any other activity that requires you to build **anchors**. Slings are typically

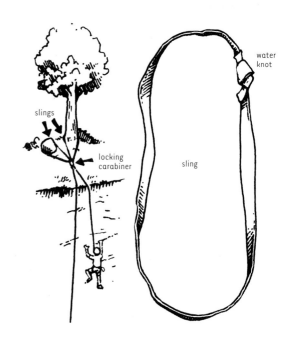

A piece of webbing tied into a loop with a water knot makes a good sling. Slings are often used to create anchors in climbing and mountaineering.

used to connect pieces of **artificial protection** or **natural protection** to other points in an anchor. To create a sling from a piece of webbing, use the **water knot** and make certain that both tails of the knot are at least 3 inches long. Sometimes slings are called *runners*.

SNAKES

Many people have an exaggerated fear of snakes given that most snakes aren't venomous and won't bite you. The few that are venomous will only bite if threatened, so if you stay away from them and take a few sensible precautions, you have little chance of being bitten. It's worth learning more about snakes if you're going into snake country, because knowledge reduces fear. Snakes are fascinating creatures that play an important part in the ecosystem by controlling the numbers of animals, including **mice and other rodents**.

Four types of venomous snakes live in North America: the copperhead, water moccasin (also called *cottonmouth*), and rattlesnake are all pit vipers. The fourth type, the coral snake, a type of cobra, is found in the southern states west to Texas; the coral snake is the most venomous North American snake. However, it's tiny, shy, and nocturnal, so there's not much chance of seeing one—let alone of being bitten.

As their name suggests, water moccasins live in rivers, creeks, and swamps. They are found in the southern states. Copperheads live in the eastern United States north to Massachusetts and in parts of the Midwest in rocky and wooded hill country.

Rattlesnakes are what come to mind when people think of venomous snakes, because these are the ones most likely to be encountered, partly because of the noise they make. There are about 30 different species of rattlesnake, which are found in Mexico, southern Canada, and throughout the United States (except Alaska, Maine, and Hawaii, the only states with no venomous snakes).

Snakes you can see are easy to avoid; just walk around them at a distance. This may seem obvious, but many bites are due to people approaching

Thick socks, above-the-ankle boots, and careful hand and foot placement are your best protection against snakebites.

or even handling snakes. The snakes that may be dangerous are the hidden ones, because if you startle one or inadvertently touch it you may be bitten. In snake country, be wary around bushes and dense vegetation and don't put your hands or feet behind rocks or under logs. It's best to step on low logs rather than over them in case there's a snake on the other side. Generally, the vibrations from your footsteps will warn snakes you are there so they can hide or move away, but you can't rely on this. Wearing high **boots** and thick **socks** when you're hiking protects your feet and ankles somewhat, but some snakes can strike as high as knee level.

Bites are rare, but if one does occur, don't panic. Fear and incorrect treatment can cause more harm than the bite. The old methods of cut and suction and applying a tourniquet are now regarded as potentially dangerous. Bear in mind that a fit, healthy adult won't die from snakebite.

Experts disagree as to the best way to treat snakebites, but there are some ground rules. If you have a venom extractor, such as the Sawyer Extractor, use it. This is a modern suction device that doesn't require cutting the wound. Otherwise, just wash the bite with soap and water and bandage it. If the bite is on an arm or leg, keep the limb hanging down so the venom doesn't spread. Any bite should be kept below the level of the heart. If the opportunity presents itself, kill the snake that inflicted the bite so a doctor can identify it later. Ideally, the victim should stay still until he can be taken to a hospital (see **rescue** and **evacuation**). This may not be possible deep in the

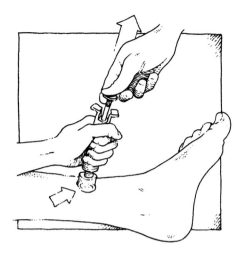

Using a venom extractor.

wilderness or when alone, however. In this case, the victim may have to walk out slowly to the nearest road or habitation.

This advice applies to snakes in North America. If you're traveling to places where there are more dangerous snakes, such as parts of Asia, Africa, South America, and Australia, be sure to get local advice.

SNOW

Snow changes the land, obliterating colors and features, smoothing out rough ground and hiding **trails**, campsites, and the scars of summer. Falling snow can fill the air, swirling around and leading to a whiteout, in which it's impossible to tell the land from the sky or whether the ground goes up or down. Then, as the snow settles, a transformed, wilder and purer landscape emerges.

Because snow has such a profound effect on an environment, knowing the patterns of snowfall for a particular area is important if you don't want to be unpleasantly surprised, either because there is no snow or because there is too much of it.

In general, snow arrives earlier and melts later farther north or at higher elevations, but this varies greatly in different locations. In high mountains, snow is possible year-round, although it usually melts quickly in the summer.

Ski touring and snowshoeing are the prime means of travel in snow-covered country, along with **glacier travel** and **mountaineering** in areas with permanent snow. **Snow camping** requires special skills, and knowing how to build **snow shelters** is useful. However, even summer hikers may have to cope with snow, so some knowledge of how to deal with snow is always useful. If there's much snow around, you should know about **avalanches**, **cornices**, **crevasses** and **crevasse rescue**, and how to use **ice axes** and **crampons**.

For small snowfields and the occasional unexpected, unseasonable snowfall, a few precautions make life more comfortable. First, remember that snow is wet, so brush it off your clothing and gear before it has an opportunity to melt and soak through anything that's not waterproof.

When **hiking** in falling snow, wear windproof clothing or rain gear that sheds the snow. Unless it's very cold, don't wear much under the shell—just a base layer and thin midlayer—or you'll overheat, soaking your inner clothes with sweat. Have a warm top (such as a thick fleece, down-fill, or synthetic-fill jacket) handy whenever you stop, however.

Hiking in whiteout conditions is difficult and potentially dangerous because visibility is greatly limited. Traveling on an accurate **compass** bearing won't necessarily keep you from going over a steep drop or cornice. Snow can drift and form a steep slope or even a cornice on surprisingly gentle terrain. So, unless you're absolutely certain of what lies ahead, stop and either pitch camp or build a snow shelter until conditions ease.

Where fallen snow covers the trail, take care if you can't see the trail emerging from the snow on the far side; it could change direction under the snow. Rather than cross the snow directly and hope to see the trail, work around the edge of the snow until the trail reappears.

Be wary of crossing snow slopes if you don't have an ice ax. Old snow can be slippery. If the snow is soft, the slope not too steep, and there's safe terrain below, use **trekking poles** for support and kick the edges of your boots into the snow to make platforms. Move slowly, make sure you have secure footing, and remember that you can't stop a slide with a trekking pole. If there's any danger, go around the snow rather than across it.

> "When I hiked the Pacific Crest Trail, I met many hikers in southern California who were dismayed at the deep snow present in the mountains, especially the High Sierra. Yet this was in April and May, when snow is likely, as any research would have revealed."—CT

If the snow is soft and deep, you'll sink in with every step and hiking will be slow and arduous. This is known, aptly, as *post-holing*. If there's an alternative route, take it. See also **snowshoeing**.

In spring the snow in open places such as meadows may form suncups, large deep depressions with narrow ridges between them. These can be awkward to cross, so go around the edge, instead.

In places exposed to strong winds, long parallel ridges of snow known as *sastrugi* can form. When they harden, these can become an impediment to skis. Cross low sastrugi at right angles, stepping across taller ones. Sastrugi are less of a problem on foot, and Chris has occasionally removed his skis and hiked across an area of sastrugi.

When climbing soft snow, kick the toes or edges of your boots into the snow; when descending, slam your heels into the snow. In both cases, keep your weight over your feet so you don't slip and, again, stay off snow slopes if there are hazards below and you don't have an ice ax.

SNOW ANCHORS

Snow anchors are simply **anchors** that rely on **snow** for their strength. Snow anchors differ from regular anchors because the integrity of snow is ever changing. Over the course of a day, snow can change from soft to hard. Furthermore, the type of snow anchor that works best in one type of snow may become utterly useless in different conditions. To accommodate for these variations, you need to familiarize yourself with different types of snow anchors, primarily deadman anchors, bollards, and pickets.

Deadman Anchor

Whoever named the deadman anchor wasn't being very fair: deadman anchors are simple to use, and they can be very strong. A deadman anchor is simply an object that is buried a few feet deep, perpendicular to the fall line of a slope. A fluke—an aluminum plate with an attached steel cable—is a popular object used for a deadman anchor. It is driven into the snow at a 40-degree angle from the anticipated direction of pull. Designed to drive itself deeper into the snow anytime it receives tension along its direction of pull, if the fluke is inserted at an angle that is too narrow or too wide, it may slide out of the snow. Practice placing the fluke correctly before you try to use one.

Flukes come in an assortment of sizes. The rule of thumb is the bigger the better (although bigger flukes add additional **weight**). If you don't have a fluke, you can improvise by burying your

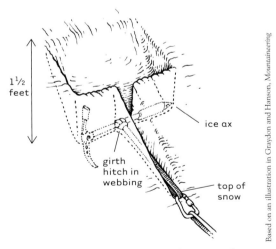

This deadman anchor utilizes a buried ice ax as the attachment point for the rope or webbing. A loop of webbing is girth hitched to the shaft of the ice ax. Deadman anchors can be built in snow or sand.

ice ax in the snow. Start by digging a narrow trench the length of the ice ax, perpendicular to the fall line of the slope. Make it at least 1½ feet deep. Lay your ice ax in the trench. Tie a piece of webbing or an accessory cord at least 3 feet long around the center of the ax's shaft using a **girth hitch**. Next, dig a ramp the length of the webbing to accommodate a gradual rise in the webbing from the depth of the ice ax to the surface of the snow. The end of the webbing is the point where you will connect the rope to the anchor with a locking **carabiner**. The deadman anchor also is useful in many situations outside of mountaineering, such as securing a **tarp** on a sandy beach.

Bollard

Another type of snow anchor is the bollard, a teardrop-shaped trench that is carved into a snowy slope. If the snow is firm, the bollard can be as little as 3 feet across. Bollards in soft snow should be much larger, however (10 to 12 feet across). As with fluke anchors, the bigger the bollard, the better. However, creating big bollards can be time consuming.

To create a bollard, dig a trench that resembles the outline of a teardrop with the tip of the drop pointing downhill. The center of the bollard should remain untouched. The depth of the trench should gradually change from 2 feet deep on the uphill rounded portion of the bollard to almost no depth at the downhill point. Once you complete the bollard, place a long piece of webbing or **rope** in the trench of the bollard (webbing is better because it's less likely to cut into the snow). Tie the webbing so that it connects into a loop several feet below the point of the bollard. The bigger the bollard, the farther downhill you'll need to extend the webbing. The end of the webbing is the point where you'll connect the rope to the anchor.

Pickets

Pickets are T-shaped aluminum stakes that can be driven into hard snow. Angle the picket about 45 degrees from the direction of pull before driving it into the snow. This angle is important, be-

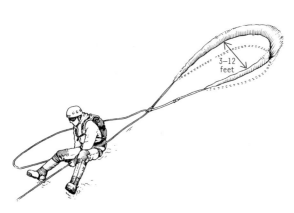

Snow bollards, tear-shaped trenches dug in the snow, make excellent anchors. Bollards should be no smaller than 3 feet across and, depending on snow conditions, can be as large as 12 feet across.

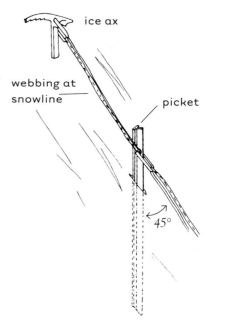

Drive pickets into the snow at a 45-degree angle to the direction of pull. To add strength and redundancy, run a piece of webbing from the first to the second picket a few feet up the slope. If necessary, use an ice ax instead of the second picket.

JERRY CINNAMON (2)

cause a poorly placed picket may slide out of the snow. Periodic holes are drilled along the spine of the picket, allowing you to attach a piece of webbing at the snowline. Avoid attaching the webbing any higher than the snowline, because this will create unnecessary torque on the picket. For a **bomber** anchor, connect two pickets together with a piece of webbing (one should be placed a few feet directly above the other). In addition to its regular function, a picket can be used instead of an ice ax for a deadman anchor.

As with rock anchors, it's best to combine multiple points of protection when building a snow anchor. In addition, practice building snow anchors on low-angle slopes in various snow conditions before relying on one with your life. One of the best ways to learn about snow anchors and **belaying** on snow is to practice with an experienced **guide** or friend. Many **outdoor schools** offer courses in **mountaineering** that include classes on snow anchors in addition to many other important skills. To augment your practical experience, consider reading *Mountaineering*, edited by Don Graydon and Kurt Hanson.

SNOW BLINDNESS

The term *snow blindness* is just a fancy name for sunburned eyes. The cornea and conjunctiva of your eyes can be exposed to the damaging effects of ultraviolet (UV) rays in all sorts of environments, not just **snow**. In fact, it doesn't even have to be sunny outside for you to fall prey to the harmful UV rays of the sun. On cloudy days, many people take off their sunglasses only to end up hours later with headaches and sensitive eyes. Eyes that are sunburned can become bloodshot, agitated, and possibly swollen. In addition, they often itch or burn and you may even find them uncomfortable to close. Some people describe the feeling as a gritty sensation, almost as if they have sand in their eyes. If you experience these symptoms after being outside all day with little or no eye protection, you have most likely sunburned your eyes. Because it can take up to 12 hours for the symptoms to appear, you may not realize that you're in trouble until it's too late. The good news is that snow blindness will spontaneously heal itself over time. The bad news is that until it does, expect to experience some discomfort or outright pain.

To relieve the pain of snow blindness, place cool compresses over the eyes. In addition, you may find a dark environment more comfortable and soothing. Eye drops, such as a saline solution, may ease the feeling of dryness, but they won't hasten recovery. Although your eyes may itch, avoid rubbing them, as this will only aggravate them more. Don't place any antibiotic ointments in the eyes.

The best way to avoid snow blindness is to wear quality sunglasses or goggles that block out UV light. Because severe snow blindness can be debilitating, carry an extra pair of sunglasses,

Emergency goggles can be fashioned from handy items such as tree bark or cardboard resupply boxes and glue. Get creative! Anything that covers most of the eyes but still allows vision will do.

particularly on long trips. Choose glasses that provide complete coverage of the eyes, including side panels. Goggles provide the best coverage but can fog easily. Nonetheless, they're often the best option, especially if you want additional protection from cold temperatures. Be particularly careful when traveling on snow or water, because these surfaces reflect UV rays and can damage your eyes from below your field of vision. In addition, be wary of UV damage in higher altitudes, where the rays become much more intense because the protective atmosphere is thinner.

If you forget or lose your glasses, there are a few emergency techniques you can use to protect your eyes. **Bandannas** can be worn "bandit-style," with small holes cut for the eyes. Or a piece of cardboard cut with slits and placed over the eyes can provide some protection. If you discover that your sunglasses aren't adequate protection, put tape over the lenses, leaving a small uncovered slit for your field of vision. While protecting your eyes in such a manner may be a nuisance, it is a far better alternative than dealing with the aftermath of severely burned eyes.

SNOWBOARDING

In recent years, snowboarding has become the fastest-growing winter sport. Most snowboarding takes place on the groomed slopes of ski areas, but an increasing number of boarders are taking to the backcountry. Backcountry snowboarding offers the same rewards as backcountry skiing (see **ski touring**). It combines the beauty and stillness of the **wilderness** under a blanket of **snow** with the rush and freedom of carving your way down fresh powder slopes.

Snowboards are designed for going downhill and are not efficient for traveling cross-country or ascending mountains. For these purposes, many snowboarders carry snowshoes. With their snowboard snug in a backpack or trailing behind them on a leash, they can ascend mountain slopes with relative ease (see **snowshoeing**). Once at the top, a quick change from snowshoe to snowboard is all they need. They don't have to switch boots, be-

cause most snowboarding boots work fine in snowshoes. Another option is to go with a split snowboard, which is built to separate lengthwise down the middle, allowing the snowboard to be broken down and worn as two mini-skis. Special climbing skins (a strip of fabric designed for skiing that allows a ski to go one direction but not the other) can be applied to the split boards for traction on ascents. Once at the top of the slope, the skins are removed and the two halves are snapped back together (see **climbing skins**).

Any winter backcountry activity, including snowboarding off groomed trails, can be dangerous. Before planning a backcountry snowboarding trip, make sure you and your party (you should never travel alone) are competent at predicting and responding to **avalanches** and preventing **hypothermia**; also be sure you have sufficient **navigation**, **first-aid**, and general winter camping skills (see **snow camping**). You also need to be an experienced snowboarder capable of handling deep powder or less-than-ideal conditions. Research your route and choose it carefully, taking into consideration the recent and predicted **weather**, the overall distance, and the terrain. Many backcountry areas require that you check in and out or get a **permit**. If not, leave your route and your anticipated time of return with a trusted friend or local authority (see **trip plan**). Make a **contingency plan** for use in the event of an emergency.

If you want to try backcountry snowboarding but you don't have the necessary skills, consider hiring a local **guide**. Local guides not only know the best places for snowboarding but can also provide you with the necessary equipment (such as avalanche transceivers) to keep you safe while you're having fun.

SNOW CAMPING

Waking to the sun sparkling on snowy mountains and crisp, bright **snow** lying all around is a wonderful experience. However, **camping** on snow requires more care and skill than summer camping if you want to be comfortable and warm.

Site Selection

Finding a campsite is easier than in summer because deep snow covers rocks, fallen trees, and other obstacles. Unless the snow is thin, you don't need to worry about trampling the ground or causing other damage. You can alter the terrain too, building snow walls and digging **camp kitchen** sites (and then knocking them down and filling them in when you leave so that your constructions don't spoil the **wilderness** for others). The main concern when choosing a site is to pick one that doesn't disturb animals, which have a hard enough time in winter. If there are signs of animals in an area, camp elsewhere. It could be an important feeding or resting area. Camp close enough to open water to be able to collect water but far enough away to allow animals easy access to the same water.

If it's windy, look for a sheltered site, but beware of camping below **cornices** or on possible **avalanche** terrain. Valley bottom sites are often sheltered but are also likely to become chilly overnight as the cold air sinks. A slightly higher site will be warmer. If possible, choose a site that gets early-morning sun. Waking to warm light glowing through the **tent** walls is a great way to start the day.

Pitching a Shelter

Once you have chosen a site, it needs preparing. If you have a floorless pyramid or tepee tent or a **tarp**, you can dig a shallow pit and pitch your shelter in it, heaping snow around the edges to stop the wind from getting in. Once inside, you can dig a deeper pit if you wish or perhaps dig out a central cold sink with sleeping benches on either side of it. You can go in and out with your boots on, cook inside without danger of setting the tent afire (make sure you have enough ventilation), and scoop up snow from inside to melt. Separate **groundcloths** or bivy bags (waterproof sleeping bag covers) can be used to keep snow off your **sleeping bag**.

With a standard floored tent, stamp out a flat platform before you pitch the tent. This can be done with skis or snowshoes. The platform should be quite a bit larger than the tent so you have room for stakes and guylines and for people to walk around the tent. When the platform is ready, leave it to harden before pitching the tent; otherwise, you will have a soft floor that gives under you and then freezes into uncomfortable lumps that you can't remove without taking the tent down.

Whatever type of shelter you use, it has to be staked out. In all but the hardest icy snow, standard stakes don't work because they just pull straight out. Snow stakes, which are long, wide, and curved, hold much better, but they can pull out too. However, good snow stakes come with holes in them for threading a guyline through before burying the stake horizontally in the snow. This can be done with ordinary stakes by tying the guyline around them, although this may not be as secure. Once the disturbed snow sets, the buried stakes will freeze into place and you may have to hack them out with an **ice ax** or **snow shovel** come morning (do this carefully, or you could damage the tent). If you plan to bury stakes like this, tie lengths of line to your shelter's stake points in advance so you're not trying to do this in a freezing **wind**.

Skis, **ice axes**, and ski poles (with the handles down) can also be used to stake out tents, although then you can't use them for any other purpose, so don't do this in base camps. You can fill stuff sacks or plastic bags with snow and bury them with the guylines tied around them, but be aware that getting the snow out of them in the morning can be difficult. An alternative is a triangle of fabric with each corner attached to the guyline and then buried in the snow. This is easier to dig out as it's not full of snow. Some tents have flaps around the edges, known as *valances*, on which you can heap snow to help hold the tent down and keep the wind out. For tents without these, you can heap snow around the edges of the tent.

If your site is exposed to the wind, build a snow wall to protect the tent. Don't build the

At this snow camp, note the pit in front of the dome tent and snow walls erected as a windbreak.

wall very close to the tent though, because snow that blows over the wall will build up on the lee side. Leave a gap of maybe 10 feet between the tent and the wall for the snow to fall into. Even more efficient are two snow walls, a tall one 15 or so feet from the tent and a lower one half that distance away. Snow should then collect in the gap between the two walls.

Living in a Snow Camp

Fresh snow must be knocked off the tent, or the latter may collapse. In heavy snow, this may have to be done every few hours. Usually, banging on the tent walls from inside is adequate, but sometimes there's so much snow you have to go out and shovel it away—carefully, so you don't damage the tent.

When making camp, be careful not to put anything down on the snow or it may get buried and lost. Instead, keep everything in your pack. Items such as skis, snowshoes, and snow shovels should be stuck in the snow, not laid down on it.

Good organization can make a snow camp efficient and pleasant. While some people are pitching shelters, others can collect water or start melting snow. It's best to plan in advance who will do which chores so everyone knows what to do.

You can use the snow to make your camp more comfortable by modifying it. For example, dig a pit in front of the tent door so you can sit in the

tent with your feet in the pit, don your boots, and then stand straight up. Build a kitchen with a table, benches, and backrests of snow to make cooking and eating relaxing. If it's sunny, build chairs or couches.

Ventilation and Condensation

Dampness can be a big problem in a snow camp. Unless it's warm and sunny, drying wet gear can be almost impossible. Dampness occurs in two ways: by bringing snow into your shelter and letting it melt and by **condensation**. The second is by far the bigger problem. Snow can be shaken or brushed off clothing before you enter a shelter and brushed out of a tent before it melts.

If the temperature is around freezing, the air may be very humid, in which case condensation and a certain degree of dampness are unavoidable. Colder temperatures are better because the air is drier. It's easier to stay warm in dry conditions at 15°F than in damp ones at 32°F. However, most condensation comes from damp gear, cooking, and body moisture.

Damp gear can be stored in your pack or a stuff sack in the vestibule or outside. Of course, it won't dry and will probably freeze like this. The alternatives are to dry it by wearing it or by storing it in your sleeping bag, both of which are fine if you are warm and can stay warm. Don't let damp clothing chill you while you try to dry it with your body heat. Small damp items, such as **socks** and **gloves**, can be hung in the tent to dry, although the moisture they give off will almost certainly condense on the tent. Damp **boots** (if your boots are leather, they will probably have moisture in them even if they feel dry) need to be kept warm or they'll freeze, making them difficult and painful to put on in the morning. Some people sleep with their boots in their sleeping bags, but if you prefer, you can put them in a stuff sack and place this on your pack or an item of clothing and then cover the stuff sack with other clothing to insulate it. Or, better yet, wear plastic boots on the trip: they don't freeze.

Cooking inside can cause a lot of condensation. Luckily, the solution is simple. Cook outside or in the vestibule with the door open so steam escapes into the open air. If a big storm forces you to cook in the vestibule with the door shut, leave the zipper open at the top, if possible. Keeping lids on pots reduces condensation somewhat. Running the stove for a while after you've finished cooking, or burning a **candle,** can dry the air at least a little.

You can do nothing about the moisture you exhale and that is given off by your body, although a **vapor barrier** will contain the latter. It's better for this moisture to pass through your clothing and sleeping bag and condense on the tent walls than to condense inside your sleeping bag, however.

Because of the cold, many people close both tent and fly-sheet doors when snow camping. Even if the tent has vents, this reduces the chances of moisture escaping and can result in copious condensation. Often, this occurs on the tent itself rather than the fly sheet, leading to a shower of frost in the morning. Leave the tent doors at least half open so that moisture vapor can escape, condensing on the fly sheet rather than on the tent. Leave the fly-sheet doors open, if the weather allows, and some of the moisture will pass into the open air, especially if you have two doorways, which allows a passage of air through the tent.

Despite all precautions on calm, cold nights, massive condensation may occur, condensation

Drying a tent before packing it away.

CHRIS TOWNSEND

that drips on you in the morning as the tent starts to warm up. In a situation like this, it's nice to have a roomy tent in which you can avoid touching the sides, and a small sponge to mop up the drips.

SNOW SHELTERS

Snow is amazing stuff. It's soft and malleable and easy to play with. You can produce all sorts of structures on its surface or by tunneling into it. Knowing how to build snow shelters is useful in emergencies—indeed, it can be a lifesaver—and also for winter camps, because snow is an excellent insulator and a snow shelter is warmer than a tent (see also **shelter, emergency**). A roomy snow shelter is better than a **tent** in stormy weather too because it's absolutely quiet and still

> "I once spent 36 comfortable hours in a snow hole while a blizzard raged outside. Camping would have been very difficult and unpleasant, and skiing was impossible."—CT

inside. There's no thrashing and cracking nylon in a snow shelter.

High in the **mountains** in a blizzard while you're trying to establish a camp isn't the time to learn how to build a shelter. Luckily, practicing is fun! A good time to practice is when you're safe and cozy in a tent or cabin and poor weather prevents you from going far. Apart from being more enjoyable than staring glumly at a storm through a window or out of your tent door, practicing in bad weather will demonstrate the difference a shelter makes to your comfort.

Tools

In an emergency, anything from pans and mugs to **ice axes** can be used to dig a shelter, but it is much quicker and easier to use a **snow shovel** or, in hard snow or **ice**, a snow saw. You should always carry a snow shovel when there is a lot of snow on the hills, but a saw is probably only worth carrying if you're intending to build a shelter. Snow saws are lightweight (around half a pound) and not very sharp. They have blunt alloy teeth that are adequate for cutting through even the hardest snow.

Types of Shelters

There are several types of snow shelter. Which is best depends on the terrain, on the snow, and on how urgently you need shelter.

Snow Caves

On steep mountainsides or where deep snow has built up on steep banks and slopes, a snow cave may be the easiest type of snow shelter to build. It's also a good one to build in a storm because it gets you out of the weather very quickly, since you can huddle in the entrance once that part is dug.

To make a snow cave, you need a bank of snow at least 6 feet deep, preferably more. A steep bank is best, with vertical being ideal. Just make sure there isn't a **cornice** or an **avalanche** slope above. If you start digging partway up the slope, you can throw the snow downhill, which is easier than piling it up. Digging is hard work, and you'll get quite hot and sweaty. You'll also be in contact with the snow, so the best clothing is rainwear worn over base layers. Whenever you stop for a rest, put on something warm because you'll quickly cool down.

Begin by digging into the bank at about head height. If there are two people or more and two shovels, make two entrances about 6 feet apart. Dig in initially for 3 or 4 feet, and then start to clear an area on either side of each entrance at about waist height. Dig upward rather than down, but make sure there is about a foot of snow for the roof, to prevent any likelihood of it collapsing. As one person digs an entrance, another person can be removing the snow. Shovel snow away, or throw it onto a **groundcloth** or a large plastic bag and then haul it outside.

The spaces cleared by the two excavators will soon join, and the final result should be two sleeping platforms with a trench between them for

CHRIS TOWNSEND

Digging a snow cave is warm, wet work. A shell over base layers is all you need to wear. Reserve your warm clothing for when you've finished.

cold air to sink into. This cold trench should be deep enough to stand up in. One of the entrances, once it is no longer needed, can be filled in with snow dug out of the cave.

The roofs of the sleeping platforms should be high enough for you to sit up comfortably, and smoothed and rounded to minimize dripping. Sloping the cave floor slightly toward the entrance will help prevent snow and cold air from entering. As you dig, you may hit rock, earth, or vegetation at the bottom or back of the cave. All you can do then is try again farther along the bank or adapt the cave to accommodate it.

A snow cave can be as big as you like, and you can even link several caves by short passages. If there are enough people and the snow is deep

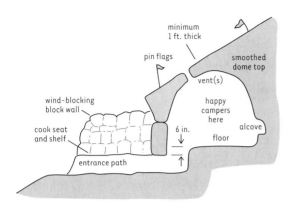

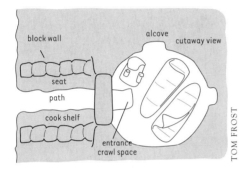

There are many kinds of snow caves; this particular one will accommodate several people.

enough, you can dig a corridor to stand up in, with caves leading off of it.

When the basic cave is complete, a shelf can be dug for use as a **camp kitchen** and niches cut in the walls for small items, such as **candles**. Keep track of where you put everything: gear dropped on the floor can quickly be buried and hard to find. Don't leave anything in the cold trench you don't want to freeze, especially your boots. When settling down for the night, close up most of the doorway with snow blocks. A **pack** can be used to fill the remaining hole to keep out wind and prevent it from filling up with snow.

Ventilation is very important, especially when cooking inside. The entrance doesn't provide adequate ventilation because snow may drift and cover it during a storm. To let air in, make a hole in the roof with a ski pole or an ice ax. Leave the pole poking out of the hole so you can wiggle it to

make sure the hole stays clear of snow. It will also act as a marker so you can find the hole again if you're away for a time. Don't leave shovels and other gear outside. They could get buried. Also, if the entrance fills with snow, you will need the shovels to dig out.

Snow Domes

Snow domes, sometimes called *instant igloos* or *quinzhees*, are simple to make. Their big advantage is that you don't need a bank or slope or even deep snow, although if the snow cover is very thin you'll have to gather snow from over a greater distance, thus creating more work and requiring more time.

Initially, just heap up a pile of snow about 10 to 15 feet across and at least 6 to 8 feet high. If the snow is deep enough, you can do this more easily by digging a circular trench around the perimeter of the intended heap. Once you have a big enough pile of snow, pat down the outside and

Snow domes are simple to construct: heap up a pile of snow, let it harden, and then dig out the center.

A completed snow dome.

then tunnel into it on the side away from the wind. Then it's simply a question of digging out the inside. The walls need to be at least a foot thick. To check this, push a ski pole or ice ax through from the outside at various points. Build a wall extending from the entrance to use up the snow from the inside and protect the door from filling up with blown snow.

Snow Trench

A snow cave or snow dome takes at least a couple of hours to build, which is fine if you don't need shelter quickly. If you do, however, a simpler shelter is better. A slot or sentry box big enough for one or two people to huddle in out of the wind can be dug in minutes and then turned into a cave if you decide to stay put.

A more roomy emergency shelter is the snow trench or snow grave. These are quick to construct and can hold one to four people. At least 5 feet of level snow is needed, however, so snow trenches can't be dug everywhere. Prod the snow with ski poles to check the depth. To build a snow trench, you'll need a **tarp** or fly sheet for the roof and skis, ski poles, or strong sticks to support the roof.

For a minimum-size trench, dig a slot about shoulder width and around 6 feet long. Only one person can dig out the trench. Others can build a wall around the windward end with the excavated snow. Once the trench is 4 or 5 feet deep,

there will be room for two people to sit inside, facing each other or back to back. If you have skis with you, make the roof by laying ski poles across the trench and then wrapping skis in a tarp and putting these over the poles. Cover the edges of the tarp with snow to hold it down, leaving one end free so you can slide the tarp out of the way and get in and out. Steps cut into the end of the trench make climbing in and out easier.

You can also use upright ski poles or skis to support the tarp like a tent roof. Again, weigh the edges down with snow.

How big you make a trench depends on how big your tarp is. Once everyone is under cover, you can extend the trench for more room as long as your roof still covers it. If you need more room and have run out of roof, you can dig slots for your legs. Note that smaller trenches are warmer than bigger ones and that the larger the roof, the more likely it is to collapse if snow is falling or the winds pick up. For a group, several trenches are better than one large one.

Fill in your snow trench when you leave, to prevent the danger that a later traveler might fall into it or catch a ski tip in it.

Igloos

Igloos are complex constructions requiring a high degree of skill and a lot of practice to build—unless, that is, you use an IceBox, a unique tool designed to make building igloos easy. With an Ice-Box, you can build an igloo in one and a half to three hours, depending on the snow. The IceBox comes in different sizes for different-sized igloos. The smallest weighs just over 5 pounds. It can be strapped to the back of a pack and is easy to assemble. Don't carry one on the off chance that it might be needed. But if you plan to build an igloo, the IceBox is more than worth its weight. An igloo is a warm, comfortable alternative to a tent or other snow shelter, especially if you intend to stay in the same area for a while

The IceBox consists of a curved form into which you pack snow, and a long pole you use to determine the radius of the igloo and to ensure

CHRIS TOWNSEND

A snow trench with a tarp roof held in place by ski poles. The interior also uses a ski pole as a center pole.

the snow blocks are correctly positioned. Using the form, you build a circle of snow blocks, each fitting next to the other, until the igloo is complete. There's no need to cut and shape blocks: the IceBox does this. And the builders don't get wet or covered in snow, as they would in digging a cave, trench, or dome.

SNOWSHOEING

If you think that your favorite backpacking route is off limits just because it's **winter**, think again! The availability of modern lightweight snowshoes has made snowshoeing one of the fastest-growing winter sports, not to mention a great way to access the backcountry. It is often said that if you can walk, you can snowshoe. Snowshoeing is an amazingly simple sport that is a good alternative for people who are uncomfortable on skis. Furthermore, snowshoes are often a better option than skis, particularly in dense forests and for tricky off-trail navigation. Without snowshoes or skis, winter travelers would sink through the **snow**—often up to their hips (known as *post-holing*). Post-holing through snow leaves you tired, sweaty, and unmotivated. If you've ever had to post-hole for any distance, you'll appreciate the ease of snowshoeing.

Equipment

Snowshoes come in many different shapes and sizes. To pick the best pair, consider how you will use them. If you're **planning a trip** to the backcountry, go with a bigger pair because you will likely be on snow that is not packed. In the backcountry it is also very likely that you will be carrying a heavy **pack** or pulling a pulk or **sled**. The weight of a pack or sled combined with the unpacked snow means that you'll need a snowshoe with significant flotation, a term that refers to how well you stay at or near the surface of the snow. Here are a few other aspects you should be familiar with.

• Bindings—Bindings keep your foot attached to the snowshoe, much like a ski binding. Unlike ski bindings, though, snowshoe bindings accept all manner of shoes and **boots**. Your binding is attached to the snowshoe with a pivot system that allows you to walk normally.

• Frames—The frame provides the structure of the snowshoe. Traditional frames are made of wood, but modern frames use strong, lightweight metals, such as aluminum, and molded, high-strength plastic.

• Decking—The decking is the material within the frame. It provides the flotation for the snowshoe and prevents you from sinking. Traditional snowshoes have rawhide deckings; modern deckings are usually made out of high-tech plastics, such as hypalon.

• Traction—You'll need lots of traction if you're on a steep slope or on **ice**. Many snowshoes come with metal cleats, just under your toe and sometimes your heel, that you can jam into the snow for traction.

While snowshoeing is relatively easy, there are a few moves that will surely land you face first in the snow. One is crossing snowshoes when you walk (stepping on one with the other). Another is trying to walk backward; it just doesn't work. Once you get past these neophyte tendencies, building confidence is easy. As you progress to more difficult terrain, you'll pick up skills that work well on steep slopes and traverses.

As with many winter sports, you need to consider a few safety issues. **Avalanches**, thin ice, **snow blindness, sunburn, hypothermia,** and **dehydration** are just a few hazards that can affect the snowshoer. Knowing how to identify potentially dangerous situations will help to ensure your safety.

SNOW SHOVELS

A snow shovel is an essential emergency item in **avalanche** terrain. Without one, digging out a victim will be very difficult if not impossible. A shovel is needed for building **snow shelters** too. Other uses are building snow walls to protect a **tent**, building snow seats and tables for a backcountry **camp kitchen**, preparing campsites, and digging small shelters for rest stops. Chris never travels without a shovel when there's **snow** on the ground.

Snow shovels are light, compact, and durable, varying in weight from 0.5 pound to 2 pounds. They may be made from aluminum or polycarbonate. Though both are strong, aluminum is better for cutting through hard snow and ice. Polycarbonate tends to bounce off. You can shift more snow more quickly with a large shovel, but it'll weigh more, be more awkward to pack, and less easy to use for digging inside a snow shelter than a small one. Unless you're planning to build a snow shelter, a lighter shovel is best. The lightest are just blades that fit onto the end of a ski pole. These are only suitable for occasional use. Shovels with telescopic shafts are useful because the shafts can be extended when digging large amounts of snow and shortened for carrying and for use inside a snow shelter. Some shovels come with a snow saw—a blunt-toothed aluminum saw used for cutting snow blocks inside a shelter—or an avalanche probe inside the shaft.

SOCKS

Socks are rarely exciting, but they're important to foot comfort. Good-quality socks should fit snugly, wick moisture, feel warm when damp, and dry quickly. They shouldn't get soggy with **rain** or sweat or have seams that rub or sag badly after a few days of wear. They should be comfortable over a wide range of temperatures. The same socks may not work for different lengths of trips and different activities.

Materials

When you're active, your feet can yield up to a pint of water over 12 hours as sweat. That's a lot of moisture, and it all has to go somewhere. A little will escape from your boot tops. Most, however, will work its way through your socks and then, more slowly, your **boots**. This means your socks will be at least slightly damp much of the time. To deal with this, socks should be made from a fiber that feels warm and holds its shape

when damp. **Wool** is arguably best for this. Not only is wool warm when damp, but it wicks moisture rapidly off your skin and absorbs it into its fibers. Another property of wool socks is that they keep your feet comfortable over a wide range of temperatures. Finally, wool doesn't smell too bad, even after many days of wear. You might get a whiff of damp sheep but not the chemical stink of many synthetics.

Wool comes in different varieties. The coarser types feel harsh against the skin and aren't suitable for socks unless you wear liners under them. Top-grade wool such as merino, used by Smart-Wool, has long, fine strands that are very soft, which means it doesn't itch or scratch. Merino wool feels luxurious against the foot and is excellent for socks, even in hot weather. The only fiber that compares to it is alpaca, the long, woolly hair from a kind of **llama**.

Although very durable, wool can wear as a result of friction, so good wool socks have synthetics added at the toe and heel. Many also have stretch synthetic fibers knitted in for a close fit and to prevent sagging. The higher the wool content, the better, even in warm weather. (And don't assume that a "wool" sock actually has a high percentage of wool—check the content label carefully.)

What about synthetic socks? The claim is that they wick moisture fast and dry quickly when damp. This is partly true when they are worn with **sandals** and trail shoes, and to some extent lightweight boots without waterproof-breathable linings. In these types of footwear, moisture passes through to the air fairly quickly. However, in medium and heavyweight boots and in any footwear with a waterproof-breathable lining, the moisture can't escape quickly, so it stays in the socks. Because synthetics aren't absorbent, they can quickly become quite wet and feel unpleasantly clammy and sticky. Once damp, they aren't as warm as wool either.

Synthetic socks also mat down quicker than wool ones and really need washing every day. They don't fluff up after washing as well as wool and aren't as durable overall. Also, you simply don't get the cosseted feel that merino wool gives. Many synthetics are used in socks, mostly acrylics and polyesters, including brands like CoolMax.

The fiber to avoid is **cotton**, which is found in some warm-weather socks. Cotton may help keep your feet cool, but it does this by absorbing lots of sweat and then drying slowly, which means you have wet socks next to your feet, leading to soft skin that blisters easily. This is made worse because cotton sags and wrinkles when wet.

Silk is sometimes found in small quantities in some socks and on its own in liner socks. It performs a little like wool, absorbing moisture but still feeling quite warm.

Designs

Modern socks are often laden with impressive-sounding features. Some of these can be quite useful, but fit and fiber content are most important. Virtually all quality socks now have inners of soft terry loops that cushion the feet. The denser the loops, the more they resist matting. Thick pads under the heels or balls of the feet can provide more warmth in these areas and a little more cushioning. Thicker socks are warmer than thin ones, of course.

Front seams should be flat and set back from the toes so they don't rub. Heels should be shaped so they fit closely.

Stretch sections around the top of the legs and the ankles and insteps help hold the socks in place and prevent them from slipping or sagging.

Warmth and Weight

Heavy, thick socks are great in very cold weather but likely to be too hot at other times unless you suffer from cold feet. Medium-weight socks are the best all-around socks, keeping feet comfortable in all but the hottest or coldest weather. In the heat, lightweight or even liner socks are all you need.

As well as how warm they are, the thickness of your socks relates to your footwear too. You may need thick socks to fill out your boots, or it may be that only thin socks will fit without feeling too

tight. Be sure to fit footwear while wearing the socks you'll wear in the backcountry. Socks also can be changed during the day to accommodate feet that swell when they get hot.

Washing

Dirty socks aren't as warm or as comfortable as clean ones and can cause **blisters** if they sag or rub and have bits of dirt in them. On trips of no more than a few days, it's worth carrying a pair of clean socks for each day. On longer trips, rinse your socks in cold water and then hang them up to dry —for example, on the back of your **pack** if you're hiking. Rinsing them gets rid of some of the grime and sweat, and drying them in the sun helps fluff them up, especially if you turn them inside out.

Waterproof-Breathable Socks

Socks aren't thought of as clothing to keep your feet dry, but waterproof-breathable socks are available (see **breathability**). Some are just thin synthetic socks designed to be worn over thicker ones, but some are quite thick and have terry loop inners and are fully shaped for a good fit. Early models weren't very comfortable, but they have improved and are now almost as comfortable as standard socks. They extend the use of sandals and trail shoes because you don't have to worry about cold, wet feet. SealSkinz makes waterproof-breathable socks in a variety of lengths and weights; socks made with Gore-Tex are sometimes available too. Waterproof-breathable socks are a better way to keep your feet dry than boots or shoes with waterproof-breathable linings, because you only need to wear them when it's wet.

"I now carry a pair of waterproof-breathable socks on any trips where cold, wet conditions are likely. I've also used them to keep my feet warm after a cold creek ford where I've worn my shoes and wool socks to protect my feet. I then change socks, hang the wool ones on my pack to dry, and hike on in waterproof socks and sodden shoes."—CT

Fit

Overall, socks should have a snug rather than a baggy fit. Loose material can rub, will wear more quickly, and may droop.

Sock sizes are measured by length, not volume. If you have broad, high-volume feet, you might need a larger size than someone with the same shoe size who has skinny, low-volume feet. The stretch materials found in most socks help them hug the feet, but you still need the right fit.

Liner Socks

Thin liner socks, usually made of a wicking synthetic fabric or perhaps of silk or thin wool, are designed to be worn under thick socks. The idea is that they wick moisture away from your foot and into the thick sock, keeping a dry layer next to your skin. In theory, the two socks then rub against each other rather than against your skin. Because they absorb moisture and are so thin, liner socks need washing frequently, usually at least once a day, or they become stiff with dried sweat. They work well worn under coarse knit socks but aren't really necessary with terry loop wool socks, which are very comfortable next to the skin anyway. Liner socks can also be worn on their own with trail shoes and sandals.

SOFT SHELLS

The garment industry started using the term *soft shell* in the late 1990s. The phrase doesn't mean, as you might think, something fluffy and cuddly (like **fleece**) but rather **clothing** that is windproof, very breathable, quick drying, and water resistant but not waterproof. (Rainwear is designated *hard shell*.) The idea is that because soft shells are far more breathable than hard shells, they can be worn most or even all of the time, with waterproof shells only being needed in prolonged wet weather (see **breathability**). Because soft shells don't have membranes or coatings, they're more comfortable than fully waterproof garments over a wide range of temperatures and weather conditions and can be worn in all but the hottest

weather. **Condensation** is minimal, even when working hard, unlike with even the best waterproof-breathable fabrics.

This isn't a new idea, of course. Water-resistant, windproof, breathable garments have always been around. However, they used to be ignored in favor of fully waterproof gear. Now it's becoming understood that soft-shell garments are ideal most of the time.

> "In my view, single-skin windproof garments are the most versatile soft shells because they can be worn over everything from a thin wicking T-shirt to a thick pile jacket, depending on the conditions. A simple windproof top adds a surprising amount of warmth. Pull one on over a fleece top, and even in calm conditions you'll notice the difference."—CT

The soft-shell category is very broad. It includes synthetic insulated garments, windproof fleece, windproof shells lined with fleece, windproof pile and wicking base layer fabrics, and single-skin windproof shells in various thicknesses. The last covers simple nylon or polyester wind shells as well as thicker, brushed, stretch nylon garments and windproof membranes sandwiched between windproof nylon outers and soft wicking inners.

As well as being more breathable than any waterproof garment, soft shells are lightweight, quick drying, and very durable—and they have no easily damaged membranes or coatings to rip or peel off. Tear a soft shell, and you can just patch it or sew it up without any loss in performance. The latest soft-shell fabrics are highly water resistant too, the best keeping out all but the very heaviest **rain**. This means that you need only a lightweight basic waterproof layer rather than a fully specified one. The combination of a soft shell and a lightweight rain jacket can be more versatile than, and just as protective as, a heavy rain jacket. The weight is usually quite a bit less too. The lightest soft-shell fabrics are silicone treated to be very water resistant, such as EPIC by Nextec. Slightly heavier are ones with windproof membranes, such as Gore Windstopper and Polartec Power Shield. Stretch fabrics include many from the Swiss company, Schoeller, such as Dynamic Extreme.

The breathability of soft-shell fabrics means that they also work well as midlayers. Some can even be worn as base layers. The lightest, thinnest soft shells are **insect** proof and cool enough to wear in summer, although the thickest ones are definitely cold weather–only garments. All in all, soft shells are perhaps the most useful outdoor garments.

SOLOING

Soloing, also called *free soloing*, is a type of rock climbing that employs no ropes or protection. A solo climber who falls is at the mercy of luck and gravity. The choice to solo should be reserved for only the most experienced climbers who are willing (and insane enough?) to risk their lives to explore the fringes of the sport. It is an extremely dangerous activity in which every move, and every hold, is a matter of life or death. Soloing is not to be confused with **free climbing**, which uses ropes as well as **artificial protection** and **natural protection** to mitigate the consequences of a fall.

SOLO TRAVEL

Traveling solo is dangerous and irresponsible according to the common wisdom. However, many of the greatest **wilderness** journeys that resonate most strongly with us have been done solo, from Reinhold Messner's ascent of Mount Everest to Colin Fletcher's first-ever continuous hike through the Grand Canyon.

Solo travel is qualitatively different from traveling with companions. Companionship and camaraderie can be very enjoyable but can cut you off from the real reasons for going to the backcountry: to be part of the wilderness and to become aware of the rhythms and details of nature.

Alone, you can become aware of so much more—a delicate spider's web shining with early morning dew, a squirrel watching from a branch, the play of light on a rock face, the curve of a creek mirroring the curve of the mountain ridge high above. In company, you may notice these things but often only superficially, because it's more difficult to stop, look, and absorb the beauty and to ponder the wonder of nature. Also, when solo, you make less noise and are less conspicuous than a group and therefore are more likely to come upon wildlife.

> "I can feel very alone in a strange city or when waiting at a large airport, and there's nothing more lonely than a hotel room in a soulless concrete block. But in the wilderness, I never feel alone. Nature is my companion."—CT

Obviously, some wilderness activities are more dangerous than others, and with some, such as **glacier travel**, going solo makes them even more hazardous. **Rock climbing**, which is pretty safe with a partner and **rope** and protection competency, becomes extremely dangerous done solo, because one slip could be fatal. Other activities, such as **hiking** and **ski touring**, can be as safe or as dangerous as you make them. Stick to clear **trails** and easy terrain with no **avalanche** danger, and they are very safe indeed. Go off trail in rugged country or ski steep slopes, and the risk increases. With all of these activities, practitioners need to know their own strengths and weaknesses and the risks they take by going solo.

Part of the pleasure of going solo comes from the freedom it gives. There's no one to discuss plans with, no one to object when you want to stop and stare at a lake for an hour or hike long into the evening. You can go for 12 hours on a day when you just flow over the land or water and movement seems effortless and a pure joy, while on another day you can spend hours in camp watching animals or **clouds** or simply soaking up the wilderness. Over the days, you can slip into a natural rhythm that suits you perfectly—waking, resting, traveling, eating, and sleeping when your body, not your companion, says it is time to do so.

Going solo also develops self-reliance and backcountry skills. There's no one else to route find, make camp, cook dinner, decide whether it's safe to cross a stream, climb a ridge, or ski a slope. You make mistakes, of course, but you learn from them and soon become more knowledgeable and skilled. Indeed, going solo can lead to safer travel because soloists have to be responsible for themselves and think carefully about every decision and its possible consequences.

The sense of adventure increases when you are alone. The wilderness seems bigger and more intense. Learn to cope with this, and you'll feel confident in a way that you never will if you always travel with a group. You'll also never have to rely on the abilities of others again, even when in a group.

Many people fear being alone. The wealth of life, both plant and animal, the vagaries of the weather, and the splendor of the landscape should all keep you occupied and content. It all comes down to feeling at home in the wilderness.

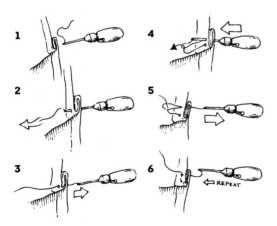

The Speedy Stitcher is a manual sewing awl that puts a sturdy lock stitch in tough materials like canvas and heavy nylon. The waxed thread and burly needle will handle most trail repair jobs, making this tool a must for a well-stocked repair kit.

SPEEDY STITCHER

The Speedy Stitcher is a handy sewing awl for formidable materials that would break a regular needle. The Speedy Stitcher is perfect for repairing canvas, leather, thick nylon, or webbing. This is one tool that should always be in your **repair kit**! The Speedy Stitcher can usually be found at outdoor stores or on many on-line outdoor retailers.

SPIDERS AND SCORPIONS

Spiders and scorpions are arachnids, along with **ticks**. They aren't insects, despite what many people think. They are also fascinating creatures and ones you needn't fear if you take some precautions.

Spiders

The vast majority of spiders are harmless to humans, although some may bite if handled or threatened. Two spiders do have bites that may need medical treatment: the brown recluse, found in the southern United States, and the black widow, found throughout much of North America except the far north. Both types of spiders are shy and avoid people.

If you're bitten by a spider and have a venom extractor (see **snakes**), use it. Not much else can be done in the backcountry, so you'll need to leave the **wilderness** and seek medical help. Analgesics can be used to relieve any pain. Note, though, that healthy adults are extremely unlikely to have any serious complications from a spider bite. Only small children, elderly people, or those with an illness are at real risk.

The female black widow spider—the one that bites—is quite distinctive: she is jet black with a large, round abdomen that has a red or orange marking underneath, often shaped like an hourglass. If bitten by one, you might feel awful and have muscle spasms for a couple of days. Brown recluse spiders are harder to identify. They're brown spiders with long legs and have a dark violin-shaped marking on the upper back. Because medical treatment for a brown recluse bite is very

Black widow spider.

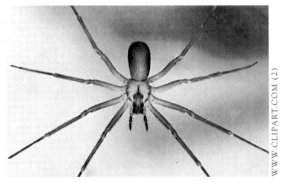

Brown recluse spider.

WWW.CLIPART.COM (2)

specific, try to catch any spider that bites you so it can be identified. A brown recluse bite might make you physically sick, and the bite may **blister**. There are also potential long-term complications if a recluse bite is not treated.

Scorpions

Although scorpions are found throughout North America except in the far north, the only species with a potentially deadly sting lives in the southwestern states and Mexico. Scorpions don't bite; they sting with their tails, which curl over their bodies. The dangerous bark scorpion is pale greenish yellow, yellow, or tan and measures 0.5 to 3 inches long.

If you're stung by a scorpion, use a venom extractor to try to remove some of the poison. You are likely to be very agitated physically and unable to keep still. Only young children, elderly people, and the infirm are at risk from scorpion bites and should be evacuated to a hospital (see

evacuation). Healthy adults should recover quickly. Not much can be done in the backcountry for a scorpion sting. Ice can relieve pain at the site of the sting, although it's unlikely any will be available.

Avoidance

To avoid being bitten or stung by spiders and scorpions, be careful where you put your hands. These creatures hide under rocks and pieces of bark and in brush piles, so don't disturb these with bare hands. Be careful with gear too. Shake out any **clothing**, **sleeping bags**, **sleeping pads**, or other items that have been lying flat on the ground. Turn footwear upside down and tap the outside to encourage any creatures to vacate, though more often than not, scorpions will be under your boots rather than in them.

Traveling Abroad

Some countries, including Mexico, have spiders and scorpions that are much more dangerous than those found in the United States and Canada. If going abroad, check in advance to see what the potential hazards are and what you should do.

SPLINTS

When an injury occurs in the backcountry, proper treatment is critical. If the injury is to a bone, joint, or muscle, a splint may be required to immobilize the affected area. In the **wilderness**, a splint can be made from almost anything: a snowshoe, **sleeping pad**, paddle, stick, even a **rope**! Because you don't have many resources, you need to think creatively. Often the best splint is an anatomical one (such as two fingers taped together).

A few golden rules apply to splinting. If the injury is to a bone, splint the joints above and below the bone (in addition to the bone itself). This is the only way to ensure immobility. If the injury is to a joint, splint the bone above and below the joint (in addition to the joint itself). The splint should be well padded on all sides of the injury. Padding not only protects the injury but also prevents uncomfortable parts of the splint from aggravating the patient. Materials good for padding include soft **clothing, sleeping bags,** even stuff sacks!

A splint should be snug and secure but never so tight that it restricts circulation. If circulation is compromised, the injury will become complicated, because tissue can survive only a few hours without adequate circulation. To ensure that you haven't splinted an injury too tightly, frequently check for circulation below the splint (away from the heart) by feeling for a pulse or depressing the nail bed of a finger or toe and watching to see if the pink color immediately returns to the nail. This means you must leave the fingers and toes accessible, not covered by the splint (although covering them with a sock or mitten will help maintain warmth). You should also check with the patient to determine if she has feeling in the fingers or toes below the splint. If she doesn't, loosen the splint. In addition, as swelling occurs, reevaluate the circulation and loosen the splint as necessary.

Splints should be well padded and secure, but not so cumbersome that they are difficult to wear. This is especially important if the injured person wants to remain mobile. For example, you may have the ultimate splint for a twisted ankle, but if it prevents the person from being able to perform basic tasks (such as going to the bathroom), you may need to reconsider. Also take into account how easy it is to remove or adjust the splint. Splints often need to be adjusted, either for changes in swelling or for simple changes of clothing.

SPORT CLIMBING

Sport climbing is a style of indoor or outdoor **rock climbing** that uses routes laced with permanent bolts into which you clip your quickdraws (short loops of webbing) and **rope.** Because you don't need to think about placing protection (or carry the heavy gear), you're able to concentrate on solving challenging moves or improving your technique and efficiency. While there are some sport routes in the **wilderness,** wilderness climbing is usually traditional (often referred to as *trad* climbing), which requires you to build solid **anchors** and, unlike sport climbing, place **artificial protection** as you ascend the route.

SPRAINS AND STRAINS

Sprains and strains are difficult to diagnose in the backcountry. The activities that cause sprains and strains are often the same that cause fractures. Indeed fractures, sprains, and strains have very similar signs and symptoms, including swelling, pain, and discoloration. Unless you have X-ray vision, you may not be able to determine if an injury is a fracture, a sprain, or a strain. If this is the case, always treat the injury as a fracture and either begin an **evacuation,** if the injury is severe, or allow a few days of rest to see if the injury improves. (See also **fractures.**)

To treat any musculoskeletal injury, remember the acronym RICE (Rest, Ice, Compression, Elevation). Rest involves avoiding major activity, although gently moving the injured area occasionally can be beneficial. Apply ice in 15- or 20-minute periods every hour or two. Compression involves wrapping the injured area in a flex-

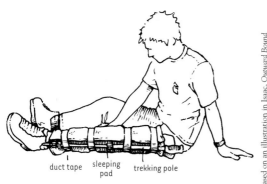

duct tape   sleeping pad   trekking pole

Based on an illustration in Isaac, *Outward Bound Wilderness First-Aid Handbook*

The golden rule of splinting is to immobilize and splint the joint above and below the injured bone (or the bone above and below an injured joint). Check that the splint is snug, comfortable, and well padded. Leave fingers and toes accessible so you can check for adequate circulation. Splints can be made from many materials —here, a trekking pole and sleeping pad.

ible bandage, like an ace bandage. Elevating the injured part above the heart will help control swelling. RICE helps control swelling and fosters natural healing. Most of the swelling will occur within the first 24 hours after the incident. If you don't have ice handy, use **snow** or even a **bandanna** dipped into a cold river or lake. An anti-inflammatory drug, such as ibuprofen, can also be administered. If the injury isn't severe, you should be able to resume use of the injured joint or muscle after a day or two of rest. However, limit its use to only those activities that don't cause pain. If necessary, you can tape or splint the injury to prevent unnecessary movement (see **splints**), but make sure you don't restrict circulation in the process by always checking for an adequate pulse below the splint. If the injury doesn't seem to be improving, or if adequate circulation is reduced, continue RICE and plan an immediate evacuation to advanced medical care.

SPRAYSKIRTS

A sprayskirt is a fabric barrier that covers the open portion of a canoe or kayak and prevents excessive water from entering the boat. Kayaking sprayskirts are most commonly made of neoprene or nylon, and all are equipped with a grab loop sewn into the front of the sprayskirt. The grab loop allows the wearer to pop the skirt off the cockpit, for example to perform a **wet exit**.

In kayaking, the paddler wears the sprayskirt around her waist and attaches it to the coaming (the rim of the cockpit) upon entering the boat. To attach it, start at the rear of the cockpit and tuck the sprayskirt under the coaming, working your way to the front. Be careful to ensure that the grab loop at the front of the sprayskirt ends up outside the cockpit. Depending on the sprayskirt and the size of your cockpit, this simple process can be an aerobic workout involving many foul words. As you get more accustomed to your skirt, and as it stretches out a bit, the whole process will take but a few seconds.

Sprayskirts for canoes are less common, although they are often used for extended **wilderness** tripping. This is especially true when the route calls for travel on remote rivers. In addition to keeping out the heaving spray of white-

This canoe sprayskirt is attached to the canoe with snaps and covers the entire length. The paddlers step in and out of the sprayskirt as they enter or exit the canoe.

The kayak sprayskirt is worn by the paddler, who attaches it to the kayak when she sits in the boat.

water, canoe sprayskirts add tremendous warmth on cold days and help keep your gear dry when it's raining. Unlike kayaking sprayskirts, **canoeing** sprayskirts generally stay attached to the canoe rather than the paddler. The paddler steps into a canoe that has been rigged with a sprayskirt and then tightens the sprayskirt around his body. An exception is made for canoeists paddling decked canoes, also called *C1s* or *C2s*. These canoeists wear sprayskirts much as kayakers do.

Anytime you plan to use a sprayskirt, either canoeing or kayaking, learn how to perform a wet exit in the event of a capsize. For beginning paddlers, wet exits can be quite scary! Practice the motions until they're second nature. If you're kayaking, also practice reattaching the sprayskirt while you're on the water. You'll use this skill when you perform a **self-rescue** or an assisted rescue. If you're canoeing, you'll probably have to go to shore to reassemble your sprayskirt. Nonetheless, practice performing a rescue on a canoe outfitted with a sprayskirt. This is especially true if you'll be paddling in cold water or any distance from shore.

STANDING WAVES

A standing wave is a wave formed by a feature in moving water, such as a rock, a constriction, or a sudden change in the speed of the current. Unlike ocean **waves**, which move across the surface of the water and often cover great distances, standing waves do not move. Rather, they remain in one location, even as water passes through them.

Standing waves are usually formed as water rushes over a rock that lies just beneath the surface. They can also form when fast-moving water runs into slow or stationary water, as is often the case at the end of rapids. Paddlers scouting a set of rapids or backpackers looking for the best river crossing can use the presence of standing waves to decipher what is going on beneath the surface of the water. (See **scouting rapids** and **river crossings**.)

The standing waves formed by constrictions in the river, or those found at the ends of rapids, often signify deep water, although you should always be on the lookout for a renegade rock hiding below the surface. The one-wave-after-another formation (often called *haystacks* or a *wave train*) can make for a fun ride in a canoe or kayak, but if the waves are too big, they can easily overwhelm the paddler and swamp the canoe or kayak.

When is a wave too big? That's a relative question. What's big to one person may not be big to another. In addition, what's big to an open boat, such as a canoe, can be a piece of cake for an inflatable raft or a decked boat, such as a kayak. One thing you can be sure of is that standing waves feel a lot bigger when you're in the middle of them than they look from shore. If you think a

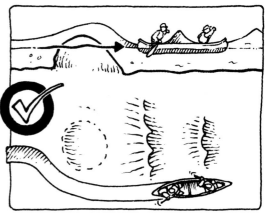

Big standing waves can be difficult to negotiate, especially in a canoe. To avoid swamping, stay away from the wave entirely or paddle along its outer edge.

standing wave looks big from shore, it's guaranteed to look even bigger when you're rapidly approaching it. If this is the case, try avoiding the brunt of the wave by paddling just off to its side. This is often called *skirting* the wave, or *riding its shoulder*.

Some standing waves signify **moving-water hazards** that you should avoid. For example, a standing wave that curls back on itself in a continuous mass of aerated white foam generally indicates a rock or ledge immediately upstream. If the velocity of the water below the rock is less than that of the water pouring over the rock, you can end up with a churning mass of recirculating water, which is known as a **hole** or a **hydraulic**. Until you can identify the harmless hydraulics from the deadly ones, you should plan on leaving them alone.

The size of a standing wave can change depending on the river's water level. It is also possible for the wave to be washed out completely if the water is very high. Therefore, don't expect a set of rapids, or a certain wave, to look the same as when you last saw it. If a set of rapids appears more technical than you remember, there's a good chance it actually is. Water levels can have dramatic effects on the appearance and difficulty of rapids. For this reason, always make a habit of scouting rapids before committing yourself to running them.

STOVES

Hardy hikers can get by without a stove, at least in warm weather. When it's cold or wet, though, hot **food** and drink can be a morale booster and a great aid to warming up if you get really chilled.

> "I remember one ultralight overnight where we didn't bother with a stove and ended the day huddled in our sleeping bags under a tarp, eating cold snacks and drinking cold water while the lashing rain turned to sleet and then snow. I won't leave the stove behind again."—CT

In freezing conditions, you may also need a stove to melt **snow**. Stoves are an environmentally friendly alternative to campfires: they're cleaner, more efficient, and produce hot food much more quickly.

Stove Types

The criteria for a portable stove are light weight, low bulk, ease of use, stability, durability, and ease of maintenance in the field. How fast a stove brings water to a boil is commonly cited as the most important feature, and books and catalogs often contain tables showing the relative performance of different stoves. These data can be useful but may be misleading because they're often gathered under ideal conditions. It's unrealistic to expect a stove to bring cold creek water to a boil in a storm as quickly as it brings tap water to a boil in still air. Also, boiling times aren't as important as many people think: it's better to have a reliable lightweight stove and good fuel efficiency and wait a couple of minutes for water to boil.

Tests, both in the backcountry and in the kitchen, show that one of the big differences in stoves is between those that use pressurized fuel (white gas or kerosene in liquid-fuel stoves; butane/propane in canister stoves) and those that use nonpressurized fuel (alcohol and solid-fuel tablets). (See **fuel**.) Pressurized stoves should bring a pint of water to a boil within 5 minutes if sheltered from the wind. Nonpressurized stoves can take 15 minutes or more, and in some conditions the water may not reach a boil.

Another big difference among stoves is the amount of heat control, if any. For quick-cooking meals and hot drinks that require only boiling water, this doesn't matter, but for simmering, frying, or baking it does. Butane/propane canister stoves usually have good flame control and can be turned down very low. Liquid-fuel stoves vary enormously: some simmer quite well, while some don't simmer at all. The ones that simmer best have separate flame controls linked directly to the burner rather than just fuel-line controls. Nonpressurized fuels are almost impossible to control, though some alcohol stoves have crude simmer rings that dampen the flame when dropped over the burner.

Which stove is best depends on the type of **cooking** you'll do, when you'll use the stove, and how much you like tinkering with machinery. If you want to do any real cooking rather than just boiling, you'll need good flame control, which eliminates alcohol and solid-fuel stoves as well as many liquid-fuel ones. If you'll be melting snow or using the stove in below-freezing conditions, then you want one that will run efficiently for long periods in the cold, which means a liquid-fuel stove. If you're into **ultralight hiking**, the ones to look at are canister, solid-fuel, or alcohol stoves.

An advantage of nonpressurized stoves is that they have no moving parts (thus nothing to go wrong) and therefore continue working unless smashed with a rock. Liquid-fuel stoves are complex and need regular maintenance. With the latter, carrying a maintenance kit is a good idea; with the former, there's no such thing. Canister stoves are relatively maintenance free. Solid-fuel and alcohol stoves are silent; canister and liquid-fuel burners roar.

People sometimes point out that certain stoves pollute because they burn petroleum. That's true, but the amount of fuel involved is minute compared to what your car burned getting you to the trailhead. If pollution concerns you that much, use an alcohol stove.

Solid-Fuel Stoves

These are the most minimalist stoves, consisting of no more than pot supports and a metal platform on which to put a fuel tablet. This makes them very light: a typical commercial solid-fuel stove weighs 3½ ounces, while a homemade titanium one can weigh as little as ⅓ ounce. Their light weight is one of their few advantages, however. They have no flame control and they take longer than pressurized stoves to heat food or water. If all you require is small amounts of hot water, a solid-fuel stove is adequate.

Alcohol Stoves

Alcohol stoves are small, double-walled fuel reservoirs with a ring of jets around the top. The reservoir may be open, or enclosed with just a hole for pouring in the fuel. On their own, these stoves are vulnerable to wind, but some come with solid metal windscreens that will resist gales. In Sweden, where many of these stoves are made, they're known as *stormcookers*. The windscreens have holes in them: turn these into the wind, and the heat output increases greatly. For simmering, you can drop a damper ring over the burner and knock it into position with a stick, although the ring is not very effective.

Alcohol burners alone are very light, at around 2½ ounces. The solid metal windscreens can add another 11 to 15 ounces. These stoves sometimes come with a pot as well, with a solo unit including burner, screen, and pot weighing 33 to 35 ounces. A simpler version with a small windscreen and one pot weighs 12 ounces, while one without a pot weighs less than 7 ounces.

Homemade alcohol burners have become popular with various groups, from Boy Scouts to ultralight long-distance hikers. They're made from food and drink cans and are very light in weight. Construction and usage details can be found on the World Wide Web.

Alcohol stove with pan set. Alcohol doesn't need pressurizing, which allows you to use your stove in a tent vestibule or inside a shelter.

Natural-Fuel Stoves

This type of stove runs on twigs, pine cones, bits of bark—even dried dung. The Sierra Stove by ZZ Manufacturing consists of a hollow-walled combustion chamber set above a fan powered by a single AA battery. It works like a blacksmith's forge, the fan acting like a bellows, blowing air into the hollow walls; from there, the air passes through a ring of holes and into the fire in the main chamber, which then burns very hot. The power of the fan is adjustable; a battery is said to last six hours.

Butane/Propane Stoves

Butane/propane canister stoves are the easiest and cleanest pressurized stoves. They are quick to light, have an easily controlled flame for simmering, and are much lighter and smaller than liquid-fuel stoves. There are several different types of canister on the market, and some stoves take only one canister type.

There are two common types of canister stoves: screw-in and hose-connected. The first type screws directly into the top of the canister. Compact and very lightweight, some weighing less than 3 ounces, these stoves are great for solo and duo use but not for larger groups, because they aren't very stable with big pots.

Hose-connected stoves have long, flexible fuel lines running from the canister to the stove, which sits on the ground. This means it can be totally surrounded by a windscreen for maximum weather protection, a tactic that is potentially dangerous with screw-in stoves because the canister could overheat. (You can put a windscreen around three sides of a screw-in stove, as long as you check regularly that the canister remains cool.) Another advantage of hose-connected stoves is that they're very stable due to their low profile and thus can be used with large pans.

Both types of stoves can be removed from the canister for packing. Occasionally, you may still find the old-fashioned type of stove that pierces the canister and can't be removed until the canister is empty, making for a bulky unit to pack. A standard canister weighing about 12 ounces and carrying 8 ounces of fuel will last three to four days for solo cooking; this is comparable to liquid fuel.

With all of these advantages, why would you bother with any other type of stove? For short three-season **backpacking** trips close to home, there's no reason at all. However, canisters aren't available everywhere, especially in remote areas, and even when they are, the ones you find may not fit your stove.

Another disadvantage is that as fuel is used, the pressure in the canister drops and boiling time increases. This problem is aggravated in cold weather. Butane/propane mixtures work far better in the cold than butane alone does, but even so, in below-freezing temperatures, a canister less than half full may not produce enough heat to boil water. Warming the canister with your hands helps, but for really cold conditions, other fuels are better. Another problem is that the canister cools as it releases fuel, so running the stove continuously for a long period of time leads to a much more rapid drop-off in performance than does running it in short bursts. This makes these stoves less efficient for melting snow or for group cooking than ones that run on other fuels. Some canister stove models have preheat tubes that run through the flame to help the fuel vaporize in the cold and minimize the fall in heat output as the canister empties.

Liquid-Fuel Stoves

For cold-weather cooking, pressurized stoves that run on white gas, kerosene, and other petroleum liquid fuels are the most efficient because they work at full power whatever the temperature. These stoves are also a good choice for long-distance hikes and trips to remote places because the fuel can be found almost everywhere. This is especially so if you have a multifuel stove that will run on just about any petroleum product you can find.

Liquid-fuel stoves aren't quite as easy to use as butane/propane canister stoves, however.

They generally need priming, which means pre-heating the burner with a small amount of fuel (or alcohol, preheating paste, or solid fuel tablets). This ensures that the fuel will vaporize before reaching the burner, so that it burns as a gas rather than a liquid. Priming isn't difficult, but it does require a little practice. Stoves may flare when primed. Some stoves need less priming and are less prone to flaring than others, but the risk is always there.

Generally, these stoves should always be used outside. In stormy weather, you can light the stove just outside the tent and then bring it into the tent porch, if the porch is large enough. Always leave a door zipper open, and make sure there is plenty of space around and above the stove and that no gear is nearby.

There are two types of liquid-fuel stoves: those with built-in fuel tanks sitting under the burners and those with fuel lines or hoses lead-

Lighting a Liquid-Fuel Stove

Ensure that the stove is set up in a safe place, that all connections are secure, and that there are no leaks. All stoves are slightly different, but the following is a general description of how to light a low-profile liquid-fuel stove with a pump.

1. Pump the fuel bottle until you meet firm resist-ance—usually after 20 to 30 strokes when the bottle is full, more when it is partly empty. Once the bottle is pressurized, attach it to the stove.

2. Open the control valve slightly and allow about a teaspoon of fuel to run down into the priming cup situated below the burner. Close the valve.

3. Light the fuel in the priming cup. When it has almost burned out, open the valve slowly: the stove should light with a healthy roar and burn with a blue flame. If the priming fuel burns out before you open the valve, apply a match to the burner as you open it. If the flames are yellow or the stove burns erratically, it's not hot enough. Close the valve, let the yellow flames die down, and light it again. If it still doesn't burn properly, close the valve again, wait for the stove to cool, and then prime it again.

4. Let the stove burn at a low flame for a minute or so before opening the valve fully. This makes flar-ing less likely.

5. If the power of the flame starts to drop, pump the fuel bottle a few times to maintain the pressure.

ing to pumps that plug into fuel bottles. Both types work well, but the latter design has some advantages: it's more stable, weighs less, and takes up less room in your **pack**. The size of fuel bottle can be varied according to the length of the trip. Perhaps most important, you can use fully encircling windshields because there's no danger of the fuel tank overheating (when the tank lies under the burner, the stove must not be fully shielded).

All stoves that use fuel bottles as tanks have pumps, because pressure is required to force the fuel along the hose to the burner. Stoves with tanks below the burner may have pumps for increased efficiency and ease of lighting, but these aren't essential.

Simmering can be difficult, especially with stoves whose only control is on the pump. If you simmer regularly, look for a stove with a flame control at the burner. With any stove that has a pump, simmering is easier if you pump only a few strokes and if the fuel bottle or tank is half empty.

These stoves are complex beasts that need proper treatment if they are to function efficiently and safely. On trips of more than a few days, you should carry a maintenance kit. All seals should be regularly checked and replaced if they are cracked or worn. If a leak appears and you don't have a spare seal, don't use the stove. The most common problems are blocked jets and pumps that don't pressurize the fuel (see **repairs**). Not all liquid-fuel stoves are fully maintainable in the field. For long trips or ventures into remote places, don't consider ones that aren't.

Liquid-fuel stoves range in weight from 8 ounces to over 2 pounds, so they're not that light. They are fuel efficient, however, so the longer the trip or the greater the number of people, the less the weight matters.

Windscreens

Some stoves come with separate windscreens, but many don't. In anything but a dead calm, a windscreen makes a big difference. In strong **winds**, a screen can make the difference between a stove that stays lit and one that doesn't. You can buy a lightweight foil windscreen for a stove that doesn't have one. Some stoves are advertised to be wind resistant due to the shape of the pot supports, small built-in windscreens, or other features, but these aren't very efficient.

Safety

Naked flames are potentially hazardous, and naked flames under pressure and attached to a highly flammable fuel are even more so. Any stove requires care and attention while it is lit. Learn how your stove works, and practice so you can use it almost automatically.

Always check that fuel lines and canisters are attached properly and that no fuel is leaking out. Before lighting a stove, make sure you have put the caps back on fuel bottles. Any pressure stove can flare—it even happens with canisters, though rarely—so don't have your face over it when you light it.

When refilling a pressure stove or changing canisters, make sure there are no naked flames, such as a campfire or a candle, anywhere near because some fuel always escapes. Always refuel outside, and try not to spill any of the fuel.

If storms force you to use a stove in a tent porch with the doors shut or inside a **snow shelter**, be sure you have some ventilation. Stoves give off carbon monoxide, which can kill.

Transporting a Stove

When traveling by air with a stove, find out airline policy in advance. Although Federal Aviation Administration regulations don't forbid stoves on aircraft, many airlines have stricter rules. Some allow only new stoves in their original packaging; some allow only used stoves without permanently attached fuel tanks and some canister stoves but not liquid-fuel stoves. Whatever the rules, always air your stove well so that, if it's checked, it will have no fuel smell. Buy fuel at your destination: it is illegal and dangerous to carry fuel on an aircraft.

STRAINERS

Strainers are objects in rivers, either partially or fully submerged, that allow water but little else to pass through. More often than not, strainers are downed trees that extend into a river from a nearby bank. They are commonly found on the outside of river bends where the current has eroded the shore. In addition to fallen trees, strainers can take the form of submerged fences, old docks, and even industrial debris! If a boat gets pushed into a strainer, it will become stuck in the sieve or capsize and get sucked underwater.

A capsize is bad for the boat but much worse for the paddler. This is where things get really ugly. Now in the water, the paddler is forced against the strainer before getting sucked under the surface of the water. Trying to swim through a strainer is a gamble against the odds. Imagine trying to push your way through the branches of a bushy tree. Now imagine the same thing, only underwater, where you can't see or breathe; that's how a strainer feels. Thus strainers should be avoided under all circumstances. They are death traps.

If you find yourself unavoidably heading toward a strainer, try to build up enough momentum to propel yourself over the top of it. If you're swimming, quickly change from the traditional

Strainers, such as this fallen tree, are deadly: they can capsize boats and trap swimmers, forcing them underwater. Always avoid strainers.

feet-first position into a crawl stroke. Swim toward the strainer vigorously, building enough speed to push your body up and over the object (see **swimming in rivers**). If you're able to get your torso and hips out of the water, it will improve your chance of survival significantly. Strainers do not require much current to be dangerous. They should be considered hazardous even when they look benign.

SUN PROTECTION

Since the beginning of recorded history, humans have worshiped the sun. Indeed, the sun is the source of all life on earth. Without it, we would not exist. Outdoor enthusiasts come to appreciate all **weather**, but it's hard to deny that bright, sunny days are the most welcome. While the sun can be comfortingly warm and uplifting, you also need to guard against its many hazards.

The most common sun-related injury is sunburn. Sunburns are partial-thickness **burns** that occur when your skin is exposed to the sun's damaging ultraviolet (UV) rays. UV rays can cause considerable cellular damage to the body's largest organ, your skin. If the cellular damage is severe, anticipate pain, swelling, and **blisters**. While none of these effects are life threatening, they can cause serious complications on a backcountry trip. Sunburned hands, feet, shoulders, or hips can prevent you from walking, paddling, or carrying a backpack. In addition, an infected blister may be cause for an **evacuation**. Unless they're protected, your eyes can suffer from the debilitating effects of **snow blindness**. Despite its name, snow blindness can occur in any environment any time of year. It's a painful condition that will restrict your ability to see.

The sun's UV rays can be found anywhere there is sunlight. Because they penetrate clouds, they're present even on cloudy days. They are most intense at the lower **latitudes** and higher altitudes. In fact, the intensity of UV rays is compounded by 4 percent for every 1,000-foot gain in altitude. They are further enhanced when they're reflected off of **snow**, water, **ice**, or rock.

The sun (and its accompanying UV rays) is most intense between 10 A.M. and 4 P.M. This happens to coincide with prime traveling hours (unless you are in the **desert**), so be sure to take adequate sun precautions during this time. If you aren't wearing a watch, look at your shadow. If it is shorter than you are, the UV rays are still intense. Only when your shadow is longer than your full height can you let down your guard.

When the sun's intensity combines with severe heat, anticipate additional problems. As your body begins to sweat profusely, it will require copious amounts of water to keep hydrated. Inattention, or the lack of a **water** source, can quickly result in severe **dehydration**. In addition, many heat-related illnesses are provoked by intense heat and direct sunlight.

To protect yourself from the dangers of the sun, practice these simple techniques.

• Wear sunscreen (minimum SPF 30) anytime you are outside. Start applying it about half an hour before you need the protection. This allows it to be absorbed by your skin. Reapply sunscreen at least every three hours (more frequently if you sweat a lot or go swimming).

• Wear a hat that covers your ears and the back of your neck, such as a wide-brimmed hat. If you're **backpacking**, you may prefer a baseball or desert-style cap with a flap that extends over your ears and neck; these hats are less likely to rub against tall backpacks.

• Buy good sunglasses (or goggles) that wrap around your face to provide maximum coverage. They should offer 99 to 100 percent UVA and UVB protection, the two types of ultraviolet rays that penetrate the earth's ozone layer. They should also block at least 75 to 95 percent of the visible light. Polarized lenses work well for reducing glare on snow, ice, and water.

• Wear long-sleeved shirts and long pants. Tightly woven **fabrics** repel UV rays the best. Some are even rated with their own SPF.

• Wear a sunscreen that provides total block-age on your nose, ears, and lips. Many sunscreen manufacturers produce products that contain zinc oxide (which offers 100 percent protection) in easy-to-apply sticks.

• Research any medications you take to ensure that they don't make your skin hypersensitive to the sun. Many photosensitizing drugs, such as certain antibiotics, are commonly prescribed and may put you at risk.

Protecting yourself from the sun should be a priority in any environment.

Reflections from water and snow can increase your chances for sunburning skin and eyes. This skier has made a sun shade from his jacket to protect himself on a winter day.

CHRIS TOWNSEND

• Drink a lot of water (at least a gallon a day). In arid environments, increase your intake appropriately.

• In hot environments, restrict the bulk of your travel to the morning and evening hours. Avoid working hard when the sun is intense. Take rests in the shade, even if it means taking the time to set up a tarp.

• When traveling on snow or ice remember to protect yourself against reflected UV rays. Wear lip protection, and apply sunscreen in unlikely places, such as the area around your nostrils and the underside of your chin. Also consider wearing goggles.

The dangers of the sun are not to be taken lightly. Several people die every year from dehydration and heat-related illnesses that are exacerbated by the sun. In addition, it is estimated that one in six Americans will develop skin cancer over the course of his lifetime, and 1 million new cases of skin cancer are diagnosed every year. Those at the highest risk are people who spend a considerable amount of time outdoors. Be especially concerned if you have light skin, blonde or red hair, light-colored eyes, lots of freckles, or a history of skin cancer in your family. The good news is that most skin cancers are preventable. By taking a few sun safety precautions, you can guard against this deadly disease.

SURFING

Anytime you paddle a large body of water, you may encounter surf—that is, waves that are breaking. Surf develops both in surf zones, usually along the coast, and in open water. In either case it is important to know how to negotiate surf to prevent capsizing.

Surf Zones

A surf zone is any area along a coastline where **waves** continually break, such as on a beach, sandbar, or coral reef. Surf zones present special challenges for sea kayakers launching or landing their boats.

As waves approach shore they slow down and build in height. When a wave's height reaches approximately one seventh of its length, the wave breaks. If the shoreline has a gentle incline, the wave will break as a *spilling wave*, gradually spilling its way toward shore. Spilling waves are the easiest to navigate in a kayak.

When the bottom is steep, as in a sudden drop-off, the wave will approach shore and change from a swell to a crashing wave in an instant, breaking as a *dumping wave*. Dumping waves release tremendous energy in a small area. They can damage kayaks and injure paddlers. They also tend to produce strong undertow currents.

A surf zone has two main parts: the *impact zone* and the *soup zone*. The impact zone is where the waves actually break, expending most of their energy. Because dumping waves tend to crash at the last minute, their impact zone is relatively short and intense. This is a place to avoid. The impact zone for spilling waves is more spread out. Impact zones shift depending on the size of the waves, with bigger waves breaking farther from shore and smaller waves closer in.

On the shore side of the impact zone is an accumulation of foamy water, the soup zone, consisting of the remnants of the wave after it breaks. The soup zone is a relatively benign area that is generally easy to negotiate in a kayak; the zone acts as a buffer between the high-energy impact zone and the shore. A shore with a long soup zone allows you to launch and land your kayak with relative ease. On a gradually sloped beach, the soup zone may extend over a hundred feet. If the slope is abrupt, you may find a soup zone that is as short as a few feet or, worse, nonexistent. Avoid landings in surf without a soup zone.

Also important in the surf zone are rip currents (rip tides) that carry water away from shore. Rip currents and other **coastal currents** also affect the way you launch or land.

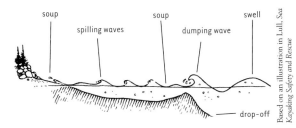

soup   soup   swell

spilling waves   dumping wave

drop-off

Based on an illustration in Lull, *Sea Kayaking Safety and Rescue*

The anatomy of the surf zone. When deep-water waves suddenly reach shallow ground, expect large dumping waves—and avoid them! Gradual beaches offer spilling waves that are much better for surfing. Soup zones can be found wherever waves dissipate. The relative calm of a soup zone can be a welcome break after a wild ride through the surf.

Because the geography of every beach is different, you may find two beaches next to each other with completely different surf zones: one may have wonderful spilling waves that are great for surfing, and the other may have huge dumping waves that spell trouble. You may even come across a surf zone with both types: dumping waves at one end and spilling waves at the other. If there's a sandbar off shore, you may see an impact zone followed by a soup zone followed by a second impact zone and finally a second soup zone. In this scenario, the second impact zone (the one closest to the beach) will be less threatening than the first, as the waves will have already dispersed most of their energy.

Surf can also develop away from shore. Surf that develops in open water usually suggests local or approaching strong winds—a good reason to get off the water.

Paddling in Surf

When paddling in surf, you can either let the waves pass under your kayak or you can ride them. Allowing each wave to pass beneath your kayak is a very controlled way to paddle that keeps the wave from picking up your boat and pushing it forward. But you can also choose to go surfing: hitching a ride on the face of the wave and letting it push you toward shore, much like surfboarders do.

Because it's easy to capsize when you're surfing, many kayakers avoid it when their boat is loaded with food and gear. They opt instead for controlled paddling that keeps them out of the surf. To accomplish this, paddle forward (toward shore) in the lull between waves; paddle backward (away from shore) as soon as a wave begins to lift the stern of your kayak. Paddling backward counters the forward motion of the wave and lets it pass beneath your hull. As soon as the crest of the wave passes, resume paddling forward until the next wave lifts the stern. Keep an eye over your shoulder for incoming waves.

Before you decide to try surfing waves, make sure you have a **bombproof** high **brace** and good control of your kayak. Start out by surfing the small waves within the soup of the surf zone. Paddle out a short distance, and turn around so you are facing shore. As soon as a wave breaks a few feet behind your stern, paddle forward, fast. You'll feel the wave pick up the stern as you begin to surf down its face. Once you become comfortable with the smaller waves, move out to the larger waves in deeper water.

You'll soon realize that surfing makes your kayak turn one way or the other. If you let the wave turn your kayak, you'll end up broaching—turning sideways, or parallel, to the wave. And broaching can capsize the boat. To avoid broaching, use the stern rudder stroke to correct your direction and to stay on the leading face of the wave (see **kayaking strokes**). Be prepared to alternate the stern rudder stroke quickly from one side of the kayak to the other, in order to move straight ahead.

If you find that you're broaching, perform a quick brace into the breaking face of the wave. Bracing into the face utilizes the wave's surging water to support your paddle and keep you upright. If you brace on the opposite side of the kayak (the shore side), the same surging water will flip the kayak. When you brace successfully against a wave, it will push you toward shore in a movement known as *side surfing*. Skilled kayakers side-surf on purpose; it can be a great way to get to shore. But unless you've practiced it many times, on both sides of the kayak, be prepared to capsize.

Whenever you paddle on coastal water or large lakes, be aware of your proximity to surf zones. They can form far from shore over shoals, sandbars, and pockets of coral. If you need to launch or land through a surf zone, spend some time determining the type of waves you'll be contending with. Learn and practice surfing techniques until you're confident in launching and landing through moderate surf. In addition, it helps to have a solid roll that you can execute in rough water (see **rolling a kayak**).

Surf Landings

Surf landings can be tricky. Plan your route to take advantage of the most protected launching and landing sites, often behind headlands, on the back sides of islands, or in bays. Depending on the geography of the surf zone, you may be dealing with spilling waves, dumping waves, and/or coastal currents. If you're lucky you'll be landing on a nice sandy beach—but you may be landing on rock.

While you're still outside the surf zone, watch the waves and try to identify periodic lulls in the swells. Time your landing to take advantage of such lulls. If the lulls are too short (as is sometimes the case), approach the beach carefully using a controlled landing, paddling to let the waves pass beneath the kayak. If the waves are small and spilling, you may decide to surf them instead. But if the waves are dumping, avoid surfing and remain with the controlled landing. Paddle in on the backside of the wave. Be prepared to feel your kayak suddenly drop when the wave breaks. If the wave breaks directly on shore, get out of the kayak as quickly as possible, grab the bow toggle, and run the boat up onto the beach. If the kayak remains in the path of another dumping wave it could sustain serious damage (and so could you).

If you're with a group, send the most experienced person through the surf first. Once that person lands she can observe the surf zone from

Being comfortable in surf is important for open-water sea kayak trips.

ANNIE AGGENS

shore (a superior vantage point) and locate the best route through the surf. She can guide other paddlers toward shore and help pull their kayaks out of the water. The second-most-experienced paddler should remain with the group and be the last person to land. Once you land, assist other paddlers in getting out of their kayaks. Don't get yourself between a kayak and the shore: waves can push the kayak toward shore with great force, and you don't want to be in the way.

Knowing how to handle your kayak in surf is a critical skill. Classes in surf kayaking can be found in most coastal regions. To locate a course near you, contact the American Canoe Association or the British Canoe Union (see resources section).

SURVIVAL

So what happens if you lose your **pack**? What do you do if your canoe tips over and gets washed downstream? What goes on when everything is lost? Easy—you survive. *Survival* is a catchy term. As a society, we have a fascination with survival situations. You may entertain fantasies of being stuck on an island or in the Alaskan wilderness. Could you hack it? If you're diligent in all your planning, if you develop **contingency plans** and know how to react to an emergency situation, you should never find yourself in a survival situation. With today's high-tech gear and with more options than ever for learning **wilderness** skills, a person would have to make a series of critical and yet completely preventable (some might even say negligent) mistakes in order to find himself in a true survival mode. Still, it's possible that even the most prepared, well-trained wilderness traveler could have some freak accident or natural disaster that would require a survival frame of mind. If this were to happen to you, you would need to start thinking creatively in order to make use of all your resources.

As in any other emergency situation, remember the acronym STOP—Stop, Think, Organize, and Plan. In survival mode, conserving energy becomes important. Prioritize what you need immediately. Most people can survive for a while without **food** but can't go for more than a day or two without water. If you are near a lake or river, consider yourself lucky. Before you drink the water, purify it. If you don't have iodine or a pump, boil your water. If you can't purify the water, drink it anyway. While diseases caused by waterborne creatures such as *Giardia* or *Cryptosporidium* can cause diarrhea, you'll die much faster if you drink nothing at all. (See also **water**.)

If no visible water is around, you'll need to search for water. Look at the base of gullies and valleys and along the bottom of cliffs. Trees, bushes, and vegetation clinging to rock walls or cliffs are a good sign that water is nearby. Mosses are also a good indicator. If water isn't pooling on the ground, you may need to dig. Dig straight down, but stop if you get farther than a foot with no signs of moisture: all this energy you're exerting is soaking up the water you have in your body. Conserve your energy as much as possible to stay hydrated.

If animals are around, watch their behavior. Also keep your eyes peeled for flocking birds, which may lead you to water. Animal tracks that converge are also a good sign that water is present, as are flocking bees and migrating ants. Keep watch on the **weather**, and be prepared to make use of any rainstorms. If it rains, collect water in any manner possible. Also try to collect the moisture from early-morning dew. If you find a bog or even a pile of mud, swish your **bandanna** in the muck and then wring it out, collecting any water that is expelled. Intricate solar stills are interesting to read about and are sometimes advocated for dire situations, but you'll likely lose more sweat building one than you could replace with water acquired from it. If you're in a hot environment, restrict your searching to the morning and evening hours. Spend the afternoon relaxing under the shade of an emergency shelter (see **shelter, emergency**).

As for food, you should be able to survive off of your surroundings (although it may not be pleasant). The good news is that if you filed a **trip plan** with someone before your departure, you may be rescued before long. In the meantime, you can find nourishment in plants, berries, fruits, insects, fish, and animals. Depending on supplies and skill, you should be able to catch something, even if only a few frogs or worms. Start by taking an inventory of your surroundings. Have you seen any animals in the last few days? What about fish? Have you seen any nesting birds? If you find a nest, check it for eggs or immature birds that haven't yet begun to fly. Either are OK to eat. Older birds make good food, but they generally fly away when you approach them.

Fish are hard to catch unless you have a hook and line. Nonetheless, if you're near a river or lake, you may be able to spear a fish with a sharpened stick or trick it into swimming into a trap made out of branches. Small animals may be snared or clubbed, especially if they're slow. Porcupines are notoriously easy to kill with a boulder or log. Animals may not be the easiest catch, however. Don't waste your energy on difficult or improbable tasks; instead, try to get the easiest nourishment possible. **Edible plants** require a certain familiarity on your part, although some are easily recognized. Coconuts, for example, are easy to identify, so if you have the misfortune of getting stranded on a tropical island you aren't doing too badly! Berries (especially raspberries, strawberries, and blueberries) are easy to identify, although they're both seasonal and regional. Don't eat any berries you can't identify—some are harmful. Insects and bugs can be collected off trees and from the underside of rocks and downed logs.

Obviously, your survival depends on the gear you have with you and what you can fashion from your surroundings. The other big factor is your attitude—it helps to be a natural optimist. Hard as it may be, you must think and act rationally, even optimistically. More people have died from lost hope rather than from inadequate resources.

Unlike the **Leave No Trace** creed of the wilderness traveler, most survival skills require damaging alterations to the environment. Needless to say, you should never use such skills unless you are in a true survival situation.

SURVIVAL KIT

Many people who venture into the wilderness don't go without a survival kit. Survival kits carry an assortment of items that may prove invaluable in a **survival** situation, such as **fishing** line, hooks, waterproof matches, and a **signaling** mirror. Most people would agree that a survival kit doesn't do much good unless it is on your person at all times. Sure, you could keep a survival kit in your backpack, but if your **pack** is swept away by a **flash flood** (or lost or stolen by a **wild animal**), you may be looking at a lengthy hike to the trailhead with no food or shelter. However unlikely that situation may be, you'll be glad your survival kit is in your pocket, not with your pack. For this reason, many people make their survival kits small enough to fit in a pocket or wear on a belt.

There are many commercial survival kits available, although some are more attractive than they are practical. Before you invest in a survival kit, examine the contents thoroughly. Better yet, create your own survival kit with items that you know are durable, practical, and difficult to improvise.

Survival kits range from having one or two items to being the size of a shoebox. When building a survival kit, consider including the following items.

- 10 feet parachute cord
- 30 feet of 20-pound fishing line
- 3 fishing hooks
- 2 lead sinkers
- 1 small bobber
- Flint and steel or waterproof matches
- 5 feet **duct tape**
- 1 garbage bag
- 1 razor blade
- Potable Aqua tablets
- Loud whistle
- Small squeeze light (credit card size works well)
- 1 foot flexible tubing (to use as a straw or siphon for hard-to-reach water)

- 2 needles
- 5 feet waxed dental floss (for use as thread and cord)
- 1 pencil
- 3 sheets waterproof paper (for emergency notes or messages)
- 1 latex glove (as a water container)
- Small mirror (if the container holding the kit cannot be used as a signaling device)

No two survival kits will look exactly alike, unless they're commercial. You may get some great ideas from another person's kit, so look around and don't be afraid to add to or change your contents. Keep in mind that you may already carry important survival tools, such as a good **knife** or a **compass**, on your person. If this is the case, there is no need to be overly redundant. Good containers include the tins from Altoids, Sucrets, or Band-Aids; old makeup compacts (including the mirror); and small plastic jars, such as those made by Nalgene.

SWAMPED

Swamped describes a canoe or kayak so filled with water that it has become virtually useless. When boats take on a lot of water, they quickly become overwhelmingly heavy. This makes them a night-

Swamped after a large set of rapids in Saskatchewan. A more conservative route through the whitewater would have prevented this swamping. Swamping isn't just a pain, it can also be dangerous.

mare to navigate. Simple turns can take extreme amounts of energy. In addition to lack of response, a swamped canoe or kayak becomes very tippy. This can be a serious problem if you take on a load of water when you're only halfway down a set of rapids! In fact, taking on too much water is often the cause of a capsize, especially in **canoeing**. Once you get about 6 inches of water in the bottom of your canoe, things can deteriorate quickly.

Paddlers have various techniques and equipment to prevent taking on water. **Sprayskirts** are a necessity for any kayaker planning to paddle beyond a relaxing float in a peaceful pond. While sprayskirts are not as common on canoes, they have their place in **wilderness** tripping. Most paddlers concerned about swamping also outfit their canoes or kayaks with **flotation**. Flotation, or float bags, are nylon or rubber bags that are inflated and then secured in the hull of the boat. These bags reduce the amount of space water can occupy. In heavily loaded canoes or kayaks, your packs may do this job just fine. In addition to the above equipment, many sea kayaks have built-in bulkheads that prevent water from flooding the entire hull.

Most canoes and kayaks won't sink, because the materials they are made of have a degree of buoyancy. However, a swamped canoe or kayak is more than a hassle: it's dangerous, particularly when traveling on a river. When a canoe or kayak swamps, the likelihood that it will wrap around a rock or pin the paddler increases considerably. To prevent such accidents, many rivers have regulations that require a minimum amount of flotation for every boat. If you plan to paddle a river with lots of whitewater, check with a local paddle shop or river authority to determine the rules regarding flotation. If there are no rules, be smart and use it anyway. Remember, if you swamp your canoe or kayak, it will become a hazard to everyone on the river, not just to you! Be prepared to rescue a swamped canoe or kayak by familiarizing yourself with a variety of rescues, including the **T-rescue.**

SWAMPS (OR WETLANDS)

Swamps are lowlands saturated with water. They are home to countless plants, animals, and insects. In the United States alone, swamps and wetlands cover over 100,000 square miles. They're great places to look for birds and other wildlife.

If your route takes you through a swamp, be careful where you walk. Step on durable surfaces whenever possible. Not only will this protect the fragile swamp ecosystem, but it will also prevent you from getting stuck in muck. When part of your body becomes submerged in saturated muck, suction can form around the body part and make it hard to extricate. Keep your shoes tied securely, because loose shoes can be pulled right off your feet. Plan ahead by filling water bottles before you arrive, and don't plan to camp at the swamp. As breeding grounds for many **insects**, swamps are notoriously buggy. In addition, the soft, wet ground usually doesn't offer good **camping**, but you can use a flat-bottomed boat or hammocks for sleeping accommodations, if necessary.

Nonetheless, some swamps make excellent backcountry destinations. The cypress swamps of Everglades National Park are a popular destination for backcountry travelers interested in exploring a tropical wilderness. For backpackers, the Florida Trail covers over 1,000 miles of swamps, grassy corridors, and subtropical environments. Other hiking trails and canoe and kayak routes that explore swampy regions can be found throughout the southeastern United States.

SWEEP STROKE

The sweep stroke is a paddle stroke used to turn a canoe or kayak or to correct it from veering off a straight course.

Kayak Sweep Stroke

To execute a sweep stroke in your kayak, place your paddle in the water near the bow of your kayak. To do this, rotate your on-side shoulder (the side on which you're paddling) toward the bow. This will cause your torso to wind up. You may need to bend and tuck your off-side arm against your chest. During this process, don't shift the position of your hands. Instead, if you feel the urge to move your hands, rotate your whole body to get the desired result.

Once the paddle is in the water, create an arch from the bow of your boat all the way to the stern by unwinding your torso. The wider your arch, the more effect you create. Ideally, the blade of

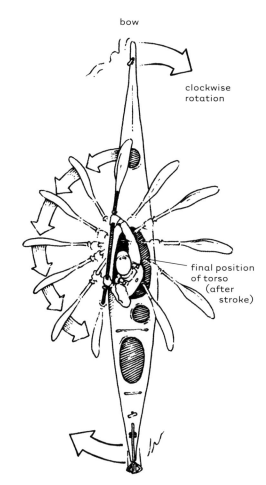

Bird's-eye view of the sweep stroke, showing the paddle's final position. To maximize the sweep stroke, rotate your torso to follow your paddle. At the end of this stroke your shoulders should be parallel to the side of the kayak.

your paddle should be almost a full paddle's length away from your kayak by the time it passes your hip. By using **torso rotation** to propel your stroke, you are in effect turning the kayak around the paddle, which remains relatively stationary. At the end of the stroke, you should be able to drop your paddle in the water so it's floating parallel to your kayak. To turn the kayak in the opposite direction, simply repeat the process on the other side. Many people lose out on a lot of power by ending their sweep stroke too early. To avoid this, perform a full sweep stroke with your paddle starting at the bow and ending all the way at the stern.

Experienced paddlers will edge their kayaks when using the sweep stroke. Though edging is a somewhat more advanced technique, you should at least know what it is. When you "edge" a kayak, you lean it on its edge, or **gunwale**. This reduces the kayak's waterline (the amount of the kayak that is actually in the water) and makes it easier to pivot. First try edging in warm water with a partner nearby, because it's likely that you'll capsize in your first few attempts.

Canoeing Sweep Stroke

As in kayaking, the most effective way to turn a canoe is to perform a corrective stroke as close to the bow or stern of the canoe as possible. Because tandem canoeists generally sit closer to the ends of the canoe than to its center, rarely is a full sweep stroke used. Instead, canoeists perform only the beginning or the end of the stroke (depending on whether they're in the bow or the stern). Only a solo canoeist uses the full sweep stroke. Therefore, in canoeing, this stroke is often referred to as the *quarter sweep*.

To perform a quarter sweep in the bow of a tandem canoe, rotate your on-side shoulder until you can place your paddle in the water near the bow. The thumb of your top hand (the one on the grip) should be facing up, while the thumb of your lower hand (the one on the shaft) should point toward the water. This will position the blade to optimize its contact with the water. Bring the paddle through the water in an arc by unwinding

your torso. Stop the blade before it reaches 90 degrees, or before it passes your hip.

If you're in the stern, start the quarter sweep by placing the paddle in the water straight out from your hip. Once again, the thumb on your grip hand will be facing up, and the thumb of your shaft hand will be pointing toward the water. Bring the paddle back to the stern of the canoe by rotating your torso and keeping your shoulders parallel to the shaft of your paddle. Repeat this stroke as necessary.

The solo canoeist will use the full sweep stroke. This is accomplished by combining the entry of the bow quarter sweep with the exit and recovery of the stern quarter sweep. The wider

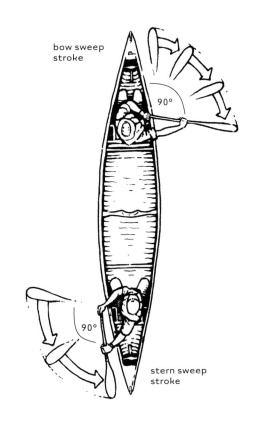

Bird's-eye view of a sweep stroke as executed by the bow and stern paddlers in a canoe. Each paddler's stroke completes only 90 degrees of an arc (hence the stroke is known as the "quarter sweep"). Anything beyond that is wasted energy.

you can make the arc of your stroke, the better. To extend the paddle farther into the water, consider choking up on your paddle shaft by sliding your shaft hand toward your grip hand. In addition, leaning the boat onto its edge will help you achieve a tighter turn.

Both the kayak and canoe sweep strokes can be reversed to provide the opposite effect. For example, in a kayak or solo canoe a forward sweep on the right side makes you turn left, while a reverse sweep on the same side will turn you to the right. In addition, portions of the full sweep (like the quarter sweep) can be used in both canoeing and kayaking to provide small corrections while maintaining a forward direction of travel.

SWIMMING IN RIVERS

A swim down a remote section of river or through a set of whitewater rapids is usually the result of an unexpected capsize of a canoe or kayak or a loss of footing during a **river crossing**. These unintentional excursions are at best unpleasant and always have the potential to become very dangerous. Because you may encounter **moving-water hazards** before you reach the security of shore, you must know specific swimming techniques that will maximize your safety.

There are a number of immediate actions you should take if you accidentally end up in the water. If you have been crossing a river while hiking, you'll need to jettison your **pack** before it weighs you down. This should be fairly easy, especially if you took the important preventive measures of unclipping your hip belt and sternum strap before you began the crossing. Don't worry about your pack at this point. If it has any measure of buoyancy, you can look for it after you get out of the water.

If you capsized a canoe or kayak, immediately locate your boat and get upstream of it. Swimming downstream of a **swamped** boat spells disaster. All it takes is one rock in your path to leave you pinned between the rock and your boat. With 1,000 pounds or more of pressure sandwiching you in this position, survival is unlikely.

The next step is to get your body into the defensive swimming position. This is on your back and facing downstream. Your feet should be at the surface of the water, ready to fend off any rocks. Use your arms to keep yourself afloat. As you pass over rocks, raise your butt and arch your back to stay as close to the surface of the water as possible. If you're floating through big **waves**, time your breaths so you inhale when you're in the trough (or base) of a wave. Hold your breath as you pass through the crests.

The defensive swimming position is important for a few reasons. First, it allows you to see approaching hazards and meet them feet first. Second, it keeps your feet away from the bottom of the river, where they can become entrapped by rocks. Third, it is the most energy-efficient way to swim in a river. The defensive swimming position is the safest way to get through a stretch of difficult water. However, this position makes it very difficult to get to shore or to change your lateral location in a river.

Because of this, there are a few situations in which you should avoid the defensive swimming position. If you suddenly realize you're submerged in freezing-cold water, you may have only moments to act before **hypothermia** makes you begin to lose control of your body. In this scenario, shift into an aggressive swimming position by rolling onto your stomach with your head upstream. Perform an aggressive crawl stroke toward shore. This can be exhausting and time consuming, so time your aggressive swimming to take advantage

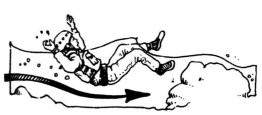

The defensive swimming position keeps the feet downstream and near the surface, away from possible entrapments.

Based on an illustration in Bechdel and Ray, *River Rescue*

of **eddies** in the river or along the banks. An aggressive swimming position will also help you avoid **holes**, ledges, and strainers in the river.

If you're heading directly toward an unavoidable strainer, shift into a crawl-style swimming

> "Even after years of training, I once lost my cool and tried to stand up in a particularly nasty stretch of waist-deep river. Thankfully, I caught myself in the act and quickly brought my feet to the surface of the water."—AA

position with your head downstream. Swim aggressively toward the strainer, and try to generate enough momentum to propel yourself over the strainer (or at least onto it). It is critical to get your upper body and hips out of the water and onto the strainer. If you're unable to accomplish this, it is very likely that the current will pull you back into the water and through the strainer. (See also **strainers**.)

Anytime you're paddling a river you should be wearing a **PFD** (personal flotation device). Your PFD will perform the critical task of keeping you afloat, allowing you to use your energy to get to shore. Because backpackers typically don't carry PFDs, they must use excellent **judgment** when selecting river crossings. Some backpackers carry an inflatable PFD on trips that require difficult crossings. Along with a PFD, a helmet can significantly increase your chances of surviving a nasty swim.

The urge to stand up in a river can be very strong. However, your feet can easily become entrapped in rocks. If you're in water over knee depth and a foot becomes trapped, you can easily be forced beneath the surface of the water. Don't let your fear and your desire for control override your judgment: never put your feet down until you can touch the river bottom with your hands. This means that you should look like an alligator as you approach shore.

Several paddling organizations, such as the American Canoe Association, offer courses that cover swimming in rapids (see resources section). Every so often you should practice swimming a safe stretch of whitewater (make sure you're with people experienced in whitewater rescue). Not only will your skills benefit from the drill, but you will also be reminded of the awesome power of the river and the caution that you must exercise when paddling a river or choosing a river crossing.

SWITCHBACKS

Switchbacks are **trails** that zigzag their way up and down **mountain** slopes. By traversing the slope at a slight incline, instead of **hiking** directly up or down the fall line, you can conserve a lot of energy. Switchbacks are almost always present if a trail exists. While hiking up or down a slope, always travel on the switchbacks. Ignoring the switchbacks or taking short cuts damages the slope by increasing erosion. If a trail does not exist, traverse the slope at a gradual incline, just as you would if switchbacks were present.

T-RESCUE

The T-rescue is a convenient way to rescue a capsized canoe or kayak and drain it of any unwanted water. It uses a second, noncapsized canoe or kayak as the rescue boat and thus is an assisted rescue. In other words, you couldn't use this rescue if you were by yourself. Relatively easy to execute, the T-rescue is best used in situations where the boats are not heavily loaded and where both the rescue boat and the **swamped** boat are free from hazards. Therefore, the T-rescue is not the best rescue to use if you're in the middle of a set of rapids.

When performing a T-rescue in a canoe, paddle over to the capsized boat and locate the paddler(s). Assess their situation. Are they composed? Can they assist you in the rescue? If so, stow their paddles in your canoe, and instruct them to rotate their canoe so that it's upside down in the water. Position your canoe so that is it perpendicular to theirs. Establish and maintain contact with their canoe (if there are two paddlers in the water, one of them can be given this role). Move toward the center of your canoe, maintaining a low center of gravity. If there are two paddlers in the rescue boat, have one person complete their move to the center before the second starts.

When you are in the center, reach over the **gunwale** of your boat and lift the capsized canoe out of the water and across your gunwales. To help you, direct the person(s) in the water to push down on the opposite end of the capsized canoe to help break the suction on the surface of the water. Bring the capsized canoe entirely out of the water onto your gunwales, allowing it to drain. Once it's emptied of water, flip the canoe over and slowly push it back into the water, making sure you avoid the paddlers. When the canoe is in the water, maneuver it alongside your own and stabilize it while the paddlers reenter one at a time. Wait until the paddlers are in their appropriate positions and ready to paddle before you let go.

The T-rescue for a kayak differs only slightly. When you encounter the swamped kayak, first locate the paddler and assess the paddler's situation. Does he have his paddle? Is he exhibiting signs of **hypothermia**? Is he just goofing around? Establish contact with the bow of the swamped kayak; then stow your paddle under your deck lines so you can use both hands. Offer to stow the paddle of the person being rescued. If you need assistance raising a heavy kayak out of the water, direct the paddler to push down on the stern. Beware of the **rudder** bobbing around—metal rudders and fragile heads don't mix well! If you don't require the paddler's assistance, have him hold onto the bow of your kayak, where you can easily see him.

Next, draw the kayak up and over the cockpit of your own boat. If it isn't upside down at this point, roll it over to allow the water to drain. Lift the bow of the boat in this step: lifting the stern first will result in water draining into the cockpit instead of out of the boat. Once the water is emptied, slowly push the kayak back into the water right side up, making sure to avoid the paddler. Align the boats so they're next to each other, bow to stern, and direct the paddler in the water to come alongside the stern of his boat. Lean over the recovered kayak and stabilize it for reentry.

The easiest way to reenter a kayak is for the paddler to kick his way onto the rear deck of his kayak until he is resting on his stomach, behind the cockpit. Keeping a low profile, the paddler then rotates on his stomach and places his feet into the cockpit. By sliding into the cockpit and rotating into the sitting position, he can replace his **sprayskirt** and regain his composure. Again, the rescuer holds on to the rescued boat until the paddler is prepared and ready to begin paddling.

The T-rescue is a simple technique that all paddlers should know. If conditions on the water are causing boats to capsize, performing this rescue may not be easy. Be prepared by practicing several different rescues so you don't have to rely on just one. For more information on rescues check out *Canoeing Safety and Rescue* by Doug

The T-rescue is a quick, easy way to drain a canoe or kayak of water. This rescuer has pulled the overturned, swamped kayak across her cockpit, rolled it over, and allowed it to drain. The capsized paddler is hanging onto the bow of the rescuer's kayak, where rescuers can easily see her.

McKown, *Sea Kayaking Safety and Rescue* by John Lull, and *River Rescue: A Manual for Whitewater Safety* by Les Bechdel and Slim Ray.

TALUS

Talus refers to the rocks found spreading out from the base of a cliff. The word is probably derived from the Latin *talutium*, meaning "slope." Talus is similar to **scree**, although it includes larger rocks, and the same techniques are required to negotiate it.

TARPS

A tarp is simply a sheet of waterproof material used as protection from the **weather**. In the **wilderness** context, a tarp is a basic shelter, rather like a tent fly sheet without doors. Once you add doors, zippers, and other features, it's no longer a tarp: it's a tent.

Tarps are lightweight, roomy, easy to ventilate, versatile, and inexpensive. However, they lack insect protection, although you can hang a netting shelter inside, and they offer slightly less weather protection than a tent. The latter isn't as significant as many people believe. Once you are well practiced in erecting tarps, you can cope with just about any weather. Some people argue that tarps are actually better in storms than tents because they're more versatile and the profile can be lowered for better wind resistance. Tarps can be easier to pitch than tents, but it does require practice. A tent has one fixed shape, while a tarp can have many configurations. Practice pitching several of these, and you should be able to deal with any weather conditions.

Many tarps are too heavy to carry far, but some lightweight ones are available, usually made from silicone-treated nylon, which is strong and durable. Weights range from 8 ounces for an 8- by 5-foot one, which is just big enough for one person, to several pounds for ones that can hold four or more.

One of the joys of tarp camping is that you needn't feel closed in, as you do in a tent. Unless it's really wet and windy, leave at least one side of the tarp open. That way you can be under cover and still have a great view. Ventilation is good too, making **condensation** less likely. Additionally, **cooking** under a tarp is much safer than cooking in a tent porch.

> "In grizzly bear country, where sleeping in an enclosed tent is advisable, I've carried a small tarp for use as a kitchen shelter in wet weather."—CT

The versatility of a tarp means you can adapt the shape to the weather, the terrain, or just your whim. A tarp can be a pyramid, an open-ended ridge, a sloping ridge, a lean-to, and many other shapes.

Pitching a Tarp

To pitch a tarp, you need stakes, cord, and supports. When pitching a tarp with a ridge, you can use **trekking poles** inside the tarp for support, making for a more stable structure. Sticks picked up in the forest will probably be too sharp and rough for this and are better used on the outside, attached to the tarp with guylines.

In fair weather, a tarp can be pitched as an open-ended ridge with a pole at each end and the sides well above the ground. If the weather changes, you can lower the sides and reduce the height of the adjustable-length trekking poles, perhaps staking one end of the tarp to the ground with the pole at its minimum height. This makes a sloping ridge, which is more weather resistant than an open-ended one.

If the weather looks threatening or is already wet and windy, a pyramid design with a single pole in the middle of the tarp and three sides staked down at ground level makes a good shelter. If the weather is really rough, have a low entrance, maybe a foot high, on the remaining side. Otherwise, use a second pole here, shorter in length than the central one. Again, if the weather worsens, lower both poles. If the wind shifts during the night, you can move the door

from one end of the tarp to the other, staking down the old door end to keep the weather out. You can do all of this without getting out of the tarp. Try doing that with a tent!

For these different configurations, a tarp needs stake points round the edges with lengths of line attached to them. Then you can either stake the edge of the tarp down to the ground or use the

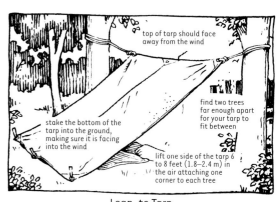

Lean-to Tarp

Open-Ended Ridge Using Trees

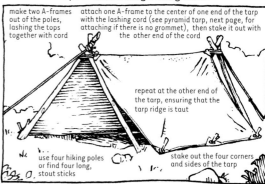

Open-Ended Ridge Using Four Sticks or Poles

Tarps.

lines and have the sides above the ground for ventilation. Some tarps come with lines in the middle of the sides. These pull the sides out, giving more room inside and shedding **rain** and **wind**. However, you do need something to attach them to, such as sticks, trees, or rocks. You can stake them to the ground, although they won't be as effective then.

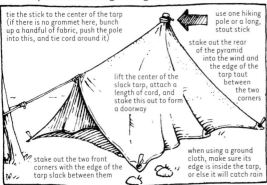

Open-Ended Ridge Using Two Sticks or Poles

use two hiking poles or find two long, stout sticks

tie one pole to the center of one end of the tarp (see pyramid tarp, below, for attaching if there is no grommet)

stand the stick upright and stake it out with the other end of the cord

repeat at the other end of the tarp, ensuring that the tarp ridge is taut

when using a ground cloth, make sure its edge is inside the tarp, or else it will catch rain

stake out the four corners and sides of the tarp

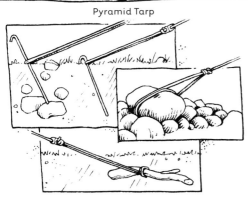

Pyramid Tarp

tie the stick to the center of the tarp (if there is no grommet here, bunch up a handful of fabric, push the pole into this, and tie cord around it)

use one hiking pole or a long, stout stick

stake out the rear of the pyramid into the wind and the edge of the tarp taut between the two corners

lift the center of the slack tarp, attach a length of cord, and stake this out to form a doorway

stake out the two front corners with the edge of the tarp slack between them

when using a ground cloth, make sure its edge is inside the tarp, or else it will catch rain

Top: Drive stake into ground at 45°, buried to the head if possible; if not, guyline should tie around the stake at ground level. Middle and Bottom: Two ways to tie down tarp lines without stakes.

Condensation

On calm, humid nights, condensation can form even in a tarp pitched as a lean-to with three sides open to the air. Any wind coming under the edges will remove most of it. Condensation certainly isn't the problem in a tarp that it can be in a tent. Any that does form can run down the walls into

Tarp pitched as a raised ridge with plenty of ventilation.

Tarp pitched as a sloping ridge for protection against wind-driven rain.

Tarp pitched with a low profile to resist wind.

CHRIS TOWNSEND (3)

the ground. Because tarps are roomy, brushing against wet walls shouldn't be a problem either.

Insects

Mosquitoes and other biting **insects** are a big problem with tarps. You can't just zip yourself inside as you can with a tent. There are various netting shelters you can get to hang or pitch inside a tarp, but few are available that don't look restrictive and awkward to use. They also add weight to your **pack**.

Groundcloth

Unless the ground is dry, you'll need to use a **groundcloth** with a tarp. This is useful for keeping gear clean and fending off insects and other crawling creatures, which tend to go under rather than over it.

TAUT-LINE HITCH

Often used to secure **tarps** and rainflies, the taut-line hitch is a very practical knot. It's handy because it can be tightened or loosened without

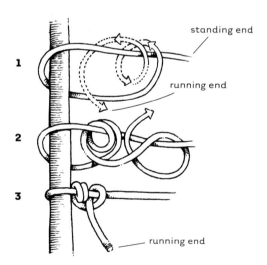

Taut-line hitch: 1. Wrap the rope around an object to create a loop. Feed the running end (see knots) of the rope over the standing end and through the loop at least twice. 2. Bring the running end out of the loop and over the standing end. Secure the running end as shown. 3. Tighten the wraps so they lie flat and close together.

having to retie the hitch. This means that when the rain or **snow** really falls and your tarp begins to sag, you can run out and tighten the guylines with a simple slide of the knot. What a convenience!

TELEMARK SKIING

See **ski touring**.

TENTS

Tents are iconic symbols of **wilderness** exploration. Images of tents in remote places, from the Arctic to the Himalaya, conjure up thoughts of adventure amid spectacular scenery. At the same time, tents are standard tools for any outdoor enthusiast who goes into the wilderness for more than a day at a time.

Tents come in a wide variety of shapes and sizes. Many are designed for car camping and therefore aren't really usable for backcountry **camping**, but this still leaves a large selection.

The main criteria for a wilderness tent are that it should be weatherproof, roomy, easy to pitch, compact to carry, and as light as possible. Unfortunately, these criteria conflict with one another, so compromises have to be made, depending on when and where the tent will be used. For above-timberline and **winter** mountain camping, wind and snow resistance is paramount, which means extra weight and bulk. However, for three-season **forest** and valley camping, with perhaps the occasional above-timberline camp in good weather, a less stable but much lighter tent is adequate. **Desert** camping usually demands maximum airflow for coolness.

Condensation

The prime function of a tent is to keep the weather off you. Unfortunately, keeping moisture in the form of **rain** and **snow** out of a tent will also keep moisture in the form of **condensation** in the tent. Condensation occurs when the air in the tent contains moisture vapor that can't escape. When this vapor hits cold tent walls, it condenses into liquid. Moisture vapor is given off by your body, by wet gear that is slowly drying, and by steam from **cooking**. To minimize condensation, cook outside and store wet gear in waterproof bags so moisture can't escape. There's nothing you can do about body moisture, also known as *invisible perspiration*.

Condensation is worst in humid conditions and on calm nights, because there's no air movement to take the moisture vapor away. It can also occur on breezy nights if you have all the tent doors and vents shut. In dry climates, it's much less of a problem than in damp ones. Go to the Olympic Peninsula in Washington state, and your tent may drip with condensation every night. Camp in the deserts of the southwestern United States, however, and the dry air will easily absorb moisture vapor and leave your tent dry. Unfortunately, it's in the wet places that tents are most necessary.

The best way to deal with condensation is to have as much airflow through a tent as possible. Because warm air, which holds the most moisture, rises, vents should be high up the tent wall so cool air can enter under the edge of the fly sheet and replace the moist air. A vent at each end of the tent is best because then air can flow through the tent whichever way the wind blows. Vents should have waterproof covers so rain can't get in and should either be made of mesh or have zipper-closed mesh panels so mosquitoes can't enter. On some tents, the top of the fly-sheet door can be unzipped for ventilation and may have a hood for protection. Vents may have to be closed in severe storms, but generally it's best to leave them open. The tent will be warmer if you shut them, but the condensation will be worse. It's better to rely on **clothing** and **sleeping bags** for warmth and allow cool air into the tent to remove moisture vapor. Of course if there's no **wind**, the vents won't be much use and you'll just have to be careful not to push against the wet tent walls and to mop up any drips that occur.

Tents come in double- and single-wall construction. The first type handles condensation by having an inner, breathable, nonwaterproof tent through which moisture vapor can easily pass, topped by a waterproof fly sheet on which the moisture can condense and then run down into the ground (see **breathability**). This works quite well as long as a separation is maintained between the two layers; if you push them together, it will transfer moisture from the fly sheet onto the inner tent. On clear nights when rain is unlikely, you can use just the inner tent, so that moisture vapor passes into the air. This system can break down in very cold weather when the inner tent becomes so cold that moisture condenses on it instead of passing through it. The condensation then usually freezes, leading to a shower of frost in the morning.

Single-skin tents may be made from waterproof-breathable fabrics, with the idea being that moisture vapor passes through the walls. This works in fairly cold, dry places, and such tents are popular with high-altitude mountaineers (see also **mountaineering**). In humid conditions, however, it's easy to overload the fabric so that condensation occurs. If the tent has a sewn-in groundcloth, as most do, the condensation has nowhere to go.

Some single-skin tents are really just fly sheets without inner tents. These are made from nonbreathable, waterproof fabrics, but because there's no floor, moisture can run into the ground. Condensation can still be a nuisance though.

Structure

Tents are made from a variety of materials. The quality of these in part determines both the performance and the life of a tent.

Fabrics

Tents are made from nylon or polyester. Often, when looking at tents, you'll see no perceptible difference between two models except the cost. However, the quality of the fabrics is probably the reason for the price difference. Basic polyurethane-coated nylon is the least expensive tent fabric and also the least durable. It isn't very resistant to ultraviolet (UV) light and will degrade quickly if left in the sun for long. Add UV treatment and the fabric will last much longer.

Polyester is more UV resistant than nylon and doesn't stretch when wet like nylon. Polyurethane coatings will eventually wear off both nylon and polyester.

Perhaps the best, and undoubtedly the most expensive, tent fabric is silicone-treated nylon. It's very strong, and the treatment won't wear off because it impregnates the material rather than just lying on the surface. Because it has a high-tear strength, silnylon, as it's called, can be used in very light weights, thus making it ideal for ultralight tents.

Ripstop nylon, in which a grid of extra-strong threads is woven into the fabric, is stronger and more tear resistant than plain nylon.

Inner tents are usually made from very thin, lightweight, unproofed nylon, sometimes with large mesh panels to allow better airflow. Mesh is fine in warm weather, but your tent will be warmer if you can cover it up with solid fabric in the cold. Some tents have zippered panels for this purpose.

Tent floors are made from polyurethane-coated nylon in a heavier weight than that used for fly sheets. Silnylon is too slippery for floors. Floors get harder usage than any other part of the tent and are easily damaged if care isn't taken. You can put a **groundcloth** under the floor to protect it, but that does add weight to your load. Some tent makers make groundcloths shaped to fit under their tents (known as *footprints*). If you use one of these, be sure the edges of the groundsheet don't stick out, or they could catch rain and create a puddle between the two layers. Fold any protruding part under rather than up, to make rain more likely to flow beneath the groundcloth.

Poles

Your choice in pole material is between aluminum alloy and fiberglass. The first is by far the stronger and is used in all good-quality tents. It's also much lighter. Flexible poles for hoop tents need to have shockcord running through them to keep the sections connected and make them manageable. Rigid poles, found in pyramid tents, may have shockcord too, but it isn't as essential.

Stakes

Often, the stakes that come with tents are chosen for lightness or compactness rather than function. Different stakes work best in different types of ground. For soft terrain, half-moon or angle stakes are best; pins and skewers are likely to pull out. In very soft sand or snow, long, wide half-moon stakes, known as *snow stakes*, may be needed. In hard ground, thin pins and skewers are best because they can be pushed in more easily.

Most stakes are made of aluminum alloy and weigh from 0.5 ounce to 2 ounces. If you want a much stronger and slightly lighter stake, purchase titanium ones. These are almost impossible to bend, making them excellent for really hard ground, and weigh as little as 0.25 ounce.

Because stakes are easy to mislay and they break occasionally, carrying a few spares is wise. This will add only a few ounces to your load.

Where tent stakes do become heavy is when your tent requires large numbers of them. At most, a backcountry tent should have 15 to 20 stake points. When purchasing a new tent, check that enough stakes have been provided. Sometimes the count can be a little short.

Guylines

Most tents have at least a couple of guylines for stability in strong winds; some have many more. Often the guylines aren't needed unless it's windy, but sometimes they're required to pull the tent into shape. Tents may have attachment points for extra guys too. If you'll be using the tent in windy places, attach these in advance.

Guylines can get into an awful tangle if packed away loose, so tie them back in bundles to avoid this. Of course, when hurriedly packing in the wet and cold, it's easy to ignore this chore. If you do, just hope that it won't still be stormy the next evening, because it's time-consuming, finger-numbing work trying to undo the mess.

Guylines are usually kept under tension when

staked out, with metal or plastic locking sliders. These are fine, but when adding or replacing guy-lines, you can use a **taut-line hitch** instead.

Seams

Seams are a potential leak point on any tent. On polyurethane-coated and waterproof-breathable tents, they should be taped. Silnylon can't be taped because it's too slippery. However, the impregnation of the fabric plus careful sewing means the seams shouldn't leak anyway.

If tape peels off seams or a silnylon seam does leak, the seam can be coated with seam sealant (there's a special one for silnylon). Do this when you have time to let the sealant dry before using the tent. In the wilderness, you could stick a piece of **duct tape** over the leaking seam or smear it with candle wax, margarine, or something else that will keep the water out (assuming you're not in bear country). (See also **seam sealing**.)

Designs

Tents come in a huge array of shapes and sizes. Which is best depends on your needs.

Ridge Tents

Traditional ridge tents, with an upright pole at each end, had just about disappeared for back-country travel until, oddly, they were rescued from oblivion by **trekking poles**, which make good tent poles. The new ridge tents are single-skin models that would be called *tarps* except for the fact that they have zipped doors. Although they may come with a groundsheet, this isn't permanently attached. The main advantage is the light weight: a two-person model can weigh under 2 pounds. They're pretty stable too, especially since the poles can be shortened to create a storm-shedding low profile. The big disadvantage is a lack of insect proofing, although mesh inner tents are available for some models.

Pyramid Tents

The pyramid or tepee tent is another design that is having a resurgence after virtually vanishing.

Stretched geodesic dome and pyramid tents are stable designs for winter and mountain camping.

These single-pole, single-skin tents are popular with snow campers because they can be dug into the snow since there's no floor to get in the way (see **snow camping**). Detachable groundcloths are available. Pyramid tents are very light for the space and have more headroom than any other portable design. A two- to three-person model you can almost stand up in can weigh as little as 3 pounds, including the pole. As with other tents without sewn-in groundcloths, however, pyramids aren't insect proof. But again, mesh inner tents with floors are available for some models, although they do add considerably to the weight.

Dome Tents

Dome tents are roomy and easy to pitch. They have flexible poles that cross each other and give the tent a firm structure so it can stand without being staked out. This is often touted as an advantage, but a freestanding tent can easily become a kite in a gust of wind, so on all but the most sheltered sites, staking a dome tent is advisable.

The simplest, lightest domes have two or three poles that cross at the apex. These are fine for sheltered sites, but the long unsupported sections of pole can deform in strong winds, pushing the sides of the tent inward. However, the most wind-resistant design is also a dome, the geodesic, in which three or four poles cross one another in several places to form a very strong geodesic structure. Four-pole geodesics are popular with high-altitude mountaineers because they will withstand heavy snowfall and very strong winds.

Dome tents are designed to hold two people and more. The design can't be made light enough for solo tents. Crossover pole domes start at around 5 pounds; geodesics, at 6 pounds for single-skin models and 8 or more pounds for double-skin ones. Three-pole semigeodesics are also available that weigh slightly less, 5.5 pounds and upward, but they have less space because they taper to the rear.

Tunnels

Tunnel tents give more room for the weight than any other double-skin design. They're also very easy to pitch, especially if the poles are all the same length. Usually, two stakes at each end will set a tunnel up. They aren't freestanding though, nor are they as stable as geodesic domes, although the best ones are far more stable than crossover pole domes. For maximum wind resistance, pitch tunnel tents with the rear into the wind because they can deform in side winds. Ones with the poles close together are more wind resistant than those with large, unsupported panels between the poles. Pitched properly, a good tunnel tent will withstand very strong winds.

Tunnels come in many weights and sizes. The lightest two-pole tunnels weigh 3 to 4 pounds and will sleep two people. Four-pole models that sleep four can weigh 12 pounds or more. The lightest tunnels usually slope to the rear and have poles of different lengths. The big ones tend to have same-length poles.

Single Hoop

Although tunnel tents can be made light enough for solo use, this usually involves a loss of headroom. The roomiest solo tents are single-hoop models, which have one long pole that may run across or along the tent. Single-hoop tents are quite roomy and surprisingly stable and can weigh as little as 3 pounds for one with enough room to sit up in and a large vestibule.

Other Designs

Flexible poles allow designers to come up with all sorts of hybrid tents. There are plenty of models that don't fit into neat categories. Some of these are simply bizarre, while others are functional.

Size and Weight

Tents range in size from tiny tunnels without room to sit up to massive domes in which you can walk around. Weight and space are of course related. The first of those tents is easily carried but might make you feel claustrophobic and certainly won't have room for storing gear, cooking, or doing anything much other than sleeping. The second would make a great base camp for a group, but no one would want to carry it anywhere in a **pack**.

Everyone needs enough room to lie down without pushing against the walls of the tent. After that, it's a personal matter. Some like a solo tent to have enough room to sit up in and enough porch space to store gear and cook safely. When sharing, enough headroom for each person and room for all the gear is ideal. Some people can make do with less space than this. Be wary of manufacturer claims. Some "two-person" tents assume you are both quite small and very friendly with each other!

Exoskeleton tunnel tents are useful in rain because you pitch the fly sheet first or the fly and tent as a unit, keeping the tent itself dry.

CHRIS TOWNSEND

Consider the length, width, and floor area. Around 30 square feet should be adequate for two people, as long as the tent is at least 55 inches wide at the widest point. Solo tents should have around 25 square feet of space and be about 36 inches wide. Length should be at least 7 feet in both cases, more if you're over 6 feet tall. If you want to sit up, you need a tent taller than the distance between the floor and the top of your head when you sit cross-legged. You can't judge this by how tall you are, because it depends on your back length, not your overall height.

The size of the porch matters too. In **bear** country, where you won't be cooking in your porch, having a porch big enough to cook in is probably a waste of weight. Elsewhere, it's worth having, especially in bad weather or for winter camping. Otherwise, being able to store your gear in the porch and still get in and out of the tent is worthwhile. For twosomes, two porches are worth having, so each person has a separate entrance or so you can store gear and cook at one end and go in and out the other.

In winter, consider larger tents. You'll spend much more time inside and will probably do some cooking in the porch. Winter sleeping bags and clothing are bulkier than summer items too.

Tent weights vary greatly even among models of the same size and design. Heavier fabrics and extra features can make a big difference. When looking at weights, check what information the manufacturer includes. Some give minimum weights that include tent and poles but not stakes and stuff sacks, and maximum weights covering everything that comes with the tent, including tubes of seam sealant and instruction booklets. The weight carried won't be either of these but is likely to be nearer the maximum.

Inner or Outer Pitching

Most tents pitch in the traditional manner, in which you erect the tent and then throw the fly sheet over the top. Some, however, pitch the other way around. You erect the fly sheet and then hang the inner inside. These tents also may

go up as a unit, although you should always be able to separate inner and outer for drying. Because the poles on a tent that pitches fly sheet first are on the outside, these tents are sometimes known as *exoskeleton tents*. Advantages are that, in rain, the inner tent won't get wet as it's being set up, and you have a shelter very quickly. You can even use the fly sheet alone to save weight. When taking the tent down in wet conditions, you can pack everything except fly, poles, and stakes before going outside. The disadvantages are that getting a taut set to the inner tent can be difficult, and it can be hard or even impossible to pitch the inner tent on its own.

For wet areas, exoskeleton tents are a good idea. For dry areas, a tent that pitches inner first might be better.

Pitching the Tent

There are many ways of pitching a tent, depending on the design, but a few points hold true for all types. First, make sure there is nothing sharp on the site that could tear the groundcloth. Pitch the tent so that the door is facing away from the wind, if any, or else toward the east, so the rising sun will shine in at dawn. Stake out the tent tautly, with few wrinkles, because these can rattle in a wind. Tighten all guylines.

Most tents can be pitched in just a few minutes as long as the stakes go easily into the ground. On rocky or very hard ground, however, this may not be the case. If the stakes really won't go in, attach lengths of cord to the stake points and tie these around rocks, logs, or trees. Sometimes just attaching a loop of cord to the stake point so you have more options on where to place the stake is enough.

Wind can make pitching a tent much more difficult. You need to ensure that nothing blows away, so put stuff sacks in your pack or in a pocket and don't let go of the tent until you've staked down the rear facing into the wind. Then get the poles in place before raising the tent. Stake it out quickly to stop it thrashing in the wind, which can cause damage.

Taking the tent down is the last thing you should do before leaving a camp. This allows any condensation time to dry.

Care

Tents are most likely to be damaged by sharp objects, so be careful with anything like **knives** or **ice axes** around tents. Don't track in sharp twigs or rocks, and keep tent floors as clean as possible. Hiking footwear should never come into the tent: leave it in the porch. If debris does accumulate inside, shake the tent out before packing it. If you tear a tent, a piece of sticky-backed nylon tape or duct tape will patch it (see **repairs**).

Dry the tent before packing it. If you can't, take it out of your pack and air it during the day, if the weather permits. When packing a tent, simply stuff it into the stuff sack. There's no need to fold or roll it; doing so usually just makes it harder to shove into the stuff sack.

When your trip is over, the tent should be dry before you store it to prevent mildew. Even if the tent seems dry, airing it before storing is still a good idea. Dry the poles and stakes to discourage corrosion.

Otherwise, tents require little care. Eventually, with polyurethane-coated tents, the outer water repellency will wear off and the fly sheet will start to absorb moisture. This doesn't mean it's leaking, but it does increase moisture weight and drying time. There are various sprays that will restore the water repellency. This isn't a problem with silnylon.

Eventually, with waterproof tents, the waterproof coating will wear out and the tent will leak. You can't repair this, so it's time for a new tent.

THIN ICE

See **ice**.

THROW BAGS

A capsize in moving water can happen in an instant (see **moving-water hazards**). One moment, you're performing an **eddy** turn, and the next moment the canoe has flipped and you're bobbing downriver, struggling to get into the defensive swimming position and gasping for breath. If the river is gentle, you can easily swim to shore. If, however, the river is more demanding, having somebody toss you a throw bag will help you get to shore as soon as possible. Throw bags (sometimes called *rescue bags*) are small nylon bags stuffed with 30 to 70 feet of buoyant **rope**. The rope is attached at one end to the inside of the throw bag, then stacked inside the bag for easy deployment as the bag is thrown (see **coiling a rope**). The rescuer holds the free end of the rope in one hand and with the other arm throws the bag to the person in the water. Used correctly, the throw bag is a fast, accurate, and effective way to reach a person in the water.

Any river rat can tell you a hundred stories about throw bags ending up in trees, in power lines, and in the rocks lining the riverbank. To botch a throw in a crisis situation is the worst nightmare of any shoreline rescuer. The panic in the eyes of the swimmer says it all: "You missed?!" Hitting your target on the first throw takes a lot of practice. And practice you must. A reliable throw is a prerequisite for any moving-water adventure.

The three basic throws are the underhand, side arm, and overhand. Each throw has its own merits. As you practice, you'll discover which works best for you. Before you throw the bag, ensure you have an adequate amount of line in your nonthrowing hand. When the swimmer grabs the rope, you'll feel a significant pull. If you have only a few inches to hold on to, the end of the rope might slide through your fingers. Avoid throwing the bag upstream or downstream of the swimmer, who may not be able to grab the rope. Rather, throw the bag *beyond* the swimmer so the rope falls directly in front of her face or on her head. Shout her name and "Rope!" as you throw the line.

Once the swimmer grabs the line, she will begin to pendulum in toward shore, so pick a rescue location that has a benign shoreline or an eddy downstream of your position. Prepare yourself for the weight of the swimmer by getting into

Tossing a throw bag accurately at a moving target is a skill well worth practicing, as these paddlers are doing in turn. It's not as easy as it looks!

ANNIE AGGENS

a strong stance with a low center of gravity. Look for footing that can withstand a good deal of shock. If necessary, have another person help hold the line or act as ballast. **Belaying** the rope (with the line running behind the rescuer's back) adds stability, but be careful not to be pulled into the water. A tree can also be used if the strength of a belay is required.

Wilderness trips demand significant caution. In particular, whitewater emergencies require a fast, precise response. Always be prepared to use your throw bag. The throw bag should be accessible, and everyone on the trip should know how to use it. If you're scouting a set of rapids that could result in an upset, consider **lining** or **portaging** (see **scouting rapids**). If you decide to shoot the rapids, make a plan for what to do if you should dump or become **swamped**. Where should the people with the throw bags stand? What happens if they miss their throws? Where should the person in the water swim? What is the run-out like?

Like any other rope, carefully maintaining your throw bag will increase its longevity. Keep it out of direct sunlight, and clean dirt and sand from it after every use. Store the line dry and free from any knots. If you plan on paddling in remote areas, knowing how to prevent and respond to moving-water emergencies is critical. Consider taking a course in swift water rescue prior to your

departure. Courses are regularly offered by organizations such as the American Canoe Association (see resources section). You can also read more about river-rescue techniques in *The Whitewater Rescue Manual*, by Charles Walbridge and Wayne Sundmacher, or *River Rescue*, by Les Bechdel and Slim Ray.

THROWING A CLIMBING ROPE

Throwing a **rock climbing** rope down a rock face so it ends up where you want it (and not in a tree or jammed in a crack) is not always easy. **Wind**, wet or icy **ropes**, and obstacles in your path can make even the simplest toss difficult. In addition, when a good throw really counts, such as during a rapid descent from a mountain, you may not get a second chance.

Climbing ropes generally need to be thrown on two occasions: at top-roping sites and at **rappelling** sites. The first step in either scenario is to build a solid **anchor** and clip the center of your rope to the anchor using a **carabiner**. If the center of the rope is not marked, you can easily find it by stacking the rope. Stacking the rope will also ensure that it is free of knots or kinks. Throwing a climbing rope as one big bundle will usually result in a mess. Separate the rope into two sections: the section of rope nearest the anchor, and the section of rope containing the two loose ends. Begin by coiling the portion of the rope closest to the anchor. You want to coil about 40 feet in a loose butterfly coil (see **coiling a rope**). Once you have completed the first coil, set it aside and begin the second coil. There should be several feet of rope between the two coils.

To throw the rope, pick up the first coil (the one closest to the anchor), shout "Rope!" and, using a forceful side-arm throw, toss the coil over the cliff. This should be the middle portion of the rope. Now pick up the second coil, and throw it over in the same fashion. The weight of the second coil will help pull the rope straight. If you have an extra person near the anchor, have her hold the rope so it doesn't slide through the carabiner (which holds it to the anchor). You can also

AMY DUCHELLE

Throwing a climbing rope correctly on the first try takes practice. Climbers often split the rope into two coiled piles that are thrown separately. The weight of the second thrown coil helps straighten out the rope. This climber has just thrown the first coil; the second coil is in her right hand.

secure the rope to the biner with a **clove hitch**. **Throw bags** designed specifically for climbing ropes eliminate the need to throw coils. Instead, the bag can simply be tossed over the side and the rope will feed out as the bag descends.

Whichever method you use to throw your rope, be sure to yell "Rope!" as loud as you can before your toss. This warns anyone below that a cascade of rope will be descending. A piece of rope thrown from a height of 60 or 70 feet can do some damage. In addition, throwing a rope down a rock face can dislodge unsettled rocks and other debris. Anyone below will be glad for the warning. Yell "Rope!" even if you suspect nobody is beneath you.

To ensure that you can throw a rope effectively, practice throwing and retrieving ropes in a variety of situations.

THRU-HIKING

Strictly speaking, thru-hiking means **hiking** a **trail** or route from one end to the other in one continuous trip. However, the term can also be used for hiking part of a trail and then returning and thru-hiking the remainder sometime later. Since there's no absolute definition of thru-hiking, you make your own rules. You don't have to stick to the official route, if there is one, although some people may tell you so. Some hikers hike a long-distance trail in one season but do it in sections, sometimes changing direction, so they may start off heading north but finish heading south. This is known as *flip-flopping*. How you do your thru-hike is up to you.

> "I was once told that my walk along a trail 'didn't count' because I was leaving it temporarily to visit an interesting historic site close by. Another hiker was told his hike wasn't valid because he was going in the opposite direction than that described in the standard trail guide!"—CT

The great joy of thru-hiking is the experience of being on the trail and living in the **wilderness** for weeks and months at a time. Reaching the end of the trail is, of course, a reason to celebrate, but it's what happens along the way that matters.

See also **long-distance hiking** and **long-distance trails**.

TICKS

There aren't many things people dislike about the **wilderness**, but ticks often make it onto that short list. Ticks are arachnids—they're in the same family as **spiders and scorpions**, mites, and other eight-legged arthropods. As parasites, they cling to "host" animals, which supply them with warm blood for food and reproduction. Usually, the host animal is a rodent, small mammal, or reptile, but humans can be hosts as well.

By clinging to tall grasses and brush with their hind legs, ticks are able to seize passing animals with their front legs. Once on the animal, the tick draws blood by taking a small bite from the host's flesh and inserting a barbed anchor that keeps it strongly attached. The bite is usually undetected by the host, and the tick can continue to draw blood until the feeding process is complete, usually within 24 to 48 hours. At this point, the tick, which has become considerably engorged with blood, will detach itself from the host, fall to the ground, molt, and repeat the process. A female tick, if she has mated, will drop to the ground after feeding and lay many eggs.

Because ticks travel from one host to another, they can acquire and transmit diseases. The most well-known disease is Lyme disease, but the wilderness traveler should also be aware of babesiosis, ehrlichosis, and Rocky Mountain spotted fever. If detected early, all of these are easy to treat with antibiotics. Lyme disease, babesiosis, ehrlichosis, and Rocky Mountain spotted fever share many flulike symptoms: joint and muscle pain, headache, fatigue, fever, and occasionally gastrointestinal discomfort. Rashes often precede or accompany these symptoms, but not always. The rash from Lyme disease is red and often looks like a bull's-eye. The rash caused by Rocky Mountain spotted fever is, not surprisingly, spotty and can appear after other initial symptoms. If you develop symptoms after you have been exposed to ticks, see your doctor for a test. While treating these infections is relatively easy, delayed diagnosis makes treatment more difficult. This is especially true for Rocky Mountain spotted fever, which often requires hospitalization and can be fatal if untreated.

Despite their names, Rocky Mountain spotted fever and Lyme disease (named after Lyme, Connecticut, the site of the first major outbreak) can be found across the United States and around the world. Cases of Rocky Mountain spotted fever, for example, rarely occur in the Rocky Mountains (in

fact, over half the cases are reported in the southern Atlantic states). Because you can be exposed to ticks just about anywhere, prevention is key. Follow these general guidelines to help protect yourself from a tick-borne disease.

- Limit your exposure to ticks by wearing long pants tucked into your socks anytime you're in tick territory.
- Wear light-colored clothing so you can better see ticks crawling on your clothes.
- Examine yourself often for ticks. Pay close attention to your head and groin, which are often overlooked. Keep in mind that some ticks, like the deer tick, can be as small as a pinhead.
- Brush off gear before you bring it into your **tent**.
- Check children and pets thoroughly and regularly.
- Use repellents as desired for additional protection.

Repellents have been proven to deter, and even kill, ticks. Products containing **DEET** or permethrin are most commonly used. Both of these products are potent chemicals, and users should read the directions carefully and take adequate precautions, especially with children. Many wilderness travelers feel the chemicals in most repellents are too toxic to use on their clothing, let alone their skin.

If you discover a tick on your body, remove it carefully. Use tweezers to pull the tick out of your skin by its mouth, *not* its body. The mouth is the part of the tick closest to your skin. Squeezing the tick's body may inject you with toxins. When removing the tick, pull up and outward with steady pressure. Try not to twist or crush the tick because this may leave parts of the tick's body in your flesh. If you're concerned that the tick is infected and you want to find out for sure, save the tick in a plastic bag for future diagnosis.

A vaccine against Lyme disease is available to people who are at high risk of becoming infected. Given in three doses over the course of a year, the vaccine has proven effective, although its longevity has not been determined, and the need for booster shots is likely. The vaccine is recommended for individuals between ages 15 and 70 who have frequent or prolonged exposure to tick-infested habitats. The vaccine is not recommended for children under age 15, pregnant women, or individuals with little or no risk of becoming infected.

A wealth of information about ticks and tick-borne diseases can be found on the Internet and in medical newsletters. Visit the Centers for Disease Control and Prevention website for updated information (see resources section).

TIDES

As part of your plans to travel on coastal waters or along coastal beaches, get information on the local tides. Depending on your location, tides can significantly alter your course or can go undetected. On portions of Hudson Bay, where the difference between low and high tide can be 12 feet, the water retreats a whopping 5 miles from shore (that's well out of sight). You may go to bed with water lapping a few feet away and wake up to find that the ocean has drained, literally! Then again, you may be at a location where the tide is imperceptible. For example, paddling the island of Crete in the Libyan Sea, or off portions of Belize, it is hard to discern whether the tide is high or low.

Knowing the tidal schedule of your area is extremely important. Let's say you're **backpacking** along the coast and you decide to set up camp on the beach. Understanding the local tides could prevent you from waking to cold water seeping into your tent. If you're a paddler, you should know that high tide is notorious for stealing equipment that is not tied to shore or stowed on high ground. Kayaks literally float away, along with paddles, food sacks, and everything else. In addition to stowing your gear correctly, make sure the landings you plan aren't underwater during high tide. Likewise, if there is a large tidal range, plan your arrival at camp during high tide.

There's nothing worse than having to drag your heavy kayak several hundred feet through the muck of a tidal flat. Paddling on tides often means timing your departure precisely to take advantage of incoming or outgoing tides.

Tides can be calculated because they conveniently run on a schedule of sorts. Each day, the tidal cycle occurs 50 minutes later than the day before. For example, if high tide was at 10 A.M. today, it will occur at 10:50 A.M. tomorrow. In addition, when there are two tidal cycles in a day, as is the case in most parts of the world, the tides will be approximately 6 hours and 15 minutes apart. In other words, if the first high tide is at 12 A.M., low tide will be at 6:15 A.M. and high tide will return again at 12:30 P.M. In areas that have only one daily tidal cycle (less common), the tides will be 12 hours and 30 minutes apart. In this case, high tide will be at 12 A.M. and low tide will be at 12:30 P.M.

> "I once encountered a group of paddlers wading in the flats of Hudson Bay looking for three of their food bags. They had portaged their gear out onto the extensive flats with the intention of meeting the incoming tide (this is sometimes necessary to save time). Unfortunately, when they had returned to their camp for another load, the tide quickly crept in and snatched up their gear. What a nightmare!"—AA

If the moon is full or new, expect the tidal range to be greater than normal (potentially as much as a few feet). This is called a *spring tide*. When the moon only shows half, expect the range to be less than normal. This is called *neap tide*. If the date is near June 21 or December 21, the solstices, the spring tide will be at its greatest. If the date is near March 21 or September 21, the equinoxes, expect the neap tide to be at its greatest.

To avoid getting tricked by the tide, do your research ahead of time but be ready for variations

Portaging on tidal flats is mucky and undesirable work. It can be prevented by researching the local tidal schedule. The tidal range on the Hudson Bay is so great that these paddlers portaged to meet the incoming tide in order to maximize their paddling hours.

in your predictions. A strong **wind** or significant change in the barometric pressure can unexpectedly increase the tidal range. When you're **camping** along the shore, find the high-water mark (usually a line of kelp and other ocean debris) and camp several feet above this point. Stow your important gear (such as your kayak or backpack) higher than your tent. This way, if the tide rises higher than predicted, you'll awaken in time to salvage your gear. Remember, if the land is flat, the incoming and outgoing tides will move quickly. To avoid trouble, never let down your guard, especially in areas with a large tidal range.

If you're traveling off the beaten path, you'll need to calculate the tidal schedule for your specific location. This can be accomplished by locating the nearest port, or station, whose tides are predicted by an organization such as NOAA (National Oceanic and Atmospheric Administration) and deducing your distance from that location. There is an excellent description of how to use tide tables in David Burch's *Fundamentals of Sea Kayak Navigation*. In addition, you can find a lot of helpful information on the Internet regarding tide tables and tidal currents (see resources section). If you lose your tidal information, or if it appears to be wrong, it may be worth hanging out for a day to make your own observations.

See also **coastal currents**.

TITANIUM

Found all over the earth, titanium is the fourth most common metal. Processing it is a complex and expensive process, however, so titanium products are quite costly. Its big advantage is that it's very strong for its weight, so it can be used for ultralight products. In the outdoors industry, it's used for a wide range of gear, including **ice axes**, ice screws, **tent** stakes, camp **stoves**, and **cooking** pots. Titanium dioxide is used in sunblock and as a coating for tent fly sheets because it resists ultraviolet light well (see also **sun protection**).

TOILET PAPER

Despite common belief, toilet paper is not a necessity in the **wilderness**. There are plenty of natural alternatives to toilet paper that do the job just fine. Nor does taking a roll of toilet paper on the trail mean it will be available when you need it. Rolls of toilet paper more often than not end up as big loaves of white pudding due to moisture exposure. Furthermore, bringing toilet paper means you have to pack it out. For some people, that fact alone is enough to persuade them to "go natural."

When selecting natural toilet paper, look for items that are soft and free of sap or other sticky drippings. A working knowledge of **poisonous plants** is essential. Don't limit yourself to just leaves. There are abundant alternatives that may be just the right size, shape, or consistency for your needs. While unlikely in appearance, rounded rocks and thick twigs can come in handy. This is especially true if you are above treeline or in the **tundra**, where leafy green plant life is minimal. In the winter, you can wipe with a big wad of snow—while some people would rather have a root canal, others swear by this method.

Whatever your preference, make sure you do the job completely without wiping yourself raw. Rashes from poor hygiene (often referred to as *butt fire*) can be uncomfortable or downright painful. It is an especially horrible affliction to have on a **hiking** or skiing trip. A little ointment and better selection of wiping material can usually cure this problem in a day. (See also **sanitation**.)

TOP ROPING

Top roping is a type of **rock climbing** that originated when climbers had access to the top of a climb but not to its base. To access the pitch, the climbers would set up an anchor at the top of the climb, rappel to its base, and then climb back up. Nowadays, top roping generally refers to any climb whose anchor you are able to place by **hiking** to the top of the climb instead of leading the pitch. Top-roping sites are easy to identify because the rope will most likely run from the climber on the rock up to the anchor system and then back down to the belayer. Top roping is great for beginners or people working difficult routes because it lessens the likelihood of a significant fall. Because it feels secure and therefore allows people to build their confidence, top roping is often a stepping-stone to more advanced climbing techniques, such as leading.

Locating a good top-roping site is easy at popular climbing hangouts but can be more difficult in the backcountry. When choosing a site, look for an anchor that is relatively easy to access. In addition, avoid sites that have a lot of loose debris, such as rocks and boulders, near the top. Remember, you will likely have limited equipment, so pick a spot that allows you to build a **bomber** anchor with the protection that you have. Rig the anchor so it equally displaces the weight of the climber on at least three solid pieces of protection. Remember, everything about your anchor should be redundant (see **anchors**). Once you have the anchor built, attach your rope at its midpoint and prepare to throw it to the base (see **throwing a climbing rope**). When the rope is hung, rappel down the climb and clear it of any loose rocks or other debris that could become dislodged while climbing (see **rappelling**). Make sure nobody is below you while you are doing this.

As with any rock climbing activity, ensure that all systems are go before you leave the ground.

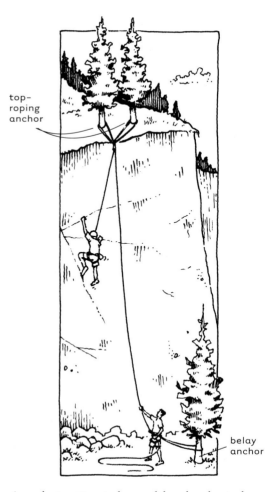

A good top-roping site has a solid anchor that is close to the climbing pitch, a safe area below the pitch for the belayer, and, if necessary, an object that can be used as a belay anchor (see belaying).

Are your knots tied correctly? Are they dressed (see **knots**)? Is your harness securely fastened? Is the buckle double backed? Is your helmet secured? Are your **carabiners** locked? In addition, establish a clear communication system with your climbing partner (see **climbing communication**).

Top roping is a great way to learn the basics of climbing. If you're looking to get into the sport, study under an experienced friend or **guide**. There are also a number of **outdoor schools** that have rock climbing courses geared toward beginning or intermediate climbers.

TORSO ROTATION

No matter what type of paddling you enjoy, you'll be able to perform your best if you learn to tap into the strength of your torso instead of simply relying on your arms. The muscle groups in your torso are much larger than those in your arms and can therefore be used as the driving force behind your paddle strokes. Confused? Think about how a major-league baseball pitcher throws the ball. Does he use only his arm? No, because he needs much more power than he can generate with his arm alone. Instead, he winds up his torso, squaring his shoulders to third base, and then propels the ball forward with a powerful unwinding of his torso. The same thing happens in paddling.

> "To be honest, the first time I tried torso rotation I felt a little like a robot in a boat. But I stuck with the regimen, and the payoff was huge. Soon I was whipping myself in and out of eddies and getting the power I needed when it really counted."—AA

When you first learn to paddle using the various muscles in your torso, you may feel awkward and tempted to revert to your old, trusted methods. To practice using your torso muscles while paddling, try to keep your arms relatively straight, but not locked. Imagine that you have a big barrel between your chest and the paddle. This makes it necessary to rotate your whole body to execute a stroke. Eventually, it will become second nature to use your torso as the driving force behind your strokes, and you'll feel the difference with every dip of your paddle.

TOWING

On a paddling trip, exhaustion, injury, illness, fear, or even a broken paddle could make someone lose their ability to paddle adequately. Whatever the reason, the disabled paddler may require a tow to get to shore. This is primarily true with single kayaks, which, unlike canoes or tandem

When a kayaker can no longer paddle, a tow may be necessary. In this single tow, a third kayaker is stabilizing the incapacitated paddler.

kayaks, don't have the benefit of two paddlers. Towing a person is easy in calm conditions, but when circumstances deteriorate, the tow becomes more challenging. **Wind, waves,** and other **open-water hazards** can conspire to make towing a difficult and sometimes dangerous task.

There are several ways to tow a kayak. The quickest is to have the incapacitated paddler hold onto your kayak as you paddle to shore. Known as a *contact tow*, this process is good only for short distances on flat water. Another type of tow is the single-kayak tow. To set up the single-kayak tow the rescuer attaches her tow line to the bow of the kayak to be towed, and then continues paddling. This one-person tow is simple to set up but can quickly become tiresome. The pace of the tower will be reduced to half speed at best.

"Once, while sea kayaking on Lake Superior, my paddling partner became incapacitated with seasickness. After vomiting over the side of the kayak, he was overcome with weakness and was unable to continue paddling. The wind was blowing steady at 15 knots out of the north, and the swells were increasing. Luckily, we were only three-quarters of a mile from camp. I attached my towrope to the bow of his kayak and towed him to camp, where he soon recovered."—AA

If there are multiple kayaks in the party, two or more can work together to tow the same boat. In this scenario, they can either perform an in-line tow or a fan tow. The in-line tow positions all the kayaks in a line with at least 20 feet between each kayak. The first paddler tows the second paddler, who tows the third, and so forth. The last kayak to be towed is the disabled kayak. This system distributes the load over several paddlers. While an in-line tow keeps all of the boats well spaced, communication can be a problem. The fan system has several kayaks lined up horizontally, all towing the same boat. This is similar to the fan hitch used in arctic **dogsledding**. The fan tow works well in calm conditions, but the paddlers have to concentrate on keeping themselves spread out. It's common for the towers to run into one another or bump paddles.

ANNIE AGGENS

If you don't have a tow rig attached to your kayak, you can use a tow belt, which can be deployed quickly. The quick-release buckle allows you to release the belt in an instant if necessary.

In order to tow a kayak, you must have a towrope. Paddlers with fully outfitted kayaks will have a towrope attached to the rear deck of their kayaks. The rope is positioned so that it can be deployed from the cockpit without difficulty. Another type of towrope is coiled into a pouch and can be worn as a belt. A tow belt (a belt that contains a towrope) is convenient because you can take it with you from one boat to another, and you can easily deploy it. The tow belt is designed with a quick-release buckle that allows an easy escape from the belt should the rope itself become a danger. At no time should you ever tie yourself directly to a towrope. You should always be able to escape the towing system. Towing may sound simple, but it requires practice. You'll appreciate your advanced preparation the first time you have to tow someone in rough conditions.

TRAIL ETIQUETTE

Most backcountry campers would agree that an ethical code accompanies traveling in the **wilderness**. For instance, a responsible hiker will not discard snack wrappers onto the trail or blast loud songs from a radio. Proper trail etiquette helps protect the natural and aesthetic value of the wilderness. To ensure that you display appropriate trail etiquette, practice the following techniques (see also **Leave No Trace**).

- Aspire to be invisible on the trail by traveling quietly and leaving no trace of your path. Always pack out your trash, no matter how minimal (or seemingly biodegradable).
- Hike on trails whenever possible. In a group, travel in a single-file line to prevent widening the trail.
- If the trail goes through a puddle or patch of mud, walk right through it. Avoid walking around it, because this will create an ever-widening path.
- Where no trail exists, spread out and walk a few feet abreast so as not to create a new trail.

- Take breaks off the trail on durable surfaces. Taking a break on the trail blocks the way for others.
- If you encounter other people on the trail, step aside to let them pass. Allow faster hikers to get by.
- Never go to the bathroom on a trail. Instead, move off the trail and out of sight.
- Don't make a lot of noise. Traveling quietly allows others to enjoy the natural surroundings.
- Don't cut the corners on **switchbacks**. This creates damaging erosion.
- Step off the trail well before horsepackers or pack animals approach you. If you're on a slope, step on the downhill side of the trail. Talk softly among your group or to the horsepackers to let the horses know that you aren't a threat. (See also **horsepacking**.)

As anywhere else, common sense and common courtesy goes a long way in the wilderness. By practicing trail etiquette you help ensure good-natured relationships among all backcountry users.

TRAIL MAGIC

> "I've met friendly, encouraging, and helpful people everywhere from arctic Sweden to the Arizona desert."—CT

Proper trail etiquette includes traveling in single file while on the trail and avoiding shortcuts. Be alert for fast-moving mountain bikers and horsepackers.

Trail magic occurs when you're thirsty and you meet someone who offers you **water**, when you arrive in a town and a stranger offers you accommodation, or when you reach a road crossing and you're offered a ride to a supply point. It's a heartening experience that gives you a warm feeling and a positive view of humanity that is inspiring and uplifting. Trail magic is particularly associated with the **Appalachian Trail**, where it's well established in many places, but it can occur anywhere. Indeed, there's a danger of hikers taking it for granted. The age-old belief that one should help travelers—a belief that in the past became a requirement, a duty even, with some people—still seems alive and well when you go on foot.

TRAIL MARKERS

Trail markers are found the world over, often indicating the start of **trails**. They can range from somewhat obtrusive metal poles with brightly painted signs showing the direction and distance to trail junctions, backcountry huts, and trailheads, to more discreet wooden signs with just an arrow or a name on them that blend in with the tree to which they are attached. In many areas, such trail markers are being phased out as not in accord with wilderness values. Old wooden ones are often left to collapse and slowly decay. These old signs are not to be relied on, of course, but even new ones can be misleading. If you don't want to make a mistake, it's better to check your map at junctions, however new and confident the signs may look.

> "Following a well-signed section of the Arizona Trail in the Superstition Mountains, I missed a trail junction and had to backtrack. I assumed it wasn't signed, but when I found the junction there was a neat new sign on a tree pointing the wrong way. I'd probably glanced at this in passing and not noticed the junction at all. Luckily, the sign was screwed onto the tree, and I was able to realign it so it pointed the correct way."—CT

Trails are often marked with blazes or other waymarks. A common blaze is an ax cut in a tree, often in the form of a T or a slash with a dot above. Old blazes can sometimes be difficult to distinguish from scars and other marks in the tree. Named trails may have specific blazes that distinguish them from other trails. The most famous of these is the white diamond of the **Appalachian Trail**, which is attached to trees and posts along the route. In areas where there are no trees, piles of stones known as *cairns* or *ducks* are used to mark trails. In some countries, paint splashes

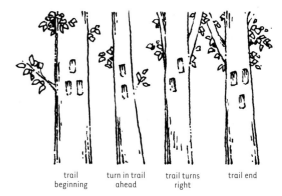

trail beginning   turn in trail ahead   trail turns right   trail end

Trail marker "language" is generally intuitive. A single blaze indicates the trail continues straight ahead.

mark routes. In the Alps, different combinations of red, yellow, and white stripes are used to mark different long-distance trails.

While blazes and waymarks aid navigation, they also can detract from a feeling of wilderness. For that reason, new permanent markings should not be made. If you must mark a route so you can find your way back, do so in a way that can be removed afterward. Arrows drawn in the dust or made with stones or twigs and small cairns can easily be erased or dismantled, unlike paint spots or ax cuts. Keep in mind, however, that in climates like the **desert**, the **wind** will cover most discrete markings within a few hours—unless the cairn is substantial.

TRAIL RUNNING

For some **wilderness** travelers, **hiking** just isn't fast enough. Instead, they like to run. Trail running covers everything from short, gentle runs along local **trails** to multiday endeavors.

If you like being part of a big event, you can participate in one of the many organized running events, ranging from short runs of a few hours to weekend events covering 100 miles or more. The best and most competitive runners set out to win, but for most entrants, just finishing is enough. Highly structured and safety conscious, organized events feature medical checks, marked routes, food and drink points, and more.

Many runners never take part in such events,

however. The longest runs of all, such as running the length of the **Grand Canyon** or a **long-distance trail** like the **Appalachian Trail**, tend to be solo affairs, although runners usually have a support team to meet them with food and supplies and perhaps to act as pace setters, navigators, and gear carriers. Such multiday runs require great stamina and determination.

The majority of trail runners do it primarily to keep fit for **backpacking** and **mountaineering** trips. They go out for regular runs on local trails, runs that can be as long as they like and at whatever pace they fancy.

The growing popularity of trail running has led to the development of a range of ultralight equipment. Runners heading into the wilderness still need to carry some gear, but the less it weighs, the easier the run. You can't run in **boots**, of course, at least not easily or comfortably, so trail runners use lightweight running shoes with good cushioning and grip. Rather than a full **pack**, runners often carry **fanny packs**, which bounce and impede motion less—although there are ultralight packs designed for longer runs that require more equipment, such as **camping** gear (see also **ultralight hiking**). **Dehydration** is a real threat to runners, so hydration systems with drinking hoses (that allow you to drink as you run) are popular. **Clothing** should be of fabric that is fast wicking and thin, designed to shed sweat and keep you dry rather than provide insulation. Warmer items are needed on longer runs and in cold weather. There is even an ultralight aluminum **crampon** designed to fit trail running shoes. Running snowshoes are available too.

For more information on trail running in the United States, contact the All American Trail Running Association (see resources section).

TRAILS

Standing at a trailhead looking down the thin brown line of the trail snaking off into the backcountry is an exciting, magical moment—the start of a journey into the **wilderness**, into the unknown. Trails lace wilderness and backcountry worldwide, serving as footpaths into nature for those willing to go and look.

Trails that are well located and well constructed can withstand much traffic. However, many trails are not that well designed or built and are easily damaged. This is often because originally they were game trails, old mining or wagon roads, or even mere lines that hikers took that turned into trails.

The ideal trail is only wide enough for one person, so hikers should walk single file. If you walk side by side, you break down the edges, widening the trail, damaging vegetation, and leading to erosion and unsightly scars. Multiple trails through meadows and soft ground mar many places. The original trail sinks slowly under the pressure of feet, horses' hooves, and sometimes **mountain bike** tires, and water begins to gather in places, forming puddles and muddy sections. Hikers go around these, widening the trail and allowing the water to spread. Over time, the trail becomes a wide, muddy morass, with bypass trails curving out to the sides as hikers try to keep their feet dry. The solution is to think of the trail rather than your feet and to stick to the main line even if it does mean muddy **boots** and possibly damp feet. Where the old trail is impossible to find in deep, churned-up mud, stay on the already damaged ground without spreading out at the sides. If you really want to keep your feet dry, wear **gaiters** or waterproof **socks**. Try to avoid wet trails in spring, when snowmelt makes them very soft and vulnerable to damage.

Switchbacks make trails easier to ascend and less likely to break down from erosion. A carefully graded trail can be a joy to climb and is much easier on the knees when descending than a steep one is. Hikers sometimes choose a direct line and cut the corners of switchbacks, which damages vegetation. Eventually the soil breaks down and ruts appear, down which water runs, soon turning them into wide scars. When you encounter shortcuts, help by blocking them off with logs, brush, or rocks so that others don't use them and the land has a chance to heal.

When you meet other hikers, stand aside to let them pass rather than edging past them on the trail, widening it and breaking down the margins. With horses, move well off the trail so you don't alarm them. Wait on the downhill side of the trail, if possible.

Take your rest stops off the trail at a distance that won't impede other hikers; never sit on the trail. Sit on flat rocks if possible so you won't damage any vegetation. Bare areas of sand or stones are OK too. If you do have to sit on plants, choose dry, hardy ones, such as grass, rather than soft, easily bruised ones.

Trail maintenance is costly, and few agencies have adequate money for it, so it's often done by volunteers if it's done at all. While hiking, the only way you can do anything for badly eroded trails in need of maintenance is to go elsewhere, which is easier said than done when you encounter one halfway through a hike. Good planning in advance can help here. Trail guides often tell you which trails are at risk or deteriorating, and ranger stations can provide up-to-date information on the state of trails.

See also **Leave No Trace**.

TRANSPORTATION

When planning a backcountry trip, consider transportation to and from your destination or point of departure. If your route is a simple loop, you can drive to the location and leave your car at the trailhead. This assumes that the trailhead has parking, which isn't always the case. If your route is more elaborate, you need to plan a drop-off and a pickup, or a shuttle. If a friend or family member can do this for you, consider yourself lucky. If not, you may have to hire someone for the job. In well-traveled areas there likely are companies that provide shuttle services. If your route is short, the shuttle service might meet you at the end of the route (where you leave your car) and then drive you to the beginning of your route. If the route is longer, you'll need an alternative solution, which usually involves hiring someone to drive your car to the end of your route, where

they leave it for you to retrieve. If this is the case, figure out how many sets of keys you need and hire someone you trust.

Out-of-state plates often indicate that a person is going to be on the **trail** for a few days—good to know if you're a thief! Anytime you intend to leave a vehicle at a trailhead, thief proof it first. Take a look at your car. Is there alluring gear inside? If so, hide it beneath the seats or, better yet, leave it at home. Ask local officials about the safety of leaving your car at any given site. If there is a fire hazard, consider leaving your car in town and arranging transportation to the trailhead. Don't leave anything in the car that's sensitive to heat. Also, ensure that you have enough gas to get you to and from the trailhead. More than a few people have miscalculated this critical factor, resulting in long, humbling hikes to town. Finally, consider taking a spare key. After-hour locksmith visits to distant trailheads are costly—if you can contact a locksmith at all.

If your route goes to a remote region, you may require a bush plane or floatplane for a resupply or pickup (see **resupplying**). If so, start planning early because flight schedules are often booked months in advance. In addition, budget your trip carefully: charter air is not cheap. Always be prepared with a **contingency plan** for a delayed rendezvous. Keep in mind that poor weather and aviation restrictions (such as occurred after September 11, 2001) may significantly delay a plane from reaching your location.

See also **planning a trip**.

TREKKING

Trekking is another word for *hiking* and refers especially to arduous or **long-distance hiking**. In the past, it applied only to hikes in the Himalaya, but it slowly spread to cover other areas, such as the Andes, and is now used all over the world.

Trekking doesn't actually mean hiking or walking but is an Afrikaans word meaning "to travel by ox wagon"; it comes originally from the Dutch *trekken*, which means "to pull, draw, or travel." The original trekkers, or Voortrekkers (as they were known), were Afrikaans pioneers who, during the Great Trek of 1834–38, traveled with their wagons into areas of South Africa, then under British rule, where they settled.

The word wasn't applied to hiking until 1964, when a former British Gurkha officer, Lieutenant Colonel Jimmy Roberts, organized the first-ever hiking holiday in Nepal. He advertised it as a trek, three American women signed up, and Himalayan trekking had begun. Roberts's company, Mountain Travel Nepal, still exists, as part of the Tiger Mountain group.

The word *trekking* is still used particularly for organized, commercial treks, especially in the Himalaya. However, it's also now used for independent ventures as well.

TREKKING POLES

Trekking poles were almost unknown in North America until the 1990s, when they suddenly became very popular. They're still controversial items that some people dislike intensely—even though using a staff or stick for support is as old as humanity. Shepherds and others who work in the hills have always used them. **Hiking** and **mountaineering** photographs from the early twentieth century show long alpenstocks and wooden staffs in use.

In Europe, particularly in the Alps, trekking poles have been used for decades, especially by professional guides, who discovered that the poles took the strain off their knees on long, steep descents.

Why Poles?

Trekking poles provide balance on steep, rugged terrain, making crossing such ground safer and often faster. On descents, they allow for three points of contact, which is more secure. During **river crossings** a third leg can be essential for safety, and a fourth leg is also useful. Hiking uphill is faster and less tiring with poles because you can push down on them for power and stability. On marshy and **snow**-covered ground, poles can be used to probe depth and to look for hidden rocks

to stand on. If they have snow baskets (discussed below), poles also provide support in these environments. In dense vegetation and along overgrown **trails**, poles can hold back plants, especially **poisonous and stinging plants**, such as poison ivy, stinging nettles, and devil's club. A by-product of using poles is that you use your upper body more than you otherwise would, which results in better overall fitness. Finally, poles can be used to ward off aggressive dogs and some **wild animals**.

The best reason for using poles is that discovered by those alpine guides: poles take some of the weight off your legs, especially the knees, reducing wear and tear. Many hikers whose knee and leg problems were curtailing their activities have found that using poles enabled them to do much more again. Because poles transfer some of the weight to your arms and upper body, you may find your shoulders and arms ache when you first use them. This should disappear once your muscles get used to the work.

Poles are especially useful with heavy **packs**, and they can serve as a safety item in two ways. First, they make it less likely that you will slip and injure yourself. Second, if you do injure a knee or ankle, poles can provide support, enabling you to hike out rather than waiting for help.

Poles are useful for more than just hiking. In camp, they can be used as supports for a **tarp** or to turn a **tent** door into an awning. They can also prop your pack up so you can use it as a backrest.

One or Two?

Two poles are better than one. It's easier to achieve a rhythm with two, and they take weight off both legs and transfer it to both arms. However, one pole is better than no pole. A single pole on day trips with a light load is fine, but two poles are preferable with a heavy load on longer treks.

Pole Designs

Most trekking poles are actually modified ski mountaineering poles, because those are the poles alpine guides first used for hiking. With some poles, only the graphics make them different from poles used for **ski touring**.

An adjustable-length trekking pole isn't as strong as a pole made from a single length of metal. But for hiking, adjustable-length poles are plenty strong enough, unless you really abuse them. The advantages are that you can adjust them to suit the terrain (shortening them for uphill hiking and lengthening them on the downhill) and close them when you need to strap them to your pack. Adjustable poles are also easier to transport to and from the trailhead.

Most adjustable trekking poles have internal expansion plugs that tighten when you twist the poles in one direction and loosen when you twist them the other way. Others have an external locking mechanism. Both sorts can slip and need adjusting periodically.

Trekking poles come with small, solid baskets that are fine on dry, snow-free terrain. However, for snow or boggy ground, wider snow baskets are much better because they support the pole and stop it from sinking in too far. These baskets can be bought separately. Be aware that in vegetation, however, snow baskets can be a nuisance because they catch on plants and twigs.

The material used in the pole handle is more important than the handle design or shape. Foam and cork are the most comfortable and least sweaty, followed by rubber. Plastic is hard and can get sticky. Handles that angle forward allow a slightly more relaxed wrist position. Wrist straps need to be adjustable so they will fit when you're wearing bulky mitts. The softer the fabric, the more comfortable the strap is.

Trekking poles have metal tips. Carbide is the toughest material and useful if you'll be using your poles on **ice**, which other tips tend to slip on. Thin metal tips can poke holes in the side of the trail and scratch rocks, so if you don't need the security, it's best to cover them with a rubber or plastic tip cover. These grip adequately on most terrain, although you may lose them in muddy ground.

Many tips have short plastic shafts that are designed to break before the pole shaft does if the pole is placed under great strain. It's much less expensive to replace a tip than a pole section. Also, you can continue to use the pole even if the tip has broken.

> "When backpacking, I can walk longer and at a faster speed before my legs get tired if I use trekking poles. In particular, my knees no longer hurt during long steep descents on hard ground, descents I used to have to take slowly if I didn't want aching knees afterward."—CT

Using Poles

You have to use poles properly if they are to be of any benefit. Many people seem to wave them about limply, prodding the ground softly every few steps. Used like this, they're nothing more than wrist ornaments. Other people grip them tightly and stab at the ground in short staccato bursts, which is a good way to give your arms a workout but doesn't help your legs.

To use poles effectively, the weight should be on the straps so you don't have to hold the handles tightly. Put your hand through the wrist loop from below, and then bring it down with the strap running between your thumb and fingers and over the back of your wrist. Now you can push down on the pole with your hand open and relaxed. On flat or undulating terrain, swing the pole forward, plant the tip with the pole handle slanting away from you—if it's toward you, the pole acts as a brake—and walk past the pole before releasing the pressure, swinging the other pole forward as you do so. It's easy to get a good rhythm going. Whether the pole swings forward with the leg on the same side or the other side doesn't seem to matter. Both work.

On flat or undulating terrain, the ideal pole length has the pole just touching the ground as you hold your forearm parallel to the ground and grip the handle. Any longer than this, and you'll

CHRIS TOWNSEND

Correct grip for trekking poles. Place your hand up through the strap so the strap runs down between your thumb and fingers, then over the back of your hand. This way, the strap supports your hand, and you don't need to grip the pole tightly.

have to lift your arms in order to plant the poles, which is tiring. Any shorter, and you won't be able to apply as much force, so they won't be effective.

When the terrain starts to go steeply upward, adjust your technique: rather than swinging a pole up from behind you with each step, keep the poles in front of you. With each step, press down hard on one of the poles, gaining uphill propulsion. This is easier to do with shorter poles, so hold them lower down the shaft or shorten them if they're adjustable. Long poles tend to push you backward because you have to lift your arms high in the air to use them. On descents, long poles are better because you can plant them down the slope without having to lean so far forward that you feel off balance. When traversing a slope, use a short uphill pole, which won't push you away from the slope, and a long downhill pole, which will stop you from leaning down the slope.

On slopes where you need your hands and you are scrambling or even climbing, poles are a nuisance and can be dangerous. Strap them on your pack (shortening them first, if they're adjustable).

TRIM

Trim describes the way a canoe or kayak is loaded. A well-trimmed boat is evenly balanced and rides level in the water. A poorly trimmed canoe or kayak leans to one side or feels exceptionally bow or stern heavy.

Usually you trim your canoe or kayak so it floats completely level in the water. There are exceptions to this rule, however. If you anticipate **waves**, either from **wind** or whitewater, you may want to trim the boat with slightly more weight in the stern. This helps prevent the bow from plowing into the waves and may keep you a little drier. If there's a significant weight variance between the bow and the stern paddler, compensate for the difference by packing more weight near the lighter paddler. This is usually more of a concern when the bow paddler outweighs the stern paddler.

When you've finished packing a canoe or kayak, and before paddling, float the boat in calm water to determine how it is trimmed. If it looks lopsided, repack. A boat that is poorly trimmed is difficult to paddle. It's much easier to fix the problem right away than to paddle with a modified posture.

See also **packing a canoe** and **packing a sea kayak**.

TRIPLE CROWN

The Triple Crown is an award given by the American Long Distance Hiking Association–West to hikers who complete the **Appalachian Trail**, the **Pacific Crest Trail**, and the **Continental Divide Trail**. Very few hikers (35 as of early 2003) have earned this award, which involves hiking some 7,800 miles.

TRIP PLAN

Anytime you are going on a wilderness trip, you should create a trip plan and leave a copy with a trusted friend, relative, or local authority. A trip plan outlines your route and includes the estimated date of your return. It gives the description and color of your equipment, the amount of **food** you are carrying, and the skill level of your party. It also suggests an appropriate time to begin a search if you haven't returned. In the unlikely event that you run into serious trouble on your trip, rescuers will use your trip plan to focus their search. Without one, rescuers won't know where to look or what to look for. Creating a trip plan is not only responsible but also helps you organize your route and equipment. On paddling trips, trip plans are often called *float plans*. Your plan should include the following information.

- Names of party members
- Ages and medical histories
- Emergency contact information
- Route description
- Alternate route (if applicable)
- **Bailout points**
- Equipment (include color and quantity—e.g., "3 yellow tents, 2 stoves, 3 quarts fuel"; also mention any **communication devices**, such as a **cell phone** or radio)
- Skill level of participants
- **First-aid** training
- Amount of food
- Vehicle description and license plate number
- Estimated return date and suggested time to begin search if you haven't returned

National parks and provincial parks may require you to file a trip plan before departure. If your destination doesn't require a trip plan, be smart and file one anyway. When you finish your trip, always remember to check in with the person who has your plan. Forgetting to do this could result in an unnecessary, costly, hazardous, and embarrassing rescue operation.

TRUCKER'S HITCH

The trucker's hitch is useful when you need to make a **rope** very tight. By creating a mechanical advantage, this hitch allows you to really crank down on a rope. The trucker's hitch is particularly good for tying boats or bikes to the roof rack of your car. (The illustration shows how to tie the trucker's hitch.) See also **knots**.

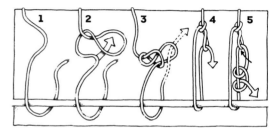

Trucker's hitch. 1. Wrap the running end (see knots*) around the object (roof rack, tree, stake). 2. Grab a bight of the rope and twist twice, creating a loop. Grab another bight from below the loop. 3. Feed the bight through the loop; you now have a new loop. 4. Feed the running end through the new loop. Pull the running end down to winch the system. 5. Tie off the loose running end with two half hitches. Tighten the first half hitch until it's snug against the loop before tying the second.*

TUMP LINE

A tump line is a long strip of material that runs across the forehead and down to the base of a heavy load. Sometimes, the tump line may be used across the chest rather than the brow. Horace Kephart, in his classic book *Camping and Woodcraft*, suggests that a tump line can be used to take the strain off your shoulders when carrying a heavy **pack**. That was in the days before hip belts, of course.

Tump lines are a traditional means of carrying heavy loads. They were used by Native Americans, fur traders, and mountain men, but in North America they were long ago replaced by packs. Tump lines are still in use in some countries. Porters use them regularly in the Himalaya, often with the traditional, large cone-shaped basket called a *doko*, and also with duffle bags and packs.

TUNDRA

The word *tundra* comes from the Finnish *tunturia*, meaning "treeless plain." Indeed, the tundra is a vast treeless expanse that covers the northern **latitudes**. Its lack of apparent plant life led early explorers to dub this region the "barren lands." In reality, however, the tundra is anything but barren. While extreme temperatures, high **wind**, and a short growing season of 50 to 60 days a year limit the growth of plant life, the sheer tenacity of hearty shrubs, lichens, mosses, and flowers makes up for their size.

Traveling on the tundra is exhilarating. It often feels as if you are floating on an ocean of grasses. The horizon stretches far into the distance, and you can see **clouds** and whole **weather** systems long before they arrive. While the tundra may appear completely flat, the ground is often covered with thousands of little mounds called *hummocks*. Hummock fields, while interesting, can make for uncomfortable **camping** and uneasy walking.

The tundra offers little protection from the wind—and how the wind can blow! Make sure that everything in camp is secure (including your **tent**, your **packs**, and even your canoes or kayaks). Beneath a thin layer of tundra topsoil lies several feet of permafrost (or permanently frozen ground), which makes staking your tent almost impossible. Be prepared to move boulders as necessary to secure your guylines, and always replace the rocks when you're finished with them.

The tundra—as shown here in the Northwest Territories, Canada—is a sea of grasses, lichens, and wildflowers. Often your tent is the highest object for miles, which can be disconcerting in thunderstorms.

True tundra exists only in the northern latitudes. However, alpine tundra—which exists in mountainous regions throughout the world—lies above the treeline and features plant life similar to that of northern tundra. In alpine tundra, employ tundra camping techniques, such as securing your campsite in case the wind kicks up.

TURNAROUND TIME

Turnaround time is a traditional **mountaineering** term. It refers to the predesignated time a party will turn around and retreat from their attempt on a mountain summit, whether they have reached the summit or not. As any mountaineer knows, timing is critical to any successful ascent. As the warmth of daylight begins to affect the structure of **snow** and **ice**, conditions on a mountain become unstable, increasing the likelihood of an **avalanche** of snow or rocks as the day wears on. In addition, afternoon **weather** tends to bring stronger **winds** and storms. For this reason, climbing parties often begin their approach to the summit in the early hours before dawn. This allows them to begin climbing at first light in the hopes of reaching the summit and beginning the descent while conditions are still favorable.

It is important for mountaineers to stick to the turnaround time once they're on the mountain; without one, they may fall prey to poor **judgment** brought on by **dehydration,** exhaustion, **altitude sickness,** or over zealousness. This can be difficult if the summit appears to be just steps away and the desire to reach the top is strong.

Setting a turnaround time is a good idea for any party striving to achieve a goal, regardless of the activity. For many backcountry users, a day hike to a local lookout or a paddle to a nearby island can offer the seductive lure of a lofty peak. Establishing a time frame for your outing and carrying enough gear to keep you safe and comfortable in the event of a delay can be as critical in the foothills as on the side of a mountain.

U

ULTRALIGHT HIKING

Ultralight hikers cut every bit of possible **weight** from every item of gear. The resulting loads are more like day packs than overnight backpacks. By choosing the very lightest gear and carrying only the absolute essentials, an ultralight hiker can get the weight of a basic load down to 20 pounds or less, including food and water. The ultralight philosophy says that there's no need to carry heavy loads, that **pack** weights can be cut drastically without compromising safety or comfort, and that by doing so **hiking** can become more enjoyable.

A Bit of History

Ultralight hiking isn't new. When Hamish Brown made the first continuous 1,600-mile traverse of all the Scottish 3,000-foot mountains in 1974, his load averaged 23 pounds, including food. Some of the ways he achieved this low weight are similar to those used by ultralighters today. His **pack** had no frame, hip belt, padding, or pockets. His **tent** was single-skin nylon, weighing just over 3 pounds. His **sleeping pad** weighed nothing: he didn't have one. "Except on **snow** these are just bulky extras," he wrote in his account of the trip, *Hamish's Mountain Walk*. He paid attention to the little details too, using his pot lid as a mug and sharpening the edge of his spoon so that he didn't need a **knife**. For part of the walk, he used a solid-fuel **stove**, an item now popular with ultralight hikers.

Jumping a decade to 1984, Colin Fletcher wrote in the third edition of his classic **backpacking** handbook, *The Complete Walker III*, that "a tide race has set in toward ultralight gear." In fact, that tide receded for over a decade before surging forward again in the late 1990s. Wanting to see what it was about, Fletcher made an ultralight trip sometime before 1984 with a load that weighed 15 pounds, 11 ounces without food and 19 pounds total. That included a frameless pack weighing just 22 ounces and a **tarp** weighing 20 ounces. Fletcher found that the "light load was a joy, especially uphill and obstacle-crossing." However, he remained concerned about the performance of ultralight gear in severe conditions, writing that "if you know you may find yourself alone in a mountain storm, three days from road-head, then false weight-economy could prove fatal; and you had better forget the gossamer game and lean heavily towards Old Wave ruggedness."

When recreational backpacking was in its infancy, there was an interest in lightweight travel too. In his 1917 book *Camping and Woodcraft*, Horace Kephart describes a summer backpacking load weighing 18 pounds, 3 ounces without food. This included a pack that weighed 2 pounds, 4 ounces and a 3-pound blanket that was used as back padding in the pack as well as for sleeping. It also included a 2-pound, 4-ounce tarp and, for cutting wood for **fires**, a 12-ounce tomahawk. Kephart called this load "medium weight."

The current ultralight movement began with Ray Jardine and his book *The Pacific Crest Trail Hiker's Handbook*. In 1994, Ray and Jenny Jardine hiked the **Pacific Crest Trail** with packs weighing 8.44 and 7.12 pounds, respectively, excluding food and clothing worn. How they did this is described in the book, and Jardine further expanded the ideas in *Beyond Backpacking*.

Pros and Cons

The attractions of a light load are obvious. Backpacking with what feels like a day pack means you can go farther with less effort, with little risk of sore shoulders, hips, or back. It also permits greater mobility, especially when crossing rough terrain, making the walker a light dancer rather than a lumbering dinosaur. You can enjoy the hills without noticing the weight on your back. Proponents of ultralight hiking argue that it can be safer too, because a heavy load can lead to injury as it makes you less mobile and puts more stress on your body. With a light load, you can move fast if the **weather** changes, descending more rapidly when a thunderstorm erupts or strong **winds** blow in than you can with a heavy pack.

Those who favor more standard loads respond by saying that you have to move fast with an ultralight load because you don't have the gear to cope with a storm. And if an injury slows you down or forces you to stop, you could be in trouble with only the limited ultralight gear. Traditionalists point out that heavier loads can mean more comfort in camp and a more enjoyable trip. A roomy tent, a thick self-inflating sleeping pad, books to read, and luxury items of food and drink are worth the weight to many people. They say backpacking is about more than load carrying— that there is more to it than just covering the miles easily and quickly.

The ultralight approach is more likely to appeal to those with a spartan approach to backpacking than to hedonists. It also appeals to those for whom the walking is more important than the **camping**. For someone who wants to cover a lot of miles each day, an ultralight load offers a great benefit.

Ultralighters say light loads are a good idea whatever distance you cover or speed you travel, and you don't have to be a high-mileage hiker to appreciate a light pack. The fact is that it's possible to carry an ultralight load without compromising safety by carefully selecting items suited to the conditions, but this requires experience and skill.

Durability

A big concern with ultralight gear is whether it's durable enough. With modern materials, this isn't really a problem as long as items are well made and aren't abused. And ultralight gear doesn't just mean using lightweight materials; it also involves simple designs with minimal features.

Much standard gear is needlessly complicated and made from unnecessarily heavy materials. Packs offer a classic example. For backpacking, 1,000-denier heavy-duty fabric that will withstand being hauled up rocky gullies just isn't needed. Neither are masses of pockets and compartments. These may be nice for organizing gear, but every zipper, flap, and panel of fabric adds weight. And for loads under 30 pounds, complicated frames and back systems are not needed.

Some ultralight fabrics are stronger than heavier ones. The silicone nylon (silnylon) used in the lightest tents and tarps is actually much tougher and longer lasting than the polyurethane-coated nylon and polyester found in heavier tents. Some traditional materials are durable too. An ultralight down **sleeping bag** will last far longer than a heavy, bulky synthetic one.

Waterproof clothing is probably the only area where ultralight gear won't last as long as heavyweight stuff. It's still tougher than the standard-weight garments of a few decades ago and is much less expensive than top-quality heavy garments. If you wear a windproof top and pants in breezy, showery weather and save your rain gear for continuous **rain**, it will last much longer. The latest developments in fabrics, with each fiber given a water-repellent coating, mean that windproof garments are becoming increasingly water resistant while staying breathable too, so that waterproofs are needed less often (see **breathability** and **clothing**).

Food and Water

However light your pack and basic gear may be, you still have to add in food and fuel, plus water unless it's always readily available. Most people can get by with about 2 pounds of food per day; some can manage on 1½ pounds. But it's easy to end up carrying more than 2 pounds per day if you don't choose carefully. Canned and fresh food is heavy.

If you're heading out for more than two or three days, the weight of food you need to carry will quickly add up. At 2 pounds a day, a week's food weighs 14 pounds. Add that weight to a pack, and it can cease to be ultralight, especially when you add in stove fuel and any water. The answer is to frequently resupply with food, fuel, and water during a long trip (see **resupplying**). To go ultralight on a long hike, you will need to find a resupply point for food at least once a week, and not carry much water.

Adopting the Ultralight Approach

Ultralight backpacking is not something most hikers can undertake without a good deal of thought or practice. It may well be easiest for those who have never backpacked and therefore don't have set notions about what is desirable and what is possible. However, a truly ultralight load is not for novices. To cope safely while using minimal equipment, you need basic hiking and camping skills. It's not advisable for even an experienced backpacker to head off into the wilderness with ultralight gear without having tried it close to home. At first, it's best to err on the side of cau-

tion and take that extra item, just in case you need it.

If you find the ultralight approach appealing, start by going through your gear and ruthlessly pruning excess weight. Just putting an item on the scale and discovering how much it weighs may give you the incentive to modify it or replace it with something that works just as well, at a lighter weight. Think about what you really need. As Ray Jardine says, not taking an item reduces its weight by 100 percent.

> "My first step toward ultralight backpacking was when I first changed from heavy boots to very light ones. That was the only change I made for over a decade, but then I made two long trips (a round of the Scottish mountains and the Arizona Trail) on which, for very different reasons (the amount of ascent on one, the amount of water I would have to carry on the other), heavy gear seemed inadvisable. On both those trips, I reduced my basic loads by some 10 to 13 pounds from what I'd carried on previous long walks, a significant amount."—CT

Replacing heavy essential items with lighter ones is the principal way to substantially reduce the weight you carry. Most weight lies in big items: tent, pack, stove, pots, sleeping bag, sleeping pad. Reduce the weight of these substantially, and your total load will be much lighter. You don't have to replace everything at once. Although ultralight gear works well as a system and some is designed to be used this way, it can still be integrated with standard gear.

Ultralight backpacking can be described as a state of mind, an attitude, as much as an activity. Those with an ultralight mind-set will consider the weight of an item first, putting this ahead of function, performance, and durability. They will always question whether an item is needed at all. The ultralight point of view looks at limiting the weight of the load as the first requirement. Conversely, if you favor a more standard approach to backpacking, you will consider safety and comfort first and end up with a relatively heavy pack.

In the end it comes down to a personal choice of how you want to enjoy the wilderness.

UMBRELLAS

Umbrellas aren't the first items you think of for **hiking**, but they are surprisingly useful in both wet and sunny **weather**. Keeping off the **rain** is their obvious use, and they do this well as long as it isn't very windy. Because you don't need to wear rain gear under an umbrella, you have no **condensation** problems and you stay drier and more comfortable. If the **wind** picks up, however, an umbrella can become awkward. You have to point it into the wind to keep out the rain, and some will still get past and start to dampen your **clothing**. In really gusty winds, umbrellas thrash about. Eventually, they break.

Umbrellas work wonderfully in the **desert** because they make great sunshades, keeping you far cooler than a **hat**. They're even better if you put a layer of Mylar (a type of silver foil) over the outside to reflect the heat. As well as hiking with an umbrella, you can shelter from the rain or the sun under one. (See also **sun protection**.)

Umbrellas are easiest to carry in open terrain and on clear trails. Once the terrain becomes rough, holding an umbrella can affect stability, and in dense vegetation it can catch and snag. At those times, it's best strapped to your **pack**.

For the backcountry, small, lightweight umbrellas are best. Good ones need weigh no more than 10 ounces.

UTM

UTM, or the Universal Transverse Mercator, is a rectangular grid system used to plot locations on the earth's surface. Developed by the military, the UTM system is considered by many to be much more user friendly than traditional **latitude** and **longitude** coordinates. It is of particular interest to **GPS** users because many GPS units give their coordinates using the UTM grid system.

With UTM, the earth is divided into 60 zones numbered 1 to 60. Each zone is 6 degrees wide and runs from 80 degrees south latitude to 84 degrees north latitude (the polar regions are excluded). Unlike lines of longitude, UTM zones do not converge. Instead, they remain rectangular, a feature that makes the UTM system easy to use. The first UTM zone (zone 1) starts at the international date line (180 degrees longitude) and runs 6 degrees to the east (ending at 174 degrees west longitude). Most of North America is covered by zones 10 to 19.

There are two UTM coordinates for every location on earth. They are called the *northing* coordinate and the *easting* coordinate (similar to

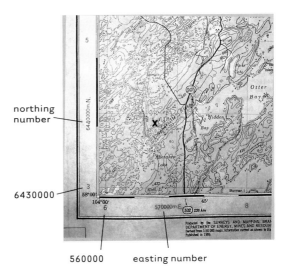

Deciphering UTM: The easting number of 570000 means that the easting line is 570,000 meters east of the zone's western edge. The northing number of 6440000 means that the northing line is 6,440,000 meters north of the equator. Because the X is 7/10 of the way between easting numbers 560000 and 570000, the easting number of the X is 567000. Because the X is 9/10 of the way between northing numbers 6430000 and 6440000, the northing number of the X is 6439000. The map is in zone 13 (noted in the map legend, not shown), so the UTM coordinates of the X are 13567000 E, 6439000 N (the easting number is always the first given, and the zone precedes the easting number).

latitude and longitude). The northing coordinate denotes how many meters the position is from the equator, while the easting coordinate denotes how many meters the position is away from the zone's longitudinal origin. When giving coordinates, easting always comes first. For example, a position with the coordinates 13 670000 2440500 tells you that the position is in zone 13 (the mountain states) and that the position is 670,000 meters from the zone's western edge and 2,440,500 meters from the equator.

The high numbers that are used as UTM coordinates take some getting used to. Once you have the hang of it, you will find that UTM is very fast and easy—one reason it's the choice among **search and rescue** crews and many backcountry travelers. Most topographical **maps** have UTM coordinates located in the margins of the map.

V–W

VAPOR BARRIERS

Vapor barriers are articles of **clothing** made out of impermeable material, such as coated nylon. When you wear a vapor barrier next to your skin or over a thin liner, it prevents your perspiration from dampening your other clothing. Vapor barriers are used in extremely cold **weather**, when even the slightest amount of moisture can cause your clothes to freeze. For example, many people wear vapor barrier **socks** under their **wool** or synthetic socks. **Boots** these days are pretty good at protecting your feet from outside moisture, but they can easily overheat and sweat. Vapor barriers prevent the sweat from getting to your sock and making it cold and clammy.

Vapor barriers aren't just for your feet; they can also be found as shirts, pants, and sleeping sacks to use inside your sleeping bag. Vapor barriers aren't for everyone, but if you sweat a lot and have a hard time keeping your insulating layers dry, you might find them helpful.

WASHING

Because unclean hands could pass on *Giardia* and other bugs that cause stomach upsets, washing your hands after going to the toilet and before handling food and cooking utensils is essential. How much other washing you do in the **wilderness** is a personal choice. Many people get by with minimal or no washing, apart from their hands, even when they spend weeks at a time in the wilderness. Where you wash, what you use, and where you dump the wastewater does matter though. Bathing in large rivers and lakes is OK as long as you don't use soap and you aren't covered in bug juice or sunscreen. Wear your clothes to give them a rinse as well. If the creeks and pools are small, wash at least a few hundred feet away from them (you can carry **water** in **cooking** pots or water containers).

Soap, even the biodegradable sort, should be kept out of wilderness water. Soap isn't essential, but if you do use it, be sparing and make sure to scatter wastewater far from creeks or lakes, ideally in sand or gravel. This should filter the soap out before the water returns to a stream. Soap is useful for ensuring clean hands, but you can also use moist wipes, which can be packed out, or hand sanitizer.

Clothing can be rinsed out in large strongly flowing creeks as long as soap isn't required. While this may not remove stains and other marks, it's enough to get rid of sweat and surface dirt. If there are no sizable creeks around, you can wash your clothing in cooking pots, again a few hundred feet from any water source.

See also **Leave No Trace** and **sanitation**.

WATCHES

Feeling free from the constraints of the clock is one of the many pleasures of life in the **wilderness**. Instead of the regimented hours of meetings, schedules, and other controls of urban life, you can live by nature's time, rising with the dawn, going to sleep when it gets dark, eating when you're hungry, and resting when you're tired. Or you can ignore the sun and rise late in the morning and stay up late at night watching the moon and the stars and listening to the sounds of the dark—owls, **coyotes**, **wolves**. Your time is your own to do with as you will.

In casting off urban life, it's tempting to leave your watch behind and be totally liberated from the ticking of the clock. On an easy trip in known terrain, this could work out OK but usually a watch or other time piece is surprisingly useful in the wilderness.

First, knowing the time helps you monitor your progress, which can help with deciding where to camp. Do you have enough time to reach the next site before dark? If the sun is visible, you might be able to work this out from its position in the sky, but on cloudy days you may have no way of estimating the time.

A watch is even more important when navigating in poor visibility (see **navigation**). Then you can use timings to plot your progress. Say it's a mile across open country shrouded in featureless mist to a lake and you know from your watch that you've been traveling 2 miles an hour. It should then take half an hour to reach the lake. If the lake doesn't appear after half an hour, you need to check whether you've gone astray. For more critical navigation in difficult or dangerous terrain, accurate timing of different legs of your route can be essential.

Some people like to take rests at regular intervals and to stop for set periods of time. Without a watch, this is impossible. Even if you don't do this, a watch is useful as a nudge to get you going when you realize your short stop has stretched to half an hour or more.

On the last day of a trip, knowing the time may be necessary if you are to make a pickup or rendezvous. On long trips, it can be important when you need to reach a supply point by a certain day or time (see **resupplying**). Needing to get to the post office before it closes at 4 P.M. isn't much use if you don't know what time it is. A watch that tells you the date helps too; when you're out for weeks at a time, you can easily forget which day it is, only to find out when you amble into a town on a Saturday afternoon and discover that the post office doesn't open again until Monday or that the weekly bus went yesterday.

Alarms are horrid things anywhere, but in the wilderness they're a real intrusion. It's far better to wake up gradually to the sound of bird song. However, if you need an early start so you can be off summits and high passes before the sun heats up the snow and increases the **avalanche** danger or before the first afternoon thunderstorm begins, then an alarm is useful.

A simple wristwatch is all you need. However, if you have an electronic **altimeter**, a watch will be part of it, and knowing both the time and the altitude is very useful when navigating in mountains. **GPS** receivers tell the time too, although these aren't as good for regular use unless you have them switched on all the time. However, if you only need to know the time occasionally, this could be enough.

Having a watch on your wrist isn't always convenient. The strap can get quite sweaty and may catch on vegetation. When you're scrambling, the face of the watch can get scratched or even broken. Carry the watch in a pocket or hang it from a pack shoulder strap so you can look at it easily. If you do the latter, remember the watch is there when you take your **pack** off, so you don't bang it against anything.

WATER

In the **wilderness**, the most refreshing drink is water. It's also essential for survival (see **dehydration**). Drink regularly for enjoyment, and you shouldn't need to worry about a lack of water.

The problem with water is that it's heavy. Carry all you need on a hot day, and you'll have a heavy load. Carry enough for a few days out, and your load will be backbreaking. Water weighs a little over 2 pounds per quart, and on a hot day you might drink a quart an hour.

> "I reckon I need 5 to 12 quarts of water a day, depending on how hot it is and how hard I've been working. That's 10 to 24 pounds of water. Clearly, carrying much water is something you don't want to do unless you have to, and carrying water for more than a few days is just impossible. On a 55-mile hike across a waterless section of the Sonoran Desert in Arizona, my companion and I put out two 9-gallon caches for the three-and-a-half-day hike. Although we drank plenty at each cache, we still each carried 3 gallons—24 pounds—at times."—CT

Locating Water

On most journeys, water is available—you just need to know where it is. In snowy country, there's no problem as long as you have enough fuel to melt snow. In most **mountain** ranges, you can find ample water too, although it can be far between sources, especially if you're following ridges. The **desert**, however, is a different story.

Maps and trail guides usually identify possible water sources. If a map is splashed with blue, you probably don't need to worry about finding water. Do check where the water is in relation to your route. It's better to carry some water than to make repeated long descents to get some. Blue dashes rather than solid lines indicate intermittent streams, so don't assume there will be water there. In areas where water is scarce, it's best to get up-to-date local information as well. Many water sources are unreliable or seasonal.

Learn where water is likely to be found. Trees, especially cottonwoods, line watercourses

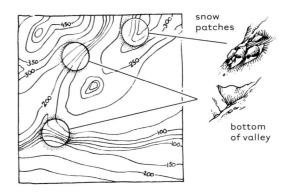

Looking for water: In any area, look at the landscape and at the map for places where water might flow or settle, and search in those areas.

in arid areas, although the water may not be on the surface year-round. Hollows trap water after **rain**. Rocks are particularly good for this, but any dip in the terrain may collect at least a puddle. Look for depressions and low points both on the ground and on the map—you may find water there. Following a valley downward may reveal water eventually, even if only tiny pools in an otherwise dry streambed. If you can't see any water, listen. Even trickles can make quite a noise if they're running over stones or falling fast.

If water sources are far apart and uncertain, carry more than you need between sources, just in case one is dry. Plan your itinerary around water sources to minimize how much water you need to carry and for how long.

Collecting Water

Collecting water usually consists of dipping a container, or the end of a water filter, into a creek or pool. It's quickest to fill containers from tiny cascades and waterfalls, especially if the containers have narrow mouths or are made from flexible plastic. Wide-mouthed rigid bottles are the easiest to fill in still water.

Where there is only a tiny trickle of water or a very shallow pool, gathering water is more difficult. A mug or cooking pot can be used to dip

You can use a water bottle attached to the end of a ski pole to collect water from a partially open stream in winter. Be careful when doing this to ensure that you're standing on firm ground and not on an overhanging snow bank that could collapse.

CHRIS TOWNSEND

water from a puddle or can be placed in a trickle to collect water. When you can't fit even a mug into a seep or crevice, use a curved piece of plastic, foil, thick paper, or bark to make a channel for the water to flow along. If the water is below a steep bank or in a deep hole, you can attach your water bottle to a hiking pole or stout stick and dip water out. If you still can't reach, attach the bottle to a length of cord and lower it into the

dip a mug into a shallow puddle, then pour into your container

lower a bottle with a rope (rocks inside to help the bottle sink)

channeling with foil/bark; plastic or stiff paper can also be used

Water collection methods.

water. A few pebbles placed in the bottom of the bottle will help it sink so it can fill with water.

Water Containers

Carrying water used to be straightforward. Plastic bottles in various sizes were standard. Water bags—thin, flexible plastic bladders inside a nylon cover—were used for **camping**. The use of water bottles for backpacking still works fine, although there are many other options now, and the bottles seem quite old-fashioned compared to modern hydration systems.

Rigid bottles come in various sizes, but anything larger than 2 quarts is too big to carry. Quart sizes tend to be the most convenient. Lexan plastic bottles from an outdoor store are very tough and weigh around 5 ounces in the quart size. Plastic soda bottles are surprisingly durable and weigh less, around 3 ounces for a quart size. They cost less too—and come filled with soda.

Flexible water bags for camp use come in various sizes. The gallon size is perhaps the most useful and weighs around 4 ounces. These bags don't carry well when full (and they're even more awkward to handle when half full), so they're not good for transporting water. The older styles, with thin inner bladders, are easily punctured. Single-layer ones made from textured nylon lined with polyurethane are much tougher.

A good alternative to both rigid plastic bottles and water bags is offered by flexible bottles, which come in every size from a pint to a gallon and more, are made from thicker plastic than water bags, and have welded seams. These are much lighter than rigid bottles and pack down very small when empty. They stand upright like a rigid bottle.

For carrying in a **pack**, water containers need secure caps that don't leak. Attached caps are less likely to be lost. Many cheap bottles leak when shaken. Caps you can drink through often leak too. These are fine for carrying in water pouches on the outside of the pack, and it's easy to see why they're popular for **trail running** and **mountain biking**, but you wouldn't want one inside your pack. Fill and shake any new bottle to check for leaks. Carry your bottles upright in the pack.

Flexible water bottles and water bags become hydration systems when they have long drinking hoses rather than caps. Many packs and fanny packs come with internal pouches for hydration systems, a hole for the hose to exit through so you can drape it over your shoulder and have it ready to drink from, and clips for fastening the hose to your shoulder strap. Hydration systems come in various sizes, usually 2 to 3 quarts. With the most versatile ones, you can replace the hose with a standard cap so the bottle can be used in camp and at other times when you don't want the hose.

> "I was initially dubious about the durability of flexible bottles, but having used several of them on the Arizona Trail without any problems, I'm now happy to use them as my main containers. I carry two 2.5-quart ones, whose combined weight is just 2.7 ounces, less than a 1-quart rigid bottle. These are big enough for camp and can be carried full. I usually back them up with a 1-quart flexible bottle (weight, 0.9 ounce) to use while hiking."—CT

An alternative to a hydration system is a pack with bottle holders on the side that can be accessed without having to remove the pack.

Good-quality water containers are worth buying because failure of water bottles far from a water source could be a serious problem. Also, cheap bottles may not be made of food-grade plastic, which means they can impart an unpleasant chemical taste to the water.

You need enough containers to hold all the water required between water sources. This could be one 1-quart bottle in wet areas or enough containers to hold a gallon in the desert. For camping, enough containers to hold all of the water you need overnight are useful and also environ-mentally friendly because you need to collect water only once, which avoids creating a trail, damaging the bank, or disturbing wildlife with repeated trips. With enough containers, you can fill up during the day and camp far away from water as well. (See also **Leave No Trace**.)

Treating Water

Many backcountry travelers use some method of treating water in order to kill harmful organisms or remove contaminants. But the first step in securing safe drinking water is to seek out sources that are likely to be clean anyway. Wilderness treatment procedures are not foolproof and can easily be done incorrectly. There is a danger in thinking that if you filter water or treat it with chemicals or even boil it, that it's guaranteed to be pure.

The cleanest water is usually that which has not been contaminated by people or domestic animals. Look for water upstream from campsites, grazing grounds, and **trails**. Check the map to see what lies upstream if you're taking water from a big river or creek. With lakes, the inlet or outlet is probably the best place. You can also consider side creeks tumbling down from steep mountainsides. Springs often produce fresh, cold, clean water. Try to find a source of water that is not cloudy, dirty, or smelly.

The standard wisdom is that wilderness water must be treated before it is safe to drink, and warnings abound of the dangers of untreated water. Some voices are being raised to temper that view. In an online *Nature Notes* article for the Yosemite Association, engineer and mountaineer Robert L. Rockwell takes issue with the need to treat water in the Sierra Nevada range of California for that feared microscopic bug *Giardia lamblia*, which causes the intestinal disorder giardiasis. In the article, Rockwell reported that "San Francisco water can contain a concentration of 0.12 [*giardia*] cysts per liter, a figure now seen to be higher than that measured anywhere in the Sierra" (www.yosemite.org/naturenotes/Giardia.htm).

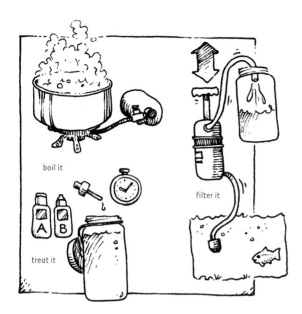

boil it

filter it

treat it

A B

Water can be treated by boiling, filtering, or purifying with chemicals.

Many people assume that drinking untreated water is the most likely way of encountering *Giardia*. However, you are more likely to catch giardiasis and other water-borne diseases from unclean **food** or utensils than from untreated water. It is essential to wash your hands before handling food or **cooking**. It's surprising how many people treat their water but don't bother about personal hygiene. (See also *Giardia* and **sanitation**.)

There are three ways to treat water in the backcountry: boiling, filtering, and treating with chemicals.

Boiling

Boiling kills everything in water and so is a good way to purify it. Achieving a rolling boil is enough to kill off any organisms present, but bear in mind that boiling will not remove chemicals, poisons, or metal contaminants. In camp, treating water by boiling does double-duty because you'll probably also need hot water for cooking and drinks. Boiling is not practical for all your water, however, due to the amount of **fuel** that would

be needed and the time it would take. If you're going to drink boiled water straight, shake it and pour it in and out of different containers to reaerate it so it doesn't taste flat.

Filtering

Filters are a popular way of treating water, perhaps because there is something reassuring about using one, or perhaps because they have been so heavily promoted. It's certainly not because they're convenient. Filters are heavy, bulky, complex, slow to operate, and prone to clogging. Keeping them clean in the wilderness is difficult yet essential if they are to be effective.

If you do use a filter, study the instructions carefully and practice with it at home. Work out how to clean and store the filter properly. Just jamming it all in a pack pocket that probably isn't clean anyway or wrapping it in an old cloth won't do.

When choosing a filter, the size of the pores is important in determining what they will block. Filtering water can remove bugs that can make you ill, such as *Cryptosporidium* and *Giardia*. Filters don't disinfect water, however, and won't remove viruses unless there is a chemical component added. This isn't a problem in North America and Western Europe, but in places like the Himalaya, Kilimanjaro, or the Andes, chemical treatment or boiling must be done because it's the only way to kill viruses. (See also **Cryptosporidium** and *Giardia*.)

Most filters use pumps. You put one hose in the water to be treated, put the other in a clean water container, and pump the water through the filter. This can be slow—a quart a minute is quite good—and even hard work, but it can be used for any amount of water. An alternative design that is much slower—it can take 10 minutes to filter a quart—but which leaves you free to do other things is the gravity filter. This involves hanging up a bag of water with the filter unit below it and a hose below that leading into a water container. For solo use and when on the move, you can get filters built into the lids of

CHRIS TOWNSEND

When using a water filter, always ensure that the output hose doesn't come into contact with the water to be filtered or the input hose. Your hands should be clean before handling the filter.

water containers. These are quite light and easy to use, but you get only a bottleful of water at a time.

All filters clog eventually. The dirtier the water, the sooner this will occur. Water that is visibly dirty can be filtered through a **bandanna** or coffee filter to remove the worst of the muck. Some filters have a prefilter for this purpose. Any filter designed for wilderness use should be field maintainable so you can clean it and get it working again when it clogs. Filter cartridges will only pass a certain amount of water before they are worn out, however. Then you need to replace the cartridge. A lightweight filter might work for 50 quarts. Some filters, however, are good for 13,000 quarts. Spare cartridges are heavy, but a group

could carry a spare. Otherwise, a chemical treatment is worth carrying as a lightweight backup.

Chemical Purification

Chemical purification can be very effective if done properly. It's available in tablet and liquid form, in three types: chlorine, iodine, and chlorine dioxide.

Chemical treatments are lightweight, low in bulk, and easy to use. However, they take time to work and some of them leave an aftertaste in the water. Water may also need filtering through a bandanna or coffee filter first, because chemicals don't remove sediment.

Chlorine is disappearing as a chemical treatment for wilderness water because it takes longer than other treatments to work and may be adversely affected by organic debris or alkalis in the water.

Available in various forms, iodine is a more reliable treatment against *Giardia*, but it's unknown whether it's effective against *Cryptosporidium*. Iodine tablets are easy to use and very light, but once a bottle has been opened the tablets need to be used within a few weeks or discarded, because they start to deteriorate after contact with the air.

Iodine crystals don't have this problem. Water is added to the crystals to produce an iodine solution, a measured amount of which is then added to the water to be treated. Be sure, however, not to let the crystals themselves into drinking water. One popular make of iodine treatment, Polar Pure, has a filter cone inside the bottle to stop the crystals from coming out. Polar Pure also has a thermometer on the side of the bottle that shows the temperature of the solution and tells you how much solution to add to a quart of water. This is dependent on the temperature because the colder the water, the more iodine that is needed. A bottle of Polar Pure weighs 3 ounces before any water is added and will purify 2,000 quarts of water before the crystals are used up. A bottle of 50 tablets, which weighs a total of 3.5 ounces, will purify 50 quarts. However, iodine can only be carried in a glass bottle; if the bottle is broken, iodine solution could make quite a mess because it leaves a stain.

With iodine treatment, you need to wait at least 20 minutes before the water is safe to drink. It will then taste of iodine, which some people strongly dislike. The taste can be neutralized by adding ascorbic acid (vitamin C) tablets. Iodine is safe for most people in low doses, although those with thyroid problems should consult their doctors before ingesting it.

The most recently developed chemical treatment uses chlorine dioxide, sold as AquaMira and Pristine, which when activated releases oxygen into the water, killing everything. The treatment comes in two plastic bottles—one containing the chlorine dioxide, the other the activator—plus a small mixing cap. The bottles weigh 2.5 ounces and will purify 120 quarts. To use it, put seven drops from each bottle in the mixing cap and then wait 5 minutes before adding it to the water to be treated; then wait another 15 minutes. Once ready, the water tastes fine, with no chemical taste, and the makers of the treatment say that no chemicals remain in the water.

Choices

How effective any water treatment is can't be judged by field use. Just because you didn't get sick doesn't mean that your filter or chemical treatment worked. The water may have been clean anyway. For confirmation of effectiveness, you have to rely on the U.S. Environmental Protection Agency and the manufacturers' research. What is clear is that any form of treatment must be used properly if it is to have a chance of working, which includes ensuring that water containers and your hands are clean.

WATER KNOT

The water knot is the ideal knot to use when you need to tie pieces of webbing together. Used frequently by climbers and mountaineers, this handy knot is often used to make **slings** out of webbing. The strength of the water knot can be severely

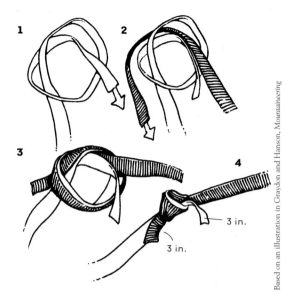

Based on an illustration in Graydon and Hanson, Mountaineering

Water knot. 1. Tie an overhand knot at one end of the webbing, making sure it lies flat. 2. With the other end of the webbing, follow the path of the overhand knot in reverse, starting with the free end. 3. Dress the knot (see knots) to ensure the knot lies flat, with no twist in the webbing. 4. The tails on a water knot should be at least 3 inches.

compromised if it is not properly dressed (see **knots**). Likewise, it is critical that both tails of the knot are over 3 inches. This prevents the knot from working itself loose. The water knot is best used on flat webbing, not on circular rope.

WATERMELON SNOW

If you thought that **snow** could only be white, think again. In many snowfields above 10,000 feet, snow is pink. Pink? Strange as it sounds, large sections of snowfields are stained with a pink tint that resembles the color of watermelon flesh. The coloration is caused by millions of microscopic algae that thrive in the melting snow. These algae have a bright red pigment that helps protect them against the sun's intense ultraviolet rays. They lie dormant during the winter months and spring into action when the snow starts to melt.

Watermelon snow is intriguing to look at, but don't be tempted to taste it or melt it into **water**.

Reports suggest that it causes diarrhea and intestinal discomfort. For drinking purposes, avoid snow that has any coloration, especially yellow!

WATERPROOFING

Ask any person who dislikes **camping** how they got turned off, and their answer will likely include being wet and cold. There's no doubt that being wet when you would rather be dry puts a damper on your day (no pun intended). While becoming wet can't be eliminated, there are some waterproofing techniques that can help you stay drier.

Start by looking at the seams of your equipment. Almost all gear, including **boots, packs,** and certainly **tents,** has seams that piece it together. Seams are riddled with tiny holes that can leak, but sealed seams keep you dry. If they aren't factory sealed with a clear tape, you may have to seal them yourself (see **seam sealing**). This process works on jackets, tents, **tarps,** and any other kind of gear with a seam.

If an article of **clothing** came with factory-sealed seams but still leaks, there are a few things that you can do to restore water repellency. Start by keeping your gear as clean as possible. Little particles of dirt, sweat, food, and bug juice can break down the water repellency of any garment. Always clean it before you store it, and wash it occasionally following the manufacturer's directions. If a **Gore-Tex** garment is leaking (most do eventually), wash it with a commercial "wash-in" water repellant treatment, such as Nikwax TX-Direct. Then machine dry it in medium heat. You can also iron your Gore-Tex using a medium heat setting. This adds a good amount of water repellency. Make sure the iron is clean. Scotchguard and other spray repellants will help make water bead up rather than soaking in. When applying them, first ensure that the garment is clean and dry. Then follow the directions.

Boots are even more susceptible to getting wet. Once wet, they make your feet cold and vulnerable to **blisters** and **cold-weather injuries,** such as **frostbite.** Protect your feet by wearing **gaiters** over your boots. Gaiters will repel water, dirt, and sand—the culprits that result in blisters. Like garments, boots can (and should) be treated on occasion. Treat your boots with oils, waxes, or silicone spray to help them repel water. In the case of leather boots, treatment also helps prevent the leather from becoming dry and brittle. Many good commercial boot treatments are available, including Tektron Boot Protector, Aquaseal Classic Cream, Biwell Classic Leather Treatment, and Nikwax Aqueous Wax (or for leather-nylon combinations, use Nikwax Fabric and Leather Waterproofing).

For heavy-duty items, such as packs, treat the seams with seam grip, a thicker version of seam sealant. When using seam grip, you need only one coat. Make sure the pack is free of dirt and any previous sealer. Also apply seam grip to all patches and minor tears in the pack. Packs can also be sprayed with Scotchguard or another type of fabric treatment. A less expensive alternative is Thompson's Water Seal (available at the hardware store), which you can apply with a paintbrush or spray bottle. In either case, saturate the pack and then allow to dry.

WATERPROOFING MAPS

There are several ways to keep your **maps** and **nautical charts** dry and protected from the deteriorating effects of dirt, rain, sand, and sweat. The easiest way is to use a map case, the simplest of which is nothing more than a clear, zippered food storage bag. Zippered bags won't hold up for very long, but they certainly can do the job for overnight or weekend trips. To reinforce this type of map case, cover the seams with **duct tape.** Commercial map cases use heavy-duty material and secure closures to keep your contents dry.

Usually, map cases are large enough to hold a map or two as well as a **compass** and any other notes you might want to stash inside. Carrying a map case will add some **weight** to your outfit. However, if it prevents your map from becoming waterlogged and torn, it is worth its weight in gold. Map cases are especially important on **canoeing** and kayaking trips.

Another way to waterproof maps is to treat them with a commercial **waterproofing** sealant. Chemically sealed maps are more water resistant than waterproof. Unless you plan to submerge your map in water (in which case you should have a map case), treating your maps with a chemical sealant will do the job. Most sealants come in a liquid form that can be sprayed or painted on maps. The chemical completely impregnates the map, repelling water and causing it to bead. Sealants are more convenient than laminating the map with contact paper, because laminated maps are difficult to fold; most sealed maps can be easily folded and unfolded without cracking. In addition, you can write on them. Some good map sealants available at any outdoor store are Aquaseal Mapseal and Nikwax Map Proof. An inexpensive alternative is Thompson's Water Seal (available at the hardware store).

WAVES

Anytime you're traveling on a waterway, be it a river, lake, or ocean, pay close attention to the development and pattern of the waves. Learning to read waves will afford you a wealth of information not accessible to the untrained eye. Waves can indicate the depth of the water, rocks beneath the surface, currents, and **tides**. They can even give you clues to incoming **weather**.

Open-Water Waves

Waves in oceans (or big lakes) are a bit different from the **standing waves** found in rivers. Ocean waves undulate along the surface of the water, sometimes at great speed, while the water stays in the same location. The source of a wave can be a storm, an earthquake, or simply an object falling into the water (such as a calving **glacier**). Indeed, the wave is nothing more than a pulse of energy flowing through the water, away from its source. A wave on an ocean may travel hundreds of miles in a day without transporting any water. The water in any given location will simply rise as

the wave passes and then settle back down again. This is called a *swell*, a wave that does not break. If a swell is small enough, you may not even detect that it has passed.

Waves are measured in height and length. Height is the distance from the top of the wave (the crest) to the bottom of the wave (the trough). A wave can be 30 feet high and still not appear steep if the wavelength is long. Wavelength is measured from the crest of one wave to the crest of the next wave. The longer the wave, the faster it travels. Wavelengths in small bodies of water can be as short as 1 or 2 feet, while the wavelengths in oceans can exceed several thousand feet. When they're this long, they can travel as fast as 70 miles an hour, with a different wave passing you every 20 seconds. Because waves can travel such great distances, you may be the recipient of a wave that was formed across the ocean!

"A friend of mine tells a harrowing story about paddling on Hudson Bay. Taking advantage of the high tide sometimes requires you to paddle in the wee hours of the morning. It was still quite dark when they set out, and the color of the water blended in with the horizon. Still, the route was very straightforward, they were all competent paddlers, and the weather looked promising—so they set out. A few stars were visible above the horizon, but after paddling for a while, the light from several stars seemed to be blinking. Before too long, they realized that they were paddling on huge swells that occasionally blocked the view of the stars. Horrified by the thought that the swells might start to break, they turned and blasted toward shore, only to have to deal with a difficult surf landing!"—AA

Hazards

When the height of a wave reaches approximately one-seventh of its length, it will no longer be able to support itself. At this point, the wave will crest and the water will tumble down its leading face. This is known as a *breaking wave*. Breaking waves are very powerful and should be considered dangerous. Waves will also break when they trip over objects, such as rocks or coral reefs, or when they finally reach land. Boomers—waves that break upon submerged rocks—often cause exploding waves that send spray flying into the air.

Another type of violent wave pattern is formed when a swell hits a cliff. This encounter will cause the wave to rebound off the cliff, much like a ball thrown against a wall. As the deflected wave makes its way back toward open water, it may slam into the next approaching wave. The combined energy of the two waves can furiously heave water into the air, a condition known as *clapotis*. Clapotis can occur anywhere that wave patterns collide. It is often found where a strong river current drains into an ocean (or lake) that has surging waves or a rising tide.

A swell that is approaching land encounters the friction of the ocean floor. This slows the momentum of the wave and creates excess energy. The abundant energy, which needs to go somewhere, finds an outlet by increasing the height of the wave. A wave can handle only so much height before it breaks, which is why waves in shallow water will break. For paddling close to shore, this can be a problem. For more information on near-shore wave forms, see **surfing**.

Windswept Waves

While deep-water swells are usually formed many miles from your location, local weather has an immediate effect on the waves in your vicinity. Windswept waves are formed when **wind** pushes against the surface of the water. The size of the wave depends on the velocity of the wind and the distance that the wind is able to travel unimpeded along the surface of the water (known as the *fetch*). A lake with a 20-mile fetch can develop much larger waves than one with a 1-mile fetch. If you're on the ocean, windswept waves

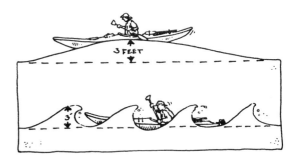

Waves can become difficult at 2 or 3 feet. A swell 2 or 3 feet high is usually no problem (top), but 2- or 3-foot shorter waves (such as found on lakes or in sudden winds) will drench you and can swamp your canoe or kayak.

can develop on top of swells. Local windswept waves are much shorter than swells and are therefore steeper. A windswept wave that is 3 feet tall will feel much different than a swell of 3 feet. A 3-foot swell will gently raise your boat, while a 3-foot windswept wave will likely soak you.

Paddling in Waves

Anytime you're paddling, be acutely aware of your surroundings, including your proximity to surf zones (see **surfing**), land, submerged objects that cause boomers, and currents that promote clapotis. Sometimes submerged rocks or patches of coral are marked on your **nautical chart**; plan your route around them. You should also be able to find tidal currents, rip currents, and river openings on your chart, although this is not always the case. Paddlers often venture into areas inaccessible to larger vessels, for which nautical charts are sometimes less than complete.

Also keep track of the condition of the water. Swells can creep up on you without much notice. This is especially true if you're in deep water and aren't paying close attention. This isn't much of a problem if you intend to stay in deep water (unless they continue to build), but big swells usually mean big surf. If you can't find a protected landing site, you may have your work cut out for you. Because shallow-water waves break so frequently, it is hard to ignore them. This is also true for waves found on bodies of water with a small fetch. If you're caught off guard as a storm approaches when you're far offshore, you'll be much better off in a decked boat, such as a kayak, than in an open boat, such as a canoe. An open canoe caught in wavy conditions can easily become **swamped**. Unless you're an experienced canoeist looking for a challenge (and a canoe full of soaked gear), stay off the water when waves build above 1 or 2 feet.

To predict wave heights, pay close attention to the local weather patterns. A VHF or **weather radio** should provide marine forecasts if you're on an ocean or one of the **Great Lakes** along the U.S.–Canada border. Always be prepared for an encounter with foul weather. Locate the best landing sites on your map, and note the portions of your route that are particularly exposed or difficult. Practice surfing techniques and canoe or kayak rescues until they become second nature (see **surfing** and **T-rescue**). In addition, choose equipment that is designed to remain seaworthy in waves. This rules out many recreational kayaks and most open canoes. Remember that in a matter of minutes, waves several feet in height can develop on inland lakes as well as coastal regions.

A healthy amount of respect and a good dose of **judgment** will help you enjoy the benefits of waves without getting caught in their fury. If you awaken to pounding surf or spray flying off the crests of waves, plan on declaring yourself **windbound**. This way you can enjoy the awesome power of crashing waves from the safety of shore, along with a pot of coffee and a good book.

WEATHER

In many ways, weather is the biggest variable on a **wilderness** trip. It can make your day beautiful or dreary; it can keep you awake at night with a great view of the stars or prevent you from leaving the **tent** in the morning. Just about every other part of a trip can be planned, but you have no control over the weather. If you've ever been caught off guard by **lightning**, or confined to your tent while the **wind** howled, you know the incredible power

of the weather. You need to be familiar with weather patterns and how they develop in order to keep safe and comfortable in the wilderness. Luckily, weather is a fascinating subject!

Weather Basics

Backcountry travelers should learn and understand the four W's: warmth, weight, wind, and wetness. These are responsible for the weather that develops over your head and how it affects you on the ground.

Warmth

The weather on the earth is primarily driven by the sun. The sun heats up the earth in an uneven pattern, partly because some geological features absorb more heat than others. As the earth heats up, the warm air rises and expands. Hot air will eventually rise so far from the earth's warm surface that it will cool down, condense, and begin its descent back to earth. This cycle of rising and falling, expanding and contracting air leads to the second W, weight.

Weight

Although it can be hard to conceptualize, air molecules actually have weight. In fact, at sea level the average weight of 1 square inch of air is a whopping 14.7 pounds! Called *air pressure*, this weight is measured with a barometer. A good way to understand pressure is to imagine each air molecule as a snowflake. One snowflake doesn't weigh much, but if you were under a few hundred thousand snowflakes, say a snowdrift, you would definitely feel the weight.

Air is most compact and heaviest at the surface of the earth. You can understand this by considering how snowflakes are much more compressed at the bottom of a snowdrift than at the top. As air rises, it expands and becomes lighter. In weather terminology, its pressure decreases. For example, if you take the square inch of air that weighs 14.7 pounds at sea level and hike to the top of a 1,000-foot hill, it will weigh only 14.1 pounds there; at 18,000 feet, it will weigh only 7.3

pounds. Thus the weight and density of air depends in part on its elevation. The air at the top of Mount Everest weighs a lot less than the air at the mountain's base. By the time the air reaches the towering heights of the summit, it has expanded so much it has become "thin." This is why mountaineers need supplemental oxygen there.

All of this pressure in the air determines how it moves, because air molecules always flow from areas of high pressure to areas of low pressure, leading to the third W, wind.

Wind

Wind is simply air moving from areas of high pressure to areas of low pressure. The greater the difference in pressure, the stronger the wind will be. You might think that wind travels in a straight line. On the contrary, as wind sweeps along the surface of the earth, it encounters obstacles, such as **mountains** and **forests**, that decrease its speed and sometimes divert its direction. Furthermore, because the earth rotates in a counterclockwise direction on its north polar axis, everything in the Northern Hemisphere veers to the east, including the wind, while everything in the Southern Hemisphere veers to the west. This is called

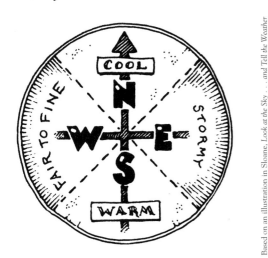

Based on an illustration in Sloane, Look at the Sky . . . and Tell the Weather

In North America, this basic but easy-to-remember illustration helps you predict the weather from wind direction. If the wind blows from the north then it will likely be cool; if the wind is from the east a storm may be due.

the *Coriolis effect.* It gives the Northern Hemisphere weather systems that tend to move from west to east. Despite national weather patterns that move in this direction, local pressure and temperature variations often have a dramatic impact on local winds. They also impact our final W, wetness.

Wetness

Moisture in the air can be found in a gaseous or liquid state. When in a gaseous state, it's called *humidity* and you can't see it. In *Eric Sloane's Weather Book* (an old, out-of-print favorite), he likens moisture in its gaseous state to a wet towel. If you pour a large glass of water onto a towel, you know that the towel is wet but you can't actually see the water. But if you wring or squeeze the towel, or in some other way condense it, the water becomes visible. Air is the same way. Usually, you can't see moisture in the air, but if you condense the air, the water will become visible. Hence the name **condensation.** So what condenses air? The first W, warmth!

When an air molecule becomes cool, it can shrink to the point where it can no longer retain water. This causes the water to condense into a liquid state, such as fog, rain, snow, or clouds. You may have seen an example of this when you have taken your hiking boots off on a cold day and your socks were steaming. When the warm, moist air from your feet is suddenly cooled, the air molecules shrink and the moisture from your sock condenses into steam. All air has a temperature at which it can no longer retain water (known as its *dew point*). If you sleep outside and your sleeping bag is soaking wet in the morning, it's because the temperature of the air dipped below its dew point.

The four W's of weather provide a basic idea of how weather works. Any dramatic change in any of the W's (such as a sudden change in the direction or velocity of the wind or a sudden drop in temperature) will surely bring a dramatic change in the weather. As you observe weather patterns, you will begin to learn more about the four W's and how they are all connected. You will notice that when the weight (or pressure) is high, the weather is usually nice. This is because high-pressure air molecules are so dense that they cannot contain much water. You'll also notice that low-pressure weather systems bring cloudy, rainy days.

Weather Forecasting

Making an accurate forecast of the weather isn't easy. Professional forecasters use computer models and satellite imaging to help them produce an accurate prediction. In the backcountry, however, you have to rely on your own observations and meteorological detective skills. Carrying a small barometer is helpful. So is carrying a **compass**, which can show you the direction of the wind. Even without these tools, you should be able to gather information from the clouds overhead.

Let's assume that you have no tools beyond your own observations. Your insight into the weather is derived from what you can see and feel. Look at the clouds, which are your biggest clue to immediate weather. Learn to read them like you do the topography on a **map**. If the clouds are becoming progressively lower in the sky, expect rain to follow within a day. Also expect rain when the sun has a vague glow or soft edges. If the clouds are billowing and becoming very tall, be wary of a thunderstorm soon. Small, puffy clouds that dot the sky are common afternoon signs of fair weather. However, if you experience significant puffy clouds in the early morning, prepare for potential foul weather in the afternoon. (See also **clouds**.)

The wind offers another clue to changing weather. Any significant change in the direction or velocity of wind is a sure sign that a change in weather (usually a storm) is on the way. Even subtle changes can signify approaching changes in the weather.

If you have a barometer, you can monitor the rising or falling trends in air pressure. The trends in pressure (whether it is rising or falling) are what matter, not the actual pressure itself. Rising pressure tends to bring fair weather, and falling pressure brings diminishing weather. The faster the change in the barometer, the more quickly the weather is approaching.

Certain geographic regions have unique weather patterns. For instance, in the mountains it is common to have afternoon storms, and in coastal areas it is common to have afternoon on-

What's Up?

Signs of Worsening Weather

Falling barometer (carry an altimeter to provide pressure readings)

Rapidly building cumulus clouds

Lenticular clouds and lowering clouds

Signs of Improving Weather

Rising barometer

Cloud breaks

Cloud bases rising

Signs of Continued Fair Weather

No clouds, steadily rising barometer

Barometer high and steady

Cumulus clouds

Dew or frost in the morning, with no fog

Morning fog that burns off rapidly

No afternoon clouds

Source of text: Jim Woodmencey, Reading Weather

If you pay attention to the clues, you can predict incoming weather from certain signs, such as changing clouds and barometric trends.

shore breezes. Keep a weather log during your trip so you can identify local weather patterns. As a part of trip preparations, research forecasts and weather patterns for your trip location. Many online weather sites have forecasts for national parks and popular outdoor destinations (see resources section).

A good forecaster is always making observations of the sky and sensing the slightest changes in the wind. If you become lazy or disinterested, you are sure to miss the subtle clues that something is on the way. Don't forget to consult the sky when planning your route for the day or even when choosing your campsite. A line of billowing clouds on the horizon should make you think twice about **camping** on high ground, hiking an exposed ridge, or paddling across an open expanse of water.

If your observations suggest that a storm is brewing, don't hesitate to take action. If you're in the mountains, get off ridges and move to low ground. If you're on open water, get to shore. When storms approach, they're often accompanied by strong winds and lightning. Get out your rain gear, throw on an extra layer, and prepare to wait it out in a safe location.

Weather Lore

In addition to using scientific methods to track the weather, many people rely on easy-to-remember folklore. Here are a few tried-and-true favorites.

When grass is dry at morning light, look for rain before the night.

When dew is on the grass, no rain will come to pass.

When halo rings the moon or sun, rain's approaching on the run.

Red sky at night, sailors' delight; red sky at morning, sailors take warning.

When campfire smoke does descend, your spell of good weather is sure to end.

When the ditch and pond offend the nose, then look for rain and stormy blows.

When joints ache with throbbing pain, you will surely get some rain.

Learning about weather is a lot of fun, and there are many good resources to consult. If you can't find *Eric Sloane's Weather Book*, try *The Weather Book* from *USA Today*, or the Audubon Society's *Field Guide to North American Weather*. There's great satisfaction in being able to identify clouds and correctly predict the weather for the next day, and in knowing the meaning behind a halo in the sky. By understanding weather, you can test all the old weather lore you learned as a child—and perhaps even come up with some of your own!

See also **wind**, **lightning**, **rain**, **Beaufort scale**, **fog**, and **snow**.

WEATHER RADIO

See **communication devices**.

WEIGHT

The weight of equipment and supplies has always been a matter of concern to outdoors people. Lists of equipment and notes on what can be made lighter or done without are common features of journals and accounts from the early days of exploration. Weight is of particular concern for hikers, skiers, and mountaineers who have to carry gear on their backs. Paddlers can carry heavier items, as long as they fit in the boat, while those with pack animals can bring almost anything they like, including the kitchen sink. Go **trekking** in the Himalaya with a team of porters to carry your gear, and you don't have to worry too much about weight either. Large canvas **tents**, cast-iron **stoves**, and sacks of fresh vegetables can all be carried when they aren't on your back.

Most foot travelers carry their own gear, and to them weight matters a great deal. Skiers and mountaineers sometimes use **sleds** for their gear, which enables them to carry more weight, although sled hauling is not an easy task.

The weight of your load affects how fast you can walk (especially uphill), how often you need to rest, and how soon you tire. Given this influence, it's surprising how many people don't know what their gear weighs or how much they usually carry. Staggering along under a massive load doesn't make for a fun time. Of course, if you're hiking only a short distance to a base camp where you'll stay for a while, the extra weight of luxuries, fresh **food**, and a larger tent could be worth the effort. But in general, a lighter load will make for a more enjoyable time.

What constitutes a light load depends on where you're going, when you're going, and what you're doing. If you need technical climbing gear, you'll have a heavier load than a hiker does. If you're **winter** camping in high mountains, you'll have a much heavier load than if you're **forest** camping in summer.

Whatever you're doing and wherever and whenever you're going, as light as possible is a good maxim as long as you're confident that you can cope with expected and unexpected weather and terrain conditions. Even easy trips with a low daily mileage are more enjoyable the lighter your load. The more distance you want to cover, the more important it is to keep the weight down. Steep, rough terrain also is easier to tackle with a light load.

See also **backpacking**, **hiking**, **thru-hiking**, **ultralight hiking**, **mountaineering**, and **skiing**.

What's "Heavy?"

Any load over 20 pounds is noticeable and has an effect on your activity. The less prepared you are, the bigger the effect it has. Set off with a 25-pound pack and without any prior training, and by the end of the day the pack will seem to have doubled in weight. It's best to build up to a load-carrying trip by taking progressively longer day hikes with progressively heavier packs until you can hike comfortably all day with the weight you expect to carry.

How Much to Carry

The rule of thumb for how much you should carry is no more than a third of your body weight.

That's fine if you weigh 200 pounds and you're all sinew and muscle. But what if 20 pounds of that is excess weight? If that's the case, presumably you should then work on the basis of 180 pounds, a third of which is 60 pounds, and then deduct the 20 extra pounds you're already carrying from that. And what if you weigh 110 pounds? By this formula, the 200-pound man can carry 66 pounds, but the 110-pound woman only 36 pounds.

In reality, what you can carry depends as much on your fitness level and strength as on body weight. Desire comes into it too. Some people are prepared to carry big weights in order to access very remote areas, stay in the **wilderness** a long time, or even just have extra luxuries along. At the same time, our bodies are simply not designed to carry heavy loads, and doing so puts a great strain on them, especially the back and the legs. That in itself is good reason to keep the weight as low as possible.

Surveys have shown that 30 pounds is a critical figure. Below this weight, a load doesn't have much of an effect on how far you can comfortably hike in a day. Above 30 pounds, you'll notice the load and it will have a significant effect on your trip. From interviews with thru-hikers on the **Appalachian Trail**, researcher Roland Mueser found that hikers who carried more than 30 pounds averaged 14.5 miles a day, while those who carried less than 30 pounds averaged 17 miles a day. You may not be planning to hike 14.5 miles a day, let alone 17, but what these figures indicate is that a load of 30-plus pounds affects your performance, which will be true however far you hike.

Most hikers and mountaineers can reduce the weight of their loads without reducing their comfort or safety and without going to the extremes of ultralight hikers. Leaving out an extra sweater is worth doing; weighing every Band-Aid and cutting the handle off your toothbrush isn't, unless every fraction of an ounce counts.

First of all, you need to know the weight of the gear you carry and get into the habit of checking weights when you buy new gear. There can be a pound or more difference in weight between

fleece jackets that provide identical warmth. Heavier ones will have more features, but ask yourself whether these are worth the weight.

When buying new items, you can choose the lightest available rather than the most highly specified or heavily advertised. Be wary of claims made by stores or companies. "Ultralight," "super-light," and "lightweight" have become buzzwords, used to attract customers, and often have no real meaning. How often do you see an item described as heavy? Weigh gear yourself, and make comparisons.

WET EXITS

Contrary to how it may look, wearing a **sprayskirt** while paddling a kayak does *not* trap you in the kayak. This is usually a major concern for beginners who are afraid they'll get stuck in a capsized kayak. For obvious reasons, they're relieved when they realize how easy it is to wet exit a kayak. A wet exit is the act of popping your sprayskirt off an overturned kayak and exiting into the water. The technique is simple, but it's good to practice since at first it's easy to become disoriented.

Your first task once your boat is overturned is to remove the sprayskirt. To get the sprayskirt off, place your hands at your hips and run them along the edge of the skirt until they meet at the grab loop. Pull the grab loop out (toward the bow) and then back toward you. This will pop the skirt off the coaming (the edge of the cockpit). Next, run your hands along the coaming back to your hips, pushing the skirt off the kayak as you go. If necessary, also run your hands behind you to lift the skirt off the back of the coaming. At this point, the sprayskirt is off the kayak, and you just have to exit the boat.

To exit, place your hands on the coaming at your hips and push your body away from the boat, sliding your legs out as if you were taking off a pair of pants. You may find it convenient to roll forward as you're doing this. When you resurface, take hold of your paddle and the boat. Also, if you are in any current, get upstream of your boat as fast as possible (see **swimming in rivers**).

Now that you've read about the wet exit, get out there and practice putting on and popping off your sprayskirt. When you're familiar with the technique above water, try tipping over.

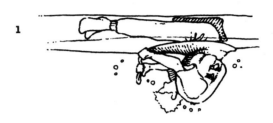

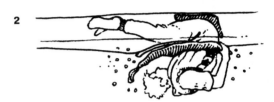

Based on an illustration in Hutchinson, *Complete Book of Sea Kayaking*

Making a wet exit is easy. 1. The paddler runs both hands forward along the cockpit coaming until they reach the sprayskirt grab loop. The paddler pulls the grab loop toward the bow and then away from the kayak. 2. The paddler runs both hands back along the cockpit coaming to his hips, freeing the rest of the sprayskirt. 3. The paddler pushes the kayak away from his hips and slides out, swimming to the surface. 4. The paddler uses one arm to control the kayak and the other to hold the paddle.

Becoming comfortable underwater and learning not to wet exit immediately will prepare you for more advanced kayak rescues, including the Eskimo roll.

WHISTLE

A simple plastic whistle is an important safety item. Weighing less than an ounce, a good whistle can make a noise approaching 100 decibels and is a far more efficient way of attracting attention than yelling. Three blasts–pause–three blasts is the recognized distress signal (six blasts is standard in British Commonwealth countries).

WHITE MOUNTAINS

There are ranges called the White Mountains all over the world, and many single White Mountains, too, of which the most famous is Mont Blanc, the highest peak in the European Alps. By far, the best-known White Mountains in the United States are those in New Hampshire, which are part of the Appalachians. The **Appalachian Trail** runs along the crest of the mountains, including the summit of the highest peak, 6,288-foot Mount Washington, which can be reached by foot, cog railway, or road.

The White Mountains are the one range in the Appalachians with a large area of above-timberline terrain. The area has notoriously stormy and windy weather, and hikers should be prepared for severe conditions, even in summer. On April 12, 1934, the highest **wind** speed ever recorded—231 miles an hour—occurred on Mount Washington. The terrain is very rocky too, which can make progress slow. A system of mountain huts run by the Appalachian Mountain Club lines the range, so camping isn't necessary (see resources section for contact information).

Far less well known are the White Mountains that lie along the Nevada–California border, which make up the east wall of Owens Valley, rising abruptly and magnificently some 10,000 feet from the **desert** floor, and are visible from much of the High Sierra. The highest summit is 14,246-foot White Mountain Peak; the range also includes the highest peak in Nevada, 13,143-foot Boundary Peak. North of White Mountain Peak, the range is little visited and quite wild, but south of the summit a road runs along the mountain crest. Lying in the **rain** shadow of the **Sierra Nevada**, these White Mountains are desert mountains, part of the Great Basin. They have very low rainfall, but enough snow for **ski touring** usually falls in winter. These White Mountains are best known for the ancient, gnarled bristlecone pines, which are found between 9,000 and 11,000 feet. These are the oldest living things on earth, with one having an incredible 5,000 years of growth rings.

WHITEWATER CANOEING

Many **wilderness** canoe trips include stretches of whitewater that range from easy class I runs to remote, difficult drops. While it may look like fun, running whitewater in the wilderness can be a risky endeavor. On remote rivers, a simple mistake can quickly turn into a dangerous situation. From losing **cooking** utensils, pots, pans, **packs**, **tents**, and even kayaks and canoes, dumping in rapids can, at the very least, be an inconvenience to paddlers. If you unexpectedly dump in a set of rapids, the consequences can be severe. And, unfortunately, some paddlers don't get off so easy;

"I've had friends lose food, cooking utensils, and pots and pans when their packs floated away. Another unlucky paddler I know lost his tent and his head net in the same upset. What a miserable combination! I myself lost my whole canoe for seven hours after dumping in a difficult run. I was lucky enough to find it floating in a large eddy a mile downriver (whew!). All of these mistakes made for good lessons in the risks of paddling remote whitewater. Humbled and more than a little shook up, I think in the end we all considered ourselves lucky."—AA many wilderness paddlers have paid for their whitewater mistakes with their lives.

Despite the risks, or perhaps because of them, many wilderness trippers find themselves paddling rivers with incredible stretches of whitewater. Indeed, if you know what you're doing, remote whitewater canoeing can be wildly fun. Here are some tips you should know before you hit the waves.

- You don't have to run the rapids. **Portaging** or **lining** is a completely acceptable alternative to paddling whitewater. On remote rivers, a better question than "Why *shouldn't* I paddle these rapids?" is often "Why *should* I?"
- Always scout the rapids. *Always.* It's the only way to discover the dangerous and sometimes hidden hazards that may exist, before it's too late. (See **scouting rapids**.)
- Don't paddle a set of rapids unless you're willing and able to perform a **rescue** in them.
- On many remote rivers, **sprayskirts** are a necessity for keeping the heaving water out of your canoe. If your canoe isn't heavily loaded, you may want to consider using **flotation** as well.
- Remember that a heavily loaded canoe doesn't respond as quickly as an empty canoe. It'll take more time to maneuver around or power past any given hazard.
- Consider using a tie-in system to keep your gear in the boat. In the event of an upset, it will prevent your gear from sinking or floating away.
- Have a person on shore spot you with a **throw bag** whenever possible. Throwing a throw bag takes practice if you want to get it right when it really counts.
- Keep your focus downriver. You need to perpetually focus two moves ahead of the one you're performing.
- Stay upright. It's the whole point of the game.

If you think you'd like to try whitewater canoeing, seek instruction and practice before you rely on your skills to get you, and all your gear, down a wilderness river. In fact, you don't need to

Whitewater canoeing in the wilderness is a lot of fun, but it can be risky. Paddlers should be proficient in reading rapids, scouting, paddling, and performing river rescues.

be in the wilderness to enjoy whitewater canoeing. Some great whitewater runs are within a half-hour drive of major metropolitan areas. Before you take on a set of rapids, spend some time to refine your **canoeing strokes** and learn the many additional skills that are specific to whitewater. In addition, you'll need to spend some time learning about rivers and **reading rapids**. There are a lot of **moving-water hazards** that can turn any whitewater run into a terrifying struggle for survival. You need to be confident that you can identify and avoid these before you even step into your canoe.

There are instructional programs across the country that can teach you whitewater skills. To locate one near you, ask around at your local paddling shop or contact the American Canoe Association (see resources section). If you're going to learn to paddle in whitewater, also take a swiftwater rescue course, which teaches you how to handle yourself in whitewater when things don't go as planned.

WICKING

Wicking is the movement of moisture away from the body and through a fabric. Base-layer fabrics such as polyester and polypropylene all wick moisture away from the skin. This occurs in two ways. First, fabrics may have a hydrophilic (water-loving) layer next to the skin that attracts moisture, lifting it off the skin. Second, body heat pushes moisture away from the body and through the fabric. Not all fabrics wick, which is why some can feel clammy next to the skin. (See **clothing**.)

However fast they wick moisture, all fabrics can be overloaded when you're sweating hard. The best fabrics remove the excess moisture quickly once you stop exercising, leaving a dry layer next to the skin.

WIDOW MAKERS

Widow makers are dead trees or branches that can fall at any moment. If you happen to be beneath a widow maker when this happens, you can easily be injured or killed. It's a bad feeling to wake up in the middle of a windy night to the creaking and groaning of an old tree. Instead, scan any likely campsite for potential widow makers before you decide to make that spot home for the night. Look a distance into the woods. Trees that are 30 feet away can still fall on you if they're that tall. If you find a widow maker at your campsite (which you frequently will), avoid placing your **tent** or **tarp** anywhere near it unless you can easily determine the path where it will fall.

Trees aren't the only objects that can make a "widow" of your loved one. Anything that can fall on you while you relax or sleep is just as dangerous. Coconuts are a perfect example of such a hazard. If you have ever seen a mature coconut fall out of a palm tree, you know that its bomblike descent could cause serious damage. If you're enjoying a tropical night under the stars, stay away from coconut-laden palm trees, especially if the coconuts are brown; these are the ones that are ripe enough to fall.

WILD ANIMALS

Watching wild animals can be the highlight of a **wilderness** trip: otters playing in a pool, a **coyote** hunting, **wolves** prowling the edge of a meadow, mule deer grazing outside your tent, a black bear and cubs eating berries. The sounds of animals can be wonderful too. The weird sounds of elk bugling in the fall, the eerie howling of wolves, and the whistle of a marmot all conjure up the wild. The more time you spend in the wilderness, especially alone, the more wildlife you will see.

Not all animal encounters are quite so enjoyable, of course, and some animals can be a nuisance and even a danger. **Bears** are the animals that people fear most, although this fear is mostly misplaced, as long as sensible precautions are taken. **Snakes** are probably the next creatures that people would most like to avoid. But, again, they aren't as big a threat as many people think. **Mice**, raccoons, and squirrels don't frighten many people, but they can be very irritating, especially if they spend every night trying to get into your **food** bags or gnawing holes in your **pack** or **tent**. Mice also can be annoying when they keep run-

> "I was memorably kept awake by a porcupine once, chewing on the wood of the hut I was sleeping in, which sounded like a chain saw. Eventually I went outside, barefoot and wearing just a fleece top, and threw snowballs at it and then chased it through the snow until it climbed a tree. I've also had a porcupine walk into the closed door of my tent over and over again, presumably in the hope that this strange, soft material would eventually give way and it could get at the salt in my sweaty boots."—CT

ning over your sleeping bag. Porcupines aren't frightening either, although you don't want to get too close to them.

Hearing strange snuffles and grunts at night can be alarming, especially in bear country. The darkness amplifies sound, and a mouse creeping around can sound huge. But after a few nights out, you'll remember and become familiar with certain sounds, such as a mouse in the grass, the **wind** in the trees, deer grazing, and other night sounds. Then you'll wake up only when the sound is unusual. Don't forget that the wilderness is home to these animals and that *you* are the visitor. You have brought the food that attracts them, and it's your responsibility to ensure they don't get it, for their sake.

Animals accustomed to eating human food are at risk. Bears who associate humans with the food they carry may become dangerous and have to be destroyed or relocated. Animals will eat plastic bags and containers if there is food inside, and these can kill them. Human food isn't good for animals anyway. Resist the temptation to feed animals, however cute that squirrel may be and however much you want to take its photograph. Be aware that any food scraps you leave will attract animals and could cause problems for the next people who visit the area. Respecting wildlife means being careful where you camp too. In arid areas, avoid camping close to or within sight of water. The water could be vital for

---

"I remember waking up in a small backcountry shelter to hear the door latch rattle. 'It's unlocked,' I called out, assuming it was another hiker. There was no reply. The rattling went on. I spoke again, more loudly. No reply. The rattling continued. Eventually, I decided I'd rather know what it was than lie there sleepless while my imagination went crazy, so I tiptoed to the door, flashlight in hand, and yanked it abruptly open. A startled deer jumped backward. We stared at each other for a few seconds, then the deer slid silently into the darkness. I guess it was scratching itself on the door handle."—CT

---

wildlife, and your presence may keep them away. (See also **Leave No Trace**.)

Don't deliberately disturb wildlife, either. Watch animals and birds from far enough away that they don't notice you. A small pair of **binoculars** is useful for this and helps you resist the temptation to go just that little bit closer. Photographers should take care, too. When you want

to get a better photograph, it's easy to forget how dangerous a bear or moose can be. If you want to take closeups of animals, carry a telephoto lens so you can do so from a safe distance.

Before visiting an area, it's worth learning about the wildlife that live there: What should you look out for? Where are animals found? What problems are likely? What can you do to avoid disturbing wildlife? Knowing about the wildlife can make a trip more interesting and also reduce the likelihood you will cause problems for the wildlife.

WILDERNESS

Wilderness is an inspiring, wonderful word that conjures up images of natural beauty, wildlife, silence, and peace. The 1964 Wilderness Act led to the creation of designated wilderness areas all over the United States (see **Wilderness Act**). Wilderness also exists outside these official enclaves, of course. Even small natural areas can be called *wilderness*, as can areas that were once exploited but which have now recovered or are in the process of recovery. Secondary-growth **forests** can be as wild as old-growth ones.

The word *wilderness* comes from the Anglo-Saxon *wildeorness*, meaning "place of the wild animals," and the presence of **wild animals** is indeed a sign that a place is still wild. Knowing that **bears** or **wolves** are out there is a sign that the land is not tame, not controlled, not fenced in or restrained.

Humanity comes from the wilderness and depends on the wilderness, despite what many, separated from nature, think. We need it both physically and spiritually. Wilderness is the source of life, providing essential water and the plants and animals that make up our food. It is also a source of inspiration, beauty, and freedom. It is possible that human life could continue without wilderness, although never without nature, but it would be a poorer, sadder, degraded, and uncivilized world.

Wilderness is self-renewing and sustainable but also easily damaged and destroyed by human technology. If we want wilderness to exist in the future, we can't take it for granted. It needs defending and protecting from those who would develop and degrade it.

However, wilderness also needs protection from being "loved to death." The very popularity of some wilderness places, while protecting them from development, also threatens them with too many people, too many pairs of **boots** trampling the land, too many campsites flattening the ground. The wilderness can start to wear out if overused. To save the wilderness from ourselves, **Leave No Trace** techniques are essential. The aim should always be to leave as little impact as possible. The old saying, "Take only memories, leave nothing but footprints," is attributed to Chief Seattle (1786–1866) of the Suquamish in Washington; the modern version was popularized by Terry and Renny Russell as "Take only photographs and leave only footprints." Today we need to be careful about where we leave those footprints too.

However, the real threat to wilderness comes from industrial development in the form of mining, dams, logging, overgrazing, ski resorts, and mass tourism facilities—not from wilderness travelers. The land can recover from eroded **trails** and campsites much more easily than it can from being clear-cut, strip-mined, or drowned.

Those who love the wilderness can work toward its preservation so that future generations can enjoy it too by joining and working with such organizations as the **Sierra Club** and the **Wilderness Society** (see resources section).

WILDERNESS ACT

"In wildness is the preservation of the Earth." So said Henry David Thoreau back in the mid-nineteenth century (against strong popular belief to the contrary). In that brief statement, Thoreau verbalized a growing belief that many individuals would soon come to share. Without the early vision and committed efforts of such conservationists as Aldo Leopold, Bob Marshall, John Muir (see **Muir, John**), Stephen Mather, and Arthur Carhart, many **wilderness** areas that we enjoy today might instead be urban sprawl or strip

mines. Unfortunately, many wild lands that deserved to be saved did not receive protection. Indeed, by the 1950s, wild lands were vanishing at an alarming rate. This significant and permanent loss of vast wilderness areas commanded the attention, energy, and dollars of people everywhere who committed themselves to the preservation of wilderness and its values.

In 1964, after eight years of debate, President Lyndon B. Johnson signed into law the Wilderness Act, which allowed the U.S. Congress to set aside federal lands as designated wilderness. The act defined wilderness as follows: "A wilderness, in contrast with those areas where man and his own works dominate the landscape, is hereby recognized as an area where the Earth and its community of life are untrammeled by man, where man himself is a visitor who does not remain."

The Wilderness Act did not come easy, and even today the very definition of wilderness that Congress outlined in 1964 is challenged and threatened. Many people are unaware of the intellectual, political, and legal battles that have been fought—and continue to be fought—in the name of wilderness. The hard work of such organizations as the **Sierra Club**, the **Nature Conservancy**, and the **Wilderness Society** have made it possible for millions of outdoor enthusiasts to experience the wilderness without realizing how fragile its existence is (see resources section).

The job of protecting the wilderness should not be left to conservationists and preservationists alone; it must be the responsibility of every person who uses this precious resource for **hiking**, biking, climbing, **canoeing**, **camping**, or any other outdoor pursuit. Keep informed regarding the preservation of your favorite wilderness area, and participate in conservation efforts. Research various conservation organizations, and become a member of those whose practices you support. Write your elected representatives on issues pertaining to wilderness areas, and preserve the wilderness by always practicing **Leave No Trace** camping techniques.

WILDERNESS SOCIETY

An "organization of spirited people who will fight for the freedom of the wilderness" was called for in 1930 by Bob Marshall. As head of the Division of Recreation and Lands in the U.S. Forest Service, Marshall worked for the creation of more **wilderness** reserves. He was a prodigious hiker, often walking more than 30 miles a day and occasionally up to 70. In 1934, Marshall—along with a small group of others, including Benton MacKaye, who came up with the idea of the **Appalachian Trail**—founded the Wilderness Society with the purpose of protecting wilderness and promoting appreciation of it. Marshall anonymously paid for the launch with a donation. The founders of the Wilderness Society believed that preserving wilderness was "a serious human need rather than a luxury and a plaything."

Since its founding, the Wilderness Society has played a major part in defending wilderness and in working for more wilderness preservation. It continues this work today. (For contact information for the Wilderness Society, see the resources section.)

WIND

All backcountry travelers have at one time cursed the wind. Wind can cause your nylon **tent** to flap loudly all night long or prevent you from making progress along your route. On the other hand, having no wind can cause problems as well. If you have ever tried to eat your dinner in an **insect**-infested meadow without a hint of wind, you know how great a breeze can be. Wind can be a blessing or a challenge, and sooner or later you'll have to deal with it at both ends of the scale.

If you're traveling in strong wind, it may be easier, smarter, and safer to stay put and wait for the wind to subside. This is called being **windbound.** Traveling into a very strong wind can be exhausting. It can also expose you to harsh **wind chill** temperatures that can lead to **hypothermia**. On open water, strong winds can generate large waves that can result in your canoe or kayak being **swamped** and make rescues difficult or impossible.

When selecting a campsite, make sure to find an area that is free from dead trees or branches. These are called **widow makers** for obvious reasons. While it is unlikely, even healthy trees can snap in a strong wind.

> "Once while I was leading a canoe trip, a completely healthy white pine tree snapped 8 feet off the ground during a wild windstorm. When it fell, it landed right on top of a tent sleeping four teenage girls. The tent collapsed, trapping the girls inside. Because the tree was alive, its many branches helped break the fall. Amazingly, the only injuries were one big bump on the head and a non-threatening asthma attack."—AA

Erecting a tent in ferocious wind can be an Olympian feat. First, make sure you've chosen a tent with many heavily stitched tie-down points or grommets (but keep in mind that grommets can rip right off of tent flies in severe wind). If your tent doesn't have many tie-down points, it will be hard to secure it in a strong wind. As you unfold your tent, keep your eye on every miscellaneous piece of fabric: the **groundcloth**, the fly, the stuff sack, and even the tent itself. Start by staking—or better yet, tying—one corner of the tent to the ground or a nearby object. If you start to erect the tent before it is anchored to the ground, it may very well take flight the minute you connect the poles—so be prepared! To avoid losing your tent to the wind, think of it as a big sail that wants to fly away, and don't underestimate the force that can be exerted against it in a strong wind. If you think that tossing your **sleeping bag, sleeping pad,** or **clothing** into your tent will keep it from blowing away, you're in for a big surprise. Rely on this method of tent control, and you could lose all your belongings in one strong gust—a dangerous predicament, and one that your friends would never let you live down!

Once the tent is erected, place it with the narrowest end into the wind, which is the most aerodynamic position.

> "One of my friends once temporarily lost her tent when it blew out of her grasp while she was setting it up. The partially assembled tent flew through the air and into the middle of a small mountain lake. Another time, while I was camping at Devil's Tower National Monument in Wyoming, a sudden strong wind picked up a two-person tent and tossed it 15 feet into the air before carrying it several hundred yards away. It just bounced along the range like tumbleweed."—AA

When **cooking**, place your **stove** on the **leeward** side of a rock or use a windscreen, if you have one. Windscreens are lightweight nylon or aluminum screens that protect the flame from the wind. If necessary, a makeshift windscreen can be fashioned out of tent stakes (or sharp sticks), a stuff sack, and some **duct tape**. If a fire hazard (such as extremely dry weather) exists, avoid building a **fire**. Wind can carry embers and sparks through the air, heightening the risk of **forest fires** or brush fires.

If you're **backpacking**, avoid exposed areas on windy days. It is amazing how nerve-racking and exhausting it can be to hike a narrow ridge on a windy day. On paddling trips, wind should be a major factor in your every decision regarding travel. Wind-generated **waves** can build quickly and make even the shortest outing a fight for survival. Big waves create dangerous surf zones that can be difficult to negotiate (see **surfing**). If you're paddling on open water and have access to **weather** forecasts, find out in advance the predicted wave heights and strength of the wind. Become familiar with the **Beaufort scale** so you can visualize the impact of wind on the water. (See also **open-water hazards**.)

On rivers, wind and current can combine to make paddling difficult and dangerous. This is especially true when the wind is blowing against the current. Always use extra caution when paddling on rivers or in **coastal currents** on windy days.

Wind tends to build in the afternoon as the earth begins to radiate heat. Sudden shifts in the wind or changes in wind strength can indicate an approaching storm. If you detect such a change, move to a secure location. If you're on the water, paddle to shore; if you're in the **mountains**, get off high ridges. Keep an eye toward the sky for signs that a storm may be brewing nearby.

With all this talk about the risks associated with strong wind, it can be easy to forget that wind is often a wonderful asset. A good tailwind can make for great sailing in your canoe or kayak. While you're sailing, you can also appreciate the fact that there are no bugs. Finally, when the wind becomes so strong that you have to stop traveling, you can rest and enjoy the day or haul out a small lightweight kite and watch it dance in the sky.

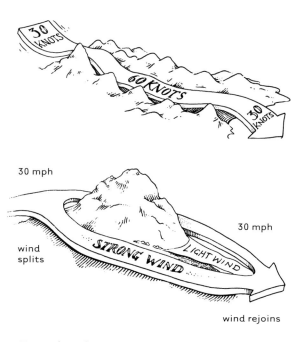

Terrain has a big impact on wind velocity. Plan your route to avoid dangerously strong winds.

WINDBOUND

Sometimes the **wind** can be your friend, and sometimes it becomes your enemy. When it's the latter, you may decide that it is safer, smarter, or just plain easier to stay put. If this is the case, you are windbound. Sometimes being windbound is annoying (especially if you are on a tight schedule). Other times, it can offer a relaxing break for your body (see also **rest days**). Only one thing is certain: there's no telling how long the wind will blow. It can last for a morning or for several days. On or about the second day of being windbound, you'll probably develop a serious case of cabin fever. This is especially true if the wind is accompanied by driving **rain** or **snow** that keeps you in your tent, as is often the case. This can be dreadfully boring, but often you'll discover creative ways to pass the time. Try reading a book, making yet another meal, or offering small sacrifices to the weather gods.

While the term *windbound* is most commonly used in paddle sports, such as **canoeing** and **sea kayaking**, it is a circumstance that can affect any outdoor enthusiast. A mountaineer who wakes to howling winds may be wiser to declare himself windbound rather than get blown off the mountain. If you're lucky, the wind will be so strong when you awaken that there's no question regarding whether you should stay put. It's much more likely, however, that you'll struggle to break camp and make it only a short distance before you realize the battle is futile. If you have been paddling or hiking your brains out and the scenery hasn't changed a bit, it's time to get the heck off the water or trail and make yourself comfortable.

WIND CHILL

The wind-chill factor measures how cold it feels outside when the **wind** is blowing. For instance, if it is 25°F but there is a 15-mile-an-hour wind, the temperature will feel like 13°F. This is because the wind carries away some of the heat your body generates. The stronger the wind, the more quickly your body loses its heat and the colder it

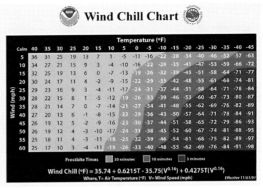

In 2001 the National Weather Service introduced this new wind-chill chart.

will feel. Wind chill can be especially devastating in cold temperatures because the risk of both **hypothermia** and **frostbite** increases.

To protect yourself from the effects of wind chill, include a wind shell such as a thin nylon jacket and pants in your layering system as your outermost layer (see **clothing**). With the invention of waterproof-breathable fabric (see **breathability**), it is quite common to have a wind shell double as your **rain** gear. This works fine, but it can make for an expensive shell. If you think that you will be wearing your wind shell all of the time (many people do), you may want to invest in a less expensive windbreaker. This will protect your rain gear from daily wear and tear and will help you stay drier when it rains.

When the temperature is low and the wind is howling, make sure to protect yourself from **cold-weather injuries**, such as hypothermia and frostbite. Cover exposed skin, and limit the amount of time you spend directly in the wind, if at all possible. While the wind chill table (updated in 2001) suggests that the wind robs our body of heat slower than we earlier suspected, it can still be quite a surprise to discover how quickly you become cold.

WINDWARD

Windward is the side of an object or landmass that faces the wind. It is the opposite of **leeward**. It can be used in a sentence as follows: "We paddled to the windward side of the island so we could surf the big waves." Because the windward side of a geologic feature is more exposed to the elements, it may present more difficult traveling conditions. In most cases, it is smart to find a lee-ward alternative, if possible (although it may be more buggy). An exception would be if you're traveling in a mountainous region in the **winter** or spring and find yourself needing to traverse a snowy slope. In this scenario, strongly consider choosing the windward side because it will have less **snow** accumulation and therefore may be a safer alternative than the leeward side. (See also **avalanches** and **cornices**.)

WINTER

A silent frozen land, the ground bone hard with days of frost, trees bowed with snow, icicles on a cliff, a keen **wind** whipping across the dead yellow grass. Winter is a time of hard, cold beauty, of splendor and harshness. Venturing into the win-ter wilderness is only for the experienced, the well equipped, and the hardy. It isn't easy, but the re-wards are many.

Not all winters are equal. For real cold, long hours of darkness, and a weak sun with no warmth, head north. If even the thought of that makes you shiver, head south, especially south-west, where winter can be the best time for **hiking** in the low **desert** (and summer is the season to fear).

The higher you go into the **mountains**, the more winter grips, even in the southwestern United States—you'll find ski resorts in Arizona. But the far north is the coldest and darkest. North of the Arctic Circle, there's no daylight at all in winter.

Dealing with winter in the north and in the mountains means dealing with cold, often ex-treme cold, and temperatures well below freezing even on the warmest days. In temperatures like this, high-quality cold-weather equipment is re-quired, along with the ability to use it regardless of conditions. **Down** and **vapor barrier** clothing makes the best sense in bitter cold, because the

air will be dry. **Tents** that can be pitched while wearing thick mitts (see **gloves and mitts**) make life in the cold much easier, and a warm **sleeping bag** is essential.

You need great care to stay warm and to avoid **cold-weather injuries**. Don't handle anything metal—such as tent poles, tent stakes, **ice axes**, **stoves**, or pots—with bare hands, or your skin will freeze and stick to it. Be careful with stove **fuel** too. If you spill white gas on your skin, it's likely to cause **frostbite**. Liner gloves are useful when handling metal, although you won't want to wear them on their own for long or your hands will get very cold.

In winter, do everything methodically and carefully. You can't afford to make mistakes. Take particular care not to get wet, and make sure your warm clothing and sleeping bag stay dry. Take care not to get cold too, putting on warm clothing as soon as you stop and living in your sleeping bag in camp, if necessary. Don't get too hot either; especially try not to sweat much because perspira-tion will dampen your clothing and then freeze. When on the move, adjust clothing whenever you start to overheat or cool down. Remember that a **hat** makes a huge difference. Just putting one on or taking it off can be enough to warm you up or cool you down. If there's any wind at all, even just a light breeze, wear windproof clothing. (See also **clothing**.)

The environmental impacts of winter travel are few compared with summer, unless the snow cover is thin. Your main concern should be not to disturb animals, which have enough difficulty surviving winter, due to the cold and a shortage of food, without having to expend energy running away from humans. Once an animal is aware of you, move away before you startle it even more.

See also **snow**, **snow camping**, **snow shelters**, and **snow shovels**.

WOLVES

Wolves are iconic **wilderness** animals. To hear the eerily beautiful howl of a wolf is to know you are in the wilderness. To see a wolf in the wild is a wonderful experience, one that leaves you shivering with delight.

> "Once in the Yukon, while crossing a meadow in the half light of evening, I watched a pack of wolves drifting along the edge of the forest. When they slipped into the shadows of the trees and were gone, I was left standing in the meadow, stunned and delighted."—CT

Wolves live in our subconscious, unfortunately usually as symbols of evil, such as in the story of Red Riding Hood and in the legend of the werewolf. From humanity's beginnings, wolves competed with us for prey; when we domesticated animals, wolves preyed on them too, except for the wolves we domesticated and turned into dogs to defend our herds against their relatives. Now our view of this magnificent **wild animal** is changing, and just in time in the United States, where the wolf was nearly wiped out. It's too late in much of Europe, however, where it has already disappeared.

The gray wolf, *Canis lupus*, used to live throughout North America, feeding on deer and elk and other mammals. During the nineteenth century and much of the twentieth, wolves were persecuted in much of the United States, until only a few hundred remained in the lower 48 states; there are far more in Alaska and in Canada (where current populations are estimated at 8,000 and 50,000, respectively).

The Endangered Species Act gave the last few wolves protection; their numbers began to increase again, and now there are some 2,200 wolves in Minnesota and a few hundred in Michigan and Wisconsin. In other areas where wolves had been completely eradicated, they have been reintroduced in small numbers, most notably in **Yellowstone** National Park and central Idaho. There are now around 160 wolves in this area, plus another 75 or so in northwestern Montana, where wolves have spread down from Canada. The return of the wolves has been due in part to their popularity with the general public, who like the idea of seeing and hearing them, and in part to the offer of compensation to ranchers and farmers for any loss of livestock.

Further south in Arizona, Mexican gray wolves, a subspecies, have been reintroduced from Mexico, while in the southeastern United States, particularly North Carolina, a different species, the red wolf (*Canis rufus*) has been released back into the wild after a breeding program of captive animals.

No human deaths from wolf attack have been recorded in North America. However, this doesn't mean wolves are completely safe. There have been a few attacks that resulted in minor injuries. The chances of being attacked are miniscule, however. Even seeing one isn't that likely, and many "wolf" sightings are actually coyotes. The two look similar, but wolves are bigger and run with their tails held straight out rather than hanging down. Wolves also have shorter ears and blunter muzzles. They vary enormously in color, from almost white to gray and brown to nearly black.

WOODCRAFT

All **wilderness** skills related to **forest** travel and **camping** could be called *woodcraft*: "skill and practice in anything relating to the woods and especially in maintaining oneself and making one's way in the woods." However, the term, also known as *bushcraft*, is usually used for the traditional skills of forest living, such as shelter building, **fire** lighting, and living off the land. These days, these skills are often grouped under the heading of survival, although they are about far more than that. Horace Kephart, author of the classic *Camping and Woodcraft*, defines woodcraft as "the art of finding one's way in the wilderness and getting along well by utilizing Nature's storehouse."

Until the second half of the twentieth century, woodcraft was standard practice because there were no other ways of living in the forest. *Camping and Woodcraft* was first published in the early 1900s yet was still in print in the 1950s. More recent books, such as Tom Brown's *Field Guide to Wilderness Survival*, cover the same material, including ax use, **knife** use, cordage techniques, shelters, fires, **edible plants**, snares and traps, and how to prepare animals for cooking. This is how the mountain men and the trappers in Canada lived. The original experts were the Native Americans, who had lived this way for generations.

Some of the skills are useful in an emergency. However, the problem with much of woodcraft is its high impact. When the number of wilderness wanderers was small, breaking branches off trees to make a bough bed, chopping down saplings to build a shelter, and lighting a fire to keep warm were acceptable. There was no alternative, given the equipment of the day. Today, there are too many of us to all live like this. If everyone who ventured into the Appalachians, the **Rocky Mountains**, or the **Sierra Nevada** carried axes and constructed natural shelters and beds, the woods would soon be devastated. We have the equipment to be more comfortable than we would be with just woodcraft techniques, so there is no need to pretend it's 1850.

In a few remote areas, woodcraft techniques are still acceptable. In the little-known Monts Groulx in northern Québec, Chris has stayed in a trapper's **tent** with poles made from felled trees, sleeping on a bough bed and cooking over a wood-burning stove. But only 200 people a year visit the region, so the impact is small, especially because most use the same tents, which the **guide** moves each year to spread out (and thus lessen) the damage.

A fascination with woodcraft is understandable. It's a means to survive without all the modern high-tech gear. If we were to lose our gear, or if it were damaged, what would we do? But for the mountain men, the same question was what would they do if they lost their ax or ran out of ammunition. They didn't live that way by choice.

The most useful woodcraft technique is undoubtedly **navigation** and route finding, followed by fire lighting. A fire could save your life and is an excellent way of **signaling** in an emergency. Shelter building could be useful too (see **shelter, emergency**).

There are many woodcraft, bushcraft, and survival schools that teach the necessary techniques. The best known of these is Tom Brown's Tracker School (see resources section). The best schools also teach the philosophy behind the skills—the respect for nature and the working with the wilderness that should lie at the heart of woodcraft.

WOOL

Wool was the main fiber used for providing warmth in the outdoors until the 1980s, when modern synthetics began to replace it. Look at any photos of outdoors people before the 1980s, and you'll see wool shirts, wool sweaters, wool pants, wool **gloves**, and wool **hats**. A checked-wool shirt was the badge of many outdoor folk. Soon, wool gave way to new synthetic materials. Why? Because these fabrics weighed less, dried more quickly, and were easier to care for.

Today, though, wool is creeping back into the outdoor **clothing** market. Why the reversion to wool? Partly it's because wool just about disappeared from the stores, except for **socks**, so for many years there wasn't really any choice. But it's mainly because of developments that mean the latest wool doesn't itch when worn next to

Canvas tent with log poles at a remote camp in northern Québec.

CHRIS TOWNSEND

the skin and it can be machine washed. Very fine knits are available too, suitable for warm-weather wear and aerobic activities.

> "On my first long-distance hike in the 1970s, I wore wool socks, a lambswool base layer, a wool shirt and wool trousers, and I carried wool mitts, a wool balaclava, and a heavy wool sweater. Five years later, all the wool had gone except for the socks, replaced by polycotton, polypropylene, acrylic, and fleece."—CT

Wool has many advantages. It absorbs moisture vapor into its fibers, leaving the surface next to the skin dry, and it can absorb up to a third of its weight before it feels cold or damp. Wool fibers are very fine, especially in top-quality wools (such as merino), and are twisted or crimped, which makes them stand apart from one another so that warm air is trapped between them. Because moisture is absorbed into the fibers, it doesn't fill these spaces, so wool is still warm when damp. These spaces also allow moisture vapor to move through the wool to the outside, making wool very breathable (see **breathability**). By absorbing and releasing moisture, both liquid and vapor, wool can keep you comfortable in a wide range of temperatures. With a wool base layer, you can stay cool when working hard, but keep warm when you stop. Wool is naturally stretchy too—up to 30 percent when dry, 60 to 70 percent when wet—so garments give great freedom of movement.

For long trips, wool is useful because it stays clean and fresh longer than many synthetics. This is because the fibers have scales on the outside that keep dirt from penetrating as well as natural antimicrobial properties. Wool that gets wet, especially socks, can sometimes smell a bit like sheep, but that's far preferable to the chemical stink of synthetics.

Wool is also fire resistant, so a wool garment won't melt or burn you if a spark from a campfire lands on it or if you brush against a hot **stove**.

And even in the thinnest knits, it's resistant to ultraviolet rays, with a **sun protection** factor of 25.

Environmentally, wool is friendly in that it's biodegradable and can also be recycled. However, sheep do cause problems with overgrazing in some areas, and some of the chemicals, especially pesticides, used to treat sheep are toxic. These chemicals are being phased out by many farmers in favor of biodegradable ones. Harsh chemicals may also be used to clean and treat the wool after the sheep has been shorn. There is a belief that the itchiness of some wool is due to residues of these chemicals rather than to the wool itself. Organic wool is available.

Wool isn't perfect, of course. The disadvantages are a slower drying time, especially in thicker knit and felted wool, and a heavier weight than synthetics, which may preclude carrying a thick wool sweater for warmth. Felted wool garments are fairly wind and water resistant, but again they are heavy. But for the extremities (socks, hats, gloves), next-to-skin wear, and light midlayers, wool is a superb fabric.

WRAPPED CANOE

Anytime a canoe is on a river, there's the possibility that it could become wrapped around a rock. Wrapping occurs when a canoe hits a rock broadside. As the current pushes on the ends of the canoe, they begin to fold around the side of the rock. This is a problem on several levels. For starters, this situation usually occurs after an upset in whitewater, which means that somebody had to swim the rapids. This can be a traumatic experience in and of itself. Before you worry about your canoe, ensure the safety of any paddling partners who swam the rapids. Are they warm? Have they been injured? (See also **swimming in rivers** and **whitewater canoeing**.)

Although staring at your canoe sitting in the middle of the rapids can feel like an emergency, it generally is not life threatening. The best thing to do is use the old acronym STOP (Stop, Think, Organize, Plan). **Retrieving a canoe or kayak** from a set of rapids can take a while, so consider spending the night at the site. If your canoe is plastic, it may rebound into a usable shape with some heat (put it in the sun) and some brute force. If your canoe is aluminum, only brute force will work. Have your **repair kit** on standby for the inevitable cracks and holes after the accident.

The real emergency with a wrapped canoe comes when people get trapped between the rock and the canoe. This is a nasty situation that often results in the death of the paddler(s). Because the canoe is being bombarded with the force of the current, it can literally crush the paddler(s) or, at the very least, prevent an easy escape. To avoid getting pinned, paddlers must immediately get upstream of their canoe or kayak if they tip over. In addition, the use of **flotation** in a canoe (air bags) or kayak (bulkheads or air bags) will significantly decrease the chance that it will get pinned in the first place.

Y

YARD SALE

Yard sale is a **skiing** term that refers to a serious wipeout that results in an ever-widening path of the skier's gear spread across the slope. Upon pulling your head out of the snow, you'll have to endure an assortment of wisecrack comments, such as "That was a serious yard sale!" and "Nice yard sale, buddy."

YELLOWSTONE

Yellowstone National Park, in the **Rocky Mountains** in northwestern Wyoming and parts of Montana and Idaho, is most famous for its geysers, bubbling mudpots, hot springs, and other thermal features. These are set in a large upland plateau mostly forested with lodgepole pine and split by the dramatic and colorful Grand Canyon of the Yellowstone River, with its tremendous 308-foot Lower Falls. There are far more active thermal volcanic features in Yellowstone than anywhere else in the world, with some 10,000 hot springs in various forms, including 200 geysers, some of which shoot thousands of gallons of steaming water over 100 feet into the air. Some geysers, such as the famous Old Faithful, are in developed areas, but many lie in the **wilderness**.

The heart of Yellowstone is a huge caldera, the remnants of a massive volcano that erupted around 600,000 years ago. Hot liquid rock called *magma* lies a few thousand feet below the earth's surface in Yellowstone. When water sinks down and hits the magma, it boils and the pressure of the steam sends up the huge spurts of the geysers. Most of the thermal features are strung out along the aptly named Firehole River and can be visited by road and boardwalk.

Yellowstone also has impressive **mountains** and beautiful high-altitude lakes, plus a large population of **wild animals**, including grizzly **bears**, bison, **moose**, elk, pronghorn and, due to recent releases, **wolves**. Aside from the thermal features and the canyon, Yellowstone isn't the most scenic area of the Rockies, however, and much of the hiking is in level **forest**. The attractions are perhaps more subtle than elsewhere, but they're present and well worth experiencing. The park is big too, some 3,468 square miles, with an average elevation of 8,000 feet, and it's easy to leave the crowds behind and experience the wilderness alone.

Native Americans lived in this area for centuries; white explorers didn't reach Yellowstone until 1807–8, when a trapper called John Colter, who had been with the **Lewis and Clark expedition** but left to stay in the mountains, made a long hike through the region. Because no one back east had ever seen geysers and steaming creeks in America, his reports on what he had seen were regarded as exaggerated traveler's tales rather than truth. The famous mountain man

Jim Bridger visited the area sometime after Colter, and his stories were also dismissed as lies.

Yellowstone became the world's first **national park** on March 1, 1872, a crucial moment in the history of **wilderness** preservation and a magnificent commitment by the U.S. government on behalf of the nation. The proposal for a park came first from judge Cornelius Hedges, whose intention was to prevent the area from being taken over by private businesses and instead preserve it for the public. Appropriately, the idea came while sitting around a campfire during an expedition to the area. Support for a park came from the Northern Pacific Railroad, who could see it becoming a major tourist destination to which they would transport people. A campaign using the

Making Your Own Yoke Pads

If you'd like to make your own set of yoke pads, the process is relatively simple and cheap, and results in a customizable fit. A pair of quick and easy rectangular yoke pads can be assembled with the following items.

2 pieces of plywood approximately
    4 by 7 in.
enough closed-cell foam padding (such as
    Ensolite) to layer 3 in. of padding for
    each piece of plywood
fabric or duct tape, enough to cover
4 ¼ in. carriage bolts (about 3 in. long)
5 carriage wing nuts to fit the bolts
2 steel brackets about 4 in. long with 2 holes
    in each to accommodate the bolts (the
    holes must be far enough apart to fit on
    either side of the yoke or thwart)

To start, lay the steel bracket in the center of the wood, and mark the holes. Drill holes through the wood at these two spots, and insert the bolts. Next, cut the foam padding to match the size of the wood frame. Place layer upon layer until you have just over 3 inches of padding on top of the wood. Now place the whole yoke assembly in the center of a generous rectangle of durable fabric, as if you were going to wrap a present (see illustration 1). Staple the fabric into place, securing one side at a time (2–3). Attach the bracket to the backside of the yoke pads (this clamps it onto

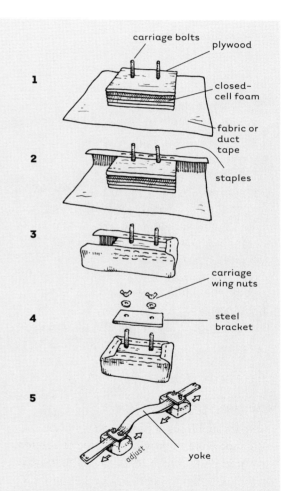

1   carriage bolts   plywood   closed-cell foam   fabric or duct tape

2   staples

3

4   carriage wing nuts   steel bracket

5   adjust   yoke

the yoke), and securely fasten with the wing nuts (4). Repeat steps to make the second yoke pad. To secure the pads to your yoke, slide them over the yoke in a position comfortable for your shoulders (5). These movable yoke pads can shift, so you may need to realign them every so often.

spectacular photographs of William H. Jackson, which showed that Colter and Bridges hadn't been lying, and the paintings of Thomas Moran helped win support. The act that created Yellowstone was for "a public park or pleasuring ground" rather than for wilderness preservation, although it did say that the landscape and features of the park should be left "in their natural condition." The value of the park as wilderness soon came to the fore though, when Congress voted, for the first time anywhere, not to allow mining there.

YOKE

A yoke is a bar (usually wooden) that lies across the **gunwales** at the center of a canoe. By resting the yoke against your shoulders, you are able to balance the canoe overhead and carry it alone with relative ease. This is called *portaging*.

Some canoes come with preexisting yokes, while others don't. If your canoe doesn't have a yoke (or has one you don't like), you can easily purchase a new yoke at a canoe specialty store or make your own at home. There is a detailed description of how to make a yoke in the book *Expedition Canoeing*, by Cliff Jacobson. Many new canoes come with center thwarts that act as yokes. These are commonly cut to accommodate the curvature of the neck but usually do not provide padding. For hard-core portagers, this is no problem, but for the rest of us, a little padding makes a big difference. See also **yoke pads**.

YOKE PADS

Yoke pads are blocks of padding that are attached to a canoe **yoke** to provide a degree of comfort while **portaging**. There are several types of yoke pads on the market, and finding a comfortable pair is well worth the trouble of shopping around. Some yoke pads are simple rectangular blocks, while others are contoured foam pads that fit the curvature of your shoulder.

When purchasing yoke pads, look for a pair that's comfortable regardless of the position of the canoe. For example, the yoke pads may feel great when the canoe is balanced directly overhead,

but consider how they will feel when you have to portage up a steep hill and the canoe is severely tilted. Will they slide off your shoulders? Will they become uncomfortable? Also look for durability. Yoke pads should be built to withstand a fair amount of abuse. Find a pair that can hold up to the rigors of **canoe tripping**.

> "I find the good old-fashioned rectangular blocks to be the most versatile yoke pads. In addition, I like yoke pads that can slide along the yoke to accommodate the different neck sizes of portagers."—AA

If you forget to pack the yoke pads, you can get some padding by wearing your **PFD** while you portage. A trick to get more padding out of your PFD is to put your head through one or both of the armholes instead of wearing it like a vest.

YOSEMITE

Yosemite National Park, in California, is one of the most spectacular natural regions and one of the most famous **national parks** in the world. Yosemite Valley, the heart of the park, is walled by huge granite cliffs down which tumble tremendous waterfalls. The valley can be reached by road and is very popular, but only a few hours of walking will take you away from the crowds and into the **wilderness**.

Yosemite is a stunning region of granite domes, deep canyons, high peaks, timberline lakes, waterfalls, and beautiful **forests**. The valley itself, just 7 miles long and 1 mile wide, consists of flat meadow and forest through which winds the placid Merced River. Above tower granite walls and domes, the most famous being 3,000-foot El Capitan, perhaps the biggest single block of granite in the world, and Half Dome, both of which are venues for serious **big-wall** rock climbing. Superb waterfalls cascade down the giant cliffs —1,612-foot Ribbon Fall; spreading, delicate Bridalveil Fall; 1,430-foot Upper and 1,000-foot Lower Yosemite Fall; and many more. Beyond the

The Yosemite wilderness is home to granite domes, timberline lakes, and waterfalls.

valley lies the Yosemite wilderness, which is part of the High Sierra and a wonderful place for **hiking**, scrambling, **rock climbing**, and, in **winter, ski touring**.

Native Americans lived in the valley for hundreds of years before the first white explorers arrived in the nineteenth century. White men may first have seen the valley in 1833, when a party led by Joseph R. Walker crossed the **Sierra Nevada** and came to the edge of a valley with precipices "more than a mile high." The first whites known for certain to have entered Yosemite were the soldiers of the Mariposa Battalion in 1851. This party gave the valley its name, calling it "Yosemity," mistakenly believing that this was what the Miwok Indians who lived there called it.

Just four years after the Mariposa Battalion's visit, the first tourists came to the valley and publisher James Hutchings began to extol its beauty and wonders in his *California Magazine*. Toll roads and trails were soon built, and hotels quickly followed. In 1860 the first appeals were made for Yosemite to be designated a park, to protect it from homesteading and commercial development; in 1864 the U.S. Congress passed a bill giving Yosemite Valley to the State of California "for public use, resort and recreation." Yosemite thus became the first state park. But the designation did little to stem continuing damage from tourism and other developments.

John Muir first came to Yosemite in 1868 and worked as a shepherd, an occupation that showed him the damage done to the land by the "hooved locusts," as he called sheep. He began a decades-long effort to learn more about Yosemite and to protect it, exploring the region's grand peaks and canyons and writing influential articles about its splendor. His articles in *Century* magazine and the work of its editor, Robert Underwood Johnson, made the case for preserving Yosemite as a national park.

In 1890 the Yosemite Act created Yosemite National Park for the protection of the "natural curiosities or wonders, and their retention in their natural condition." Although **Yellowstone** was the first national park, Yosemite was the first national park created specifically to conserve wilderness. Yosemite Valley itself remained the property of California, but was incorporated into the park in 1906 after a campaign by Muir and the **Sierra Club**.

Muir was instrumental in saving Yosemite Valley, but he lost the battle to prevent the magnificent valley of the Hetch Hetchy, which lay in the park, from being dammed to provide water for San Francisco. "As well dam for water-tanks the people's cathedrals and churches," Muir said, "for no holier temple has ever been consecrated by the heart of man." A campaign is now under way to dismantle the dam and restore the valley.

See also **Muir, John**.

YOSEMITE DECIMAL SYSTEM

See **climbing ratings**.

Z

Z-DRAG

The z-drag is a type of **rope** hauling system that creates a 3:1 mechanical advantage, which theoretically gives you three times more power than you'd have if you were pulling on a rope with no mechanical advantage. In the **wilderness**, the z-drag is most commonly used in **glacier** settings to perform **crevasse rescues** or when **retrieving a canoe or kayak** from a river.

To set up a z-drag, you need a long rope (the exact length is discussed below), webbing for your **anchor**, accessory cord to create **prusik hitches**, and at least three **carabiners**. In addition, having two pulleys makes the z-drag much easier, although they aren't necessary.

Setting up a z-drag is fairly easy once you know the finer points. Start off by building a **bomber** anchor. If you're rescuing a climber from a **crevasse**, the anchor will likely be built in the **snow** at a safe distance from the crevasse. If you're retrieving a canoe or kayak, your anchor will probably be a tree, boulder, or some other type of **natural protection** found somewhere along the shore. The amount of rope you need will end up being a little more than twice the distance from your anchor to the object you're trying to move, also known as your *load*.

After building your anchor, attach one end of the rope securely to your load. Take the rest of the rope and form the shape of the letter Z (a really big Z) on the ground near your anchor, with one bend in the Z pointing to your anchor and the other bend pointing in the direction of your load. Take the bend in the Z that's pointing toward your anchor and attach it to your anchor with a carabiner. Or, if you have a pulley, clip the pulley to the anchor and run the rope through the pulley. Now take your accessory cord and tie a prusik hitch around the portion of rope leading from the anchor directly to your load. The loop of the prusik hitch should be clipped into the same anchor with a second biner.

At the other bend in the Z, clip a carabiner to the rope (or use a pulley if you have one). Tie another prusik hitch, again around the line that runs directly to your load, and clip the loop of the prusik hitch to the carabiner at this bend in the Z. When you're finished, you should have two prusik hitches tied to the line leading to your load. One of them should be attached by pulley or carabiner to your anchor, and the other should be attached by pulley or carabiner to the free end of the rope.

To use the z-drag, pull on the free end of the rope. This will cause all parts of the system to move. You'll likely need an additional person to stand by the anchor and manage the first prusik hitch, making sure the hitch doesn't get jammed in the pulley. In addition, this person can ensure that the rope leading to your load is able to slide through the prusik hitch. As you pull, the sec-

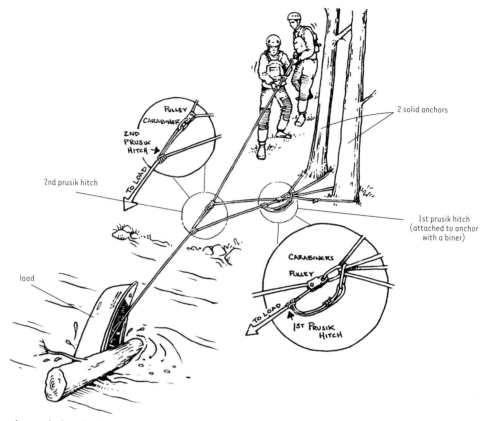

When the z-drag is deployed, the rope forms the letter Z or a backward Z. This hauling system provides a 3:1 mechanical advantage, making it easier to move heavy loads.

ond prusik hitch will move closer to the first. Eventually, you will need to let go of the rope slowly and allow the first prusik hitch (the one by the anchor) to act as a brake. Once the brake is holding the system, slide the second prusik hitch back down the line toward your load. This allows you to repeat the whole process.

Working with hauling systems is notoriously confusing until you have done it a few times. If, while reading this, you're thinking "Huh?" don't be alarmed. A few practice sessions will prepare you for the real thing. In addition to practicing the setup, you should understand the dangers of ropes under tension. The amount of energy held in a mechanical hauling system is immense. If any part of the system should fail (that is, if your rope snaps or your load breaks free), the rope and all the biners will fly through the air like shrapnel.

If you have helmets or **PFDs**, wear them. Otherwise, you can reduce the potential rebound effect of the rope by attaching a lightweight, bulky object (such as a **fleece** jacket) to the line leading directly to your load. This object, often called a *snubber*, can absorb some of the energy created by a snap in the system.

The z-drag can move very heavy objects with relative ease. Nonetheless, try out simpler methods to move an object (see **crevasse rescue** and **retrieving a canoe or kayak**) before you decide to make a z-drag. In general, it is best to move from the least complicated rescue or hauling system to the most complicated. If you're unfamiliar with the z-drag, it can take a while to learn. Therefore, if you think you may ever have cause to use this technique, be sure you have practiced it until you are competent.

Resources

BOOKS

Abbey, Edward. *Abbey's Road*. New York: Plume, 1991.

———. *Desert Solitaire: A Season in the Wilderness*. New York: Simon & Schuster, 1990.

———. *Down the River*. New York: Plume, 1991.

———. *The Journey Home: Some Words in Defense of the American West*. New York: Perennial Classics, 2000.

———. *The Monkey Wrench Gang*. New York: Perennial Classics, 2000.

Alden, Peter, et al. *National Audubon Society Field Guide to the Southwestern States*. New York: Knopf, 1999.

Alderson, Doug. *Sea Kayaker's Savvy Paddler: More than 500 Tips for Better Kayaking*. Camden ME: Ragged Mountain Press, 2001.

American Canoe Association and Laurie Guillion, ed. *Canoeing and Kayaking Instruction Manual*. Menasha Ridge Press, 1987.

Anderson, Sheridan. *Curtis Creek Manifesto: A Fully Illustrated Guide to the Strategy, Finesse, Tactics and Paraphernalia of Fly Fishing*. Portland OR: Frank Amato Publications, 1978.

Annerino, John. *Hiking the Grand Canyon*. Rev. and expanded. San Francisco: Sierra Club Books, 1993.

———. *Running Wild: An Extraordinary Adventure of the Human Spirit*. New York: Thunder's Mouth, 1997.

Appalachian Trail Conference Guidebooks. Birmingham AL: Menasha Ridge Press.

Bane, Michael. *Trail Safe: Averting Threatening Human Behavior in the Outdoors*. Berkeley: Wilderness Press, 2000.

Bechdel, Les, and Slim Ray. *River Rescue: A Manual for Whitewater Safety*. 3rd ed. Boston: Appalachian Mountain Club Books, 1997.

Bennett, Jeff. *The Essential Whitewater Kayaker: A Complete Course*. Camden ME: Ragged Mountain Press, 1999.

Berger, Karen. *Advanced Backpacking: A Trailside Guide*. New York: Norton, 1998.

———. *Hiking the Triple Crown: How to Hike America's Longest Trails: Appalachian Trail, Pacific Crest Trail, Continental Divide Trail*. Seattle: Mountaineers, 2001.

Berger, Karen, and Daniel R. Smith. *Along the Pacific Crest Trail*. Englewood CO: Westcliffe, 1998.

———. *The Pacific Crest Trail: A Hiker's Companion*. Woodstock VT: Countryman, 2000.

———. *Where the Waters Divide: A Three-Thousand-Mile Trek Along America's Continental Divide*. Woodstock VT: Countryman, 1997.

Bergin, Edward J. *A Star to Steer Her By: A Self-Teaching Guide to Offshore Navigation*. Centreville MD: Cornell Maritime Press, 1983.

Birkett, Bill, ed. *Classic Treks: The Thirty Most Spectacular Hikes in the World*. Boston: Little, Brown, 2000.

Breyfogle, Newell D., *Commonsense Outdoor Medicine and Emergency Companion*. 3rd ed. Camden ME: Ragged Mountain Press, 1993.

British Canoe Union and Franco Ferrero, ed. *Canoe and Kayak Handbook*. 3rd ed. Bangor UK: Presda, 2002.

Brower, David R., with Steve Chapple. *Let the Mountains Talk, Let the Rivers Run: A Call to Those Who Would Save the Earth*. San Francisco: HarperCollins, 1995.

Brown, Hamish M. *Climbing the Corbetts: Scotland's 2,500-Foot Summits*. London: Gollancz, 1988.

————. *Hamish's Mountain Walk: The First Traverse of All the Scottish Munros in One Journey.* London: Gollancz, 1978.

Brown, Tom, Jr., with Brandt Morgan. *Tom Brown's Field Guide to Wilderness Survival.* New York: Berkley, 1983.

Broze, Matt, and George Gronseth. *Sea Kayaker's Deep Trouble: True Stories and Their Lessons from Sea Kayaker Magazine.* Christopher Cunningham, ed. Camden ME: Ragged Mountain Press, 1997.

Bruce, Dan. *The Thru-Hiker's Handbook.* Hot Springs NC: Center for Appalachian Trail Studies, 1996.

Burch, David. *Fundamentals of Kayak Navigation.* 3rd ed. Guilford CT: Globe Pequot, 1999.

Calder, Nigel. *How to Read a Nautical Chart: A Complete Guide to the Symbols, Abbreviations, and Data Displayed on Nautical Charts.* Camden ME: International Marine, 2003.

Cary, Bob. *The Big Wilderness Canoe Manual.* New York: Arco, 1983.

Chouinard, Yvon. *Climbing Ice.* San Francisco: Sierra Club Books, 1978.

Cinnamon, Jerry. *The Complete Climber's Handbook.* Rev. ed. Camden ME: Ragged Mountain Press, 2000.

Cohen, Michael P. *The Pathless Way: John Muir and American Wilderness.* Madison: University of Wisconsin Press, 1984.

Colorado Trail Foundation. *The Colorado Trail: The Official Guidebook.* 5th ed. Golden: Colorado Mountain Club Press, 2000.

Conover, Garrett. *Beyond the Paddle: A Canoeist's Guide to Expedition Skills—Poling, Lining, Portaging, and Maneuvering through Ice.* Gardiner ME: Tilbury House, 1991.

Conover, Garrett, and Alexandra Conover. *Winter Wilderness Companion: Traditional and Native American Skills for the Undiscovered Season.* Rev. ed. Camden ME: Ragged Mountain Press, 2001.

Copeland, Kathy, and Craig Copeland. *Don't Waste Your Time in the Canadian Rockies: An Opinionated Hiking Guide to Help You Get the Most from This Magnificent Wilderness.* Riondell BC: Voice in the Wilderness Press, 1998.

————. *Don't Waste Your Time in the North Cascades: An Opinionated Hiking Guide to Help You Get the Most from This Magnificent Wilderness.* Berkeley: Wilderness Press, 1996.

Crane, Nicholas. *Clear Waters Rising: A Mountain Walk Across Europe.* New York: Penguin, 1997.

Daffern, Tony. *Avalanche Safety for Skiers and Climbers.* 2nd ed. Seattle: Mountaineers, 1992.

Dowd, John. *Sea Kayaking: A Manual for Long-Distance Touring.* 4th ed. Seattle: University of Washington Press, 1997.

Dudley, Ellen. *The Savvy Adventure Traveler: What to Know Before You Go.* Camden ME: Ragged Mountain Press, 1999.

Etling, Kathy. *Cougar Attacks: Encounters of the Worst Kind.* Guilford CT: Lyons Press, 2001.

Farrand, John. *National Audubon Society Pocket Guide: Familiar Animal Tracks of North America.* New York: Knopf, 1993.

Fayhee, M. John. *Along the Arizona Trail.* Englewood CO: Westcliffe, 1998.

Ferguson, Michael. *GPS Land Navigation: A Complete Guidebook for Backcountry Users of the NAVSTAR Satellite System.* Boise: Glassford, 1997.

Fletcher, Colin. *The Complete Walker III: The Joys and Techniques of Hiking and Backpacking.* 3rd ed. rev. New York: Knopf, 1984. 4th rev. ed. published in 2002 as *The Complete Walker IV* and coauthored with Chip Rawlins.

————. *The Man Who Walked through Time.* New York: Vintage, 1989.

————. *River: One Man's Journey Down the Colorado, Source to Sea.* New York: Knopf, 1997.

————. *The Secret Worlds of Colin Fletcher.* New York: Vintage, 1990.

————. *The Thousand-Mile Summer.* New York: Vintage, 1987.

Fredston, Jill A., and Doug Fesler. *Snow Sense: A Guide to Evaluating Snow Avalanche Hazard.* 4th ed. Anchorage: Alaska Mountain Safety Center, 1994.

Gadd, Ben. *Handbook of the Canadian Rockies.* 2nd ed. Jasper AB: Corax, 1995.

Getchell, Annie, and Dave Getchell Jr. *The Essential Outdoor Gear Manual: Equipment Care, Repair, and Selection.* 2nd ed. Camden ME: Ragged Mountain Press, 2000.

Gorman, Stephen. *AMC Guide to Winter Camping: Wilderness Travel and Adventure in the Cold-Weather Months.* Boston: Appalachian Mountain Club Books, 1991.

Graydon, Don, and Kurt Hanson, eds. *Mountaineering: The Freedom of the Hills.* 6th ed. Seattle: Mountaineers, 1997.

Guillion, Laurie. *Canoeing and Kayaking: Instruction Manual.* Newington VA: American Canoe Association, 1987.

Hampton, Bruce, and David Cole. *Soft Paths: How to Enjoy the Wilderness without Harming It.* Rev. ed. Molly Absolon and Tom Reed, ed. Mechanicsburg PA: Stackpole, 1995.

Harvey, Mark. *The National Outdoor Leadership School Wilderness Guide: The Classic Handbook.* Rev. ed. New York: Simon & Schuster, 1999.

Hazard, Joseph T. *Pacific Crest Trails from Alaska to Cape Horn.* Rev. ed. Seattle: Superior, 1948.

Herrero, Stephen. *Bear Attacks: Their Causes and Avoidance.* New York: Nick Lyons Books, 1985.

Hever, Karsten. *Walking the Big Wild: From Yellowstone to the Yukon on the Grizzly Bears' Trail.* Toronto: McClelland & Stewart, 2002.

Hodgson, Michael. *America's Secret Recreation Areas: Your Recreation Guide to the Bureau of Land Management's Wild Lands of the West.* San Francisco: Foghorn Press, 1995.

Hutchinson, Derek C. *The Complete Book of Sea Kayaking.* 4th ed. Old Saybrook CT: Globe Pequot, 1995.

Isaac, Jeffrey. *The Outward Bound Wilderness First-Aid Handbook.* Rev. ed. New York: Lyons Press, 1998.

Jacobson, Cliff. *Camping's Top Secrets: A Lexicon of Camping Tips Only the Experts Know.* 2nd ed. Old Saybrook CT: Globe Pequot, 1998.

———. *Expedition Canoeing: A Guide to Canoeing Wild Rivers in North America.* 3rd ed. Guilford CT: Globe Pequot, 2001.

Jardine, Ray. *Beyond Backpacking: Ray Jardine's Guide to Lightweight Hiking: Practical Methods for All Who Love the Out-of-Doors, from Walkers and Backpackers, to Long-Distance Hikers.* LaPine OR: AdventureLore Press, 2000.

———. *The Pacific Crest Trail Hiker's Handbook.* 3rd ed. LaPine OR: AdventureLore Press, 2000.

Jones, Steve. *Mountain Bike Technique.* Birmingham AL: Menasha Ridge Press, 1997.

Jones, Tom Lorang. *Colorado's Continental Divide Trail: The Official Guide.* Englewood CO: Westcliffe, 1997.

Kephart, Horace. *Camping and Woodcraft: A Handbook for Vacation Campers and for Travelers in the Wilderness.* Knoxville: University of Tennessee Press, 1988.

Krakauer, Jon. *Eiger Dreams: Ventures among Men and Mountains.* New York: Anchor, 1997.

———. *Into the Wild.* New York: Anchor, 1997.

———. *Into Thin Air: A Personal Account of the Mount Everest Disaster.* New York: Villard, 1998.

Leopold, Aldo. *A Sand County Almanac: With Essays on Conservation.* New York: Oxford University Press, 2001.

Letham, Lawrence. *GPS Made Easy: Using Global Positioning Systems in the Outdoors.* 3rd ed. Seattle: Mountaineers, 2001.

Long, John. *Climbing Anchors.* Evergreen CO: Chockstone Press, 1993.

———. *How to Rock Climb!.* 4th ed. Guilford CT: Globe Pequot, 2002.

Long, John, and Craig Luebben. *Advanced Rock Climbing.* Helena MT: Falcon, 1999.

Lopez, Barry. *Arctic Dreams: Imagination and Desire in a Northern Landscape.* New York: Vintage, 2001.

Loughman, Michael. *Learning to Rock Climb.* San Francisco: Sierra Club Books, 1981.

Lowe, Jeff. *Ice World: Techniques and Experiences of Modern Ice Climbing.* Seattle: Mountaineers, 1996.

Ludlum, David M. *The Audubon Society Field Guide to North American Weather.* New York: Knopf, 1991.

Luebben, Craig. *How to Ice Climb!* Helena MT: Falcon, 1999.

Lull, John. *Sea Kayaking Safety and Rescue.* Berkeley: Wilderness Press, 2001.

Lynx, Dustin. *Hiking Canada's Great Divide Trail.* Calgary AB: Rocky Mountain Books, 2000.

Mason, Bill. *Path of the Paddle: An Illustrated Guide to the Art of Canoeing.* Rev. ed. Minocqua WI: NorthWord Press, 1995.

Matthiessen, Peter. *The Snow Leopard.* New York: Penguin, 1996.

McClung, David, and Peter Schaerer. *The Avalanche Handbook.* Seattle: Mountaineers, 1993.

McGivney, Annette. Leave No Trace: A Practical Guide to the New Wilderness Etiquette. Seattle: Mountaineers, 1998.

McKown, Doug. *Canoeing Safety and Rescue.* Calgary AB: Rocky Mountain Books, 1992.

McNeish, Cameron. *The Wilderness World of Cameron McNeish: Essays from Beyond the Black Stump.* Glasgow Scotland: In Pinn, 2001.

McPhee, John. *Encounters with the Archdruid.* New York: Farrar, Straus & Giroux, 1971.

Meyer, Kathleen. *How to Shit in the Woods: An Environmentally Sound Approach to a Lost Art.* 2nd ed. rev. Berkeley: Ten Speed Press, 1994.

Miller, Arthur P., and Marjorie L. Miller. *Trails Across America: Traveler's Guide to Our National Scenic and Historic Trails.* Golden CO: Fulcrum, 1996.

Miller, Dorcas (S.). *Backcountry Cooking: From Pack to Plate in Ten Minutes.* Seattle: Mountaineers, 1998.

———. *Good Food for Camp and Trail: All-Natural Recipes for Delicious Meals Outdoors.* Boulder CO: Pruett, 1993.

Milligan, John E. *Celestial Navigation by H.O. 249.* Cambridge MD: Cornell Maritime Press, 1974.

Molvar, Erik. *Alaska on Foot: Wilderness Techniques for the Far North.* Woodstock VT: Countryman, 1996.

Mortlock, Colin. *Beyond Adventure*. Milnthrope UK: Cicerone, 2001.

Morton, Keith. *Planning a Wilderness Trip in Canada and Alaska*. Calgary AB: Rocky Mountain Books, 1997.

Mueser, Roland. *Long-Distance Hiking: Lessons from the Appalachian Trail*. Camden ME: Ragged Mountain Press, 1998.

Muir, John. *John Muir: The Eight Wilderness Discovery Books*. Seattle: Mountaineers, 1992.

———. *The Mountains of California*. New York: Modern Library, 2001.

———. *My First Summer in the Sierra*. Boston: Houghton Mifflin, 1998.

———. *Sacred Summits: John Muir's Greatest Climbs*. Graham White, ed. Edinburgh Scotland: Canongate, 1999.

———. *A Thousand-Mile Walk to the Gulf*. William Frederic Badè, ed. Boston: Houghton Mifflin, 1998.

Murie, Olaus J., editor. *A Field Guide to Animal Tracks*. 2nd ed. Boston: Houghton Mifflin, 1975.

Nash, Roderick Frazier. *Wilderness and the American Mind*. 4th ed. New Haven: Yale University Press, 2001.

Nealy, William. *Mountain Bike! A Manual of Beginning to Advanced Technique*. Birmingham AL: Menasha Ridge Press, 1992.

North Woods Animal Scat Guide. Wevertown NY: Northwoods Field Guides, n.d.

O'Bannon, Allen. *Allen and Mike's Really Cool Backpackin' Book*. Helena MT: Falcon, 2001.

O'Bannon, Allen, and Mike Clelland. *Allen and Mike's Really Cool Backcountry Ski Book: Traveling and Camping Skills for a Winter Environment*. Helena MT: Falcon, 1996.

———. *Allen and Mike's Really Cool Telemark Tips: 109 Amazing Tips to Improve Your Tele-Skiing*. Helena MT: Falcon, 1998.

Olson, Sigurd F. *Listening Point*. Minneapolis: University of Minnesota Press, 1997.

———. *The Lonely Land*. Minneapolis: University of Minnesota Press, 1997.

———. *Reflections from the North Country*. Minneapolis: University of Minnesota Press, 1998.

Owen, Peter. *The Book of Outdoor Knots*. New York: Lyons & Burford, 1993.

Parker, Paul. *Free-Heel Skiing: Telemark and Parallel Techniques for All Conditions*. 3rd ed. Seattle: Mountaineers, 2001.

Peacock, Doug. *Grizzly Years: In Search of the American Wilderness*. New York: H. Holt, 1990.

Pearson, Claudia, ed. *NOLS Cookery*. 4th ed. Mechanicsburg PA: Stackpole, 1997.

Pielou, E. C. *A Naturalist's Guide to the Arctic*. Chicago: University of Chicago Press, 1994.

Powell, John Wesley. *The Exploration of the Colorado River and Its Canyons*. Washington DC: Adventure Classics/National Geographic, 2002.

Raleigh, Duane. *Ice: Tools and Technique*. Carbondale CO: Elk Mountain Press, 1995.

Reynolds, Kev. *Walking in the Alps*. New York: Interlink Books, 2000.

Rezendes, Paul. *Tracking and the Art of Seeing: How to Read Animal Tracks and Sign*. 2nd ed. New York: HarperCollins, 1999.

Robbins, Royal. *Basic Rockcraft*. Glendale CA: La Siesta Press, 1971, 1985.

Rock, Harry. *The Basic Essentials of Canoe Poling*. Merrillville IN: ICS Books, 1992.

Roper, Steve. *The Sierra High Route: Traversing Timberline Country*. Seattle: Mountaineers, 1997.

Ross, Cindy. *Journey on the Crest: Walking 2,600 Miles from Mexico to Canada*. Seattle: Mountaineers, 1987.

Rowell, Galen. *The Art of Adventure*. San Francisco: Sierra Club Books, 1996.

———. *Galen Rowell's Vision: The Art of Adventure Photography*. San Francisco: Sierra Club Books, 1993.

———. *High and Wild: Essays and Photographs on Wilderness Adventure*. Bishop CA: Spotted Dog Press, 2002.

———. *Mountain Light: In Search of the Dynamic Landscape*. San Francisco: Sierra Club Books, 1986.

———. *In the Throne Room of the Mountain Gods*. San Francisco: Sierra Club Books, 1986.

Russell, Terry, and Renny Russell. *On the Loose*. San Francisco: Sierra Club, 1967, reprint 1979; Salt Lake City: Gibbs-Smith, 2001.

Schaffer, Jeffrey P., and Andy Selters. *The Pacific Crest Trail*. 5th ed. Berkeley: Wilderness Press, 1990.

Secor, R. J. *The High Sierra: Peaks, Passes, and Trails*. 2nd ed. Seattle: Mountaineers, 1999.

Seidman, David, with Paul Cleveland. *The Essential Wilderness Navigator: How to Find Your Way in the Great Outdoors*. 2nd ed. Camden ME: Ragged Mountain Press, 2001.

Selters, Andy. *Glacier Travel and Crevasse Rescue*. 2nd ed. Seattle: Mountaineers, 1999.

Seton, Ernest Thompson. *Wild Animals at Home*. Garden City NY: Doubleday, Page, 1913.

Simpson, Joe. *Touching the Void*. New York: Harper & Row, 1988.

Sloane, Eric. *Eric Sloane's Weather Book*. New York: Hawthorn, 1977.

———. *Look at the Sky . . . and Tell the Weather*. Rev. and enl. ed. New York: World, 1970.

Smith, Dave. *Backcountry Bear Basics: The Definitive Guide to Avoiding Unpleasant Encounters*. Seattle: Mountaineers, 1997.

Snyder, Gary. *The Practice of the Wild: Essays*. San Francisco: North Point Press, 1990.

Sobey, Ed. *The Whole Backpacker's Catalog: Tools and Resources for the Foot Traveler*. Camden ME: Ragged Mountain Press, 1999.

Soles, Clyde. *Rock and Ice Gear: Equipment for the Vertical World*. Seattle: Mountaineers, 2000.

Starr, Walter A., Jr. *Starr's Guide to the John Muir Trail and the High Sierra Region*. 12th ed. rev. San Francisco: Sierra Club Books, 1977.

Stegner, Wallace. *Beyond the Hundreth Meridian: John Wesley Powell and the Second Opening of the West*. Lincoln: University of Nebraska Press, 1982.

Storer, Tracy I., and Robert L. Usinger. *Sierra Nevada Natural History: An Illustrated Handbook*. Berkeley: University of California Press, 1963.

Strauss, Robert. *Adventure Trekking: A Handbook for Independent Travelers*. Seattle: Mountaineers, 1996.

Sweet, Robert J. *GPS for Mariners*. Camden ME: International Marine, 2003.

Thoreau, Henry David. *A Week on the Concord and Merrimack Rivers/Walden, Or, Life in the Woods/The Maine Woods/Cape Cod*. New York: Literary Classics of the United States, 1985.

Tighe, Kelly, and Susan Moran. *On the Arizona Trail: A Guide for Hikers, Cyclists, and Equestrians*. Boulder CO: Pruett, 1998.

Townsend, Chris. *The Advanced Backpacker: A Handbook of Year-Round, Long-Distance Hiking*. Camden ME: Ragged Mountain Press, 2001.

———. *The Backpacker's Handbook*. 2nd ed. Camden ME: Ragged Mountain Press, 1997.

———. *Backpacker's Pocket Guide*. Camden ME: Ragged Mountain Press, 2002.

———. *Crossing Arizona: A Solo Hike through the Sky Islands and Deserts of the Arizona Trail*. Woodstock VT: Countryman, 2002.

———. *The Great Backpacking Adventure*. Sparkford UK: Oxford Illustrated, 1987.

———. *High Summer: Backpacking the Canadian Rockies*. Seattle: Cloudcap, 1989.

———. *The Munros and Tops*. Edinburgh UK: Mainstream Press, 1997.

———. *Walking the Yukon: A Solo Trek through the Land of Beyond*. Camden ME: Ragged Mountain Press, 1993.

———. *Wilderness Skiing and Winter Camping*. Camden ME: Ragged Mountain Press, 1994.

Turner, Frederick. *Rediscovering America: John Muir in His Time and Ours*. San Francisco: Sierra Club Books, 1985.

Wagner, Ronald L., and Bill Adler Jr. *The Weather Sourcebook: Your One-Stop Resource for Everything You Need to Feed Your Weather Habit*. 2nd ed. Old Saybrook CT: Globe Pequot, 1997.

Walbridge, Charles, and Wayne A. Sundmacher Sr. *Whitewater Rescue Manual: New Techniques for Canoeists, Kayakers, and Rafters*. Camden ME: Ragged Mountain Press, 1995.

Walbridge, Charlie, and Jody Tinsley. *The American Canoe Associations's River Safety Anthology*. Birmingham AL: Menasha Ridge Press, 1996.

Whitney, Stephen. *A Sierra Club Naturalist's Guide to the Sierra Nevada*. San Francisco: Sierra Club Books, 1979.

Wilkerson, James A., ed. *Medicine for Mountaineering and Other Wilderness Activities*. 5th ed. Seattle: Mountaineers, 2001.

Wilkinson, Ernest. *Snow Caves for Fun and Survival*. Rev. ed. Boulder CO: Johnson, 1992.

Williams, Jack. *The Weather Book*. 2nd ed. rev. New York: Vintage, 1997.

Wolf, James R. *Guide to the Continental Divide Trail*. Rev. ed., 6 vols. Bethesda: Continental Divide Trail Society, 1991–98.

Wyckoff, Jerome. *The Story of Geology: Our Changing Earth through the Ages*. Rev. ed. New York: Golden Press, 1976.

PERIODICALS

Backcountry, 802-644-6606, www.backcountrymagazine.com

Backpacker, 800-666-3439, www.backpacker.com

Canoe and Kayak, 800-692-2663, www.canoekayak.com

Couloir, 530-582-1884, www.couloirmag.com

National Geographic Adventure, 800-647-5463, www.nationalgeographic.com/adventure

Outside, 505-989-7100, www.outsidemag.com

Paddler, 888-774-7554, www.paddlermagazine.com

Rock and Ice, 970-704-1442, www.rockandice.com

Sea Kayaker, 206-789-9536, www.seakayakermag.com

ORGANIZATIONS

All American Trail Running Association, 719-573-4405, www.trailrunner.com

American Avalanche Association, 970-946-0822, www.americanavalancheassociation.org

American Canoe Association, 703-451-0141, www.acanet.org/acanet.htm

American Canyoneering Association, 435-590-8889, www.canyoneering.net

American Heart Association, 800-242-8721, www.americanheart.org

American Long Distance Hiking Association–West, www.aldhawest.org

American Mountain Guide Association, 303-271-0984, www.amga.com

American Red Cross, 202-639-3520, www.redcross.org

Appalachian Long Distance Hikers Association, www.aldha.org

Appalachian Mountain Club, 617-523-0636, www.outdoors.org

Appalachian Trail Conference, 304-535-6331, www.atconf.org

British Canoe Union, www.bcu.org.uk

Bureau of Land Management, 202-452-5125, www.blm.gov

Canadian Avalanche Association, 250-837-2435, www.avalanche.ca

Centers for Disease Control and Prevention, International Travelers' Hotline, 404-332-4559, www.cdc.gov/travel

Commission Europeenne de Canyon, www.cec-canyoning.org/e/

Continental Divide Trail Alliance, www.cdtrail.org

Continental Divide Trail Society, www.cdtsociety.org

Highpointers Club, www.highpointers.org

International Federation of Mountain Guides Association (IFMGA), www.ivbv.info/en/index.asp

Leave No Trace, 800-332-4100, www.lnt.org

The Long Trail, 802-244-7037 (Green Mountain Club), www.longtrail.org

National Oceanic and Atmospheric Administration, 202-482-6090, www.noaa.gov

National Outdoor Leadership School (NOLS), 800-710-6657, www.nols.edu

National Park Service, 888-GO PARKS (888-467-2757), 202-208-6843, www.nps.gov

National Parks Reservation Center, (888-467-2757) 800-365-2267, http://reservations.nps.gov

National Speleological Society, 256-852-1300, www.caves.org

Nature Conservancy, 800-628-6860, www.nature.org

Outward Bound, 866-467-7651, www.outwardbound.org

Professional Paddlesports Association, 800-789-2202, www.propaddle.com

Sierra Club, 415-977-5500, www.sierraclub.org

SOLO, 603-447-6711, www.soloschools.com

Union Internationale des Associations d'Alpinisme (UIAA), www.uiaa.ch

U.S. Coast Guard, 202-267-2229, www.uscg.mil

USDA Forest Service, 202-205-8333, www.fs.fed.us

Wilderness Medical Associates, 888-945-3633, www.wildmed.com

Wilderness Medicine Institute, 800-710-6657, www.wmi.nols.edu

The Wilderness Society, 800-843-9453, www.wilderness.org

MAPS

Fresh Tracks Map Store, www.freshtracksmaps.com

Map Link, 800-627-7768, www.maplink.com

Topo USA, 800-561-5105, www.delorme.com/topousa

TopoZone, 978-251-4242, www.topozone.com

Trails Illustrated, 800-962-1643, http://maps.nationalgeographic.com/trails/

USGS Topographic Maps, 888-ASK-USGS (888-275-8747), http://mcmcweb.er.usgs.gov/topomaps/

WEB RESOURCES

America's Roof, www.americasroof.com

GORP, www.gorp.com

Intellicast.com, www.intellicast.com

National Park Foundation, 202-238-4200, www.nationalparks.org

Peakware World Mountain Encyclopedia, www.peakware.com

Tide's Online, http://tidesonline.nos.noaa.gov

Tom Brown's Tracker School, 908-479-4681, www.trackerschool.com

VIDEOS

Grace under Pressure

The Kayak Roll (a Kent Ford performance video)

Metric Conversion Table

$(F - 32) \times 0.556 = °C$
acre $\times$ 2.47 = hectare
cubic inch $\times$ 163 = cubic millimeters
foot $\times$ 0.3048 = meters
gallon $\times$ 4.2268 = liters
inch $\times$ 2.54 = centimeters
mile $\times$ 1.6093 = kilometers
ounce $\times$ 28.35 = grams
pound $\times$ 0.4536 = kilograms
quart $\times$ 0.94635 = liters
square inch $\times$ 64.5 = square millimeters
square mile $\times$ 2.580 = square kilometers
yard $\times$ 0.91440 = meters

Index